HENRY MORE. THE IMMORTALITY OF THE SOUL

ARCHIVES INTERNATIONALES D'HISTOIRE DES IDÉES

INTERNATIONAL ARCHIVES OF THE HISTORY OF IDEAS

122

ALEXANDER JACOB

(editor)

HENRY MORE.
THE IMMORTALITY OF THE SOUL

HENRY MORE.
THE IMMORTALITY
OF THE SOUL

Edited by
A. JACOB

1987 **MARTINUS NIJHOFF PUBLISHERS**
a member of the KLUWER ACADEMIC PUBLISHERS GROUP
DORDRECHT / BOSTON / LANCASTER

Distributors

for the United States and Canada: Kluwer Academic Publishers, P.O. Box 358, Accord Station, Hingham, MA 02018-0358, USA
for the UK and Ireland: Kluwer Academic Publishers, MTP Press Limited, Falcon House, Queen Square, Lancaster LA1 1RN, UK
for all other countries: Kluwer Academic Publishers Group, Distribution Center, P.O. Box 322, 3300 AH Dordrecht, The Netherlands

Library of Congress Cataloging in Publication Data

ISBN 90-247-3512-2
ISBN 90-247-2433-3 (series)

Copyright

PRINTED IN THE NETHERLANDS

Horatio: O day and night, but this is wondrous strange!
Hamlet: And therefore as a stranger give it welcome.
There are more things in heaven and earth, Horatio,
Than are dreamt of in your philosophy.

Hamlet, Act I, Sc. V, ll.164-167.

To Horatio.

Preface

The significance of Henry More's vitalist philosophy in the history of ideas has been realized relatively recently, as the bibliography will reveal. The general neglect of the Cambridge Platonist movement may be attributed to the common prejudice that its chief exponents, especially More, were obscure mystics who were neither coherent in their philosophical system nor attractive in their prose style. I hope that this modern edition of More's principal treatise will help to correct this unjust impression and reveal the keenness and originality of More's intellect, which sought to demonstrate the relevance of classical philosophy in an age of empirical science. The wealth of learning -- ranging as it does from Greek antiquity to 17th-century science and philosophy -- that informs More' s intellectual system of the universe should, in itself, be a recommendation to students of the history of ideas. Though, for those in search of literary satisfaction, too, there is not wanting, in More's style, the humour, and grace, of a man whose erudition did not divorce him from a sympathetic understanding of human contradictions. As for More's elaborate speculations concerning the spirit world in the final book of this treatise, I think that we would indeed be justified in regarding their combination of classical mythology amd scientific naturalism as the literary and philosophical counterpart of the great celestial frescoes of the Baroque masters.

*

In the preparation of this edition, I am indebted to the Departments of Philosophy, Classics, and English of the Pennsylvania State University for the valuable learning I derived from them. Particularly, Prof. Emily Grosholz and Prof. Michael Kiernan helped me with many suggestions on the philosophical and textual aspects of this edition. I should also like to thank the two readers for Martinus Nijhoff for their perspicacious comments on my edition.

My thanks are due also to Prof. Charles Mann, Mrs. Noelene Martin and Mrs. Grace Perez of the Pennsylvania State University Library, and to the Librarians of Columbia University Library, the New York Academy of Medicine

Library, the Folger Renaissance Library, and the Library of Congress, for their kindness in facilitating my research. The figure of the brain from Charles Singer's transcription of Vesalius' *De Humani Corporis Fabrica* that I have used in my Introduction is reproduced by courtesy of the Wellcome Medical Historical Museum, London.

Finally, I must thank Mrs. P. M. Sawchuk for heroically typing the manuscript of this edition, and Mr. Thomas Minsker, of the University Computation Center, for his expert assistance in printing it.

University Park, Pennsylvania   Alexander Jacob
July,1986

Contents

Biographical Introduction

> But for the better Understanding of all this, we are
> to take ... our Rise a little higher and to premise
> some things which fell out in my Youth; if not also in
> my Childhood itself. To the End that it may more
> fully appear that the things which I have written,
> are not any borrowed, or far-fetch'd Opinions, owing
> unto Education and the Reading of Books; but the
> proper Sentiments of my own Mind, drawn and
> derived from my most intimate Nature -- Henry
> More, Preface to *Opera Omnia* (1679) [1]

The intellectual individuality which characterized Henry
More, the principal representative of the group of Platonist
philosophers that distinguished the University of Cambridge in
the middle of the seventeenth century,[2] is evidenced in the
earliest stages of his life. More was born at Grantham in
Lincolnshire, and was baptized at the parish church,
St.Wulfram's, on October 10, 1614.[3] His father, Alexander
More, was a Calvinist,and was alderman and, later,mayor of
Grantham for several years. Henry More was the seventh son
of Alexander More and, from his childhood, he displayed an
"anxious and thoughtful genius" which manifested itself in a
considerable proficiency in French and Latin at Grantham
School as well as a keen sensitivity to the Platonic harmony of
Spenser's poetry, which his father read to him "entertaining us
on winter nights, with that incomparable Peice of his, the *Fairy*

---

1 Tr. Richard Ward in *The Life of the learned and pious Dr. Henry More*, ed.
M. F. Howard, London:Theosophical Publishing Co., 1911, p. 58.

2 Of the other Cambridge Platonists, the most important are Benjamin
Whichcote (1609-1683), John Smith (1618-1652), and Ralph Cudworth (
1617-1688).

3 The Parchment Roll at Grantham, entitled 'A true Certificate of all such
as were baptized in the Parish Church of Grantham, Anno Domini 1614'
indicates the baptism date of Henry More thus "October 10, Henry the
Sonne of Mr.[Alexander] More" (Folio Register Parchment). See A.B.
Grosart, *The Complete Poems of Dr. Henry More*, Edinburgh, 1878, rpt. N.Y.:
AMS Press, 1967, p.xiin.

Queen, a Poem as richly fraught with divine Morality as Phansy."[4] This humanistic temperament could not be reconciled with the harsh doctrine of predestination which his Calvinist upbringing had forced upon him, and already by the time of his entry to Eton (1627 or 1628), he was revolting against it. He remembers in his autobiographical sketch that he vehemently disputed against the Calvinist interpretation of fate that his paternal uncle,[5] who accompanied him to Eton, imposed on the words of Epictetus," ἄγε με ὦ Ζεῦ καὶ σὺ ἡ πεπρωμένη."[6] until his uncle had to threaten him with the rod for his "immature Forwardness in philosophizing concerning such matters." For, indeed, as he says, "I had such deep Aversion in my Temper to this Opinion, and so firm and unshaken a perswasion of the Divine Justice and Goodness, that on a certain Day, in a Ground belonging to Aeton College, where the Boys us'd to play, and exercise themselves, musing concerning these Things with my self ... I did seriously and deliberately conclude within myself viz; 'If I am one of those that are predestinated unto Hell, where all Things are full of nothing but Cursing and Blasphemy, yet will I behave myself there patiently and submissively towards God; and if there be any one Thing more than another, that is acceptable to him, that will I set myself to do with a sincere Heart, and to the utmost of my Power': Being certainly persuaded that if I thus demeaned my self, he would hardly keep me long in that Place."[7] Opposed to the frightening God of Calvin, More was inbred with a more spiritual awareness of Divinity, an "exceeding hail and entire Sense of God, which Nature herself had planted deeply in me."[8]

This "boniform faculty" in him, as he was to call it later[9]

---

4 More, "To his dear Father Alexander More, Esquire," in Grosart, *op. cit.*,p. 4.

5 This was probably Gabriel More D.D. who, in March 1631-2, was installed Prebendary of Westminster, see Grosart, *op. cit.*, p.xn.

6 "Lead me, O Jupiter, and thou, Fate."

7 Ward, *op. cit.*, p. 59.

8 Ward, *op.cit.*, p. 60.

9 cf. *Enchiridion Ethicum*, Bk I, Ch. 5, Art. 7: "Wherefore as it is now plain, that something there is which of its own nature, and incontestably is *true*.

was allowed to develop rapidly at Cambridge which he entered in 1631. Masson, in his *Life of John Milton,* presents a piquant evocation of More's arrival at Christ's in the last year of Milton's residence there: "Among the new admissions at Christ's, besides a Ralph Widdrington, afterwards of some note as a physician, a Charles Hotham, and others whose subsequent history might be traced, there was one youth at whcm Milton, had he foreseen what he was to be, would certainly have looked with more than common attention. This was a tall thin sapling, of clear olive complexion, and a mild and rapt expresion, whose admission into the College is recorded in the entrybook thus:

> *December* 31,1631 -- Henry More, son of Alexander, born at Grantham in the County of Lincoln, grounded in letters at Eton by Mr. Harrison, was admitted, in the 17th year of his age a lesser pensioner under Mr. Gell.[10]

This new student, whose connexion with Christ's thus began just as that of Milton was drawing to a close, was the Henry More afterwards so famous as the Cambridge Platonist, and so memorable in the history of the College.[11] More was especially fortunate in being tutored by Robert Gell, whom he describes as "a Person both learned and pious and, what I was not a little sollicitous about, not at all a Calvinist."[12] Gell was a friend of

---

So is there somewhat which of its own nature is simply *good.* Also that as the former is comprehended by the Intellect, so the sweetness and delight of the latter is relished by the *Boniform Faculty.* (Tr.Edward Southwell in *An Account of Virtue; or, Dr.Henry More' s Abridgement of Morals,put into English,* London, 1690, p. 31).

10 This is an English rendering of the original Latin :
"Decemb. 31, 1631
Henricus More, Filius Alexander, natus Granthamiae in agro Lincolinensi literis institutus Etonae a M^{ro} Harrison, anno aetatis 17. admissus est Pensionarius minor sub M^{ro} Gell." (Grosart,*op. cit.,* p. xv)

11 David Masson, *The Life of John Milton,* London: Macmillan, 1881, I: 248f.

the liberal divine Joseph Mede, (who, until his death in 1638, was a very influential figure in the College) and was, even more than Mede, interested in the Cabala and Hermetism. It is quite probable that, as Geoffrey Bullough conjectures, he contributed to the development of similar esoteric interests in the young More.[13] The intimate connection in More's mind between Divinity and Nature is seen in his account of the "mighty and almost immoderate Thirst after Knowledge" which dominated him as a student, especially for "that which was Natural; and above all others, that which was said to drive into the deepest Cause of Things, and Aristotle calls the first and highest Philosophy, or Wisdom ... For even at that Time, the Knowledge of natural and divine Things seem'd to me the highest Pleasure and Felicity imaginable."[14]

This enthusiasm for philosophy led him first to the study of Aristotle and Cardano and Scaliger, but he was quickly disillusioned with their teachings, which seemed to him "either so false or uncertain, or else so obvious and trivial, that I looked upon myself as having plainly lost my time in the Reading of such Authors."[15] By the time of taking his bachelor's degree in 1635, he was beginning to ponder seriously "whether the Knowledge of things was really that Supreme Felicity of Man; or something Greater and more Divine was; Or, supposing it to be so, whether it was to be acquired by such an Eagerness and Intentness in the reading of Authors, and contemplating of Things; or by the Purging of the Mind from all sorts of Vices whatsoever; Especially having begun to read now the Platonick Writers, Marsilius Ficinus, Plotinus himself, Mercurius Trismegistus, and the Mystical Divines, among whom there was frequent mention made of the Purification of the Soul, and of the Purgative Course that is previous to the Illuminative."[16] More was also deeply influenced by the mediaeval mystical work attributed to Tauler, or disciple of his, *Theologia Germanica* which had been edited and popularized by

---

12 Ward, *op. cit.*, p. 61.

13 Bullough, *Philosophical Poems of Henry More*, Manchester, 1931, p. xv.

14 Ward, *op. cit.*, p. 62

15 Ward, *op. cit.*, p. 63.

16 *Ibid.*, p. 64f.

Luther, and which detailed the process of spiritual purification. However, although More may have been encouraged in his Platonic and mystical learning by Mead, Gell, and Benjamin Whichcote -- the influential Platonist Puritan of Emmanuel College who was appointed Sunday Afternoon Lecturer in Trinity Church in 1636 and, later, Provost of King's College in 1644 -- More was indeed the first to undertake a detailed philosophical study of Neoplatonism. The young More's extraordinary enthusiasm for Platonist learning is evident from the fact he was the first to possess a copy of Plotinus at Cambridge. As he himself declares in his letter of December 27,1673 to Rev. E. Elys, "I bought one copy of Plotinus when I was a *Junior* Master for 16 shillings and I think I was the first that had either the luck or the courage to buy him."[17] Whichcote, who used to be considered the founder of the C bridge Platonist movement[18], was never deeply philosophical, and the incidental Platonism of his sermons can scarcely be compared to the elaborate Neoplatonic metaphysics that More reconstructed from the ancients in his *Psychodia Platonica*, which is, indeed, the first major philosophical document of the movement.[19]

The *Psychodia Platonica* was the literary culmination of More's spiritual efforts to achieve mystical enlightenment, "a more full Union with this Divine and Celestiall Principle, the inward flowing Wellspring of Life eternal." These efforts seem, indeed, to have been successful, for, as he reports, "When this inordinate Desire after the Knowledge of things was thus allay'd in me, and I aspir'd after nothing but this sole Purity and Simplicity of Mind, there shone upon me daily a greater Assurance than ever I could have expected, even of those things which before I had greatest Desire to know. Insomuch that within a few years, I was got into a most Joyous and

---

17 More, *Letters on Several Subjects*, London, 1694, p. 27.

18 See J. D. Roberts' book on Whichcote, *From Puritanism to Platonism in Seventeenth Century England*, The Hague: Martinus Nijhoff, 1968.

19 See C. A. Staudenbaur's convincing refutation of Robert's championing of Whichcote as the father of the Cambridge Platonists in his review article ,"Platonism, Theosophy and Immaterialism: Recent views of the Cambridge Platonists," *JHI*, (1974), 157-63.

Lucid State of Mind, and such plainly as is ineffable."[20]This
state of intellectual radiance he immediately recorded in a short
poem called Εὐπορία (which answered an earlier poem
expressing his spiritual perplexity, called Ἀπορία) However,
the first major fruit of his Neoplatonic enlightenment was the
long poem called 'Psychozoia, or the Life of the Soul,' which he
composed in 1640, probably while he was a non-regent M.A. at
the the college[21]and before he was elected Fellow and Tutor of
Christ's -- a position he occupied for the rest of his life.[22] Later
followed companion pieces, 'Psychathanasia, or the Immortality
of the Soul,' 'Antipsychopannychia, or the confutation of the
Sleep of the Soul', and 'Antimonopsychia, containing a
confutation of the unity of Souls' which, together with
'Psychozoia', were published as Ψυχοδία Platonica: or a
Platonicall Song of the Soul in 1642. Four years later, under
the impulse of his discovery of Cartesian philosophy, he wrote
a new poem called Democritus Platonissans, or an essay upon
the Infinity of Worlds out of Platonick principles. He appended
this to 'Psychathanasia' in his second edition of A Platonick
Song of the Soul (published in his Philosophicall Poems of 1647)
along with an appendix to 'Antipsychopannychia' on 'The
Praexistency of the Soul.'

The enthusiasm with which More greeted Descartes'
philosophical principles is evident in the letters he wrote to
Descartes between December 1648 and October 1649 as well

---

20 Ward, op. cit., p. 67.

21 See C. C. Brown, "Henry More's 'Deep retirement': New material on
the early years of the Cambridge Platonist," RES, (NS) xx,(1969) 445-54.

22 Ward, in his Life, declares that More was so devoted to "Contemplation
and Solitude that he turned down every preferment offered to him
including the Deanery of Christchurch, the Provostship of Dublin College
with the Deanery of St. Patrick's, two Bishoprics, and even the Mastership
of Christ's College, Cambridge (Ward,op. cit., Ch. 4). More was fortunate in
inheriting considerable property on the death of his father (cf. Alexander
More's will, proved 23 April, 1649, in Consistory Court Lincoln, 1649, fol.
236). It is with reason, therefore, that he says in his Epistle Dedicatory to
Lady Conway in An Antidote against Atheism: "For the best result of Riches, I
mean in reference to our selves, is, that finding ourselves already well provided
for, we may be fully Masters of our own time" (Sig. A3).

as in most of the philosophical works he published in the two decades after the poems of 1647.[23] However, even in the letter, More is careful to indicate the points on which he differed from the French philosopher, such as the latter's restriction of extension to matter and his denial of souls to beasts. So that, although More benefitted greatly from his exposure to the discipline of the Cartesian system -- reflected, chiefly in the axiomatic method of demonstration adopted in *An Antidote against Atheisme* (1653) and *The Immortality of the Soul* (1659) -- it is not surprising that his increasingly religious concerns after 1660 and the dangers posed by the rise of several atheistic Cartesian philosophers on the continent[24] led him to turn against his former idol in his final philosophical treatise of 1671, *Enchiridion Metaphysicum*, where the Cartesians are mocked as 'Nullibists.'[25]

Apart from his correspondence with Descartes, More's involvement in contemporary intellectual controversies is reflected in his attacks on Thomas Vaughan's theurgic treatises, *Anthroposophia Theomagica* and *Anima magica abscondita* (1650). Vaughan, twin brother of the poet Henry Vaughan, was a Rosicrucian, and More considered his magical mysticism an enthusiastic distortion of Platonism. More was angered, too, by Vaughan's criticism of Descartes in these works since he himself was still an ardent admirer of the French philosopher. Further, Vaughan' s claim that he was a Platonist seemed to More a threat to his own reputation since

---

23 See *Epistolae Quatuor ad Renatum Descartes* in *A Collection of Several Philosophical Writings of Dr. Henry More*, London, 1662.

24 More may have had in mind, particularly, such Cartesians works as Lambert van Velthuysen's, *Tractatus de Initiis Primae Philosophiae* (1664), Louis de la Forge's *Tractatus de Mente Humana* (1669), and Lodewijk Meyer's *Philosophia S. Scripturae interpres Exercitatio paradoxa* (1666), and Adriaan Koerbagh's *Een Bloemhof van allerley lieflikheyd sonder verdriet* (1668), which exhibited increasing degrees of atheism. (see A. Gabbey "Philosophia Cartesiana Triumphata:Henry More (1646-1671)" in *Problems of Cartesianism*, ed. T. M. Lennon, J. M. Nichols, J. W. Davis, Kingston: McGill-Queen's Univ. Press, 1982, pp. 239ff.).

25 The term 'nullibists' refers to the Cartesian denial of extension to *res cogitans* and the consequent denial of place to it.

he was, at that time, the most important Platonist philosopher in England and was liable to be linked with Vaughan; for, as he said, there being "nobody else besides us two dealing with these kinds of notions, men might yoke me with so disordered a companion as yourself."[26] More's first attack on Vaughan, *Observations upon Anthroposophia Theomagica* and *Anima Magica Abscondita*, (1650) under the pseudonym 'Alazonomastix' (Vaughan had called himself 'Eugenius Philalethes') was answered by Vaughan in *The man-mouse taken in a Trap* (1650). More replied to this in *The Second Lash of Alazonomastix* (1651), and Vaughan retaliated scurrilously with *The Second Wash; or The Moor Scour'd Again* (1651). More refused to answer this work and thereby brought the quarrel to a close. However, his rationalist disdain for the whole phenomenon of religious "Fantastry and Enthusiasme" was so great that he decided to republish his two tracts against Vaughan, along with an extended discussion of the subject which he called *Enthusiasmus Triumphatus*, in 1656.

"Enthusiasm" was not the only danger that More had to combat. While the Platonist movement was growing in Christ's College with the arrival of George Rust[27] in 1649 and Ralph Cudworth as Master of Christ's in 1654, there developed a strong opposition to the new 'Latitude men' as they were derisively called, from orthodox divines. More was "rayl'd at and bluster'd against for an Heretick,"[28] and in December 1665 Ralph Widdrington (also of Christ's) even petitioned the Archbishop against the college as "a seminary of Heretics."[29] The rational theology of More and his advocacy of religious toleration rather than dogmatism in *An Explanation of the Grand Mystery of Godliness* (1660) provoked an angry response from Joseph Beaumont, Master of Peterhouse and author of

---

26 More, *The Second Book of Alazonomastix*, Cambridge, 1651, p. 35.

27 Rust was a disciple of More and author of *A Letter of Resolution Concerning Origen and the Chief of His Opinions* (London,1661) and *A Discourse of Truth* (London, 1682).

28 More, letter to Lady Conway, December 31,1663,in M.H.Nicolson, ed., *Conway Letters*,(New Haven:Yale Univ. Press,1930) No.141,p. 220.

29 See More, letter to Lady Conway, June 29, 1665, *Conway Letters*, No.161, p. 242.

Psyche (1668), in a set of 'Objections' which he privately communicated to More. More defended himself in *The Apology of Dr.Henry More* (1664) in which he insisted that "there is no real clashing at all betwixt any genuine spirit of Christianity and what true Philosophy and right Reason does determine or allow." Beaumont replied with *Some Observations upon the Apologie of Dr.Henry More* (1665) which, however, as Grosart puts it, "never gets at More's meaning, and More crushes him ... in his iron grasp and strangely piercing though mystical logic."[30]

Most of More's writings after 1660 were predominantly theological and dealt mostly with Scriptural and Apocalyptic exegesis, such as *An Exposition of the seven Epistles to the seven Churches* (1669), *Apocalypsis Apocalypseos* (1680), and *Paralipomena Prophetica* (1685), or anti-papist polemics such as *A Modest Enquiry into the Mystery of Iniquity* (1664), and *An Antidote against Idolatry* (1672-73). His translation of his philosophical works into Latin, *Opera Omnia*(1675-79), also contains several scholia of a Christian Cabalist nature. This does not mean that he abandoned all interest in philosophical issues in his later works. In the *Divine Dialogues* (1668), he elegantly united science, philosophy, and theology in a series of Platonic dialogues, while the *Enchiridion Metaphysicum* (1671) was a renewed exposition of his anti-mechanistic system. His polemical writings of this period included the *Philosophiae Teutonicae Censura* against Jacob Boehme (written in 1670 and published in the *Opera Omnia*), and the *Epistola altera ad V. C.* and *Demonstrationum duarum Propositionum* against Spinoza (written between 1677-78 and published in the *Opera Omnia*). Apart from these, More also published a treatise of morality, *Enchiridion Ethicum* (1668), which is one of his finest works.

Although most of his works were written at Cambridge, his intellectual life gained considerable extension through his frequent visits to Ragley Hall in Warwickshire, the seat of the Conways. Lady Anne Conway (1631-1689) was the sister of one of his pupils, John Finch (1626-1682) and, ever since her first acquaintance with More, she remained an ardent student

---

30 A.B. Grosart, *The Complete Poems of Joseph Beaumont*,Edinburgh:1880, rpt. N.Y.: AMS Press, 1967, I:xxxii.

of his, and a devoted friend.[31] It was at her home that More
met the Cabalist Frans Mercurius van Helmont, son of the
alchemist Jan-Baptista van Helmont, and friend of Leibniz.
Through Helmont, More was introduced to the Christian
Cabalist, Baron Christian Knorr von Rosenroth, and
contributed articles to the latter's Latin translation of the
Zohar, *Kabbala Denudata* (Frankfurt, 1677). However, in spite
of his varied intellectual contacts, More's metaphysical system
was an original one and changed little in its essentials
throughout his philosophical career. The extraordinary wide-
ranging scope of his reading in both ancient and contemporary
philosophy and science only prompted interesting modulations
and elaborations from time to time of the principal theme of the
reality and primacy of spirit in the universe.

Despite the many controversies that attended his
philosophical career, More concluded his life with a sense of
fulfillment, and one of his last statements before his death was
"That he had with great sincerity offer'd what he had written
to the world" and "That he had spent all his time in the state of
those Words, *Quid Verum sit et quid Bonum quaero et rogo; et in
hoc* omnis sum.[32] More's death was peaceful and, according to
Ward, he expressed his sense of death to his close friend, Dr.
John Davies[33] who attended him constantly in his last days,
"in those first Words of that famous Sentence *of Tully's: 'O
Praeclarum illum Diem:' ... O mõst Blessed Day: When I shall
come to that Company of Divine Souls above, and shall depart
from this Sink and Rout below*"[34] More died on September 1,
1687, and was buried two day later, in the Chapel of Christ's
College, Cambridge.

---

31 The relationship between More and Lady Conway -- which resembled
Descartes' friendship with Princess Elizabeth of Bohemia -- has been
elaborately discussed in Nicolson's edition of the *Conway Letters* and A.
Gabbey's article, "Anne Conway et Henry More," *Archives de Philosophie*,
48 *(1977),379-404.*

32 Ward, *op.cit.*, p. 225.

33 John Davies, D. D. (Oxon.) 1678, was rector of Heydon, Essex.

34 Ward,*op. cit.*, p. 227.

The intellectual background of *The Immortality of the Soul.*

Although *The Immortality of the Soul* is the most complete exposition of More's philosophical system, it is anticipated in many of its themes by the five long poems that constitute his *A Platonick Song of the Soul*, (1647). More's earliest meditations on the soul and its immortality were inspired primarily by the desire to establish the spiritual reality of God and thus counter the scepticism of the atheists of the age. In this respect, his philosophical writings form a major contriction to the abundant apologetic literature of the sixteenth and seventeenth centuries which, ever since the injunction of the fifth Lateran Council (1512-17) under Pope Leo X to attempt demonstrations of the existence of God and of the immortality of the soul, sought to counter the rise of atheism amongst those imbued with Epicurean learning and the new science. The first of the poems of the *Platonick Song of the Soul* (or *Psychodia Platonica*, as I shall call it, for convenience, after the title of the first edition), 'Psychozoia,' moves from a macrocosmic to a microcosmic representation of the soul, the first part detailing the metaphysical movements of Psyche, the World Soul, and the second describing the spiritual progress of an individual human soul, Mnemon. The allegorical form of 'Psychozoia' was derived from Spenser's *Faerie Queene* (1590-1609), but More's hero, Mnemon, is of a loftier spirituality than even the Red Cross Kight and attains a state of mystical union with God, Theoprepy, whereas the Red Cross Kight is allowed only a glimpse of the City of God in *The Faerie Queen*, X, 55-67. This difference is due mainly to the Neoplatonist cast of More's mind, which, in fact, tired so easily of earthly adventures that, after 'Psychozoia,' he abandoned the Spenserian allegorical method, and expounded philosophical concepts in discursive verse in the next four poems of his *Psychodia Platonica*.

C. A. Staudenbaur has shown that the structure of More's *Psychodia Platonica* is to a large extent derived from Ficino's *Theologia Platonica de immortalitate animorum.*[35] While this may be true of parts of Psycathanasia, the contents of More's

---

35 See C. A. Staudenbaur, "Galileo, Ficino, and Henry More's Psychathanasia," *JHI*, 29 (1968), 567-578.

poems are not exactly the same as Ficino's, More having
formulated his notion of Psyche and the individual spirit from
the more ancient sources of the Chaldean oracles, Hermes Tris-
megestus, Plotinus and the Alexandrian Neoplatonists, as well
as from later Platonists like Psellus and Ficino.[36] Another
poetic precedent closer to home that has been little noted by
critics is Sir John Davies' *Nosce Teipsum* (1599, 4th ed. 1622),
whose second elegy treats 'Of the souls of man, and the
immortalitie thereof.'[37] Davies, like More, insists that "[The
Soule] *is a substance* , and a reall thing," (273) which is distinct
from the body which "yet she *survives , although the Bodie dies*"
(272).[38] He proves the separate reality of the soul by
theoretical arguments such as the independence of the soul in
its peculiar acts of ratiocination and judgement. Unlike More,
however, Davies believes that the soul is created individually in
every man (the 'Creationist' hypothesis). He even specifically
denies the theory that More was to maintain about the origin of
souls.[39]

> *Then neither* from eternitie before,
> Nor from the time when *Times* first point begun
> Made he all *Soules*, which now he keeps in store
> Some in the Moone, and others in the Sunne
>
> (ll. 593-6)

since it comes dangerously close to the theory of
metempsychosis:

---

36 cf. A. Jacob, "Henry More's *Psychodia Platonica* and its relationship to
Marsilio Ficino's *Theologia Platonica*," *JHI*, 46, No. 4 (1985), pp. 503-22.

37 It is not my intention in this section to suggest possible influences on
More's work so much as to give the reader an overview of the major 17th
century treatises on the immortality of the soul before More's own contribution to the subject. For a survey of the controversy about the immortality of the soul from the Middle Ages to the Renaissance, see G. T.
Buckley, *Atheism in the English Renaissance*, Chicago: Univ. of Chicago
Press, 1932, Ch. II.

38 All quotations from Davies are from *The Poems of Sir John Davies*, ed.R.
Krueger, Oxford: O.U.P., 1975.

39 cf. 'The Praeexistency of the Soul,'95.

Nor did he first a certain number make,
Infusing part in *beasts*, and part in *men*,
And, as unwilling farther paines to take,
Would made no more then those he formed then:

So that the widow *Soule*, her *body* dying,
Unto the next borne *body* married was
And so by often chaunging and supplying,
Mens *soules* to *beasts*, and beasts to men did passe:

(ll. 601-8)

Davies' explanation of the reason why the soul is infused into the body by God shows him to be one of the typical anthropocentric Renaissance Platonists such as Ficino and Mirandola:

This substance, and this *spirit*, of Gods owne making
Is in the bodie plac't, and planted here,
"That both of God, and of the world partaking,
"Of all that is, man might the image beare.

God first made Angels bodilesse, pure, minds;
Then other things, which mindlesse bodies bee;
Last he made Man, th' *Horizon* twixt both kinds,
In Whom we do the worlds abridgement see.

(ll. 877-84)

The particular manner in which the union of soul and body is effected is illustrated through the characteristic Neoplatonist metaphor of light

But as the faire, and cheerefull *morning light*,
Doth here, and there, her silver beames impart,
And in an instant doth her self unite
To the transparent Aire, in all and part:

So doth the piercing *Soule* the bodie fill:.
Being all in all, and all in part diffus'd,
Indivisible, incorruptible still,
Not forc't encountred, troubled or confus'd.

(ll. 909-12, 917-20)

The diversity of the soul's phenomenal effects, too, is explained with the Neoplatonist analogy of the sun:.

> And as the Sunne *above* the light doth bring
> Though we behold it in the Aire below,
> So from th' eternall light the *Soule* doth spring,
> Though in the bodie she her powers do show
>
> *But as* this worlds *Sunne* doth effects beget
> Diverse, in divers places every day,
> Here *Autumnes* temperature, there *Summers* heate,
> Here flowrie *Spring-tide* and there *Winter* gray.
> (ll. 921-28)

Davies divides the powers of the soul within the body into three main sorts, the vegetative or quickening powers, the powers of sense, and the intellective powers. The first corresponds to More's 'plastic' faculty, the second includes the five senses and imagination, or the common sense, as well as phantasy, sensative memory ,the emotions, and motions, vital and local. The intellectual powers are wit (reason and understanding, opinion and judgement) and will.

The arguments that Davies offers for the soul's immortality are entirely theoretical, such as its desire for knowledge, its motions "of both will and wit," which lead it to the eternal God, its contempt of bodily death, and the universal thought of immortality amongst men even those who doubt it:

> *And though* some impious wits do questions move
> And doubt if *Soules* immortal be or no
> That *doubt* then immortalitie doth prove
> Because they seeme immortall things to know.
> (ll. 1521-4)

Davies clinches his arguments for the soul's immortality by declaring that the soul is incorruptible and indestructible, since no material or temporal agents might affect her spiritual nature, and her divine cause, God, will never cease to exist.

Like most other works of this kind, the last part of *Nosce Teipsum* answers objections to the immortality of the soul. The apparent evidence of the soul's degeneration in senility and insanity Davies counters by attributing this change to the clouding of the brain by humours of *"Phrensie"* which "so disturbes, and blots the formes of things"(1.1650). But the soul itself is left intact, and once the humours are purged, "Then shall the *wit*, which never had disease, Discourse, and Judge, discreetly as it ought" (ll.1659-60). In answering the next objection, that the soul is impotent after death since it has no more organs to operate with, Davies reiterates the soul's independence of the body in its higher activities of judgement and choice. The soul's efficiency is, in fact, heightened after its release from the body, and Davies describes the perfect knowledge of the disembodied soul in a manner quite similar to More's at the end of 'The Praeexistency of the Soul':[40]

> So when the *Soule* is borne (for death is nought
> But the *Soules* birth, and so we should it call)
> Ten thousand things she sees beyond her thought,
> And in an unknowne manner knowes them all.
>
> Then doth she see by Spectacles no more,
> She heares not by report of double spies
> Her selfe in instants doth all things explore,
> For each thing present, and before her lyes.
> (ll. 1773-80)

The next objection, too, is one discussed by More in his *Immortality of the Soul*,[41] namely, the fact that souls do not return to bring us news of the other world. To this Davies replies;

> The *Soule* hath here on earth no more to do,

---

40 cf. 'The Praeexistency of the Soul,' 102:

> ... But when she's gone from hence,
> Like naked lamp she is one shining sphear.
> And round about has perfect cognoscence
> Whatever in her Horizon doth appear:
> She is one Orb of sense all eye all airy ear.

41 cf. *The Immortality of the Soul*, Bk. III, Ch. 15.

> Then we have businesse in our mothers wombe;
> What child doth covet to returne thereto?
> Although all children first from thence do come.
>
> (ll. 1789-92)

To the last objection, that the rewards and punishments of heaven and hell are merely fictitious, Davies simply replies that it is a common notion amongst all mankind and

> ... *how* can that be false which every tong
> Of every mortall man affirms for true;
> Which truth hath in all ages been so strong,
> As lodestone-line, all harts it ever drew.
>
> (ll. 1825-28)

Davies concludes his poem with a reminder of the soul's three essential powers and, since the first, the vegetative, is exercised in the womb, the second, the sensitive, in the world, and the third, the rational, if properly directed, in the company of God, it is imperative that human beings concentrate their attention on overcoming the hindrances of the flesh and strive to realize the divinity of the rational soul.

*

Most of the basic issues of Davies' poem reappear, with greater elaboration, in More's song of the soul. More's first poem, 'Psychozoia' begins on a more cosmic level than Davies', with an account (Bk I, and Bk II, Stanzas 1-23) of the various phases of the world-soul, Psyche, the third of the Plotinian hypostases. Psyche is the daughter of Ahad or the One, and she is symbolically married to Aeon, the intelligible universe of forms, also begotten of Ahad. At her marriage she is vested with several veils that represent the multiplicity of the phenomenal world. These include Semele (intellectual imagination), Arachnea(the web of sense-perception) with her chief, Haphe, (touch), Physis (vegetative nature) Proteus and Idothea (the changeability of forms), Tasis (extension) and, finally, Hyle (matter). This is the basis of all differentiation:

> Upon this universall Ogdoas
> Is founded every particularment:

From this same universall Diapase
Each harmony is fram'd and sweet concent.[42]

(II,15)

This orb is the vital equivalent of the radiant sun, and the individual souls are its rays:

Now deem this universall Round alone,
And rayes no rayes but a first all-spred light,
And centrick all like one pellucid Sun;
A Sun that's free, not bound by Natures might,
That where he lists exerts his rayes outright,
Both when he lists, and what, and eke how long,
And then retracts so as he thinketh meet,
These rayes he that particular creature-throng;
Their number none can tell, but that all-making tongue.

(16)

The process by which Psyche is differentiated into individual creatures is described in Canto I, 41-47. Her garment of Nature is "all besprinkled with centrall spots" which are, as it were, impregnated with aetherial darts, and

... when the hot bright dart doth pierce these Knots,
Each one dispreads it self according to their lots.
When they dispread themselves, then gins to swell
Dame *Psyches* outward vest, as th'inward wind
Softly gives forth, full softly doth it well
Forth from the centrall spot; yet as confin'd
To certain shape, according to the mind
Of the first centre, not perfect cir'clar-wise
It shoots it self ...

(42-43)

This process is governed by the laws of "true Symmetry," except that the realization of the seminal forms contained in

---

42 All citations from the *Psychodia Platonica* are from *The Complete Poems of Dr. Henry More*, ed. A. B. Grosart, Edinburgh, 1878, rpt. N.Y.: AMS Press, 1967.

Psyche is hindered by "that old Hag that hight/ Foul Hyle mistresse of the miry strond" (44) who "From her foul eben-box, all tinctures staines." (45). It is interesting also to observe in More's description of Psyche's extension a prefiguration of More's peculiar notion of spirit developed in *The Immortality of the Soul*, Bk I, Chs. 2-7.

The rest of 'Psychozoia,' after Bk II, Stanza 23, is devoted to a narration of the life of individual souls and particularly of one, Mnemon, who is aided in his spiritual ascent by Simon, the Christian. More, however, resumes his discussion of the soul *per se* without its allegorical framework in his next poem, 'Psychathanasia.' He begins with a description of "the state of th' evermoving soul/ Whirling about upon her circling wheel;" (I, ii, 8).The soul's manifestation in the phenomenal realm as beast and plant is obviously flawed by their lack of higher intelligence, which is peculiar to man alone. Man is, besides, endued with the radiant force of "True Justice" (I, ii, 19),the supra-rational power which More otherwise called "divine sagacity" and John Smith, his fellow Cambridge Platonist, "divine irradiations."[43]It is this "*Deiform* intellective in man that gives him a sense of eternity (I, ii, 47).

In Canto iii More employs the symbolic device of a nymph appearing to him in a vision to explain to him the immortal nature of the "orb Unitive" from which emanate all other forms, intellectual, psychical, imaginative, sensitive, spermatical and quantitative. The limit of these emanations is marked by Hyle, which in Canto iv is described as mere potentiality. The union of weak souls to particular bodies is explained by the activity of the "Plastick might," which he was later to call the 'Spirit of Nature':[44]

> This is that strange form'd statue magicall
> That hovering souls unto it can allure
> When it's right fitted; down those spirits fall
> Like Eagle to her prey, and so endure
> While that low life is in good temperature.
>
> (II, i, 10)

---

43 cf. below p.xxxiv.

44 See *The Immortality of the Soul*, Bk. III, Chs. 12-13.

The stronger souls, however, resist this decline:

> Others disdain this so near unity,
> So farre they be from thinking they be born
> Of such low parentage, so base degree,
> And fleshes foul attraction they do scorn.
> They be th' outgoings of the *Eastern morn*,
> Alli'd unto th' eternall Deity,
>
> (II, i, 12)

More then emphasizes the distinctness of the soul from its body by insisting on the non-corporeality of spiritual substance and the difference between material and spiritual extention:

> Thus maugre all th' obmurmurings of sense
> We have found an essence incorporeall,
> A shifting centre with circumference
> But she not only sits in midst of all,
> But is also in a manner centrall
> In her outflowing lines. For the extension
> Of th' outshot rayes circumferentiall
> Be not gone from her by distrought distension,
> Her point is at each point of all that spread dimension
>
> (II, ii, 10)

The difficulty of a geometrical demonstration of this abstruse Plotinian idea is alleviated somewhat by the familiar Neoplatonic metaphor of light that precedes it:

> The term of latitude is breadthless line;
> A point the line doth manfully retrude
> From infinite processe; site doth confine
> This point: take site away it's straight a spark divine
>
> . . . .
>
> If yet you understand not, let the soul
> Which you suppose extended with this masse
> Be all contract and close together roll
> Into the centre of the hearts compasse:
> As the sunsbeams that by a concave glasse

Be strangely strengthned with their strait constraint
Into one point, that thence they stoutly passe,
First all before, then withouten restraint,
The high arch'd roof of heaven with smouldry smoke they taint.

But now that grosnesse, which we call the heart
Quite take away, and leave that spark alone
Without that sensible corporeall part
Of humane body: so when that is gone
One nimble point of life that's all at one
In its own self, doth wonderfully move,
Indispers'd, quick, close with self-union,
Hot, sparkling, active, mounting high above
In bignesse nought, in virtue like to thundring Jove.

(II, ii, 6-9)

More further distinguishes spirit from body by their different modes of perception:.

For see how little share hath guantite
In act of seeing, when we comprehend
The heavens vast compasse in our straitned eye
. . . .
. . . . . . So that if outward sense
In his low acts doth not at all depend
On quantity, how shall the common sense
That is farre more spirituall, depend from thence?

(II, ii, 27),

and by the spirit's unique quality of 'self-reduplication' which allows it to totally infuse the body:

... Therefore one spirit goes
Through all this bulk, not by extension
But by a totall *Self-reduplication*.

(II, ii, 33)

This feature of the soul also proves its absolute indivisibility.

The next canto adduces further evidences of the soul's independence of the body in its intuition of God (10), its natural desire for truth (17), its powers of intellectual abstraction (18), its innate mathematical idea of unity, which cannot be an extended entity, its powers of synthesis of contraries, and the marvellous range of its intellection from introspection to "Th'all comprehension of eternity" (23-28).

Book III begins with a review of the soul's three "essences," plantal, imaginative, and deiform. The second canto is more interesting in its discussion of the state of the soul before its entry into the body (1-8). The three theories he considers are 1. souls in a state of wakefulness drawn down by "a magick might" i.e. the plastic nature, or else dragged unconsciously in their sleep by fancy; 2. souls in a"tri-centrall" form, the highest centre being that of intellect, the next a dormant one, and the last that which tends earthwards, and 3. souls with one center but quite asleep until their lower faculty drives them to this earth. Though he is not able to decide on any one of these possibilities as representing the exact nature of the soul's pre-existence, he has no doubts of its ability to outlive the body. The soul's aspiration to God reveals that "her spring is God: thence doth she 'pend,/ Thence did she flow, thither again she's fled" (12). Like Davies, More points to the indivisibility and independence of the soul in its higher activities of intellect and will (23-42). Also, like Davies, More believes that "our Souls be counite/ With the worlds spright and body" (44),which is the *Anima Mundi*.

Although fancy perception and memory are really independent of the external world and are, rather, innate ideas that "Of old Gods hand did all forms write/ In humane Souls, which waken at the knock/ Of *Mundane* shapes" (45), the fact that the soul is partly allied to the "mundane spright" renders it liable to decay in old age and distemper. Fortunately, the soul is not totally identical with the world-soul, since the soul has a direct connection with "the *ever-live-Idees*, the lamping fire/ Of lasting *Intellect*" (50). Thus the human soul has the power of *"animadversion"* which the worldsoul is deprived of: "She knows that spright, that spright our soul can never know" (55). Especially in sleep or ecstasy, the soul is joined with her eternal ideas and the "spright of God." This state of illumination is contrasted to the deceptive knowledge provided by the senses.

The last two cantos of 'Psychathanasia' discuss the fallacy of the Ptolemaic theory of the universe as a particular proof of the fallibility of sense impressions. In doing so, More recovers the Neoplatonic notion of the sun as the cosmic image of God in

its brilliance, centrality and stability. This leads to a hymn to
God and His providential workings in the universe. More
considers, in this connection, the questions raised by sceptics
regarding, among other things, the duration of the world. He
resolutely declares that world was not existent *ab aeterno* since
that makes impossible any calculations whatsoever of time:

> For things that we conceive are infinite
> One th'other no'te surpasse in quantity
> So I have prov'd with clear convincing light,
> This world could never from infinity
> Been made. Certain deficiency
> Doth always follow evolution;
> Nought' s infinite but tight eternity,
> Close thrust into itself; extension
> That's infinite implies a contradiction.

(35)

He is willing to grant only that the world might have come into
being simultaneously with Nature and his a "long future" left
to exist before its final dissolution in "this worlds shining
conflagration."(37)

This view of the finitude of the world More reversed
entirely in 'Democritus Platonissans,' which he first published
in 1646. Hoping to furnish *"mens minds with variety of
apprehensions concerning the most weighty points of Philosophie
that they may not seem rashly to have settled in the truth, though
it be the truth,"* he resorts now to -- of all people -- the
materialistic philosophers, Epicurus, Democritus, and
Lucretius, in order that he may *"if justice may reach the dead,
do them the right as to shew that though they be hooted at, by the
rout of the learned, as men of monstrous conceits, they were either
very wise or exceeding fortunate to light on so probable and
specious an opinion, in which notwithstanding there is so much
difficulty and inconsistencie"* ('To the Reader'). He even forces
Descartes' view of a *mundus indefinitè extensus*[45] imply nothing
else but *extensus infinitè*.

---

45 cf. Descartes, *Principia*, II, 21.

The real reason for More's new belief in an infinity of worlds is his belief that God's plenitude must express itself infinitely. Matter is described here as the final degeneration of spirit "fixt, grosse by conspissation" (Stanza 13). The emanative virtue of spirit causes an instantaneous outflow of a "precious sweet Ethereall dew"(50) which "streight" is turned into an infinite matter and "matter infinite needs infinite worlds must give"(50). Thus there is infinite matter from eternity and,

> ... in each atom of the matter wide
> The total Deity doth entirely won,
> His infinite presence doth therein reside,
> And in this presence infinite powers do ever abide
>
> (69)

This matter, it must be noted, is not Hyle, which in 'Psychathanasia,' I, i, iv , 2, he had defined as "plain potentialitie." The underlying matter of the sensible world is due especially to Tasis (or, extension) which is the "reall cuspis of the Cone even infinitely multiplied and reiterated" (Note to 'Psychozoia,' II, 9). Since it is an "actuall centrality, though as low as next to nothing," it is given a place above Hyle -- which is nothing -- in his series of emanations in 'Psychozoia' II, 13. But his note ends with the piquant remark, "But what inconvenience is in *Tasis*, or the corporeall sensible nature, to spring from *Hyle*, or the scant capacity, or incompossibility of the creature" -- showing that the last two elements are inextricably bound to each other. The actual process of conversion of divine spirit into matter is explained in the very first stanzas where More describes the life that flows out of God as a light which in its last proection is "liquid fire" (or "aether", called also, by More,"Tasis"). Out of this is formed "each shining globe and clumperd mire/Of dimmer orbs," which constitute the

> ... knots of the universall stole
> Of sacred *Psyche*; which at first was fine,
> Pure, thin, and pervious till hid powers did pull
> Together in severall points and did encline
> The nearer parts in one clod to combine.
> Those centrall spirits that the parts did draw
> The measure of each globe did then define,

> Made things impenetrable here below,
> Gave colour, figure, motion, and each usuall law.
>
> (12)

The extension of matter in the universe is, however, not indivisibly total, as the spiritual extension of the higher forms is:

> But totall presence without all defect
> 'Longs only to that Trinity by right,
> *Ahad, Aeon, Psyche* with all graces deckt,
> Whose nature well this riddle will detect;
> A circle whose circumference no where
> Is circumscrib'd, whose Centre's each where set,
> But the low Cusp's a figure circular,
> Whose compasse is bound, but centre's every where.
>
> (8)

Material extension, on the other hand, is

> Onely a,Creaturall projection,
> Which flowing yet from God hath ever been,
> Fill'd the vast empty space with its large streem.
> But yet it is not totall every where
> As was even now by reason rightly seen;
> Wherefore not God, whose nature doth appear
> Entirely omnipresent, weigh'd with judgement clear
>
> (67)

The symbol of a cone constituted of a primary circle at its base with uncircumscribed circumference and a material cusp, also circular, but with limited compass -- both having spiritual centres that are ubiquitous -- is a bewildering one. But it is the closest More can get to a geometric representation of the emanation of a primal matter from God that is as manifest as God's infinite power and yet restricted in its pervasiveness on account of its material nature. At any rate, this is the material from which the various planets and stars are molded, and these infinite worlds will last as endlessly as God's eternal power will. This commitment to the endless duration of the universe also compels More to renounce his earlier view of the end of the world. Instead, he embraces now Origen's heretical theory of cycles of generation and destruction:[46]

> Ne ought we doubt how Nature may recover
> In her own ashes long time buried.
> For naught can e'er consume that centrall power
> Of hid spermatick life, which lies not dead
> In that rude heap, but safely covered,;
> And doth by secret force suck from above
> Sweet heavenly juice, and therewith nourished
> Till her just bulk, she doth her life emprove;
> Made mother of much children that about her move.
>
> (101)

In the next poem, 'Antipsychopannychia,' More reaffirms the immortality of the soul, by stressing the persistence of consciousness in the after-life. The intellect and will are not deprived of their power when the body perishes since they, unlike the senses and fancy, work independently of matter. He reinforces this fact by reminding us, through his cone image, of the contrary infinites of spirit and matter:

> Lo! Here's the figure of that mighty Cone
> From the strait Cuspsis to the wide-spread Base
> Which is even all in comprehension
> What's infinitely nothing here hath place;
> What's infinitely all things steddy stayes
> At the wide basis of this Cone inverse
> Yet its own essence doth it swiftly chace,
> Oretakes at once; so swiftly doth it pierce
> That motion here's no motion.
>
> (II, 9)

This image of the transformation of divine spirit into matter is used by More to highlight the solar brilliance of the base and the nocturnal darkness of the material cusp:

> Suppose the Sunne so much to mend his pace,
> That in a moment he did round the skie

---

46 See Origen, *De Principiis*, Bk. I, Ch. 6.

> The nimble Night how swiftly would he chace
> About the earth? so swift that scarce thine eye
> Could ought but light discern. But let him be
> So fast, that swiftnesse hath grown infinite
> In a pure point of time so must he flie
> Around this ball, and the vast shade of Night
> Quite swallow up, ever steddy stand in open sight
> (II, 10)

This analogy is designed to remind us of the need to remain steadfast within our divine selves and avoid diffusion in the sense world:

> Wherefore the soul cut off from lowly sense
> By harmlesse fate, farre greater liberty
> Must gain.
> (II,14)

The state of the soul after its liberation from the body is conditioned by the ideas it expresses in this life:

> The manner of her life on earth may cause
> Diversity of those eruptions.
> For will, desire, or custome so dispose
> The soul to such like figurations:
> (II, 25)

These ideas are formal extensions of the soul from its "centrall self-vitality" which render her 'omniform' and allow her to either expand to the Divine form in herself or constrict herself into the Infernal Night which is next to the nothingness of matter. If we guard against immersion in earthly life which awakens "th' *Idee*/ of innate darkness" (III, 46) in the soul, the soul will follow its natural inclination to the idea of God(which is "perfect *Unity*/ And therefore must all things more strongly bind" (III, 18). When it actually is united with God, the freedom it achieves is infinite:

> ... For there the faster she doth strive
> To tie her selfe, the greater liberty
> And freer welcome, brighter purity
> She finds, and more enlargement, joy and pleasure

O'er flowing, yet without satietie;
Sight without end, and love withouten measure
(III, 19)

The 'Praeexistency of the Soul' relates the adventures of
the soul before its entry into this earthly life in order to confirm
the possibility of the soul's post-mortem existence without its
bodily adjuncts. The invocation to Plotinus at the beginning of
the poem reveals More's firm commitment to Neoplatonist
philosophy, and the rest of the poem is iformed with notions
borrowed from other Neoplatonists such as Proclus and Psellus.
The process by which the individual souls already differentiated
from Psyche enter the various bodies is explained with the
theory of the soul' s three vehicles -- celestial, aerial, and
terrestrial -- which Proclus developed in his *Theologia
Platonica*,111,125 ff. The souls that await generation have a
choice of either the flery chariot which is "the Orb of pure quick
life and sense," (13) the light vehicle of air which is "more
grosse subject to grief and fear/ And most what soil'd with
bodily delight", (15) ,or earthly vehicles which "be but the souls
live sepulchres/ Where least of all she acts." More believes
that air is the medium from which all earthly bodies are
fabricated and to which they return (23-28):

Shew fitly how the preexistent soul
Inacts and enters bodies here below,
And then entire, unhurt, can leave this moul
And thence her airy vehicle can draw
In which by sense and motion they may know
Better then we what things transacted be
Upon the Earth; and when they list, may show
Themselves to friend or foe, their phantasie
Moulding their airy Orb to grosse consistency

(24)

This magical quality of the soul's aerial vehicle is substantiated
by More with the stock Renaissance examples of signatures
caused by the imagination as well as the strange physical
transformations   effected   by   vehement   dreams

(29-34).[47]Turning to Psellus for inspiration, next, More begins a detailed description of the six types of spirits and their various activities (35- 83) which he was to repeat with many of the same examples in his prose treatises, *An Antidote against Atheisme*(l653) and *The Immortality of the Soul* (1659). The rational religious purpose of More's interest in spiritualism is evident in his Preface to the collected edition of Philosophical Poems of 1647 where he declares:.

> I have also added another [Canto] of the Praeexistency of the Soul, where I have set out the nature of Spirits, and given an account of Apparitions and Witch-craft, very answerable I conceive to experience and story, united to that task by the frequent discoveries of this very Age. Which if they were publickly recorded, and that course continued in every Parish, it would prove one of the best Antidotes against that earthly and cold disease of Sadducisme and Atheisme, which may easily grow upon us if not prevented, to the hazard of all Religion, and the best kinds of Philosophy.[48]

Interestingly, against those who are satisfied with nothing less than "a Demonstration," More defends himself by citing the failure of other philosophers in this regard: "For [their] satisfaction, *Mounsieur des Chartes* hath attempted bravely, but yet methinks on this side of mathematicall evidence. He and that learned Knight our own Countryman[i.e. Sir Kenelm Digby] had done a great deal more if they had promised lesse. So high confidence might become the heat and scheme of Poetry much better then sober Philosophy"[49]

All the stories "of Ghosts, of Goblins, and drad sorcery" that he quotes are provided, he says, "to prove that souls dismist/ From these grosse bodies may be cloth'd in air,/ Scape free (although they did not praeexist)/ And in these airy orbs

---

47 cf. *The Immortality of the Soul* Bk. III Ch. 6-7, as well as my Commentary Notes to these sections.

48 Grosart, *op. cit.,* p. 6.

49 *Ibid.*p.7.

feel,see,and hear"(84). Although he is still as diffident of the
theory of pre-existence as he was in 'Psychathanasia'(III, ii,
1-9), he offers it here as a strong rational possibility. The
alternative theories of the origin of souls, namely creationism
and traducianism, he dismisses since the one imagines the soul
to be of the same substance as the seed, and the other sullies
the purity of God in abominable acts of lust. More posits his
own theory of emanation as the most sensible explanation of
the movements of the soul:

> By flowing forth from that eternall store
> Of lives and souls ycleep'd the World of life.
> Which was, and shall endure for evermore.
> Hence done all bodies vitall fire derive
> And matter never lost catch life and still revive
>
> (95)

Although he is not quite sure what impels souls to descend so
low from their original habitation in "this immense orb of vast
vitality" and vaguely attributes this fall to "choice or Nemesis,"
he believes that

> A praeexistency of souls entire
> And due Returns in courses circular,
> This course all difficulties with ease away would bear
>
> (98)

Our oblivion of our pre-natal existence is easily explained by
the fact that, even in this life, "fierce disease/ Can so empair
the strongest memory" (100). At any rate, we can be sure that
the soul, liberated from the body, will retain memory of this
life, since, much like Davies' disembodied soul,

> Lie naked lamp she is one shining sphear.
> And round about has perfect cognoscence
> Whatere in her Horizon doth appear,;
> She is one Orb of sense, all eye, all airy ear.
>
> (102)

A point raised in passing towards the end of 'The
Praeexistency of the Soul' that "Each where this Orb of life's
with every soul;/ Which doth imply the souls ubiquity" (97)

might lead us to wonder if More's philosophy is not very much
akin to an Averrostic one, which maintains that there is but
one Soul in the universe "though many seem in show." More's
suggestion that there might well be "a praeexistency of souls
entire" is an indication that he believed in a real multiplicity of
souls that exist as such, even before their various incarnations.
But since he has not been very forthright in his doctrine of pre-
existency, he attempts to absolve himself of any suspicion of
Averroism in his last poem, 'Antimonopsychia.' The first proof
of the marked differentiation of souls is the fact of individual
ratiocination, which cannot exist if there be but one soul. For,
forms, which are the source of all knowledge, will then be
unique, and if one man at any mcment withdraws from the
idea of, say, fire, that form will be lost to all men at that
moment, and no one else can think of fire. Instead, More
insists that God creates a plurality of souls and that every
created soul is "indew'd/ with a self-centrall essence which from
[God's]/ Doth issue forth, with proper raies embew'd"(20). This
essence is "deiform" and informed with a natural desire to
reunite with its source:

> And deep desire is the deepest act
> The most profound and centrall energie,
> The very selfnesse of the soul, which backt
> With piercing might, she breaks out, forth doth flie
> From dark contracting death, and doth descry
> Herself unto herself. . .
>
> (36)

And this desire is indeed fulfilled once the soul is free of her
dangerous attachment to the body:

> So though the soul, the time she doth advert
> The bodies passions takes her self to die
> Yet death now finish'd, she can well convert
> Herself to other thoughts. And if the eye
> Of her adversion were fast fixt on high,
> In midst of death 'twere no more fear or pain,
> Then 'twas unto Elias to let flie
> His useless mantle to the Hebrew swain.
> While he rode up to heaven in a bright fiery wain
>
> (39).

*

The *Psychodia Platonica* was the only major work that More wrote in verse. Henceforth he devoted his energies to stricter exposition of his philosophy in prose. One of the reasons for this change may have been his admiration for the concision of Descartes' style. Also, the example of other contemporary treatises on the soul such as Sir Kenelm Digby's may have forced him to formulate his theories in the more philosophical mode of prose. However, apart from the greater precision of prose expression and a reduction of speculations regarding the cosmic career of Psyche, More's philosophy altered little in its fundamentals. In fact, the considerable independence of More's philosophical views is seen in his general indifference to the views of the soul held by other philosophers, both on the continent and in England, who had tried to establish the immortality of the soul by other means. Descartes had avoided any detailed discussion of the immortality of the soul in his *Meditationes* of 1641, even though he claimed to have written this work in an effort to subscribe to the recommendation of the Lateran Council ("Epistle to the deans and doctors"). His reasons for not elaborating the topic are stated in the synopses of the meditations. He believes that he will have already achieved a convenient proof of the soul's immortality if he can show that the soul is a substance distinct from the body, which he has indeed proved by the end of the sixth meditation. In this meditation he has also demonstrated that the soul is indivisible whereas the body is divisible. He declares that these proofs of the special nature of the soul are all he is willing to undertake since it would require a total explanation of physics to be more definite in his argument. This explanation would entail a demonstration of the manner in which substances created by God could be by their nature incorruptible, even if God could reduce them to nothingness. Hence it must be shown that matter is a primal substance that never perishes and, also, that the soul never changes like the extended body, even though it, too, is a substance. But these are subjects not appropriate to geometrical demonstration.

More, however, was little deterred by the reasoning of
Descartes with regard to the difficulty of establishing the soul's
immortality, and it may be argued that *Democritus Platonissans*
(1646) was an answer to Descartes' reticence. Even the
publication of 'Psychathanasia' and the other poems together in
1647 may have been inspired by a desire to prove superior to
the problem faced by the French philosopher. Though, More
may have also had in mind the other work published in France
on the soul, Sir Kenelm Digby's *Two Treatises* (1644), for its
second treatise dealt with 'The nature of mans soule ... in way
of discovery, of the immortality of reasonable soules.' Digby's
adherence to the Aristotelian view of the soul as the form of the
body led to some contradictions such as the theory that the
soul, though a substance, is in no place or time once separated
from the body: "her activity requireth no application to place
or time; but she is, of her selfe, mistresse of both,
comprehending all quantity whatsoever, in an indivisible
apprehension; and ranking all the partes of motion, in their
complete order; and knowing at once, what is to happen in
every one of them" (Ch XI). This impersonal immortality of the
rational soul is, however, difficult to reconcile with Digby's
belief in the persistence of individual memory in the after-life,
since memory, according to Aristotle, depends on the
phantasms produced by sense-perceptions. Digby is forced to
become quasi-Platonist in this case and admit that the soul
"worketh by much more, then what hath any actuall
correspondence in the fansie and that all thinges are united to
her by the force of *Being*: from which last, it followeth that all
thinges she knoweth, are *her selfe*, and she,*is, all that she
knoweth:* wherefore, if she keepeth *her selfe* and her owne
Being, she must needs keepe the knowledge of all that she
knew in this world" (Ch X). However, the liberated soul in
Digby's philosophy, unlike the liberated soul of the Platonists,
is absolutely unchanging in its post-mortem condition since
immortal reason can hardly alter. This means that "there can
be no change made in her, after the first instant of her parting
from her body; but, what happinesse or misery betideth her in
that instant continueth with her or all eternity" (Ch XI). Such
a harsh doctrine of eternal torment could scarcely have been
agreeable to an Origenist like More.

More elaborate, though less original a discussion of the soul's immortality was that of the Gassendist, Walter Charleton, in his dialogue, *The Immortality of the Human Soul* (1647). Charleton, through the person of Athanasius, refutes Lucretius' division of the soul into *Animus* and *Anima* and maintains that there is only one soul. Like More, Charleton is undeterred by the difficulty of producing geometrical demonstrations of the soul's immortality, and, spurred by the Lateran Council, he attempts to prove it analytically or *a priori*. The incorporeality of the soul he establishes in the usual way by emphasizing the soul's higher functions of volition and intellection as well as moral phenomena such as the universal desire of immortality and the divine justice that must be fulfilled in the after-life. He answers, too, the familiar objections about the apparent decay of the soul in old age and distemper. His explanation of the diffusion of the soul throughout the body is more interesting. He seems to approach More's conception of spiritual extension when he declares that this diffusion is "not by extension of bulk, but by Reduplication (as the Schools speak) by *position of the same Entity in each part of the body*" (Dialogue 2). The example he gives of such diffusion, however, is the scholastic favorite of "*intentional species* or *visible Image* Which all men allow to be diffused through the whole medium or space, as that it is at the same time whole in every part of that space; because in what part soever of the space the eye of the spectatour be posited, the whole image is visible therein" *(Ibid.)* -- a theory which More, like Descartes, repudiated. The union of the incorporeal soul to the body is further illustrated by the analogy of Epicurus' doctrine of "an Eternal and Incorporeal Inanity, or space diffused through the world, and commixed with all Bodies or Concretions, which are yet dissoluble" *(Ibid.)* and by the *anima mundi* of Plato and Aristotle "that being diffused through all parts of the Universe, it associateth and mixeth itself with all things" *(Ibid.)*. Though Charleton resembles More in these explanations, he differs widely from him in identifying the medium through which this union is effected as the blood. Adducing the authority of Aristotle and Harvey, he maintains that the soul is first "enkindled" from the blood which transmits her "conserving and invigorating influence" into all parts of the body. The union which the blood effects between soul and body is not difficult to understand since the union of corporeal and incorporeal substance does not need mutual contact but merely "an *Intimate Praesence*, which is yet a kind of Contact" *(Ibid.)*.

The most Neoplatonist of all the treatises on the immortality of the soul that preceded More's was that of More's fellow Cambridge divine, John Smith, in 'A discourse demonstrating the immortality of the Soul'(edited by John Worthington in *Select Discourses*,1660).[50] Smith begins by declaring that the immortality of the soul does not need any demonstration but might be assumed "as a Principle or *Postulatum*" from the *consensus gentium* regarding it (Ch 2). Though Smith presents several rational arguments since he must please his skeptical opponents, he prefers to rely on the divine nature of the soul, above all, to prove its immortality. The state of illumination wherein the purified reason is irradiated by"the Light of divine goodness" Smith calls 'true Sanctity'(Ch 7).

Directed mainly against the Epicureans, Smith's short treatise relies heavily on Plotinus as well as Plato and the pre-Socratics. Smith's first argument for the soul' s immortality is, predictably, from its incorporeal nature and its control of sense, cognition, memory and foresight, which cannot be produced by a fortuitous concourse of atoms as the Epicureans believe. Similarly, spontaneous motion and the frequent conflict between reason and sensual appetites argue the separateness of the soul from the body. Mathematical notions are not dependent on matter but contained within the soul which expresses them by virtue of its peculiar extension and power of self-penetration: "The Soul can easily pyle the vastest number up together in her self, and be her own force sustain them all, and make them all couch together in the same space." Furthermore, this proves "how all that which we call *Body*

---

50 This discourse was probably written in 1658 or 1651 since it refers to Descartes as "a late sagacious philosopher." Descartes had died in Feb. 1658 and, according to R. A. Greene ('Introduction' to Nathaniel Culverwell, *An Elegant and Learned Discourse of the Light of Nature*, Toronto: Univ. of Toronto Press, 1971, p. xlix), Smith delivered the discourses collected by Worthington between 1651 and 1652, as sermons, while serving as dean and catechist of Queen's College.

rather issued forth by an infinite projection from some *Mind,* then that it should exalt it self into the nature of any Mental Being, and, as the *Platonists* and *Pythagoreans* have long since well observed, how our bodies should rather be in our Souls then our Souls in them" (Ch 5). Similarly, the innate ideas of moral, physical, and metaphysical sorts such as justice, wisdom, eternity, truth, etc., reveal the distinct nature of the soul.

In an appendix concerning Aristotle's notion of immortality, Smith points to the contradiction involved in Aristotle's assertion that the soul is an intelligible entity and that *"in those beings which are purely abstracted from matter, that which understands is the same with that which is understood"* at the same time as he insists that "the Understanding beholds all things in the glass of Phansie; and then questioning how our πρῶτα νοήματα or First principles of knowledge, should be *Phantasmes,* he grants *that they are not indeed phantasmes,* ἀλλ᾽ οὐκ ἄνευ φαντασμάτων, *but yet they are not without phantasmes*; which he thinks is enough to say, and so by his meer dictate, without any further discussion to solve that knot" (Ch 8).

The union of the soul to the body must, according to Smith, be intimate, or else the soul would never attend the body. Quoting Proclus and Heraclitus, he declares it must be "some subtile *vinculum* that knits and unites it to it in a more physical way, which *Proclus* sometimes calls πνευματικὸν ὄχημα τῆς ψυχῆς *a spiritual kind of vehicle*, whereby corporeal impressions are transferr'd to the mind, and the dictates and secrets of that are carried back again into the body to act and move it. *Heraclitus* wittingly glancing at these mutual aspects and entercourses calls them ἀμοιβὰς ἀναγκαίας ἐκ τῶν ἐναντίων the Responsals or Antiphons wherein each of them catcheth up the others part and keeps time with it; and so he tells us that there is ὁδὸς ἄνω καὶ κάτω, *a way that leads upwards and downwards* between the Soul and the body, whereby their affairs are made known to one another" (Ch 9). He agrees with "a late sagacious Philosopher," namely, Descartes,[51]who had localized the union of soul an body in "that part of the brain from whence all those

---

51 cf. Descartes, *Les Passions de L'Âme*, Arts. 12, 13.

nerves that conduct the animal spirits up and down the body take their first original" *(Ibid.)*. Like most Neoplatonists, Smith believes, too, that not only do the animal spirits maintain "a conspiration and consent of all its [the body's] own parts, but also it bears a like relation to other mundane bodies with which it is conversant, as being a part of the whole Universe" *(Ibid.)*.

We see in,Smith's little discourse a clear foreshadowing of More's enormous treatise on the same subject. But More came to his work with a much wider range of ideas about the soul, many of which he had already developed in his *Psychodia Platonica*. Especially provoked by the threats to religion posed by the materialist philosophy of Hobbes, whose major works had already been published by 1656,[52] More sought to quash, once and for all, the materialists' denial of a spiritual substance distinct from matter. In doing so, he considerably sophisticated the notions of spirit and of the soul that he had been developing since his *Psychodia Platonica*.

The context in which More first crystallised his original notions of spiritual extension and its peculiar virtue of "spissitude" was the correspondence with Descartes beginning in December 1648. Even in his first letter of 11 December, he points to impenetrability and penetrability as the distinguishing characteristics of matter and spirit, rather than extension, as Descartes had maintained:

> the difference between the divine nature and corporeal is clear, for the former can penetrate the latter, but the latter cannot penetrate itself.[53]

He further clarifies the special emanative quality of spiritual extension in his next letter to Descartes of 5 March 1649, where he declares that there is

---

52 These included *Leviathan*(1651), the 'Tripos'--*Human Nature*(1658), *De Corpore* (1658) and *Of Liberty and Necessity* (1654) -- and *Elements of Philosophy*(1656).

53 See *Epistolae Quatuor ad Renatum Descartes* in More, *A Collection*. The translations are mine.

> an infinite difference between the divine amplitude
> and the corporeal ... in that the former arises from
> the repetition in every part of the total and integral
> essence, while the latter from the external and
> immediate application of parts one against the other.

The same letter also points tentatively at the peculiar quality of "spissitude" that More definitely attributes to spirit in *The Immortality of the Soul:*

> Finally, since the incorporeal substance possesses
> such a wonderful virtue that by the mere application
> of itself without links, hooks, wedges or other
> instruments, it constricts, expands and divides
> matter, pushes it out, and at the same time draws it
> in, does it not seem probable that it can enter into
> itself, since it is obstructed by no impenetrability,
> and expand itself again, and do other similer things?

A more confident explanation of "spissitude" appears in his letter of 23 July 1649 where he declares:

> That something real can be confined (without any
> diminution of itself) within lesser or greater limits is
> confirmed by motion, from your own Principles
> [II,36]. For, according to your sometimes a greater,
> sometimes a lesser subject. Indeed I conceive with
> the same facility and clarity that there may be a
> substance which without any diminution of itself
> might dilate or contract itself, whether this is
> occasioned by itself or something else.

In his next major published work *Antidote against Atheisme*(1653), however he offers only a partial definition of spirit as -- as including the properties of "*Self-penetration, Self-motion, Self-contraction* and *Dilation*, and *Indivisibility*", to which he added the "power of *Penetrating, Moving,* and *Altering the Matter*" (Bk I, Ch 4, Sec 3). He does not elaborate his conception any further except for a general description of its workings in the body in Bk I, Ch II. However, in Chs. 3 and 10 of *An Appendix to the foregoing antidote* (1655), he discusses the mathematical validity of his definition of spirit in almost the same detail as in *The Immortality of the Soul*, Bk I, Ch 6:

> If by *Extension* be meant *Juxta-position of parts*, or
> placing of them one by another, as it is in *Matter*, I
> utterly deny that a *Spirit* is at all in this sense
> *extended*. But if you mean only a certain *Amplitude
> of presence*, that it can be at every part of so much
> *Matter* at once, I say it is *extended*, but that this kind
> of *Extension* does not imply any *divisibility* in the
> substance thus *extended*; for *Juxta-position* of parts,
> *Impenetrability* and *Divisibility* goe together, and
> therefore where the two former are wanting,
> *Extension* implyes not the Third.
> But when I speak of *Indivisibility*, that
> Imagination create not new troubles to her self, I
> mean not such an *Indivisibility* as is fancied in a
> Mathematical point; but as we conceive in a *Sphere
> of light* made from one lucid point or radiant Center.
> For that *Sphere* or *Orbe of light*, though it be in some
> sense *extended*, yet it is truly *indivisible*, supposing
> the *Center* such: For there is no means imaginable
> to discerp or separate any one ray of this *Orbe*, and
> keep it apart by it self disjoyned from the *Center*.(Ch
> 10, Sec 9)

Yet, despite these various prefigurations, none of More's
writings so far achieved the comprehensive scheme of *The
Immortality of the Soul*. For, in it, he succeeded in developing
not only an axiomatic demonstration of his emanational theory
of spiritual substance but also an inclusive intellectual system
of the universe, far more original and complete than that
presented by his Cambridge friend, Ralph Cudworth, in *The
True Intellectual System of the Universe*(1678). *The Immortality
of the Soul* was, in fact, the first major philosophical treatise
that attempted an adaptation of the metaphysics of the ancient
Neoplatonist philosophers to all the discoveries of modern
science, ranging from the physics and psychology of Descartes
to the natural science of Henri de Roy, Sennert, and Harvey,
and from the anatomical studies of Spiegel, Wharton, and
Bartholin to the alchemical theories of van Helmont the elder.

The composition and reception of
The Immortality of the Soul

The first reference to the composition of *The Immortality of the Soul* in the letters of More to Lady Conway[54] is in a letter dated April 27, (No. 89, p. 149). Nicolson conjectures that this letter may have been written in 1658, but is clearly misguided in her calculation. For one thing, More's reference to a recent illness in this letter is continued in a letter dated by him May 11, 1657 (No. 82, p. 143). The letter of April says: "I am much obliged for your kinde congratulating of my health, but I profess I have been, since my last, as sick as I was upon the seas in our voyage to France. Which was by riding a journey beyond my ordinary pace," and in the letter of May, 1657 he reports, "I am far better in health then I was, God be thanked but methinks it is exceeding hott weather here at Cambridge, far hotter then it was in France in June." The repeated references to his trip to France[55] find an echo in the 'Epistle Dedicatory of *The Immortality of the Soul* which indicates that "the first occasion of busying my thoughts upon this Subject" was "then when I had the honour and pleasure of reading *Des-Cartes* his *Passions* with your Lordship in the Garden of *Luxenburg*."[56] Besides, the letter of April 27 contains the first mention of the commencement of this treatise: This present world is so full of vexations and disturbances, that I am up to the hard eares in computing the certainty of that which is to come, severely demonstrating to my selfe in dry prose that the soul of man is immortale and that there are enjoyments attainable after this earth."

---

54 Edited by Marjorie Hope Nicolson in *Conway Letters*, New Haven: Yale Univ. Press, 1938.

55 More accompanied Lady Conway to France in May, 1656, where she expected to be 'trepanned' in order to be cured of her debilitating migraine. There they were joined by Lord Conway in July, and, though the operation was never carried out, the remainder of their sojourn in Paris was apparently a reposeful one (cf. Nicolson, op. cit., pp.117-118).

56 'The Epistle Dedicatory,' in *A Collection of Several Philosophical Writings of Dr. Henry More*, Sig. Ff6 .

In another letter dated February 8 which Nicolson rightly dates to 1658[57] (No. 84, p. 144) More reports on the progress of a "Discourse" he is working on "I have wrote so much already on the subject I am on, that if I had not been mistaken in my account, less then this had finish'd the whole Discourse, but I am just now come to the third book." Since More did not produce any large-scale work containing three books between *An Antidote against Atheisme*(1653) and *The Immortality of the Soul* (1659) the reference in this letter is surely to the present work. This confirms my judgement that the treatise was begun much earlier, in April 1657, since he has already written two-thirds of it by February 1658.

By March 1658, More had completed the work, and was busy transcribing it, as he indicates in his letter of March (No. 85, p. 145): "I have finish'd my Discourse, but shall be much troubled in reading of it over and getting of it transcrib'd. It will be at least a 3d part of the pains I tooke in writing of it," and April 5 (No. 86, p. 146): "The continuall Transcription of my Treatise is something tedious, and will not be finished till May." This book was not printed until March 1659 and it is with great relief that More declares in his letter of March 28 to Lady Conway (No. 95, p. 155):

> I have at length gott some copies to present your Ladiship, my old Lady Conway, and my Lord with all. I write not to him this time, because the book includes a letter to him. I have enclos'd one here to my lady your mother. I have sent Madame Clifton[58] also a book, that has nothing of mine written in the margin, though there be nothing in the pages but what is in some sort mine; if you will do me the favour to present it to her with my service. I wrote not to her because I thought the book would be as

---

57 The reference in this letter to 'Elphicke' whom More recommends as a servant to Lady Conway makes it certain that it was written in 1658 since Lady Conway's letter of April 9, 1658 to her husband says "Elficke came to me this afternoon, you cannot expect I shold give you any character of him as yet because I can have no knowledge of him in so short a time."
58 Lady Francis Clifton, sister of Lady Conway.

much if not more then she will have the patience to
read, which is the reason that I send Mr. Whitby
also with out a letter, but I hope my Lord will
recommend both Castellio and that copy I sent to Mr.
Whitby with a line or two of his. Every thing takes
away a mans moisture, and this is a very dry
starveling Spring. I used as much as I could to gett
these copies bound, and not with the best speed, for
the binding of them this new mode the preface looks
something duskishly by the breaking of them, but the
Treatise it self is very well.

In spite of the distressing personal circumstances which
attended the inception of the work[59] and the strain of
composing and transcribing such a long and complicated work,
More's spiritual ardour was unflagging, and in the same letter
he announces, "I am now wholly taken up with my Treatise of
Christian Religion, and I can not for my life study any thing
els, nor I think leave of till I have finish'd it."[60]
Ward, in his biography, reveals that although the
composition of his works was extremely painful ("Being deeply
once engag'd, he said to a friend, that when he got his Hands
out of the Fire, he would not very suddenly thrust them in
afresh"),[61]More wrote carefully and "had this Particular in his
Way, that what he did, must go usually as he first wrote it;
and he could not well make Changes in it. His First Draught,
he would say, must stand. And he was so Warm (as it should
seem) and in the midst of his Business at the time of his
composures, and carried them all on with so Even a hand; that
if anything slipt amiss unawares from him, or was omitted by
him, he could not afterwards correct it so easily, or supply it to

---

59 See his letter to Lady Conway, April 27 (cited above p.xxxix). His
worries included not only his own illness but also the anxiety caused by
relatives (particularly his nephew, Gabriel): "I am very full of perplexity
and vexation touching my young kindred, because Vertue, Witt and Health
will not meet in any of them, so far as I see."
60 This was *An Explanation of the Grand Mystery of Godliness*, published in
the following year.
61 Ward, *op. cit.*, p. 168.

his Mind." He could it, (as he said) but it seldom seem'd so savoury to him as the rest.' And indeed the very Course of his MSS[62] doth in a high Measure shew this; there being generally in all of them, English or Latin, a very even Thread, and much Clearness of writing as well as Clearness of Expression, throughout."[63] More said of his style writing (in a conversation with Ward) that "he affected nothing in writing but to represent his full mind, and to be understood." But Ward's comment on this remark is significant; "But certainly then he had a very Happy way of doing this; and a sort of natural Rhetorick, Elegance and Propriety in his Constitution."[64] For, More's prose is always vivid, and even the most abstract scientific or philosophical concepts are often reinforced by picturesque images drawn from human life and society. In the discussion of the seat of the soul in *The Immortality of the Soul*, for example, the absurdity of animal spirits possessing powers of cogitation is pointed to with a humorous illustration: "they having no means of *communicating* one with another, but justling one against another which is as much to the purpose, as if men should knock heads to communicate to each other conceits of Wit" (Bk II, Ch 6, sec 5), while More's final comment on the general inscrutability of the grand patterns of Providence in the universe is highlighted by the splendid metaphor of a dance:

> This is a small glance at the Mysteries of Providence, whose fetches are so large, and Circuits so immense, that they may very well seem utterly incomprehensible to the *Incredulous* and *Idiots*, who are exceeding prone to think that all things will ever be as they are, and desire they should be so; though it be as rude and irrational, as if one that comes into a *Ball* and is taken much with the first Dance he sees, would have none danced but that, or have them

---

62 According to M.F. Howard, the editor of Ward's biography of More, "The actual MSS of the Doctor, published or unpublished seem to have disappeared." (Ward, *op. cit.*, p. 241).

63 Ward,*op.cit.* p. 170.

64 *Ibid.*, p. 171.

move no further one from another then they did when
he first came into the room; whereas they are to
trace nearer one another, or further off, according to
the measures of the musick, and the law of the
Dance they are in. And the whole Matter of the
Universe, and all the parts thereof, are ever upon
Motion, and in such a Dance, as whose traces
backwards and forwards take a vast compass, and
what seems to have made the longest stand, must
again move, according to the modulations and
accents of the musick, that is indeed out of the
hearing of the acutest ears, but yet perceptible by
the purest Minds and the surest Wits (Bk III, Ch 19,
sec 7).

Apart from such frequent comparisons to familiar phenomena,
the texture of More's work is enriched by numerous allusions to
classical mythology and history. Even the plan of the work is
very imaginatively designed, beginning as it does with a bare
axiomatic definition of spirit and matter, and leading, through
an intricate study of man's psychology and his relation to the
universe, to a final Neoplatonic vision of the apotheosis of the
soul.

*

The reception of *The Immortality of the Soul* was
generally enthusiastic. One of the first to read the work was
Samuel Hartlib, the Comenian reformer and philanthropist,
and his letter of April 20, 1659 to John Worthington, a
colleague of More's at Cambridge, declares his appreciation of
the treatise as an "accurate comment made upon the
immortality of the Soul, the like I am verily persuaded hath
never been unfolden upon paper in any language whatsoever."
He expresses, too, his eagerness to spread interest in it: "I
have recommended that book to several people already, and
shall continue to do, whether any occasions be offered or not ...
I hope the Latin Translation will shortly follow with the other
Treatises of that divine soul."[65] Already in his letter of May 5,

Hartlib reports so success in his efforts: "By some lines here adjoined from Paris, you will see how I have begun to spread the fame of the Treatise concerning the Immortality of the Soul, on which some friends of mine have begun to make their observations..."[66]   That   the   book   was   not   easy   of understanding is clear from the fact that one of the friends to whom Hartlib had given a copy had begun to make observations upon the book, but was wary of addressing them to More before the appearance of More's next treatise of Christian religion. "For," as Hartlib tells Worthington in his letter of June 26, "it may be he thinks (and perhaps not impertinently) that both these Treatises being compared together, will give a mutual light to many passages which seem now obscure and very paradoxal."[67]

To others, the work seemed not sufficiently Christian and even atheistical. In Hartlib's letter to John Worthington, dated Feb 22, 1660, he quotes John Beale's apprehensions with regard to *The Immortality of the Soul:* "There [in an earlier letter to Hartlib] I shew'd, that Mr. More's Immortality could not involve Atheism, as some over sharply object. In a former which answered to yours of Jan 12, as respecting to your correspondent at Paris, I shew'd that on the other hand I was far from the opinion, that Mr. More's arguments were clear demonstrations, and in that I shew'd, that all our discourses of separate substances, first matter, or atoms, or purest air or spirit, and most of all when they fall upon God's incomprehensible attributes of immensity, eternity, etc., whether in the notions of Sir Kenelm Digby, or of Cartesians, of Arminians or Calvinians, are in my account so far from demonstrations and philosophical or theological aphorisms that I cannot acquit them from shallowness, presumption, and indeed prophanation."[68] This criticism of one of the early members of the Royal Society highlights the boldness of More's venture to give a rational and scientific account of spiritual truths when most people fought

---

65 *The Diary and Correspondence of Dr. John Worthington,* ed. James Crossley, Manchester; Chetham Society, 1847, p. 120 ff.
66 *Ibid.,*p.131.
67 *Ibid.,*p.136.
68 *Ibid.,*p.185.

shy of such demonstrations for either theological or scientific reasons.

The general interest of the work, however, seems to have been little affected by the religious scruples of the orthodox, and Worthington's letter of May 8, 1661, indicates the esteem in which More's philosophy was held amongst the learned: "He [More] is desired to reprint his former discourses viz. of Atheism, of the Immortality of the Soul, and Conjectura Cabbalistica on Genesis Ch 1, 2, 3, and to put them all into one folio; the bookseller[69] is urgent with him about it and that the poems may not be omitted."[70] Hartlib's heartfelt approval of this idea is recorded in two of his letters to Worthington, of May 14 and May 28: "I am glad that Mr. More intends to put his several Discourses into one Fol[io]. I wish other learned men would do the like ..."[71] Hartlib's enthusiasm for the propagation of More's phiiosophy is, in fact, so great that, on hearing that Descartes' royal friend, the Princess Elizabeth of Bohemia,was likely to marry Lord Craven, he writes to Worthington, "I wish she were in England, that she might marry Dr. More's Cartesian Notions which would beget a noble off-spring of many excellent and fruitful truths.[72] The efforts of Worthington and Hartlib to get More to republish his major works in a collected edition bore fruit in the *Collection of Several Philosophical Writings* of 1662 which contained all the works mentioned in Worthington's letter except the poems, which More considered in his maturity to be the extravagances of his youth and much inferior to his prose writings. Besides these, it included the *Appendix to the Said Antidote*, *Enthusiasmus Triumphatus* and his *Epistolae Quatuor ad Renatum Descartes* as well as the *Epistola ad V.C.* The satisfaction that the production of the collected edi tion gave him is evident in his letter of March 15, 1662 to Lady Conway (Nicolson, p. 198, No. 123):

---

69 This was William Morden who had published the 1659 edition of *The Immortality of the Soul.*

70 *Diary*, pp.305f.

71 *Ibid.*, p.314 (letter of May *28).*

72 *Ibid.*, p. 317.

I have been exceeding busy this great whyle, and now I will tell your Ladiship what it is about. I had granted Morden the leave of printing my *Antidote* with the *Appendix*, my *Enthusiasmus Triumphatus*, all my letters to Descartes with that to W.C., my *Treatise of the Immortality of the Soule*, and my *Conjectura Cabbalistica* in such a Folio as my *Mystery of Godliness*,[73] and therefore I took the opportunity to perfect the Treatises to greater exactness in severall thinges then before, especially my *Cabbala Philosophica*, where I have added ten chapters for a further defense thereof. One maine thing that I pleased my self in among the rest was that I had the opportunity, whenever I thought there might be the least occasion of offence (which my eyes discovered to be but very seldome) to alter thinges so as would be most passable and inoffensive. The [Impression?][74] is now almost finished, and I have almost made an end of my Generall Preface I intend to prefix to the whole volume. This edition has cost me a third part of the paines of writing the books, but I have completed all thinges so exquisitely to my minde that I would not for all the world but that I had had this opportunity of revising them, so fond am I of the fruits of my own minde, which yet I think I should not be, did I not hope they will be very serviceable to the world in their chiefest concernes.

*

More' s translation of his major works into Latin between 1675 and 1679 was designed to gain a wider, continental, audience for his religious philosophy.[75] The circle of Leibniz was certainly very interested in the work of the Cambridge

---

73 This appeared later in a collected edition of the theological works in 1708.

74 Nicolson's conjecture.

75 Apart from More's own translation of his works, *The Immortality of the*

Platonist, as is attested by the letters of Henri Justel to Leibniz dated Oct. 4, 1677: "Je suis bien aise que le traitté de l'ame de Henricus Morus soit en latin," and July 24, 1679: "Les oeuvres de Henricus Morus en latin sont imprimés. C'est un philosophe platonicien qui a ecrit bien des choses contre les Athees et libertins qui sont plus fortes que le livre de Mr. Huet."[76] But Leibniz himself, though generally in sympathy with the aims of the Cambridge metaphysicians, did not find it easy to accept More's substantialization of the soul. In his letter of June 22, 1715, to Rémond, he remarks, "M. Morus etoit Platonicien et Origeniste; mais il avoit de plaisantes opinions sur la nature de l'Ame, qu'on peut voir dans son livre de l'Immortalite de l'Ame, traduit de l'Anglois."[77] However, despite Leibniz's supercilious response, interest in More's principal philosophical treatise continued through the latter part of the seventeenth century and into the eighteenth.[78] Samuel Johnson' s conversation with in March, 1722 gives us an idea of the impression that it made on the staunch Anglican writer. When Boswell "ventured to lead him to the subject of our situation in a future state" and asked him if there were "any harm in our forming to ourselves conjectures as to the particulars of our happiness, though the

---

Soul was apparently translated into French by a certain M. Briot according to the note to the letter of Henri Justel to Leibniz, July 38, 1677 (in Leibniz, 'Allgemeine Politischer und Historischer Briefwechsel,' *Sämtliche Schriften und Briefe*, Reihe I, Bd. 2, Otto Reichl Verlag, Darmstadt, 1927, p. 287n). Besides this, two references in More's letters to Lady Conway, about a "translation of my Immortality of the Soul" (July 11, 1672) and "P. his epitome of my Immortality, etc." (Nov. 1, 1673) have led Marjorie Hope Nicolson to conjecture that "this seems to imply that Von Rosenroth translated More's Immortality of the Soul into German" (*Conway Letters*, p. 360n).

76 Leibniz, *op. cit.*, pp.297, 504.

77 Leibniz, *Die Philosophischen Schriften von G.W. Leibniz*, ed. C.J. Gerhardt, Berlin, 1887, vol. III, p. 646.

78 Ward (*op.cit.*, p. 177) reports that "for twenty years together, after the *Return* of King Charles the Second, the *Mystery of Godliness*, and Dr More 's other works, ruled all the Booksellers in London." In his unpublished second part of the life of More, he gives a detailed account of More's works. *The Immortality of the Soul* he describes as "a curious and a difficult work;

Scripture has said but very little on the subject," Johnson replied, "Sir, there is no harm. What philosophy suggests to us on that topick is probable. What Scripture tells us is certain. Dr. Henry More has carried it as far as philosophy can."[79]

---

and yet perhaps, if prejudice could be entirely removed, as rational as curious." ("Some account of Dr. More's Works," Christ's College MS, p. 133).

79 Boswell, *Life of Johnson*, London: O.U.P., 1953, p. 471.

Analysis of *The Immortality of the Soul*

The structure of the *The Immortality of the Soul* is extremely complex. The first chapter[80] presents the moral purpose of the treatise and the seven axioms of chapter 2 proclaim its rational methodology. The next three axioms of the second chapter and chapters 3-7 detail the distinctive characteristics of body and spirit focussing on the special virtues of spirit -- indiscerpibility, motion, penetration, and spissitude. Chapter 8 describes the four types of spirits -- God, the sole uncreated spirit, and the four species of created spirits -- angelic souls, human souls, brute souls, and the seminal forms. In chapters 9-10, More pauses to consider the objections of Hobbes to the existence of spirit and, having dismissed them, he goes on to give, in chapters 11-14, three proofs for the existence of spiritual substance -- from the absolute perfection of God, from the phenomenon of motion, and from the empirical evidence of apparitions.

The first three chapters of Book II continue the proofs of the existence of immaterial substance beginning with six axioms that rehearse the Hobbesian theory of perception as arising from matter in motion in order to expose the inadequacies of mechanism in explaining such higher human functions as ratiocination, memory, imagination, spontaneous motion, and free will. Having established the need of an incorporeal soul to carry out these functions, More attempts in chapters 4-11, to locate the seat of common sense and the operations of the soul. This accomplished, More commences the principal theme of the immortality of the separate soul. A discussion of the pre-existence of the soul in chapters 12-13 leads to a description of the manner in which the souls enter different bodies by virtue of their three vehicles. Chapters 15-17 further demonstrate the separability of the soul from

---

80 I have not included a separate analysis of the Preface, having incorporated it in my detailed analysis of the text (see below pp.lvi,lxv). The purpose of the Preface is both polemical and elucidatory. It sets forth a series of likely objections that might be raised by critical readers against some of the main issues dealt with in the treatise, and counters them with specific defences.

the body with arguments drawn, as in the concluding chapters
of Book I, from reason, history, and the virtues of God.

As in the case of Book I, More begins Book III with a
profession of his moral purpose in attempting to describe the
after-life of the soul and presents a series of related axioms --
this time to demonstrate the power of vital congruity of the
soul. More particular description of the soul's dimensions and
shape leads to a consideration of the aerial abode of souls, the
senses of aerial genii and their physical features (chapters 2-8).
Not content with these speculations about the constitution of
the daemons, More goes on to conjure up a vibrant vision of the
spirit world, its pleasures, politics, and ethics, in chapters 9-11.
In chapters 12-13, More elaborates his theory of the 'Spirit of
Nature,' the peculiar spiritual substance which explains the
formation of the diverse physical phenomena of the world as
well as their larger unity. And in the final section of the work
(chapters 14-19), More considers the various objections to the
soul's immortality and systematically refutes them all.

*

In order to facilitate the task of appreciating the ornate
baroque fabric of this work, I shall divide my analysis of it into
three parts dealing with 1. the physical elements of More's
philosophy, 2. the physiological constitution of man, the
microcosm, and, 3. the metaphysical marvels of the
macrocosm. These three sections largely correspond to the
relation ship of More's system to those of Hobbes, Descartes,
and the Neoplatonists, respectively.

I. More and Hobbes

a. Doctrine of Substances

Flora I. Mackinnon, in her edition of the *Philosophical Writings of Henry More*, suggests that "the difference in method and spirit between Hobbes and More is greater than the difference between their respective conceptions of the nature of reality" and that "Hobbes' casual admission that 'we take notice also some way or other of our conceptions',[81] which would seem to provide a basis on which More could have met Hobbes on his own ground and from which he might have demonstrated the incompleteness of this conception of reality, was aparently overlooked by More in his insistence on argumentation."[82] But this is to vastly underrate both the radical divergence of More' s conception of substance from Hobbes' notion of bodies and the significance of his strong criticism of what he perceived as Hobbes' reprehensible omissions.

More begins his critique of Hobbes' position in Bk. I, Ch. 9 by acknowledging Hobbes' special philosophical merits: "And truly I do not remember that I ever met with any one yet that may justly be suspected to be able to make good this Province [that there is nothing but body in the universe] then our Countreyman Mr. *Hobbs*, whose inexuperable confidence of the truth of the Conclusion may well assure any man that duely considers the excellency of his natural Wit and Parts, that he has made choice of the most Demonstrative Arguments that humane Invention can search out for the eviction thereof " (Sec. 2). Before answering Hobbes' objections to spiritual reality, More takes care to absolve himself from the charge of misrepresenting Hobbes' view: "And that I may not incurre the suspicion of mistaking his Assertion, or of misrepresenting the force of his Reasons, I shall have punctually set them down in the same words I find them in his own Writings, that any man may judge if I doe him any wrong" (Sec 3). The fundamental weakness of Hobbes' system was his identification of

---

81 The quotation from Hobbes is from *Human Nature*, Ch. 3, Art. 6.
82 F. 1. Mackinnon, *Philosophical Writings of Henry More*, N.Y.: Oxford Univ. Press, 1925, p.289.

substance and body. More immediately points out that "this is not to prove, but to suppose what is to be proved, That the universe is nothing else but an Aggregate of Bodies"(Ch. 10, Sec. 1). In fact, Hobbes had taken into consideration all possible constructions of the terms 'body' and 'spirit' in his discussion of their special significance in the Scripture. He realizes that body and spirit are the equivalent of corporeal and incorporeal substance in the language of the scholastics. But he deems this terminology contradictory since substance is the same as body. He arrives at this conclusion through a definition of substance as that which is "*subject* to various accidents, as sometimes to be moved; sometimes to stand still, and to seem to our senses sometimes hot, sometimes cold, sometimes of one colour, smell, taste, or sound, sometimes of another."[83] Hobbes seems to associate the word 'substance' with *subjectum* whereas it is more obviously linked to *substantia* as being the underlying essence of a thing (see Aristotle,*Categories*V, 3). Thus, Hobbes' clever conclusion that "according to this acception of the word, *substance* and *body* signify the same thing therefore *substance incorporeal* are words, which when they are joined together, destroy one another, as if a man should say, an *incorporeal body*" is less convincing than it first seems. The brunt of More's attack is that substance may have incorporeal as well as corporeal differentiae and, unless Hobbes first proves that it cannot, his mockery of incorporeal substance is premature.

More, on the other hand, begins his description of substance more cautiously as the "naked essence" of a thing which is "*utterly unconceivable to any of our Faculties*" (Bk. I, Ch. 2, Axiome 8).[84] He establishes the elusive nature of substance by the Cartesian method of divesting a body ('subject') of all its accidents and arriving at "a mere

---

83 *Leviathan*, Ch. 34. All citations are from *The English Works of Thomas Hobbes*, ed. Sir William Molesworth, London, 1839-1895.

84 In this understanding of 'substance' as the undiversificated substratum of a thing More anticipates Locke in his *Essay Concerning Human Understanding*, Bk, II, Ch. 23. Sec.2. The notion may be detected even earlier in More's account of the 'infinite matter' of the universe in *Democritus Platonissans*,68.(See above p.xxiii).

undiversificated Substance."[85]   Having done this, he rightly
claims that the immediate properties of a substance are
"indemonstrable" *for "if the* naked substance *of a* Thing be so
utterly unconceivable, there can be nothing deprehended there
to be a connexion between it and it's first Properties" (Ch. 2,
Sec.10).

The next step is to determine the characteristic attributes
of matter, which he decides are impenetrability and
discerpibility (or actual as opposed to merely intellectual
divisibility) solely on the basis of empirical evidence and
common sense: "For that it does as certainly and irresistibly
keep one part of it self from *penetrating* another it is so, we
know why" (Sec. 11).   Then, with logical coherence, he
completes the paradigm by positing another substance with the
opposite qualities of penetrability and indiscerpibility. This is
his original conception of spirit.

More later considers also the possibility of there being two
other kinds of substance between these two, with the attribute-
combinations of impenetrability and indiscerpibility and
penetrability and discerpibility, respectively (Ch. 3, Sec. 3).
But he dismisses the first as an absurdity, for impenetrability
implies some form of matter and no matter in nature is indiscerpible. If it were, it would be spirit. More does not show
any awareness of the Gassendist theory of indivisible,
impenetrable atoms propounded in *Syntagma Philosophicum* I,
55a.[86]   But, even if he had been aware of the theory, he would

---

85 cf. Descartes, *Meditationes*, II. Although More does not introduce the
notion of extension at this point, he assumes it in his description of matter
and spirit in the next axiom where the discerpibility of the one and the
penetrability of the other argue for the extensionality of both matter and
spirit. It is at this juncture that More's metaphysics diverges from the
Cartesian restriction of extension to matter.

86 That More did not read Gassendi carefully is attested by the two letters
to Hartlib,dated 5 Nov. 1649 and 28 Dec. 1649 in which he first asks
Hartlib to "procure me out of France with any tolerable spead a copy of
Gassendus his Epicurean philosophy" but later declares "Gassendus is too
tedious a philosopher for me ὁ βίος βραχύς. I am glad you did not send it
to me." See C.Webster "Henry More and Descartes: Some New Sources,"
BJHS,IV, 16 (1969) p. 375f.

have refused to accept that such atoms were the 'primordials' of the world since, as he explains in the same section, mere indiscerpibility of parts is not a sufficient basis for *"cogitation and communion of sense,"* which are the distinguishing activities of spirit in its primary phase. These functions require "a more perfect degree of union than there is in mere *Indiscerpibility of parts."* And such an integrity of substan ce is to be found only in spirit. Thus, to the Platonist, no argument is subtle enough to destroy the priority of mind to matter. As for the second possibility, of the existence of a substance that is penetrable and discerpible, More considers this, too, as just another form of matter by virtue of its divisibility and its union through juxtaposition of parts and, hence, not worthy of a distinct classification.

Although the empirical proofs of the existence of spiritual substance are not immediately offered (they are dispersed throughout the rest of the work), he does counter the objection that "it implies a contradiction that *Extended* Substance should run one part into another; for so part of the *Extension*, and consequently of the *Substance* would be lost" (Ch. 2, Sec. 11), this self-penetration seeming to negate its indivisibility. (This objection is made by Descartes in his letter of 15 April 1649 to More where he declares that one cannot understand how one part of an extended thing can penetrate another part which is equal to it, without understanding at the same time that the middle part of its extension mūst be removed or destroyed: however, a thing that is destroyed cannot penetrate another.") He defends his theory by postulating a fourth dimension called "spissitude," which includes the possibility of "the redoubling or contracting of Substance into less space then it does sometimes occupy" as well as that of the "lying of two Substances of several kinds in the same place at once." For the former he gives the examples of a piece of wax reduced from a long figure to a round, where what is lost in longitude is gained in latitude" or depth. The latter he illustrates by the example of the motion of a body and the body itself coextended within the same space, for "motion is not nothing" and any thing that is is extended.[87]

---

87 This extraordinary reification of motion is clarified in *Divine Dialogues,*

We note in More's argumentation here a rationalistic method similar to Descartes'. The otherwise problematic fourth dimension is justified on the Cartesian grounds that it is "as easy and familiar to my Understanding, as that of the *Three dimensions* to my Sense or Phansy." More relies here on clear and distinct ideas as an epistemological criterion just as Descartes did in the *Meditationes*, IV. Then, following once again Descartes' adherence to geometric demonstrations as being the most reliable, More proceeds to give a series of axiomatic proofs of the simultaneous indiscerpibility and penetrability of spirit (Chs.5-6,Axioms 11-19).

Starting from the "ancient notion of *Light*" (Ch. 5, Sec. 2) and the fact that "it is most vigorous towards its fountain and fainter by degrees," he undertakes to examine the "one lucid point" of the primary substance which constitutes its source. This point is "purely indivisible" yet it is not nothing. For, a perfect globe on a perfect plane touches the latter at a similarly infinitesimal point which is a quantity, it being impossible that "one Body should touch another, and yet touch one another in nothing" (Sec.3). Such a "first point" which geometry proves to be at once indivisble in its littleness and potentially divisible as quantity is in fact the true notion of a spirit, the "*inmost Centre of life*." This vital primary substance is "in Magnitude so

---

London, 1668, No. 25 ff. where Philotheus argues that 1. What ever has no Extension or amplitude is nothing," 2."Wherefore Extension or Amplitude is an intrinsecall or essential property of *Ens quatenus Ens*," 3."And it can as little be deny'd but that motion is an entity, I mean a Physicall Entity" [i.e. since it can be measured], 4."Therefore Extension is an intrinsecal l property of motion." However, the extension of motion is different from that of matter, for the former is "not simply the *Translation*, but the *vis agitans* that pervades the whole body that is moved." His further distinction that the extension of matter is "one single Extension not to be lessened nor increased without the lessening and increasing of the Matter itself; but the other a gradual Extension, to be lessened or augmented without any lessening or augmenting the matter. Whence again it is a sign that it has an extension of its own, *reduplicative* into it self, or reducible to thinner or weaker degrees" reveals that 'motion' as entity is really the same as 'spirit.' This identification of motion with spirit is also the basis of its vital emanative power (see below p.lvi).

little that it is *Indiscerpible* but in virtue so great that it can send forth out of itself so large a Sphere of *Secondary Substance*, as I may call it, that it is able to actuate grand proportions of *Matter*, this whole sphere of life and activity being in the mean time utterly *Indiscerpible*." (Ch. 6, Axiome 15).

The extension of the secondary substance from the first point is through the immediate emanative causality of spirit, which is instinct with self-motion (a quality he attributes to spirit in order to avoid the infinite regress which would result from attributing motion to matter -- Axiome 16).[88] And, as it implies a contradiction that an emanative effect should be disjoined from its original (by virtue of Axiome 17, which maintains that an emanative effect is coexistent with the substance that is the cause of it), it follows that the vital sphere is utterly indiscerpible from the centre to the circumference. But the parts within it, being of an inferior substance, by Axiome 19, are only "closely coherent" through "immediate union of these parts." The conceptualization of this as physical phenomenon is certainly difficult. And More himself recognizes this in his Preface. Sec. 3, where he attempts a more precise explanation of his conception of spirit. He describes the *"parts indiscerpible"* that constitute the spiritual atoms as having

---

88 More elaborates on the absurd consequences of matter possessing innate motion in Ch. 11. If motion is coexistent with matter (as Gassendi for example, attempted to prove by asserting a *materia actuoso* [*Syntagma Philosophicum* I 335 b]) then it must be an emanative effect, by More's definition in Axiome 17, and motion must be equally distributed in all parts of matter. This would mean that the planets would have a "common *Dividend* of all the motion which themselves and the Sun and Stars, and all the Aetherial matter possess." And since the matter of the planets is far less than that of the others, it would possess a disproportionately high amount of activity whereby every Planet could not faile of melting itself into little less finer substance then the purest Aether" (Sec.3). Throughout this argument More is closely following Socrates' in *Phaedrus* 245 E: "Thus that which moves itself must be the beginning of motion. And this can be neither destroyed nor generated, otherwise all the heavens and all generations must fall in ruin and stop and never again have any source of motion or origin" (Tr.H.N. Fowler, Loeb Classical Library).

"real extension, but so little, that they cannot have less and be any thing at all, and therefore cannot be actually divided." This sort of minute spiritual extension he calls "Essential (*as being such that without that measure of it, the very Being* of Matter *cannot be conserved)." The extension of matter composed of these parts is* called 'Integral' extension, *"these parts of this compounded matter being actual and really separable one from another."* He again insists that a spiritual point, unlike a mathematical point, cannot be *"pure Negation or Non-entity and there being no* medium *betwixt* extended *and* non-extended, *no more then there is betwixt Entity and Non-entity, it is plain that if a thing* be at *all, it must be extended."*[89] The problem then arises that all extended things must have figure, and figures, of no matter what size, must have parts that are divisible. To this More replies, *"I say, those* indiscerpible *particles of* Matter *have no* Figure *at all: As* infinite Greatness *has no Figure, so* infinite Littleness *has none also. And a* Cube infinitely little *in the exactest sense, is as perfect a contradiction as a* Cube infinitely great *in the same sense of* Infinity; *for the Angles would be equal in magnitude to the* Hedrae *thereof."*

However, despite his mathematical demonstrations of the differing natures of spirit and matter, the transition from 'essential' extension to 'integral' is still difficult to comprehend except with intuitive intelligence, what Aristotle calls νοῦς in

---

89 cf., Leibniz's distinction between spiritual points and mathematical in 'Système nouveau de la nature et de la communication des substances, aussi bien que de l'union qu'il y a entre l'âme et le corps'(1695):"Mais les Atomes de matiere sont contraires à la raison: outre qu'ils sont encor composés de parties, puisque l'attachement invincible d'une partie à l'autre (quand on le pouvait concevoir ou supposer avec raison) ne detruiront point leur diversité Il n'y a que les Atomes de substance, c'est à dire, les unités réelles et absolument destituées de parties, qui soyent les sources des actions, et les premiers principes absolus de la composition des choses, et comme les derniers elemens de l'analyse des choses substantielles. On les pourroit appeler *points metaphysiques*: ils ont quelque chose de vital et une espece de perception, et les points mathematiques sont leurs points de veue, pour exprimer l'univers" (*Die Philosophischen Schriften von Gottfried Wilheim Leibniz*, ed. C. J. Gerhardt, Berlin, 1888, Vol. IV, ii, p. 482f).

Ethica Nichomachea, VI, 6-7. The transformation of the primary substance of spirit into its secondary substance is of the same mysterious mathematical nature as the conversion of an infinitesimal point into a line by repetition of itself (Axiomes 13, 14). So More fittingly concludes with the example of the human mind, quoting Aristotle: Ει γὰρ καὶ τῶι ὄγκωι μικρόν ἐστι, δυνάμει καὶ τιμιότητι πολὺ μᾶλλον ὑπερεχει παντῶν ,[90] and juxtaposes it to the more perceptible physical phenomenon of a little spark of light that infuses a large sphere of air.

As this notion of the emanation of a secondary essence from the primary indivisible substance of spirit is ultimately derived from Plotinus, I think it would be useful to present here Plotinus' description of the Soul in *Enneades*, IV, ii, 1:

> But on the other hand, that first utterly indivisible Kind must be accompanied by a subsequent Essence, engendered by it and holding indivisibility from it, but, in virtue of the necessary outgo from source, tending firmly towards the contrary, the wholly partible; this secondary Essence will take an intermediate place between the first substance, the undivided, and that which is divisible in material things and resides in them ... The Essence, very near to the impartible, which we assert to belong to the Kind we are now dealing with, is at once an Essence and an entrant into body; upon embodiment, it experiences a partition unknown before it bestowed itself.
>
> In whatsoever bodies it occupies -- even the vastest of all, that in which the entire universe is included -- it gives itself to the whole without abdicating its unity nature, at once divisible and indivisible, which we affirm to be soul, has not the unity of an extended thing: it does not consist of separate sections; its divisibility lies in its presence at every point of the recipient, but it is indivisible as dwelling entire in every part.

---

90 Aristotle, *Ethica Nichomachea*, X, 7: "For though this be small in bulk, in power and value it far surpasses all the rest" (Tr. H. Rackham).

> To have penetrated this idea is to know the
> greatness of the Soul and its power, the divinity and
> wonder of its being, as a nature transcending the
> sphere of Things.[91]

More's comparison of the primal spiritual entity to a point
also has a counterpart in Plotinus (IV, vii, 8): ". . . it must still
be admitted that there do exist intellections of intellectual
objects and perceptions of objects not possessing magnitude;
how, we may then ask, can a thing of magnitude [i.e. if we
assume the mind to be extended] know a thing that has no
magnitude, or how can the partless be known by means of
what has parts? We will be told, 'By some partless part.' But,
at this, the intellective will not be body: for contact does not
need a whole; one point suffices."

Ralph Cudworth, in commenting on this section of the
Enneades, interprets Plotinus as an 'unextended Incorporealist'
and differentiates him from More who asserted "another
extension specifically differing from that of bodies."[92] But this
observation is only partly correct. Plotinus is indeed careful to
deprive soul of any quality that would imply a corporeal
nature, including extension. However, having distinguished
two 'phases' in the Soul, an indivisible one and a divisible, he is
faced with the problem of determining "whether these and the
other powers which we call 'parts' of the Soul are situated all
in place; or whether some have place and standpoint, others
not; or whether again none are situated in place" (IV, iii, 20).
He quickly dismisses the possibility of the soul's being
contained in the body as in a space: "Space is a container, a
container of body; it is the home of such things as consist of
isolated parts, and is never, therefore, found whole in any part;
now, the Soul is not a body and is no more contained than
containing ... Besides (if the Soul were contained as in space)
contact would be only at the surface of the body, not
throughout the entire mass" (*Ibid.*). But the answer he gives

---

91 All citations from Plotinus are from *The Enneads*, tr. S. Mackenna,
London, 1956.
92 Ralph Cudworth, *The True Intellectual System of the Universe*, ed. T.
Birch, 4 vols., London, 1820, vol. IV, p. 81.

to the problem is strikingly like More's: "May we think that
the mode of the Soul's presence to body is that of the presence
of light to the air? This certainly is presence with distinction:
the light penetrates through and through but nowhere
coalesces, the light is the stable thing, the air flows in and out;
when the air passes beyond the lit area it is dark; under the
light it is lit. We have a true parallel to what we have been
saying of body and soul, for the air is in the light rather than
the light in the air"(IV, iii, 22). And in his later elaboration of
the union of Soul and body he even, accidentally, grants it the
same extension (ὄγκος) as the body, in his effort to establish
the non-corporeal nature of the Soul: "Two bodies (i.e. by
hypothesis, the Soul and the human body) are blended, each
entire through the entirety of the other; where the one is, the
other is also; *each occupies an equal extension and each the
whole extension* no increase of size has been caused by the
juncture: the one body thus inblended can have left in the
other nothing undivided. This is no case of mixing in the sense
of considerable portions alternating; that would be described as
collocation. No, the incoming entity goes through the other to
the very minutest point ... an impossibility, of course ... body
cannot traverse anything as a whole traversing a whole. But
soul does this. It is therefore incorporeal." (IV, vii, 8, my
italics).

*

   More's neo-Plotinian conception of spirit, to be fully
defended in an age of empirical science, required solid proof of
the existence of spiritual substance. Consequently, More was
comitted to a belief in daemonic aparitions and sought
vigorously to demonstrate their reality (see below pp.lxxxivff.)
Hobbes' objection in Part IV of his *Elements of Philosophy* (Ch.
25, Art. that "ghosts and incorporeal substances" are mere
vivid dreams "especially such as some men have when they are
between sleeping and waking, and such as happen to those that
have no knowledge of the nature of dreams and are withal
superstitious" was quite misguided, according to More. He
dismisses Hobbes' view as based on the false assumption that
such phenomena are to be witnessed only in the minds of
superstitious men. For "Philosophers and Christians alike"
have argued for the existence of spirits and immaterial

substance "from the evidence of Externall Objects of Sense, that is, the ordinary *Phaenomena* of Nature. " (Ch. 10, Sec. 2): He adduces the example of atheistic philosophers like Pomponazzi, Cardano and Vanini to demonstrate the universality of the belief in supernatural phenomena. Hobbes' other objection in Part I of *Elements of Philosophy* that those things seen in sleep do not have real existence (Ch. 5, Sec. 4) is based on the unproved assumption that everything (including space) is imaginary that is not body.

The next argument that More finds in Hobbes against spirit (in his *Human Nature*, Ch. 11, Sec. 4) is built on the Aristotelian notion that all conceptions are supported by phantasms produced by the action of the senses and the imagination, and since we cannot have any phantasms of a spirit which does not have any dimensions, the only knowledge we have of spirits can be that accepted on "faith from supernatural revelation given to the holy writers of the Scripture." Not only is this way of reasoning manifestly contradictory (if miracles and spirits can occur in biblical history, how can we rule out the existence of spirits altogether in modern?), but More does not, in the first place, subscribe to the view that dimension is the exclusive predicate of body. For, spirit, too, is extended, and differs from body merely in that it lacks impenetrability. It must be noted that Hobbes did offer a solution to the problem of spirits in the Bible in *Leviathan*, Ch. 34 and Ch. 45, by suggesting that angels and apparitions are corporeal too, though of subtler matter. But the linguistic and scientific awkwardness of allowing "spiritual bodies" in the empirical-materialistic universe of Hobbes only highlights the distinction of More's concept of spirit as the primordial substance that infuses different forms of matter.

In attempting to account for ancient religious belief in supernatural agents such as the *imagines* and *umbrae* of the Romans (*Leviathan, Ch.* 12.), Hobbes once again decries the deluded belief in spirits. More replies that the *secundae notiones* of the mind, which include logical and mathematical terms, are evidence of intellection that is not dependent on sense impressions. Hobbes' objection that such universals are mere names (*Human Nature*, Ch. 5) More rejects by pointing to the historical evidence of similar common notions arising amongst nations speaking different languages which proves that universals are real existents and not mere effects of

language. This repetition of the Herbertian theory of common
notions rests largely on the rationalistic conviction of the
immutability of mathematical truths (cf. Descartes,
Meditationes I, *Regulae* II), a conception mostlyignored by
Hobbes in his restriction of 'computation' to a knowledge of the
causes of corporeal effects (Part I of *Elements of Philosophy*,
Ch. 1', 2-5).

More interesting is More's example of the freewill as
evidence of intellectual activity that is free of material
influence. Evidences of heroic conduct such as the adherence to
virtue at the cost of physical pain to oneself argue the existence
of a faculty that cannot be explained by the action and reaction
of one art of matter against another. In Bk. II, Ch. 3, More
attacks Hobbes' deterministic view of life by considering the
various arguments expressed in Hobbes' treatise *Of liberty and
necessity*. The first argument that, since nothing in the
universe is *sui generis* but is caused by the action of an external
agent, *"the Will is also caused by other things"* More counters by
focussing on the falseness of the materialist's theory of change:

> But that *Motion* in a large sense, taking it for
> mutation or change, may proceed from that very
> Essence in which it is found, seems to me plain by
> Experience: For there is an Essence in us, whatever
> we call it, which we find endued with this property
> [of varying its modifications] as appears from hence,
> that it has variety of perceptions, *Mathematical*,
> *Logical*, and I may adde also *Moral*, that are not any
> impresses nor footsteps of Corporeal Motions(Sec. 7).

In Hobbes' reasoning that willing is caused by the Will,
More keenly perceives Hobbes' hidden scholasticism in believing
in *"Faculties* and *Operations...* as separate and distinct from the
Essence they belong to" (Sec. 8). Having established the soul of
man as a spiritual substance whose motive power naturally
results in willing and understanding, he avoids the "sophistry"
of Hobbes' identification of "necessary" with "necessitated," for
the soul is not necessitated by any external cause to will but by
itself in the form of the understanding, "by the displaying of
certain notions and perceptions [which the soul] raises in
herself that be purely intellectual" (Sec. 10).

More exposes the flaw of Hobbes' second argument that every sufficient cause is a necessary cause for *"if it be impossible that a sufficient cause should not produce the effect, then is a sufficient cause a necessary cause, for that is said to produce an effect necessarily that cannot but produce it"* by stressing the special virtue of voluntary causality, which can abstain from producing an effect even when it his sufficient power to produce it. The reason for this, of course, is that it is directed by the understanding, which is part of the soul, as indicated above.

Hobbes' third argument for determinism from the logical example of 'Future disjunctions' is clearly a weak one, for he considers the disjunct proposition 'It shall rain or not rain,' as though it were a connex axiom, which is necessary in its connected entirety, whereas a disjunct proposition is necessary only if both its parts are individually shown to be necessary. Thus Hobbes' example could be broken up into its parts as follows: 'If it be necessary it shall rain, it shall rain' and 'If it be necessary it shall not rain, it shall not.' And Hobbes would then have little evidence of universally necessitated actions, since the first part of both these propositions would still have to be proved to be true. Hobbes, however, maneuvers the parts so that they read as follows: 'If it be not necessary it shall rain, it is necessary it shall not rain,' whereas the most he could have rightly asserted is that 'If it be not necessary it shall rain, it shall or shall not rain,' which is quite contrary to what he set out to prove.

The "diffidence" of Hobbes' fourth argument *"That the denying of Necessity destroyeth both the decrees and the prescience of God Almighty"* More immediately traces to the contradiction involved in Hobbes' assumption of a omniscient divinity in a system that proclaims that there is "nothing but *Body* or *Matter* in the whole comprehension of things." More's defen ce of freewill takes into account those rare instances where the liberty of will may degenerate so far that it causes predictable automatic responses, as in a hungry dog, or may ascend to such a level of heroism that we may accurately foretell the actions of a virtuous person in a crisis. But, for the rest, the freewill of man does not contradict the prescience of God which extends so far "as to know precisely and fully whatever implies no contradiction to be Known" (Sec. 20). This definition of God's omniscience seems to come dangerously close to limiting his omnipotence, which is only "able to doe whatever imples no contradiction to be done." But More's God is a rational more than a transcendent being (cf. Bk. I, Ch. 4, Sec. 2), and, as in Descartes' *Meditationes* (III, V), it would be absurd (even if not impossible) for the guarantor of all logical ideas to contradict the law of contradiction with his power.

Hobbes' last objection to spiritual substance is that it is partly derived from the scholastic reification of "separated essences" or "Forms." In particular, he is appalled at the resultant riddle of the soul as being *tota in toto et tota in qualibet parte (Leviathan*, Ch. 24; *Human Nature*, Ch. 11). Although More too is scornful of this paradoxical formula, he attempts to save the authors of it by interpreting it in a Platonic manner; "I suppose they may mean nothing by it, but what *Plato* did by his making the Soul to consist ἐκ μεριστῆς καὶ ἀμερίστου οὐσίας (Bk. I, Ch. 10, Sec. 8), which, according to him, implies "an Essence that is intellectually divisible, but really indiscerpible." As we have already seen, this is the definition of a spiritual point (Axiome 15, see above p.liii).

As for Hobbes' objection to the scholastics' allocation of spirit to place in the definitive sense of it on the nominalist grounds that the distinction between 'circumscriptive' and 'definitive' place is merely a linguistic quibble (*Leviathan*, Ch. 46), More once again defends the schoolmen by showing how it is indeed possible to have two different definitions of place, as *"the Concave Superficies of one Body immediately environing another Body "* or as *" Imaginary Space* that is coincident with the magnitude of any body," Hobbes' own definition in Part II of *Elements of Philosophy* Ch. 7, Art. 2. Since the latter is indeed what the scholastics meant by definitive place, More sees no reason why Hobbes should quarrel with them or with More himself, whose notion of spirit is such that it can occupy the same space along with a body.

b. Psychology

Book II of *The Immortality of the Soul* begins with a demonstration of the existence of spiritual substance from the inadequacy of matter to explain all the processes of sense and perception. Hobbes' explanation of sense as being due to "some internal motion in the sentient generated by some internal motion of the parts of the object, and propagated through all the media to the innermost part of the organ "(Part IV of

Elements of Philosophy, Ch. 25, Art. 2) More considers as being sound as far as it goes. For, all perception is generally preceded by corporeal motion and so too is cogitation *"from the* heat *that* Thinking *casts a man into* (Preface, Sec. 5). And, *"as* heat *is lost ... so our* Understanding *and* Imagination *decayes and our* Senses *themselves fail, as not being able to be moved by the impression of outward Objects, or as not being in a due degree of liquidity and agility, and therefore in death our Bodies become as senseless as a lump of* clay" (*Ibid.*). But he refuses to believe that "a *general agitation* onely of the particles of the *Matter* will suffice to *excite* them to *thinking*, and that they being thus *excited*, can freely run out to other *cogitations* and *Phantasmes* then what adequately arise from the impress of *Motion"* (Bk Ch. 1, sec.3). The intellectual processes of man are far too complex to be produced by the mere motion of matter. The animadversion of material particles, if at all they be capable of it, would be limited to the immediate sensible phantasms that are produced by their random collisions and could never diversify their operations automatically into the great "Variety of thoughts, the exercise of *Inventions, Judgement* and *Memory"* that are characteristic of the intellect. Matter is, besides, "a principle *purely passive* and no otherwise *moved* or *modified* than as some other thing *moves* and *modifies* it, but canot move itself at all." More gives a humorous illustration of the absurdity of attributing self-motion to matter: "For if it had any such *Perception*, it would by virtue of its *Self-motion* withdraw it self from under the knocks of hammers or fury of the fire, or of its own accord approach to such things as are most agreeable to it and pleasing." This further argues the existence of a substance capable of self-motion. Of course, Hobbes himself had qualified his materialistic view of perceptions by maintaining that not all bodies are endued with sense but only those "fit for the retaining of such motion as is made in them" (Part IV of *Elements of Philosophy*, Ch. 25, Art. 5). For sense "hath necessarily some *memory* adhering to it, by which former and later phantasms may be compared together, and distinguished from one another" (*Ibid*). But the weakness of this theory is revealed by More's example of a bell, in which every stroke produces a tremor "which decaying, must (according to his Philosophie)[93] be *Imagination*, and to the

stroke past must be Memory;and if a stroke overtake it within
the compass of this *Memory*, what hinders but *Discrimination* or
Judgment may follow?" (Bk.II, Ch. 2, Sec.1).

More then turns to the faculty of sight in particular
(Axiome 24) and demonstrates the impossibility of a point of
matter perceiving, through the sole means of physical contact,
large objects, the view of "half an horizon at once," or different
colours at the same time. More here employs Descartes'
theory of colours as arising from the contrary modifications of
motion in the globules of subtle matter between the object and
the sentient *(Météores*, Ch. 8). As colours cannot be
communicated at once to one and the same round particle of
matter (i.e. of the sentient) contrary colours such as red and
black can be perceived only successively and never
simultaneously. Moreover, if perception were produced merely
by the impressions made on a bare point of matter, all colours
would be contaminated, due to the fact that perceptions require
"a *considerable* stay upon the *percipient Matter*" and "*some
leisurely continuance* of this or that Motion before it be wiped
out." The crucial necessity of a perceptive principle that is
naturally stable leads More to discount also Hobbes' description
of the heart as "the fountain of all sense" (Part IV of *Elements
of Philosophy*, Ch. 25, Art. 4), following the Aristotelian theory
of *De Juventute et Senectute*, Ch. 3. For, even if one granted
that there be a soul in the heart (that the heart can cause local
motions by itself More is not for a moment willing to concede),
perceptions would be "horribly disturbed by [the heart's]
sgueezing of it self, and then flagging again by vicissitudes.
Neither would Objects appear in the same place, or at least our
sight not fixt on the same part of the Object when the *Heart* is
drawn up and when it is let down again" (Bk. II, Ch. 7, Sec. 8).

All these various limitations of the materialist hypothesis
led More to investigate the real nature of the "I myself" which
perceives, imagines, remembers, reasons, and is the source of
spontaneous motion and freewill. Hobbes' failure to consider
the question of the intellectual self in any detail thus
constituted for More a fatal flaw in an otherwise coherent
system. And while he greatly preferred Descartes'

---

93 In Part IV of *Elements of Philosophy*,Ch. 25, Art. 7, 8.

identification of a *res cogitans* distinct from matter, he was resolved to go much farther than the French philosopher in establishing the reality of such a *res* with his definite notion of spirit as extended entity.

II. More and Descartes

Psychology

The 'Epistle Dedicatory' to Lord Conway reveals that *The Immortality of the Soul* was partly inspired by More's reading of Descartes' *Les Passions de l'âme* (1649),[94] in the summer of 1656 in the Garden of Luxembourg, "to pass away the time." Descartes' physiological analysis of the passions struck him as being "handsome and witty." Yet, "all did not seem so perfectly solid and satisfactory to me but that I was forced in some principal things to seek satisfaction from my self." The particular fault that More focusses on in *The Immortality of the Soul* is the tenuous nature of Descartes' establishment of a thinking substance distinct from body (*Discours*,IV; *Meditationes*,II). "For," as he says in Bk. I, Ch. 8, Sec. 9,"being there may be *Modes* common to more subjects then one, and this of *Cogitation* may be pretended to be such as is competible as well to Substance *Corporeal* as *Incorporeal*, it may be conceived apart from either, though not from both. And therefore his Argument does not prove That that in us which does *think* or *perceive* is a Substance distinct from one Body, but onely That there may be such a Substance which has the power of *thinking* or *perceiving*, which yet is not a *Body*." Whereas, More focusses the definition of the *ego cogitans* by emphasizing the ultimate independence of cogitation of any form of corporeal substance whatsoever and thereby ascertains the existence of another substance "which must needs be a Substance *Incorporeal*," of which thinking is a mode.

Descartes' refusal to discuss the substantial nature of the *res cogitans* had led to some awkward problems in his physiological study of human activity. While maintaining that the soul is characterized by thought alone *(Passions*, Art.4), he divides intellection into two kinds (Art. 17), the voluntary actions of the soul and its passive perceptions. But sense

---

94 More read the book in the Latin translation of 1650 as is evident from his references to *'De Passion[ibus Animae]'* in his marginal notes to *The Immortality of the Soul*. But I quote for convenience from the English translation of Descartes' French original in *The Philosophical Writings of Descartes*. tr. J. Cottingham, R. Stoothoff, P.Murdoch, Cambridge: C.U.P, 1985, I, 325ff.

perceptions depend on the interaction between objects outside the body and the nerves which contain animal spirits that transmit impressions to the brain. This necessitates the inclusion of the animal spirits at least (if not the nerves which contain them and the blood which produces them)[95] in a general description of the powers of the soul. But the soul in Descartes' view is not extended: "it is of such a nature that it has no relation to extension, or to the dimensions or other properties of the matter of which the body is composed" (Art 30). However, he maintains that "the soul is really joined to the whole body and that we cannot properly say that it exists in any one part of the body to the exclusion of the others" *(Ibid.)*. His description of the activity of the soul, consequently, belies his original refusal of extension to spirit: "The soul has its principal seat in the small gland located in the middle of the brain. From there it radiates through the rest of the body by means of the animal spirits, the nerves, and even the blood" (Art. 34). The contradiction involved in fixing the soul in one part of the brain and then expecting it to be "really joined" to the rest of the body through the aid of animal spirits is not much clarified in Article 41, which details the exact manner in which the soul acts: "The activity of the soul consists entirely in the fact that simply by willing something it brings it about that the little gland to which it is closely joined moves in the manner required to produce the effect corresponding to this volition."

More was quick to perceive the problems inherent in Descartes' mechanistic psychology and in Bk. II, Ch. 5, he set out to refute it as well as he could. He first attacks Descartes' location of the soul in the conarion in much the same way as he did Hobbes' psychological system, which differed from Descartes' only in its omission of an immaterial soul. The faculty of vision is the clearest evidence of the inadequacy of Descartes' theory. If, as Descartes believes,[96] in the act of seeing "the Image that is propagated from the Object to the *Conarion*, is impressed thereupon in some latitude of space ... it is manifest that the *Conarion* does not, nor can perceive the whole Object, though several parts may be acknowledged to

---

95 See Art. 10.

96 *Les Passions de l'âme*, Art. 35.

have the *perception* of the several parts thereof. But something *perceives* the whole which therefore cannot be the *Conarion.*" (*Sec. 2).* Being a material body, the conarion cannot integrate the diverse impressions it receives in its various parts into a single visual image.

Also, spontaneous motion[97] cannot be explained by the action of "so weak and so small a thing as that *glandula* is" which is obviously "unable to *determine* the *Spirits* with that force and violence we find they are determined in *running, striking, thrusting* and the like." This is especially evident in that "sometimes scarce the thousandth part of the *Conarion* shall be director of this force; viz, when the Object of Sight, suppose, is as little as a pin's point, or when a man is pricked with a needle, these receptions must be as little in the *glandula* as in the exterior Sense " (Sec. 3). In other words, Descartes' conception of the soul's instrument does not properly explain the directive power of the soul. To those who may reply that the animal spirits are so subtle that they can be propelled through any particular course with such rapidity as to be able to cause these violent physical actions, More gives a diagrammatic demonstration -- employing a model used by Descartes' disciple Henri de Roy in his *Philosophia Naturalis* (Amsterdam, 1661) of the impossibility of the spirits moving in any specific direction merely through mechanical action without the express "*Imperium* of our *Soul* that does *determine* the *Spirits* to this *Muscle* rather than the other, and holds them there in despite of external force."[98] The crucial ability of the soul to control the spirits at every part of their course through the body is absent in Descartes' description of motion (Art.41 & Art.11-16). In fact, Descartes' account of the production of different motions due to the differences in the external objects that impinge on the nerves or in the quality of the animal spirits themselves is little different from that of Hobbes.[99]

---

97 *Ibid.,* Art. 11.

98 From this More infers, also, that brutes too must have souls -- another point of quarrel with Descartes (See his *Epistolae Quatuor ad Renatum Descartes,* and L.D. Cohen's discussion, "Descartes and Henry More on the Beast-Machine," *Annals of Science,* I(1936),48-61).

99 cf. Part IV of *Elements of Philosophy,*Ch. 25, Art. 12.

More next attacks Descartes' theory of memory in Art. 42 of the *Passions*. Descartes had suggested that objects leave traces in the form of pores in the brain which are found by the animal spirits at the command or "inclination" of the conarion. This explanation, says More, accounts for only the figure of a thing, not its colours according to Descartes' own theory of colours (see above p.lxvi). Also, the fact that we can distinctly remember many objects exposed to our view "at the same distance, the Eye keeping exactly in the same posture, insomuch that it shall be necessary for these images to take up the very same place of the *Brain*" shows that such memories are produced by a substance endowed with a power "perfectly beyond the bounds of *mere Matter*, for there would be a necessary confusion of all" (sec. 7). Moreover, the conarion cannot by mechanical means alone invert the position of images on the retina. For this, it must have the power of raising motions in itself, "such as are not necessarily conveighed by any corporeal impress of another body" (Sec. 8). But this contradicts Descartes' own laws of movement in *Principia*, II, Arts, 36, 37.

More sought to avoid these problems of the interaction between the rational soul and the inferior part of it by including as the distinctive qualities of noncorporeal substance indivisibility and self-motion, with its resulting power of extension, either in the form of self-penetration, self-contraction and dilatation or the power of penetrating, moving and altering matter. From the combination of indivisibility, self-motion and penetration, "it is plain that such *a Spirit* as we define, having the power of Motion upon the Whole extent of its essence, may also determine this Motion according to the property of its own nature"(Bk. I, Ch. 7, Sec. 2).

In Bk II, Chs,10 and 11, More sets forth his conception of the human soul, its infusion of the body and its various activities. He returns to a Stoic and Neoplatonic understanding of sympathetic connexion between various forms of spirit.[100] The soul of the world or *anima mundi* is one everywhere, though it forms itself into different human and animal souls

---

100 cf. for example, Plotinus, *Enneades*, III, 8; IV, 3, 4, and 9; Origen, *De Principiis*, II, i, 3.

through the agency of the *spiritus naturae* or spirit of nature,which he otherwise recognizes as "the *Unity* of the *Soul of the Universe*, which is interessed in all plastick powers" (Ch. 10, Sec. 7). This unity and heterogeneity of spiritual substance is repeated within the human body by the sympathy that exists between the rational soul in the common sensorium and the rest of the soul which fully pervades the body. The soul informs the body in the following manner: "the Soul, which is a *Spirit*, and therefore *contractible* and *dilatable*, begins within less compass at first in organizing the fitlyprepared Matter, and so bears itself on in the same tenour of work till the Body has attained its full growth; and ... the soul dilates it self in the dilating of the Body, and so possesses it through all the members thereof" (Ch. 10, Sec. 2). The rational soul planted in matter by the world-soul sends forth from itself "such an *Essential Emanation from it self* as is utterly devoid of all *Sense* and *Perception*; which you may call, if you will *the Exteriour branches of the Soul*, or *the Rayes of the Soul.*" (Ch. 11, Sec. 10). Once this is accomplished, the various faculties of the soul continue to function until "satiety or fatigue" breaks the bonds between the soul and the body (See below p. lxxxv).

The lowest faculty of the soul is the plastic or vegetative part of the soul whose operations More had described in *Enthusiasmus Triumphatus* ,Sec.4,as being "fatall and naturall to [the soul] so long as she is in the body" . These include the automatic functions of the body such as the "perpetual *Systole* and *Diastole* of the *Heart*," as well as respiration. According to More, (Ch. 11) sensation is caused in much the same way as Descartes had indicated, but More insists on the importance of the essential continuity of the soul throughout the body to explain the peculiar fact that pain is felt not in the common sensorium but in the external organ affected. Also, he gives a detailed proof (Ch. 10, Sec. 9) of the necessity of the soul's being present at "the bottom of the eye" or retina, where the image of an object is made in order that the figure and the colour may be retained intact when it conveys it to the centre of perception "intirely in the same circumstances." If this activity were left to the nerves and the "bare laws of Matter," the restriction of the image into the narrow range of the optic nerve would result in distortion of both figure and colour in the image, just as the opacity of the brain would rob it of its "splendour or entireness." "Wherefore," he concludes, "I do not doubt but that the image which the Soul perceives is that in the Eye and not any other corporeally producted to the inside of the Brain"(*Ibid.*).

In his explanation of memory, More differs from Descartes in refusing to believe "that the *Brain* should be stored with *distinct images* (whether they consist of the Flexures of the supposed *Fibrillae*, or the orderly puncture of Pores, or in a continued Motion of the parts thereof, some in this manner, and others in that)" (Ch. 11, Sec. 4). Rather, the only marks that might be present in the brain must be "a kind of *Brachygraphie*," mnemonic devices for the soul to remind itself of objects and events. These marks must be made by the plastic part of the soul, since the rational soul has "no perception of them distinct from the representation of those things which they are to remind her of." Memory is, in other words, not a function of the material brain but "a *Promptitude*" in the rational soul "to think of this or that Phantasm, with the circumstances thereof, which were raised in her upon some occasion" (Sec. 5). While this promptitude might arise from frequency or novelty of impression of an image, the soul can also by itself through "*voluntary attention* ... very carefully and on set purpose [imprint] the *Idea* as deeply as she can into her inward Sense." In such an action, as also in the recovery of images, she is assisted by her plastic faculty.

Spontaneous motion, too, reveals the continuous presence of the soul throughout the body. Having already established the soul's power of moving matter as well as its ubiquity, More has little difficulty in explaining the way in which, at the command of the will in the common sensorium, "that part of the Soul that resides in the *Muscles*, "by its plastic power, guides the spirits into "the *Fibrous* parts of the *Muscle* as the main Engine of motion," where the "subtle liquor of the *Animal Spirits*, makes them swell and shrink like Lute-strings in rainy weather: And in this chiefly consists that notable strength of our Limbs in *Spontaneous motion*" (Ch. 11, Sec. 7).

In spite of the diffusion of the soul through the body, the primary functions of the soul that enable her to "*Imagine, Remember, Reason,* and be the fountain of *Spontaneous Motion,* as also the Seat of what the Greeks call τὸ αὐτεξούσιον or *liberty of Will*" are located in a single part of the brain, (Bk II, Ch. 2, Sec.2). However, this "immediate instrument" of the soul is not the conarion, for the reasons already indicated above.

Having dismissed the possibility of the common *sensorium* being any form of recognizable matter, however liquid, More then identifies it as being a substance "so *yielding* and *passive*, that it easily feels the several assaults and impresses of other Bodies upon it, or in it" which for want of more precise terminology he calls "subtile matter" which is tenuous, passive nearly homogeneous and registering no perceptibie change "from the playing together of its own tenuious particles" (Sec. 3). Such "matter" can scarcely be distinguished from spirit.

In trying to locate such a substance in the body that could serve as the seat of the soul, More considers, apart from Descartes' theory of the conarion, the opinions of many contemporary anatomists and philosophers. The spinal marrow and the animal spirits of the fourth ventricle of the brain are first discarded, the first as being too gross and the second as too liquid a conglomeration of particles (Bk. II, Ch. 6). Among those that placed the seat of the soul outside the head, Jan Baptista van Helmont had chosen the upper orifice of the stomach (in his treatise, *De Sede Animae* and Hobbes the heart (in Part IV of *Elements of Philosophy*, Ch. 25). Van Helmont's misconception More sagaciously attributes to the "great *Sympathy* betwixt the *Orifice of the Stomack* and the *Heart*, whose *Pathemata* are so alike and conjoyned that the Ancients have given one name to both parts, calling them promiscuously καρδία (Ch. 7, Sec. 6). This intimate connection often causes a wound "About *the mouth of the Stomack*" to be more fatal than a wound in the head, which does not affect the pulse as quickly, and so people wrongly tend to believe that the stomach is the source of life as well as of sensation. As for Hobbes' view, we have already seen the main reason for More's rejection (see above p.lxvi). He adds to this the evidence of animals which continue to live for a while even after their heart has been removed.

Further anatomical evidence is adduced to prove that the seat of common sense must be in the head (Sec. 10). Since the whole brain is not the source of common sense (Sec. 11), it must be one particular part of it. Henri de Roy's location of the centre of perception in a "small solid particle" (*Philosophia Naturalis* Bk. V, Ch. 1) is easily refuted on the basis of its hardness, and so, too, are the external and internal membranes of the head which are not conveniently enough located for the reception of all sense impressions (Sec. 14). Descartes' opinion

More valiantly defends against the criticisms of Caspar
Bartholin   and   Joseph   Wharton   (in   the   latter's
Adenographia,Ch. 23), but finally discounts on account of the
fact that the conarion is too weak to direct the animal spirits
into particular pores of the brain (See above pp.lxxff). Besides,
the stones that have been discovered in it as well as the net of
veins and arteries around it are signs of grossness incompatible
with the superior functions of the rational soul.[101] Wharton's
location of the common sensorium in the concourse of nerves in
the fourth ventricle is close to the actual location but errs in
suggesting that the material "pitch of the Brain" itself, where
the nerves meet, could be the centre of perception.

This clears the way for More's own choice of the pure
spirits in the fourth ventricle of the brain as the common
sensorium.[102] For,these spirits are of the finest texture and
abundant enough to serve as the agents of sense, spontaneous
motion, and cogitation. More's choice of the fourth ventricle is
apparently based on Bartholin's anatomical discoveries in
Institutiones Anatomicae, III, 4:

> We consider the use of this ventricle is to be the
> place of generation and elaboration of the animal
> spirits. For this ventricle is 1. very pure and subtle,
> 2. It has a sufficient cavity for this, and 3. It is
> situated in a convenient place for spreading the
> animal spirits all around it into all the nerves,
> Hierophil was, consequently, right in thinking this to
> be the most important ventricle of all.

Examples of the visible manifestations of spiritous activity
in animals include such phenomena as the bubbles that move
through the body of a snail observed in a glass by Henri de Roy

------

101 See Bartholin, *Institutiones Anatomicae* (Oxford, 1633), Bk. III, Ch. 6:
[The pineal gland] is of a harder substance and yellowish colour, and is
covered with a fine membrane ... A small net of nerves holds this gland
firmly on both sides" (my translation).
102 See the diagram of the brain from Vesalius' *De humani corporis fabrica*
(1542) reproduced below p.lxxvi from *Vesalius on the human brain*, tr.
C.Singer, London: OUP., 1952, pp. 104f.

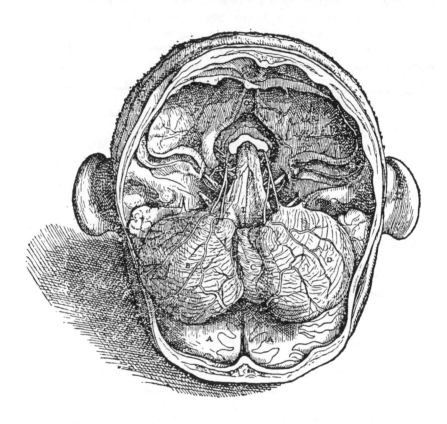

... I That depression in the medulla dorsalis which is
likened to the pointed part of a scribe's quill ··· which constitutes the middle
cavity of that ventricle common to medulla dorsalis and cerebellum. This the
experts in dissection have called the 'fourth ventricle'...

(in *Philosophia Naturalis*, IV, Ch. 17) and the ebb and flow of spirits in the eye according to the passions "insomuch that the Soul even seems to speak through them, in that silent voice of Angels" (Ch. 8, Sec. 9). That the rational soul uses these spirits in intellection too is obvious from the fact that even the *"Inventive* and purely *Intellectual Operations"* are influenced by "change of Air, or Distemper or Diseasedness" (sec 10). This need of fine spirits is due to the fact that the soul has "exceeding little" power of moving matter though it readily directs matter in motion.

The extreme subtlety of the pure spirits in the fourth ventricle as opposed to the rest of the animal spirits in the body is highlighted by More's comparison of the swiftness of their motion to that of light in answering objections to his theory of the ventricular spirits (Ch. 9, Sec. 4). And, as we have already observed, the example of light in More is always indicative of the transformation of the primary substance of non-corporeal spirit into its secondary substance (see above p. lv).This is borne out by his larger identification of the pure spirits of the fourth ventricle to the aethereal matter on which the *spiritus naturae* acts first in fashioning the universe (Ch.9, Sec.6).His additional reference here to the fire of Hermes Trismegistus (in *Poemander*, Chap 10), which is both "the most inward vehicle of the Mind" and "the instrument that God used in forming the world" is of the utmost importance, I think, in suggesting the vital continuity of different forms of substance both within and without the body. The animal spirits of the body are sympathetically allied to the aerial element (Descartes' second element) of the universe, just as the fine spirits of the fourth ventricle are part of the aethereal (or Descartes' first element). This leads to the inevitable conclusion that the incorporeal spiritual substance in man that More calls "Soul" must be really consubstantial with the rational part of the *divina anima* or else it could not participate in the Intellect which constitutes the second hypostasis of the Neoplatonic triad.[103] However, as this seems to come very close to Averr oistic pantheism More refused to elaborate such

---

103 cf. also More' s emanational triads in *Philosophiae Teutonicae Censura*, Quaestio IV, where there is only one intellectual stage in the two triads:

a suggestion further and preferred to expound,instead, a modified system of Plotinan monism which insisted on the vitalistic unity of the Soul, but left the Intellect beyond philosophic consideration.

Supremum Bonum
Aeternus Intellectus } Trinitas purae Divinitatis
Divina Anima

Anima Mundi
Spiritus Naturae } Trinitas Universalis Naturae
Abyssus physicum Monadum

More, *Opera Omnia*, II, i, rpt.,George Olms, Hildesheim, p. 547.

III. More and Neoplatonism

a. Metaphysics

In the Preface, Sec. 10, More addresses himself to the problem of the 'monopsychism' implicit in his psychology. He realizes that he may have made an "*over-favorable representation of their Opinion that make but one Soul in the whole Universe, induing her with* Sense, Reason, *and* Understanding: *which* Soul *they will have to act in all Animals,* Daemons *themselves not excepted.*" His assertion in Bk. II, Ch. 15, Sec. 8, in particular, that there is a "*Magick Sympathy* that is seated in the Unity of the Spirit of the World, and the continuity of the subtle Matter dispersed throughout; the Universe in some sense being, as the *Stoicks* and *Platonists* define it, one vast entire *Animal*" seems to bear this out. However, already in his discussion of the pre-existence of the soul (Bk. II, Ch. 12) he had distinguished the rational soul from the *anima mundi* (Sec. 11). In fact, the theory of pre-existence itself is a special proof that the human soul goes through several individual existences and is not an universally undifferentiated entity. More's opinion is that every human soul is *a mundo condito* (Sec. 6), the *anima mundi* being the "perfective Architect thereof" (Ch. 10, Sec. 2) so that all souls including the souls of animals "do bear the same date with the Creation of the World."(Ch. 12, Sec. 6). But as the particular material form of human bodies has evolved through "many Millions of Alterations and Modifications, before it lighted into such a contexture as to prove the entire Body of any one person in the world, has been in places unimaginably distant, has filed, it may be, through the triangular passages of as many Vortices as we see Stars in a clear frosty night, and has shone once as bright as the Sun (as the *Cartesian* Hypothesis would have all the Earth to have done,[104] inasmuch that we eat, and drink, and cloath our selves with that which was once pure Light and Fire" (Sec. 6), so too, particular souls have undergone subtle transformations through time and infused different forms of matter. Such spiritual changes, though bewildering, are compatible with his notion of spirit as a substance that is

---

104 cf. *Principia*, IV, Art. 2.

indiscerpible, yet divisible into matter (see above pp.liiiff).

According to More, one of the most incontrovertible proofs of the differentiation of the world-soul into individual human beings and animals is memory, which is peculiar to the individual and not to place (Pref., Sec. 10). This would be obvious if one were to accept the mechanistic theory of reminisence maintained by Descartes and Hobbes. But since More himself did not fully subscribe to this view (see above p.lxxii) and held, instead, that "Memory is wholly in the Soul herself"(Preface, Sec. 10), we wonder why the rational part of the *anima mundi* too, unknown to the individual soul, might not perceive or remember the same things as the latter. The absolute indiscerpibility of spiritual substance must include such a possibility. However, the clear evidence that we cannot remember things which were never experienced by us at one place, at another, merely because someone else experiences them in the other place reveals that individual souls are barred from total participation in the Intellect on account of their immersion in material bodies. "By reason of her interest and vitall union with the body" (*Ibid.*), the soul depends on its own animal spirits for parception and memory. Thus, although there be just one Intellect, the fractioning of the world-soul prevents individual souls from possessing it entirely. This misfortune of the soul also explains its loss of memory of its own pre-existence (Bk. II, Ch. 13).

More also considers the related opinion of those that follow ancient authors such as Epictetus, Philo, and Hermes Trismegistus in maintaining that souls are vital rays of the *anima mundi* (Bk. III, Ch. 16)[105]. Though he is rather more sympathetic to this delicate division of individual souls from the world-soul, he insists on reinterpreting this theory according to his notion of individuation as resulting from *"an emanation of a secondary substance from the several parts of the Soul of the World resembling the Rayes of the Sun"* (Sec. 8). One reason for this is that More prefers to think that the human soul is "independent on any thing but the Will and Essence of her Creator; which being exactly the same every Where, as also his

---

105 cf. Epictetus, *Dissertationes*, I, Ch. 14; Philo, *De Opificio Mundi*, 146; *Hermes Trismegistus*,Poemander,XII, 1.

Power is, her emanative support is exactly the same to what she had in the very first point of her production and station in the World" (*Ibid.*). This further confirms the impression that, in More's philosophy, the rational soul is continuous with the eternal Mind which pervades the universe as Nemesis (or the law of equivalence between moral action and reaction), while the numerous lesser souls are distinct expressions of the Divine Soul, first through time (as world-soul), and then in matter (as individual souls).

The agent whereby the *anima mundi* diversifies itself while remaining a unity is the *spiritus naturae*. This entity is an evidence of the same "unity of the soul of the universe" that manifests itself as the plastic faculty in the individual soul. It is defined by More in Bk. III, Ch. 5, Sec. 1, as "*A Substance incorporeal, but without Sense and Animadversion, pervading the whole Matter of the Universe, and exercising a Plastical power therein according to the sundry predispositions and occasions in the parts it works upon, raising such phaenomena in the World, by directing the parts of the Matter and their Motion, as cannot be resolved into mere Mechanical powers.*"[106] We may conclude from this description that the soul of the world, like the human soul, has a superior part to it (the rational) and an inferior (the plastic), and we may attribute this division to the basic distinction between the primary substance of spirit and its secondary substance (see above p.lvi)[107] Thus, while the eternal mind of God proceeds in a direct line through the *anima mundi* to the souls of angels, genii and men, the plastic faculty of the *anima mundi* (the Divine Soul, of course, has no inferior

---

106 This definition is, in fact, much the same as that of the seminal forms of things in Bk. I, Ch. 8, Sec. 3 as "*a created Spirit organizing duly*prepared matter unto life and vegetation proper to this or the other kind of Plant." The basic feature of both these spiritual entities is vegetative formation by moving or directing matter.

107 The Spirit of Nature (φύσις) is not to be identified with the *Anima Mundi* (ψυχή) since the former is the "inferior soul of the world" (Bk. III, Ch. 12, Sec. 2). As early as in the 'Notes upon Psychozoia' More had differentiated '*Physis*' as "a kind of life eradiating from Intellect and *Psyche*,"(Note to I, 41) from *Psyche* which he defines as "the Soul of the World" (Note to I, i, 7).

plastic part in itself and expresses itself only in time as World Soul) branches off into the bodies of angels, genii, men, animals and even plants. As it immerses itself in increasingly gross forms of matter, it gradually loses first, its rational adjunct, beneath the level of man, and then, itself, beneath the level of plants, where there is nothing but mineral matter and the *Abyssus physicum monadum* (see above p.lxxviii).

Being deprived of sensation and ratiocination, the spirit of nature works "fatally or naturally, as several *Gamaieu's* we meet withall in Nature seem somewhat obscurely to subindicate" (Bk.II, Ch.10, Sec.7). The special virtue of the spirit of nature is sympathetic attraction ("in this sense it is that *Plotinus* sayes, that the World is ὁ μέγας γόης, the great Magus or *Enchanter*") and its most obvious biological manifestation is as instinct in birds and beasts (Bk. III, Ch. 13). That this "*Vicarious power of God* upon the Universal Matter of the World" is a real existent rather than "an obscure Principle" introduced by him "*for Ignorance and Sloth to take sanctuary in*" (Preface, Sec. 11) More demonstrates through the inadequacy of mechanical explanations in the case of such a common physical phenomenon as gravity. He refers in particular to the theories suggested by Descartes and Hobbes. Descartes in Part IV of the *Principia* had attributed the descent of heavy bodies to the continual movement of the particles of the second element *(globuli coelestes)* around the surface of the earth which force all the bodies around it towards its centre -- just as the natural tendency of the aetherial particles in and around a drop of water to move in straight lines renders the waterdrop round (Art. 19).[108] More considered neither of these accounts valid since "there must be some *Immaterial* cause, such as we call *The Spirit of Nature* or *Inferior Soul of the World, that must direct the motions of the Aethereal* particles to act upon these grosser Bodies to drive them towards the Earth" (Bk.III, Ch. 13, Sec. 1). The crucial surplus of agitation in the celestial globules that Descartes had pointed to in Art. 22 was inadequate in accounting for the centrifugal ascent of these globules which according to Descartes (Art. 23), caused the

---

108 cf. E.J.Aiton's discussion of "The Cartesian Theory of Gravity" in *Annals of Science*,1,(1959), 27-49.

descent of those bodies constituted of the third element which accidentally happened to find themselves in the atmosphere. By itself such subtle matter cannot rise to "the middle Region of the Aire and further" (Sec. 2) and cause bodies to descend. Again, as in the case of his objection to Descartes' theory of spontaneous motion (see above p.lxix), More insists on the fact that no matter, however subtle, can effect movement beyond its material limitations unless motivated and directed by a potent spiritual substance that is in immediate contact with it. As for the drop of water, even though it be turned round by the action of the aetherial particles, it will also necessarily be rendered stationary and "hang *in aequilibrio*, as a piece of Cork rests on the water, where there is neither winde nor stream, but is equally plaied against by the particles of water on all sides" (Sec. 1) -- which is contrary to experience.

Hobbes' effort to save the Cartesian theory by emphasizing the diurnal motion of the earth as the cause of the rise of the aetherial matter (in Part IV of his *Elements of Philosophy*, Ch. 30) leads him to the absurd conclusion that, as there is less motion in the latitudes above the equator than at it, "heavy bodies must descend with less and less velocity as they are more and more remote from the equator; and that at the poles themselves, they will either not descend at all, or not descend by the axis" (Art. 4). Hobbes stalls at this point saying that "Whether it be true or false, experience must determine. But it is hard to make the experiment, both because the times of their descents cannot be easily measured with sufficient exactness, and also because the places near the poles are inaccessible." The folly of this theory, More promptly points out, is evident even from ordinary experience "in the very Clime where we live in"(Sec. 3). For, according to Hobbes' explanation there would not only be no descent of heavy bodies at the poles, but, even in latitudes below them, "men cannot walk upright but declining" (Sec.4).[109] This simple geometric demonstration allows More to deride opponent for confidently rejecting all immaterial substance in the world "whenas in the mean time he does not produce so much as possible Corporeal causes of the most ordinary effects in

---

109 See also More's diagrammatic representation of the problem on p.261.

Nature" (Sec. 5).

b. Demonology

More similarly dismisses the explanation offered by Descartes of the ascent of fire, of magnetism, and of the formation of "a *round Sun* or *Star*" as being beyond the capacity of brute matter (Bk. II, Ch. 15, Sec. 5 and Bk. III, Ch. 13, Sec. 6). The further examples that he gives of the power of the *spiritus naturae*, however, are more curious and constitute More's contribu tion to the current theories on various sorts of attraction and biological formation propounded by such thinkers as Kircher, Digby, Helmont, Harvey and Sennert. More employs the *spiritus naturae* to explain the sympathetic vibrations of strings without the air in between being vibrated (Bk. III, Ch. 12, Sec. 6), sympathetic cures such as magnetic remedies that alter the temparature of a wound at a great distance (Sec. 3), and the appearance of signatures on foetuses owing to the secret desires or fears of the mother (Sec. 5).[110] The last example is especially interesting since it shows that the plastic part of the soul is not only responsible for the formation of the foetus in the body, but also underlies the unity of the rational soul in the common *sensorium* and the extended parts of it over the rest of the body. I think that all these various examples reveal that the basic action of the plastic power is indeed motion,[111] within the limits of the matter in which it operates. In this respect we might usefully compare the Plotinian notion of τόλμὰ (daring), which seeks to explain the difference of the One into many and

---

110 Earlier (Bk. I, Ch. 14, Secs. 10-13), More had adduced the case of signatures to disprove the possibility of direct astrological influence on human affairs, a concern equally evident in Plotinus' *Enneades*, II, iii, 'Whether the stars are causes.'

111 More himself seems to have come to this understanding of the Spirit of Nature by the time he prepared his Latin edition of *The Immortality of the Soul*, where, in his *Scholium* to Bk. I, Ch. 11, Sec. 9, he says: "Whereas it is much more likely, that God immediately imparted Motion, and that not mechanical, but *vital*, to the *Spirit of Nature*..." The translation is that of the 1713 edition of the work in *A Collection of Several Philosophical Writings of Dr. Henry More*, London, 1712-1713.

the various forms that result from this differentiation. The
first movement away from the One is through a daring self-
assertion which consttutes the infinite desire of the Intellect.
But this desire is also directed simultaneously back to the One,
in an almost static dual process reminiscent of the
Empedoclean doctrine of Strife and Love.[112] The result of this
tension of primal extension is the world of intellectual Forms.
The emanation of Soul from Intellect is similar to that of the
latter from the One. But the τόλμὰ of the Soul results in a
movement in time, which, in Plato's description, (*Timaeus* 37d)
is 'a moving image of eternity.' In this Soul (More's *anima
mundi*) are contained the seeds of nature which are the λόγοι
which it derives from contemplating the Intellect. The Soul's
continuous movement towards Nature (corresponding to More's
spiritus naturae) under the guidance of Intellectual forms thus
produces the various individual souls found in the universe.
That More attributed this movement to τόλμὰ too is confirmed
by his reference to the individual soul's' "wild and *audacious*
ramble from a more secure state" (Bk. III, Ch. 14, Sec.10). The
contemplation of Soul by the individual forms or souls of nature
is the weakest of all possible contemplations and ,so, results
only in sterile material forms which are lifeless and
unproductive. This realm of matter is indeed the furthest
remove from the One and represents absolute privation of
reality and goodness.

The concept of the *spiritus naturae* as the pervasive
inferior soul of the world allowed More to develop his own
modern version of Neoplatonic demonology. It is by the plastic
power that the soul, leaving the terresterial body either during
a disease or at death, extends itself into the aerial matter
around it and activates it in the form of beasts (Bk. III, Ch.
12, Sec. 4) or genii (Bk.II, Chs. 15-17, Bk.III, *passim*). The
seat of the plastic faculty in the body is the heart, and so,
passions, rather than the will or imagination, can act
effectively upon the vital congruity that binds soul to body.
During a distemper the bonds of the soul are loosened -- though
not entirely severed -- so that the aerial vehicle of the plastic

---

112 cf. Empedocles, Fragments 17-22, 26-36 in *Die Fragmente der
Vorsokratiker*, ed. H. Diels and W. Kranz, Berlin, 1951-1952.

part of the soul is free to exert itself and "pass in the Aire, as other Inhabitants of that Element doe, and act the part of separate Spirits, and exarcise such Functions of the *Perceptive* faculty as they do that are quite released from Terrestrial Matter" (Bk. II, Ch. 15, Sec. 10). The continuity of the plastic part of the soul and that of the world-soul however ensures that the "damp in the Body that loosed the Union of the Soul being spent, the Soul, by that natural *Magick* I have more then once intimated, will certainly return to the Body, and unite with it again as firm as ever"(*Ibid.*).

The theory of the three vehicles of the plastic part of the human soul can be traced back to Proclus (*Platonic Theology*, III, 125f)[113] but More is careful to show that Aristotle, too, maintained a theory of an aetherial element in the sperm of the body, φύσις ἀνάλογου οὖσα τῶι τῶν ἄστρων στοίχειωι (*De Generatione Animalium*, II, 3). But since Aristotle restricted the elements to two, aetherial and terrestrial, More prefers the late Platonist formulation and what he considers its most recent manifestation in Descartes' first and second elements (*Principia* IV, Art. 2). The conception of three vehicles that could bear the soul allowed a gradation according to Nemesis from earth-bound souls through aerial ones to angelic (Bk. II, Ch. 14, Sec. 6). For "Eternal Wisdome and Justice has forecast that which is the best" and so fashioned our faculties that "When we have rightly prepared ourselves for the use of them, they will have a right *correspondency* with those things that are offered to them to contemplate in the world" (Ch. 15, Sec. 4).

Another reason for More's insistence on the embodiment of souls in different forms of subtle matter is the fact that he cannot bring himself to believe in totally disembodied souls such as those "the Platonists call Νόες or *pure Intellects*"(Bk. III, Ch. 1, Sec. 3). This probably refers to the gods in *Enneades*, IV, iii, 11, which are never separated from the inteligible world. But More's rejection of this notion is hardly convincing: "This must seem hard and incongruous, especially if we consider what

---

113 For a full discussion of the Platonic and Neoplatonic theories of the soul's vehicles, see E. R. Dodds, 'The Astral Body in Neoplatonism', Appendix II, *The Elements of Theology*, Oxford: Clarendon Press, 1963, pp. 313-21.

noble Beings there are on this side the Νόος or Νόες, that all the Philosophers that ever treated of them acknowledge to be vitally united with either *Aëreal* or *Aethereal* Vehicles" (*Ibid.*). He also denies the existence of Proclus' ἑνάδες[114] ,although this doctrine is really a very original explanation of the simultaneous existence of any member of a hypostasis as independent entity and participated divinity. The ἑνάδες, which constitute the direct link with the One at the level of every hypostasis below the One as well as every series that proceeds from each hypostasis, are real existents and identified by Proclus with the Hellenic gods. More's suspicion of these metaphysical entities which were, according to E.R. Dodds, "a last desperate attempt to carry out the policy of Iamblichus and maintain the united front of Hellenic philosophy and Hellenic religion against the inroads of Christianity,"[115] is thus partly theological.

More's universe is strictly monotheistic, but the plenitude of Divine power nevertheless demands that the entire cosmos be replete with life:

> For this Earth that is replenisht with living Ceatures, nay put in all the Planets too that are in the world, and fancy them inhabited, they all joyned together bear not so great a proportion to the rest of the liquid Matter of the Universe (that is in a nearer capacity of being the Vehicle of Life) as a single Cumminseed to the Globe of the Earth. But how ridiculous a thing would it be, that all the Earth beside being neglected, only one piece thereof, no better then the, rest, not bigger then the smallest seed, should be inhabited? The same may be said also of the compass of the Aire; and therefore it is necessary to enlarge their Territories, and confidently to pronounce there are *Aetherial Animals*, as well as *Terrestrial* and *Aereal*." (Bk. II, Ch. 15, Sec. 3).

---

114 cf. *Elements of Theology*, Props. 113-165.
115 E.R. Dodds, ed. *The Elements of Theology*, Oxford, 1963, p. 259.

We are reminded here of the Pythagorean epigraph of the title-pege proclaiming Πάντα τὸν ἀέρα ἔμπλεον εἶναι ψυχῶν. These diverse souls are possible precisely because of the different vehicles that the plastic faculty of the soul possesses. More further clarifies the notion of the soul's vehicles by analogy with the range of powers present in the perceptive faculty of the soul. Some of our perceptions are "the very same with those of Beasts; others little inferiour to those that belong to *Angels*, as we ordinarily call them; some perfectly brutish, others purely divine: why therefore may there not reside so great a Latitude of capacities in the *Plastick* part of the Soul, as that she may have in her all those three *Vital Congruities*, whereby she may be able livingly to unite as well with the *Celestial* and *Aereal* body as with this *Terrestrial* one?" (Ch. 15, Sec. 4). Just as the cessation of one thought is immediately followed by the rise of another, so, too, when the lowest vital congruity, the terrestrial, is destroyed, the aerial vehicle is awakened, and, the air outside the body being purer than that within, the perceptive faculty of the soul begins to operate with greater vigour than before. This persistence of the perceptive part of the soul as well as of its plastic part in extra-terrestrial conditions is further proof, I think, of the continuous nature of the intellectual substance that emanates from the eternal Mind, for it is hard to see how the higher perceptions can be carried out in the air any more than in the body without the *res cogitans* couched in subtle spirits such as those of the fourth ventricle.

The empirical 'proofs' that More offers of the supernatural voyages of the soul are drawn from either classical historians such as Pliny and Herodotus, Renaissance polymaths such as Cardano and Scaliger, or demonologists such as Bodin and Weyer. All these examples (Bk. II, Chs. 15ff.) reveal the peculiar mythologizing nature of More's mind, a quality he shares with most of the Neoplatonists of antiquity as well as of the Middle Ages and the Renaissance.[116] He first dismisses the possibility of the souls of brutes having aerial or aetherial

---

116 See, for example, the different aspects of demonology developed in Plotinus, *Enneades*, III; V, 5-7; Porphyry, *De abstinentia*, II, 36ff.; Iamblichus,*De Mysteriis*; Proclus' Commentaries on *Timaeus*, *Alcibiades*

vehicles so as to produce animal apparitions. For "the Souls of Brutes seem to have a more passive nature then to be able to manage or enjoy this escape of Death, that free and commanding Imagination belonging only to us, as also Reminiscency" (Ch. 17, Sec. 7). In other words, though they possess animal spirits, they lack the finer spirits of the brain which are necessary for imagination and reminiscence, which are the bases of the desires which determine the after-life of "*intellectual Creatures.*" This is borne out by such phenomena as divine ecstasies and dreams, where the mind, struggling to be free of the body, makes use solely of the pure spirits in the fourth ventricle and "performs some preludious Excercises, conformable to those in her Aiery Vehicle"(Ch. 17, Sec. 9). This impossibility of the existence of 'animal' genii means the apparitions of animals are due to the transformation of 'human' genii into such shapes at will. For, if a person can move his foot or finger by a mere action of the will which directs the animal spirits to the appropriate part of the body, then the soul in its aerial vehicle will be able not only to direct the motions of its fluid particles but also to change their conformation since "the whole Vehicle of the Soul is in a manner nothing else but Spirits" (Bk. III, Ch. 1, Sec. 11).[117]

The series of axioms that begin Book III detail the particular qualities that the soul possesses by virtue of her three vehicles. Apart from the obvious fact of continued sensation through the animal spirits, we also note an increased ability to exert her innate power of self-motion in the aerial and aethereal vehicles(Axioms 31, 32, 34) as also to carry out intellectual activity. The sensitive powers of aerial daemons bear a remarkable resemblance to their terrestrial counterparts and this ensures that "whatever is the *Custome* and *Desire* of the soul in this life ... sticks and adheres to her in that which is to come " (Ch. 4, Sec. 4). Since memory is located in the soul

---

I,Republic; Michael Psellus,*De operatione daimonum;* Dante,*Purgatorio*,25; Ficino,*Theologia Platonica*,XVII,XVIII; Cudworth,*True Intellectual System*, III,IV.

117 More elaborates here the familiar Renaissance analogy of the power of the mother's imagination to cause signatures on the foetus as well as monstrous births (Ch. 5, Sec. 11-Ch. 7, Sec. 6).

itself and needs only the spirits to help it, there is nothing to hinder its continuation in the soul's aerial condition. At the same time, conscience is heightened and the passions it produces in the extremely sensitive aerial body serve as worse punishment than death. Conversely, good conduct in this life results in "a certain *Health* and *Beauty* of the *Aereal* Vehicles; also better Company and Converse, and more pleasant Tracts and Regions to inhabit" (Ch. 11, Sec. 8). In this view of the larger workings of providence, as in his view of the origin and development of souls, More follows Plotinus' account in *Enneades*, IV, iv, 45:

> Anyone that adds his evil to the total of things is known for what he is and, in accordance with his kind, is pressed down into the evil which he has made his own, and hence, upon death, goes to whatever region fits his quality -- and all this happens under the pull of natural forces -- Thus this universe of ours is a wonder of power and wisdom, everything by a noiseless road coming to pass according to a law which none may elude -- which the base man never conceives though it is leading him, all unknowingly, to that place in the All where his lot must be cast -- which the just man knows, and knowing, sets out to the place he must, understanding, even as he begins the journey, where he is to be housed at the end, and having the good hope that he will be with the gods.

The Platonic aristocracy of More's morality, too, is reflected, in the conclusion of his paraphrase of this Plotinian passage: "Of so great consequence is it, while we have opportunity, to aspire to the Best things" (Ch. 11, Sec. 12).

The rarefied bodies of demons approximate more nearly to the spiritual substance that gives them life and activity: "For they have no less Body then we our selves have, only this Body is far more active then ours, being more spiritualized, that is to say, having greater degrees of Motion communicated unto it; which the whole Matter of the world receives from some Spiritual Being or other, and therefore in this regard may be said the more to symbolize with that Immaterial Being, the more Motion is communicated to it" (Ch.2, Sec.9). This increased capacity for motion in the aereal daemons allows them not only to withstand winds and storms but also to derive enjoyment therefrom (Ch.3, Sec.10-15).

The aerial condition of the soul is not eternal, however. This is because there is an "intrinsecall Principle" in the soul which determines the "*Periodical terms* of her *Vital Congruity*" (Ch. 17, Sec. 3), and these periods the Platonists have ascertained to be the shortest in the terrestrial condition, many ages long in the aerial, and for ever in the aetherial. At the termination of the aerial congruity, the souls that have continued in their vices are punished with a descent back into the terrestrial state which is "the profoundest pitch of *Death*" while the virtuous rise into an aethereal state. The aetherial vehicle is one of light and fire corresponding to the fine spirits of the fourth ventricle. The life of the aetherial beings is almost divine and cannot be destroyed by either the conflagration of the world or the extinction of the sun which were predicted by the ancients and which More believed as being not impossible (Chs. 18, 19). This freedom from mundane catastrophies is due to the fact that the soul in its aetherial vehicle has an extraordinary power not only of directing but also of moderating the motion of its spherical particles "by adding or diminishing the degrees of agitation ... whereby she is also able to temper the solidity thereof" (Ch. 19, Sec. 5). This allows her to pass from one 'vortex' (or solar system) to another and "receive the warmth of a new *Vesta*" (*Ibid.*).The aetherial soul is in fact above the reach of Fate, the worklngs of the Evil Principle of darkness which the Persians called 'Arimanius' (Ahriman).In this state where the Divine Mind shines forth through "pure and transparent light," the soul has achieved its "true Ἀποθέωσις."

More's carefully-wrought fantasia on the after-life of the soul constitutes as important a part of his endeavor to formulate a comprehensive and coherent system of the universe as his preoccupation with contemporary physics and physiology. To those that object against the excessive particularity in his descriptions of the social, political, and moral circumstances of the aerial amd aetherial beings in Book III, More replies that his "punctual *and* rational *Description of this* future *state*" is indeed nothing but "an intelligible *Hypothesis*" and supports himself with the precedent of the Platonists " *whose imaginative presages I have often observed to hold a faithful compliance with the severest Reason"* (Preface, Sec. 7). J.A.Stewart, in his book on *The Myths of Plato,* derides More for his "facility of scientific explanation" in his treatment of spirits.[118] But we have already seen that the theory of the soul's vehicles and the unifying power of the *spiritus naturae* is carefully and elaborately worked out.[119] Besides, "the skillful use of 'modern science'," which Stewart recognizes in Plato as "one of the marks of the great master"[120] finds a striking correspondence in More's clever deployment of the most influential concepts of contemporary science, namely those of Descartes and Hobbes, for the purposes of his Christian Platonist eschatology. In fact, all that Stewart says of Plato's use of the cosmological speculations of his age for his illustrative myth in the *Phaedo* might be legitimately applied to the final book of *The Immortality of the Soul:*

> The true object of the *Phaedo* myth is, indeed, moral and religious, not in any way scientific -- its true object is to give expression to man's sense of responsibility, which it does in the form of a vivid history, or spectacle, of the connected life-stages of an immortal personality. This moral and religious object, however, is served best, if the history or spectacle, though carefully presented as a creation of fancy, is not made too fantastical, but is kept at least consistent with 'modern science.'

More's moral aim, too, is the same as that of the Platonists.[121] For, knowledge of the true nature of the soul and its immortality is conducive not only to an aspiration for the good but also to a rational and god-like detachment from the passions of the world:

---

118 J.A.Stewart,*The Myths of Plato,* Carbondale: S.Illinois Univ. Press, 1960, p. 118.

119 Ralph Cudworth, incidentally, whom Stewart praises for being less credulous than More, repeats these theories in his sprawling *True Intellectual System of the Universe* (1678), Vol. I, Ch. 3.

120 Stewart, *op. cit.,* p. 113.

121 cf. Plotinus, *Enneades,* III, ii, 15.

The *fear* and abhorrency therefore we have *of Death*, and the *sorrow* that accompanies it, is no argument but that we may live after it, and are but due affections for those that are to be spectatours of the great *Tragick-Comedy* of the World; the whole plot thereof being contrived by Infinite Wisdome amd Godness, we cannot but surmise that the most sad representations are but a *shew*, but the delight *real* to such as are not wicked and impious; and that what the ignorant call *Evil* in this Universe is but as the shadowy strokes in a fair picture, or the mournful notes in Musick, by which the Beauty of the one is more lively and express, and the Melody of the other more pleasing and melting (Bk. III, Ch. 15, Sec. 9).

Textual Introduction

There are three editions of *The Immortality of the Soul* which were published during More's lifetime, two in English, (the original of 1659 and the second revised edition of 1662) and a third in Latin, (*Immortalitas Animae*, included in the *Operā Omnia*, London,1675-1679). The Latin edition was posthumously translated into English in the fourth edition of his *Collection of Several Philosophical Writings* (1712-1713). All three editions prepared by More differ substantially from one another. This is especially true of the Latin edition which contains several additional *Scholia*, many of a Christian Cabalist nature, representative of the increasingly theological orientation of More's writings in the 1660's and after. Consequently I have chosen to consider the first two English editions as a group in the preparation of my edition, since they constitute the climactic expression of More's philosophical thought, before it became overtly theological.

Of the two English editions of *The Immortality of the Soul*, the first edition is in octavo and has a title page that reads: [In black and {red}]
The / {IMMORTALITY} / OF / THE / SOUL. / {So farre forth as it is demon-} / strable from the knowledge of NATURE and the Light / of REASON / [rule] / {By HENRY MORE Fellow of Christ's / College in Cambridge} / [rule] / Πάντα τὸν ἀέρα ἔμπλεον εἶναι ψυχῶν, καὶ τούτας / δαίμονάς τε καὶ ἥρωας νομίζεσθαι. *Pythag.* / *Quid jucundius quàm scire quid simus, quid / fuerimus,quid erimus; atque cum his etiam / divina atque suprema illa post obitum Mundi- / que vicissitudines?* Cardanus. / [rule] / {*LONDON*}, / Printed by *J. Flesher,* for *William Morden* / Bookseller in *Cambridge,* 1659.
Collation: 8°, A2, A$^{3-4}$, a-b^8, B-Z^8, 2A-20^8, 2P$^{1-4}$ [$4 signed; leaving A4 and 2P4 unsigned] 311 leaves, pp. *i-xxxviii,* 1-549, *550-584.*(*S.T.C.* M2663, Copy: PSU.)

I have used as my copy-text the second edition, "more correct and much enlarged" which appeared in the 1662 folio edition of More's philosophical writings, the title-page of which reads:
[In black and {red}]
A / {COLLECTION} / of Several / Philosophical Writings / Of / {D^{ro} HENRY MORE} / Fellow of *Christ's* Colledge in *Cambridge.* / As Namely, /

His{
Antidote Against Atheism.
Appendix to the said Antidote.
Enthusiasmus Triumphatus.
Letters to Des-Cartes, Ec.
Immortality of the Soul.
Conjectura Cabbalistica.

The second Edition more correct and much enlarged / [rule] / {Aristot.Ethic. lib. 10}./ Εἰ δὴ θεῖον ὁ νοῦς πρὸς τὸν ἄνθρωπον, καὶ ὁ κατὰ τοῦτον βίος θεῖος πρὸς τὸν ἀνθρώπινον βίον. / χρὴ ἡ κατὰ τοὺς παραινοῦντας ἀνθρώπινα ·φροωεῖν ἀνθρώπου ὄντας, ἀλλ᾿ ἐφ᾿ ὅσον ἐνδέχεται, / ἀπαθανατίζειν, καὶ ἅπαντα ποιεῖν πρὸς τὸ ζῶν κατὰ τὸ κράτιστον τῶν ἐν ἡμῖν / \{And again Ch. 8 and 7}./ »Ηδὲ τελεία εὐδαιμονία ὅτι θεωρητική τίς ἐτιν ἐνέργια, καὶ ἐντεῦθεν ἂν φανείη, ὅτι τοὺ θεοὺς / μάλιστα ὑπειλήφαμεν μακαρίους καὶ εὐδαίμονας εἶναι ./ οὐδὲ γὰρ ἦι ἄνθρωπός ἐστιν, οὕτω βιώσεταί τις, ἀλλ᾿ ἦι θεῖόν τι ἐν αὐτῶι ὑπάρχει. / / {LONDON}, / Printed by *James Flesher,* for *William Morden* Book-Seller in Cambridge, / MDCLXII.

The works in the edition have individual title-pages and that of the present treatise reads:
THE / IMMORTALITY / OF / THE / SOUL,/ so farre forth as it is demonstrable from / the Knowledge of NATURE and the Light of REASON. / [rule] / by *HENRY MORE*, D.D. /Fellow of *Christ's* College in *Cambridge.* / [rule] / Pythag. Πάντα τὸν ἀέρα ἔμπλεον εἶναι ψυχῶν, καὶ τούτοις δαίμονάς τε καὶ ἥρωας νομίζεσθαι. / Cardanus. / *Quid jucundius quàm* scire quid simus, quid *fuerimus, quid erimus, atque* / *cum his etiam divina atque suprema illa post obitum Mundique vicissi-* / *tudines?*/ [rule] / [ornament:vine openwork] / [rule] / *London,* / Printed by *James Flesher,* for *William Morden* Book-seller in *Cambridge,* / MDCLXII.

Collation: 2° ,2F$^{5-6}$, 2G-2Z^6, 3A-3C^6,3D$^{1-4}$ [$4 signed; leaving 3D4 unsigned] 243 leaves, pp. *i-iii, 1-234, 235-245 (misprinting 88-89 as 78-79).* Title, 2F5(2F5^V blank). Dedicatory Epistle, headed 'To the Right Honourable Edward,Lord Viscount Conway and Kilulta, 2F7-2Gl(2Gl^V blank). Preface, headed 'The Contents of the Preface,' 2G2-2H2 (2H2^V blank). Text, headed 'The Immortality of the Soul,' 2H3-3C4 . Contents, headed 'The Contents of the several Chapters,' 3C5-3D4. Catchwords: 2F6 - 3D3 . Irregular 216 Plant,] Plant; and 206 1.THAT] 1. HAT (*S.T.C.*

M2646, Copy: PSU.).

*

   As More himself declares in letter of March 15, 1662, to
Lady Conway, he took considerable care to revise his writings
for the collected edition: "... I took the opportunity to perfect
the Treatises to greater exactness in severall thinges then
before ... one maine thing that I pleased my self in among the
rest was that I had the opportunity, whenever I thought there
might be the least occasion of offense (which my eyes
discovered to be but very seldome) to alter things so as would
be most passable and inoffensive."[122] My collation of the 1659
and 1662 editions of *The Immortality of the Soul*[123] has
revealed that More added several sections to the original,
sometimes inserting an entire article into a chapter, and, at
others, modifying or expanding an original article. In addition,
he provided marginal references identifying the sources of
many of the numerous references in the text to contemporary
and classical authors.
   While some of the revisions involve the addition of large
sections, many of them entail the change of merely one word or
phrase[124] as in as in Bk.II, Ch.I, Sec. 8 (p.82) where the
sentence beginning "Which being ..." originally began "This
being ...," or in Bk. II, Ch. 8, Sec. 7,(p.127)where the
transposition of source references from the text in *1659* to
marginal notes in *1662* forces More to add the phrase "into
view" in order to conceal the exclusion elegantly. Most of these
small changes are corrections of errors of grammar or of style.
In Bk.I, Ch. 9, Sec. 9 (p. 52), for example, the second sentence
in *1659* had a redundant 'he' in the main clause after the
parenthetical phrase "again ...*Formes*" and, similarly, in Bk. II,
Ch. 10, Sec. 8,(p.137) where the clause after the parenthesis in
the second sentence originally began with an extra relative
'that'. Likewise, in Bk. I, Ch.14, Sec.8 (p.75) the addition of

---

122 Nicolson,*Conway Letters*, No. 123, p. 198.
123 Hereafter referred to as *1659* and *1662*.
124 The reader is advised to consult the Textual Notes for complete
citations of textual variants.

'yet' to the second part of the sentence beginning "But if ..."
strengthens the sense of the sentence since the second part of it
actually contradicts the first. So, too, in Bk. II, Ch. 6, Sec. 5
(p.114), the addition of the final phrase "that is the cause
thereof" in the second edition clarifies the grammatical
construction of the last sentence.

Sometimes the changes are more than grammatical
corrections and effect stylistic improvements. In Bk. II, Ch.
17, Sec. 9 (p.182), for instance, More altered the epithet
'hoppled' to 'entangled', since 'hoppled' is too close in meaning
to 'fettered,' which follows it. In Bk. II, Ch. 1, Sec. 8, (p.82)
the original phrase " the *least reality* of which matter can
consist" is deftly reduced to "the *least Reality of Matter*" in
1662. So too, in Bk. II, Ch. 16, Sec. 6 (p.174), the more
elaborate paraphrase of Baronio in *1659* is trimmed of its
circumlocution in the second edition. In Bk. III, Ch. 9, Sec. 8
(p.241), the alteration of the phrase "such a white splendour as
is discovered in the full Moon" to "such a White faint splendour
as is discovered in the Moon" is both more poetic and more
accurate in that it allows More to contrast the general faintness
of the earth's sphere as observed by the aerial spirits with the
brighter marks on it owing to the "distinction of Land and
Water." In Bk. III, Ch. 16, Sec. 8 (p.283), too, the addition of
the example of the great distances covered during the earth's
revolution to that of the distances traversed by human beings
on the planet is both an imaginative exaggeration for the
purpose of ridicule and a valid scientific observation.

Not all the changes are merely stylistic, however, some of
the revisions indicate either a greater certainty regarding an
issue or, conversely, a greater hesitancy. In Bk. I, Ch. 11, Sec.
6 (p.61), for example, More's conviction of the insignificance of
the planets in relation to the vast amplitude of the universe is
shown to have increased by the time of the 1662 revision, for,
whereas he originally likened them to an "apple" when
compared to "the whole ball of the Earth," he now considers
them to be "as an ordinary grain of Sand." So too, in Bk. I,
Ch. 11, Sec. 9 (p.64), the change of "Matter of its own Nature
has no active Principle of Motion" in the 1659 edition to "no
Matter whatsoever of its own Nature has any active Principle of
Motion" bears witness to his increased antipathy towards the
contrary doctrine. On the other hand, the change of "is" in the
last sentence of Bk. I, Ch. 11, Sec. 6 (p.62), to "seems" reveals

a greater caution on the part of More in offering historical precedent as evidence against a scientific possibility. That the question of the self-destruction of the world if matter were instinct with motion exercised him considerably at the time of the revision is seen from his insertion of another sentence relating to it in the next article, "For thus they would avoid that hasty and universal Conflagration there inferred," and, more importantly from the addition of an entire article (No. 8, p.63) designed to dismiss the hypothesis of the existence of a divine matter that can circumvent the destruction of the world. The addition of Sec. 3 in Bk. II, Ch. 1 (p.78), which denies the power of cogi tation to matter is also directed by the same aversion to any form of matter being considered divine.

In Bk. III, Ch. 12, Sec. 3 (p.256), the addition of the qualification "if it will prove true" to his example of the sympathetic fermentation of wines shows that More was indeed less credulous than some readers may infer from a rapid reading of his works and was careful in his revision to make evident his judicious use of stories of supernatural effects. This is confirmed by his new division of Sec. 10 (p.268) in the next chapter, dealing also with the sympathetic powers of the Spirit of Nature, where he juxtaposes the more acceptable scientific example of magnetic motion to that of the working of wines in order to highlight the innate similarity between these two actions.

One other form of stylistic change needs to be mentioned: the reduced use of the term "Your Lordship" in the 1662 Epistle Dedicatory to Lord Conway, and the change of the valediction from "Your Honours humbly devoted Servant" to " *Your Lordships humbly devoted Servant*" (p.3). This rephrasing of the original letter can scarcely be attributed to any new republican tendencies in More, for, throughout his life, monarchical order was a rational ideal for him.[125] The only plausible reason for this change is that More sought to render his formal style more concise in the later edition and, also, to effect a certain symmetry between the valediction of this Epistle Dedicatory and that to Lady Conway in *An Antidote*

---

125 cf. Nicolson, "Christ's College and the Latitude Men," *MP*, 27, (August 1929), p.39.

against Atheisme which, in both 1653 and 1662, is signed "Your Ladiships humbly-devoted Servant."

In one or two instances, the revisions correct errors of meaning in the original edition, as in Bk II Ch. 16 Sec 7 (p.175), where "they" is substituted for "it" in the last part of the third sentence since the pronoun in this case should refer to the "others" whose opinions is being discussed here, whereas "it" would tend towards "the Soul" for its antecedent, thereby making nonsense of the sentence. Similarly, in Bk. III, Ch. 15, Sec. 7 (p.277), the inadvertent fusion of the two words "in, clogg'd" in the 1659 edition is corrected in the second edition, though this is already noted in the Errata listed at the end of *1659*. Since the sentence would not be grammatically wrong even with the mistake -- though it would not have signified what More intended -- it is probable that this error and the other seven included in the Errata of the 1659 edition were recorded by More himself.

Among the larger additions to the 1662 edition, two are in the form of answers to possible objections to his views. For example, in the Preface, Sec 10 (p.16), he elaborates on the contradictions involved in the notion of a single, percipient, world-soul by focussing on the physiological mechanism of individuals. In Bk. II, Ch. 1, Secs. 3 and 4, are added to discuss more comprehensively the materialists' assumption of a single, corporeal principle in the universe. The additions thus form a continuation of More's treatment of this subject in Sec.5 of the Preface. Most of the other additions are clarifications of scientific or philosophical points, as in Bk. II, Ch. 1, Sec. 14 (p.85), where he emphasizes the contamination of colours that would result if the percipient were a corporeal point in the optic nerve by adding the condition "especially if it [i.e. the object] be nigh and very small."

In Bk. II, Ch. 5, Sec. 8 (p.110), his addition of the phrase "Some (suppose) before and others behinde" to the remark that imaginations are formed of impressions received in the brain shows a more precise knowledge of current physiological theories. While, in Bk. II, Ch. 8, Sec. 13 (p.130) , his further description of the nerves as "one continued Receptacle or Case of that immediate instrument of the sensiferous motions of the Soul, the *Animal Spirits*, wherein also lies her hidden Vehicle of life in this mortal body," is both a reiteration of the pervasive activity of the animal spirits as the instrument of the rational soul and a more profound, Platonic, conclusion to the Chapter. Also helpful are the short passage added in Bk. II Ch. 10, Sec. 8(p.137), in which he demonstrates the sensible explanation of the experience of pain that the continuity of animal spirits in the body affords, and the phrase "which is interested in all Plastick powers" in the first sentence of Bk. II, Ch.10, Sec, 7 (p.137), which reveals that the correspondence between the *Anima mundi* and the animal spirits is by virtue of the plastic and motive powers of both.

Not all the clarifications are highly significant, however. The addition of the sentence "Whence the Sun, the Stars and Planets would appear to us in that bigness they really are of, they being perceiv'd in that bigness by those parts of the *Soul of the World* that are at a convenient nearness to them" in Bk. III, Ch. 16, Sec 7 (p.283), is a repetition of a point made in many similar ways earlier in the same chapter and in Sec. 10 of the Preface, too. On the other hand, the inclusion of a section describing "the Will and Essence of her [i.e. the soul's] Creator" in the next section (p.283) is indeed of special importance in understanding the skillful approximation that More effects between emanation and creation (cf. Commentary Notes, p.37 5).

Apart from these additions, there is one very long elaboration of the diverse ways in which the Spirit of Nature operates through the instincts of animals (Bk. III, Ch. 13, Sec. 9). It may seem curious that More should have added a whole article at this point since in the original edition, even with his briefer discussion of the same subject, he had felt that he had tired his audience, saying, "But this argument being too lubricous, I will not much insist upon it." But the detailed discussion of the instinctual habits of birds and insects shows that More realized that this manifestation of the Spirit of Nature was the most convincing proof of its existence. Particularly, the evidence of the use of nidification for the preservation of the species rather than the individual seemed to point to the working of a providential agent geared to "the Conservation of the Whole." In another instance (Bk. II, Ch. 1, Sec. 8), More's revision of the 1662 edition involves the omission of an article from the original and the substitution of a new passage. The original is, in fact, the record of an interesting physical experiment he seems to have conducted himself proving the ultimate distortion of images when reduced to an infinitesimal point. The revision, on the other hand, is -- apart from its specific reference to "one *real* line of motion" directed to the point -- a more far -fetched and derisive dismissal of the alternative theory.

The revisions that More made for the second edition are thus present throughout the work and often involve, as we have seen, the change of just one word or phrase either to correct some grammatical or stylistic error or to suit some newly added material. The latter form of revision is due, also, in a couple of instances, to the different paragraphing of the 1662 edition. For instance, in Bk. II, Ch. 11, Sec. 5 (p.142), the second paragraph beginning "Wherefore I shall conclude ... " was part of the first paragraph in *1659* and read "And therefore I shall conclude..." So too in the opening of Bk. III, Ch. 3, Sec.14 (p.209). The rearrangement of the paragraphs into smaller units results in a clearer and more logical pattern of exposition, as in Bk. I, Ch. 2, Sec. 11 -- to give but one example -- where all three paragraphs of the article were originally run into one paragraph, whereas the new scheme effectively moves from an initial discussion of the essential properties of a spirit, penetrability and indiscerpibility, to an explanation of the resulting "fourth Mode" of spissitude, and on to the extraordinary final example of 'motion' as spiritual extension. Similarly, the punctuation of the revised edition is, also, clearer and more careful, as in Bk. I, Ch. 2, Sec. 12 (p.28), where the second parenthesis in the first sentence originally included the clause beginning "which with ... " when it should be restricted, as it is in *1662*, to the discussion of 'Indiscerpibility' and 'Impenetrability.'

Given the minute nature and ubiquity of the revisions, it is tempting to think that More actually provided the printer with a new manuscript. The reference to the great strain of revision in his letter to Lady Conway (cited above p.xlvi) seems to point to a transcription of the entire treatise, especially since the expression he uses to describe it, "This edition has cost me a third part of the paines of writing the books" is the same as that used in his letter of March, 1658,[126] in relation to the transcription original version of the *Immortality of the Soul*

---

126 cf. Nicolson, *Conway Letters*, No. 85, p. 145.

shortly after its composition. However, since More's manuscripts are apparently not extant, it is difficult to ascertain whether More transcribed the entire work again for his printer or allowed him to work from the original edition along with a list of revisions submitted in manuscript.

This question is further obscured by the fact that the orthography of *1662* is altered considerably from that of *1659*. The first edition has a greater number of words with doubled final consonants, such as "aethereall," "vitall," or "universall," and verbs and substantives with the archaic addition of a mute 'e,' such as "finde," "doe," and "soule." As these 'quainter' spellings reflect More's own spelling habits as revealed in his letters -- habits that persisted right through the sixties and seventies.[127]it is likely that the spelling changes evident in *1662* are due to the inclination of the printer or his need to justify the lines. Another feature of the second edition which may be attributed to More with a little more certainty (unless the printer were an especially perceptive reader) is the more consistent capitalization and italicization of substantives and their attributes for the sake of emphasis) especially when they represent metaphysical or scientific entities such as *Motion*, *Sight*, or *Incorporeal*.

In my edition, I have followed the paragraph scheme, the punctuation and the spelling of the 1662 edition without, in any instance, indicating their original forms. In a few cases where the spelling or numbering of the second edition is clearly faulty, I have emended the text.[128] I have also made certain typographical alterations silently: display capitals have been replaced by ordinary ones, long 's' by modern 's', and Renaissance Greek contractions have been expanded.

I have removed all of More's marginal references from my text, and have reproduced them in my Commentary Notes.

---

127 cf. More's letters in Nicolson, *op. cit., passim.*

128 The four instances where I have emended the text are the erroneous spellings *Definitivé* in Bk. I, Ch.9, Sec.10 (p.53) and Victualle'rs in Bk. II, Ch. 16, Sec. 1 (p.170), and the misprinting of Sec. 10 as 15 in Bk.II , Ch. 12(p.150) and Sec. 13 as 12 in the summary of sections at the head of Bk. III, Ch. 1 (p.191).

To facilitate reading, I have translated in my Notes all Greek and Latin quotations not translated or closely paraphrased by More himself.

THE
IMMORTALITY
OF
THE SOUL,

So farre forth as it is demonſtrable from
the Knowledge of N A T U R E and
the Light of R E A S O N.

By *HENRY MORE*, D.D.
Fellow of *Chriſt*'s College in *Cambridge*.

Pythag.

Γ´άντα τ´ άέρα έμπλεον ἔἰ ψυχῶν, ὃ τύτοις δαίμοναί τε ϗ ήρωας
νομίζεϑ.

Cardanus.

*Quid jucundius quàm ſcire quid ſimus, quid fuerimus, quid erimus; atque
cum bis etiam divina atque ſuprema illa poſt obitum Mundique viciſſi-
tudines?*

LONDON,
Printed by *James Fleſher*, for *William Morden* Book-ſeller in *Cambridge*,
MDCLXII.

To the Right Honourable
EDWARD,
Lord Viscount
CONWAY and KILULTA.

My Lord,
Though I be not ignorant of your Lordships aversness from all
Addresses of this kinde, (whether it be that your Lordship has
taken notice of that usual Vanity of those that dedicate Books,
in endeavouring to oblige their Patrons by over-lavish praises,
such as much exceed the worth of the party they thus
ummeasurably commend; or whether it be from a natural
Modesty that cannot bear, no not so much as a just
representation of your own Vertues and Abilities; or lastly from
a most true Observation, That there are very few Treatises
writ which are any thing more then mere Transcriptions or
Collections out of other Authors whose Writings have already
been consecrated to the Name and Memory of some other
worthy Persons long since deceased; so that they do but after a
manner rob the dead to furnish themselves with Presents to
offer to the living) Yet notwithstanding this your averseness, or
whatever grounds there may be surmised thereof, I could not
abstain from making this present Dedication. Not so much I
confess to gratify your Lordship (though it be none of the best
Complements) as for mine own satisfaction and content. For I
do not take so great pleasure in any thing as in the sense and
conscience of the fitness and sutableness of mine own actions;
amongst which I can finde none more exactly just and befitting
then this; there being many Considerations that give you a
peculiar right and title to the Patronage of this present
Discourse. For besides your skill in Philosophy and real
sense of Piety, two such Endowments as are rarely to be found
together (especially in Persons of high quality) and yet without
which matters of this nature can neither be read with any
relish nor easily understood; there are also other things still
more peculiar, and which naturally do direct and determine me
to the choice I have made. For whether I consider the many
civilities from your self and nearest Relations, especially from
your noble and vertuous Lady, whom I can never think on but
with admiration, nor mention without the highest respect: or
whether I recollect with my self the first occasion of busying
my thoughts upon this Subject, which was then when I had the

honour and pleasure of reading *Des-Cartes* his *Passions* with
your Lordship in the Garden of *Luxenburg* to pass away the
time, (in which Treatise though there be nothing but what is
handsome and witty, yet all did not seem so perfectly solid and
5   satisfactory to me but that I was forced in some principal
things to seek satisfaction from my self:) or lastly, call to
minde that pleasant retirement I enjoyed at *Ragley* during my
abode with you there; my civil treatment from that perfect and
unexceptionable pattern of a truly Noble and Christian Matron,
10   the Right Honourable your Mother; the solemness of the Place,
those shady Walks, those Hills & Woods, wherein often having
lost the sight of the rest of the World, and the World of me, I
found out in that hidden solitude the choicest Theories in the
following Discourse: I say, whether I considered all these
15   circumstances, or any of them, I could not but judge them more
then enough to determine my choice to so Worthy a Patron.

    Nor could the above-mentioned surmises beat me from my
design, as not at all reaching the present case. For as for my
part, I am so great a Lover of the Truth, and so small an
20   Admirer of vulgar Eloquence, that neither the presage of any
gross advantage could ever make me stoop so low as to expose
my self to the vile infamy or suspicion of turning *Flatterer*, nor
yet the tickling sense of applause and vain-glory, to affect the
puffy name and title of an Orator. So that your Lordship
25   might be secure as touching the First surmise.

    And verily for the Second, though I confess I might not be
at all averse from making a just and true representation of
your Vertues and Accomplishments; yet considering the
greatness of them, & the meanness of mine own Rhetorick, I
30   found it not so much as within my power, if I would, to
entrench upon your Modesty; and therefore I must leave it to
some more able Pen to doe you and the World that right
whether you will or no.

    And lastly, for that scruple concerning the theft or petty
35   sacriledge of several *Plagiaries*, who, as it were, rob the
Monuments of the dead to adorn the living; it is the onely thing
that I can without vanity profess, that what I offer to you is
properly my own, that is to say, that the invention, application
and management of the Reasons and Arguments comprised in
40   this Book, whether for confutation or confirmation, is the
genuine result of my own anxious and thoughtful Mind, no old
stuff purloined or borrowed from other Writers. What truth

and solidity there is in my Principles and Reasonings were too great a piece of arrogance for me to predetermine. This must be left to the judgements of such free and discerning spirits as your Lordship: With whom if what I have writ my find acceptance or a favourable censure, it will be the greater 5 obligation and encouragement to,

My Lord,

Your Lordships humbly devoted Servant, 10

HENRY MORE.

The CONTENTS *of the* Preface

I. The Title of the Discourse how it is to be understood. 2. The Author's submission of his whole Treatise to the infallible Rule of Sacred Writ. 3. A plain and compendious Demonstration that *Matter* consists of parts *indiscerpible.* 4. An Answer to an Objection touching his Demonstration against the Sun's superintendency over the affairs of the Earth. 5. A confirmation of Mr. *Hobbs* his Opinion, That Perception is really one with Corporeal Motion and Re-action, if there be nothing but *Matter* in the World. 6. An Apologie for the Vehicles of *Daemons* and Souls separate. 7. As also for his so punctually describing the State of the other life, and so curiously defining the nature of a particular Spirit. 8. That his *Elysiums* he describes are not at all *Sensual*, but *Divine.* 9. That he has not made the State of the wicked too easy for them in the other world. 10. That it is not *one Universal* Soul that hears, sees and reasons in every man, demonstrated from the Acts of Memory. 11. Of the *Spirit of Nature*; that it is no obscure Principle, nor unseasonably introduced. 12. That he has absolutely demonstrated the Existence thereof. 13. That the admission of that Principle need be no hinderance to the progress of *Mechanick* Philosophy. 14. The great pleasure of that study to pious and rational persons. 15. Of what concernment it would be if *Des-Cartes* were generally read in all the Universities of Christendome. 16. An excuse of the prolixity of his Preface from his earnest desire of gratifying the publick, without the least offence to any rational or ingenuous Spirit.

That the present Treatise may pass more freely and smoothly through the hands of men, without any offence or scruple to the good and pious, or any real exception or probable cavil from those whose Pretensions are greater to Reason then Religion; I shall endeavour in this Preface to prevent them, by bringing here into view, and more fully explaining and clearing, whatever I conceive obnoxious to their mistakes and obloquies.

1. And indeed I cannot be well assured but that the very Title of my Discourse may seem liable to both their dislikes. To the dislike of the one, as being confident of the contrary Conclusion, and therefore secure That that cannot be demonstrated to be true, which they have long since judged not worthy to be reckoned in the rank of things probable; *it may be not so much as of things* possible. *To the dislike of the other, as being already perswaded of the truth of our Conclusion upon other and better grounds: which would not be better, if the natural light of Reason could afford Demonstration in this matter. And therefore they may* 5 *haply pretend, that so ambitious a Title seems to justle with the high Prerogative of Christianity, which has* brought life and immortality to light.

But of the former I demand, By what Faculty they are made so secure of their being wholly mortal. For unless they will 10 *ridiculously conceit themselves inspired, whenas they almost as little believe there is either God or Spirit, as that they have in them an Immortal Soul, they must either pretend to the* experience of Sense, *or the* clearness of Reason. *The former whereof is impossible; because these bold deniers of the* 15 *Immortality of the Soul have not yet exprienced whether we subsist after Death or no. But if they would have us believe they have thus concluded upon rational grounds; I dare appeal unto them, if they can produce any stronger Reasons for their Cause then what I have set down for them, and if I have not fully and* 20 *fundamentally answered them. If they will say their confidence proceeds from the weak arguings of the adverse party; I answer, it is weakly done of them, (their own Arguments being as unconcluding as they can fancy their adversaries) to be so secure, that Truth is on their own part rather then on theirs. But this* 25 *can touch onely such managements of this Cause as they have seen already and censured. But that is nothing to me, who could never think I stood safe but upon my own legs. Wherefore I shall require them onely to peruse what I have written before they venture to judge thereof; and after they have read, if they will* 30 *declare that I have not demonstrated the Cause I have undertook, I think it reasonable and just, that the punctually shew in what part or joynt of my Demonstration they discern so weak a coherence as should embolden them still to dissent from the Conclusion.* 35

But to the other I answer with more modesty and submission, That the Title of My Book doth not necessarily imply an promise of so full and perfect a Demonstration, that nothing *can be added for the firmer assurance of the Truth; but onely that there may be expected as clear a Proof as* Natural Reason *will* 40 *afford us. From which they should rather inferre, That I do acknowledge a further and a more palpable evidence*

comprehended in Christian Religion, *and more intelligible and convictive to the generality of the World, who have neither leisure nor inclination to deal with the spinosities and anxieties of humane Reason and Philosophy. But I declined the making use*
5 *of that Argument at this time; partly because I have a design to speak more fully thereof in my Treatise* Of the Mystery of Christian Religion, *if God so permit; and partly because it was unsutable to the present Title, which pretends to handle the matter onely within the bounds of* Natural Light, *unassisted and*
10 *unguided by any miraculous Revelation.*

2. *Which will be a pleasant spectacle to such as have a Genius to these kinde of Contemplations, and wholly without danger; they still remembring that it is the voice of Reason and Nature, (which being too subject to corruption may very well be*
15 *defectuous or erroneous in some things,) and therefore never trusting their dictates and suggestions, where they clash with the Divine Oracles, they must needs be safe from all seduction: though, I profess, I do not know any thing which I assert in this Treatise that doth disagree with them. But if quicker-sighted*
20 *then my self do discover any thing not according to that Rule, it may be an occasion of humble thankfulness to God for that great priviledge of our being born under an higher and exacter light: whereby those that are the most perfectly exercis'd therein, are inabled as well to rectifie what is perverse, as to supply what is*
25 *defectuous in the light of Nature; and they have my free leave afore-hand to doe both throughly all along the ensuing Discourse.*

And this may serve by way of a more general Defence. But that nothing may be wanting, I shall descend to the making good also of certain Particulars, as many as it is of any consequence
30 *further to clear and confirm.*

3. *In the First Book there occurre onely these Two that I am aware of. The one concerning the* Center *of a particular Spirit, whose Idea I have described, and demonstrated possible. The other concerns my Demonstration of the* Impossibility *of the*
35 Sun's *seeing any thing upon Earth, supposing him merely corporeal. In the making good the former, I have taken the boldness to assert, That* Matter *consists of parts* indiscerpible, *understanding by* indiscerpible *parts, particles that have indeed real extension, but so little, that they cannot have less and be any*
40 *thing at all, and therefore cannot be actually divided. Which minute Extension, if you will, you may call Essential (as being such that without that measure of it, the very Being of* Matter

cannot be conserved,) as the extension of any Matter compounded
of these you may, if you please, term Integral; these parts of this
compounded Matter being actually and really separable one
from another. The Assertion, I confess, cannot but seem
paradoxical at first sight, even to the ingenious and judicious. 5
But that there are such indiscerpible particles into which Matter
is divisible, viz. such as have Essential extension, and yet have
parts utterly inseparable, I shall plainly and compendiously here
demonstrate (besides what I have said in the Treatise it self) by
this short Syllogism. 10

That which is actually divisible so farre as actual division
any way can be made, is divisible into parts indiscerpible.

But Matter(I mean that Integral or Compound Matter) is
actually divisible as farre as actual division any way can be
made. 15

It were a folly to goe to prove either my Proposition or
Assumption, they being both so clear, that no common notion in
Euclide is more clear, into which all Mathematical
Demonstrations are resolved.

It cannot but be confessed therefore, That Matter consists of 20
indiscerpible particles, and that Physically and really it is not
divisible in infinitum, though the parts that constitute an
indiscerpible particle are real, but divisible onely intellectually;
it being of the very essence of whatsoever is to have Parts or
Extension in some measure or other. For, to take away all 25
Extension, is to reduce a thing onely to a Mathematical point,
which is nothing else but pure Negation or Non-entity; and there
being no medium betwixt extended and not-extended, no more
then there is betwixt Entity and Nonentity, it is plain that if a
thing be at all, it must be extended, And therefore there is an 30
Essential Extension belonging to these indiscerpible particles of
Matter; which was the other Property which was to be
demonstrated.

I know unruly Fancy will make mad work here, and
clamour against the Conclusion as impossible. For Finite 35
Extension (will she say) must needs have Figure, and Figure
extuberancy of parts at such a distance, that we cannot but
conceive them still actually divisible. But we answer, That when
Matter is once actually divided as farre as possibly it can, it is a
perfect contradiction it should be divided any further; as it is also 40
that it cannot be divided actually as farre as it can actually be
divided. And no stronger Demonstration then this against them

can be brought against us by either Fancy or Reason : and
therefore supposing we were but equal in our reasoning, this is
enough to give me the day, who onely contend for the possibility
of the thing. For if I bring but fully as good Demonstration that
5   it is, as the other that it is not, none can deny me but that the
thing is possible on my side.

But to answer the above-recited Argument, though they can
never answer ours; I say, those indiscerpible particles of Matter
have no Figure at all: As infinite Greatness has no Figure, so
10   infinite Littleness has none also. And a Cube infinitely little in
the exactest sense, is as perfect a contradiction as a Cube
infinitely great in the same sense of Infinity; for the Angles
would be equal in magnitude to the Hedrae thereof. Besides, wise
men are assured of many things that their Fancy cannot but play
15   tricks with them in; as in the Infinity of Duration and of Matter,
or at least of Space. Of the truth whereof though they are never
so certain, yet if they consider this infinite Matter, Space, or
Duration, as divided, suppose, into three equal parts (all which
must needs be infinite, or else the whole will not be so) the middle
20   part of each will seem both finite and infinite; for it is bounded at
both ends. But every thing has two handles, as Epictetus notes;
and he is a fool that will burn his fingers with the hot handle,
when he may hold safe by the other that is more tractable and
cool.

25   4. Concerning my Demonstration of the Impossibility of the
Suns being a Spectator of our particular affairs upon Earth,
there is onely this one objection, viz. That though the Sun
indeed, by reason of his great distance, cannot see any particular
thing upon Earth, if he kept always in that ordinary shape in
30   which we should suppose that, if he were devoid of sense, he
would doe; yet he having life and perception, he may change some
part of his Body (as we do our Eye in contracting or dilating the
pupil thereof) into so advantageous a Figure that the Earth may
be made to appear to him as bigge as he pleases.

35   Though some would be more ready to laugh at, then answer
to, so odde a surmise, which supposes the Sun blinking and
peering so curiously into our affairs, as through a Telescope; yet
because it comes in the way of reasoning, I shall have the patience
seriously to return this Reply.

40   First, That this Objection can pretend to no strength at all,
unless the Body of the Sun were Organical, as ours is; whenas he
is nothing but fluid Light: so that unless he hath a spiritual

Being in him, to which this Light should be but the Vehicle, this arbitrarious figuring of his fluid Matter cannot be effected. But to grant there is any such incorporeal *Substance in the* Sun, *is to yield what I contend for,viz. That there are* Immaterial Substances *in the World. World.* 5

But that there is no such Divine Principle in him, whereby he can either see us, or aim at the producing any apparition on the Earth in reference to any one of us, by the activity of that Spirit in him, it is apparent from the scum and spots that lie on him: Which is as great an Argument that there is no such Divinity in 10 *him as some would attribute to him, (such as* Pomponatius, Cardan, Vaninus *and others) as the dung of Owls and Sparrows, that is found on the faces and shoulders of Idols in Temples, are clear evidences thet they are but dead Images, no true Deities.*

Lastly, though we should suppose he had a particular 15 sentient *and* intelligent *Spirit in him, yet the consideration of the vast distance of the Earth from him, and the thickness of her* Atmosphere, *with other disadvantages I have already mentioned in my Treatise, makes it incredible that he should be able to frame his Body into any Figure so exquisite as will compensate* 20 *these insuperable difficulties.*

5. In my Second Book the first Exception is concerning the 20th *Axiome, which, say they, I have not proved, but onely brought in the testimony of Mr* Hobbs *for the support thereof; which therefore onely enables me to argue with him upon his own* 25 *Principles, wherin others will hold themselves unconcerned. But I answer, first, that it will concern all his followers as well as hinself, so that it is no contemptible victory to demonstrate against all those so confident Exploders of* Immaterial Substances, *That their own acknowledged Principles will necessarily inferre the* 30 *Existence of them in the World. But in the next place, it will not be hard to produce undeniable Reasons to evince the truth of the above-named Axiome, viz.* That Sense and Perception in *Matter,* and supposing nothing but *Matter* in the World, is really the same with Corporeal Motion and Re-action. 35

For it is plain in Sensation, *there being always* external motion *from objects when our Senses are affected. And that inward* Cogitation *is thus performed, appears from the* heat *that* Thinking *casts a man into: Wherefore generally all* Cogitation *is accompanied with* motion corporeal. *And if there be nothing but* 40 Body *or* Matter *in the World,* Cogitation *it self is really the same thing with* Corporeal Motion.

Moreover as in Sensation *the* Corporeal Motion *is first, and* Perception *follows; so it is necessary that universally in all* internal Cogitations *also certain* Corporeal Motions *immediately precede those* Perceptions, *though we did admit that* Matter
5 *moved it self: For no* Sense *would thence arise without resistance of something it hit against. Insomuch that the* subtilest Matter *unresisted or not imprest upon, would be no more capable of* Cogitation *then a* Wedge of Gold *or* Pig of Lead. *And therefore if we will but* confess *(what none but mad men would venture to*
10 *deny) that a* Pig of Lead *or* Wedge of Gold *has not any* Thought *or* Perception *at all without some knock or allision proportionable to their bigness and solidity, the* subtilest Matter *must likewise have none without some proportionable impression or resistance. Whence it is plain that alwaies* corporeal Re-action *or* Collision
15 *precedes* Perception, *and that every* Perception *is a kind of* feeling, *which lasts so long as this resistance or impress of motion lasts; but that ceasing, is extinguish'd, the* Matter *being then as stupid as in a* Pig of Lead. *And that therefore as in general there is alwaies* Corporeal *motion where there is*
20 Cogitation, *so the diversification of this motion and collision causes the diversification of cogitations, and so they run hand in hand perpetually; the one never being introduced without the fore-leading of the other, nor lasting longer then the other lasteth. But as* heat *is lost: (which implies as considerable* motion *or*
25 *agitation of some very subtile* Matter,*) so our* Understanding *and* Imagination *decayes, and our* Senses *themselves fail,as not being able to be moved by the impression of outward* Objects, *or as not being in a due degree of liquidity and agility, and therefore in death our* Bodies *become as senseless as a lump of clay.*

30   *All* Sensation *therefore and* Perception *is really the same with* Motion *and* Re-action *of* Matter, *if there be nothing but* Matter *in the world.*

    And that every piece of Matter *must perceive according as it self is moved, whether by it self (if it were possible) or by*
35 *corporeal impress from other parts, is plain, in that* Matter *has no subtile rayes, or any power or efflux streaming beyond it self, like that which the* Schools *call* species intentionales, *nor yet any union more mysterious then the mere* Juxta-position *of parts.*

    For hence it is manifest that there can be no communication
40 *of any impress that one part of the* Matter *receives or is affected with from another at a distance, but it must be by jogging or crouding the parts interjacent. So that in every regard* corporeal

Motion *or* Re-action, *with sufficient tenuity of parts and due duration, will be the adequate cause of all perception, if there be nothing but* Matter *in the world. This I think may suffice to assure any indifferent man of the truth of this part of* Mr Hobbs *his Assertion, if himself could make the other part true, That* 5 *there is nothing existent in Nature but what is purely corporeal. But out of the former part, which is his own acknowledged Principle, I have undeniably demonstrated that there is.*

    6. *The other Exception is against that Opinion I seem to* 10 *embrace touching the* Vehicles of Daemons and Souls separate, *as having herein offended against the authority of the* Schools. *And I profess this is all the reason I can imagine that they can have against my Assertion. But they may, if they please, remember that the Schools trespass against a more ancient* 15 *authority then thamselves, that is to say, the* Pythagoreans, Platonists, Jewish Doctours, *and the* Fathers *of the Church, who all hold* That even the purest Angels have corporeal Vehicles. *But it will be hard for the* Schools *to alledge any ancient Authority for their Opinion. For* Aristotle *their great* 20 *Oracle is utterly silent in this matter, as not so much as believing the Existence of* Daemons *in the world (as* Pomponatius *and* Vaninus *his sworn disciples have to their great contentment taken notice of:) And therefore being left to their own dry subtilties, they have made all* Intellectual *Beings that are not grossly terrestrial,* 25 *as* Man *is,* purely Immaterial. *Whereby they make a very hideous Chasme or gaping breach in the order of things, such as no moderate judgment will ever allow of, and have become very obnoxious to be foiled by Atheistical wits, who are forward and skilful enough to draw forth the absurd consequences that lye hid* 30 *in false supossitions, as* Vaninus *does in this. For he does not foolishly collect from the supossed pure Immateriality of* Daemons, *that they have no knowledge of particular things upon Earth; such purely Incorporeal Essences being uncapable of impression from Corporeal Objects, and therefore have not the* 35 Species *of any particular thing that is corporeal in their mind. Whence he infers that all* Apparitions, Prophecies, Prodigies, *and whatsoever* miraculous *is recorded in ancient History, is not to be attributed to these, but to the influence of the Stars; and so concludes that there are indeed no such things as* Daemons *in the* 40 *Universe.*

By which kinde of reasoning also it is easy for the
Psychopannychites *to support their Opinion of the* Sleep of the
Soul. *For the Soul be utterly rescinded from all that is corporeal,
and having no vital union therewith at all, they will be very prone*
5   *to infer, that it is possible she should know any thing* ad extra, *if
she can so much as* dream. *For even the power also may seem
incompetible to her in such a state, she having such an essential
aptitude for vital union with* Matter. *Of so great consequence is
it sometimes to desert the opinion of the* Schools, *when something*
10   *more rational and more safe and useful offers it self unto us.*

     7. *These are the main Objections my First and Second Book
seem liable unto. My last I cannot but suspect to be more
obnoxious. But the most common Exception I foresee that will be
against it, is, That I have taken upon me to describe* the state of
15   the other World *so punctually and particularly, as if I had been
lately in it: For over-exquisiteness may seem to smell of art and
fraud. And as there is a diffidency many times in us when we
hear something that is extremely sutable to our desire, being then
most ready to think it too good to be true; so also in Notions that*
20   *seem over-accurately fitted to our Intellectual faculties, and agree
the most naturally therewith, we are prone many times to suspect
them to be too easy to be true; especially in things that seemed at
first to us very obscure and intricate.   For which cause also it is
very likely that the Notion of a particular Spirit, which I have so*
25   *accurately described in my First Book, may seem the less credible
to some, because it is now made so clearly intelligible, they
thinking it utterly improbable that these things, that have been
held alwaies such inextricable perplexities, should be thus of a
suddain made manifest and familiar to any that has but a*
30   *competency of Patience and Reason to peruse the Theory.*

     *But for my own part, I shall not assume so much to my self,
as peremptorily to affirm that the* Indiscerpibility *of a Spirit
arises that way that I have set down, that is to say, that* God *has
made a particular Spirit just in that manner that I have*
35   *delineated. For his* Wisdome *is infinite, and therefore it were an
impious piece of boldness to confine him to one certain way of
framing the nature of a Being, that is, of endowing it with such
Attributes as are essential to it, as* Indiscerpibility *is to the* Soul
of Man. *But onely to have said in general, It is possible there*
40   *may be a particular Essence of its immediate nature* penetrable
and indiscerpible, *and* notparticularly *to have described the
manner how it may be so; might have seemed to many more*

slight and unsatisfactory, Deceit lurking in Universals, as the Proverb has it. And therefore for the more fully convincing of the adverse party, I thought fit to pitch upon a punctual description *of some one way, how the* Soul *of Man or of a* Daemon *may be conceived necessarily* indiscerpible, *though* dilatable; *not being* 5 *very sollicitous whether it be just that way or no, but yet well assured that it is either* that way *or* some better. *But this one way shews the thing* possible *at large:* (As that mean *contrivance of an Indian* Canoa *might prove the possibility of Navigation.) And that is all that I was to aim at in that place;* 10 *saving that I had also a zeal for the credit of the* Platonists, *whose imaginative presages I have often observed to hold a faithful compliance with the severest Reason. And I think I have here demonstrated that their Fancy is not at all irrational in so usually comparing* Form *or* Spirit *to the radiant* Light. 15

So in my description of the state of the other world, *I am not very sollicitous whether things be just so as I have set them down: but because some men utterly misbelieve the thing, because they can frame no particular conceit what the Receptions and Entertains of those Aerial Inhabitants may be, or how they pass* 20 *away their time; with many other intricacies which use to entangle this Theory; I thought it of main concernment to take away this Objection against the* Life to come *(viz,* That no man can conceive what it is, and therefore it is not at all, *which is the ordinary Exception also against the* Existence of all 25 Incorporeal Substances*) by a* punctual *and* rational *Description of this* future state. *Which I exhibit to the world as an* intelligible *hypothesis, and such as may very well be, even according to the dictates of our own Faculties, being in the mean time fully asssured, that things* are either thus, *or after a* better 30 *or* more exact *order. But, as I said, to propound some* particular probable *way, I thought it of no small service to those who totally distrust all these things for that reason mainly, as being such as we can make no rational representation of to the Understandings of men.* 35

8. But there are also particular Objections. The first whereof is against our aerial and Aethereal Elysiums, *which forsooth, to make their reproach more witty, they will parallel with the* Mahometan *Paradise. But besides that I do in the very place where I treat of these things suspend my assent after the* 40 description *of them, there is nothing there offered in their* description, *but, if it were assented to, might become the most*

*refined spirit in the World.   For there is nothing more certain
then* That the Love of God and our Neighbour is the greatest
Happiness that we can arrive unto, either in this life, or that
which is to come. *And whatever things are* there described, *are*
5   *either the* Causes, Effects *or* Concomitants *of that noble and
divine Passion.   Neither are the* External incitements *thereto,
which̄ I there mention, rightly to be deemed* Sensual, *but*
Intellectual*: For even such is also* sensible Beauty, *whether it
shew it self in* Feature, Musick, *or whatever* graceful
10   Deportments *and* comely Actions, *as* Plotinus *has well defined.
And those things that are not properly* Intellectual, *suppose*
Odours *and* Sapours, *yet such a Spirit may be transfused into the
Vehicles of these* Aerial *Inhabitants thereby, that may more
then ordinarily raise into act their* Intellectual *Faculties. Which
15   he that observes how our* Thoughts *and* Inclinations *depend
immediately on a certain subtile Matter in our* Bodies, *will not at
all stick to acknowledge to be true.   And therefore whatever our*
Elysiums *seem to the rash and injudicious, they are really no
other thing then* pure Paradises of Intellectual pleasure, Divine
20   Love *and* blameless Friendship *being the onely delight of those
places.*
 9. The next objection is concerning the state of the Wicked,
as if I had made their condition too easy *for them.   But this
methinks any man might be kept off from, if he would but*
25   *consider, that I make* the rack of Conscience *worse then a*
perpetually-repeated death. *(Which is too-too credible to come to
pass there, whenas we finde what execution* Passions *will doe
upon us even in this life; the* Sicilian *Tyrants having not found
out a more exquisite torture then they.   And as for those Souls*
30   *that have lost* the sense of Conscience, *if any can doe so, I have
allotted* other punishments *that are* more corporeal, *and little
inferiour to* the fire *of that great Hell that is prophesied of, as the
portion of the Devils and the damned at the last Day.   By which
neither then nor before could they be tortured (if we appeal to
35   humane Reason, whom alone we appeal to,as judge in this
Treatise) if they were not vitally united with* corporeal Vehicles.
 10. The two last Exceptions are, the one touching the Soul of
the World, *the other the* Spirit of Nature. *The first is against
our over-favourable representation of their Opinion that make but*
40   one Soul *in the whole Universe, induing her with* Sense, Reason,
and Understanding: *which Soul they will have to act in all*
Animals, Daemons *themselves not excepted.   In all which, say*

they, it is One and the same Universal Soul *that* Hears, Sees, Reasons, Understands, *Ec. This Opinion I think I have confuted in this Third Book, as sufficiently as any one Error can be confuted in all Natural Philosophy. And that favourable representation I have made there of it, has that in it, whereby* 5 *unless a man be very remiss and mindless, he may easily demonstrate the falsness of the supposition. For though we may well enough imagine how, the* Body *being* unchanged, *and this* Soul of the Universe *exquisitely the* same *every where that though the party change place, and shift into another part of the* 10 Soul of the World, *he may retain the* same *Opinions, Imaginations and Reasonings, so farre forth as they depend not on* Memory *(this* Universal Soul *raising her self into the* same *Thoughts upon the* same *Occasions;) yet* Memory *is incompetible unto that part which has not had the* Perception *before of what is* 15 *remembered. For there is necessarily comprehended in Memory a Sense or* Perception *that we have had a* Perception *or Sense afore of the thing which we conceive ourselves to* remember.

To be short therefore, and to strike this Opinion dead at one stroke; They that say there is but one Soul of the World, *whose* 20 perceptive *Power is every where they must assert, that what one part thereof perceives, all the rest perceives; or else that perceptions in* Daemons, *Men and Brutes are confined to that part of this Soul that is in them, while they perceive this or that. If the former, they are confutable by Sense and Experience. For* 25 *though all Animals lie steeped, as it were, in that subtile* Matter *which runs through all things, and is the immediate Instrument of Sense and Perception; yet we are not conscious of one anothers thoughts, nor feel one anothers pains, nor the pains and pleasures of Brutes, when they are in them at the highest. Nor yet do the* 30 Daemons *feel one anothers affections, or necessarily assent to one anothers opinions, though their Vehicles be exceeding pervious; else they would be all* Avenroists, *as well as those that appeared to* Facius Cardanus, *supposing any were. Wherefore we may generally conclude, that if there were such an* Universal Soul, *yet* 35 *the particular perceptions thereof are restrained to this or that part in which they are made: which is contrary to the* Unity of a Soul, *as I have already said in its due place.*

But let us grant the thing (for indeed we have demonstrated it to be so, if there be such an Universal Soul, *and none but it)* 40 *then the grand Absurdity comes in, which I was intimating before, to wit, That that part of* the Soul of the World *that never*

perceived a thing, shall notwithstanding remember *it, that is to say, that it shall perceive it has perceived that which it never perceived: And yet one at* Japan *may remember a countreyman arrived thither that he had not seen nor thought of for twenty*
5   *years before. Nay, which is more to the purpose, supposing the* Earth move, *what I write now, the Earth being in the beginning of* Aries, *I shall remember that I have written when she is in the beginning of* Libra, *though that part of the Soul of the World that possesses my Body then will be twice as distant from what does*
10   *guide my hand to write now, as the Earth is from the Sun.*

      Nor can the plainness of this Demonstration be eluded by any Evasion whatsoever. For First, if we should admit that there be certain Marks sealed in the Brain *in the seeing or considering this or that Object, whereby the Soul would impress the* Memory
15   *thereof upon her more deeply; the virtue of remembring by this would be in that she had once joyned such a Thought or Representation with such an impress or Mark, otherwise it would avail nothing. Wherefore the* Soul of the World, *in B suppose, not having joyned such a Representation with this Mark in the*
20   *Brain as she did in A, can remember nothing thereby. For it is utterly unconceivable how any Figuration or Motion whatsoever in the Brain can represent to the Soul a Perception as perceiv'd heretofore, if the Soul her self has heretofore had no such Perception. For there can be no* Basis of this reflexive *and*
25   comparative *Act but the foregoing Perception of which the Soul is still conscious: Of which she cannot be conscious, if she never perceiv'd it. Whence it is plain that these supposed Marks have not a capacity in them to impose upon* the Soul of the World *in B, so as to make her conceit she had a Perception of a thing,*
30   *when indeed she never had.*

      But then again in the Second place, It is very evident That the power of Memory *does not consist in such* Marks *or* Figures *in the Brain, nor in any* Vibration *or* Motion *there, as I have sufficiently proved in the following discourse. Which further*
35   *assures us, That Memory is wholly in the Soul her self, and that She is the sole Repository of all the Perceptions she has had; and that therefore the* Soul of the World *cannot perceive her self to have perceived a thing when she has not perceived it.*

      And Thirdly and lastly, It is hence also manifest (I mean
40   *from* Memory *being seated only in the Soul her self, she acting in this, as in all other functions, only by virtue of a fit tenour of Spirits and due temper of Brain) That the Body changing place*

from A to B, that part of the Soul of the World *in it at B will have the remembrance of such things as were never perceived in A, and forget, or rather have no knowledge of, what the Soul perceived there; and that therefore by changing place a man may chance to become in a moment an excellent Physician,* 5 *Mathematician, or the like, or of a sudden become a Sott, and lose all his learning; which is the likelier of the two. For the Fruits of that Meditation and Study are lost, when once the Body has left that part of the Soul of the World which did thus study and meditate. So possible is it that every man should not have a* 10 particular *Soul of his own.*

Nor can this Errour in the Soul of the World, of perceiving she has perceived when she has not be argued possible in her from the adherence of that perpetual deemed mistake in our Outward Senses; as that we feel a pain, *suppose, in our finger, or* 15 white *upon the wall; whenas there is neither* white *in the one, nor* pain *in the other, but only in our* Common Percipient *which is confined within our Brain. For it is apparent that if this be an Errour, yet there is a plain and necessary Foundation thereof.*

For as when we thrust a Cane against the ground, we 20 *necessarily feel different feelings; one when against Gravel, another against Stone, and a third against Mud or Earth, and feel them also at tha distance of the Cane: So also is it in* Colours; *the* Medium *betwixt the Object and the Eye being as the Cane, and the variety of feeling at the end of the Cane like that* 25 *variety of Colours; of which there is a necessary causality in the variety of the surfaces of the objects; which the* Common Percipient *must needs perceive, and at such a distance as the* Medium *engages, as it was before in the length of the Cane. So that to perceive such differences at that distance they are and* 30 *where they doe causally exist, is not so much an Errour as a Truth. And there is the same reason in ticklings or prickings in any part of the Body: For it is true that those differences are also causally there; and therefore our* Perception *is rightly carried thither: For there is there that harshness and dis-harmony to* 35 *Nature, which the Soul cannot perceive but with an harsh and painfull perception, not only by reason of her interest and vitall union with the Body, but also from the speciall nature of the* Perception *it self.*

So that it seems to me an hard Censure to say the Soul does 40 *mistake in these* Perceptions: *and if she do in some sort, yet we can trace the necessary and determinate Cause, and that both very*

*palpable and very intelligible. But for this Errour of the Soul of
the World perceiving, suppose in B, that she has perceived
what notwithstanding she never perceived, it is a thing quite of
another kind, and an entire and undoubted mistake of which no*
5   *imaginable Cause can be produced that should lead her into it.
Whence it follows that she never commits it; and that therefore the*
reflexive *Art of* Memory, *which does firmly assure us of a
foregoing Perception, (no other Faculty having any power or
pretence to evidence the contrary,) does necessarily inferr, That*
10   *every man has a* Particular Soul *of his own, and that such an*
Universal Soul, *as the* Avenroists *fancy, will not salve all*
Phaenomena.

        *And yet I dare say this wild Opinion is more tenable then
theirs that make nothing but mere* Matter *in the world. But I*
15   *thought it worth the while with all diligence to confute them both,
the better of them being but a more refined kinde of* Atheism,
*tending to the subversion of all the Fundamentals of Religion and
Piety amongst men.*

        11. As for the Spirit of Nature, *the greatest exceptions are,*
20   *That I have introduced an* obscure Principle *for Ignorance and
Sloth to take sanctuary in, and so to enervate or foreslack the
useful endeavours of curious Wits, and hinder that expected
progress that may be made in the* Mechanick Philosophy; *and
this, to aggravate the crime, before a competent search be made*
25   *what the* Mechanical powers of Matter *can doe. For what*
Mechanical *solutions the present or foregoing Ages could not
light upon, the succeeding may; and therefore it is as yet
unseasonable to bring in any such Principle into* Natural
Philosophy.

30   *To which I answer, That the* Principle *we speak of is neither*
obscure *nor* unseasonable; *nor so much introduced by me, as
forced upon me by inevitable evidence of Reason. That it is no*
obscure Principle, *the clear Description I have given of it in my
Treatise will make good. Against which I know no imaginable*
35   *exception, unless it may seem harsh to any one that a* Substance
devoid of all sense and perception, *and therefore uncapable of
premeditated contrivance, should be supposed fit to form the*
Matter *into such exquisite organization. But this can appear no
difficulty to him that duly considers that what* Phantasme *is to*
40   *our* Soul, *that* Fabrick *is to the* Spirit of Nature: *and that as the
tenour of our Spirits (which are but subtile matter) will cause the*
Soul *immediately to exert it self into this or that* Imagination, *no*

knowledge or premeditation interceding; so such or such a
preparation or predisposition of the Matter of the World will cause
the Spirit of Nature *to fall upon this or that kinde of* Fabrication
or Organization, *no perception or consultation being interposed.*

 Those that pretend that the introduction of this Principle is 5
unseasonable, *I demand of them when they will think it to be*
seasonable. *For this simple surmise, That although all the*
Mechanical *solutions of some* Phaenomena *which have been*
hitherto offer'd to the world be demonstrably false, yet future Ages
may light upon what is true; can be held nothing else by the 10
judicious, but a pitiful subterfuge of fearful Souls, that are very
loath to let in any such affrightful Notion as an Immaterial *or*
Spiritual Substance *into the world, for fear the next step must be*
the acknowledgment also of a God; from whom they would fain
hide themselves by this poor and precarious pretence. *But I say,* 15
if the introduction of this Principle be not seasonable *now, it will*
never be seasonable. For that admirable Master of Mechanicks
Des-Cartes *has improved this way to the highest, I dare say, that*
the Wit *of man can reach to in such* Phaenomena *as he has*
attempted to render the Causes of. *But how in sundry passages* 20
he falls short in his account, I have both in the forenamed and
following Chapter, as also elsewhere, taken notice. I will instance
here onely in the Phaenomenon *of* Gravity, *wherein I think I*
have perfectly demonstrated that both He and M^r. Hobbs *are quite*
out of the story, and that the Causes they assign are plainly 25
false. *And that I have not mentioned the Opinions of others in*
this way, it was onely because I look'd upon them as less
considerable.

 12. But you'l say that though these be all mistaken, yet it
does not follow but that there may arise some happy Wit that will 30
be a true Mechanical *solution of this Probleme. But I answer,*
That I have not onely confuted their Reasons, but also from
Mechanical *Principles granted on all sides and confirmed by*
Experience, demonstrated that the Descent (suppose) of a Stone,
or Bullet, or any such like heavy Body, is enormously contrary to 35
the Laws of Mechanicks; *and that according to them they would*
necessarily, if they lye loose, recede from the Earth, and be
carried away out of our sight into the farthest parts of the Aire, if
some Power *more then* Mechanical *did not curb that Motion,*
and force them downwards towards the Earth, so that it is plaim 40
that we have not arbitrariously introduced a Principle, but that it
is forced uppn us by the undeniable evidence of Demonstration.

From which to suspend our assent till future Ages have improved this Mechanical Philosophy *to greater height, is as ridiculous, as to doubt of the truth of any one plain and easy Demostration in the first Book of* Euclide, *till we have travelled*
5   *through the whole field of that immense study of Mathematicks.*

     13. Nor lastly needs the acknowledgment of this Principle to damp our endeavours in the search of the Mechanical *causes of the* Phaenomena *of Nature, but rather make us more circumspect to distinguish what is the result of the* mere Mechanical *powers*
10 *of* Matter *and* Motion, *and what of an* Higher Principle. *For questionless this secure presumption in some,* That there is nothing but *Matter* in the world, *has emboldened them too rashly to venture on* Mechanical *solutions where they would not hold, because they were confident there were no other solutions to be*
15 *had but those of this kinde.*

     14. Besides that to the Rational and Religious there is a double Pleasure to carry them on in this way of Philosophy: The one from the observation how far in everything the Concatenation of Mechanical *causes will reach; which will wonderfully gratifie*
20 *their Reason: the other frcm a distinct deprehension where they must needs break off, as not being able alone to reach the Effect; which necessarily leads them to a more confirmed discovery of the Principle we contend for, namely the* Spirit of Nature, *which is the* Vicarious power of God *upon the Matter, and the first step to*
25 *the abstrusest* Mysteries in Natural Theologie; *which must needs highly gratifie them in point of Religion.*

     15. And truly for this very cause, I think it is the most sober and faithful advice that can be offered to the Christian World, that they would encourage the reading of Des-Cartes *in all*
30 *publick Schools or Universities. That the students of philosophy may be throughly exercised in the just extent of the* Mechanical *powers of Matter, how farre they will reach, and where they fall short. Which will be the best assistance to Religion that Reason and the Knowledge of Nature can afford.*
35 *For by this means such as are intended to serve the Church will be armed betimes with sufficient strength to grapple with their proudest Deriders or Opposers. Whenas for want of this, we see how liable they are to be contemned and born down by every bold, though weak, pretender to the* Mechanick Philosophy.
40   *16. These are the main Passages I could any way conceive might be excepted against in the ensuing Discourse: which yet are so innocent and firm in themselves, and so advantageously*

circumstantiated in the places where they are found, that I fear
the Reader may suspect my judgement and discretion in putting
myself to the trouble of writing, and him of reading, so long and
needless a Preface. Which oversight though it be an argument of
no great Wit, yet it may be of such Humanity, and of an earnest 5
desire of doing a publick good without the least offence or dis-
satisfaction to any that are but tolerable Retainers to Reason and
Ingenuity. But for those have bid a dieu to both, and measure all
Truths by their own humour some fancy, making every thing
ridiculous that is not sutable to their own ignorant conceptions; I 10
think no serious man will hold himself bound to take notice of
their perverse constructions and mis-representations of things
more then a religious Eremite or devout Pilgrim to heed the ugly
mows and grimaces of Apes and Monkies he may haply meet with
in his wearisome passage through the Wilderness. 15

The
IMMORTALITY
of
THE SOUL

Chap. I.

10

I. *The Usefulness of the present Speculation for the understanding of Providence, and the management of our lives for our greatest Happiness;* 2. *For the moderate bearing the death and disasters of our Friends,* 3. *For the begetting true Magnanimity in us,* 4.
15 *and Peace and Tranquillity of Mind.* 5. *That so weighty a Theory is not to be handled perfunctorily.*

1. Of all the Speculations the *Soul* of man can entertain her self withall, there is none of greater moment, or of closer
20 concernment to her, then this of her own *Immortality,* and *Independence* on this *Terrestriall Body.* For hereby not onely the intricacies and perplexities of *Providence* are made more easy and smooth to her, and she becomes able, by unravelling this clue from end to end, to pass and repass safe through this
25 Labyrinth, wherein many both anxious and careless Spirits have lost themselves; but also (which touches her own interest more particularly) being once raised into the knowledge and belief of so weighty a Conclusion, she may view from this Prospect the most certain and most compendious way to her
30 own *Happiness;* which is, the bearing a very moderate affection to whatever tempts her, during the time of this her Pilgrimage, and a carefull preparing of her self for her future condition, by such Noble actions and Heroicall qualifications of Mind as shall render her most welcome to her own Countrey.
35 2. Which Belief and Purpose of hers will put her in an utter incapacity of either *envying* the *life* or *successes* of her most imbittered *Enemies,* or of *over-lamenting* the *death* or *misfortunes* of her dearest *Friends;* she having no Friends but such as are Friends to God and Vertue, and whose Afflictions
40 will prove advantages for their future Felicity, and their departure hence a passage to present possession thereof.

3. Wherefore, being fully grounded and rooted in this so concerning a Perswasion, she is freed from all *poor* and *abject* thoughts and designs; and as little admires him that gets the most of this World, be it by Industry, Fortune or Policy, as a discreet and serious, man does the spoils of School-boyes, it 5 being very inconsiderable to him who got the victory at Cocks or Cob-nut, or whose bag returned home the fullest stuffed with Counters or Cherry-stones.

4. She has therefore no *aemulation,* unless it be of doing good, and of out-stripping, if it were possible, the noblest 10 examples of either the present or past Ages; nor any *contest,* unless it be with her self, that she has made no greater proficiency towards the scope she aimes at: and aiming at nothing but what is not in the power of men to confer upon her, with courage she sets upon the main work; and being still more 15 faithfull to her self,and to that Light that assists her, at last tasts the *first fruits* of her future *Harvest,* and does more then presage that *great Happiness* that is accrewing to her. And so quite from the troubles and anxieties of this present world, staies in it with *Tranquillity* and *Content,* and at last *leaves* it 20 with *Joy.*

5. The Knowledge therefore and belief of the *Immortality of the Soul* being of so grand Importance, we are engaged more carefully and punctually to handle this so weighty a Theory: which will not be performed by multiplying of words, but by a 25 more frugall use of them; letting nothing fall from our pen, but what makes closely to the matter, nor omittimg any thing materiall for the evincing the truth thereof.

30

Chap. II.

1. And to stop all Creep-holes, and leave no place for the subterfuges and evasions of confuted and cavilling spirits, I shall prefix some few *Axiomes*, of that plainness and evidence, that no man in has wits but will be ashamed to deny them, if
5   he will admit any thing at all to be true. But as for perfect *Scepticisme*,it is a disease incurable, and a thing rather to be pitied or laught at, then seriously opposed. For when a man is so fugitive and unsetled, that he will not stand to the verdict of his own Faculties, one can no more fasten any thing upon him,
10 then he can write in the water, or tye knots of the wind. But for those that are not in such a strange despondency, but that they think they know something already and may learn more, I do not doubt, but by a seasonable recourse to these few Rules, with others I shall set down in their due place, that they will be
15 perswaded, if not forced, to reckon this Truth, of *the Immortality of the Soul*, amongst such as must needs appear undeniable to those that have parts and leisure enough accurately to examine, and throughly to understand that I have here written for the demonstration thereof.
20

AXIOME I.

What ever things are in themselves, they are nothing to us, but so far forth as they become known to our Faculties or Cognitive powers.
25

2. This *Axiome* is plain of it self, at the very first proposal. For as nothing, for example, can concern the *Visive* faculty, but so far forth as it is *visible*; so there is nothing that can challenge any stroke to so much as a touching, much less
30 determining, our *Cognitive* powers in generall, but so far forth as it is *cognoscible*.

AXIOME II.

Whatsoever is unknown to us, or is known but as merely possible,
35 *is not to move us or determine us any way, or make us undetermined; but we are to rest in the present light and plain determination of our owne Faculties.*

3. This is an evident Consectary from the foregoing
40 Axiome. For the Existence of that that is *merely possible* is utterly unknown to us to be, and therefore is to have no weight against any Conclusion, unless we will condemn our selves to

eternall *Scepticisme.* As for example, If after a man has argued
for a *God* and *Providence,* from the wise contrivance in the
frame of all the Bodies of Animals upon earth, one should
reply, That there may be, for all this, Animals in *Saturn,*
Jupiter, or some other of the Planets, of very inept fabricks; 5
Horses, suppose, and other Creatures, with onely one Eye, and
one Eare, (and that both on a side, the Eye placed also where
the Eare should be,) and with onely three Leggs; Bulls and
Rams with horns on their backs, and the like: Such allegations
as these, according to this Axiome, are to be held of no force at 10
all for the enervating the Conclusion.

AXIOME III.
All our Faculties have not a right of suffrage for determining of
Truth, but onely Common Notions, Externall Sense, and evident 15
and undeniable Deductions of Reason.

4. By *Common Notions* I understand whatever is
Noematically true, that is to say, true at first sight to all men in
their wits, upon a clear perception of the Terms, without any 20
further discourse or reasoning. (From *Externall Sense* I exclude
not *Memory,* as it is a faithfull Register thereof.) And by
undeniable Deduction of Reason, I mean such a collection of one
Truth from another, that no man can discover any looseness or
disjoyntedness in the cohesion of the Argument.   25

AXIOME IV.
What is not consonant to all or some of these, is mere Fancy, and
is of no moment for the evincing of Truth or Falsehood, by either
it's Vigour or Perplexiveness.   30

5. I say *mere Fancy,* in Counter-distinction to such
Representations as, although they be not the pure Impresses of
some reall Object, yet are made by *Rationall deduction* from
them, or from *Common Notions,* or from both. Those 35
Representations that are not framed upon such grounds, I call
mere Fancies; which are of no value at all in determining of
Truth. For if *Vigour of Fancy* will argue a thing true, then all
the dreams of mad-men must goe for Oracles: and if the
Perplexiveness of *Imagination* may hinder assent, we must not 40
believe Mathemanatical demonstration, and the 16th
Proposition of the 3^{d} Book of *Euclide* will be confidently

concluded to contain a contradiction.

AXIOME V.

Whatever is clear to any one of these Three Faculties, is to be held undoubtedly true, the other having nothing to evidence to the
5   *contrary.*

6. Or else a man shall not be assured of any sensible Object that he meets with, nor can give firm assent to such Truths as these, *It is impossible the same thing should be, and*
10   *not be, at once Whatever is, is either finite, or infinite*; and the like.

AXIOME VI

What is rejected by one, none of the other Faculties giving
15   *evidence for it, ought to goe for a Falsehood.*

7. Or else a man may let pass such Impossibilities as these for Truth, or doubt whether they be not true or no, viz. *The part is greater then the Whole; There is something that is*
20   *neither finite nor infinite*; Socrates *is invisible*; and the like.

AXIOME VII.

What is plainly and manifestly concluded, ought to be held undeniable, When no difficulties are alledged against it, but such
25   *as are acknowledged to be found in other Conclusions held by all men undeniably true.*

8. As for example, suppose one should conclude, *That there may be Infinite Matter*, or, *That there is Infinite Space*, by
30   very rationall arguments; and that it were objected onely, that then the *Tenth* part of that *Matter* would be Infinite; it being most certain That there is *Infinite Duration* of something or other in the world, and that the *Tenth* part of this *Duration* is Infinite; it is no enervating at all of the former Conclusion, it
35   being incumbred with no greater incongruity then is acknowledged to consist with an undeniable Truth.

AXIOME VIII.

The Subject, or naked Essence or Substance of a thing, is utterly
40   *unconceivable to any of our Faculties.*

9. For the evidencing of this Truth, there needs nothing more then a silent appeal to a mans owne Mind, if he do not find it so; and that if he take away all *Aptitudes, Operations, Properties* and *Modifications* from a *Subject*, that his conception thereof vanishes into nothing, but into the *Idea* of a mere 5 *Undiversificated* Substance; so that one *Substance* is not then distinguishable from another, but onely from *Accidents* or *Modes*, to which *properly belongs no subsistence.*

AXIOME IX.   10

There are some Properties, Powers and Operations, immediately appertaining to a thing, of which no reasons can be given, nor ought to be demanded, nor the Way or Manner of the cohesion of the Attribute with the Subject can by any means be fancyed or imagined.   15

10. The evidence of this Axiome appears from the former. For if the *naked substance* of a Thing be so utterly unconceivable, there can be nothing deprehended there to be a connexion betwixt it and it's first Properties. Such is *Actual* 20 *Divisibility* and *Impenenetrability* in *Matter*. By *Actual Divisibility* I understand *Discerpibility*, gross tearing or cutting one part from another. These are *Immediate Properties of Matter*; but why they should be there, rather then in any other Subject, no man can pretend to give, or with any credit aske, 25 the reason. For *Immediate Attributes* are indemonstrable, otherwise they would not be *Immediate*.

11. So the *Immediate Properties* of a *Spirit* or Immateriel Substance are *Penetrability* and *Indiscerpibility*. The necessary cohesion of which Attributes with the Subject is as little 30 demonstrable as the former. For supposing that, which I cannot but assert, to be evidently true, That there is no Substance but it has in some sort or other the Three dimensions; This Substance, which we call *Matter*, might as well have been *penetrable* as *impenetrable*, and yet have been 35 Substance: But now that it does so certainly and irresistibly keep one part of it self from *penetrating* another, it is so, we know not why. For there is no necessary connexion discernible betwixt *Substance* with *three dimensions*, and *Impenetrability.* For what some alledge, that it implies a contradiction, that 40 *Extended* Substance should run one part into another; for so part of the *Extension*, and consequently of the *Substance*, would

be lost; that, I say, (if nearly looked into) is of no force. For the *Substance* is no more lost in this case, then when a string is doubled and redoubled, or a piece of wax reduced from a long figure to a round: The dimension of *Longitude* is in some part
5   lost, but without detriment to the *Substance* of the wax. In like manner when one part of an *Extended* Substance runs into another, something both of *Longitude, Latitude* and *Profundity* may be lost, and yet all the *Substance* there still; as well as *Longitude* lost in the other case without any loss of the
10   *Substance.*

And as what was lost in *Longitude* was gotten in *Latitude* or *Profundity* before; so what is lost here in all or any two of the dimensions, is kept safe in *Essential Spissitude*: For so I will call this *Mode* or *Property of a Substance*,that is able to
15   receive one part of it self into another. Which *fourth Mode* is as easy and familiar to my Understanding, as that of the *Three dimensions* to my Sense or Phansy. For I mean nothing else by *Spissitude*, but the redoubling or contracting of Substance into less space then it does sometimes occupy. And Analogous to
20   this is the lying of two Substances of several kinds in the same place at once.

To both these may be applied the termes of *Reduplication and Saturation*: The former, when Essence or Substance is but once redoubled into it self into another; the latter, when so oft,
25   that it will not easily admit any thing more. And that more *Extensions* then one may be commensurate, at the same time, to the same Place, is plain, in that *Motion* is coextended with the Subject wherein it is, and both with *Space*, And *Motion* is not nothing; wherefore two things may be commensurate to one
30   Space at once.

12. Now then *Extended Substance* (and all Substances are extended) being of it self indifferent to *Penetrability* or *Impenetrability* and we finding one kind of Substance so *impenetrable*, that one part will not enter at all into another,
35   which with as much reason we might expect to find so irresistibly united one part with another that nothing in the world could dissever them (For this *Indiscerpibility* has as good a connexion with Substance as *Impenetrability* has, they neither falling under the cognoscence of Reason or Demonstration, but
40   being *Immediate* Attributes of such a Subject. For a man can no more argue from the *Extension* of Substance, that it is *Discerpible*, then that it is *Penetrable*; there being as good a

capacity in *Extension* for *Penetration* as *Discerption*) I conceive,
I say, from hence we may as easily admit that *some Substance*
may be of it self *Indiscerpible*, as well as others *Impenetrable*;
and that as there is one kind of *Substance*, which of it's own
nature is *Impenetrable* and *Discerpible*, so there may be another 5
Indiscerpible and *Penetrable*. Neither of which a man can give
any other account of, then that they have the Immediate
Properties of such a Subject.

AXIOME X.   10
The   discovery   of   some   Power,   Property,   or   Operation,
incompetible to one Subject, is an infallible argument of the
Existence of some other, to which it must be competible.

13. As when *Pythagoras* was spoken unto by the River 15
Nessus, when he passed over it, and a Tree by the command of
Thespesion the chief of the *Gymnosophists* saluted *Apollonius* in
a distinct and articulate voice, but small as a womans; it is
evident, I say, That there was something there that was
neither *River* nor *Tree*, to which these salutations must be 20
attributed, no *Tree* nor *River* having any Faculty of *Reason* nor
Speech.

25

Chap. III.

1. *The general Notions of* Body *and* Spirit. 2. *That the Notion*
of Spirit *is altogether as intelligible as that of* Body. 3. *Whether*
there be any substance of a mixt *nature, betwixt* Body *and* Spirit. 30

1. The greatest and grossest Obstacle to the belief of *the*
Immortality of the Soul, is that confident opinion in some, as if
the very notion of *a Spirit* were a piece of Non-sense and
perfect Incongruity in the conception thereof. Wherefore to 35
proceed by degrees to our maine designe, and to lay our
foundation low and sure, we will in the first place expose to
view the genuine notion of *a Spirit*, in the *generall* acception
thereof; and aftewards of *severall kinds* of *Spirits*: that it may
appear to all, how unjust that cavill is against *Incorporeal* 40
Substances, as if they were mere Impossibilities and
contradictious Inconsistencies. I will define therefore a *Spirit* in

generall thus, A *substance penetrable and indiscerpible*. The fitness of which Definition will be the better understood, if we divide *Substance* in generall into these first kindes, viz. *Body* and *Spirit*, and then define *Body* to be A *Substance impenetrable*
5   *and discerpible*. Whence the contrary kind to this is fitly defined, *A Substance penetrable and indiscerpible*.

2. Now I appeal to any man that can set aside prejudice, and has the free use of has Facultles, whether every term in the Definition of a *Spirit* be not as intelligible and congruous to
10 Reason, as in that of a *Body*. For the precise Notion of *Substance* is the same in both, in which, I conceive, is comprised *Extension* and *Activity* either connate or communicated. For *Matter* it self once moved can move other *Matter* And it is easy to understand what *Penetrable* is as
15 *Impenetrable*, and what *Indiscerpible* as *Discerpible* and *Penetrability* and *Indiscerpibility* being as *immediate* to *Spirit*, as *Impenetrability* and *Discerpibility* to *Body*, there is as much reason to be given for the Attributes of the one as of the other, by Axiome 9. And *Substance* in its precise notion including no
20 more of *Impenetrability* then *Indiscerpibility*, we may as well wonder how one kind of Substance can so firmly and irresistibly keep out another. Substance (as *Matter*, for example, does the parts of *Matter)* as that the parts of another Substance hold so fast together, that they are by no means
25 *Discerpible*, as we have already intimated. And therefore this *holding out* in one being as difficult a business to conceive as the *holding together* in the other, this can be no prejudice to the notion of a *Spirit*. For there may be very fast union where we cannot at all imagine the cause thereof, as in such Bodies
30 which are exceeding hard, where no man can fancy what holds the parts together so strongly; and there being no greater difficulty here, then that a man cannot imagine what holds the parts of a *Spirit* together, it will follow by Axiome 7. that the Notion of a *Spirit* is not to be excepted against as an
35 incongruous notion, but is to be admitted for the notion of a thing that may really exist.

3. It may be doubted, whether there may not be Essences of a *middle* condition betwixt these *Corporeal* and *Incorporeal* Substances we have described, and that of two sorts, The one
40 *Impenetrable and Indiscerpible*, the other *Penetrable and Discerpible*. But concerning the first, if *Impenetrability* be understood in reference to *Matter*, it is plain there can be no

such Essence in the world; and if in reference to its own parts, though it may then look like a possible *Idea* in it self, yet there is no footsteps of the existence thereof in Nature, the Souls of men and Daemons implying contraction and dilatation in them.

As for the latter, it has no priviledge for any thing more 5 then *Matter* it self has, or some *Mode* of *Matter*. For it being *Discerpible*, it is plain it's union is by *Juxtaposition* of parts, and the more *penetrable*, the less likely to conveigh Sense and Motion to any distance. Besides the ridiculous sequel of this supposition, that will fill the Universe with an infinite number 10 of shreds and rags of Souls and Spirits, never to be reduced again to any use or order. And lastly, the proper Notion of a Substance *Incorporeal* fully counter-distinct to a *Corporeal* Substance, necessarily including in it so strong and indissoluble union of parts, that it is utterly *Indiscerpible*, whenas yet for all 15 that in this general notion thereof neither *Sense* nor *Cogitation* is implied, it is most rational to conceive, that that *Substance* wherein they are must assuredly be *Incorporeal* in the strictest signification; the nature of *Cogitation* and *communion of Sense* arguing a more perfect degree of union then is in mere 20 *Indiscerpibility of parts*.

But all this Scrupulosity might have been saved for I confidently promise my self, that there are none so perversly given to tergiversations and subterfuges, but that they will acknowledge, whereever I can prove that there is *a Substance* 25 *distinct from Body or Matter*, that it is in the most full and proper sense *Incorporeal*.

30

Chap. IV.

1. *That the Notions of the several kinds of* Immaterial Beings *have no Inconsistency nor Incongruity in them.* 2. *That the Nature of God is as int*elligible as the Nature of any Being 35 whatsoever. 3. *The true Notion of his* Ubiquity, *and how intelligible it is.* 4. *Of the Union of the Divine Essence.* 5. *Of his Power of Creation.*

1. We have shewn that the Notion of a *Spirit* in general is 40 not at all incongruous nor impossible: And it is as congruous, consistent and intelligible in the *sundry kinds*

thereof; as for example that of God, of Angels, of the Souls of Men and Brutes, and of the λόγοι σπερματικοὶ or *Seminal Forms* of things.

2. The Notion of God, though the knowledge thereof be
5   much prejudiced by the confoundedness and stupidity of either superstitious or profane men, that please themselves in their large Rhetorications concerning the uconceiveableness and utter incomprehensibleness of the Deity; the one by way of a devotional exaltation of the transcendency of has Nature, the
10 other to make the belief of his Existence ridiculous, and craftily and perversly to intimate that there is no God at all, the very conception of him being made to appear nothing else but a bundle of inconsistencies and impossibilities: Nevertheless I shall not at all stick to affirm, that his *Idea* or Notion is as easy
15 as any Notion else whatsoever, and that we may know as much of him as of any thing else in the world. For the very *Essence* or *naked Substance* of nothing can possibly be known, by Axiome 8. But for His *Attributes*, they are as conspicuous as the Attributes of any Subject or Substance whatever: From
20 Which a man may easily define Him thus; *God is a Spirit Eternal, Infinite in Essence and Goodness, Omniscient, Omnipotent, and of himself necessarily Existent.*

I appeal to any man, if every term in this Definition be not sufficiently intelligible. For as for *Spirit*, that has been already
25 defined and explained. By *Eternal* I understand nothing here but Duration without end or beginning: by *Infiniteness of Essence*, that has Essence or Substance has no bounds, no more then his Duration: by *Infinite in Goodness*, such a benign Will in God as is carried out to boundless and innumerable
30 benefactions: by *Omnisciency* and *Omnipotency*, the ability of knowing or doing any thing that can be conceived without a plain contradiction: by *Self-existency*, that he has his Being from none other: and by *necessary Existence*, that he cannot fail to be. What terms of any Definition are more plain then these of
35 this? or what Subject can be more accurately defined then this is? For the naked Subject or Substance of any thing is no otherwise to be known then thus. And they that gape after any other Speculative knowledge of God then what is from his *Attributes* and *Operations*, they may have their heads and
40 mouths filled with many hot scalding fancies and words, and run mad with the boisterousness of their own Imagination, but they will never hit upon any sober Truth.

3. Thus have I delivered a very explicite and intelligible Notion of *the Nature of God*; which I might also more conpendiously define, *An Essence absolutely Perfect*, in which all the terms of the former Definition are comprehended, and more then I have named, or thought needful to name, much less to insist upon; as his *Power of Creation*, and his *Omniprescence* or *Ubiquity*, which are necessarily included in the *Idea* of *absolute Perfeciton*. The latter whereof some ancient Philosophers endeavouring to set out, have defined God to be *a Circle whose Centre is every where and circumference no where*. By which Description certainly nothing else can be meant, but that the Divine Essence is *every where present* with all those adorable Attributes of *Infinite* and *absolutely-Perfect Goodness, Knowledge and Power*, according to that sense in which I have explained them. Which *Ubiquity* or *Omnipresence* of God is every whit as intelligible as the overspreading of *Matter* into all places.

4. But if here any one demand, How the Parts, as I may so call them, of the Divine Amplitude hold together, that of *Matter* being so discerpible; it might be sufficient to re-mind him of what we have already spoken of the general Notion of a *Spirit*. But besides that, here may be also a peculiar rational account given thereof, it implying a contradiction, that an *Essence absolutely Perfect* should be either limited in presence, or change place in part or whole, they being both notorious Effects *or Symptoms of Imperfection, which is inconsis*tent with the Nature of God. And no better nor more cogent reason can be given of any thing, then that it implies a contradiction to be otherwise.

5. That *Power* also *of creating things of nothing,* there is a very close connexion betwixt it and the *Idea* of *God*, or of a *Being absolutely Perfect*. For this Being would not be what it is conceived to be, if it were destitute of the *Power of Creation*; and therefore this Attribute has no less coherence with the Subject, then that it is a contradiction it should not be in it, as was observed of the foregoing Attribute of *Indiscerpibility* in God. But to alledge that a man cannot imagine how God should create something of nothing, or how the Divine Essence holds so closely and invincibly together, is to transgress against the 3, 4, and 5. Axiomes, and to appeal to a Faculty that has no right to determine the case.

Chap. V.

1. *The Definition belonging to all* Finite *and* Created Spirits. 2.
5   *Of* Indiscerpibility, *a Symbolical representation thereof.* 3. *An*
objection answered against that representation.

1. We have done with the Notion of that *Infinite* and
Uncreated Spirit we usually call *God*: we come now to those
10   that are *Created* and *Finite*, as the *Spirits of Angels, Men* and
Brutes; *we will cast in* the *Seminal Forms* also, or *Archei*, as the
Chymists call them, though haply the world stands in no need
of them. The *Properties* of a *Spirit*, as it is a Notion common to
all these, I have already enumerated in my Antidote, *Self-*
15   *motion, Self-penetration, Self-contraction and dilatation,* and
Indivisibility, by which I mean *Indiscerpibility*: to Which I added
Penetrating, Moving and *Altering the matter.* We may therefore
define *This kind* of *Spirit* we speak of, to be *A substance*
Indiscerpible, that can move it self, that can penetrate, contract,
20   *and dilate it self, and can also penetrate, move, and alter the*
Matter. We will now examine every term of this Definition,
from whence it shall appear, that it is as congruous and
intelligible, as those Definitions that are made of such things as
all men without any scruple acknowledge to exist.
25   2. Of the *Indiscerpibility* of a *Spirit* we have already given
rational grounds to evince it not impossible, it being an
Immediate Attribute thereof, as *Impenetrability* is of a *Body*; and
as conceivable or imaginable, that one *Substance* of its own
nature may invincibly *hold its parts together*, so that they
30   cannot be disunited nor dissevered, as that another may *keep*
out so stoutly and irresistibly another Substance from entring
into the same space or place with it self. For this ἀντιτυπία or
Impenetrability is not at all contained in the preciee conception
of a *Substance as Substance*, as I have already signified.
35   But besides that *Reason* may thus easily apprehend that it
may be so, I shall a little gratifie *Imagination*, and it may be
Reason too, in offering the *manner* how it is so, in this kind of
Spirit we now speak of. That ancient notion of *Light* and
Intentional species is so far from a plain impossibility, that it
40   has been heretofore generally, and is still by very many
persons, looked upon as a Truth, that is, That *Light* and *Colour*
do ray in such sort as they are described in the Peripatetical

Philosophie. Now it is observable in *Light*, that it is most vigorous towards its fountain, and fainter by degrees. But we will reduce the matter to *one lucid point*, which, according to the acknowledged Principles of Opticks, will fill a distance of space with its *rays of light*: Which *rayes* may indeed be 5 reverberated back towards their Centre by interposing some opake body, and so this *Orbe of light* contracted; but, according to the *Aristotelean* Hypothesis, it was always accounted impossible that they should be clipt off, or cut from this *lucid point*, and be kept apart by themselves. Those whom dry 10 Reason will not satisfy, may, if they please, entertain their Phansy with such a Representation as this, which may a little ease the anxious importunity of their Mind, when it too eagerly would comprehend the manner how this *Spirit* we speak of may be said to be *Indiscerpible*. For think of any *ray* of this *Orbe of* 15 *light*, it does sufficiently set out to the *Imagination* how *Extension* and *Indiscerpibility* may consist together.

    3. But if any object, That the *lucid Centre of this Orbe*, or the *Primary Substance*, as I elsewhere call it, is either *divisible* or *absolutely indivisible*; and if it be *divisible*, that as concerning 20 that *Inmost* of a *Spirit*, this Representation is not at all serviceable to set off the nature thereof, by shewing how the parts there may hold together so *indiscerpibly*; but if *absolutely indivisible*, that it seems to be nothing: To this I answer, what *Scaliger* somewhere has noted, *That what is infinitely great or* 25 *infinitely small, the Imagination of man is at a loss to conceive it.* Which certainly is the ground of the perplexedness of that Probleme concerning *Matter*, whether it consists of points, or onely of particles divisible *in infinitum*.

    But to come more closely to the business; I say that though 30 we should acknowledg the *Inmost Centre of life*, or the very First point, as I may so call it, of the *Primary Substance* (for this *Primary Substance* is in some sort gradual) to be *purely indivisible*, it does not at all follow, no not according to *Imagination* it self, that it must be nothing. For let us imagine 35 a perfect *Plane*, and on this *Plane* a perfect *Globe*, we cannot conceive but this *Globe* touches the *Plane*, and that in what we ordinarily call a *point*, else the one would not be a *Globe*, or the other not a *Plane*. Now it is impossible that one Body should touch another, and yet touch one another in nothing. This 40 *inmost Centre* therefore *of life* is something, and something so full of essential vigour and virtue, that though gradually it diminish, yet can fill a certain Sphere of Space with its own presence and activity, as a spark of light illuminates the duskish aire.

5   Wherefore there being no greater perplexity nor subtilty in the consideration of this *Centre of life* or *Inmost of a Spirit*, then there is in the *Atomes of Matter*, we may by Axiome 7. rightly conclude, That *Indiscerpibility* has nothing in the notion thereof, but what may well consist with the possibility of the existence of the Subject whereunto it belongs.

10

Chap. VI.

15   1. *Axiomes that tend to the demonstrating how the Centre or First point of the* Primary Substance *of a* Spirit *may be* Indiscerpible. 2. *Several others that demonstrate how the* Secondary Substance *of a* Spirit *may be* Indiscerpible. 3. *An application of these Principles.* 4. *Of the union of the* Secondary

20   Substance *considered transversly.* 5. *That the Notion of a* Spirit *has less difficulty then that of* Matter. 6. *An answer to an Objection from the Rational faculty.* 7. *Answers to Objections suggested from Fancy.* 8. *A more compendious satisfaction concerning the Notion of a* Spirit.

25

      1. And thus we have fairly well gratified the *Fancy* of the Curious concerning the *Extension* and *Indiscerpibility* of a *Spirit*; but we shall advance yet higher, and demonstrate the possibility of this Notion to the severest Reason, out of these

30   following Principles.

AXIOME XI.
A Globe touches a Plane in something, though in the least that is conceivable to be reall.

35

AXIOME XII.
The least that is conceivable is so little, that it cannot be conceived to be discerpible into less.

40   ### AXIOME XIII.
As little as this is, the repetition of it will amount to considerable magnitudes.

As for example, if this Globe be drawn upon a Plane, it constitutes a *Llne*; and a *Cylinder* drawn upon a *Plane*, or this same *Line* described by the Globe multiplied into it self, constitutes a *superficies*, etc. This a man cannot deny, but 5 the more he thinks of it, the more certainly true he will find it.

AXIOME XIV.
Magnitude cannot arise out of mere Non-Magnitudes.

10

For multiply *Nothing* ten thousand millions of times into nothing, the Product will be still *Nothing*. Besides, if that wherein the Globe touches a Plane were more then *Indiscerpible*, that is, *purely Indivisible*, it is manifest that a *Line* will consist of *Points* Mathematically so called, that is, 15 *purely Indivisible*; which is the grandest absurdity that can be admitted in Philosophy, and the most contradictious thing imaginable.

AXIOME XV.   20
The same thing by reason of its extreme littleness may be utterly Indiscerpible, *though* intellectually Divisible.

This plainly arises out of the foregoing Principles: For every Quantity is *intellectually* divisible; but something Indiscerpible 25 was afore demonstrated to be Quantity, and consequently divisible, otherwise Magnitude would consist of Mathematicall points. Thus have I found a possibility for the Notion of *the Center of a Spirit*, which is not a Mathematicall point, but Substance, in Magnitude so little, that it is *Indiscerpible*; but in 30 virtue so great, that it can send forth out of it self so large a Sphere of *Secondary Substance*, as I may so *Indiscerpible*.

2. This I have said, and shall now prove it by adding a few more Principles of that evidence, as the most rigorous Reason shall not be able to deny them.   35

AXIOME XVI.
An Emanative Cause is the Notion of a thing possible.

By an *Emanative Cause* is understood such a Cause as merely 40 by Being, no other activity or causality interposed, produces an Effect. That this is possible is manifest, it being demonstrable

that there is *de facto* some such Cause in the world; because
something must move it self. Now if there be no *Spirit, Matter*
must of necessity move it self, where you cannot imagine any
activity or causality, but the bare essence of the *Matter* from
5   whence this motion comes. For if you would suppose some
forme motion that might be the cause of this, then we might
with as good reason suppose some forme to be the cause of
that, and so *in infinitum*.

10   AXIOME XVII.
An Emanative Effect is coexistent with the very Substance of that
which is said to be the Cause thereof.

This must needs be true, because that very Substance which is
15   said to be the Cause, is the adequate and immediate Cause,
and wants nothing to be adjoyned to its bare essence for the
production of the Effect; and therefore by the same reason the
Effect is at any time, it must be at all times, or so long as that
Substance does exist.
20

                    AXIOME XVIII.
No Emanative Effect, that exceeds not the virtues and powers of
the Cause, can be said to be impossible to be produced by it.

25   This is so plain, that nothing need be added for either
explanation or proof.

                    AXIOME XIX.
There may be a Substance of that high Virtue and Excellency,
30   *that it may produce another Substance by Emanative causality,*
provided that Substance produced be in due gradual proportions
inferiour to that which causes it.

This is plain out of the foregoing Principle. For there is no
35   contraexceed the capacity of its own powers: Nor is there any
incongruity, that one Substance should cause something else
which we may in some sense call Substance, though but
Secondary or *Emanatory*; acknowledging the *Primary Substance*
to be the more adequate Object of Divine Creation, but the
40   *Secondary* to be referrible also to the *Primary* or *Centrall*
Substance by way of causall relation. For suppose God created
the *Matter* with an immediate power of *moving* it self, God

indeed is the Prime Cause as well of the *Motion* as of the *Matter*, and yet nevertheless the *Matter* is rightly said to *move* it self. Finally, this *Secondary* or *Emanatory* Substance may be rightly called *Substance*, because it is a Subject indued with certain powers and activities, and that it does not inhere as an 5 *Accident* in any other Substance or Matter, but could maintain its place, though all Matter or what other Substance soever were removed out of that space it is extended through, provided its *Primary Substance* be but safe.

3. From these four Principles I have here added, we may 10 have not an imaginative but rationall apprehension of that part of a *Spirit* which we call the *Secondary Substance* thereof. Whose *Extension* arising by graduall Emanation from the First and Primest Essence, which we call the *Centre of the Spirit* (which is no impossible supposition by the 16, 18, and 19. 15 Axiomes) we are led from hence to a necessary acknowledgment of perfect *Indiscerpibility* of parts, though not intellectuall Indivisibility, by Axiome 17. For it implies a contradiction that an *Emanative* effect should be disjoyned from its originall.   20

4. Thus have I demonstrated how a *Spirit*, considering the lineaments of it (as I may so call them) from the Centre to the Circumference, is utterly *indiscerpible*. But now if any be so curious as to ask how the parts thereof hold together in a line drawn cross to these from the Centre, (for *Imagination*, it may 25 be, will suggest they lye all loose:) I answer, that the conjecture of *Imagination* is here partly true and partly false, or is true or false as she shall be interpreted. For if she mean by loose, actually disunited, it is false and ridiculous: but if only so discerpible, that one part may be disunited from another, that 30 may not only be true, but, upon supposition the essential rayes are not fully enough redoubled within, plainly necessary; otherwise a *Spirit* could not contract one part and extend another, which is yet an Hypothesis necessary to be admitted. Wherefore this Objection is so far from weakening the 35 possibility of this Notion, that it gives occasion more fully to declare the exact concinnity thereof.

To be brief therefore, a *Spirit* from the Centre to the Circumference is utterly *indiscerpible*, but in lines cross to this it is closely coherent, but need not be indiscerpibly; which 40 cohesion may consist in an immediate union of these parts, and transverse penetration and transcursion of *Secondary Substance* through this whole Sphere of life which we call a *Spirit*.

Nor need we wonder that so full an Orbe should swell out from so subtil and small a point as the *Centre of this Spirit* is supposed. Εἰ γὰρ καὶ τῶι ὄγκωι μικρόν ἐστι.δυνάμει καὶ τιμιότητι
5   πολὺ μᾶλλον ὑπερέχει πάντων. as *Aristotle* speaks of the mind of man. And besides, it is but what is seen in some sort to the very eye in light, how large a spheare of Aire a little spark will illuminate.

5. This is the pure *Idea* of a *created Spirit* in general,
10   concerning which if there be yet any cavil to be made, it can be none other then what is perfectly common to it and to *Matter*,that is, the unimaginableness of Points and smallest Particles, and how what is discerpible or divisible can at all hang together: but this not hindering *Matter* from actual
15   existence, there is no reason that it should any way pretend to the inferring of the impossibility of the existence of a *Spirit*, by Axiome 7.

But the most lubricous supposition that we goe upon here, is not altogether so intricate as those difficulties in *Matter*. For
20   if that be but granted, in which I find no absurdity, That a Particle of *Matter* may be so little that it is utterly uncapable of being made less, it is plain that one and the same thing, though intellectually divisible, may yet be really indiscerpible. And Indeed it is not only possible, but it seems necessary that this
25   should be true: For though we should acknowledge that *Matter* were discerpible *in infinitum*, yet supposing a Cause of Infinite distinct perception and as Infinite power, (and God is such) this Cause can reduce this capacity of infinite discerpibleness of *Matter* into act, that is to say, actually and at once discerp it or
30   disjoyn it into so many particles as it is discerpible into. From whence it will follow, that one of these particles reduced to this perfect Parvitude is then utterly indiscerpible, and yet intellectually divisible, otherwise Magnitude would consist of mere points, which would imply a contradiction.
35   We have therefore plainly demonstrated by reason, that *Matter* consists of parts indiscerpible; and therefore there being no other Faculty to give suffrage against it, for neither Sense nor any Common Notion can contradict it, it remains by Axiome 5. that the Conclusion is true.
40   6. What some would object from Reason, that these *perfect Parvitudes* being acknowledged still intellectually divisible, must still have parts into which they are divisible,

and therefore be still discerpible; To this it is answered, That *division into parts* does not imply any *discerpibility*, because the parts conceived in one of these *Minima Corporalia* (as I may so call them) are rather *essential* or *formal* parts then *integral*, and can no more actually be dissevered, then Sense and Reason 5
from the Soul of a man. For it is of the very Essence of *Matter* to be *divisible*, but it is not at all included in the essence thereof to be *discerpible*; and therefore where *discerpibility* fails there is no necessity that *divisibility* should fail also. See the Preface, Sect. 3.   10

7.   As   for   the   trouble   of   spurious   suggestions   or representations from the *Phansy*, as if these *perfect Parvitudes* were   *Round*   bodies,   and   that   therefore   there   would   be *Triangular intervalls betwixt*, void of Matter; they are of no moment in this case, she always representing a *Discerpible* 15
magnitude   instead   of   an   *Indiscerpible*   one.   Wherefore   she bringlng in a false evidence, her testimony is to be rejected; nay if she could perplex the cause far worse, she was not to be heard, by Axiome the 4.

Wherefore *Phansy* being unable to exhibit the Object we 20
consider, in its due advantages, for ought we know these *perfect Parvitudes* may   lye   so   close   together,   that   they   have   no *intervalls betwixt*: nay it seems necessary to be so; For if there were any such *intervalls*, they were capable of particles less then these least of all; which is a contradiction in Reason, and a 25
thing utterly impossible.

But if we should gratifie *Phansy* so far as to admit of these *intervalls*, the greatest absurdity would be, that we must admit an insensible *Vacuum*, which no Faculty will be able ever to confute. But it is most rationall to admit none, and more 30
consonant   to   our   determination   concerning   these   *Minima Corporalia*, as I call them, whose largeness is to be limited to the least real touch of either a Globe on a Plane, or a Cone on a Plane, or a Globe on a Globe: if you conceive any real touch less then another, let that be the measure of these *Minute* 35
Realities in *Matter*.   From whence it will follow, they must touch a whole side at once, and therefore can never leave any empty *intervalls*.

Nor   can   we   imagine   any   Angulosities   or   Round protuberancies in a quantity infinitely little, more then we can 40
in one infinitely great, as I have already declared in my Preface. I must confess, a mans *Reason* in this speculation is

mounted far beyond his *Imagination*; but there being worse
intricacies in Theories acknowledged constantly to be true, it
can be no prejudice to the present Conclusion, by the 4. and 7.
Axiomes.

5   8. Thus have we cleared up *a full and distinct Notion of a
Spirit*, with so unexceptionable accuracy, that no Reason can
pretend to assert it impossible nor unintelligible. But if the
Theory thereof may seem more operose and tedious to
impatient wits, and the punctuality of the Description the more
10   hazardous and incredible, as if it were beyond our Faculties to
make so precise a Conclusion in a Subject to obscure, they may
ease their Understanding, by contenting themselves, with what
we have set down Chap. 2, Sect. 11, 12. and remember that
that Wisdome and Power that created all things, can make
15   them of what nature He pleases; and that if God will that there
shall be a Creature that is *penetrable and indiscerpible*, that it
is as easy a thing for him to make one so of its own nature, as
one *impenetrable and discerpible*, and indue it with what other
Properties he pleases, according to his own will and purpose:
20   which induments being immediately united with the Subject
they are in, Reason can make no further demand how they are
there, by the 9. Axiome.

25

Chap. VII.

1.*Of the Self-motion of a Spirit.* 2.*Of Self-penetration.* 3.*Of Self-
contraction and dilatation.* 4.*The power of penetrating of* Matter.
30   5. *The power of moving.* 6. *And of altering the* Matter.

1. We have proved the *Indiscerpibility* of a *Spirit* as well
in *Centre* as *Circumference*, as well in the *Primary* as *Secondary*
Substance thereof, to be a very consistent and congruous
35   Notion, The next Property is *Self-motion*, which must of
necessity be an Attribute of something or other; For by *Self-
motion* I understand nothing else but *Self-activity*, which must
appertain to a Subject active in it self. Now what is simply
active of it self, can no more cease to be active then to Be;
40   which is a sign that *Matter* is not active of it self, because it is
reducible to Rest: Which is an Argument not only that Self-ac
tivity belongs to *a Spirit*, but that there is such a thing as *a*

Spirit, *in the world, from which* activity *is communicated to* Matter. And indeed if *Matter* as *Matter* had motion, nothing would hold together; but Flints, Adamant, Brass, Iron, yea this Sole Earth would suddenly melt into a thinner Substance then the subtle Aire, or rather it never had been condensated 5 together to this consistency we finde it. But this is to anticipate my future purpose of proving That there are Spirits existing in the world: It had been sufficient here to have asserted, That *Self-motion* or *Self-activity* is as conceivable to appertain to *Spirit* as to *Body*, which is plain at first sight to 10 any man that appeals to his own Faculties. Nor is it at all to be scrupled at, that any thing should be allowed to *move it self* because our Adversaries, that say there is nothing but *Matter* In the world, must of necessity (as I have intimated already) confess that *this Matter moves it self*, though it be very 15 incongruous so to affirm.

2. The congruity and possibility of *Self-penetration* in a *created Spirit* is to be conceived, partly from the limitableness of the *Subject*, and partly from the foregoing Attributes of *Indiscerpibility* and *Self-motion*. For *Self-penetration* cannot 20 belong to God, because it is impossible any thing should belong to him that implies imperfection, and *Self-penetration* cannot be without the lessening of the presence of that which does penetrate it self, or the implication that some parts of that Essence are not so well as they may be; which is a 25 contradiction in a Being which is *absolutely Perfect*. From the Attributes of *Indiscerpibility* and *Self-motion* (to which you may adde *Penetrability* from the general notion of a *Spirit*) it is plain that such *a Spirit* as we define, having the power of Motion upon the whole extent of its essence, may also determine this 30 Motion according to the Property of its own nature: and therefore if it determine the motion of the exteriour parts inward, they will return inward towards the Centre of essential power; which they may easily doe without resistance, the whole Subject being *penetrable*, and without damage, it being also 35 *indiscerpible*.

3. From this *Self-penetration* we do not only easily, but necessarily, understand *Self-contraction* and *dilatation* to arise. For this *Self-moving Substance*, which we call a *Spirit*, cannot penetrate it self, but it must needs therewith contract it self; 40 nor restore it self again to its former state, but it does thereby dilate it self: so that we need not at all insist upon these

Termes.

4. That power which *a Spirit* has to *penetrate Matter* we may easily understand if we consider *a Spirit* only as a Substance, whose immediate property is *Activity*. For then it is
5 not harder to imagine this Active Substance to pervade this or the other part of *Matter*, then it is to conceive the parvading or disspreading of motion it self therein.

5. The greatest difficulty is to fancy how this *Spirit*, being so *Incorporeal*, can be able to move the *Matter*, though it be in
10 it. For it seems so subtile, that it will pass through, leaving no more footsteps of its being there, then the Lightening does in the Scabbard, though it may haply melt the Sword, because it there findes resistance. But a *Spirit* can find no resistance any where, the closest *Matter* being easily penetrable and pervious
15 to an *Incorporeal* Substance. The ground of this difficulty is founded upon the unconceivableness of any *Union* that can be betwixt the *Matter*, and a Substance that can so *easily pass through it*. For if we could but once imagine an Union betwixt *Matter* and a *Spirit*, the activity then of the *Spirit* would
20 certainly have influence upon *Matter*, either for *begetting*, or *increasing*, or *directing* the *motion* thereof.

But notwithstanding the *Penetrability* and easy passage of a *Spirit* through *Matter*, there is yet for all that a capacity of a strong union betwixt them, and every whit as conceivable as
25 betwixt the parts of *Matter* themselves. For what glue or Cement holds the parts of hard matter in stones and metalls together, or, if you will, of what is absolutely hard, that has no pores or particles, but is one continued and perfectly homogeneous body, not only to *Sense*, but according to the exact
30 *Idea* of Reason? What Cement holds together the parts of such a body as this? Certainly nothing but *immediate Union and Rest*. Now for *Union*, there is no comparison betwixt that of *Matter* with *Matter*, and this of *Spirit* with *Matter*. For the first is only superficiall; in this latter the very inward parts are
35 united point to point throughout. Nor is there any feare it will not take hold, because it has a capacity of passing through. For in this absolutely solid hard Body, which let be A, in which let us conceive some inward superficies, suppose E A C, this superficies is so smooth as nothing can be conceived smoother:
40 why does not therefore the upper E D C side upon the neather part E F C upon the least motion imaginable, especially E F C being supposed to be held fast whilst the other is thrust

against? This facility therefore of some Body passing upon another without any sticking, seeming as necessary to our Phansy as a *Spirit*'s passing through all Bodies without taking hold of them, it is plain by Axiome 7. That a firm union of *Spirit* and *Matter* is very possible, though we cannot conceive 5 the manner thereof.

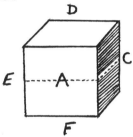

And as for *Rest*, it is competible also to this conjunction of *Matter* with *Spirit*, as well as of *Matter* with *Matter*. For suppose the whole body A moved with like swiftness in every part, the parts of A then are according to that sense of *Rest*, by which 10 they would explain the adhesion of the parts of *Matter* one with another, truly quiescent. So say I that in the *Union* of *Matter* and *Spirit*, the parts of the *Matter* receiving from the *Spirit* just such a velocity of motion as the *Spirit* exerts, and no more, they both rest in firm *Union* one with another. That which 15 comes to pass even then when there is far less immediate *Union* then we speak of. For if we do but lay a Book on our Hand, provided our Hand be not moved with a swifter motion then it communicates to the Book, nor the Book be pusht on faster then the swiftness of our Hand; the Book and our Hand 20 will most certainly retain their Union and goe together. So naturall and easy is it to conceive how *a Spirit* may move *a Body* without any more perplexity or contradiction then is found in the *Union* and *Motion* of the parts of *Matter* it self. See the Appendix to my Antidote.   25

6. The last Terme I put in the Definition of a *Spirit* is, *the power of altering the Matter*; which will necessarily follow from its *power of moving it* or *directing its motion*. For *Alteration* is nothing else but the varying of either the Figures, or postures, or the degrees of motion in the particles; all which are nothing 30 else but the results of *Local motion*. Thus have we cleared the *intelligibility* and *possibility* of all the *Terms that belong to the Motion of* a created *Spirit* in general, at least of such as may be

rationally conceived to be the causes of any visible *Phaenomena*
in the world. We will now descend to the defining of the chief
Species thereof.

5

Chap. VIII.

I. *Four main* Species *of* Spirits. 2. *How they are to be defined.*
10 *3. The definition of a Seminal Form*; 4. *Of the Soul of a Brute*;
*5. Of the Soul of a Man. 6. The difference betwixt the Soul of
an Angel and an Humane Soul. 7. The definition of an Angelical
Soul. 8. Of the Platonical* Νόες *and* Ενάδες. *9. That* Des-Cartes
his Demonstration of the Existence of the Humane Soul does at
15 *least conclude the possibility of a Spirit.*

I. We have enumerated *Four kinds of Spirits*, viz. *The*
λόγοι σπερματικοὶ or *Seminal Forms, the Souls of Brutes, the
Humane Soul, and that Soul or Spirit which actuates or informes*
20 *the vehicles of Angels*: For I look upon *Angels* to be as truly a
compound Being, consisting of Soul and Body, as that of Men &
Brutes. Their Existence we shall not now goe about to prove,
for that belongs to another place. My present designe is onely
to expound or define the notion of these things, so far forth as
25 is needful for the evincing that they are the Ideas or Notions of
things which imply no contradiction or impossibility in their
conception; which will be very easy for us to perform: the chief
difficulty lying in that *more General notion* of a *Spirit*, which we
have so fully explained in the foregoing Chapters.
30   2. Now this *General notion* can be contracted into *Kindes*,
by no other *Differences* then such as may be called peculiar
Powers or properties belonging to one *Spirit* and excluded from
another, by the 8. Axiome. From whence it will follow, that if
we describe these *several kindes of Spirits* by *immediate* and
35 *intrinsecal* Properties, we have given as good Definitions of
them as any one can give any thing in the world.
3. We will begin with what is most simple, *the Seminal
Forms* of things which, for the present, deciding nothing of their
existence, according to their ἰδέα *possibilis*, we define thus; *A*
40 *Seminal Form is a created Spirit organizing duly-prepared Matter
into life and vegetation proper to this or the other kind of Plant.*
It is beyond my imagination wnat can be excepted against this

Description, it containing nothing but what is very coherent and intelligible. For in that it is a *Spirit*, it can *move Matter* intrinsecally, or at least *direct the motion* thereof: But in that it is not an *Omnipotent* Spirit, but *Finite* and Created, its power may well be restrained to *duly-prepared Matter* both for vital 5 union and motion; He that has made *these Particular Spirits*, varying their Faculties of Vital union according to the diversity of the preparation of *Matter*, and so limiting the whole comprehension of them all, that none of them may be able to be vitally joyned with any *Matter* whatever: And the same first 10 Cause of all things that gives them a power of uniting with & moving of *matter duly prepared*, may also set such laws to this motion, that when it lights on matter fit for it, it will produce such and such a Plant, that is to say, it will shape the matter into such Figure, Colour and other properties, as we discover 15 in them by our Senses.

4.   This is the First degree of *Particular Life* in the world, if there be any purely of this degree *Particular*. But now, as *Aristotle* has somewhere noted, the Essences of things are like Numbers, whose *Species* are changed by adding or taking away 20 an Unite: adde therefore another *Intrinsecall power* to this of *Vegetation*, viz. *Sensation*, and it becomes *the Soul of a Beast*. For in truth the bare Substance it self is not to be computed in explicite knowledg, it being utterly in it self unconceivable, and therefore we will onely reckon upon the Powers. *A Subject* 25 *therefore from whence is both Vegetation and Sensation is the* *general notion of the Soul of a Brute*. Which is distributed into a number of kindes, the effect of every *Intrinsecall power* being discernible in the constant shape and properties of every distinct kind of Brute Creatures.   30

5.   If we adde to *Vegetation* and *Sensation Reason* properly so called, we have then a settled notion of the *Soul of* *Man*;which we may more compleatly describe thus: *A created* *Spirit indued with Sense and Reason, and a power of organizing* *terrestrial Matter into humane shape by vital union therewith*.   35

6.   And herein alone, I conceive, does the *Spirit* or *Soul* of an *Angel* (for I take the boldness to call that *Soul*, whatever it is, that has a power of vitally actuating the *Matter*) differ from the *Soul* of a *Man*, in that the Soul of an *Angel* may vitally actuate an *Aerial* or *Aethereal* Body, but cannot be born 40 into his world in a *Terrestrial* one.

7. To make an end therefore of our Definitions: an
Angelical Soul is very intelligibly described thus; *A created
Spirit indued with Reason, Sensation, and a power of being
vitally united with and actuating of a Body of Aire or Aether*
5   *onely.* Which power over an *Aereal* or *Aethereal* Body is very
easily to be understood out of that *general notion of a Spirit* in
the foregoing Chapters. For it being there made good, that
union with *Matter* is not incompetible to a *Spirit*, and
consequently nor moving of it, nor that kind of motion in a
10   *Spirit* which we call *Contraction* and *Dilatation*; these Powers, if
carefully considered, will necessarily infer the possibility of the
Actuation and Union of an *Angelical Soul* with an Aethereal or
Airey Body.

8. The *Platonists* write of other Orders of *Spirits* or
15   *Immaterial Substances*, as the Νόες and Ενάδες. But there being
more Subtilty then either usefulness or assurance in such like
Speculations, I shall pass them over at this time; having
already, I think, irrefutably mede good, That there is no
incongruity nor incompossibili*ty comprised* in the Notion of
20   *Spirit* or *Incorporeal Substance.*

9. But there is yet another way of inferring the same, and
it is the Arguments of *Des Cartes*, whereby he would conclude
that there is *de facto* a *Substance in us distinct from Matter*, viz.
our own *Mind.* For every Real Affection or Property being the
25   *Mode* of some Substance or other, and *real Modes* being
unconceivable without their *Subject*, he inferres that, seeing we
can doubt whether there be any such thing as *Body* in the
world (by which doubting we seclude *Cogitation* from *Body)*
there must be some other Substance distinct from the *Body,*to
30   which *Cogitation* belongs.

But I must confess this Argument will not reach home to
DesCartes his purpose, who would prove in Man a *Substance
distinct from his Body.*For being there may be *Modes* common to
more Subjects then one, and this of *Cogitation* may be
35   pretended to be such as is competible as well to Substance
Corporeal as *Incorporeal,* it may be conceived apart from
either, though not from both. And therefore has Argument
does not prove That that in us which does *think* or *perceive* is a
Substance distinct from our Body, but onely That there may be
40   such a Substance which has the power of *thinking* or *perceiving,*
which yet is not a *Body.* For it being impossible that there
should be any *real Mode* which is in no Subject, and we clearly

conceiving *Cogitation* independent for existence on *Corporeal* Substance; it is necessary, That there may be some other Substance on which it may depend; which must needs be a Substance *Incorporeal.*

5

Chap. IX.

I. *That it is of no small conseqence to have proved the* Possibility 10
of the *Existence of a Spirit.* 2. *The necessity of examining of Mr.* Hobbs *his Reasons to the contrary.* 3. *The first Excerption out of Mr.* Hobbs. 4. *The second Excerption.* 5. *The third.* 6. *The fourth.* 7. *The fifth.* 8. *The sixth.* 9. *The seventh.* 10. *The eighth and last Excerption.*   15

1. I have been I believe, to admiration curious and sollicitous to make good, That the Existence of a *Spirit* or *Incorporeal Substance* is possible. But there is no reason any one should wonder that I have spent so much pains to make 20
so small and inconsiderable a progresse, as to bring the thing onely to *a bare possibility.* For though I may seem to have gained little to my self, yet I have thereby given a very signal overthrow to the adverse party, whose strongest hold seems to be an unshaken confidence, That the very Notion of a *Spirit* or 25
Substance Immaterial is a perfect Incompossibility and pure Non-sense. From whence are insinuated no better Consequences then these: That it is impossible that there should be any God, or Soul, or Angel, Good or Bad; or any Immortality or Life to come. That there is no Religion, no 30
Piety nor Impiety, no Vertue nor Vice, Justice nor Injustice, but what it pleases him that has the longest Sword to call so. That there is no Freedome of Will, nor consequently any Rational remorse of Conscience in any Being whatsoever, but that all that is, is nothing but *Matter* and *corporeal Motion*; and 35
that therefore every trace of mans life is as necessary as the tracts of Lightning and the fallings of Thunder; the blind *impetus* of the *Matter* breaking through or being stopt every where, with as certain and determinate *necessity* as the course of a Torrent after mighty storms and showers of Rain.   40

2. And verily considering of what exceeding great consequence it is to root out this sullen conceit that some have taken up concerning *Incorporeal Substance,* as if it bore a contradiction in the very termes, I think I shall be wanting to
5 so weighty a Cause if I shall content my self with a bare recitation of the Reasons whereby I prove it possible, and not produce their Arguments that seem most able to maintain the contrary. And truly I do not remember that I ever met with any one yet that may justly be suspected to be more able to
10 make good this Province then our Countreyman Mr. *Hobbs,* whose inexuperable confidence of the truth of the Conclusion may well assure any man that duely considers the excellency of his natural Wit and Parts, that he has made choice of the most Demonstrative Arguments that humane Invention can search
15 out for the eviction thereof.

3. And that I may not incurre the suspicion of mistaking his Assertion, or of misrepresenting the force of his Reasons, I shall here punctually set them down in the same words I find them in his own Writings, that any man may judge if I doe him
20 any wrong. The first place I shall take notice of is in his *Leviathan. The word* Body *in the most general acceptation signifies that which filleth or occupieth some certain room or imagined place; and dependeth not on the Imagination, but is a real part of that we call the Universe. For the Universe being the*
25 *Aggregate of all* Bodies, *there is no real part thereof that is not also* Body; *nor any thing properly a* Body, *that is not also part of (that Aggregate of all* Bodies) *the Universe. The same also because Bodies are subject to change, that is to say, to variety of appearance to the sense of living Creatures, is called* Substance,
30 *that is to say, subject to various Accidents; as sometimes to be moved, sometimes to stand still, and to seem to our Senses sometimes Hot, sometimes Cold, sometimes of one Colour, Smell, Tast, or Sound, sometimes of another. And this diversity of seeming, (produced by the diversity of the operation of Boies on*
35 *the Organs of our Sense) we attribute to alterations of the Bodies that operate, and call them* Accidents *of those Bodies. And according to this acception of the word,* Substance *and* Body *signifie the same thing; and therefore* Substance Incorporeal *are words which when they are joyned together destroy one another,*
40 *as if a man should say an* Incorporeal *Body.*

4. The second place is in his *Physicks*. *But it is here to be observed that certain Dreams, especially such as some men have when they are betwixt sleeping and waking, and such as happen to those that have no knowledge of the nature of Dreams, and are withall superstitious, were not heretofore nor are now accounted* 5 *Dreams. For the Apparitions men thought they saw, and the voices they thought they heard in sleep, were not believed to be Phantasmes, but things subsisting of themselves, and objects without those that Dreamed. For to some men, as well sleeping as waking, but especially to guilty men, and in the night, and in* 10 *hallowed places, Fear alone, helped a little with the stories of such Apparitions, hath raised in their mindes terrible Phantasmes, which have been and are still deceitfully received for things really true, under the names of Ghosts and Incorporeal Substances.* 15

5. We adde a third out of the same Book. *For seeing Ghosts, sensible species, a shadow, light, colour, sound, space, etc. appear to us no less sleeping then waking , they cannot be things without us, but onely Phantasmes of the mind that imagines them.* 20

6. And a fourth out of his Humane Nature. *But Spirits supernatural commonly signifie some substance without dimension, which two words do flatly contradict one another.* And Artic. 5. *Nor I think is that word* Incorporeal *at all in the Bible, but it is said of the Spirit, that it abideth in men, sometimes that* 25 *it dwelleth in them, sometimes that it cometh on them, that it descendeth, and goeth, and cometh, and that Spirits are Angels, that is to say, Messengers;all which words do imply Locality, and locality is Dimension, and whatsoever hath dimension is Body, be it never so subtile.* 30

7. The fifth Excerption shall be again out of his Leviathan. *And for the Matter or Substance of the Invisible agents so fancyed, they could not by natural cogitation fall upon any other conceit, but that it was the same with that of the Soul of Man, and that the Soul of Man was of the same Substance with* 35 *that which appeareth in a Dream to one that sleepeth, or in a Looking-glass to one that is awake: Which, men not knowing that such Apparitions are nothing else but creatures of the Fancy, think to be real and external Substances, and therefore call them Ghosts, as the Latines called them* Imagines *and* Umbrae; *and* 40 *thought them Spirits, that is, thin aerial bodies; and those invisible Agents, which they feared, to be like them, save that they*

*appear and vanish when they please. But the opinion that such
Spirits were Incorporeal or Immaterial could never enter into the
mind of any man by nature; because though men may put
together words of contradictory signification, as* Spirit *and*
5   Incorporeal, *yet they can never have the imagination of any thing
answering to them.*

We will help out this further from what he also writes in
his Humane Nature. *To know that a Spirit is, that is to say, to
have natural evidence of the same, it is impossible. For all*
10   *evidence is conception, and all conception is imagination, and
proceedeth from Sense; and Spirits we suppose to be those
Substances which work not upon the Sense, and therefore are not
conceptible.*

8. The sixth, out of Chap. 45. where he writes thus: *This*
15   *nature of Sight having never been discovered by the ancient
pretenders to Natural knowledge, much less by those that
consider not things so remote (as that Knowledge is) from their
present use; it was hard for men to conceive of those Images in
the Fancy and in the Sense, otherwise then of things really*
20   *without us. Which some (because they vanish away they know
not whither nor how) will have to be absolutely Incorporeal, that
is to say, Immaterial, or Forms without Matter, Colour and
Figure, without any coloured or figured body, and that they can
put on aiery bodies, (as a garment) to make them visible when*
25   *they will to our bodily eyes; and others say, are Bodies and living
Creatures, but mode of Aire, or other more subtile and aethereal
matter, which is then, when they will be seen, condensed. But
both of them agree on one general appellation of them,* Daemons.
As if the dead of whom they dreamed were not the Innabitants of
30   *their own Brain, but of the Aire, or of Heaven or Hell, not
Phantasmes, but Ghosts; with just as much reason as if one
should say he saw his own Ghost in a Looking-glass, or the
Ghosts of the stars in a River, or call the ordinary Apparition of
the sun of the quantity of about a foot, the Daemon or Ghost of*
35   *that great Sun that enlightneth the whole visible world.*

9. The seventh is out of the next Chapter of the same
book. Where he again taking to task that *Jargon,* as he calls it,
of *Abstract Essences* and *Substantial Formes,* writes thus: *The
world (I mean not the Earth onely, but the Universe, that is,*
40   *the whole mass of all things that are) is Corporeal, that is to say,
Body, and hath the Dimensions of Magnitude, namely Length,
Breadth and Depth; also every part of Body is likewise Body, and*

hath the like dimensions; and consequently every part of the Universe is Body, and that which is not Body is no part of the Universe: And because the Universe is all, that which is no part of it is nothing, and consequently no where.

10. The eighth and last we have a little after in the same Chapter, which runs thus; *Being once fallen into this errour of Separated Essences, they are thereby necessarily imavolved in many other absurdities that follow it. For seeing they will have these Forms to be real, they are obliged to assign them some place. But because they hold them Incorporeal without all dimension of Quantity, and all men know that Place is Dimension, and not to be filled but by that which is corporeal, they are driven to uphold their credit with a distinction, that they are not indeed any where* Circumscriptivè, *but* Definitivè. *Which termes, being mere words, and in this occasion insignificant, pass onely in Latine, that the vanity of them might be concealed. For the Circumscription of a thing is nothing else but the determination or defining of its place, and so both the termes of distinction are the same. And in particular of the essence of a man, which they say is his Soul, they affirm it to be all of it in his little finger, and all of it in every other part (how small soever) of his Body, and yet no more Soul in the whole Body then in any one of these parts. Can any man think that God is served with such Absurdities? And yet all this is necessary to believe to those that will believe the existence of an Incorporeal Soul separated from the Body.*

Chap. X.   30

I. *An Answer to the first Excerption.* 2. *To the second.* 3. *An Answer to the third.* 4. *To the fourth Excerption.* 5. *An Answer to the fifth.* 6. *To the sixth.* 7. *To the seventh.* 8. *An Answer to the eighth and last.* 9. *A brief Recapitulation of what has been said hitherto.*

I. We have set down the chiefest passages in the Writings of Mr. *Hobbs,* that confident Exploder of *Immaterial Substances* out of the world. It remains now that we examine them, and see whether the force of his Arguments bears any proportion to the firmness of his belief, or rather mis-belief, concerning these

things. To strip therefore the first Excerption of that long
Ambages of words, and to reduce it to a more plain and
compendious forme of reasoning, the force of his Argument lies
thus: *That seeing every thing in the Universe is* Body (*the*
5 *Universe being nothing else but an Aggregate of Bodies*) Body
and Substance *are but names of one and the same thing it being
called* Body *as it fills a place, and* Substance *as it is the subject
of several Alterations and Accidents. Wherefore* Body *and*
Substance *being all one,* Incorporeal Substance *is no better sense
10 then an Incorporeal Body, which is a contradiction in the very
termes.* But it is plain to all the world that this is not to prove,
but to suppose what is to be proved, That the Universe is
nothing else but an Aggregate of Bodies: When he has proved
that, we will acknowledge the sequel; till then, he has proved
15 nothing, and therefore this first argumentation must pass for
nought.
     2. Let us examine the strength of the second, which
certainly must be this, if any at all; *That which has its original
merely from Dreams, Fears and Superstitious Fancies, has no
20 reall existence in the world: But Incorporeal Substances have no
other Original.* The Proposition is a Truth indubitable, but the
Assumption is as weak as the other is strong; whether you
understand it of the real Original of these Substances, or of the
Principles of our knowledge That they are. And be their
25 Original what it will, it is nothing to us, but so far forth as it is
cognoscible to us, by Axiome first. And therefore when he
sayes, they have no other Original then that of our own
Phansy, he must be understood to affirme that there is no
other Principle of the Knowledge of their Existence then that
30 we vainly imagine them to be; which is grossly false.
     For it is not the *Dreams* and *Fears* of Melancholick and
Superstitious persons, from which Philosophers and Christians
have argued the Existence of *Spirits* and *Immaterial Substances*;
but from the evidence of Externall Objects of Sense, that is, the
35 ordinary *Phaenomena* of *Nature*, in which there is discoverable
so profound Wisdome and Counsell, that they could not but
conclude that the Order of things in the world was from a
higher Principle then the blind motions and jumblings of *Matter*
and *mere Corporeal* Beings.
40   To Which you may adde what usually they call
Apparitions, which are so far from being merely the *Dreams*
and *Fancies* of the Superstitious, that they are acknowledged

by such as cannot but be deemed by most men over-Atheistical, I mean *Pomponatius* and *Cardan*, nay by *Vaninus* himself, though so devoted to Atheisme, that out of a perfect mad zeale to that despicable cause he died for it. I omit to name the *Operations of the Soul*, which ever appeared to the wisest of all 5 Ages of such a transcendent condition, that they could not judge them to spring from so contemptible a Principle as *bare Body* or *Matter*. Wherefore to decline all these, and to make representation onely of *Dreams* and *Fancies* to be the occasions of the world's concluding that there are *Incorporeal Substances*, 10 is to fancy his Reader a mere fool, and publickly to profess that he has a mind to impose upon him.

3. The third argumentation is this: *That which appears to us as well sleeping as waking, is nothing without us: But Ghosts, that is Immaterial Substances, appear to us as well* 15 *sleeping as waking.* This is the weakest Argument that has been yet produced: for both the Proposition and Assumption are false. For if the Proposition were true, the Sun, Moon, Stars, Clouds, Rivers, Meadows, Men, Women, and other living creatures were nothing without us: For all these appear to us 20 as well when we are *sleeping* as *waking*. But *Incorporeal Substances* do not appear to us as well *sleeping* as *waking*. For the Notion of an *Incorporeal Substance* is so subtile and refined, that it leaving little or no impression on the *Phansy*, its representation is merely supported by the free power of 25 *Reason*, which seldome exercises it self in sleep, unless upon easy imaginable Phantasmes.

4. The force of the fourth Argument is briefly this: *Every* Substance has dimensions; but a Spirit has no dimensions. Here I confidently deny the Assumption. For it is not the 30 Characteristicall of *a Body* to have *dimensions*, but to be *Impenetrable*. All Substance has *Dimensions*, that is, Length, Breadth, and Depth: but all has not *Impenetrability*. See my Letters to Monsieur *Des-Cartes*, besides what I have here writ in this present Treatise.   35

5. In the Excerptions belonging to the fifth place these Arguments are comprised. 1. *That we have no principle of knowledge of any Immaterial Being, but such as a Dream or a Looking-Glass furnisheth us withall.* 2. *That the word* Spirit *or* Incorporeal *implies a contradiction, and cannot be conceived to be* 40 *sense by as natural Understanding.* 3. *That nothing is conceived by the Understanding but what comes in at the Senses, and*

therefore Spirits not acting upon the Senses must remain unknown and unconceivable.

We have already answered to the first in what we have returned to has second Argument in the second Excerption.

5   To the second I answer, That *Spirit* or *Incorporeal* implies no contradiction, there being nothing understood thereby but *Extended Substance* with *Activity* and *Indiscerpibility*, leaving out *Impenetrability*: Which I have above demonstrated to be the Notion of a *thing possible*, and need not repeat what I have

10   already written.

To the third I answer, That *Spirits* do act really upon the *Senses*, by acting upon *Matter* that affects the *Senses*; and some of these Operations being such, that they cannot be rationally attributed to the *Matter* alone, *Reason* by the information of the

15   *Senses* concludes that there is some other more noble Principle distinct from the *Matter*. And as for that part of the Argument that asserts that there is nothing in the Understanding but what comes in at the Senses, I have, and shall again in its due place demonstrate it to be a very gross Errour.

20   But in the mean time I conclude, that the Substance of everything being utterly unconceivable, by Axiome 8. and it being onely the *Immediate Properties* by which a man conceives every   thing,   and   the   Properties   of   *Penetrability*   and *Indiscerpibility* being as easy to conceive, as of *Discerpibility*

25   and *Impenetrability*, and the power of commmunicating of motion to *Matter* as easy as the *Matter*'s reception of it, and the Union of *Matter* with *Spirit*, as of *Matter* with *Matter*; it plainly follows, that the Notion of a *Spirit* is as naturally conceivable as the Notion of a *Body*.

30   6. In this sixth Excerption he is very copious in jearing and making ridiculous the opinion of Ghosts and Daemons; but the strength of his Argument, if it have any, is this, viz. *If there be any such things as Ghosts or Daemons, then they are (according to them that hold this opinion) either those Images*

35   *reflected from water or Looking-glasses, cloathing themselves in aiery garments, and so wandring up & down; or else they are living Creatures made of nothing but Aire or some more subtile and Aethereal Matter.* One might well be amazed to observe such slight and vain arguing come from so grave a Philosopher,

40   were not a man well aware that his peculiar eminency, as himself somewhere professes, lies in *Politicks*, to which the humours and Bravadoes of Eloquence, especially amongst the

simple, is a very effectuall and serviceable instrument. And certainly such Rhetorications as this cannot be intended for any but such as are of the very weakest capacity.

Those two groundless conceits that he would obtrude upon the sober Assertors of *Spirits* and *Daemons* belong not to them, but are the genuine issue of his own Brain. For, for the former of them, it is most justly adjudged to him, as the first Author thereof; it being a Rarity, which neither my self nor (I dare say) any else ever met with out of Mr *Hobbs* his Writings. And the latter he does not onely not goe about to confute here, but makes a shew of allowing it, for fear he should seem to deny Scripture, in Chap. 34. of his *Leviathan*. But those that assert the Existence of *Spirits*, will not stand to Mr *Hobbs* his choice for defining of them, but will make use of their own Reason and Judgment for the settling of so concerning a Notion.

7. In this seventh Excerption is contained the same Argument that was found in the first; but to deal fairly and candidly, I must confess it is better back'd then before. For there he supposes, but does not prove, the chief ground of his Argument; but here he offers at a proof of it, couched, as I conceive, in these words [*and hath the dimensions of Magnitude, namely Length, Breadth and Depth*] for for hence he would infer that the whole Universe is *Corporeal*, that is to say, every thing in the Universe, because there is nothing but has *Length, Breadth and Depth*. This therefore is the very last ground has Argument is to be resolved into. But how weak it is I have already intimated, it being not *Trinal Dimension*, but *Impenetrability*, that constitutes a *Body*.

8. This last Excerption seems more considerable then any of the former, or all of them put together: but when the force of the Arguments therein contained is duly weighed, they will be found of as little efficacy to make good the Conclusion as the rest. The first Argument runs thus; *Whatsoever is real, must have some place: But Spirits can have no place.* But this is very easily answered. For if nothing else be understood by *Place*, but *Imaginary Space*, Spirits and Bodies may be in the same *Imaginary Space*, and so the Assumption is false. But if by *Place* be meant the *Concave Superficies of one Body immediately environing another Body*, so that it be conceived to be of the very Formality of a *Place*, immediately to environ the *corporeal* Superficies of that Substance which is said to be placed; then it

is impossible that a *Spirit* should be properly said to be in a *Place*, and so the Proposition will be false. Wherefore there being these two acceptions of *Place*, that Distinction of being there *Circumscriptivè* and *Definitivè* is an allowable *Distinction*,
5   *and the* terms may not signify one and the same thing. But if we will with M^r. *Hobbs* (and I know no great hurt if we should doe so) confine the Notion of *Place* to *Imaginary Space*, this distinction of the Schools will be needless here, and we may, without any more adoe, assert, That *Spirits* are as truly in
10 Place as *Bodies*.

His second Argument is drawn from that Scholastick Riddle, which I must confess seems to verge too near to profound Non-sense, That the Soul of man is *tota in toto* and *tota in qualibet parte corporis*. This mad Jingle it seems has so
15 frightened Mr *Hobbs* sometime or other that he never since could endure to come near the Notion of a *Spirit* again, not so much as to consider whether it were a mere Bug-bear, or some real Being. But if Passion had not surprised his better Faculties, he might have found a true settled meaning thereof,
20 and yet secluded these wilde intricacies that the heedless Schools seem to have charged it with: For the *Immediate Properties* of a *Spirit* are very well intelligible without these Aenigmatical flourishes, viz. That it is a *Substance Penetrable and Indiscerpible*, as I have already shewn at large.
25   Nor is that Scholastick Aenigme necessary to be believed by all those that would believe the Existence of an *Incorporeal* Soul; nor do I believe Mr *Hobbs* his interpretation of this Riddle to be so necessary. And it had been but fair play to have been assured that the Schools held such a perfect contradiction,
30 before he pronounced the belief thereof necessary to all those that would hold the Soul of Man *an Immaterial Substance, separable from the Body*. I suppose they may mean nothing by it, but what *Plato* did by his making the Soul to consist ἐκ μεριστῆς καὶ ἀμερίστου οὐσίας· nor *Plato* any thing more by that
35 *divisible* and *indivisible Substance*, then an Essence that is intellectually divisible, but really indiscerpible.

9. We have now firmly made good, that the Notion of *a Spirit* implies no contradiction nor incompossibility in it; but is the Notion or *Idea* of a thing that may possibly be. Which I
40 have done so punctually and particularly, that I have cleared every *Species* of *Substances Incorporeal* from the imputation of either obscurity or inconsistency. And that I might not seem to

take advantage in pleading their cause in the absence of the
adverse party, I have brought in the most able Advocate and
the most assured that I have hitherto ever met withall; and
dare now appeal to any indifferent Judge, whether I have not
demonstrated all his Allegations to be weak and inconclusive. 5
Wherefore having so clearly evinced the *possibility* of the
Existence of a Spirit, we shall now make a step further, and
prove That it is not onely a thing *possible*, but that it is *really*
and *actually* in Nature.

10

Chap. XI.

I. *Three grounds to prove the Existence of an* Immaterial 15
Substance, *whereof the first is fetch'd from the Nature of God.* 2.
The second from the Phaenomenon *of Motion in the World.* 3.
That the Matter is not Self-moveable. 4. *An Objection that the
Matter may be part Self-moved, part not.* 5. *The first answer to
the Objection.* 6. *The second Answer.* 7. *Other Evasions* 20
answered. 8. *The last Evasion of all answered.* 9. *The
Conclusion, That no Matter is Self-moved, but that a certain
quantity of motion was impressed upon it at its first Creation by
God.*

25

I. There be Three main Grounds from whence a man may
be assured of the *Existence of Spiritual* or *Immaterial Substance.*
The one is the consideration of the transcendent excellency of
the Nature of God,; who being, according to the true *Idea* of
him, *an Essence absolutely Perfect* cannot possibly be *Body*, and 30
consequently must be something *Incorporeal*: and seeing that
there is no contradiction in the Notion of *a Spirit in general*, nor
in any of *those kinds of Spirits* which we have defined, (where
the Notion of God was set down amongst the rest) and that in
the very Notion of him there is contained the reason of his 35
Existence, as you may see at large in my *Antidote*; certainly if
we find any thing at all to be, we may safely conclude that He
is much more. For there is nothing besides Him of which one
can give a reason why it is, unless we suppose him to be the
Author of it. Wherefore though God be neither *Visible* nor 40
Tangible, yet his very *Idea* representing to our Intellectual
Faculties the necessary reason of his Existence, we are, by

Axiome 5. (though we had no other Argument drawn from our
Senses) confidently to conclude That He is.

2. The second ground is the ordinary *Phaenomena* of
Nature, the most general whereof is *Motion*. Now it seems to
me demonstrable from hence, That there is some Being in the
world distinct from *Matter*. For *Matter* being of one simple
homogeneal nature, and not distinguishable by specificall
differences, as the Schools speak, it must have every where the
very same Essential properties; and therefore of it self it must
all of it be either without motion, or else be self-moving, and
that in such or such a tenor, or measure of motion; there being
no reason imaginable, why one part of the *Matter* should move
of it self lesse then another; and therefore if there be any such
thing, it can onely arise from externall impediment.

3. Now I say, if *Matter* be utterly devoid of motion in it
self, it is plain it has its motion from some other Substance,
which is necessarily a Substance that is not *Matter*, that is to
say, a *Substance Incorporeal*. But if it be moved of it self, in
such or such a measure, the effect here being an *Emanative
effect*, cannot possibly fail to be whereever *Matter* is, by Axiome
17, especially if there be no external impediment: And there is
no impediment at all, but that the Terrestrial parts might
regain an activity very nigh equal to the Aethereal, or rather
never have lost it. For if the Planets had but a common
Dividend of all the motion wnich themselves and the Sun and
Stars, and all the Aethereal matter possess, (the matter of the
Planets being so little in comparison of that of the *Sun, Stars*
and *Aether*) the proportion of motion that will fall due to them
would be exceeding much above what they have. For it would
be as if four or five poor men in a very rich and populous City
should, by giving up that estate they have, in a levelling way,
get equal share with all the rest. Wherefore every Planet could
not faile of melting it self into little less finer Substance then
the purest *Aether*. But they not doing so, it is a signe they
have not that Motion nor Agitation of themselves, and
therefore rest content with what has extrinsecally accrued to
them, be it less or more.

4. But the pugnacious, to evade the stroke of our
Dilemma, will make any bold shift; and though they affront
their own Facultles in saying so, yet they will say, and must
say, That part of the *Matter* is self-moving, part without motion
of it self.

5. But to this I answer, That first, this Evasion of theirs
is not so agreeable to Experience; but, so far as either our
Sense or Reason can reach, there is the *same Matter* every
where. For consider the *subtilest parts of Matter* discoverable
here below, those which for their Subtilty are invisible, and for   5
their Activity wonderfull, I mean those particles that cause
that vehement agitation we feel in *Winds*: They in time lose
their motion, become of a visible vaporous consistency, and
turn to Clouds, then to Snow or Rain, after haply to Ice it self;
but then in process of time, first melted into Water, then   10
expelled into Vapours, after more fiercely agitated, do become
Wind again. And that we may not think that this
Reciprocation into *Motion* and *Rest* belongs onely to *Terrestrial*
particles; that the *Heavens* themselves be of the same Matter,
is apparent from the Ejections of *Comets* into our *Vortex*, and   15
the perpetuall rising of those Spots and Scum upon the Face of
the Sun.

6. But secondly, to return what is still more pungent.
This *Matter* that is *Self-moved*, in the impressing of Motion upon
other *Matter*, either looses of its own motion, or retains it still   20
entire. If the first, it may be despoiled of all its motion: and so
that whose immediate nature is to *move*, shall *rest*, the entire
cause of its motion still remaining, viz. it self: which is a plain
contradiction by Axiome 17. If the second, no meaner an
inconvenience then this will follow, That the whole world had   25
been turned into pure *Aether* by this time, if not into a perfect
flame, or at least will be in the conclusion, to the utter
destruction of all corporeal Consistencies. For, that these *Self-
moving parts of Matter* are of a considerable copiousness, the
event does testify, they having melted almost all the world   30
already into *Suns*, *Stars* and *Aether*, nothing remaining but
Planets and *Comets* to be dissolved: Which all put together
scarce beare so great a proportion to the rest of the Matter of
the Universe, as an ordinary grain of sand to the whole ball of
the Earth. Wherefore so potent a Principle of Motion still   35
adding new motion to *Matter*, and no motion once communicated
being lost, (for according to the laws of Motion, no Body loses
any more motion then it communicates to another) it plainly
follows, that either the World had been utterly burnt up ere
now, or will be at least in an infinite less time then it has   40
existed, nay, I may say absolutely in a very little time, and will
never return to any frame of things again; which though it

possibly may be, yet none but a mad-man will assert, by
Axiome 2. And that it has not yet been since the first *Epoches*
of History, seems a Demonstration that this second Hypothesis
is false.

5   7. There is yet another Evasion or two, which when they
are answered there will be no Scruple remaining touching this
point. The first is, That the *Matter* is all of it homogeneall, of
the like nature every where, and that it is the common
Property of it all to be of it self indifferent to *Motion* or *Rest*;
10 and therefore, that it is no wonder that some of it *moves*, and
other some of it *rests*, or *moves* less then other some. To which
I answer, That this *Indifferency of the Matter to Motion* or *Rest*
may be understood two wayes: Either *privately*, that is to say,
That it has not any real or active propension to *Rest* more then
15 to *Motion*, or *vice versa*, but is merely passive and susceptive of
what *Motion* or *Fixation* some other Agent confers upon it, and
keeps that modification exactly and perpetually, till again some
other Agent change it; (in which sense I allow the Assertion to
be true, but it makes nothing against us, but for us, it plainly
20 implying That there is an *Incorporeal Substance* distinct from
the *Matter*, from whence the *Matter* both is and must be *moved*.)
Or else, *this Indifferency* is to be understood *positively*, that is to
say, That the *Matter* has a real and active propension as well to
Motion as to *Rest*, so that it *moveth* it self and *fixeth* it self from
25 its own immediate nature. From whence there are but these
two Absurdities that follow: the first, That two absolutely
contrary properties are *immediately* seated in one simple
Subject; then which nothing can seem more harsh and
unhandsome to our Logical faculties; unless the second, which
30 is, That *Motion* and *Rest* being thus the *Emanative* effects of
this one simple Subject, the *Matter* will both *move* and *rest at
once;* or, if they do not understand by *Rest*, Fixation, but a
mere absence of motion, That it will both move and not move
at once. For what is *immediate* to any Subject, will not cease to
35 be, the Subject not being destroyed, by Axiome 17.

Nor will they much help themselves by fancying that
Matter necessarily exerting both these *immediate* powers or
properties at once of *Motion* and *Rest*, moves her self to such a
measure and no swifter. For this position is but coincident with
40 the second member of the *Dilemma*, Sect. 3. of this Chapter;
and therefore the same Argument will serve for both places.

The other Evasion is, by supposing part of the *Matter* to be *Selfmoving*, and part of it *Self-resting*, in a positive sense, or *Self-fixing*: Which is particularly directed against what we have argued Sect. 6. For thus they would avoid that hasty and universal Conflagration there inferred. But that this 5 Supposition is false, is manifest from Experience. For if there be any such *Self-fixing* parts of *Matter*, they are certainly in Gold and Lead and such like Metalls; but it is plain that they are not there. For what is *Self-fixing*, will immediately be reduced to *Rest*, so soon as external violence is taken off, by 10 Axiome 17. Whence it will follow, that though these *Self-fixing parts of Matter* may be carried by other Matter while they are made fast to it, yet left free they will suddainly *rest*, they having the *immediate* cause of *Fixation* in themselves. Nor can any one distrust, that the change will be so suddain, if he 15 consider how suddainly an external force puts *Matter* upon motion. But a Bullet of gold or lead put thus upon motion, swift or slow, does not suddainly reduce it self to *rest*. Whence it plainly appears that this other Evasion contradicts Experience, and therefore has no force against our former 20 Arguments.

8. The utmost Evasion the Wit of man can possibly excogitate is that Figment of a certain *Divine Matter* dispersed in the World, which some conceit the onely *Numen* thereof, whose motions they make not *necessary*, but *voluntary*; whereby 25 they would decline that exorbitant inconvienience mentioned in the sixth Section of this Chapter. But the opinion to me seems very harsh and prodigious for these reasons following.

First, they seem very absurd in imagining this to be the *Numen* of the World or God himself, it being so inconsistent 30 with *Personality* and the *Unity* of the Godhead to be made up of an Infinite number of interspersed *Atoms* amidst the Matter of the World: For this cannot be *one* God in any sense; nor a single *Divine* Atome an Entire Deity. From whence it would follow that there is no God at all. 35

And then in the second place, They acknowledging this *Divine Matter* to be *Matter*, acknowledge therewith *Impenetrability* and *Juxta-position* of parts, diversity also of figure, and, where there are no pores at all, absolute *Solidity* and *Hardness*. Whence it is manifest that whatsoever 40 Reasonings are strong against *Ordinary Matter* for making it uncapable of *Perception* and *free Action*, from the *Nature* and

Idea thereof, they are as strong against this, on which they have conferred the title of *Divine*.

And thirdly and lastly, That there is no such *Divine Matter* interspersed amongst the *subtile Matter* of the World, that can
5   act freely and knowingly, *Effects* also and *Experiments* plainly declare, as I have abundantly noted in my *Antidote against Atheism*.

9.   Wherefore it is most rational to conclude; That no *Matter* whatsoever of its own Nature has any active Principle of
10   *Motion*, though it be receptive thereof; but that when God created it, he suparadded an impress of *Motion* upon it, such a measure and proportion to all of it, which remains still much-what the same for quantity in the whole, though the parts of *Matter* in their various occursion of one to another have not
15   alwaies the same proportion of it. Nor is there any more necessity that God should reiterate this impress of *Motion* on the *Matter* created, then that he should peretually create the Matter. Neither does his conservation of this quantity of Motion any thing more imply either a repetition or an
20   augmentation of it, then the conservation of the *Matter* does the superaddition of new *Matter* thereunto. Indeed he need but conserve the *Matter*, and the *Matter* thus conserved will faithfully retain, one part with another, the whole summe of Motion first communicated to it, some small moments excepted,
25   which are not worth the mentioning in this place.

Chap. XII.

30

I. *That the Order and Nature of things in the Universe argue an* Essence Spiritual *or* Incorporeal. 2. The Evasion of this Argument. *3. A preparation of Mr* Hobbs *to answer the Evasion.* 4. The first Answer. 5. The second Answer. 6. Mr
35   Hobbs *his mistake, of making the Ignorance of Second Causes the onely Seed of Religion.*

I. We have discovered out of the simple *Phaenomenon* of Motion, the necessity of the Existence of some *Incorporeal*
40   *Essence distinct from the Matter*: But there is a further assurance of this Truth, from the consideration of the Order and admirable Effect of this Motion in the world. Suppose

Matter could move it self, would mere *Matter*, with Self-motion, amount to that admirable wise contrivance of things which we see in the World? Can a blind *impetus* produce such Effects, with that accuracy and constancy, that, the more wise a man is, the more he will be assured *That no Wisdome wan adde, take* 5 *away, or alter any thing in the works of Nature, whereby they may be bettered?* How can that therefore that has not so much as Sense, arise to the Effects of the highest pitch of *Reason* or *Intellect?* But of this I have spoke so fully and convincingly in the second Book of my *Antidote,* that it will be but a needless 10 repetition to proceed any further on this Subject.

2. All the Evasion that I can imagine our Adversaries may use here, will be this: That *Matter* is capable of *Sense,* and the finest and most subtile of the most refined Sense, and consequently of *Imagination* too, yea haply of *Reason* and 15 *Understanding.* For Sense being nothing else, as some conceit, but *Motion,* or rather *Re-action of a* Body pressed upon by another Body, *it will follow that all the Matter* in the World has in some manner or other the power of *Sensation.*

3. Let us see now what this Position will amount to. 20 Those that make *Motion* and *Sensation* thus really the same, they must of necessity acknowledge, That no longer *Motion,* no longer *Sensation,* (as Mr *Hobbs* has ingenuously confessed in his *Elements* of Philosophy:) And that every *Motion* or *Re-action* must be a new Sensation, as well as every ceasing of Re-action 25 a ceasing of Sensation.

4. Now let us give these busie active *particles* of the *Matter* that play up and down every where the advantage of *Sense,* and let us see if all their heads laid together can contrive the *Anatomical* fabrick of amy Creature that lives. Assuredly 30 when all is summ'd up that can be imagined, they will fall short of their account. For I demand, Has every one of these particles that must have an hand in the framing of the Body of an Animal, the whole design of the work by the impress of some Phantasm upon it, or, as they have several offices, so 35 have they several parts of the design? If the first, it being most certain, even according to their opinion whom we oppose, that there can be no *knowledge* nor *perception* in the *Matter,* but what arises out of the *Re-action* of one part against another, how is it conceivable that any one particle of *Matter* or many 40 together (there not existing yet in Nature any Animal) can have the *Idea* impressed of that Creature they are to frame?

Or if one or some few particles have the sense of one part of the Animal (they seeming more capable of this, the parts being far more simple then the whole *Compages* and contrivement) and other some few of other parts, how can they confer notes?
5   by what language or speech can they communicate their counsel one to another? Wherefore that they should mutually serve one another in such a design, is more impossible then that so many men blind and dumb from their nativity should joyn their forces and wits together to build a Castle, or carve a
10 Statue of such a Creature as none of them knew any more of in several then some one of the smallest parts thereof, but not the relation it bore to the whole.

5. Besides this, *Sense* being really the same with *Corporeal Motion*, it must change upon new impresses of
15 Motion; so that if a particle by Sense were carried in this line, it meeting with a counterbuffe in the way, must have qúite another Impress and Sense, and so forget what it was going about, and divert its course another way. Nay though it scaped free, *Sense* being *Re-action*, when that which it bears
20 against is removed, Sense must needs cease, and perfect Oblivion succeed. For it is not with these particles as with the Spring of a Watch or a bent Cross-bow, that they should for a considerable time retain the same *Re-action*, and so consequently the same Sense. And lastly, if they could, it is
25 still nothing to the purpose; for let their Sense be what it will, their motion is necessary, it being merely corporeal, and therefore the result of their motion cannot be from any kind of knowledge. For the corporeal motion is first, and is onely felt, not directed by feeling. And therefore whether the *Matter* have
30 any Sense or no, what is made out of it is nothing but what results from the wild jumblings and knockings of one part thereof against another, without any purpose, counsel or direction. Wherefore the ordinary *Phaenomena* of Nature being guided according to the most Exquisite Wisdome imaginable, it
35 is plain that they are not the Effects of the mere motion of *Matter*, but of some *Immaterial* Principle, by Axiome 10.

6. And therefore *the Ignorance of Second Causes* is not so rightly said to be the *Seed of Religion*, (as M^r. Hobbs would have it) as of *Irreligion* and *Atheism*. For if we did more
40 punctually and particularly search into their natures, we should clearly discern their insufficiency for such effects as we discover to be in the wcrld. But when we have looked so closely

and carefully into the nature of *Corporeal Beings*, and can finde
no Causality in them proportionable to these Effects we speak
of, still to implead ourselves rather of Ignorance, then the
Matter and *Corporeal motion* of Insufficiency, is to hold an
opinion upon humour, and to transgress against our first and 5
second Axiomes.

Chap. XIII.

10

I. *The last proof of* Incorporeal Substances, *from Apparitions.*
2. *The first Evasion of the force of such Arguings.* 3. *An
Answer to that Evasion.* 4. *The second Evasion.* 5. *The first
kind of the second Evasion.* 6. *A description out of* Virgil *of that* 15
Genius that suggests the dictates of the Epicurean *Philosophy.* 7.
The more full and refined sense of that Philosophy now-a-dayes.
8. *The great efficacy of the Stars (which they suppose to consist
of nothing but Motion and Matter) for production of all manner of
Creatures in the world.* 20

I. The Third and last ground which I would make use of,
for evincing the Existence of *Incorporeal Substances*, is such
extraordinary Effects as we cannot well imagine any natural,
but must needs conceive some free or spontaneous Agent to be 25
the Cause thereof, whenas yet it is clear that they are from
neither Man nor Beast.   Such are speakings, knockings,
opening of doors when they were fast shut, sudden lights in the
midst of a room floating in the aire, and then passing and
vanishing; nay, shapes of Men and severall sorts of Brutes, 30
that after speech and converse have suddainly disappeared.
There and many such like extraordinary Effects (which, if you
please, you may call by one generall terme of *Apparitions*)
seem to me to be an undeniable Argument, that there be such
things as *Spirits* or *Incorporeal Substances* in the world; and I 35
have demonstrated the sequel to be necessary in the last
Chapter of the *Appendix to my Treatise against Atheism*; and in
the third Book of that Treatise have produced so many and so
unexceptionable Stories concerning *Apparitions*, that I hold it
superfluous to adde anything here of that kind, taking far more 40
pleasure in exercising of my Reason then in registring of
History.   Besides that I have made so carefull choice there

already, that I cannot hope to cull out any that may prove more pertinent or convictive; I having penn'd down none but such as I had compared with those severe lawes I set my self in the first Chapter of that third Book, to prevent all
5 tergiversations & evasions of gain-sayers.

2. But, partly out of my own observation, and partly by information from others, I am well assured there are but two wayes whereby they escape the force of such evident Narrations. The first is a firm perswasion that the very *Notion*
10 of a *Spirit* or *Immaterial Substance* is an *Impossibility* or *Contradiction* in the very termes. And therefore such stories implying that which they are confident is *impossible*, the Narration at the very first hearing must needs be judged to be false; and therefore they think it more reasonable to conclude
15 all those that profess they have seen such or, such things to be mad-men or cheats, then to give credit to what implies a *Contradiction*.

3. But this Evasion I have quite taken away, by so clearly demonstrating that the *Notion of a Spirit* implies no more
20 *contradiction* then the *Notion of Matter*; and that its Attributes are as conceivable as the Attributes of *Matter*: so that I hope this creep-hole is stopt for ever.

4. The second Evasion is not properly an Evasion of the truth of these stories concerning *Apparitions*, but of our
25 deduction therefrom. For they willingly admit of these *Apparitions* and *Prodigies* recorded in History, but they deny that they are any Arguments of a truly *Spiritual* and *Incorporeal Substance* distinct from the *Matter* thus changed into this or that shape, that can walk and speak etc. but that they
30 are special Effects of the influence of the Heavenly Bodies upon this region of Generation and Corruption.

5. And these that answer thus are of two sorts. The one have great Affinity with *Aristotle* and *Avenroes*, who look not upon the Heavenly Bodies as mere Corporeal Substances, but
35 as actuated with Intelligencies, which are Essences separate and Immaterial. But this Supposition hurts not us at all in our present design; they granting that which I am arguing for, viz. *a Substance Incorporeal*. The use of this perverse Hypothesis is only to shuttle off all Arguments that are drawn from
40 *Apparitions*, to prove that the Souls of men subsist after death, or that there are any such things as *Daemons* or *Genii* of a nature permanent and immortal. But I look upon this

Supposition as confutable enough, were it worth the while to encounter it.

That of the *Sadducees* is far more firm, they supposing their ἀπόῤῥοιαὶ *nothing else but the efficacy of the presence of God* altering *Matter* into this or the other Apparition or 5 Manifestation; as if there were but one Soul in all things, and God were that Soul variously working in the Matter. But this I have already confuted in my Philosophicall Poems, and shall again in this present Treatise.

6. The other *Influenciaries* hold the same power of the 10 Heavens as these; though they do not suppose so high a Principle in them, yet they think it sufficient for the salving of all Sublunary *Phaenomena*, as well ordinary as extraordinary. Truly it is a very venerable *Secret*, and not to be uttered or communicated but by some old *Silenus* lying in his obscure Grot 15 or Cave, nor that neither but upon dumbe circumstances, and in a right humour, when one may find him with his veins swell'd out with wine, and his Garland faln off from his head through his heedless drousiness: Then if some young *Chromis* and *Mnasylus*, especially assisted by a fair and forward *Aegle*, 20 that by way of a lovefrolick will leave the tracts of her fingers in the blood of Mulberies on the temples and forehead of this aged Satyre, while he sleeps dog-sleep, and will seem to see, for fear he forfeit the pleasure of his feeling; then, I say, if these young lads importune him enough, he will again sing that old 25 song of the *Epicurean* Philosophy in an higher strain then ever, which I profess I should abhor to recite, were it not to confute; it is so monstrous and impious. But because no sore can be cured that is concealed, I must bring this *Hypothesis* into view also, which the Poet has briefly comprised in this summary. 30

> *Namque canebat, uti magnum per inane coacta*
> *Semina terrarumque animaque marisque fuissent,*
> *Et liquidi simul ignis; ut his exordia primis*
> *Omnia, et ipse tener mundi concreverit orbis.*

7. The fuller and more refined sense whereof now-a-daies 35 is this That *Matter* and *Motion* are the Principles of all things whatsoever; and that by *Motion* some *Atomes* or particles are more subtile then others, and of more nimbleness and activity. That motion of one Body against another does every where necessarily produce Sense, *Sense* being nothing else but the *Re-* 40 *action* of parts of the *Matter*. That the *subtiler* the *Matter* is, the *Sense* is more subtile. That the *subtilest Matter* of all is that

which constitutes the *Sun* and *Stars*, from whence they must
needs have the purest and *subtilest sense*. That what has the
most perfect *Sense*, has the most perfect *Imagination* and
Memory because *Memory* and *Imagination* are but the same
5   with *Sense* in reality, the latter being but certain *Modes* of the
former. That what has the *perfectest Imagination*, has the
highest Reason and *Providence; Providence* and *Reason* being
nothing else but an exacter train of Phantasmes, Sensations or
Imaginations. Wherefore the *Sun* and the *Stars* are the *most*
10 *Intellectual Beings* in the world, and in them is that *Knowledge,*
Counsel and *Wisdome* by which all Sublunary things are
framed and governed.

8. These by their several impresses and impregnations
have filled the whole Earth with vital *Motion*, raising
15 innumerable sorts of Flowers, Herbs and Trees out of the
ground. These have also generated the several Kinds of living
Creatures. These have filled the Seas with Fishes, the Fields
with Beasts, and the Aire with Fowles; the Terrestrial matter
being as easily formed into the living shapes of these several
20 *Animals* by the powerful impress of the *Imagination* of the Sun
and Stars, as the *Embryo* in the womb is marked by the strong
fancy of his Mother that bears him.   And therefore these
Celestial powers being able to frame living shapes of Earthly
matter by the impress of their *Imagination*, it will be more easy
25 for them to change the vaporous Aire into like transfigurations.

So that admitting all these Stories of *Apparitions* to be true
that are recorded in Writers, it is no Argument of the Existence
of any *Incorporeal* Principle in the world. For the piercing Foresight of these glorious Bodies, the *Sun* and *Stars*, is able to
30 raise what *Apparitions* or *Prodigies* they please, to usher in the
Births or foresignify the *Deaths* of the most considerable
persons that appear in the world; of which *Pomponatius* himself
does acknowledge that there are many true examples both in
Greek and *Latine* History. Thas is the *deepest Secret* that old
35 *Silenus* could ever sing to ensnare the ears of deceivable Youth.
And it is indeed φρικτὸν μυστήριον, in the very worst sense,
Horrendum Mysterium, a very dreadful and dangerous Mystery,
saving that there is no finall hope that it may not prove true.
Let us therefore now examine it.

Chap. XIV.

I. *That the Splendor of the Celestial Bodies prnves no Fore-*
sight nor Soveraignty that they have over us. 2. *That the Stars*
can have no knowledge of us, Mathematically demonstrated. 3. 5
The sane Conclusion again demonstrated more familiarly. 4.
That the Stars cannot communicate Thoughts, neither with the
Sun nor with one another. 5. *That the Sun has no knowledge of*
our affairs. 6. *Principles laid down for the inferring that*
Conclusion. 7. *A demonstration that he cannot see us.* 8. *That* 10
he can have no other kind of knowledge of us, nor of the frame of
any Animal on Earth. 9. *That though the Sun had the*
knowledge of the right frame of an Animal, he could not transmit
it into Terrestrial matter. 10. *An Answer to that Instance of the*
Signature of the Foetus. *11,12. Further Answers thereto.* 13. *A* 15
short Increpation of the confident Exploders of Incorporeal
Substance *out of the world.*

I. That the *Light* is a very glorious thing, and the lustre of
the *Stars* very lovely to look upon, and that the Body of the *Sun* 20
is so full of splendour and Majesty, that without flattery we
may profess our selves constrained to look aside, as not being
able to bear the brightness of his aspect; all this must be
acknowledged for Truth: but that these are as so many *Eyes* of
Heaven to watch over the Earth, so many kind and careful 25
Spectators & Intermedlers also in humane affairs, as that
phansiful Chymist *Paracelsus* conceits, who writeth that not
onely Princes and Nobles, or men of great and singular worth,
but even almost every one, near his death has some
prognostick sign or other (as knockings in the house, the dances 30
of dead men, and the like) from these compassionate Fore-seers
of has approaching Fate; this I must confess I am not so
paganly Superstitious as to believe one syllable of; but think it
may be demonstrated to be a mere fancy, especially upon this
present Hypothesis, That the *Sun* and *Stars* have no 35
immaterial Being residing in them, but are mere *Matter*
consisting of the subtilest Particles and most vehemently
agitated. For then we cannot but be assured that there is
nothing in them more Divine then what is seen in other things
that shine in the dark, suppose rotten wood, glo-worms, or 40
the flame of a rush-candle.

2. This at least we will demonstrate, That let the *Sun* and
Stars have what knowledge they will of other things, they have
just none at all of us, nor of our affairs; which will quite take
away this last Evasion. That the *Stars* can have no knowledge
5   of us is exceeding evident: For whenas the *Magnus orbis* of the
Earth is but as a Point compared with the distance thereof to a
fixed Star, that is to say, whenas that Angle which we may
imagine to be drawn from a Star, and to be subtended by the
Diameter of the *Magnus orbis*, is to Sense no Angle at all, but
10 as a mere Line; how little then is the Earth it self? and how
utterly invisible to any *Star*, whenas her Diameter is above
1100. times less then that of her *Magnus orbis*? From whence
it is clear that it is perfectly impossible that the *Stars*, though
they were endued with sight, could so much as see the *Earth* it
15 self, (much less the inhabitants thereof) to be *Spectators* and
Intermedlers in their affaires for good or evil; and there being
no higher Principle to inspire them with the knowledge of these
things, it is evident that they remain utterly ignorant of them.
3. Or if this Demonstration (though undeniably true in it
20 self) be not so intelligible to every one, we may adde what is
more easy and familiar, viz. That the *Stars* being lucid Bodies,
those of the first magnitude near an hundred times bigger then
the Earth, and yet appearing so small things to us, hence any
one may collect, that the opake Earth will either be quite
25 invisible to the *Stars*, or else at least appear so little, that it will
be impossible that they should see any distinct Countries, much
less Cities, Houses, or Inhabitants.
4. Wherefore we have plainly swept away this numerous
Company of the celestial Senators from having any thing to doe
30 to consult about, or any way to oversee the affairs of Mankind;
and therefore let them seem to wink and twinkle as
cogitabundly as they will, we may rest in assurance that they
have no plot concerning us, either for good or evill, as having
no knowledge of us. Nor if they had, could they *communicate*
35 *their thoughts* to that great deemed Soveraign of the world, the
Sun; they being ever as invisible to him, as they are to us in
the day-time. For it is nothing but has light that hinders us
from seeing so feeble Objects, and this hinderance consisteth in
nothing else but this, That that motion which by his Rayes is
40 caused in the Organ is so fierce and violent, that the gentle
vibration of the light of the *Stars* cannot master it, nor indeed
bear any considerable proportion to it: What then can it do in

reference to the very Body of the *Sun* himself, the matter whereof has the most furious motion of any thing in the world?

5. There is nothing now therefore left, but the *Sun* alone, that can possibly be conceived to have any knowledge of, or any superintendency over our terrestrial affairs. And how 5 uncapable he is also of this office, I hold it no difficult thing to demonstrate. Whence it will plainly appear, that those *Apparitions* that are seen, whether in the Aire or on Earth (which are rightly looked upon as an Argument of Providence and Existence of some *Incorporeal Essence* in the world) cannot 10 be attributed to the power and prevision of the *Sun*, supposing him purely corporeal.

6. For it is a thing agreed upon by all sides, That *mere Matter* has no *connate Ideas* in it of such things as we see in the world; but that upon *Re-action* of one part moved by another 15 arises a kind of *Sense* or *Perception*. Which opinion as it is most rational in it self to conceive (supposing *Matter* has any sense in it at all) so it is most consonant to experience, we seeing plainly that *Sense* is ever caused by some outward corporeal motion upon our Organs, which are also corporeal. For that 20 *Light* is from a corporeal motion, is plain from the reflexion of the rayes thereof; and no Sound is heard but from the motion of the Aire or some other intermediate Body; no Voice but there is first a moving of the Tongue; no Musick but there must either be the blowing of wind, or the striking upon strings, or 25 something Analogical to these; and so in the other Senses.

Wherefore if there be nothing but *Body* in the world, it is evident that Sense arises merely from the *motion* of one part of *Matter* against another, and that *Motion* is ever first, and *Perception* follows, and that therefore *Perception* must 30 necessarily follow the laws of *Motion*, and that no *Percipient* can have any thing more to conceive then what is conveighed by Corporeal motion. Now from these Principles it will be easy to prove that, though we should acknowledge a power of *Perception* in the *Sun*, yet it will not amount to any ability of his being 35 either a *Spectator* or *Governor* of our affairs here on Earth.

7. According to the Computation of *Astronomers*, even of those that speak more modestly, the *Sun* is bigger then the *Earth* above an hundred and fifty times. But how little he appears to us every eye is able to judge. How little then must 40 the *Earth* appear to him? If he see her at all, he will be so far from being able to take notice of any Persons or Families, that

he cannot have any distinct discerning of Streets, nor Cities, no
not of Fields, nor Countries; but whole Regions, though of very
great Extent, will vanish here, as *Alcibiades* his Patrimony in
that Map of the world *Socrates* shewed him, to repress the pride
5   of the young Heire. The *Earth* must appear *considerably* less to
him then the *Moon* does to us, because the *Sun* appears to us
less then the *Moon*. It were easy to demonstrate that her
discus would appear to the *Sun* near thirty, nay sixty times
less then the Moon does to us, according to *Lansbergius* his
10   computation.

Now consider how little we can discern in that broader
Object of sight, the *Moon*, when she is the nighest,
notwithstanding we be placed in the dark, under the shadow of
the *Earth*, whereby our sight is more passive and impressible.
15   How little then must the fiery eye of that *Cyclops* the
Sun,which is all Flame and Light, discern in this lesser Object
the *Earth*, his vigour and motion being so vehemently strong
and unyielding? What effect it will have upon him, we may in
some sort judge by our selves: For though our Organ be but
20   moved or agitated with the reflexion of his Rayes, we hardly
see the *Moon* when she is above the Horizon by day: What
impress then can our *Earth*, a less Object to him then the *Moon*
is to us, make upon the *Sun*, whose Body is so furiously hot,
that he is as boiling Fire, if a man may so speak, and the Spots
25   about him are, as it were, the scum of this fuming Cauldron?

Besides that our *Atmosphere* is so thick a covering over us
at that distance, that there can be the appearance of nothing
but a white mist enveloping all and shining like a bright cloud;
in which the rayes of the *Sun* will be so lost, that they can
30   never return any distinct representation of things unto him.
Wherefore it is as evident to *Reason* that he cannot see us, as it
is to *Sense* that we see him; and therefore he can be no *Overseer*
nor *Intermedler* in our actions.

8. But perhaps you will reply That though the *Sun* cannot
35   see the *Earth*, yet he may have a *Sense* and *Perception* in
himself (for he is a fine glittering thing, and some strange
matter must be presumed of him) that may amount to a
wonderful large sphere of *Understanding*, *Fore-knowledge* and
Power. But this is a mere fancyful surmise, and such as cannot
40   be made good by any of our Faculties: Nay the quite contrary
is demonstrable by such Principles as are already agreed upon.
For there are no *connate Ideas* in the *Matter*, and therefore out

of the collision and agitation of the *Solar* particles, we cannot
rationally expect any other effect in the *Sun*, then such as we
experiment in the percussion of our own eyes, out of which
ordinarily follows the sense of a confused light or flame. If the
Sun therefore has any sense of himself, it must be only the   5
perception of a very vigorous *Light* or *Fire*, which being still one
and the same representation, it is a question whether he has a
sense of it or no, any more then we have of our bones, which
we perceive not by reason of our accustomary and
uninterrupted sense of them, as Mr *Hobbs* ingeniously   10
conjectures in a like supposition.

But if you will say that there is a perception of the jogging
or justling, or of whatever touch or rubbing of one *Solar* particle
against another, the body of the *Sun* being so exceeding liquid,
and consequently the particles thereof never resting, but   15
playing and moving this way and that way; yet they hitting
and fridging so fortuitously one against another, the
perceptions that arise from hence must be so various and
fortuitous, so quick and short, so inconsistent, flitting and
impermanent, that if any man were in such a condition as the   20
Sun necessarily is, according to this Hypothesis, he would both
be, and appear to all the world to be, stark mad; he would be so
off and on, and so unsettled, and doe, and think, and speak all
things with such ungovernable rashness and temerity.

In brief, that the *Sun* by this tumultuous agitation of his   25
Fiery Atoms should hit upon any rational contrivance or right
Idea of any of these living Creatures we see here on Earth, is
utterly as hard to conceive, as that the Terrestrial particles
themselves should justle together into such contrivances and
formes, which is that which I have already sufficiently   30
confuted.

9. And if the *Sun* could light on any such true frame or
forme of any Animal, or the due rudiments or contrivance
thereof, it is yet unconceivable how he should conveigh it into
this Region of Generation here on *Earth*, partly by reason of   35
the *Earth*'s Distance and Invisibleness, and partly because the
deepest Principle of all being but mere Motion, without any
superior power to govern it, this *Imagination* of the *Sun*
working on the *Earth* can be but a simple *Rectilinear* impress
which can never arise to such an inward solid organization of   40
parts in living Creatures nor hold together these *Spectres* or
Apparitions in the Aire, in any more certain form then the

smoak of chimnies or the fume of Tobacco.

10.   Nor is that Instance of the power of the Mother's fancy on the *Foetus* in the womb, any more then a mere flourish; for the disparity is so great, that the Argument proves
5   just nothing: For whereas the Mother has an Explicite *Idea* of the *Foetus* and every part thereof, the *Sun* and *Stars* have no distinct *Idea* at all of the parts of the *Earth*; nay I dare say that what we have already intimated will amount to a Demonstration, That though they had *Sense*, yet they do not so
10   much as *know* whether this Earth we live on be *in rerum Naturâ* or no.

11.   Again, the *Mark* that is impressed on the *Foetus*, the Mother has a clear and vivid conception of; but the curious contrivance in the *Idea* of Animals, I have shewn how
15   incompetible it is to the fortuitous justling of the fiery particles of either *Sun* or *Stars*.

12.   Thirdly, the *Impress* on the *Foetus* is very simple and slight, and seldome so curious as the ordinary impresses of Seals upon Wax, which are but the modifications of the surface
20   thereof; but this supposed Impress of the *Imagination* of the *Sun* and *Stars* is more then a solid Statue, or the most curious *Automaton* that ever was invented by the wit of man; and therefore impossible to proceed from a mere *Rectilinear* impress upon the *Aether* down to the *Earth* from the *Imagination* of the
25   *Sun*, no not if he were supposed to be actuated with an *Intelligent* Soul, if the *Earth* and all the space betwixt her and him were devoid thereof. Nor do I conceive, though it be an infinitely more slight business, that the direction of the *Signature* of the *Foetus* upon such a part were to be performed
30   by the *Fancy* of the Mother, notwithstanding the advantage of the organization of her body, were not both her self and the *Foetus* animated Creatures.

13.   Wherefore we have demonstrated beyond all Evasion, from the *Phaenomena* of the Universe, That of necessity there
35   must be such a thing in the world as *Incorporeal Substance*; let inconsiderable Philosophasters hoot at it, and deride it as much as their Follies please.

The
IMMORTALITY
of
THE SOUL

The Second Book

Chap. I.

10

I. *An addition of more Axi*omes *for the demonstrating that there* is *a* Spirit *or* Immaterial Substance *in Man.* 2. *The Truth of the first of these Axiomes confirmed from the testimony* 15 *of M^r* Hobbs, *as well as demonstrated in the Preface.* 3,4. *That Demonstration further cleared and evinced by answering a certain Evasion.* 5. *The proof of the second Axiome.* 6. *The proof of the third.* 7. *The confirmation of the fourth from the testimony of M^r* Hobbs, *as also from Reason.* 8. *An explication and proof of* 20 *the fifth.* 9. *A further Proof of the Truth thereof.* 10. *An Answer to an Evasion.* 11. *Another Evasion answered.* 12. *A further mananagement of this first Answer thereto.* 13. *A second Answer.* 14. *A third Answer, wherein is mainly contained a confirmation of the first Answer to the second Evasion.* 15. *The* 25 *plainness of the sixth Axiome.* 16. *The proof of the seventh.*

1. Having cleared the way thus far as to prove That there is *no Contradiction* nor Inconsistency in the *Notion of a Spirit,* but that it *may Exist* in Nature, nay that *de facto* there are 30 *Incorporeal Substances* really Existent in the world; we shall now drive more home to our main design, and demonstrate *That there is such an Immaterial Substance in Man,* which, from the power it is conceived to have in actuating and guiding the *Body,* is usually called *the Soule.* This Truth we shall make 35 good first in a more *general* way, but not a whit the lesse stringent, by evincing That *such Faculties* or *Operations* as we are conscious of in our selves, are utterly incompetible to *Matter* considered *at large* without any *particular* organization. And then afterwards we shall more punctually consider the *Body of* 40 *man,* and every possible fitness in the structure thereof that is worth taking notice of for the perfomance of *these Operations*

we ordinarily find in our selves. And that this may be done
more plainly and convincingly, we will here adde to the number
of our Axiomes these that follow.

5   AXIOME XX.
Motion *or* Re-action *of one part of the* Matter *against another, or*
at least a due continuance thereof, is really one and the same with
Sense *and* Perception, *if there be any* Sense *or* Perception *in*
Matter.
10

    2.This Axiome, as it is plain enough of it self (supposing
there were nothing but *Body* in the world) so has it the suffrage
of our most confident and potent adversary Mr. *Hobbs* in his
Elements of Philosophy. Whose judgment I make much of in
15   such cases as these, being perswaded as well out of Reason as
Charity, that he seeing so little into the nature of *Spirits*; that
defect is compensated with and extraordinary Quicksightedness
in discerning of the best warrantable wayes of salving all
Phaenomena from the ordinary allowed properties of *Matter*.
20   Wherefore I shall not hold it impertinent to bring in his
Testimony in things of this nature, my Demonstrations
becoming thereby more recommendable to men of his own
Conclusions. But my design being not a particular victory over
such a sort of Men, but an absolute establishing of the Truth,I
25   shall lay down no Grounds that are merely *Argumenta ad*
hominem; but such as I am perswaded (upon this Hypothesis,
That there is nothing but *Body* in the world) are evident to any
one   that   can   indifferently   judge   thereof.   And   the
demonstration of this present Axiome I have prefixed in my
30   Preface, Sect. 5.
    3. Against which I cannot imagine any possible Evasion,
unless one should conceit that a *general agitation* onely of the
particles of the *Matter* will suffice to *excite* them to *thinking*,
and that they being thus *excited*, can freely run out to other
35   *cogitations* and *Phantasmes* then what adequately arise from
the impress of *Motion*.
    But to this may briefly be answered, First, That since
from the *Agitation* and Collision of these particles *Sense* must
needs arise (for they being near Upon of the same magnitude,
40   they will effectually act one upon another) the *Animadversion*
of these particles will be so taken up and fixt upon their
sensible perceptions, that though they otherwise had a power of

freely thinking, yet they would alwaies be necessarily detained
in these sensible Phantasmes.

And then, Secondly, All that is perceived, is perceived *in
common* by that which is capable of being the *Percipient*. But
nothing that is not really the same with corporeal motion, or an   5
immediate and adequate effect thereof, can be *communicated* to
the common particles of this or that *Matter*. Hence therefore it
is plain that there is not any *congeries* of *Matter* that does run
into *free cogitations*, whether *grosser* Phantasmes or *second*
Notions, for the want of mutual communication of them in one   10
Particle to another, as I have more particularly demonstrated
in its due place.

Thirdly and lastly, It is sufficiently manifest from sense
and experience that *Matter* is a principle *purely passive*, and no
otherwise *moved* or *modified* then as some other thing *moves*   15
and *modifies* it, but cannot move it self at all. Which is most
demonstrable to them that contend for *Sense* and *Perception* in
it. For if it had any such *Perception*, it would by virtue of its
Self-motion withdraw it self from under the knocks of hammers
or fury of the fire; or of its own accord approach to such things   20
as are most agreeable to it and pleasing, and that without the
help of *Muscles*, it being thus immediately endowed with a *Self-
moving* Power. But the *Matter* being so stupid as to want *this
Power*, how can it be thought a Subject wherein a Power and
activity *infinitely more divine* should reside, that is, the free   25
expatiating into *Variety of thoughts*, the exercise of *Invention*,
Judgement and *Memory*, and that in such Objects as are
supposed not to be the Impresses of the *Motion* of the particles
one upon another?

Nor would I be thought cunning and fraudulent in naming   30
such gross and *massy Matter* as uses to be struck with
Hammers or hewen with Axes, and to conclude from thence
that no *Matter* at all, no not the most subtile, does move it self:
For *Self-motion* is as competible to a *massy* piece of *Matter* as
the *most minute* particle imaginable; for Force will be to Force   35
as Magnitude to Magnitude; and therefore the most *massy*
pieces of *Matter* will move themselves the most strongly and
most irresistinly. From whence it appears that the *minutest*
particle of any Massy body separate from it has not one jot of
advantage toward *Self-motion* thereby, but onely becomes lass   40
irresistible in its *Self-motion*.

4. Nor can you help your self by recurring to the *Figment* of a *Matter specifically distinct* from what men ordinarily speak of, (which some adorn with the title of *Divine*, as if it were the very substance of the highest Godhead:) For we may easily
5   undeceive our selves if we do but contemplate some considerable quantity of this *Divine Matter*, suppose a *Globe* of some few inches Diameter, and perfectly *solid*,that is, the parts thereof immediately united without pores or intervalls; and then consider how it cannot fail of being more hard then
10 the *Pig of Lead*, or the *Wedge of Gold*, which I mention in my Demonstration of this Axiome, and as Opake as any body whatsoever. For hence this *Divine Matter* will appear to our mind as uncapable of *spontaneous Motion* and of free *Cogitations* and *Perceptions* unimpressed from corporeal motion
15 as the *Pig of Lead* and *Wedge of Gold* there mentioned; and that therefore this *Figment* is but a mere Mockery of words, and as ill put together in this sense, as a *divine* Pig of Lead or *divine* Wedge of Gold would be.

And what I have said of the *whole Globe*, there is the same
20 reason of *any particle* of the same nature with it; which will be no more capable of *free cogitation*, then the particles of that *Matter* that makes up *Gold* or *Lead*. For if there be any *perception*, it must be by *corporeal Re-action* in both, if we impartially attend to the dictates of our own Faculties. And let
25 them be as they will, *communication of free Perceptions* will not be found possible in either; the *Divinest Matter* imaginable having no other union then *Juxta-position* of parts, as our Adversaries themselves freely will acknowledge.

To which faithful presages and rational conclusions of our
30 own Mind you may finally adde the suffrage of Nature in Experiments, which do clearly assure us that there is no such *Divine Matter* endued with *free cogitation* and free Agency intermingled or interspersed in the *common Matter* of the World, as I have plainly shown in my Antidote. And
35 therefore we will conclude that no *Matter* whatsoever has any *perception* in any other manner or according to any other laws then what Mr. *Hobbs* has already defined, and my self in this twentieth Axiome have declared, if *Matter* have any *perception* at all.

AXIOME XXI.

So far as this continued Re-action *reaches, so far reaches* Sense *or* Perception, *and no further.*

5.This Axiome is to be understoed as well of Duration of
Time, as Extension of the Subject, viz. That *Sense* and
Perception spread no further in *Matter* then *Re-action* does, nor
remain any longer then this *Re-action* remains. Which Truth is
fully evident out of the foregoing Axiome.

AXIOME XXII.

That diversity there is of Sense *or* Perception *does necessarily
arise from the diversity of the Magnitude, Figure, Position,
Vigour and Direction of* Motion *in parts of the* Matter.

6. The truth of this is also clear from the 20th Axiome.
For *Perception* being really one and the same thing with *Re-
action* of *Matter* one part against another; and there being a
diversity of *Perception*, it must imply also a diversity of
medification of *Re-action*; and *Re-action* being nothing but
Motion in Matter, it cannot be varied but by such *variations* as
are competible to *Matter*, viz. such as are *Magnitude, Figure,
Posture, Local Motion*, wherein is contained any endeavour
towards it, as also the *Direction* of that either full Motion or
curb'd endeavour, and a *Vigour* thereof; which if you run to
the lowest degrees, you will at last come to *Rest*, which
therefore is some way referrible to that head, as to *Magnitude*
you are to refer *Littleness*. These are the first conceivable in
Matter, and therefore diversity of *Perception* must of necessity
arise from these.

AXIOME XXIII.

Matter *in all the variety of those* Perceptions *it is sensible of, has
none but such as are impressed by Corporeal Motions, that is to
say, that are* Perceptions *of some Actions or modificated
Impressions of parts of* Matter *bearing one against another.*

7. To this Truth Mr *Hobbs* sets his seal with all
willingness imaginable, or rather eagerness, as also his
Followers, they stoutly contending that we have not the
perception of any thing but the Phantasms of material Objects,
and of sensible words or Marks, which we make to stand for

such and such Objects. Which certainly would be most true if
there were nothing but *Matter* in the world; so that they speak
very consonantly to their own Principles: I say, this is not only
true in that School, but also rational in it self, supposing
5   nothing but *Matter* in the world, and that *Perception* and *Re-
action* is really one. For that *Re-action* being in Brutes as well
as in Men, there must not be any difference by a perception of
quite another kind, but by an external way of communication
of their perceptions. And therefore the distinction betwixt *Men*
10 and *Beasts* must consist onely in this, that the one can agree in
some common mark, whether *Voices* or *Characters*, or whatever
else, to express their *perceptions*, but the other cannot; but the
perceptions themselves must be of one kind in both, they neither
of them perceiving any thing but *corporeal impressions*, such as
15 they feel by the parts of the *Matter* beating one against
another.

AXIOME XXIV.

The distinct Impression of any considerable extent of variegated
20 *Matter cannot be received by a mere point of Matter.*

8. By *a mere point of Matter* I do not mean a mere
Mathematical point, but *a perfect Parvitude*, or the *least Reality
of Matter*, (concerning which I have spoke already). Which
25 being the least quantity that *discerpible Matter* can consist of,
no particle of *Matter* can touch it less then it self. This
Parvitude therefore that is so little that it has properly no
integral parts, really distinguishable, how can it possibly be a
Subject distinctly receptive of the view, haply, of half an
30 Horizon at once? which sight is caused by real and distinct
motion from real distinct parts of the Object that is seen. But
this *perfect Parvitude* being the minutest quantity that *Matter* is
divisible into, no more then one *real* line of motion can be
directed upon it, the rest will goe beside. To which you may
35 adde that if this so *perfect Parvitude* were distinctly parceptive
of variegated Objects, it were a miracle if it could not perceive
the particles of the *Aire* and of the Atmosphere, the *Globuli* of
light, and subtilest contexture of the parts of Opake bodies.
9. Again, this Object we speak of may be so variegated, I
40 mean with such colours, that it may imply a contradiction, that
one and the same particle of *Matter* (suppose some very small
round one, that shall be the Cuspe of the visual pyramide or

Cone) should receive them all at once; the opposite kindes of those colours being uncommunicable to this round particle otherwise then by contrariety of Motions, or by *Rest* and *Motion*, which are as contrary; as is manifest out of that excellent Theoreme concerning *Colours* in *Des-Cartes* his 5 Meteors, which if it were possible to be false, yet it is most certainly true, that seeing *Motion* is the cause of *Sight*, the contrariety of Objects for Colour must arise out of contrary modifications of Motion in this particle we speak of, that immediately communicates the *Object* to the *Sentient*: which 10 contrariety of *Motions* at the same time and within the same surface of the adequate place of a Body is utterly incompetible thereto.

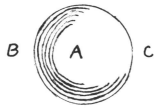

10. Nor is that Evasion any thing available, That there is not any contrariety of real Motion here, but that there is onely 15 endeavour to Motion: For it is plain that Endeavour is as real as Motion it self, and as contrary, because it does really affect the sight, and in a contrary manner. Besides, this Endeavour toward Motion is Motion it self, though of an exceeding small progress: But be it as little as it will, it is as great a 20 contradiction, for example, that the Globe A should upon the same centre, and within the same superficies (which is its adequate place according to the meaning of that Notion in *Aristotle*'s School) be turned mever so little from C to B, and from B to C, at once, as to be turned quite about in that 25 *manner*. *To which* you may adde that some Colours imply *the ones* Motion, *and the others Rest*; but a Globe if it rest in any one part from turning, rests in all.   From whence it will follow, That it is impossible to see *Red* and *Black* at once.

11. This Subterfuge therefore being thus clearly taken 30 away, they substitute another, viz. That the distinct parts of the Object do not act upon this round particle, which is the Cuspe of the visual Pyramide, at once, but successively, and so swiftly, that the Object is represented at once; as when one swings about a fire-stick very fast, it seems one continued circle 35

of fire. But we shall find this instance very little to the
purpose, if we consider, that when one swings a fire-stick in a
circle, it describes such a circle in the bottome of the Eye, not
upon one point there, but in a considerable distance; and that
5 the Optick Nerve, or the Spirits therein, are touched
successively, but left free to a kind of *Tremor* or *Vibration* as it
were, (so as it is in the playing of a Lute) till the motion has
gone round, and then touches in the same place again, so quick,
that it findes it still vigorously moved: But there being but
10 one particle to touch upon here, some such like inconveniences
will recurre as we noted in the former case.

  12. For as I demonstrated before, that some Colours
cannot be communicated at once to one and the same round
particle of *Matter*; so from thence it will follow here, That,
15 such Colours succeeding one another, the impress of the one
will take off immediately the impress of the other; from whence
we shall not be able to see such various Colours as are
discernible in a very large Object at once. For unless the
impression make some considerable stay upon that which
20 receives it, there is no Sensation; insomuch that a man may
wag his finger so fast that he can scarce see it: and if it do
make a due stay, suppose a large Object checkered with the
most opposite Colours, it were impossible that we should see
that checker-work at once in so large a compass as we do, but
25 we shall only see it by parts, the parts vanishing and coming
again in a competent swiftness, but very discernible.

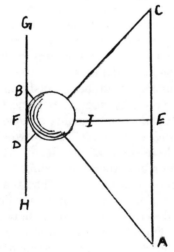

13. Again; if we could possibly imagine the *vicissitudes* of the impresses, from the distinct parts of the Basis of the visual Cone to the point of it, which we will suppose to be a very small *globulus*, such as *Des-Cartes* his second Element consists of, it being thus *successively* thrust against, things must then be 5 as I have represented them in the adjoining figure, where C A is the Object, G H the Sentient Matter, and I the *Globulus*, which will be born from E directly toward F, where there will be received such a colour in the *least Reality* of the Sentient Matter in F; but from A it will be born towards B, and with a 10 very short rowling touch in another *Reality*, or it may be more distantly from F, and impress such a colour from A upon B, or thereabout, and so from C upon D: so that hereby also it is manifest that no one *perfect Parvitude* receives the whole Object C E A.   15

14. Lastly, this quick vicissitude of impulse or impression would contaminate all the Colours, and make the whole Object as it were of one confounded colour, as a man may easily perceive in a *painted Wheel*: For what is it but a quick coming on of one colour upon the same part of the Optick nerve upon 20 which another was, immediately that makes the whole *Wheel* seem of one blended colour? But not to impose upon any one, this instance of the *Wheel* has a peculiar advantage above this present Supposition for making all seem one confounded colour, because the colours of the *Wheel* come not onely upon one and 25 the same part of the Nerve, but in one and the same line from the Object; so that in this regard the instance is less accommodate. But it is shreudly probable, that *fluid perceptive Matter* will not fail to find the colours tinctured from one another in some measure in the whole Object here also, 30 especially if it be nigh and very small, by reason of the instability of that particle that is successively plaied upon from all parts thereof. But at least this instance of the Wheel is an unexceptionable confirmation of our first Demonstration of the weakness of the second Evasion, from the *necessity* of a *con-* 35 *siderable stay* upon the *percipient Matter*, and that *Sensation* cannot be but with some *leisurely continuance* of this or that Motion before it be wiped out. We might adde also that there ought to be a due permanency of the Object that presses against the Organ, though no *new* impression suddenly 40 succeeded to wipe out the former, as one may experiment in swiftly swinging about a painted Bullet in a string, which will

still more fully confirm what we aime at. But this is more then enough for the making good of this 24. Axiome; whose evidence is so clear of it self, that I believe there are very few but will be convinced of it at the first sight.

5

AXIOME XXV.

Whatever impression or parts of any impression are not received by this perfect Parvitude *or* Real point *of Matter, are not at all perceived by it.*

10

15. This is so exceeding plain of it self, that it wants neither explication nor proof.

AXIOME XXVI.

15 *Whatever* Sense *or* Motion *there is now in* Matter, *it is a necessary impression from some other pert of* Matter, *and does necessarily continue till some part or other of* Matter *has justled it out.*

20   16. That what *Motion* there is in any part of Matter is *necessarily* there, and there continues till some other part of *Matter* change or diminish its *Motion*, is plain from the laws of *Motion* set down by *Des-Cartes* in his *Principia Philosophiae*. And that there is the same Reason of *Sense* or *Perception* (
25 supposing there is nothing but *Matter* in the world) is plain from Axiome 20. that makes *Motion* and *Sense* or *Perception* really the same.

30

Chap. II.

I. *That if* Matter *be capable of* Sense, Inanimate things *are so too: And of* Mr Hobbs *his wavering in that point* 2. *An*
35 *Enumeration of several Faculties in us that* Matter *is utterly uncapable of.* 3. *That* Matter *in no kind of Temperature is capable of* Sense. 4. *That no one point of* Matter *can be the* Common Sensorium. 5. *Nor a multitude of such Points receiving singly the entire image of the Object.* 6. *Nor yet*
40 *receiving part part, and the whole the whole* 7. *That* Memory *is incompetible to* Matter. 8. *That the* Matter *is uncapable of the notes of some circumstances of the object which we remembred.*

9. *That* Matter *cannot be the Seat of second Notions.* 10. *M*^{r}
Hobbs *his Evasion of the foregoing Demonstration clearly
confuted.* 11. *That the Freedome of our Will evinces that there
is a Substance in us distinct from* Matter. *12.* That *M*^{r} Hobbs
therefore acknowledges all our actions necessary.   5

I. *We have now made our addition of such Axiomes as are
most* useful for our present purpose. Let us therefore,
according to the order we propounded, before we consider *the
fabrick and organization of the Body,* see if *such Operations* as
we find in our selves be competible to *Matter* looked upon in a   10
more *general* manner. That *Matter* from its own nature is
uncapable of *Sense,* plainly appears from Axiome 20, and 21.
For *Motion* and *Sense* being really one and the same thing, it
will necessarily follow, that whereever there is *Motion,*
especially any considerable duration thereof, there must be   15
Sense and *Perception* Which is contrary to what we find in a
Catochus, and experience daily in dead Carkasses; in both
which, though there be *Re-action,* yet there is no *Sense.*

In brief, if any *Matter* have *Sense,* it will follow that upon
Re-action all shall have the like, and that a Bell while it is   20
ringing, and a Bow while it is bent, and every Jack-in-a-box
that Schoolboyes play with, while it is held in by the cover
pressing against it, shall be living Animals, or Sensitive
Creatures. A thing so foolish and frivolous, that the mere
recital of the opinion may well be thought confutation enough   25
with the sober.

And indeed Mr. *Hobbs* himself, though he resolve *Sense*
merely into *Re-action of Matter,* yet is ashamed of these odd
consequences thereof, and is very loth to be reckoned in the
company of those Philosophers, (though, as he saies, learned   30
men) who have maintained That *all Bodies are endued with
Sense,* and yet he can hardly abstain from saying that they are;
onely he is more shie of allowing them *Memory,* which yet they
will have whether he will or no, if he give them *Sense.* As for
Example, in the ringing of a Bell, from every stroke there   35
continues a *tremor* in the Bell, which decaying, must (according
to his Philosophie) be *Imagination,* and referring to the stroke
past must be *Memory*; and if a stroke overtake it within the
compass of this *Memory,* what hinders but *Discrimination* or
Judgment may follow? But the Conclusion is consonant enough   40
to this absurd Principle, *That there is nothing but Matter in the
Universe, and that it is capable of perception.*

2. *But we will not content our selves onely with the discovery of this one ugly inconvenience of this bold assertion, but shall* further endeavour to shew that the Hypothesis is false, and that *Matter* is utterly *uncapable of such operations as we find in* 5 *ourselves,* and that therefore there is *Something in us Immaterial* or *Incorporeal* For we find in ourselves, that one and the same thing both *heares,* and *sees,* and *tasts,* and, to be short, *perceives* all the variety of Objects that Nature manifests unto us. Wherefore *Sense* being nothing but the impress of 10 corporeal motion from Objects without, that part of *Matter* which must be the common *Sensorium,* must of necessity receive all that diversity of impulsions from Objects; it must likewise *Imagine, Remember, Reason,* and be the fountain of *spontaneous Motion,* as also the Seat of what the Greeks call 15 the τὸ αὐτεξούσιον or *liberty of Will*: Which supposition we shall finde involved in unextricable difficulties.

3. *For first, we cannot conceive of any* Portion *of* Matter *but* it is either *Hard* or *Soft.* As for that which is *Hard,* all men leave it out as umbtterly unlike to be endued with such 20 Cognitive faculties as we are conscious to our selves of. That which is Soft will prove either *opake or pellucid,* or *lucid.* If *opake,* it cannot see, the exterior superficies being a bar to the inward part. If *pellucid,* as *Aire* and *Water,* then indeed it will admit inwardly these *Particles* and that *Motion* which are the 25 conveighers of the Sense, and distinction of *Colours*; and *Sound* also will penetrate. But this *Matter* being *heterogeneall,* that is to say, consisting of parts of a different nature and office, the Aire, suppose, being proper for *Sound,* and those *Round particles* which *Cartesius* describes for *Colour* and *Light*; the 30 perception of these Objects will be differently lodged: but there is some one thing in us that perceives both. Lastly, if *lucid,* there would be much-what the same inconvenience that there is in the *opake,* for its own fieriness would send off the gentle touch of external impresses; or if it be so mild and thin that it 35 is in some measure *diaphanous,* the inconveniences will again recurre that were found in the *pellucid.*

And in brief any *liquid Matter* has such variety of particles in it, that if the Whole, as it must, (being the common *Sensorium*) be affected with any impress from without, the 40 parts thereof must be variously affected, so that no Object will seam *homogeneall,* as appears from Axiome 22. Which Truth I shall further illustrate by a homely, but very significant, representation. Suppose we should put Feathers, Bullets and Spur-rowels in a Box, Where they shall lye intermixedly, but close, one with another: upon any jog this Box receives, supposing all the stuffage thereof has *Sense*, it is evident 1 that the several things therein must be differently affected, and 5 therefore if the common *Sensorium* were such, there would seem no homogeneall Object in the world. Or at least these severall particles shall be the several *Receptives* of the several motions of the same kinde from without, as the Aire of Sounds, the *Cartesian Globuli* of Light and Colours. But what receives 10 all these, and so can judge of them all, we are again at a loss for, as before: unless we imagine it some very fine and *subtile* Matter, so *light* and *thin*, that it feels not it self, but so *yielding* and *passive*, that it easily feels the several assaults and impresses of other Bodies upon it, or in it; which yet would 15 imply, that *this Matter* alone were *Sensitive*, and the others not; and so it would be granted, that not all *Matter* (no not so much as in *Fluid* Bodies) has *Sense*.

Such a tempered *Matter* as this is analogous to the *Animal Spirits in* Man, which, if *Matter* could be the *Soul*, were the 20 very *Soul* of the *Body*; and *Common percipient* of all Motions from within or without, by reason of the tenuity, passivity and near homogeneity, and (it may be) imperceptibility of any change or alteration from the playing together of its own tenuious and light particles; and therefore very fit to receive 25 any manner of impresses from others. Whence we may rationally conclude, That some such *subtile Matter* as this is either the *Soul*, or her *immediate Instrument* for all manner of perceptions. The *latter* whereof I shall prove to be true in its due place. That the *former* part is false I shall now 30 demonstrate, by proving more stringently, That no *Matter* whatsoever is capable of such *Sense* and *Perception* as we are conscious to our selves of.

4. For concerning that part of *Matter* which is the Common *Sensorium*, I demand whether some one point of it 35 receive the whole image of the Object, or whether it is wholly received into every point of it, or finally whether the whole *Sensorium* receive the whole image by expanded parts, this part of the *Sensorium* this part of the image; and that part that. If the first, seeing that in us which *perceives* the external 40 Object *moves* also the Body, it will follow, That one little point of *Matter* will give local motion to what is innumerable millions

of times bigger then itself; of which there cannot be found nor
imagined any example in Nature.

    5. If the second, this difficulty presents it self, which also
reflects upon the former Position, How so small a point as we
5   speak of should receive the images of so vast, or so various
Objects at once, without Obliteration or Confusion; a thing
impossible, as is manifest from Axiome 24. And therefore not
receiving them, cannot perceive them, by Axiome 25. But if
every point or particle of this *Matter* could receive the whole
10   image, which of these innumerable particles, that receive the
Image entirely, may be deemed *I my self* that perceive this
Image? But if I be all those Points, it will come to pass,
especially in a small Object, and very near at hand, that the
line of impulse coming to divers and distant Points, will seem
15   to come as from several places, and so one Object will
necessarily seem a Cluster of Objects. And if I be but one of
these Points, what becomes of the rest? or *who* are they?

    6. There remains therefore onely the third way, which is
that the parts of the image of the Object be received by the
20   parts of this portion of *Matter* which is supposed the common
Sensorium. But this does perfectly contradict experience; for we
finde our selves to perceive the whole Object, when in this case
nothing could perceive the whole, every part onely perceiving
its part; and therefore there would be nothing that can judge of
25   the whole. No more then three men, if they were imagined to
sing a song of three parts, and none of them should heare any
part but his own, could judge of the Harmony of the whole.

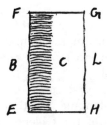

    7. As concerning the *Seat of Imagination* and *Memory*,
especially *Memory*, what kinde of *Matter* can be found fit for
30   this function? If it be *Fluid*, the images of Objects will be prone
to vanish suddainly, as also to be perverted or turned contrary
wayes. For example, C, a particle of this *fluid Matter*,
receiving an impress from B, must feel it is coming from B; but

in toying and tumbling up and down, as the particles of *fluid Matter* doe, turnes the side E F which received that impress from B towards L, whence it will feel as if the impress had been from L, for it must feel it as from the place directly opposite to it self, (if it can after the removal of the present 5 Object, against which the *Re-action* is, feel it at all:) and the same reason will be in other particles of this *fluid Matter*, which must needs force a great deal of preposterous confusion both upon the *Fancy* and *Memory*. If it be *Hard*, it will soon be composed to *Rest*, as in a Bell whose *tremor* is gone in a little 10 time; but we *remember* things some years together, though we never think of them till the end of that term. If *Viscid*, there is the like inconvenience, nay it is the unfittest of all for either receiving of *Motion* or continuing it, and therefore unlikely to be the *Seat* of either *Fancy* or *Memory*. For if *Motion* or *Re-action* 15 and *Sense*, whether internal or external, be all one, *Motion* ceasing *Memory* must needs cease, by Axiome 21. Nor can it any more *remember* when it is again moved in the same manner, then a Stone or a piece of Lead that was flung up into the Aire, can become more light or more prone to flie upwards 20 when they have once ceased from Motion; for they are both exquisitely as if they had never been moved.

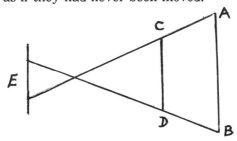

8. Lastly, we remember some things of which there can be no *Signatures* in *Matter* to represent them, as for example, *Wilderness* and *Distance*. For as for both of them, there is no 25 note can be made in the Matter E by lines from the two Objects A B and C D, whereby the difference of remoteness of A E above C E, or of the wideness of A B above C D, can be discerned; for both the Objects make one and the same signature in the Matter E.   30

9. Those that are commonly called by the name of *Secundae Notiones*, and are not any sensible Objects themselves, nor the Phantasmes of any sensible Objects, but

onely our manner of conceiving them, or reasoning about them, in which number are comprehended all *Logical* and *Mathematical* termes; these, I say, never came in at the *Senses*, they being no impresses of corporeal motion, which
5   excite in us, as in Doggs and other Brutes, the sense onely of Sounds, of Colours, of Hot, of Cold, and the like. Now *Matter* being affected by no perception but of corporeal impression, by the bearing of one Body against another; it is plain from Axiome 23. that these *Second Notions*, or *Mathematical* and
10 *Logical* conceptions, cannot be seated in *Matter*, and therefore must be in some other Substance distinct from it, by Axiome 10.

        10.   Here Mr. *Hobbs*, to avoid the force of this Demonstration, has found out a marvellous witty invention to
15 befool his followers withall, making them believe that there is no such thing as these *Secundae Notiones*, distinct from the *Names* or *Words* whereby they are said to be signified; and that there is no perception in us, but of such *Phantasmes* as are impressed from external Objects, such as are common to Us
20 and Beasts: and as for the *Names* which we give to these, or the *Phantasmes* of them, that there is the same reason of them as of other *Marks*, *Letters*, or *Characters*; all which coming in at the *Senses*, he would beare them in hand that it is a plain case, that we have the perception of nothing but what is impressed
25 from corporeal Objects. But how ridiculous an Evasion this is, may be easily discovered, if we consider, that if these *Mathematical* and *Logical Notions* we speak of be nothing but *Names*, Logical and Mathematical Truths will not be the same in all Nations, because they have not the same *names*. For
30 Example, *Similitudo* and ὁμοιότης. ἀναλογία and *Proportio*, λόγος and *Ratio*, these *names* are utterly different, the *Greek* from the *Latine*; yet the *Greeks Latines*, nor any Nation else, do vary in their conceptions couched under the these different *names*: Wherefore it is plain, that there is a *setled notion* distinct from
35 these *Words* and *Names*, as well as from those corporeal Phantasmes impressed from the Object; which was the thing to be demonstrated.

        11. Lastly, we are conscious to our selves of that Faculty which the Greeks call αὐτεξούσιον. or *a Power in our selves,*
40 notwithstanding any outward assaults or importunate temptations, *to cleave to that which is virtuous and honest, or to yield to pleasures or other vile advantages.* That we have this

Liberty and freedome in our selves; and that we refuse the good, and chuse the evil, when we might have done otherwise; that natural Sense of *Remorse of Conscience* is an evident and undeniable witness of. For when a man has done amiss, the pain, grief, or indignation that he raises in himself, or at least 5 feels raised in him, is of another kind from what we find from misfortunes or affronts we could not avoid. And that which pinches us and vexes us so severely, is the sense that we have brought such an evil upon our selves, when it was in our power to have avoided it. Now if there be no *Sense* nor *Perception* in 10 us but what arises from the *Re-action of Matter* one part against another; whatever Re-presentation of things, whatever Deliberation or Determination we fall upon, it will by Axiome 26. be *purely necessary*, there being upon this Hypothesis no more *Freedome* while we deliberate or conclude, then there is in 15 a pair of scales, which rests as *necessarily* at last as it moved before. Wherefore it is manifest that this Faculty we call *Free-will* is not found in *Matter*, but in some other Substance, by Axiome 10.

12. Mr. *Hobbs* therefore, to give him his due, consonantly 20 enough to his own principles, does very peremptorily affirm *That all our actions are necessary.* But I having proved the contrary by that Faculty which we may call *Internal Sense* or *Common Notion*, found in all men that have not done violence to their own Nature; unless by some other approved Faculty he 25 can discover the contrary, my Conclusion must stand for an undoubted Truth, by Axiome 5. He pretends therefore some Demonstration of *Reason*, which he would oppose against the dictate of this *Inward Sense*; which it will not be amiss to examine, that we may discover his Sophistry.   30

Chap. III.

35

I. *M*^{r} Hobbs *his Arguments whereby he would prove all our actions necessitated. His first Argument* 2. *His second Argument* 3. *His third Argument* 4. *His fourth Argument* 5. *That must be the meaning of these words,* Nothing taketh beginning from it self, *in the first Argument of M*^{r} Hobbs. 6. *A* 40 fuller and more determin*ate explication of the foregoing words, whose sense is evidently convinced to be,* That no Essence of it

self can vary its modification 7. That this is onely said by M^r
Hobbs, *not proved, and a full confutation of his Assertion.* 8.
Mr Hobbs *imposed upon by his own Sophistry.* 9. *That one
part of this first Argument of his is groundless,the other*
sophistical. 10. *The plain proposall of his Argument, whence
appeares more fully the weakness and sophistry thereof.* 11. *An
Answer to his second Argument .* 12. *An Answer to the third.*
13. *An Answer to a difficulty concerning the Truth and
Falsehood of future Propositions.* 14. *An Answer to Mr Hobbs
his fourth Argument, which, though slighted by himself, is the
strongest of them all.* 15. *The difficulty of reconciling Free-will
with Divine Prescience and Prophecies.* 16. *That the Faculty of
Free-will is seldome put in use.* 17. *That the use of it is properly
in Moral conflict.* 18. *That the Soul is not invincible there
neither.* 19. *That Divine decrees either finde fit Instruments or
make them.* 20. *That the more exact we make Divine Prescience,
even to the comprehension of any thing that implies no contradiction in it self to be comprehended, the more clear it is that mans
Will may be sometimes free.* 21. *Which is sufficinnt to make good
my last Argument against Mr Hobbs.*

1.His first Argument runs thus (I will repeat it in his own
words, as also the rest of them as they are to be found in his
Treatise of *Liberty and Necessity;) I conceive,* (saith he) *that
nothing taketh beginning from it self, but from the action of some
other immediate agent without it self; and that therefore, when
first a man hath an appetite or Will to something to which
immedlately before he had no appetite nor Will, the cause of his
Will is not the Will it self, but something else not in his own
disposing: So that whereas it is out of controversy, that of
voluntary actions the Will is the necessary cause, and by this
which is said the Will is also caused by other thing, whereof it
disposeth not, it followeth, that voluntary actions have all of them
necessary causes, and therefore are necessitated.*
2. His second thus; *I hold* (saith he) *that to be a sufficient
cause, to which nothing is wanting that is needful to the
producing of the effect: The same also is a necessary cause. For
if it be possible that a sufficient cause shall not bring forth the
effect, then there wanteth somewhat which was needful for the
producing of it, and so the cause was not sufficient; but if it be
impossible that a sufficient cause should not produce the effect,
then is a sufficient cause a necessary cause, for that is said to*

produce an effect necessarily that cannnot but produce it. Hence it is manifest, that whatsoever is produced, is produced necessarily. For whatsoever is produced, hath had a sufficient cause to produce it, or else it had not been. What follows is either the same, or so closely depending on this, that I need not 5 adde it.

3. His third Argument therefore shall be that which he urges from *Future disjunctions*. For example, let the case be put of the *Weather*. 'Tis necessary that to morrow it shall rain, or not rain; *If therefore*, saith he, *it be not necessary it shall rain*, 10 *it is necessary it shall not rain, otherwise there is no necessity that the Proposition*, It shall rain or not rain, *should be true.*

4. His fourth is this, *That the denying of Necessity destroyeth both the Decrees and the Prescience of God Almighty. For whatsoever God hath purposed to bring to pass by man, as* 15 *an Instrument, or foreseeth shall come to pass; a man, if he have liberty from necessitation, might frustrate, and make not to come to pass; and God should either not foreknow it, and not decree it, or he should foreknow such things shall be as shall never be, and decree that which shall never come to pass.*   20

5.The Entrance into his first Argument is something obscure and ambiguous, *Nothing taketh beginning from it self:* But I shall be as candid and faithfull an Interpreter as I may. If he mean by *beginning*, beginning of *Existence*, it is undoubtedly true, That no Substance, nor Modification of 25 Substance, taketh beginning from it self; but this will not infer the Conclusion he drives at. But if he mean, that *Nothing taketh beginning from it self, of being otherwise affected or modified then before*; he must either understand by *nothing*, no Essence, neither *Spirit* nor *Body*, or no *Modification* of Essence. 30 He cannot mean *Spirit*, as admitting no such thing in the whole comprehension of Nature. If *Body*, it will not infer what he aims at, unless there be nothing but *Body* in the Universe; which is a mere precarious Principle of his, which he beseeches his credulous followers to admit, but he proves it no where, as I 35 have already noted. If by *Modification* he mean the *Modification of Matter* or *Body*; that runs still upon the former Principle, That there is nothing but *Body* in the world, and therefore he proves nothing but upon a begg'd Hypothesis, and that a false one; as I have elsewhere demonstrated. 40 Wherefore the most favourable Interpretation I can make is, That he means by *no thing*, no Essence, nor Modification of

Essence, being willing to hide that dearly-hug'd Hypothesis of his (*That there is nothing but Body in the World*) under so general and uncertain termes.

6. The words therefore in the other senses having no pretence to conclude any thing let us see how far they will prevail in this, taking *no thing*, for *no Essence*, or *no Modification of Essence*, or what will come nearer to the matter in hand, *no Faculty of an Essence*. And from this two-fold meaning, let us examine two Propositions that will result from thence, viz. *That no Faculty of any Essence can vary its Operation from what it is, but from the action of some other immediate Agent without it self; or, That no Essence can vary its Modification or Operation by it self, but by the action of some other immediate Agent without it.* Of which two Propositions the latter seems the better sense by far, and most natural. For it is very harsh, and, if truly looked into, as false, to say, *That the Mode or Faculty of any Essence changes it self*; for it is the Essence it self that exerts it self into these variations of Modes, if no externall Agent is the cause of these changes. And Mr *Hobbs* opposing an *External Agent* to *this Thing* that he saies does not change it self, does naturally imply, That they are both not *Faculties* but *Substances* he speaks of.

7. Wherefore there remains onely the latter Proposition to be examined, *That no Essence of it self can very its Modification.* That some Essence must have had a power of moving is plain, in that there is *Motion* in the world, which must be the Effect of some Substance or other. But that *Motion* in a large sense, taking it for mutation or change, may proceed from that very Essence in which it is found, seems to me plain by Experience: For there is an Essence in us, whatever we will call it, which we find endued with this property; as appears from hence, that it has variety of perceptions, *Mathematical, Logical* and I may adde also *Moral*, that are not any impresses nor footsteps of Corporeal Motion, as I have already demonstrated: and any man may observe in himself, and discover in the writings of others, how the Mind has passed from one of these perceptions to another, in very long deductions of Demonstration; as also what stilness from bodily Motion is required in the excogitation of such series of Reasons, where the Spirits are to run into no other posture nor motion then what they are guided into by the Mind it self, where these immaterial and intellectual Notions have the leading and rule. Besides in grosser Phantasmes,

which are supposed to be somewhere impressed in the Brain,
the composition of them, and disclusion and various disposal of
them, is plainly an arbitrarious act, and implies an Essence
that can, as it lists, excite in it self the variety of such
Phantasmes as have been first exhibited to her from External 5
Objects, and change them and transpose them at her own will.
But what need I reason against this ground of Mr. *Hobbs* so
sollicitously? it being sufficient to discover, that he onely saies,
that *No Essence can change the Modifications of it self*, but does
not prove it; and therefore whatever he would infer hereupon is 10
merely upon a begg'd Principle

8. But however, from this precarious ground he will infer,
that *whenever we have a Will to a thing, the cause of this Will is
not the Will it self, but something else not in our own disposing*;
the meaning whereof must be, *That whenever we Will, some* 15
corporeal impress, which we cannot avoid, forces us thereto. But
the Illation is as weak as bold; it being built upon no
foundation, as I have already shown. I shall onely take notice
how Mr. *Hobbs*, though he has rescued himself from the
authority of the Schools, and would fain set up for himself, yet 20
he has not freed himself from their fooleries in talking of
Faculties and *Operations* (and the absurditie is alike in both) as
separate and distinct from the *Essence* they belong to, which
causes a great deal of distraction and obscurity in the
speculation of things. I speak this in reference to those 25
expressions of his, of the *Will being the cause of willing*, and of
its being the *necessary* cause of voluntary actions, and of things
not being in its disposing. Whenas, if as man would speak
properly, and desired to be understood, he would say, *That the
Subject in which is this power or act of willing, (call it Man or the* 30
Soul of Man) is the cause of this or that voluntary action. But
this would discover his Sophistry, wherewith haply he has
entrapt himself, which is this, *Something out of the power of the
Will necessarily causes the Will; the Will once caused is the
necessary cause of voluntary actions; and therefore all voluntary* 35
actions are necessitated.

9. Besides that the first part of this Argumentation is
groundless (as I have already intimated) the second is
Sophisticall, that sayes *That the Will is the necessary cause of
voluntary actions*: For by *necessary* may be understood either 40
necessitated, forced and made to act, whether it will or no; or
else it may signify that the Will is a *requisite* cause of

voluntary actions, so that there can be no voluntary actions
without it. The latter whereof may be in some sense true, but
the former is utterly false. So the Conclusion being inferred
from assertions whereof the one is groundless, the other
5 Sophisticall, the Illation cannot but be ridiculously weak and
despicable. But if he had spoke in the *Concrete* instead of the
Abstract, the Sophistry had been more grossly discoverable, or
rather the train of his reasoning languid and contemptible.
Omitting therefore to speak of the *Will* separately, which of
10 itself is but a blind Power or Operation, let us speak of that
Essence which is endued with *Will, Sense, Reason*, and other
Faculties, and see what face this Argumentation of his will
bear, which will then run thus;

   10. *Some external, irresistible Agent does ever necessarily*
15 *cause that Essence* (call it *Soul* or what you please) *which is*
endued with the Faculties of Will and Understanding, to Will:
This Essence, endued with the power of exerting it self into the act
of Willing is the necessary cause of Voluntary actions; Therefore
all voluntary actions are necessitated. The first Assertion now at
20 first sight appears a gross falshood, the *Soul* being endued with
Understanding as well as *Will*, and therefore she is not
necessarily determined to will by external impresses, but by the
displaying of certain notions and perceptions she raises in her
self, that be purely intellectual. And the second seems a very
25 slim and lank piece of Sophistry. Both which my reasons
already alledged do so easily and so plainly reach, that I need
adde nothing more, but pass to his second Argument, the form
whereof in brief is this;

   11. *Every Cause is a sufficient cause, otherwise it could not*
30 *produce its effect, otherwise something was wanting thereto, and*
it was no sufficient cause: And therefore every cause is a
necessary cause, and consequently every Effect or Action, even
those that are termed Voluntary, are necessitated. This reasoning
looks smartly at first view; but if we come closer to it, we shall
35 find it a pitifull piece of Sophistry, which is easily detected by
observing the ambiguity of that Proposition, *Every sufficient*
cause is a necessary cause: For the force lyes not so much in
that it is said to be *Sufficient*, as in that it is said to be a *Cause*;
Which if it be, it must of necessity have *an Effect*, whether it be
40 *sufficient* or *insufficient*; which discovers the Sophisme. For
these relative terms of *Cause* and *Effect* necessarily imply one
another. But every Being that is *sufficient* to act this or that *if*

it will, and so to become the *Cause* thereof, doth neither act, nor abstain from acting *necessarily*. And therefore if it do act, it addes *Will* to the *Sufficiency* of its power; and if it did not act, it is not because it had not sufficient power, but because it would not make use of it. So that we see that every *sufficient* Cause rightly understood without captiositie is not a *necessary* cause, nor will be sure to produce the Effect; and that though there be a sufficiency of power, yet there may be something wanting, to wit, the exertion of the Will; whereby it may come to pass, that what might have acted if it would, did not: but if it did, Will being added to sufficient Power, that it cannot be said to be *necessary* in any other sense, then of that Axiome in Metaphysicks, *Quicquid est, quamdiu est, necesse est esse*: The reason whereof is, because it is impossible that a thing should be and not be at once. But before it acted, it might have chosen whether it would have acted or no; but it did determine it self. And in this sense is it to be said to be a *free Agent*, and not a *necessary* one. So that it is manifest, that though there be some prettie perversness of wit in the contriving of this Argument, yet there is no solidity at all at the bottome.

12 And as little is there in his third. But in this, I must confess, I cannot so much accuse him of *Art* and *Sophistry*, as of ignorance of the rules of *Logick*; for he does plainly assert That the necessity of the truth of that Proposition there named depends on the necessity of the truth of the parts thereof; then which no grosser errour can be committed in the Art of reasoning. For he might as well say that the necessity of the truth of a *Connex* Axiome depends on the necessity of the truth of the parts, as of a *Disjunct*. But in a *Connex*, when both the parts are not onely false, but impossible, yet the Axiome is necessarily true. As for example, *If Bucephalus be a man, he is endued with humane reason*; this Axiome is necessarily true, and yet the parts are impossible. For *Alexander*'s horse can neither be a man, nor have the reason of a man, either radically or actually. The necessity therefore is only laid upon the *connexion* of the parts, not upon the parts themselves. So when I say, *Tomorrow it will rain, or it will not rain*, this *Disjunct* Proposition also is necessary, but the necessity lies upon the *Disjunction* of the parts, not upon the parts themselves: For they being immediately disjoyned, there is a necessity that one of them must be, though there be no necessity that this must ba determined rather then that. As

when a man is kept under custody where he has the use of two
rooms only, though there be a necessity that he be found in one
of the two, yet he is not confined to either one of them. And to
be brief, and prevent those frivolous both answers and replies
5   that follow in the pursuit of this Argument in Mr Hobbs; As the
necessity of this Disjunct Axiome lies upon the *Disjunction* it
self, so the truth, of which this necessity is a made, must lye
theretoo; for it is the *Disjunction* of the parts that is affirmed,
and not the parts themselves, as any one that is but
10   moderately in his wits must needs acknowledge.

13. There is a more dangerous way that Mr Hobbs might
have made use of, and with more credit, but yet scarce with
better success, which is the consideration of a simple Axiome
that pronounces of a *future Contingent*, such as this, *Cras*
15   *Socrates disputabit.* For every Axiome pronouncing either true
or false, as all do agree upon; if this Axiome be now true, it is
impossible but *Socrates* should dispute to morrow; or if it be
now false, it is impossible he should: and so his Action of
disputing or the omission thereof will be necessary, for the
20   Proposition cannot be both true and false at once. Some are
much troubled to extricate themselves out of this Nooze; but if
we more precisely enquire into the sense of the Proposition, the
difficulty will vanish. He therefore that affirms that *Socrates*
will dispute to morrow, affirms it (to use the distinction of
25   *Futurities* that *Aristotle* somewhere suggests) either as a τὸ
μέλλον. *or* τὸ ἐσόμενον. *that is,* either as a thing that is likely to
be, *but has a possibility of being otherwise* or *else as a thing
certainly to come to pass.* If this latter, the Axiome is false; if
the former, it is true: and so the liberty of *Socrates* his actions,
30   as also of all like *contingent* effects, are thus easily rescued
from this Sophistical entanglement. For every *Future* Axiome
is as incapable of our judgment, unless we determine the sense
of it by one of the forenamed modes, as an *Indefinite* Axiome is,
before we in our minds adde the notes of *Universality* or
35   *Particularity*: Neither can we say of either of them, that they
are true or false, till we have compleated and determined their
sense.

14. His fourth Argument he proposes with some diffidence
and dislike, as if he thought it *not good Logick* (they are his
40   own words) to make use of it, and adde it to the rest. And for
my own part, I cannot but approve of the consistency of his
judgment, and coherency with other parts of his Philosophie:

For if there be nothing but *Body* or *Matter* in the whole comprehension of things, it will be very hard to find out any such *Deity* as has the *knowledge* or *fore-knowledge* of any thing: And therefore I suspect that this last is onely cast in as *Argumentum ad hominem*, to puzzle such as haves not dived to 5 so profound a depth of natural knowledge, as to fancy they have discovered there is no God in the world.

15. But let him vilifie it as he will, it is the only Argument he has brought that has any tolerable sense or solidity in it; and it is a Subject that has exercised the wits of all Ages, to 10 reconcile the *Liberty* of mans Will with the *Decrees* and *Praescience* of God. But my *Freeness*, I hope, and *Moderation* shall make this matter more easy to me, then it ordinarily proves to them that venture upon it. My Answer therefore in brief shall be this;   15

16. First, That though therebe such a Faculty in the Soul of man as *Liberty of Will*, yet she is not alwaies in a state of acting according to it.   For she may either *degenerate so far*, that it may be as certainly known what she will doe upon this or that occasion, as what an hungry Dog will doe when a crust 20 is offered him; which is the general condition of almost all men in most occurrences of their lives: or else she may be so *Heroically good*, though that happen in very few, that it may be as certainly known as before what she will doe or suffer upon such or such emergencies: and in these cases the use of *Liberty* 25 *of Will* ceases.

17. Secondly, That the use of the Faculty of *Free-will* is properly there, where we finde our selves so near to an *Aequiponderancy*, being touch'd with the sense of *Vertue* on the one side, and the ease or *Pleasure* of some *vitious action* on the 30 other, that we are conscious to our selves that we ought, and that we may, if we will, abandon the one and cleave to the other.

18. Thirdly, That in this Conflict the Soul has no such absolute power to determine her self to the one or the other 35 action, but *Temptation* or *Supernatural assistance* may certainly carry her this way or that way; so that she may not be able to use that liberty of going indifferently either way.

19. Fourthly, That Divine *Decrees* either find men fit, or make them so, for the executing of whatever is absolutely 40 purposed or prophesied concerning them.

20. Fifthly, That the *Praescience* of God is so vast and exceeding the comprehension of our thoughts, that all that can be safely said of it is this. That this knowledge is most perfect and exquisite, accurately representing the Natures, Powers and Properties of the thing it does foreknow. Whence it must follow, that if there be any Creature *free* and undeterminate, and that in such circumstances and at such a time he manay either act thus or not act thus, this perfect *Fore-knowledge* must discern from all eternity, that the said Creature in such circumstances may either act thus, or so, or not. And further to declare the perfection of this *Fore-knowledge* and *Omniscience* of God; as His *omnipotence* ought to extend so far, as to be able to doe whatsoever implies no contradiction to be done; so his *Praescience* and *Omniscience* ought to extend so far, as to know precisely and fully whatever implies no contradiction to be known.

To conclude therefore briefly; *Free* or *Contingent* Effects do either imply a contradiction to be *foreknown*, or they do not imply it. If they imply a contradiction to be *foreknown*, they are no object of the *Omniscience* of God; and therefore there can be no pretence that his *Foreknowledge* does determinate them, nor can they be argued to be determined thereby. If they imply no contradiction to be *foreknown*, that is to acknowledge that Divine *Praescience* and they may very well consist together. And so either way, notwithstanding the Divine *omniscience*, the Actions of men may be *free*.

21. The sum therefore of all is this, That mens actions are sometimes *free* and sometimes *not free*; but in that they are at any time *free*, is a Demonstration that there is a Faculty in us that is incompetible to *mere Matter*: which is sufficient for my purpose.

Chap. IV.

I. *An Enumeration of sundry Opinions concerninq the Seat of Common Senee.* 2. *Upon supposition that we are nothin*g but mere Matter, *That the whole Body cannot be the Common Sensorium*; 3. *Nor the Orifice of the Stomack*; 4. *Nor the Heart*; 5. *Nor the Brain*; 6. *Nor the Membranes*; 7. *Nor the* Septum lucidum; 8. *Nor* Regius *his small and perfectly-solid Particle.* 9.

The probability of the Conarion *being the common Seat of Sense.*

1. *I have plainly proved, that neither those more Pure and Intellectual* faculties of *Will* and *Reason*, nor yet those less pure of *Memory* and *Imagination*, are competible to *mere Bodies*. Of which we may be the more secure, I having so convincingly demonstrated, That not so much as that which we call *External Sense* is competible to the same: all which Truths I have concluded concerning *Matter generally considered.*

But because there may be a suspicion in some, which are overcredulous concerning *the powers of Body*, that *Organization* may doe strange fears (which Surmise notwithstanding is as fond as if they should imagine, that though neither Silver, nor Steel, nor Iron, nor Lute-strings, have any Sense apart, yet being put together in such a manner and formed as will (suppose) make a compleat *Watch*, they may have *Sense*; that is to say, that a Watch may be a living creature, though the several parts have neither *Life* nor *Sense*;) I shall for their sakes goe more *particularly* to work, and recite every Opinion that I could ever meet with by converse with either men or books concerning *the Seat of the Common Sense*, and after trie whether any of these Hypotheses can possibly be admitted for Truth, upon supposition that we consist of nothing but *mere modified and organized Matter.*

I shall first recite the Opinions, and then examine the possibility of each in particular, which in brief are these. 1. That the whole Body is the Seat of Common Sense. 2. That the Orifice of the Stomack. 3. The Heart. 4. The Brain. 5. The Membranes. 6. The *Septum lucidum*. 7. Some very small and perfectly-solid particle in the Body. 8. The *Conarion*. 9. The concurse of the Nerves about the fourth ventricle of the Brain. 10. The Spirits in that fourth ventricle.

2. That the first Opinion is false is manifest from hence, That, upon supposition we are nothing but *mere Matter*, if we grant the *whole Body* to be one common *Sensorium*, perceptive of all Objects, *Motion* whch is impressed upon the Eye or Eare, must be transmitted into all the parts of the Body. For *Sense* is really the same with *communication of Motion*, by Axiome 20. And the variety of Sense arising from the modification of Motion, which must needs be variously modified by the different temper of the parts of the Body, by Axiome 22. it plainly follows that the Eye must be otherwise affected by the

motion of Light, then the other parts to which this motion is
transmitted. Wherefore if it be the *whole Body* that perceives,
it will perceive the Object in every part thereof several wayes
modified at once; which is against all Experience. It will also
5   appear in all likelihood in several places at once, by reason of
the many windings and turnings that must happen to the
transmission of this *Motion*, which are likely to be as so many
Refractions or Reflexions.

3. That *the Orifice of the Stomack* cannot be *the seat of*
10   *Common Sense*, is apparent from hence, That that which is the
common *Sentient* does not only *perceive* all Objects, but has the
power of *moving* the Body. Now besides that there is no
organization in the mouth of the Stomack that can elude the
strength of our Arguments laid down in the foregoing Chapters,
15   which took away all capacity from Matter of having any
perception at all in it, there is no Mechanical reason imaginable
to be found in the Body, whereby it will appear possible, that
supposing the mouth of the Stomack were the *common*
Percipient of all Objects, it could be able to *move* the rest of the
20   members of the Body, as we finde something in us does. This
is so palpably plain, that it is needless to spend any more
words upon it.

4. The same may be said concerning *the Heart*. For who
can imagine that, if the *Heart* were that *common Percipient*,
25   there is any such Mechanical connexion betwixt it and all the
parts of the Body, that it may, by such or such a perception,
command the motion of the Foot or little Finger? Besides that it
seems wholly imployed in the performance of its *Systole* and
Diastole, which causes such a great difference of the situation
30   of the *Heart* by turns, that if it were that Seat in which the
sense of all Objects centre, we should not be able to see things
steddily or fix our sight in the same place.

5. How uncapable the *Brain* is of being so active a
Principle of *Motion* as we find in our selves, the *viscidity* thereof
35   does plainly indicate. Besides that Physicians have discovered
by experience, that the *Brain* is so far from being the *common*
Seat of all senses, that it has in it none at all. And the
Arabians, that say it has, have distinguished it into such
severall offices of *Imagination, Memory, Common Sense,* etc.
40   that we are still at a loss for some one part of *Matter* that is to
be the *Common Percipient* of all these. But I have so clearly
demonstrated the impossibility of the *Brain's* being able to

perform those functions that appertain truly to what ordinarily men call the *Soul*, in my *Antidote against Atheism*, that it is enough to refer the Reader thither.

6. As for the *Membranes*, whether we would fancy them *all* the *Seat of Common Sense*, or *some one* Membrane, or *part* 5 thereof; the like difficulties will occur as have been mentioned already.   For if *all the Membranes*, the difference and situation of them will vary the aspect and sight of the Object, so that the same things will appear to us in several hues and several places at once, as is easily demonstrated from Axiome 22. If 10 *some one Membrane*, or *part* thereof, it will be impossible to excogitate any Mechanical reason, how this *one* particular Membrane, or any *part* thereof, can be able to strongly and determinately to *move* upon occasion every part of the Body.

7. And therefore for this very cause cannot the *Septum* 15 *lucidum* be the *Common Percipient* in us, because it is utterly unimaginable how it should have the power of so stoutly and distinctly *moving* our exteriour parts and limbs.

8. As for that new and marvelous Invention of *Henricus Regius*, That it may ba *a certain perfectly-solid, but very small,* 20 *particle of Matter in the Body, that is the Seat of common perception*; besides that it is as boldly asserted, that such an *hard* particle should have *Sense* in it, as that the filings of Iron and Steel should; it cannot be the spring of *Motion*: For how should so small an Atome *move* the whole Body, but by moving 25 it self? But it being more subtile then the point of any needle, when it puts it self upon motion, especially such strong thrustings as we sometimes use, it must needs passe through the Body and leave it.

9. The most pure Mechanical Invention is that of the use 30 of the *Conarion*, proposed by *Des-Cartes*; which, considered with some other organizations of the Body, bids the fairest of any thing I have met withall, or ever hope to meet withall, for the resolution of the Passions and Properties of living Creatures into mere *Corporeal* motion.   And therefore it is requisite to 35 insist a little upon the explication thereof, that we may the more punctually confute them that would abuse his Mechanical contrivances to the exclusion of all Principles but *Corporeal*, in either Man or Beast.

40

Chap. V.

I. *How Perception of external Objects, Spontaneous Motion,*
Memory and Imagination, are pretended to be performed by the
5   Conarion, *Spirits and Muscles, without a Soul.* 2. *That the*
Conarion, *devoid of a Soul, cannot be the* Common Percipient,
demonstrated out of Des-Cartes *himself.* 3. *That the* Conarion,
with the Spirits and Organiza tion of the Parts of the Body, is not
a sufficient Principle of Spontaneous motion, without a Soul. 4.
10 *A description of the use of the* Valvulae *in the Nerves of the*
Muscles for spontaneous motion. 5. *The insufficiency of this*
contrivance for that purpose. 6. *A further demonstration of the*
insufficiency thereof, from whence is clearly evinced that Brutes
have Souls. 7. *That Memory cannot be salved the way above*
15 *described.* 8. *Nor Imagination.* 9. *A distribution out of* Des-
Cartes *of the Functions in us, some appertaining to the Body and*
others to the Soul. 10. *The Author's Observations thereupon.*

I. The sum of this Abuse must in brief be this, That the
20 *Glandula Pinealis* is *the common Sentient or Percipient of all*
Objects; and without a *Soul*, by virtue of the *Spirits* and
Organization of the Body, may doe all those feats that we
ordinarily conceive to be parformed by *Soul* and *Body* joyned
together. For it being *one*, whenas the rest of the Organs of
25 Sense are *double*, and so handsomely seated as to communicate
with the *Spirits* as well of the posteriour as anteriour Cavities
of the *Brain*; by their help all the motions of the *Nerves* (as well
of those that transmit the sense of *outward* objects, as of them
that serve for the *inward* affections of the Body, such as
30 Hunger, Thirst and the like) are easily conveighed unto it: and
so being variously moved, it does variously determine the
course of the *Spirits* into such and such *Muscles*, whereby it
moves the Body.
Moreover that the transmission of Motion from the Object,
35 through the *Nerves*, into the inward concavities of the *Brain*,
and so to the *Conarion*, opens such and such Pores of the *Brain*,
in such and such order or manner, which remain as tracts or
footsteps of the presence of these Objects after they are
removed. Which tracts or signatures, consist mainly in this,
40 that the *Spirits* will have an easier passage through these
Pores then other parts of the *Brain*. And hence arises *Memory*,
when the *Spirits* be determined, by the inclining of the

Conarion, to that part of the *Brain* where these tracts are found, they moving then the *Conarion* as when the Object was present, though not so strongly.

From the hitting of the *Spirits* into such like tracts, is also the nature of *Imagination* to be explained; in which there is little difference from *Memory*, saving that the reflexion upon time as past, when we saw or perceived such or such a thing, is quite left out. But these are not all the operations we are conscious to our selves of, and yet more then can be made out by this Hypothesis, That *Perception of Objects, Spontaneous Motion, Memory* and *Imagination*, may be all perfomed by virtue of this *Glandula*, the Animal Spirits, and mere Organization of the Body; as we shall plainly find, though but upon an easy examination.

2. For that the *Conarion*, devoid of a Soul, has no *perception* of any one Object, is demonstrable from the very description *Cartesius* makes of the transmission of the image, suppose through the Eye to the Brain, and so to the *Conarion*. For it is apparent from what he sets down in his *Treatise of the Passions of the Soul*, that the Image that is propagated from the Object to the *Conarion*, is impressed thereupon in some latitude of space. Whence it is manifest that the *Conarion* does not, nor can perceive the whole Object, though severall parts may be acknowledged to have the *perception* of the several parts thereof. But something in us *perceives* the whole, which therefore cannot be the *Conarion*.

And that we do not *perceive* the external Object *double*, is not so much because the Image is united in the Organ of *Common Sense*, as that the lines come so from the Object to both the Eyes, that it is felt in one place; otherwise if the Object be very near, and the direction of our Eyes be not fitted to that nearness, it will seem *double* however. Which is a Demonstration that a man may see with both Eyes at once; and for my own part, I'me sure that I see better at distance, when I use both, then when one.

3. As for *Spontaneous Motion*, that the *Conarion* cannot be a sufficient Principle thereof, with the *Spirits* and *organization of other parts of the Body*, though we should admit it a fit seat of *Common Sense*, will easily appear, if we consider, that so weak and so small a thing as that *Glandula* is, seems utterly unable to *determine* the Spirits with that force and violence we find they are determined in *running, striking, thrusting* and the

like; and that it is evident, that sometimes scarce the
thousandth part or the *Conarion* shall be directer of this force;
viz. when the Object of Sight, suppose, is as little as a pin's
point, or when a man is prick'd with a needle, these receptions
5   must be as little in the *Glandula* as in the exteriour Sense.

But suppose the *whole Conarion* alwaies did act in the
determining the motion of the *Spirits* into this or that *Muscle*; it
is impossible that such *fluid Matter* as these *Spirits* are, that
upon the noddings of the *Conarion* toward may easily recede
10   back, should ever determine their course with that force and
strength they are determined.

But haply it will be answered, That such subtile and fluid
bodies as the *Animal Spirits*, that are in a readiness to be upon
Motion any way, the least thing will *determine* their course; and
15   that the *Muscles themselves being well replenish'd with* Spirits,
and framed with such Valvulae as will easily intromit them
from the *Brain,* and also conveigh them out of one opposite
Muscle into another upon the least redundance of Spirits in the
one above the other, and so shut them in; that that force we
20   find in *spontaneous Motion* may very well be salved by this
Mechanical Artifice.

4. That the insufficiency of this Answer may appear, let us
more accurately consider the contrivance in the following
Figure, which must be some such thing as *Regius* has ventured
25   at in his philosophy, and which may serve for the more easy
understanding of what *Des-Cartes* writes in his Book of
Passions. Here B C are two opposite Muscles, the known
Instruments of spontaneous Motion; K, some part of the Body
to be moved; D E and F G are the Nerves through which
30   Spirits are transmitted from the Brain into the foresaid
Muscles; D and F two *Valvulae* to let pass the Spirits from the
Brain into the Muscles, but stop them if they would
regurgitate; G is a Valve that lets the Spirits out of the Muscle
C into B and E another Valve that lets the Spirits out of B into
35   C. Now in brief, the result of this Mechanicall contrivance is
this, viz. That the Spirits being determined by the *Conarion*
never so little more copinusly into B then into C, those in C will
pass through the Valve G into B, and so B swelling, and
consequently shortning it self, it must needs bring up the
40   member K.

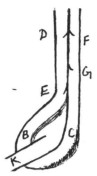

5. We will not here alledge that this may be onely a mere fancy, these Valvulae in the Nerves not being yet discovererd by any Anatomist to be part of the Organization of the Body of any Animal; but rather shew, that they would not effect what 5 is aimed at, though they were admitted. For first, it does not appear that the Spirits will make more hast out of C into B, then the pressure caused in B by the determination of the Spirits from the *Conarion* forces them to. For all places being alike to them to play in, they will goe no further then they are 10 driven or pressed, as Wind in a Bladder. And how the *Conarion* should drive or press the Spirits into B, so as to make it press those in C, and force them out so quick and smart as we find in some Actions, is a thing utterly unconceivable.

6. Besides, admit that the *Conarion* could determine them 15 with some considerable force so into B, that they would make those in C come to them through the Valve G, there being the Valve E to transmit them into C again, it is impossible but that the Tenth part of that force which we ordinarily use to open a mans hand against his will, should whether he would or no 20 easily open it. For a very ordinary strength moving K from B towards C, must needs so press the Spirits in B, that they will certainly pass by E into C, if our *Body* be nothing but *Matter Mechanically organized*. And therefore it is the mere *Imperium* of our *Soul* that does *determine* the *Spirits* to this *Muscle* rather 25 then the other, and holds them there in despite of external force. From whence it is manifest that brute Beasts must have *Souls* also.

7. Concerning *Memory* and *Imagination*, that the mere Mechanical reasons of *Des-Cartes* will not reach them, we shall 30 clearly understand, if we consider that the easy aperture of the same Pores of the *Brain*, that were opened at the presence of

such an Object, is not sufficient to represent the Object, after the *Conarion* has by inclining it self thitherward determined the course of the Spirits into the same Pores. For this could only represent the *Figure* of a thing, not the *Colours* thereof.
5   Besides, a man may bring an hundred Objects, and expose them to our view at the same distance, the Eye keeping exactly in thĕ same posture, insomuch that it shall be necessary for these images to take up the very same place of the *Brain*, and yet there shall be a *distinct remembrance* of all these; which is
10 impossible, if there be no *Soul* in us, but all be *mere Matter*. The same may be said of so many *Names* or *Words* levell'd if you will out of a Trunk into the Eare kept accurately in the same posture, so that the *Sound* shall beat perpetualiy upon the same parts of the Organ, yet if there be five hundred of
15 them, there may be a *distinct memory* for every one of them; which is a power perfectly beyond the bounds of *mere Matter*, for there would be a necessary confusion of all.

      8. Lastly, for those imaginations or representations that are of no one Object that we ever see, but made up of several
20 that have taken their distinct places in the *Brain*, some (suppose) before and others behinde, how can the *Conarion* joyn these together, and in such a posture of conjunction as it pleases? Or rather in one and the same Object, suppose this Man or that House, which we see in a right posture, and has
25 left such a signature or figure in the *Brain* as is fit to represent it so, how can the *Conarion* invert the posture of the image, and make it represent the House and Man with the heels upwards? Besides the difficulty of representing the *Distance* of an Object, or the *Breadth* thereof, concerning which we have
30 spoken already. It is impossible the *Conarion*, if it be *mere Matter*, should perform any such operations as these. For it must raise motions in it self, such as are not necessarily conveighed by any corporeal impress of another Body, which is plainly against Axiome 26.
35   9. And therefore that sober and judicious Wit *Des-Cartes* dares not stretch the power of Mechanical *organization* thus far, but doth plainly confess, That as there are *some Functions* that belong to the *Body* alone, so there are others that belong to the *Soul*, which he calls *Cogitations*; and are according to him of
40 two sorts, the one *Actions*, the other *Passions*. The *Actions* are all the operations of our *Will*, as in some sense all *Perceptions* may be termed *Actions*. And these *Actions of the Will* are

either such as are *mere Intellectual* Operations, and end in the
Soul her self, such as her stirring up her self to *love* God, or
contemplate any Immaterial Object; or they are such as have an
influence on the Body, as when by virtue of our *Will* we put our
selves upon *going* to this or that place.   5

He distinguishes again our *Perceptions* into two sorts,
whereof the one has the *Soul* for their Cause, the other the
Body. Those that are caused by the *Body* are most what such
as depend on the *Nerves.* But besides these there is one kind of
Imagination that is to be referred hither, and that property has   10
the *Body* for its cause, to wit, that Imagination that arises
merely from the hitting of the *Animal Spirits* against the tracts
of those Images that external Objects have lest in the Brain,
and so representing them to the *Conarion*; which may happen
in the day-time when our *Fancy* roves, and we do not set our   15
selves on purpose to think on things, as well as it does in sleep
by night. Those *Perceptions* that arrive to the *Soul* by the
interposition of the *Nerves* differ one from another in this, that
some of them refer to *outward objects* that strike our Sense,
others to *our Body*, such as *Hunger, Thirst, Pain*, etc. and   20
others to the *Soul* it self, as *Sorrow, Joy, Fear*, &c.

Those *Perceptions* that have the *Soul* for their Cause, are
either the *Perceptions* of her own *Acts* of *Will*, or else of her
Speculation of things purely Intelligible, or else of *Imaginations
made at pleasure*, or finally of *Reminiscency* when she searches   25
out something that she has let slip out of her Memory.

10. That which is observable in this Distribution is this,
That all those *Cogitations* that he calls *Actions*, as also those
kind of *Perceptions* whose Cause he assignes to the *Soul*, are in
themselves (and are acknowledged by him) of that nature, that   30
they cannot be imitated by any creature by the *mere
organization* of its Body. But for the other, he holds they may,
and would make us believe they are in *Bodies of Brutes*, which
he would have mere *Machinas*, that is, That from the mere
Mechanical frame of their Body, outward Objects of Sense may   35
open Pores in their Brains so, as that they may determine the
Animal Spirits into such and such Muscles for Spontaneous
Motion: That the course of the Spirits also falling into the
Nerves in the Intestines and Stomack, Spleen, Heart, Liver,
and other parts, may cause the very same effects of Passion,   40
suppose of Love, Hatred, Joy, Sorrow, in these brute *Machinas*,
as we feel in our Bodies; though they, as being senseless, feel

them not: and so the vellication of certain Tunicles and Fibres
in the Stomack and Throat may affect their Body as ours is in
the Sense of Hunger or Thirst: And finally, That the hitting of
the Spirits into the tracts of the Brain that have been signed by
5   External Objects, may act so upon their Body as it does upon
ours in *Imagination* and *Memory*.

Now adde to this *Machina* of *Des-Cartes*, the capacity in
Matter of *Sensation* and *Perception*, (which yet I have
demonstrated it to be uncapable of) and it will be exquisitely as
10 much as Mr. *Hobbs* himself can expect to arise from mere
Body, that is, All the Motions thereof being purely Mechanical,
the perceptions and propensions will be fatall, necessary and
unavoidable, as he loves to have them.

But being no *Cogitations* that *Des-Cartes* terms *Actions*, as
15 also no kind of *Perceptions* that he acknowledges the Soul to be
the Cause of, are to be resolved into any *Mechanical*
contrivance; we may take notice of them as a *peculiar* rank of
Arguments, and such, as that if it could be granted that the
Souls of Brutes were nothing but *Sentient Matter*, yet it would
20 follow that a *Substance of an higher nature*, and truly
Immaterial, must be the Principle of those *more noble
Operations* we find in our selves, as appears from Axiome 20,
and 26.

25 ——————————————————————————————————————

Chap. VI.

I. *That no part of the Spinal Marrow can be the Common*
30 Sensorium *without a Soul in the Body*. 2. *That Animal Spirits
are more likely to be that* Common Percipient. *3.* But yet it is
demonstrable *they are not:* 4. *As not being so much as capable
of Sensation;* 5. *Nor of directing Motion into the Muscles;* 6.
Much less of Imagination and rational Invention; 7. *Nor of*
35 *Memory.* 8. *An Answer to an Evasion.* 9. *The Author's reason,
why he has confuted so particularly all the suppositions of the
Seat of* Common Sense, *when few of them have been asserted
with the exclusion of a Soul.*

40   I. There remain now onely Two Opinions to be examined:
the one, *That place of the Spinal Marrow where* Anatomists
conceive there *is the nearest concurse of all the Nerves of the*

Body; the other, *the Animal Spirits in the fourth Ventricle of the Brain.* As for the former, viz. *That part of the Spinal Marrow where the concurse of the Nerves is conceived to be,* as I have answered in like case; so I say again, that besides that I have already demonstrated, that *Matter* is uncapable of *Sense,* and 5 that there is no modification thereof in the *Spinal Marrow,* that will make it more likely to be indued with that Faculty then the pith of Elder or a mess of Curds; we are also to take notice, that it is utterly inept for *Motion,* nor is it conceivable how that part of it, or in any other that is assigned to this office of being 10 the *Common Percipient* in us of all Thoughts and Objects, (which must also have the power of *moving* our members) can, having so little agitation in it self, (as appearing nothing but a kind of soft Pap or Pulp) so nimbly and strongly *move* the parts of our Body.   15

2. In this regard the *Animal Spirits* seem much more likely to perform that office; and those, the importunity of whose gross fancies constrains them to make the Soul *Corporeal,* do nevertheless usually pitch upon some *subtile thin Matter* to constitute her nature or Essence:. And therefore they 20 imagine her to be either *Aire, Fire, Light,* or some such like Body; with which the *Animal Spirits* have no small affinity.

3. But this opinion, though it may seem plausible at first sight, yet the difficulties it is involved in are insuperable. For it is manifest, that all the Arguments that were brought before 25 will recur with full force in this place. For there is no *Matter* that is so perfectly *liquid* as the *Animal Spirits,* but consists of particles onely contiguous one to another, and actually upon Motion playing and turning one by another as busy as Atomes in the Sun. Now therefore, let us consider whether that 30 Treasury of pure *Animal Spirits* contained in *the fourth Ventricle* be able to sustain so noble an office as to be the *common Percipient* in our Body, which, as I have often repeated, is so complex a Function, that it does not onely contain the *Perception of external objects,* but *Motion,* 35 *Imagination, Reason and Memory.*

4. Now at the very first dash, the transmission of the image of the Object into this crowd of particles cannot but hit variously upon them, and therefore they will have several *Perceptions* amongst them, some haply perceiving part of the 40 Object, others all, others more then all, others also perceiving of it in one place, and others in another. But the *Percipient in*

us representing no such confusion cr disorder in our beholding
of Objects, it is plain that it is not the *Animal Spirits* that is it

5. Again, That which is so confounded a *Percipient*, how
can it be a right Principle of *directing Motion* into the *Muscles*?
For besides what disorder may happen in this function upon
the distracted representation of the present Objects, the power
of *thinking, excogitating* and *deliberating*, being in these *Animal
Spirits* also, (and they having no means of *communicating* one
with another, but justling one against another; which is as
much to the purpose, as if men should knock heads to
communicate to each other their conceits of Wit,) it must needs
follow that they will have their *perceptions, inventions*, and
deliberations apart; which when they put in Execution, must
cause a marvelous confusion in the Body, some of them
commanding the parts this way, others driving them another
way: or if their factions have many divisions and subdivisions,
every one will be so weak, that none of them will be able to
command it any way. But we find no such strugling or
countermands of any thing in us, that would act our Body one
way When we would another; as if when one was a going to
write

Μῆνιν ἄειδε. θεά ...

something stronger in him, whose conceits he is *not privy* to,
should get the use of his hand, and instead of that write down

Arma virúmque cano ...

And the like may be said of any other *Spontaneous Motion*,
which being so constantly within our deliberation or command
as it is, it is a sufficient Argument to prove that it is not such a
lubricous Substance as the *Animal Spirits*, nor so disunited; but
something more *perfectly One* and *Indivisible*, that is the Cause
thereof.

6. We need not instance any further concerning the power
of *Inventions* and *Reason*, how every particle of these *Animal
Spirits* has a liberty to *think* by it self, and *consult* with it self,
as well as to *play* by it self, and how there is no possible means
of *communicating* their Thoughts one to another, unless it
should be, as I have said, by hitting one against another: but
that can onely communicate *Motion*, not their determinate
Thought; unless that these particles were conceived to figure
themselves into the shape of those things they think of, which
is impossible by Axiome 26. And suppose it were possible one
particle should shape it self, for example into a *George on*

Horse-back with a Lance in his hand, and another into an *Inchanted Castle*; this *George on Horse-back* must run against the *Castle*, to make the *Castle* receive his impress and similitude. But what then? Truly the encounter will be very unfortunate: For S. *George* indeed may easily break his Lance, 5 but it is impossible that he should be a justling against the Particle in the form of a *Castle* conveigh the entire shape of himself and his Horse thereby, such as we find our selves able to imagine of a man on horse-back. Which is a Truth as demonstrable as any Theorem in Mathematicks, but so plain at 10 first sight, that I need not use the curiosity of a longer Demonstration to make it more firm.

Nor is there any colourable Evasion by venturing upon a new way, as if this particle having transformed it self into a *Castle*, and that into an *Horseman*, all the others then would 15 see them both and they one another. For by *what light*, and *how little* would they appear, and in *what different places*, according to the different posture of the particles of *the Animal Spirits*, and with what *different faces*, some seeing one side, others another? 20

But besides this there is a further difficulty, that if such *Sensible representations* as these could be conveighed from one particle to another by corporeal encounters and justlings, or by that other way after alledged; *Logical* and *Mathematical Notions* can not. So that some of the *Animal Spirits* may think of one 25 Demonstration in *Mathematicks*, or of part of that Demonstration, and others of another: insomuch that if a *Mathematician* be to write, while he would write one thing upon the determination of these *Animal Spirits*, others may get his hand to make use of for the writing something else, to whole 30 Thoughts and Counsel he was not at all privy; nor can tell any thing, till those other *Animal Spirits* have writ it down. Which Absurdities are so mad and extravagant, that a man would scarce defile his pen by recording them, were it not to awaken those that dote so much on *the power of Matter* (as to think it of 35 it self sufficient for all *Phaenomena* in the world) into due shame and abhorrence of their foolish Principle.

7. The last Faculty I will consider is *Memory*, which is also necessarily joyned with the rest in the *Common Percipient*; of which not onely the *flüidity* of parts, but also their 40 *dissipability*, makes the *Animal Spirits* utterly uncapable. For certainly, the *Spirits* by reason of their *Subtilty* and *Activity* are

very *dissipable*, and in all likelihood remain not the same for the space of a week together; and yet things that one has not thought of for many years, will come as freshly into a mans mind as if they were transacted but yesterday.

5   8. The onely Evasion they can excogitate here is this, That as there is a continual supply of *Spirits* by degrees, so, as they come in, they are *seasoned, fermented* and *tinctured* with the same *Notions, Perceptions* and *Propensions* that the *Spirits* they find there have. These are fine words, but signifie nothing but

10   this, that the *Spirits* there present in the Brain communicate the *Notions* and *Perceptions* they have to these new comers; which is that which I have already proved impossible in the foregoing Sections. And therefore it is impossible that the *Animal Spirits* should be that *Common Percipient* that *hears,*

15   *sees, moves, remembers, understands,* and does other functions of life that we perceive performed in us or by us.

        9. We have now particularly evinced, that neither the *whole Body,* nor any of those *parts* that have been pitched upon, if we exclude the presence of a *Soul* or *Immaterial*

20   *Substance,* can be the *Seat of Common Sense.* In which I would not be so understood, as if it implied that there are none of these parts, but some or other have affirmed might be the *common Sensorium,* though we had no Soul: But because they have been stood upon, all of them, by some or other to be the

25   *Seat of Common Sense,* supposing a *Soul* in the Body, that there might no imaginable doubt or scruple be left behind, I have taken the pains thus punctually and particularly to prove, that none of them can be the place of *Common Sense* without one.

        And thus I have perfectly finished my main design, which

30   was to demonstrate *That there is a Soul or Incorporeal Substance residing in us, distinct from the Body.* But I shall not content my self here, but for a more full discovery of her *Nature* and *Faculties,* I shall advance further, and search out the *chief Seat in the Body,* where and from whence she exercises

35   her most noble Functions, and after enquire whether she be *confined* to that part thereof alone, or whether she be *spred* through all our members; and lastly consider after what manner she *sees, feels, hears, imagines, remembers, reasons,* and *moves the Body.* For beside that I shall make some good use of

40   these discoveries for further purpose, it is also in it self very pleasant to have in readiness a rational and coherent account, and a determinate apprehension of things of this nature.

Chap. VII.

5

1. *His Enquiry after the Seat of Common Sense, upon supposition there is a Soul in the Body.* 2. *That there is some particular Part in the Body that is the seat of Common Sense.* 3. *A general division of their Opinions concerning the place of Common Sense.* 4. *That of those that place it out of the Head there are two sorts.* 10 5. *The Invalidity of* Helmont' s *reasons whereby he would prove the Orifice of the Stomack to be the principle Seat of the Soul.* 6. *An answer to* Helmont's *stories for that purpose.* 7. *A further confutation out of his own concessions.* 8. *Mr.* Hobbs *his Opinion confuted, that makes the Heart the Seat of Common* 15 *Sense.* 9. *A further confutation thereof from Experience.* 10. *That the Common Sense is seated somewhere in the Head.* 11. *A caution for the choice of the particular place thereof.* 12. *That the whole Brain is not it;* 13. *Nor Regius his small solid Particle;* 14. *Nor any external Membrane of the Brain, nor the* Septum 20 Lucidum. *15.*The three most *likely places.* 16. *Objections against* Cartesius *his Opinion concerning the* Conarion *answered.* 17. *That the* Conarion *is not the Seat of Common Sense;* 18. *Nor that part of the Spinal Marrow where the Nerves are conceived to concurre, but the Spirits in fourth Ventricle of the* 25 *Brain .*

1. It will therefore be requisite for us to resume the former Opinions, altering the Hypothesis; and to examine which of them is most reasonable, supposing there be a *Substance* 30 *Immaterial* or *Soul* in man.

2. That there is *some particular* or restrain'd *Seat of the Common Sense*, is an Opinion that even all Philosophers and Physicians are agreed upon. And it is an ordinary Comparison amongst them, that the *External Senses* & the *Common Sense* 35 considered together are like a Circle with five lines drawn from the Circumference to the Centre. Wherefore as it has been obvious for them to finde out particular Organs for the *External Senses*, so they have also attempted to assign some distinct part of the Body for to be an Organ of the *Common Sense;* that 40 is to say, as they discovered Sight to be seated in the Eye, Hearing in the Eare, Smelling in the Nose, etc. so they

conceived that there is some part of the Body wherein Seeing,
Hearing and all other Perceptions meet together, as the lines of
a Circle in the Centre: and that there the Soul does also judge
and discern of the differences of the Objects of the outward
5   Senses. They have justly therefore excluded all the *External*
parts of the Body from the lightest suspicion of any capacity of
undergoing such a function as is thus general, they being all
employed in a more particular task, which is to be the Organ of
some one of these five outward Senses; and to be affected no
10   otherwise then by what is impressed upon themselves, and
chiefly from their proper Objects; amongst which five, *Touch*
properly so-called has the greatest share, it being as large as
the Skin that covers us, and reaching as deep as any
Membrane and Nerve in the limbs and trunk of the Body,
15   besides all the Exteriour parts of the Head. All which can no
more see then the Eye can hear, or the Eare can smell.

    3. Besides this, all those Arguments that do so clearly
evince that the place of *Common Sense* is somewhere in the
Head are a plain demonstration that *the whole Body* cannot be
20   the Seat thereof, and what those Arguments are you shall hear
anon. For all those Opinions that have pitched on any *one Part*
for the Seat of *Common Sense*, being to be divided into two
Ranks, to wit, either such as assign some particular place in
the *Body*, or else in the *Head*, we will proceed in this order: as
25   first to confute those that have made choice of any part for the
Seat of *Common Sense* out of the *Head*; and then in the second
place we will in general shew, that the common Sensorium
must be in *some part* of the *Head*; and lastly, of those many
opinions concerning *what part of the Head* this common
30   *Sensorium* should be, those which seem less reasonable being
rejected, we shall pitch upon what we conceive the most
unexceptionable.

    4. Those that place the Common *Sensorium* out of the
Head, have seated it either in the *upper Orifice of the Stomack*,
35   or in the *Heart*. The former is *Van-Helmont*'s Opinion, the
other M^r*Hobbs* his.

    5. As for *Van-Helmont*, there is nothing he alledges for his
Opinion but may be easily answered. That which mainly
inposed upon him was the *exceeding sensibility* of that part,
40   which Nature made so, that, as a faithful and sagacious Porter,
it might admit nothing into the *Stomack* that might prove
mischievous or troublesome to the Body. From this *tender*

Sensibility, great offences to it may very well cause *Swoonings*, and *Apoplexies*, and cessations of Sense. But *Fear* and *Joy* and *Grief* have dispatch'd some very suddainly, when yet the first entrance of that deadly stroke has been at the *Eare* or the *Eye*, from some unsupportable ill newes or horrid spectacle. And the   5
harsh handling of an angry Sore, or the treading on a Corn on the Toe, may easily cast some into a *swoon*, and yet no man will ever imagine the Seat of the *Common Sense* to be placed in the *Foot*. In fine, there is no more reason to think the Common *Sensorium* is in the *mouth of the Stomack*, because of the   10
Sensible Commotions we feel there, then that it is seated in the *Stars*, because we so clearly perceive their Light, as *Des-Cartes* has well answered upon like occasion. Nor can *Phrensies* and *Madnesses*, though they may sometimes be observed to take their rise from thence, any more prove that it is the Seat of the   15
Common Sense, then the *Furor uterinus*, Apoplexies, Epilepsies, and Syncopes proceeding from the *Wombe*, do argue that the common *Sensorium* of Women lies in that part.

6. And if we consider the great *Sympathy* betwixt the *Orifice of the Stomack* and the *Heart*, whose *Pathemata* are so   20
alike and conjoyned that the Ancients have given one name to both parts, calling them promiscuously καρδία *and the pains of the Stomack* καρδιαλγίαι and καρδιωγμόι. also that the *Heart* is that part from which manifestly are the supplies of Life, whence the *Pulse* ceasing, Life cannot long continue for want of   25
Warmth and Spirits; here is an evident reason how it may happen that a Wound about *the mouth of the Stomack* may dispatch a man more suddainly then a wound in the *Head*, they being both supposed mortal, though the seat of the *Sensitive* Soul be not chiefly in the aforesaid Orifice. For partly the   30
natural Sympathy betwixt the Orifice of the *Stomack* and the *Heart*, and partly the horrour and pain perceived by the Soul in the common *Sensorium*, which we will supose in the *Head*, does so dead the *Heart* that, as in the suddain Passions above named, it ceases to perform the ordinary functions of Life, and   35
so *Pulse* and *Sense* and all is gone in short time; whenas the *Head* being wounded mortally, *Perception* is thereby so diminished, that the *Heart* scapes the more free from the force of that lethiferous passion; and so though *Sense* be gone, can continue the *Pulse* a longer time: which is a perfect answer to   40
Helmont's stories he recites in his *Sedes Animae*.

7. To all which I may adde, That himself does
acknowledge in the end of that Treatise, that the power of
Motion, of *Will*, *Memory* and *Imagination*, is in the Brain; and
therefore unless a man will say and deny any thing, he must
5   say that the *Common Sense* is there also.

8. The Opinion of M*r* *Hobbs* bears more credit and
countenance with it, as having been asserted heretofore by
Philosophers of great fame, *Epicurus*, *Aristotle*, and the School
of the *Stoicks*: but if we look closer to it, it will prove as little
10   true as the other; especially in his way, that holds there is no
Soul in a Man, but that all is but *organized Matter*. For let him
declare any Mechanical reason whereby his *Heart* will be able
to move his *Finger*. But upon this Hypothesis I have confuted
this Opinion already. It is more maintainable, if there be
15   granted a *Soul* in the Body, that the *Heart* is the chief Seat
thereof, and place of *Common Sense*, as *Aristotle* and others
would have it, as also the Spring of *Spontaneous Motion*. But it
is very unlikely that that part that is so continually employed
in that natural Motion of *contracting and dilating* it self, should
20   be the Seat of that Principle which commands *Free* and
Spontaneous progressions: *Perceptions* also would be horribly
disturbed by its squeezing of it self, and then flagging again by
vicissitudes. Neither would Objects appear in the same place,
or at least our sight not fixt on the same part of the Object,
25   when the *Heart* is drawn up and when it is let down again, as
I have above intimated: the *extreme heat* also of it could not
admit that it be affected with the gentle motions of the Objects
of Sense, the Blood being there in a manner scalding hot. And
it is in this sense that the Aphorisme in *Aristotle* is to be
30   understood, τὸ μέσον κριτικὸν. *That which must receive the*
variety of external impresses, must not be it self in any high
temper or agitation.

9. Wherefore it is a very rash thing to assert, That the
Heart is the Seat of *Common Sense*, unless by some plain
35   experience it could be evinced to be so, whenas indeed
Experiments are recorded to the contrary. As, that if we bind
a Nerve, *Sense* and *Motion* will be betwixt the *Ligature* and the
Brain, but not betwixt the *Heart* and the *Ligature*. And that
the *Crocodile*, his *Heart* being cut out, will live for a
40   considerable time, and fight, and defend himself. The like is
observed of the *Sea-Tortoise*, and the *wild Goat*, as *Calcidius*
writes. To which you may adde what *Galen* relates of

sacrificed Beasts, that their *Hearts* being taken out and laid upon the Altar, they have been seen in the mean time not onely to breath, and roar aloud, but also to run away, till the expence of Blood has made them fall down. Which Narrations to me are the more credible, I having seen with mine own eyes a *Frog*   5 quite exenterated, heart, stomack, guts and all taken out by an ingenious friend of mine, and dexterous Anatomist; after which the *Frog* could see, and would avoid any object in its way, and skipped as freely and nimbly up and down as when it was entire, and that for a great while. But a very little wound in   10 the Head deprives them immediately of *Life* and *Motion*. Whence it is plain that the deprivation of *Sense* and *spontaneous Motion* is not from the *Heart*. For if the *Motion* be intercepted betwixt the *Brain* and *Heart*, by Mr *Hobbs* his own concession, there will be no perception of the Object. And there   15 is the same reason of the *Orifice of the Stomack*: so that this one Experiment does clearly evince these two Opinions to be erroneous.

10. And that no man hereafter may make any other unhappy choice in the parts of the Body, we shall now propose   20 such Reasons as we hope will plainly prove, That the common *Sensorium* must needs be in the *Head*; or indeed rather repeat them: For some of those whereby we proved that the *Heart* is not the Seat of *Common Sense*, will plainly evince that the *Head* is. As that out of *Laurentius*, that a *Nerve* being tied,   25 *Sense* and *Motion* will be preserved from the Ligature up towards the *Head*, but downwards they will be lost. As also that expariment of a *Frog*, whose brain if you pierce will presently be devoid of *Sense* and *Motion*, though all the Entrals being taken out it will skip up and down, and exercise its   30 Senses as before. Which is a plain evidence that *Motion* and *Sense* is derived from the *Head*; and there is now no pretence to trace any *Motion* into a farther fountain, the *Heart*, (from whence *Nerves* were conceived to branch by *Aristotle*, and from whence certainly the *Veins* and *Arteries* do, as appears by   35 every Anatomie) being so justly discharged from that office.

To which it may suffice to adde the consideration of those Diseases that seize upon all the Animal functions at once, such as are the *Lethargie, Apoplexie, Epilepsie*, and the like, the causes of which Physicians find in the *Head*, and accordingly   40 apply remedies. Which is a plain detection that the Seat of the Soul, as much as concerns the Animal Faculties, is chiefly in the *Head*. The same may be said of *Phrensy* and *Melancholy*, and such like distempers, that deprave a mans *Imagination* and *Judgment*; Physicians alwaies conclude something amiss within the *Cranium*.

5   Lastly, if it were nothing but the near attendance of the outward Senses on the *Soul*, or her *discerning Faculty*, being so fitly placed about her in the *Head*; this, unless there were some considerable Argument to the contrary, should be sufficient to determine any one that is unprejudiced, to conclude that the

10   Seat of *Common Sense, Understanding*, and *command of Motion*, is there also.

11. But now the greatest difficulty wili be to define *In what part thereof it is to be placed*. In which, unless we will goe overboldly and carelesly to work, we are to have a regard to

15   Mechanical congruities, and not pitch upon any thing that, by the advantage of this Supposal, *That there is a Soul in man*, may goe for possible; but to chuse what is most handsome and convenient.

12. That the *whole brain* is not the seat of *Common Sense*,

20   appears from the wounds and cuts it may receive without the destruction of that Faculty; for they will not take away *Sense* and *Motion*, unless they pierce so deep as to reach the *Ventricles of the Brain*, as *Galen* has observed.

13. Nor is it in *Regius* his *small solid particle*. For besides

25   that it is not likely the *Centre of Perception* is so minute, it is very incongruous to place it in a Body so perfectly *solid*, more *hard* then Marble or Iron. But this Invention being but a late freak of his petulant fancy, that has an ambition to make a blunder and confusion of all *Des-Cartes* his Metaphysical

30   Speculations, (and therefore found out this rare quirk of wit to shew, how though the *Soul* were nothing but *Matter*, yet it might be *incorruptible* and *immortal*) it was not worth the while to take notice of it here in this Hypothesis, which we have demonstrated to be true, viz. *That there is a Soul in the Body*,

35   *whose nature is Immaterial or Incorporeal*.

14. Nor are the *Membranes in the Head* the Common *Sensorium* neither those that envelop the *Brain*, (for they would be able then to see the light through the hole the *Trepan* makes though the party *Trepan'd* winked with his eyes; to say nothing

40   of the conveyance of the *Nerves*, the Organs of external Sense, that carry beyond these exteriour Membranes, and therefore point to a place more inward, that must be the *Recipient* of all

their impresses) nor any *Internal membrane*, as that which bids fairest for it, the *Septum Lucidum*, as being in the midst of the upper Ventricle. But yet if the levell of Motion through the externall Senses be accurately considered, some will shoot under, and some in a distant parallel, so that this Membrane 5 will not be struck with all the Objects of our Senses. Besides that it seems odd and ridiculous that the *Centre of Perception* should be either driven out so into plates, or spread into hollow convexities, as it must be supposed, if we make either the *external* or *internal Membranes of the Brain* the Seat of *Common* 10 *Sense*.

15. The most likely place is some one of those that the three last Opinions point at, viz. either the *Conarion*, or the *Concurse of the Nerves in the fourth Ventricle*, or *the Animal Spirits there*. 15

16. The first is *Des-cartes* Opinion, and not rashly to be refused, neither do I find any Arguments hitherto that are valid enough to deface it. Those that are recited out of *Bartholine*, and subscribed to by the learned Author of *Adenographia*, in my apprehension have not the force to ruine 20 it. We will first repeat them, and then examine them.

The first is, that this *Glandula* is too little to be able to represent the Images of all that the Soul has represented to her.

The second, That the *external Nerves* do not reach to the 25 *Glandula*, and that therefore it cannot receive the impress of sensible Objects.

The third, that it is placed in a place of excrements which would soile the *Species* of things.

The fourth, That the *Species* of things are perceived there 30 where they are carried by the *Nerves*. But the *Nerves* meet about the beginning or head of the *Spinal Marrow*, a more noble and *ample* place then the *Glandula pinealis*.

To the first I answer, That the *amplitude* of that place where the *Nerves* meet in the *Spinal Marrow* is not large 35 enough to receive the distinct impresses of all the Objects the Mind retains in *Memory*. (Besides, that the other parts of the *Brain* may serve for that purpose, as much as any of it can.) But it must be the Soul her self alone that is capable of retaining so distinct and perfect representations of things, 40 though it were admitted that she might make an occasional use of some private marks she impresses in the *Brain*, which haply may be nothing at all like the things it would *remember*, nor of any considerable magnitude nor proportion to them, such as we observe in the words *Arx* and *Atomus*, where there is no correspondency of either likeness or bigness betwixt the words 5 and the things represented by them.

To the second, thet though there be no continuation of *Nerves* to the *Conarion*, yet there is of *Spirits*; which are as able to conveigh the impresses of Motion from external Sense to the *Conarion*, as the Aire and *Aether* the impress of the Stars unto 10 the Eye.

To the third, that the *glandula* is conveniently enough placed so long as the Body is found; for no excrementitious humours will then overflow it or besmear it. But in such distempers wherein they do, *Apoplexies*, *Catalepsies*, or such 15 like diseases will arise; which we see do fall out, let the Seat of *Common Sense* be where it will.

To the last I answer, That the Nerves, when they are once got any thing far into the *Brain*, are devoid of *Tunicles*, and be so soft and spongy, that the motion of the Spirits can play 20 through them, and that therefore they may ray through the sides, and so continue their motion to the *Conarion*, whereever their extremities may seem to tend.

17. But though these Arguments do not sufficiently confute the Opinion, yet I am not so wedded to it, but I can 25 think something more unexceptionable may be found out, especially it being so much to be suspected that all Animals have not this *Conarion*; and then; that what pleased *Des-Cartes* so much in this Invention, was, that he conceited it such a marvelous fine instrument to beat the *Animal Spirits* into such 30 and such Pores of the Brain; a thing that I cannot at all close with for reasons above alledged. Besides that *Stones* have been found in this *Glandula*, and that it is apparent that it is environ'd with a net of *Veins* and *Arteries*, which are indications that it is a part assigned for some more inferiour office. But 35 yet I would not dismiss it without fair play.

18. *Wherefore that Opinion of the forecited Author, who places* the Seat of *Common Sense* in that part of the *Spinal Marrow* where the *Nerves* are suspected to meet, as it is more plain and simple, so it is more irrefutable, supposing that the 40 Soul's *Centre of perception* (whereby she does not onely apprehend all the Objects of the external Senses, but does *imagine*, *reason*, and *freely command* and *determine* the *Spirits*

into what part of the Body she pleases) could be conveniently seated in such dull pasty Matter as the *Pith of the Brain* is; a thing, I must needs profess, that pleases not my Palate at all, and therefore I will also take leave of this Opinion too, and adventure to pronounce, *That the chief Seat of the Soul, where* 5 *she perceives all Objects, where she imagines, reasons, and invents, and from whence she commands all the parts of the Body, is those purer Animal Spirits in the fourth Ventricle of the Brain.*

10

Chap. VIII.

I. *The first reason of his Opinion, the convenient Situation of* 15 *these Spirits.* 2. *The second, that the Spirits are the immediate Instrument of the Soul in all her functions.* 3. *The proof of the second Reason from the general Authority of Philosophers, and particularly of* Hippocrates; *4.* From our Sympathizing with the *changes of the Aire*; 5. *From the celerity of Motion and* 20 *Cogitation;* 6. *From what is observed generally in the Generation of things;* 7. *From* Regius *his experiment of a Snail in a glass*; 8. *From the running round of Images in a* Vertigo; *9.* From the constitution *of the Eye, and motion of the Spirits there*; 10. *From the dependency of the actions of the Soul upon the Body, whether* 25 *in Meditation or corporeal Motion*; 11. *From the recovery of Motion and Sense into a stupefied part;* 12. And lastly, from what is oberved in *swooning fits, of paleness and sharpness of visage, etc.* 13. *The inference from all this, That the Spirits in the fourth Ventricle are the Seat of Common Sense, and that the main* 30 *use of the Brain and Nerves is to preserve the Spirits.*

I. That which makes me embrace this Opinion rather then any other is this; That, first, this situation of the common *Sensorium* betwixt the *Head* and the trunk of the *Body* is the 35 most exactly convenient to receive the impresses of Objects from both, as also to impart Motion to the Muscles in both the *Head* and in the *Body*. In which I look upon it as equall with the last Opinion, and superiour to all them that went before. For whatever may be objected, is already answered in wnat I 40 have said to the last Objection against *Des-Cartes*.

2. But now in the second place, (wherein this Opinion of mine has a notorious advantage above all else that I know) It is most reasonable that that Matter which is the *immediate Instrument* of all the Animal functions of the Soul, should be the
5 chiefest Seat from whence and where she exercises these functions, and if there be any place where there is a freer plenty of the purest sort of this Matter, that her *peculiar residence* should be there. Now the *immediate Instrument* of the functions of the Soul is that *thinner Matter* which they
10 ordinarily call *Animal Spirits*, which are to be found in their greatest purity and plenty in the *fourth Ventricle of the Brain.* From whence it must follow that that precious and choice part of the Soul which we call *the Centre of perception* is to be placed in that Ventricle, not in any pith of the Brain thereabout, but in
15 the midst of these Spirits themselves; for that is the most natural situation for the commanding them into the parts of the *Head* and *Body*; besides a more delicate and subtile use of them at home, in pursuing various imaginations and inventions.

3. That this *thin and spirituous matter* is the immediate
20 engine of the Soul in all her operations, is in a manner the general opinion of all Philosophers. And even those that have placed the Common *Sensorium* in the *Heart*, have been secure of the truth of this their conceit, because they took it for granted, that the left Ventricle thereof was the fountain of
25 these pure and subtile Spirits, and please themselves very much, in that they fancied that Oracle of Physicians, the grave and wise *Hippocrates*, to speak their own sense so fully and significantly.   Γνώμη γὰρ ἡ τοῦ ἀνθρώπου πέφυκεν ἐν τῆι λαιῆι κοιλίηι· τρέφεται δε οὔτε σιτίοσιν οὔτε ποτοῖσιν ἀπο τῆς νηδύος.
30 ἀλλὰ καθαρῆι καὶ φωτοειδεῖ περιουσίαι γεγονυίη ἐκ τῆς διακρίσεως τοῦ αἵματος· that is to say, *That the Mind of man is in the left Ventricle of his Heart; and that it is not nourished from meats and drinks from the belly, but by a clear and luminous Substance that redounds by separation from the blood*: which is that which
35 happens exactly in the *Brain.* For the *Spirits* there are nothing else but more pure and subtile parts of the blood, whose tenuity and agitation makes them separate from the rest of the mass thereof, and so replenish the Ventricles of the Brain.

4. Moreover our *sympathizing* so sensibly with the *changes*
40 *of the Aire*, which *Hippocrates* also takes notice of, that in *clear Aire* our *Thoughts* are more *clear*, and in *cloudy* more *obscure* and *dull*, is no slight indication that that which conveighs

Sense, Thoughts, and *Passions* immediately to the Soul, is very tenuious and delicate, and of a nature very congenerous to the *Aire* with which it changes so easily.

5. The strange *Agility* also of *Motions* and *Cogitations* that we find in our selves, has forced the most sluggish witts, even such as have been so gross as to deem the Soul *Corporeal,* yet to chuse the freest, subtilest & most active Matter to compound her of, that their imaginations could excogitate. And *Lucretius,* the most confident of the *Epicurean Sect,* thinks he has hit the naile on the head in his choice;

> *Nunc igitur quoniam est animi natura reperta*
> *Mobilis egregie, per quam constare necesse est*
> *Corporibus parvis et laevibus atque rotundis*:

whose Testimony I account the better in this case, by how much the more crass Philosopher he is, the necessity of the tenuity of particles that are to pervade the Body of a Man being convinced hence to be so plain, that the dimmest eyes can easily discover it.

6. But we will advance higher to more forcible Arguments *amongst* which this, I think, may find some place, That we cannot discover any immediate operation of any kind of Soul in the world, but what it first works upon *that Matter* which participates in a very great measure of this *fineness* and *tenuity of parts,* which will easily yield and be guided; as may be universally observed in all *Generations,* where the *Body* is alwaies *organized* out of *thin fluid liquor,* that will easily yieid to the plastick power of the Soul. In which I do not doubt but it takes the advantage of moving the most subtile parts of all first, such as *Des-Cartes* his first and second Element, which are never excluded from any such humid and tenuious substance: which Elements of his are that true *Heavenly* or *Aethereal Matter* which is every where, as *Ficinus* somewhere saith Heaven is; and is that *Fire* which *Trismegist* affirms is the most inward vehicle of the Mind, and the instrument that God used in the forging of the world, and which the Soul of the world, whereever she acts, does most certainly still use.

7. And to make yet a step further, That ocular demonstration that *Henricus Regius* brings into view seems to me both ingenious and solid: It is in a *snail,* such as have no shells, moving in a glass: so soon as she begins to creep, certain Bubbles are discovered to move from her tail to her head; but so soon as she ceases moving, those Bubbles cease.

Whence he concludes, That a gale of Spirits that circult from her head along her back to her tail, and thence along her belly to her head again, is the cause of her progressive motion.

8. That such *thin Spirits* are the immediate Instruments of *Sense*, is also discovered by what is observed in a *Vertigo*. For the *Brain* it self is not of such a *fluid* substance as to turn round, and to make external Objects seem to doe so. Wherefore it is a sign that the immediate corporeal Instrument of conveying the images of things is the *Spirits* in the Brain.

9. And that they are the chief Organ of *Sight* is plain in the exteriour parts of the Eye: for we may easily discern how full they are of that καθαρὴ καὶ φωτοειδὴς οὐσία, *pure and lucid substance*, which *Hippocrates* speaks of, though he seat it in a wrong place; and how upon the passions of the Mind these *Spirits* ebbe or flow in the Eye, and are otherwise wonderful-significantly modified; insomuch that the Soul even seems to speak through them, in that silent voice of Angels, which some fancy to be by nothing but by dumb shews, but I do not at all believe it. It is also plain enough, that dimness of sight comes from deficiency of *these spirits*, though the parts of the Eye otherwise be entire enough. The wider opening also of the pupill of one Eye upon the shutting of the other does indicate the flux and more copious presence of *Spirits* there, as *Galen* has ingeniously collected.

10. To which we may adde that in those *more noble* operations of the Mind, when she *meditates* and excogitates various Theorems, that either she uses some part of the Body as an Instrument then, or acts freely and independently of the Body. That the latter is false is manifest from hence, that then the change of Air, or Distemper and Diseasedness, could not prejudice her in her *Inventive* and *purely Intellectual* Operations; but it is manifest that they doe, and that a mans Mind is much more cloudy one time then another, and in one Country then another, whence is that proverbial Verse,

        Boeotûm crasso jurares aëre natum.

If she uses any part of the Body, it must be either these *Animal Spirits*, or the *Brain*. That it is not the Brain, the very consistency thereof so clammy and sluggish is an evident demonstration.

Which will still have the more force, if we consider wnat is most certainly true, That the Soul has not any *power*, or else exceeding little, *of moving Matter*; but her peculiar priviledge is of *determining Matter in motion*; which the more subtile and agitated it is, the more easily by reason of its own mobility is it determined by her. For if it were an immediate faculty of the Soul *to contribute motion* to any Matter, I do not understand how that faculty never failing nor diminishing no more then the 5 Soul it self can fail or diminish, that we should ever be weary of motion. Insomuch that those nimble-footed *Maenades* or she-Priests of *Bacchus*, with other agile Virgins of the Country, which *Dionysius* describes dancing in the flowry meadows of *Maeander* and *Cayster*, might, if life and limbs would last, be 10 found dancing there to this very day, as free and frolick as wanton Kids (as he pleases to set out their activity) and that without any lassitude at all. For that immediate *motive* faculty of the Soul can still as fresh as ever impart *motion* to all the Body, and sooner consume it into air or ashes by heating and 15 agitating it, then make her self *weary*, or the Body seem so.

Wherefore it is plain that that *motion* or *heat* that the Soul voluntarily confers upon the Body is by virtue of the *Spirits*, which she, when they are playing onely and gently toying amongst themselves, sends forth into the exteriour members, 20 and so agitates and moves them: but they being so subtile and dissipable, the Soul spends them in using of them; and they being much spent, she can hardly move the Body any longer, the sense uhereof we call *Lassitude*. These are the τὰ ὁρμῶντα or ἐνορμῶντα of *Hippocrates*, and the Soul's immediate engine of 25 motion through all the parts of the Body.

11. As they are also of *Sense* in the more remote parts as well as in the Head, as *Spigelius* handsomely insinuates by that ordinary example of a mans legge being stupefied or aslaep, as some call it, by compression or whatever hinderance may be of 30 the propagation of the Spirits into that part. For as *Sense* and *Motion* is restored, a man may plainly feel something creep into it tingling and stinging like Pismires, as he compares it; which can be nothing but the *Spirits* forcing their passage into the part. Wherein what they suffer is made sensible to the 35 Soul, they being her immediate Vehicle of life and sense.

12. Lastly, In *swooning* fits, when *Motion* and *Sense* fails, th exteriour parts are *pale* and *fallen*, the Face looking more *lean* and *sharp*; of which there can be no other meaning, then that that benign gale of vital air that fill'd up the parts before, 40 is now absent and retreated from them; that is, that the *fluid Spirits* are retired, without which no *Sense* nor *Motion* can be

performed: whence it is apparent that they are the immediate
Instrument of both.

5
13. I have proved that the *Animal Spirits* are the Soul's
immediate organ for *Sense* and *Motion*. If therefore there be
any place where the *Spirits* are in the fittest plenty and purity,
and in the most convenient situation for Animal functions; that
in all reason must be concluded the chief seat and *Acropolis* of
the Soul. Now the *Spirits* in the *middle ventricle of the Brain* are
not so indifferently situated for both the *Body* and the *Head*, as
10
those in the *fourth* are; nor so pure. The Upper Ventricles,
being two, are not so fit for this office, that is so very much one
and singular. Besides that the sensiferous impresses of motion
through the eyes play under them; to say nothing how the
Spirits here are less defecate also then in the *fourth* Ventricle.

15
Wherefore there being *sufficient plenty*, and *greatest purity*,
and *fittest situation of the Spirits in this fourth Ventricle*, it is
manifest that in these is placed the *Centre of Perception*, and
that they are the *common Sensorium* of the Soul: And that as
the *Heart* pumps out *Blood* perpetually to supply the whole
20
Body with nourishment, to keep up the bulk of this Edifice for
the Soul to dwell in, and also, from the more subtile and agile
parts thereof, to replenish the *Brain* and *Nerves* with *Spirits*,
(which are the immediate Instrument of the Soul for *Sense* and
Motion;) So likewise is it plain that the main use of the *Brain*
25
and *Nerves* is to keep these *subtile Spirits* from overspeedy
dissipation; and that the *Brain* with its Caverns is but one
great round *Nerve*; as the *Nerves* with their invisible porosities
are but so many smaller productions or slenderer prolongations
of the *Brain*: And so all together are but one continued
30
Receptacle or Case of that immediate Instrument of the
sensiferous motions of the Soul, the *Animal Spirits*, wherein
also lies her hidden Vehicle of life in this mortal body.

35

Chap. IX.

I. *Several objections against* Animal Spirits. 2. *An Answer
to the first Objection touching the Porosity of the Nerves.* 3. *To*
40
*the second and third, from the Extravasation of the Spirits and
pituitous Excrements found in the Brain.* 4. *To the fourth, fetcht
from the incredible swiftness of motion in the Spirits.* 5. *To the*

last, from Ligation.   6. *Undeniable Demonstrations that there
are* Animal Spirits in the Ventricles of the Brain.

I. Before we proceed to our other two Enquiries, we are
forced to make a stop a while, and listen to some few 5
Objections made by some late Authours, who, against the
common stream of all other Philosophers, Physicians and
Anatomists, are not ashamed to deny that there are any such
things as *Spirits* in the Body; or at least that there are any in
the Ventricles of the Brain. For as for the *Nerves*, say they, 10
they have no Pores or Cavities to receive them; and besides it
is plain that what is fluid in them is nothing but a milky white
juice, as is observed in the pricking of a *Nerve.* And as for the
Ventricles of the Brain, those Cavities are too big; and the
Spirits, if they issue into them, will be as *extravasated* Blood, 15
whence they must needs be spoiled and corrupt. Besides that
they will evaporate at those passages through which the
mucous or pituitous excrements pass from the Brain. Whose
appearance there, is, say they, another great argument that
these Ventricles were intended onely for receptacles and
conveyances of such excrementitious Humours which the Brain 20
discharges it self of. Lastly, if *Spontaneous Motion* be made by
means of these *Spirits*, it could not be so extremely *sudden* as it
is; for we can wagge our finger as quick as thought, but
corporeal Motion cannot be so swift. And if the *Spirits* be 25
continued from the Head to the Finger, suppose, in the ligation
of the Nerve there would be sense from the Ligature to the
Fingers end; which is, say they, against Experience. These are
the main Objections I have met withall in *Hofman* and others;
but are such as I think are very easily answered: and indeed 30
they do in some sort clash some of them one with another.
2. For how can the *Nerves* derive juice if they have no
Pores, or are not so much as passable to these thin active
Spirits we speak of? or from whence can we better conceive
that juice to arise, then from these Spirits themselves, as they 35
lose their agitation, and flag into a more gross consistency?
3. Neither can the *Spirits* be looked upon as *extravasated* in
the Ventricles of the Brain, more then the Blood in the Auricles
or Ventricles of the Heart. Nor is there any fear of their
sliding away through the *Infundibulum*, the pituitous 40
excrements having no passage there but what they make by
their weight, as well as their insinuating moistness, which

alwaies besmearing these parts makes them more impervious
to the light Spirits, whose agility also and componderancy with
the outward Aire renders them uncapable of leaving the
Caverns in which they are.

5   That arguing from the *pituitous excrements* found there,
that they were made onely for a Receptacle of such useless
redundancy, is as ineptly inferred, as if a man should argue
from what is found in the *Intestinum rectum*, that the Stomack
and all the Intestines were made for a Receptacle of
10 Stercoreous excrement. The Spirits in the Ventricles of the
Brain, playing about and hitting against the sides of the
Caverns they are in, will in process of time abate of their
agitation, the grosser parts especially; and so necessarily come
to a more course consistency, and settle into some such like
15 moist Sediment as is found at the bottome of the Ventricles,
which nature dischargeth through fit passages, whereby the
Spirits are left more pure. But because this necessary
feculency is found in these Cavities, to conclude that that is the
only use of them, is as ridiculous as to inferre That because I
20 spit at my Mouth, and blow my Nose, that that was the chief
end and use of these two parts of my Body, or that my Eyes
were not made for seeing, but weeping.

        4. The nature of the *swiftness of Motion* in these *Spirits* is
much like that of *Light*, which is a Body as well as they. But
25 that Lucid Matter in the Sun does not, so soon as he appears
upon the Horizon, fly so many thousand miles in a moment to
salute our eyes, but Motion is propagated as it were at once
from the Sun to our Eye through the aethereal Matter betwixt.
Or suppose a long Tube, as long as you will, and one to blow in
30 it; in a moment, so soon as he blows at one end, the Motion will
be felt at the other, and that downwards as well as upwards,
and as easily; to satisfie that other frivolous Objection I find
in *Hofman*, as if it were so hard a business that these *Spirits*
should be commanded downwards into the *Nerves*. But the
35 Opposers of this ancient and solid Opinion are very simple and
careless.

        5. That of the *Ligature* proves nothing. For though the
Nerve betwixt the *Ligature* and the Finger be well enough
stored with Spirits, yet the *Centre of Perception* being not there,
40 and there being an interruption and division betwixt the Spirits
that are continued to their Common *Sensorium*, and these on
the other side of the *Ligature*; 'tis no more wonder that we feel

nothing on this side of the *Ligature*, then that we see nothing in our neighbour's garden when a wall is betwixt, though the Sun shine clearly on both sides of the wall.

6. We see how invalid their Arguments are against this received Opinion of almost all both Physicians and Philosophers: It is needless to produce any for the confirmation of it; Those which we have made use of for proving that the *Spirits* are the *immediate Instrument* of the Soul, being of equal force most of them to conclude their existence in the Body.

And yet for an overplus I will not much care to cast in a brief suggestion of the use of the *Lungs*, which the best Physicians and Anatomists adjudge to be chiefly for conveighing prepared aire to the Heart; as also of the *Rete mirabile* and *Plexus Choroides*, whose bare situation discover their use, that they may more plentifully evaporate the thinner and more agile particles of the Blood into the Ventricles of the Brain.

The *Diastole* also of the *Brain* keeping time with the *Pulse* of the *Heart*, is a manifest indication what a vehement steam of *Spirits*, by the direct and short passage of the *Arteriae Carotides*, are carried thither. For if one part of the Blood be more fiery and subtile then another, it will be sure to reach the Head. From whence considering the sponginess and laxness of the Brain, and thinness of the Tunicles in the little Arteries that are there; it will follow by Mechanical necessity that the Ventricles thereof will be filled with that καθαρὴ καὶ φωτοειδὴς περιουσία ἐκ διακρίσεως τοῦ αἵματος, which Hippocrates so fitly describes, though he fancy the Seat of it in an unfitting place.

But the purest of these Spirits being in the fourth Ventricle, as *Bartholine* and others have judiciously concluded, it follows plainly from wnat has been alledged, *That the Common* Sensorium *is to be placed in the midst of these purer Spirits of the fourth Ventricle of the Brain.*

Chap. X.

I. *That the Soul is not confined to the Common* Sensorium. *2. The first Argument from the* Plastick *power of the Soul. 3. Which is confirme d from the gradual dignity of the Soul' s Faculties, of which this* Plastick *is the lowest; 4. External*

Sensation *the next*; 5. *After that,* Imagination, *and then* Reason.
6. *The second Argument from* Passions *and* Sympathies *in*
Animals. 7. *An illustration of the manner of Natural Magick.* 8.
The third Argument from the Perception of Pain *in the exteriour*
5   *parts of the Body.* 9. *The fourth and last from the nature of*
Sight.

  I. We are now at leisure to resume the two remaining
Enquiries the forme whereof is, whether the Soul be so in this
10   *fourth Ventricle,* that it is essentially no where else in the Body,
or whether it be spread out into all the Members. *Regius* would
coup it up in the *Conarion,* which he believes to be the Common
Sensorium, and so by consequence it should be confined to the
fourth Ventricle, and not expatiate at all thence, supposing that
15   the Seat of *Common Sense.*   The reason of this conceit of his is
this, That whatever is in the rest of the Body, may come to
pass by powers merely *Mechanical*; wherein he does very
superstitiously tread in the footsteps of his Master *Des-Cartes.*
But for my own part, I cannot but dissent, I finding in neither
20   any sufficient grounds of so novel an opinion, but rather
apparent reasons to the contrary.
  2. As first, the *Frame of the Body,* of which I think most
reasonable to conclude the *Soul* her self to be the more
particular *Architect* (for I will not wholly reject *Plotinus* his
25   opinion;) and that the *Plastick power* resides in her, as also in
the Souls of Brute animals, as very learned and worthy
Writers have determined. That the *Fabrick of the Body* is out
of the concurse of *Atomes,* is a mere precarious Opinion,
without any ground or reason. For *Sense* does not discover any
30   such thing, the first rudiments of life being out of some *liquid*
homogeneal Matter; and it is against *Reason,* that the tumbling
of *Atomes* or corporeal particles should produce such exquisite
frames of creatures, wherein the acutest wit is not able to find
any thing inept, but all done exquisitely well every where,
35   where the foulness and coursness of *Matter* has not been in
fault.
  That God is not the *immediate Maker* of these *Bodies,* the
particular miscarriages demonstrate. For there is no Matter so
perverse and stubborn but his *Omnipotency* could tame; whence
40   there would be no Defects nor Monstrosities in the generation
of Animals.

Nor is it so congruous to admit, that the *Plastick* faculty of the *Soul of the World* is the *sole* contriver of these Fabricks of particular Creatures, (though I will not deny but she may give some rude preparative strokes towards Efformation;) but that in every *particular* World, such as Man is especially, his own 5 Soul is the peculiar and most perfective Architect thereof, as the Soul of the World is of it. For this *vital* Fabrication is not as in *artificial* Architecture, when an external person acts upon Matter; but implies a more particular and near union with that Matter it thus intrinsecally shapes out and organizes. And 10 what ought to have a more particular and close union with our Bodies then our Souls themselves?

My opinion is therefore, That the Soul, which is a *Spirit*, and therefore *contractible* and *dilatable*, begins within less compass at first in Organizing the fitly-prepared Matter, and so 15 bears it self on in the same tenour of work till the Bo*dy has attained its full* growth; and that the Soul *dilates* it self in the dilating of the Body, and so possesses it through all the members thereof.

3. The congruity of this Truth will further discover it self, 20 if we consider the nature of the Faculties of the Soul (of which you may read more fully in *Enthusiasmus Triumphatus*) in what a *natural graduality* they arise till they come to the *most free* of all. The *deepest* or *lowest* is this *Plastick power* we have already spoke of, in virtue whereof is continued that perpetual 25 *Systole* and *Diastole* of the *Heart*, as I am more prone to think then that it is merely Mechanical, as also that *Respiration* that is performed without the command of our Will: For the *Libration* or *Reciprocation* of the *Spirits* in the *Tensility* of the *Muscles* would not be so perpetual, but cease in a small time, 30 did not some more mystical Principle then what is merely Mechanical give Assistance; as any one may understand by observing the insufficiency of those devices that *Henricus Regius* propounds for adequate causes of such motions in the Body, These I look upon as the *First Faculties* of the Soul, 35 which may be bounded by this general character, That the exercise of them does not at all imply so much as our *Perception*.

4. Next to these is the *Sensation of any external object*, such as *Hearing, Seeing, Feeling*, etc. All which include Perception in 40 an unresistible necessity thereof, the Object being present before us, and no external Obstacle interposing.

5. *Imagination* is more free, we being able to avoid its representations for the most part, without any external help; but it is a degree on this side *Will* and *Reason*, by which we correct and silence unallowable fancies. Thus we see how the *Faculties* of the Soul rise *by Degrees* which makes it still the more easy and credible, that the *lowest* of all is compatible to her as well as the *highest*.

6. Moreover, *Passions* and *Sympathies*, in my judgment, are more easily to be resolved into this Hypothesis of the Soul's pervading the *whole Body*, then in restraining its essential presence to *one part* thereof. For to believe that such an horrible Object as, suppose, a Bear or Tiger, by transmission of Motion from it through the Eyes of an Animal to the *Conarion*, shall so reflect thence, as to determine the Spirits into such Nerves as will streighten the Orifice of the Heart, and lessen the Pulse, and cause all other symptomes of *Fear*; seems to me little better then a mere piece of *Mechanical Credulity*. Those Motions that represent the *Species* of things, being turned this way or the other way, without any such *impetus* of Matter as should doe such feats as *Des-Cartes* speaks of in his Book of *Passions*. And that which he would give us as a pledge of this Truth is so false, that it does the more animate me to disbelieve the Theorem. For the wafting of one's hand near the Eye of a mans friend, is no sufficient proof That external Objects will necessarily and Mechanically determine the Spirits into the Muscles, no Faculty of the Soul intermedling. For if one be fully assured, or rather can keep himself from the fear of any hurt, by the wafting of his friend's Hand before his Eye, he may easily abstain from winking: But if fear surprise him, the Soul is to be entitled to the action, and not the mere *Mechanism* of the Body. Wherefore this is no proof that the *Phaenomena* of *Passions*, with their consequences, may be salved in brute Beasts by pure Mechanicks; and therefore neither in Men.

But it is evident that they arise in us *against* both our *Will* and *Appetite*. For who would bear the tortures of *Fears* and *Jealousies*, if he could avoid it? And therefore the Soul sends not nor determines the Spirits thus to her own Torture, as she resides in the Head. Whence it is plain that it is the Effect of her as she resides in the *Heart* and *Stomack*, which sympathize with the horrid representation in the Common *Sensorium*; by reason of the exquisite unity of the Soul with herself, and of the continuity of Spirits in the Body, the necessary instrument of all her Functions. And there is good reason the *Heart* and *Stomack* should be so much affected, they being the chief Seats of those Faculties that maintain the *Life* of the Body; the danger whereof is the most eminent Object of *Fear* in any 5 Animal.

7. From this Principle, I conceive that not onely the *Sympathy of parts* in one particular Subject, but of *different and distant Subjects*, may be understood: such as is betwixt the party wounded, and the Knife or Sword that wounded him, 10 besmeared with the Weapon-salve, and kept in a due temper: Which certainly is not *purely Mechanical*, but *Magical*, though not in an unlawful sense; that is to say, it is not to be resolved into *mere Matter*, of what thinness or subtilty soever you please, but into the *Unity* of the *Soul of the Universe* which is interessed 15 in all Plastick powers, and into the *Continuity of the subtile Matter*, which answers to our *Animal Spirits*. And in this sense it is that *Plotinus* sayes,that the World is ὁ μέγας γόης, *the grand* Magus or *Enchanter.*And I do not question, but that upon this score merely, without the association of any Familiar 20 Spirit, several odde things may be done, for evil as well as good. For this *Spirit of the World* has Faculties that work not by Election, but fatally or naturally, as several *Gamaieu's* we meet withall in Nature seem somewhat obscurely to subindicate. Of this Principle we shall speak more fully in its 25 due place.

8. But we have yet a more clear discovery, that our Soul is *not confined to any one part* of the Head, but possesses the whole Body, from the *Perception of Pain* in the parts thereof: For it is plainly impossible that so high a torture as is felt but 30 in the pricking of a Pin, can be communicated to the *Centre of Perception* upon a mere Mechanical account. For whether the *immediate Instrument of Sense* be the *Pith of the Nerves*, as *Des-Cartes* would have it, or whether it be the *Spirits*, as is most true; it is ridiculous to think, that by the forcible parting 35 of what was joyned together at ease (when this case is not communicated to either the *Spirits*, or *Pith of the Nerves*, from the place of the Puncture, to the very seat of Common Sense) the Soul there seated should feel so smart a torment, unless that her very Essence did reach to the part where the *pain* is 40 felt to be. For then the reason of this is plain, that it is the *Unity of Soul* possessing the whole Body, and the *Continuity of*

Spirits that is the cause thereof.

And it is no wonder, if the continuation and natural composure of the Spirits be Rest and Ease to the Soul, that a violent disjoyning and bruising of them, and baring the Soul of
5   them, as I may so speak, should cause a very harsh and torturous sense in the *Centre of Perception*. This Argument bears undeniable Evidence with it, if we do but consider the fuzziness of the *Pith of the Nerves*, and the fluidity of the *Spirits*, and what little stress or crowding so small a thing as a
10   Pin or Needle can make in such soft and liquid Matter. The consideration whereof ought eternally to silence their scrupulosity who are so amused that the harms of the Body should be the pains of the Soul, the Body in the mean time being not pained. For this is infinitely more conceivable, then
15   that some par of *Matter* in my Head should feel pain by a prick in my finger, that Matter in my Head being not at all incommodated, if so much as in the least measure moved thereby; and yet that *Perception* is within the *Head* alone, has been abundantly demonstrated.

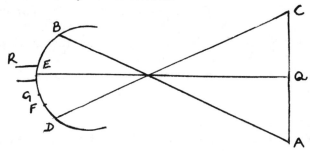

20   9. Lastly, unless the very Essence of the Soul reach from the Common *Sensorium* to the *Eye*, there will be very great difficulties how there should be so distinct a representation of any visible Object. For it is very hard to conceive that the *Colours* will not be confounded, and the bigness of the Object
25   diminished, and indeed that the image will not be quite lost before it can come to the Soul, if it be onely in the Common *Sensorium*. For it is plain, and Experience will demonstrate, that there is a very perfect Image of the Object in the bottome of the Eye, which is made by the decussation of the lines of
30   Motion from it, thus: The Line A B from the Object A C bears against that point in the bottome of the Eye in B, and the line C D against the point D; whereby C and A are felt in their

place, and in such a distance as they are in the Object C A: and
so of all the lines which come from the Object C A into the
bottome of the Eye B D. From whence the Object is felt in
such a length and breadth as it is capable of being perceived in
at such a distance from the Eye. And as the Motion that is   5
conveyed from A to B and from C to D is felt there; so the
modification of it, whereby the Object in those parts may seem
red, yellow, green, or any other colour, is felt there also.
Whence it is plain that there will be an exquisite impression,
according to all circumstances of the Object, in the bottome of   10
the Eye: so that if the Soul receive it there, and convey it
thence to her *Centre of Perception* intirely in the same
circumstances, the representation will be compleat.

But if the Soul be not there, but the conveyance thereof
must be left to the bare laws of *Matter*, the Image will be much   15
depraved, or lost, before it can come to the Common *Sensorium*.
For this Motion must be propagated from B and D till it come
to the hole E, and so pass into the Optick Nerve, to be carried
into the Brain, and so to the Seat of Common Sense: but
betwixt B and E, or D and E, there may be the depainture of   20
sundry colours, whence it will be necessary that F be tinctured
with the colour D, and G with the colour of both D and F; & so
of the rest of the Lines drawn from the Object to the Eye: so
that all their *Colours* would be blended before they came to E.
Now at that harsh flexure at E, where the visual Line is as   25
crooked as B E R, according to the experiments of *Reflexion* and
Refraction, the breadth or length of the Object C A would be
lost. For we must needs expect, that as it is in *Reflexions* and
Refractions, where the Object will appear in that Line that
immediately conveys the sense of it; so here it must be also,   30
and therefore the point C and A must appear about Q, whence
the Object will shrivel up in a manner into nothing.

And suppose it might appear in some tolerable latitude, for
all this, the *Brain* being an *opake* substance, so soon as the
Motion comes thither, it would be so either changed or lost, that   35
the Image could not pass the opacity of it in any splendour or
entireness. Wherefore I do not doubt but that the Image which
the Soul perceives is that in the Eye, and not any other
corporeally producted to the inside of the Brain (where *Colour*
and *Figure* would be so strangely depraved, if not quite   40
obliterated) I mean it is the concurse of the *lucid Spirits* in the
bottome of the Eye, with the outward Light conveyed through

the Humours thereof (which is the best sense of the Platonick συναύγεια that *Plutarch* speaks of) wherein the great Mystery of Sight consists.

5

Chap. XI.

I. *That neither the Soul without the Spirits, nor the Spirits
10 without presence of the Soul in the Organ, are sufficient Causes of*
Sensation. 2. *A brief declaration how* Sensation *is made.* 3.
How Imagination. 4. *Of* Reason *and* Memory, *and whether
there be any Marks in the Brain.* 5. *That the Spirits are the
immediate Instrument of the Soul in* Memory *also; and how*
15 Memory *arises*; 6. *As also* Forgetfulness. 7. *How*
Spontaneous Motion *is performed.* 8. *How we walk, sing, and
play, though thinking of something else.* 9. *That though the
Spirits be not alike fine every where, yet the* Sensiferous
Impression *will pass to the Common* Sensorium. 10. *That there
20 is an* Heterogeneity *in the very Soul her self; and what it is in
her we call the* Root, *the* Centre, *and the* Eye; *and what the*
Rayes *and* Branches. 11. *That the sober and allowable Distribution of her into Parts, is into* Perceptive *and* Plastick.

25   I. *After our evincing that the Soul is not confined to the
Common Sensorium,* but does essentially reach all the Organs
of the Body; it will be more easy to determine the *Nature of
Sensation* & other Operations we mentioned, which is the third
thing we proposed. For we have already demonstrated these
30 two things of main consequence; *That the Spirits are not
sufficient of themselves for these Functions; nor the Soul of her
self, without the assistance of the Spirits*: as is plain in the
interception or disjunction of the *Spirits* by *Ligature* or
Obstruction; whence it is, that *Blindness* sometimes happens
35 merely for that the Optick Nerve is obstructed.
          2. Wherefore briefly to dispatch our third Querie; I say in
general, That *Sensation* is made by the arrival of motion from
the Object to the Organ; Where it is received in all the
circumstances we perceive it in, and conveyed by virtue of the
40 Soul's presence there, assisted by her immediate Instrument
the *Spirits*, by virtue of whose continuity to those in the
Common *Sensorium*, the Image or Impress of every Object is

faithfully transmitted thither.

  3. As for *Imagination*, there is no question but that Function is mainly exercised in the chief seat of the Soul, those purer Animal Spirits in the fourth Ventricle of the Brain. I speak especially of *that Imagination which is most free*, such as 5 we use in *Romantick Inventions*, or such as accompany the *more severe Meditations* and *Disquisitions* in *Philosophy*, or any other *Intellectual* entertainments. For *Fasting, fresh Aire, moderate Wine*, and all things that tend to an handsome supply and depuration of the *Spirits*, make our thoughts more free, subtile, 10 and clear.

  4. *Reason* is so involved together with *Imagination*, that we need say nothing of it apart by it self. *Memory* is a Faculty of a more peculiar consideration; and if the *Pith of the Brain* contribute to the Functions of any power of the Mind, (more 15 then by conserving the *Animal Spirits*) it is to this. But that the *Brain* should be stored with *distinct images* (whether they consist of the Flexures of the supposed *Fibrillae* or the orderly puncture of Pores, or in a continued modified Motion of the parts thereof, some in this manner, and others in that) is a 20 thing, as I have already proved, utterly impossible.

  If there be any *Marks* in it, it must be a kind of *Brachygraphie* some small dots here and there standing for the recovering to Memory a series of things that would fill, it may be, many sheets of paper to write them at large. As if a man 25 should tie a string about a friends finger to remember a business, that a whole daies discourse, it may be, was but little enough to give him full instructions in. From whence it is plain that the *Memory* is in the *Soul*, and not in the *Brain*. And if she do make any such *Marks* as we speak of, she having no 30 perception of them distinct from the representation of those things which they are to re-mind her of, she must not make them by any *Cognitive power* but by some such as is Analogous to her *Plastick Faculty* of organizing the Body, where she acts and perceives it not.   35

  5. But whether the Soul act thus or no upon the *Brain* is a matter of uncertain determination; nor can it be demonstrated by any experiment that I know. And therefore if we will contain our selves within the capacities of the *Spirits*, which I have so often affirmed to be the immediate Instrument of the 40 Soul in all her operations, that Position will be more unexceptionable. And truly I do not understand but that they

and the Soul together will perform all the Functions of *Memory* that we are conscious to our selves of.

    Wherefore I shall conclude that *Memory* consists in this, That the Soul has acquired a greater *Promptitude* to think of
5   this or that Phantasm, with the circumstances thereof, which were raised in her upon some occasion. Which *Promptitude* is acquired by either the *often representation* of the same Phantasme to her; or else by *a more vivid impress* of it from its *novelty, excellency, mischievousness*, or some such like condition
10 that at once will pierce the Soul with an extraordinary resentment; or finally by *voluntary attention*, when she very carefully and on set purpose imprints the *Idea* as deeply as she can into her inward Sense. This *Promptitude* to think on such an *Idea* will lessen in time, and be so quite spent, that when
15 the same *Idea* is represented again to the Soul, she cannot tell that ever she saw it before.

    But before this inclination thereto be quite gone, upon this proneness to return into the same conception, with the circumstances, the *Relative Sense* of having seen it before (
20 which we call *Memory*) does necessarily emerge upon a fresh representation of the Object.

    6. But *Forgetfulness* arises either out of mere *Desuetude* of thinking on such an Object, or on others that are linked in with it, in such a Series as would represent it as past, and so
25 make it a proper Object of *Memory*. Or else for that the *Spirits*, which the Soul uses in all her Functions, be not in a due temper; which may arise from overmuch *Coolness*, or *Waterishness in the Head*, to which alone *Sennertus* ascribes *obliviousness*.

30   7. The last thing we are to consider is *Spontaneous Motion*. Which that it is performed by the continuation of the *Spirits* from the Seat of Common Sense to the *Muscles*, which is the gross Engine of *Motion* is out of doubt. The manner how it is, we partly feel and see; that is to say, we find in our selves
35 a power, at our own pleasure to *move* this or the other member with very great force, and that the *Muscle swels* that *moves* the part; which is a plain indication of influx of *Spirits*, thither directed or there guided by our mere Will: a thing admirable to consider, and worth our most serious meditation.

40   That this direction of the impresse of *Motion* is made by our mere Will, and Imagination of doing so we know and feel it so intimately, that we can be of nothing more sure. That there

is some fluid and subtile Matter, which we ordinarily call
Spirits, directed into the *Muscle* that *moves* the *Member*, its
swelling does evidence to our sight; as also the experience, that
moderate use of *Wine* which supplies Spirits *apace* will make
this motion the more strong.   5

As for the manner, whether there be any such *Valvulae* or
no in the *Nerve*, common to the opposite *Muscles*, as also in
those that are proper to each, it is not material. This great
priviledge of our Soul's *directing the motion of Matter thus*, is
wonderfull enough in either Hypothesis. But I look upon the 10
Fibrous parts of the *Muscle* as the main Engine of motion;
which the Soul moistning with that subtile liquor of the *Animal
Spirits*, makes them swell and shrink, like Lute-strings in rainy
weather: And in this chiefly consists that notable strength of
our Limbs in *Spontaneous motion*. But for those conceived 15
Valvulae that Experience has not found out yet, nor sufficient
Reason, they are to wait for admission till they bring better
evidence. For the presence of the *Animal Spirits* in this *Fibrous
flesh*, and the command of the Soul to move, is sufficient to
salve all *Phaenomena* of this kind.   For upon the Will 20
conceived in the Common *Sensorium*, that part of the Soul that
resides in the *Muscles*, by a power near akin to that by which
she *made* the Body and the Organs thereof, *guides* the Spirits
into such Pores and parts as is most requisite for the shewing
the *use* of this excellent Fabrick.   25

8. And in virtue of some such power as this do we so easily
walk, though we think not of it, as also *breath*, and *sing*, and
play on the Lute, though our Mindes be taken up with
something else. For Custome is another Nature: and though
the *Animal Spirits*, as being merely corporeal, cannot be 30
capable of any habits; yet the Soul, even in that part thereof
that is not *Cognitive*, may, and therefore may move the Body,
though *Cogitation* cease; provided the members be well
replenished with *Spirits*, whose assistance in naturall motions
of Animals is so great, that their *Heads* being taken off, their 35
Body for a long time will move as before: as *Chalcidius* relates
of *Wasps* and *Hornets*, who will fly about, and use their wings,
a good part of an houre after they have lost their Heads: which
is to be imputed to the residence of their Soul in them still, and
the intireness of the *Animal Spirits*, not easily evaporating 40
through their crustaceous Bodies.

For it is but a vulgar conceit to think, that the *Head* being taken off, the Soul must presently fly out, like a Bird out of a Basket, when the Lid is lifted up. For the whole World is as much throng'd with *Body*, as where she is; and that *Tye* of the
5 *Spirits* as yet not being lost, it is a greater engagement to her to be there then any where else. This motion therefore in the *Wasp*, that is so perfect and durable, I hold to be *Vital*; but that in the parts of dismembred creatures, that are less perfect, may be usually *Mechanical*.
10 9. We have now, so far forth as it is requisite for our design, considered the *Nature and Functions of the Soul*; and have plainly demonstrated, That she is a Substance distinct from the Body, and that her very Essence is spread throughout all the Organs thereof: as also that the generall
15 Instrument of all her Operations is the subtile *Spirits*; which though they be not in like quantity and sincerity every where, yet they make all the Body so pervious to the impresses of Objects upon the external Organs, that like Lightning they pass to the Common *Sensorium*. For it is not necessary that the
20 *Medium* be so fire and tenuious as the Matter where the most subtile motion begins. Whence Light passes both Aire and Water, though Aire alone is not sufficient for such a motion as Light, and Water almost uncapable of being the Seat of the Fountain thereof. This may serve to illustrate the passage of
25 Sense from the Membranes (or in what other seat soever the Spirits are most subtile and lucid) through thicker places of the Body to the very *Centre of Perception*.
        10. Lastly, we have discovered as kind of *Heterogeneity* in the Soul; and that she is not of the same power every where.
30 For her *Centre of Perception* is confined to the *Fourth Ventricle of the Brain*; and if the *Sensiferous Motions* we speak of be not faithfully conducted thither, we have no knowledge of the Object. That part therefore of the Soul is to be looked upon as most precious; and she not being an independent Mass, as
35 *Matter* is, but one part resulting from another, that which is the noblest is in all reason to ba deemed the cause of the rest. For which reason (as *Synesius* calls God, on whom all things depend, ῥιζῶν ῥίζαν. so) I think *this Part* may be called the Root of the Soul.
40   Which apprehension of ours will seem the less strange, if we consider that from the highest *Life*, viz. the *Deity*,there does result that which has no *Life* nor *Sense* at all, to wit the *stupid*

Matter. Wherefore in very good Analogie we may admit, that that precious part of the Soul in which resides *Perception, Sense* and *Understanding* may send forth such an *Essential Emanation from it self* as is utterly devoid of all *Sense* and *Perception*; which you may call, if you will, *the Exteriour* 5 *branches of the Soul,* or *the Rayes of the Soul,* if you call that nobler and diviner part the *Centre*; which may very well merit also the appellation of the *Eye of the Soul,* all the rest of its parts being but mere darkness without it. In which, like another *Cyclops,* it will resemble the World we live in, whose 10 one Eye is conspicuous to all that behold the light.

11. But to leave such lusorious Considerations, that rather gratifie our Fancy then satisfy our severer Faculties; we shall content our selves hereafter, from those two notorious Powers, and so perfectly different, which Philosophers acknowledge in 15 the Soul, (to wit, *Perception* and *Organization,*) onely to term that more noble part of her in the Common *Sensorium,* the *Perceptive,* and all the rest the *Plastick* part of the Soul

20

Chap. XII.

I. *An Answer to an Objection, That our Arguments will as well prove the Immortality of the Souls of Brutes as of Men.* 2. 25 *Another objection inferring the Praeexistence of Brutes Souls, and consequently of ours.* 3. *The first Answer to the Objection.* 4. *The second Answer consisting of four parts.* 5. *First, That the Hypothesis of* Praeexistence *is more agreeable to Reason then any other Hypothesis.* 6. *And not onely so, but that it is very* 30 *solid in it self.* 7. *That the Wisdome and Goodness of God argue the truth thereof.* 8. *As also the face of Providence in the World.* 9. *The second part of the second Answer, That the* Praeexistence of the Soul *has the suffrage of all Philosophers in all Ages, that held it* Incorporeal. 10. *That the* 35 Gymnosophists *of Aegpt, the* Indian Brachmans, *the* Persian Magi, *and all the learned of the* Jews *were of this Opinion.* 11. *A Catalogue of particular famous persons that held the same.* 12. *That* Aristotle *was also of the same mind.* 13. *Another more clear place in* Aristotle *to this purpose, with Sennertus his* 40 *Interpretation.* 14. *An Answer to an Evasion of that Interpretation.* 15. *The last and clearest place of all out of*

Aristotle's *Writings*.

1. Having thus discovered the Nature of the Soul, and that she is a *Substance distinct from the Body*; I should be in readiness to treat of her *Separation from it*, did I not think my self obliged first, to answer an envious Objection cast in our way, whereby they would make us believe, That the Arguments which we have used, though they be no less then Demonstration, are mere Sophisms, because some of them, and those of not the least validity, prove what is very absurd and false, *viz*, That the *Souls of Brutes* also are *Substances Incorporeal*, distinct from the Body: from whence it will follow, that they are *Immortal*. But to this I have answered already in the *Appendix to my Antidote*, and in brief concluded, That they are properly *no more Immortal* then the *stupid Matter*, which *never perishes*, and that out of a *terrestrial* Body they may have no more sense then it. For all these things are as it pleases the first Creatour of them.

2. To this they perversely reply, That if the Souls of Brutes subsist after death, and are then sensless and unactive, it will necessarily follow that they must come into Bodies again. For it is very ridiculous to think that these Souls, having a Being yet in the world, and wanting nothing but fitly-prepared *Matter* to put them in a capacity of living again, should be alwaies neglected, and never brought into play, but that new ones should be daily created in their stead: for those innumerable Myriads of Souls would lie useless in the Univefse the number still increasing even to infinity. But if they come into Bodies again, it is evident that they *praeexist*: and if the Souls of Brutes *praeexist*, then certainly the Souls of Men doe so too. Which is an Opinion so wild and extravagant, that a wry mouth and a loud laughter (*the Argument that every Fool is able to use*) is sufficient to silence it and dash it out of countenance. No *wise man* can ever harbour such a conceit as this, which every *Idiot* is able to confute by consulting but with his own *Memory*. For he is sure, if he had been before, he could *remember* something of that life past. Besides the unconceivableness of the Approach and Entrance of these *praeexistent* Souls into the *Matter* that they are to actuate.

3. To this may be answered two things. The first, That though indeed it cannot be well denied, but that the concession of the *Praeexistence* of the Souls of Brutes is a very fair

introduction to the belief of the *Praeexistence* of the Souls of
Men also; yet the sequel is not at all *necessary*, but one may be
without the other.

4. The second is this, That if the sequel were granted, no
Absurdity can be detected from thence in Reason, if the   5
prejudices of Education, and the blind suggestion of
unconcerned Faculties, that have no right to vote here be laid
aside. To speak more explicitely, I say, This consequence of
our Soul's *Praeexistence* is more agreeable to Reason then any
other Hypothesis whatever; Has been received by the most   10
learned Philosophers of all Ages, there being scarce any of
them that held the Soul of man *Immortal* upon the mere light of
Nature and Reason, but asserted also her *Praeexisttence*; That
Memory is no fit Judge to appeal to in this Controversie; and
lastly, That *Traduction* and *Creation* are as intricate and uncon-   15
ceivable as this opposed Opinion.

5. I shall make all these four parts of my Answer good in
order. The truth of the first we shall understand, if we
compare it with those Opinions that stand in competition with
it, which are but two that are considerable. The one is of those   20
that say the Soul is *ex traduce*; the other of those that say it is
created, upon occasion. The first Opinion is a plain
contradiction to the *Notion* of a Soul which is a *Spirit*, and
therefore of an *Indivisible*, that is, of an *Indiscerpible*, Essence.
The second Opinion implies both an Indignity to the Majesty of   25
God, (in making him the chief assistant and actour in the
highest, freest, and most particular way that the Divinity can
be conceived to act, in, those abominable crimes of Whoredome,
Adultery, Incest, nay Buggery it self, by supplying those foul
coitions with new created Souls for the purpose:) and also an   30
injury to the Souls themselves; that they being ever thus
created by the immediate hand of God, and therefore pure,
innocent and immaculate, should be imprisoned in unclean,
diseased and disordered Bodies, where very many of them
seem to be so fatally overmastered, and in such an utter   35
incapacity of closing with what is good and vertuous, that they
must needs be adjudged to that extreme calamity which attends
all those that forget God. Wherefore these two Opinions being
so incongruous, what is there left that can seem probable, but
the *Praeexistency* of the Soul.   40

6. But I shall not press the *Reasonableness* of this Opinion onely from comparing it with others, but also from the concinnity that is to be found in it self. For as it is no greater wonder that every *particular* mans Soul that lives now upon Earth should be *à mundo condito*, then the *particular Matter of their Bodies should,* (Which has haply undergone many Millions of Alterations and Modifications, before it lighted into such a contexture as to prove the entire Body of any one person in the world, has been in places unimaginably distant, is filed, it may be, through the triangular passages of as many *Vortices* as we see Stars in a clear frosty night, and has shone once as bright as the Sun (as the *Cartesian* Hypothesis would have all the Earth to have done) insomuch that we eat, and drink, and cloath our selves with that which was once pure Light and Flame:) So, that *de facto* they do bear the same date with the Creation of the World, that unavoidable certainty of the *Praeexistence* of the Souls of Brutes does, according to the very concession of our Adversaries, fairly insinuate.

7. But this is not all. Both the *Attributes* of God, and Face of things in the world, out of which his *Providence* is not to be excluded, are very strong Demonstrations thereof to Reason unprejudiced. For first, If it be *good* for the Souls of men to be at all, the *sooner* they are, the *better*. But we are most certain that the *Wisdome* and *Goodness* of God will doe that which is the *best*; and therefore if they can enjoy themselves before they come into these *Terrestrial* Bodies, (it being better for them to enjoy themselves then not,) they must be before they come into these Bodies; that is, they must be in a capacity of enjoying themselves without them for long periods of time, before they appeared here in this Age of the World. For nothing hinders but that they may live *before* they come into the Body, as well as they may *after* their going out of it: the latter whereof is acknowledged even by them that deny the *Praeexistence*.

Wherefore the *Praeexistence* of Souls is a necessary result of the *Wisdome* and *Goodness* of God, who can no more fail to doe that which is *best*, then he can to *understand it*: for otherwise his *Wisdome* would *exceed* his *Benignity*; nay there would be less hold to be taken of *His Goodness*, then of the *Bounty* of a very benign and *good man*, who, we may be well assured, will slip no opportunity of *doing good* that lies in his power, especially if it be neither *damage* nor *trouble* to him; both which hinderances are incompetible to the Deity.

8. Again, The face of *Providence* in the World seems very
much to sult with this Opinion; there being not any so natural
and easie account to be given of those things that seem the
most harsh in the affairs of men, as from this Hypothesis, *That
their Souls did once subsist in some other state; where, in several* 5
*manners and degrees, they they forfeited the favour of their
Creatour. And so according to that just Nemesis that He has
interwoven in the constitution of the Universe and of their own
Natures, they undergoe several calamities and asperities of
Fortune, and sad drudgeries of Fate, as a punishment inflicted,* 10
*or a disease contracted from the several Obliquities of their
Apostasie.* Which key is not onely able to unlock that recondite
mystery of some particular mens almost fatal aversness from
all Religion and Vertue, their stupidity and dumbness and even
invincible slowness to these things from their very childhood, 15
and their uncorrigible propension to all manner of Vice; but also
of that squalid forlornness and brutish Barbarity that whole
Nations for many Ages have layen under, and many do stil lie
under at this very day. Which sad Scene of things must needs
exceedingly cloud and obscure the waies of *Divine Providence,* 20
and make them utterly unintelligible; unless some light be let in
from the present Hypothesis we speak of.

It is plain therefore that there are very weighty Reasons
may be found out to conclude *the Praeexistence of Souls.* And
therefore this Opinion being so demonstrable from this Faculty, 25
and there being no other that can contradict it, (for that the
verdict of *Memory* in this case is invalid I shall prove anon) we
are according to the Light of Nature undoubtedly to conclude,
That the Souls of Men do praeexist, by Axiome 5.

9. And as this Hypothesis is *Rational* in it self, so has it 30
also gained the suffrage of all Philosophers of all Ages, of any
note, that have held the Soul of Man *Incorporeal* and *Immortal.*
And therefore I am not at all sollicitous what either the
Epicureans or *Stoicks* held concerning this matter; this contest
being betwixt those onely that agree on this Truth, *That the* 35
Soul is a Substance Immaterial. And such amongst the
Philosophers as held it so, did unanimously agree *That it does
praeexist.* This is so plain, that it is enough onely to make this
challenge; every one in the search will satisfie himself of the
Truth thereof. I shall only adde, for the better countenance of 40
the business, some few Instances herein, as a pledge of the
Truth of my general Conclusion. Let us cast our Eye therefore

into what corner of the World we will, that has been famous for *Wisdome* and Literature, and the *wisest* of those Nations you shall find the Assertours of this Opinion.

5
10. In Egypt, that ancient Nurse of all hidden Sciences, that this Opinion was in vogue amongst the wise men there, those fragments of *Trismegist* do sufficiently witness. For though there may be suspected some fraud and corruption in several passages in that Book, in reference to the interest of Christianity; yet this Opinion of the *Praeexistency of the Soul*, in
10 which Christianity did not interest it self, cannot but be judged, from the Testimony of those Writings, to have been a Branch of the *Wisdome* of that Nation: of which Opinion not onely the *Gymnosophists* and other wise men of *Egypt* were, but also the *Brachmans* of *India*, and the *Magi* of *Babylon* and *Persias*; as
15 you may plainly see by those *Oracles* that are called either *Magical* or *Chaldaical*, which *Pletho* and *Psellus* have commented upon. To these you may adde the abstruse Philosophy of the *Jews*, which they call their *Cabbala*, of which *the Soul' s Praeexistence* makes a considerable part; as all the
20 learned of the *Jews* do confess. And how naturally applicable this Theory is to those three first mysterious chapters of *Genesis*, I have, I hope, with no contemptible success, endeavoured to shew in my *Conjectura Cabbalistica*.

11. And if I should particularize in persons of this Opinion,
25 truly they are such, or so great fame for depth of Understanding and abstrusest Science, that their Testimony alone might seem sufficient to bear down any ordinary modest man into an assent to their doctrine. And in the first place, If we can believe the *Cabbala* of the *Jews*, we must assign it to
30 *Moses*, the *greatest Philosopher* certainly that ever was in the world; to whom you may adde *Zoroaster*, *Pythagoras*, *Epicharmus*, *Empedocles*, *Cebes*, *Euripides*, *Plato*, *Euclide*, *Philo*, *Virgil Marcus Cicero*, *Plotinus*, *Iamblichus*, *Proclus*, *Boethius*, *Psellus*, and severall others which it would be too long
35 to recite. And if it were fit to adde *Fathers* to *Philosophers*, we might enter into the same list *Synesius* and *Origen*:the latter of whom was surely the greatest Light and Bulwark that antient Christianity had; who, unless there had been some very great matter in it, was far from that *levity* and *vanity*, as to entertain
40 an Opinion so vulgarly slighted and neglected by other men: and the same may be said of others that were Christians, as *Boethius*, *Psellus*, and the late learned *Marsilius Ficinus*. But I

have not yet ended my Catalogue: that admirable Physician *Johannes Fernelius* is also of this perswasion, and is not content to be so himself onely, but discovers those two grand Masters of Medicine, *Hippocrates* and *Galen*, to be so too; as you may see in his *De abditis rerum causis. Cardan* also, that famous 5 Philosopher of his Age, expresly concludes, that the *Rational Soul* is both a distinct being from the *Soul of the World*, and that it does *praeexist* before it comes into the Body: and lastly *Pomponatius*, no friend to the Soul's Immortality, yet cannot but confess, that the safest way to hoid it is also therewith to 10 aknowledge her *Praeexistence.*

12. And that nothing may be wanting to shew the frivolousness of this part of the Objection, we shall also evince that *Aristotle*, that has the luck to be believed more then most Authors, was of the same opinion, in his Treatise *De Anima.* 15 Where he speaking of the necessity of the qualification of the Body that the Soul is to actuate, and blaming those that omit that consideration, saies, That they are as careless of that matter, as if it were possible that, according to the *Pythagorick fables*, any Soul might enter into any Body. Whenas every 20 Animal, as it has its proper *species*, so it is to have its peculiar *form*. But those that define otherwise παραπλήσιον λέγουσι ,saith he, ὥσπερ εἴτις φαίη τὴν τεκτονικὴν εἰς αὐλοὺς ἐνδύεσθαι δεῖ γὰρ τέχνην χρῆσθαι τοῖς ὀργάνοις. τὴν δὲ ψυχὴν τῶι σώματι. i.e. *They speak as if one should affirm that the skill of a Carpenter did* 25 *enter into a Flute or Pipe; for every Art must use its proper Instruments, and every Soul its proper Body.* Where (as *Cardan* also has observed) *Aristotle* does not find fault with the Opinion of the Soul's going out of one Body into another, (which implies their *Praeexistence*;) but that the Soul of a Beast should goe into 30 the Body of a Man, and the Soul of a Man into a Beast's Body: that is the Absurdity that *Aristotle* justly rejects, the other Opinion he seems tacitely to allow of.

13. He speaks something more plainly in his *De Generat. Animal. There are generated*, saith he, *in the Earth, and in the* 35 *moisture thereof, Plants and living Creatures; because in the Earth is the moisture, and in the moisture Spirit, and in the whole Universe an Animal warmth or heat; insomuch that in a manner all places are full of Souls*, ὥστε τρόπον τινὰ πάντα ψυχῆς εἶναι πλήρη ,*Adeo ut modo quodam omnia sint Animarum plena,* 40 as *Sennertus* interprets the place: *Aristotle* understanding by ψυχὴ. *the same that he does afterwards by* ψυχικὴ ἀρχὴ. *that*

Principle we call *Soul*, according to the nobility whereof he
asserts that Animals are more or less noble; which assertion
therefore, reaches Humane Souls as well as these of Beasts.

5 14. Nor can this Text be eluded by being so injurious to
Aristotle, as to make him to assert that there is but one Soul in
the world, because he saies ψυχῆς, not ψυχῶν. For the text
admitting of *Sennertus* his exposition as well as this other,
that which is most reasonable is to be attributed to him. Now if
his meaning was, that there is but One Soul in the World that
10 goes through all things, and makes the Universe one great
Animal, as the *Stoicks* would have it; he need not say that all
places are *in a manner* full of this Soul, but *absolutely* full of it,
as our Body is *wholly* actuated by the Soul in it. And therefore
the Sense must be, that all places indeed are *in a manner* full of
15 Souls: not that they have opportunity to actuate the *Matter*,
and shew their presence there by vital operation; but are there
dormient as to any visible energie, till *prepared Matter* engage
them to more sensible actions.

15. We will adde a third place still more clear, out of the
20 same Treatise, where he starts this very question of the
Praeexistency of Souls, of the *Sensitive* and *Rational* especially;
περὶ αἰσθητικῆς ψυχῆς καὶ περὶ νοητικῆς. whether *both kinds* do
προϋπάρχειν. *that is* praeexist, before they come into the Body,
or whether the *Rational* only: and he concludes thus, Λείπεται
25 δὲ τὸν νοῦν μόνον θύραθεν ἐπεισιέναι καὶ θεῖον εἶναι μόνον· οὐδεν
γὰρ αὐτοῦ τῆι ἐνεργείαι κοινωνεῖ σωματικὴ ἐνέργεια. i.e. *It remains
that the Rational or Intellectual Soul onely enter from without, as
being onely of a nature purely divine; with whose actions the
actions of this gross Body have no communication.* Concerning
30 which point he concludes like an Orthodox Scholar of his
excellent Master *Plato*; to whose footsteps the closer he keeps,
the less he ever wanders from the Truth. For in this very
place he does plainly profess, what many would not have him
so apartly guilty of, that the Soul of man is *Immortal*, and can
35 perform her proper Functions without the help of this
Terrestrial Body.

And thus I think I have made good the two first parts of
my Answer to the proposed Objection; and have clearly proved,
That the *Praeexistence of the Soul* is an Opinion both in it self
40 the most rational that can be maintained, and has had the
suffrage of the renownedst Philosophers in all Ages of the
World; and that therefore this Sequel from our Arguments for

the Immortality of the Soul is no discovery of any fallacy in
them.

5

Chap. XIII.

I. *The third part of the second Answer, That the forgetting of the
former state is no good Argument against the* Soule's
Praeexistence. 2. *What are the chief causes of Forgetfulness.* 3. 10
*That they all conspire, and that in the highest degree, to destroy
the memory of the other state.* 4. *That mischances and Diseases
have quite taken away the Memory of things here in this life.* 5.
*That it is impossible for the Soul to remember her former
condition without a Miracle.* 6. *The fourth part of the second* 15
*Answer, That the Entrance of a Praeexistent Soul into a Body is
as intelligible as either Creation or Traduction.*

I. As for the two last Difficulties, concerning the *Soul's*
Memory of *her former state*, and *the manner of her coming into* 20
the Body ; I hope I shall with as much ease extricate many self
here also, especially in the former. For if we consider what
things they are that either *quite take away*, or exceedingly
diminish our *Memory* in this life; we shall find the concourse of
them all, and that in a higher degree, or from stronger causes, 25
contained in our descent into this *Earthly* Body, then we can
meet with here: they none of them being so violent as to dis-
lodge us out of it.

2. Now the things that *take away our Memory* here are
chiefly these; either *The want of opportunity of being re-minded* 30
of a thing, as it happens with many, who rise confident they
slept without dreaming such a night, and yet before they go to
bed again, recover a whole Series of representations they had
in their last sleep, by something that fell out in the day,
without which it had been impossible for them to recall to mind 35
their Dream. Or else, in the second place, *Desuetude of
thinking of a matter*; whereby it comes to pass, that what we
have earnestly meditated, laboured for, and penn'd down with
our own hands when we were at School, were it not that we
saw our names written under the Exercise, we could not 40
acknowledge for ours when we are grown men. Or lastly, *Some
considerable change in the frame and temper of our Body,*

whether from some externall mischance, or from some violent
Disease, or else from old age, which is disease enough of it self:
which often do *exceedingly impair*, if not *quite take away* the
Memory, though the Soul be still in the *same* Body.

5   3. Now all these Principles of *Forgetfulness*, namely, *The
want of something to re-mind us, Desuetude of thinking*, and *an
Extraordinary change in the Body* are more eminently to be
found in the *Descent* of the Soul into these Earthly prisons, then
can happen, to her for any time of her *abode* therein. For there

10 is a greater *difference*, in all probability, betwixt that Scene of
things the Soul sees out of the Body and in it, then betwixt
what she sees *sleeping* and *waking* and the perpetuall
occursions of this present life continue a long *Desuetude* of
thinking on the former. Besides that their *Descent* hither in all

15 likelihood scarce befalls them but in their state of *Silence* and
Inactivity, in which myriads of Souls may haply be for many
Ages, as the maintainers of this Opinion may pretend, by
reason of the innumerable expirations of the *Aëreal periods of
life*, and the more narrow Lawes of *preparing Terrestrial Matter*.

20 And lastly, her coming into this *Earthly* Body is a greater and
more disadvantageous change, for the utter spoiling of the
Memory of things she was acquainted with before, then any
Mischance or *Disease* can be for the bringing upon her a
forgetfulness of what she has known in this life.

25   4. And yet that *Disease* and *Casualties* have even utterly
taken away all *memory*, is amply recorded in History. As that
Messala Corvinus forgot his own name; that one, by a blow
with a stone, forgot all his learning; another, by a fall from an
Horse, the name of his Mother and kinsfolks. A young Student

30 of *Montpelier*, by a wound, lost his Memory so, that he was
fain to be taught the letters of the Alphabet again. The like
befell a *Franciscan* after a Feaver. And *Thucydides* writes of
some, who after their recovery from that great Pestilence at
Athens, did not onely forget the names and persons of their

35 friends, but themselves too, not knowing who themselves were,
nor by what name they were called:

>   *Atque etiam quosdam cepisse obliviarerum*
>   *Cunctarum, neque se possent cognoscere ut ipsi*;

as the Poet *Lucretius* sadly sets down in his description of that
40 devouring Plague, out of the fore-named Historian.

5. Wherefore without a miracle it is impossible the Soul should *remember* any particular circumstance of her former condition, though she did really *praeexist*, and was in a capacity of acting before she came into this Body, (as *Aristotle* plainly acknowledges she was) her change being far greater by coming 5 into the Body then can ever be made while she staies in it. Which we haply shall be yet more assured of, after we have considered *the manner of her descent*, which is the last Difficulty objected.

6. I might easily decline this Controversie, by pleading 10 onely, That the *Entrance of the Soul into the Body*, supposing her *Praeexistence*, is as intelligible as in those other two wayes, of *Creation* and *Traduction*. For how this *newly-created* Soul is *infused* by God, no man Knows; nor how, if it be *traducted* from the Parents, both their Souls contribute to the making up a new 15 one. For if there be decision of part of the Soul of the Male, in the injection of his seed into the matrix of the Female, and part of the Female Soul to joyn with that of the Male's; besides that the decision of these parts of their Souls makes the Soul a *Discerpible essence*, it is unconceivable how these *two parts* 20 should make up *one Soul* for the Infant: a thing ridiculous at first view. But if there be no decision of any parts of the Soul, and yet the Soul of the Parent be the Cause of the Soul of the Child, it is perfectly an act of *Creation*; a thing that all sober men conclude incompetible to any particular Creature. It is 25 therefore plainly unintelligible, how any Soul should pass from the Parents into the Body of the seed of the *Foetus*, to actuate and inform it: which might be sufficient to stop the mouth of the Opposer, that pretends such great obscurities concerning the *entrance of Praeexistent Souls into their Bodies.* 30

Chap. XIV.

35

1. *The Knowledge of the difference of* Vehicles, *and the Soul's Union with them necessary for the understanding how she enters into this Earthly Body.* 2. *That though the Name of* Vehicle *be not in* Aristotle, *yet the Thing is there.* 3. *A clearing of Aristotle's notion of the Vehicle, out of the Philosopohy of* Des- 40 Cartes. 4. *A full interpretation of his Text.* 5. *That* Aristotle *makes onely two Vehicles,* Terrestrial *and* Aethereal; *which is*

more then sufficient to prove the Soul's oblivion of her former state. 6. That the ordinary Vehicle of the Soul after death is Aire. 7. The duration of the Soul in her several Vehicles. 8. That the Union of the Soul with her Vehicle does not consist in Mechanical *Congruity, but* Vital. 9. *In what* Vital congruity *of the Matter consists.* 10. *In what* Vital congruity *of the Soul consists, and how it changing,the Soul may be free from her Aiery Vehicle, without violent precipitation out of it.* 11. *Of the manner of the Descent of Souls into Earthly Bodies.* 12. *That there is so little absurdity in the* Praeexistence of Souls, *that the concession thereof can be but a very small prejudice to our Demonstrations of her Immortality.*

I. But I shall spend my time better in clearing the Opinion I here defend, then in perplexing at other that is so gross of it self, that none that throughly understand the nature of the Soul can so much as allow the possibility thereof: wherefore for the better conceiving how a *Praeexistent Soul* may enter this *Terrestrial Body,* there are two things to be enquired into; *the difference of the Vehicles of Soul,* and *the cause of their union with them.* The *Platonists* do chiefly take notice of *Three* kinds of *Vehicles, Aethereal, Aereal,* and *Terrestrial,* in every one whereof there may be several degrees of purity and impurity, which yet need not amount to a new *Species.*

2. This Notion of Vehicles, though it be discoursed of most in the School of *Plato,* yet is not altogether neglected by *Aristotle,* as appears in his *De Generat. Animal.* where, though he does not use the Name, yet he does expresly acknowledge the Thing it self: For he does plainly affirm, That every Soul partakes of a Body distinct from this organized terrestrial Body, and of a more divine nature then the Elements so called; and that as one Soul is more noble then another, so is the difference of this diviner Body; which yet is nothing else with him then that warmth or heat in the seed, τὸ ἐν τῶι σπέρματι ἐνυπάρχον τὸ καλούμενον θερμὸν. which is not Fire, but a Spirit contained in the spumeous seed, and in this Spirit a nature analogous to the Element of the Stars.

3. Of which neither *Aristotle* himself had, nor any one else can have, so explicite an apprehension as those that understand the first and second Element of *Des-Cartes;* which is the most subtile and active Body that is in the World, and is of the very same nature that the Heaven and Stars are, that is to

say, is the very Body of Light, (which is to be understood chiefly of the first Element) though so mingled with other Matter here below that it does not shine, but is the Basis of all that natural warmth in all generations, and the immediate Instrument of the Soul, when it organizeth any Matter into the figure or shape of an Animal; as I have also intimated elsewhere, when I proved, *That the Spirits are the immediate Instrument of the Soul in all Vital and Animal functions.* In which *Spirits* of necessity is contained this *Celestial* Substance, which keeps them from congealing, as it does also all other liquid bodies, and must needs be in the Pores of them; there being no *Vacuum* in the whole comprehension of Nature.

4. The full and express meaning therefore of *Aristotle's* text must be this, That in the spumeous and watry or terrene moisture of the seed is contained a Body of a more spirituous or aëreal consistency, and in this aëreal or spirituous consistency is comprehended φύσις ἀνάλογος οὖσα τῶι τῶν ἄστρων στοιχείωι, *a nature that is analogous or like to the Element of the stars,* namely that it of it self *aethereal* and *lucid.*

5. And it is this *Vehicle* that *Aristotle* seems to assert that the Soul does act in separate from the Body; as if she were ever either in this *Terrestrial* Body, or in her *Aethereal* one: which if it were true, so vast a change must needs obliterate all *Memory* of her former condition, when she is once plunged into this earthly prison. But it seems not so probable to me, that Nature admits of so great a Chasme; nor is it necessary to suppose it for this purpose: the descent of the Soul out of her *Aiery* Vehicle into this *terrestrial* Body, and besmearing moisture of the first rudiments of life, being sufficient to lull her into an eternal oblivion of whatever hapned to her in that other condition; to say nothing of her long state of *Silence* and Inactivity before her turn come to revive in an *earthly* body.

6. Wherefore not letting go that more orderly conceit of the *Platonists,* I shall make bold to assert, That the Soul may live and act in an *Aëreal* Vehicle as well as in the *Aethereal*; *and that there* are very few that arrive to that high Happiness, as to acquire a *Celestial* Vehicle immediately upon their quitting the *Terrestrial* one: that *Heavenly Chariot* necessarily carrying us in trimph to the greatest Happiness the Soul of man is capable of: which would arrive to all men indifferently, good and bad, if the parting with this *Earthly* Body would suddainly mount us into the *Heavenly.* Wherefore by a just *Nemesis* the

Souls of Men that are not very Heroically vertuous will find themselves restrained within the compass of this caliginous *Aire*, as both Reason it self will suggest, and the *Platonists* have unanimously determined.

5   7. We have competently described the difference of those *Three kinds of Vehicles*, for their *purity* and *consistency*. The *Platonists* adde to this the difference of *duration*, making some of them of that nature as to entertain the Soul a longer time in them, others a shorter. The shortest of all is that of the
10   *Terrestrial* Vehicle. In the *Aëreal* the Soul may inhabit, as they define, many ages, and in the *Aethereal* for ever.

        8. But this makes little to the clearing of the *manner of their* descent εἰς γένεσιν ,which cannot be better understood then by considering their *Union* with the Body generated, or
15   indeed with any kind of Body whatever, where the Soul is held captive, and cannot quit her self thereof by the free *imperium* of her own Imagination and Will. For what can be the cause of this cohaesion, the very Essence of the Soul being so easily penetrative of *Matter*, and the dimensions of all *Matter* being
20   alike penetrable every where? For there being no more *Body* or *Matter* in a Vessel filled with *Lead* then when it is full of *Water*, nor when full with *Water* then when with *Aire*, or what other subtiler *Body* soever that can be imagined in the Universe; it is manifest that the *Crassities* of *Matter* is every where alike, and
25   alike penetrable and passable to the Soul. And therefore it is unconceivable how her *Union* should be so with any of it, as that she should not be able at any time to glide freely from one part thereof to another as she pleases.

        It is plain therefore, that this *Union of the Soul with Matter*
30   does not arise from any such gross *Mechanical* way, as when two Bodies stick one in another by reason of any toughness and viscosity, or streight commissure of parts; but from a *congruity* of another nature, which I know not better how to term then *Vital*: which *Vital Congruity* is chiefly in the *Soul* it self, it being
35   the noblest Principle of Life; but is also in the *Matter*, and is there nothing but such modification thereof as fits the *Plastick* part of the Soul, and tempts out that Faculty into act.

        9. Not that there is any *Life* in the *Matter* with which this in the *Soul* should sympathize and unite; but it is termed *Vital*
40   because it makes the *Matter* a *congruous* Subject for the Soul to reside in, and exercise the functions of life. For that which has no *life* it self, may tie to it that which has. As some men are

said to be tied by the teeth, or tied by the ear, when they are
detained by the pleasure they are struck with from good
Musick or delicious Viands. But neither is that which they eat
alive, nor that which makes the Musick, neither the
Instrument, nor the Air that conveighs the found. For there is 5
nothing in all this but mere Matter and corporeal motion, and
yet our *vital* functions are affected thereby. Now as we see that
the *Perceptive* part of the Soul is thus vitally affected with that
which has no life in it, so it is reasonable that the *Plastick*, that
is utterly devoid of all *Perception*. And in this alone consists 10
that which we call *Vital Congruity* in the prepared Matter,
either to be organized, or already shaped into the perfect form
of an Animal.

10. And that *Vital Congruity* which is in the Soul, I mean
in the *Plastick* part thereof, is analogous to that Pleasure that 15
is perceived by the Sense, or rather to the capacity of receiving
it, when the Sense is by agreeable motions from without or in
the Body it self very much gratified, and that whether the
Mind will or no. For there are some Touches that will in their
Perception seem pleasant, whether our Judgement would have 20
them so or not. What this is to the *Perceptive* part of the Soul,
that other *Congruity of Matter* is to the *Plastick*. And therefore
that which ties the Soul and this or that Matter together, is an
unresistible and unperceptible pleasure, if I may so call it,
arising from the *congruity* of *Matter* to the *Plastick* faculty of 25
the Soul: which *Congruity in the Matter* not failing, nor that in
the Soul, the *Union* is at least as necessary as the continuation
of eating and drinking, so long as Hunger and Thirst continues,
and the Meat and Drink proves good. But either satiety in the
Stomack or some ill tast in the Meat may break the *congruity* 30
on either side, and then the action will cease with the pleasure
thereof. And upon this very account may a Soul be conceived
to quit her *Aiery* Vehicle within a certain period of Ages, as the
Platonists hold she does, without any violent precipitation of her
self out of it.   35

11. What are the *strings* or *cords* that tie the Soul to the
Body, or to what Vehicle else soever, I have declared as clearly
as I can. From which it will be easy to understand the *manner
of her descent.* For assuredly, the same *cords* or *strings* that tie
her there, may draw her thither: Where the carcass is, there 40
will the Eagles be gathered. Not that she need use her
Perceptive faculty in her descent, as Hawks and Kites by their

sight or smelling fly directly to the lure or the prey: but she
being within the *Atmosphere* (as I may so call it) of Generation,
and so her *Plastick* power being reached and toucht by such an
invisible reek, (as Birds of prey are, that smell out their food
5 at a distance;) she may be fatally carried, all *Perceptions*
ceasing in her, to that Matter that is so fit a receptacle for her
to exercise her efformative power upon. For this *Magick-
sphere*, as I may so term it, that has this power of conjuring
down Souls into *Earthly* Bodies, the nearer the Centre, the
10 virtue is the stronger; and therefore the Soul will never cease
till she has slided into the very Matter that sent out those rays
or subtile reek to allure her.

From whence it is easy to conceive that the Souls of Brutes
also, though they be not able to exercise their *Perceptive* faculty
15 out of a *Terrestrial* body, yet they may infallibly finde the way
again into the world, as often as *Matter* is fitly prepared for
generation. And this is one Hypothesis, and most intelligible to
those that are pleased so much with the opinion of those large
Sphears they conceive of *emissary Atomes.*

20 There is also another, which is the Power and Activity of
the *Spirit of Nature* or *Inferiour Soul of the World*, who is as fit
an Agent to transmit particular Souls, as she is to move the
parts of Matter. But of this hereafter.

12. What has been said is enough for the present to
25 illustrate the pretended obscurity and unconceivableness of this
Mystery. So that I have fully made good all the four parts of
my Answer to that Objection that would have supplanted the
force of many strongest Arguments for the Soul's Immortality;
and have clearly proved, That though this sequel did
30 necessarily result from them, *That the Souls both of Men and
Beasts did Praexist*, yet to unprejudiced reason there is no
Absurdity nor Inconvenience at all in the Opinion. And
therefore this Obstacle being removed, I shall the more
chearfully proceed to the demonstrating of the Soul's *actual*
35 *Separation* from the Body.

Chap. XV.

I. *What is meant by the* Separation *of the Soul, with a confutation of* Regius, *who would stop her in the dead Corps.* 2. *An Answer to those that profess themselves puzled how the Soul* 5 *can get out of the Body.* 3. *That there is a threefold* Vital Congruity *to be found in three several Subjects.* 4. *That this triple Congruity is also competible to one Subject, viz. the Soul of Man.* 5. *That upon this Hypothesis it is very intelligible how the Soul may leave the Body.* 6. *That her Union with the* Aereal 10 Vehicle *may be very suddain, and as it were in a moment.* 7. *That the Soul is actually separate from the Body, is to be proved either by* History *or* Reason. *Examples of the former kinde out of* Pliny, Herodotus, Ficinus. 8. *Whether the Ecstasie of Witches prove an actual separation of the Soul from the Body.* 9. *That* 15 *this real separation of the Soul in Ecstasie is very possible.* 10. *How the Soul may be loosned and leave the Body, and yet return thither again.* 11. *That though Reason and Will cannot in this life release the Soul from the Body, yet Passion may; and yet so that she may return again.* 12. *The peculiar power of Desire for* 20 *this purpose.* 13. *Of* Cardan's *Ecstasies, and the ointment of* Witches, *and what truth there may be in their confessions.*

I. Concerning the *actual and local Separation of the Soul from the Body*, it is manifest that it is to be understood of this 25 *Terrestrial Body*. For to be in such a separate state, as to be where no *Body* or *Matter* is, is to be out of the World: the whole Universe being so thick set with *Matter* or *Body*, that there is not to be found the least vacuity therein. The question therefore is only, whether upon death the Soul can pass from 30 the Corps into some other place. *Henricus Regius* seems to arrest her there by that *general law of Nature*, termed the *Law of Immutability*; whereby every thing is to continue in the same condition it once is in, till something else change it. But the application of this law is very grosly injust in this case. For, as 35 I have above intimated, the Union of the Soul with the Body is upon certain terms; neither is every piece of Matter fit for every Soul to unite with, as *Aristotle* of old has very solidly concluded. Wherefore that condition of the Matter being not kept, the Soul is no longer engaged to the Body. What he here 40 says for the justifying of himself, is so arbitrarious, so childish and ridiculous, that, according to the merit thereof, I shall utterly neglect it, and pass it by, not vouchsafing of it any Answer.

2. Others are much puzled in their imagination, how the Soul can get out of the Body, being imprisoned and lockt up in
5   so close a Castle. But these seem to forget both the *Nature of the Soul*, with the *tenuity of her Vehicle*, and also the *Anatomy of the Body*. For considering the *nature of the Soul* her self, and of Matter which is alike penetrable every where, the Soul can pass through solid Iron and Marble as well as through the soft
10   Air and Aether; so that the thickness of the Body is no impediment to her. Besides, her *Astral* Vehicle is of that tenuity, that it self can as easily pass the smallest pores of the Body as the Light does Glass, or the Lightning the Scabbard of a Sword without tearing or scorching of it. And lastly, whether
15   we look upon that principal seat of the *Plastick* power, of the *Heart*, or that of *Perception*, the *Brain*; when a man dies, the Soul may collect her self, and the small residue of Spirits (that may haply serve her in the inchoation of her new Vehicle) either into the Heart, whence is an easy passage into the
20   Lungs, and so out at the Mouth; or else into the Head, out of which there are more doors open then I will stand to number. These things are very easily imaginable, though as invisible as the Air, in whose element they are transacted.

3. But that they may still be more perfectly understood, I
25   shall resume again the consideration of that Faculty in the *Plastick* part of the Soul, which we call *Vital Congruity*. Which, according to the number of Vehicles, we will define to be threefold, *Terrestrial*, *Aereal*, and *Aethereal* or *Celestial*. That these *Vital Congruities* are found, some in some kinde of Spirits
30   and others in othersome, is very plain. For that the *Terrestrial* is in the Soul of Brutes and in our own is without controversie; as also that the *Aereal* in that kinde of Beings which the Ancients called Δαίμονες and lastly, that the *Heavenly* and *Aethereal* in those Spirits that Antiquity more properly called
35   Θεοὶ. as being Inhabitants of the Heavens. For that there are such *Aereal* and *Aethereal Beings* that are analogous to *Terrestrial* Animals, if we compare the nature of God with the *Phaenomena* of the world, it cannot prove less then a Demonstration.
40   For this Earth that is replenisht with living Creatures, nay put in all the Planets too that are in the world, and fancy them inhabited, they all joyned together bear not so great a

proportion to the rest of the liquid Matter of the Universe (that is in a nearer capacity of being the Vehicle of Life) as a single Cumin-seed to the Globe of the Earth. But how ridiculous a thing would it be, that all the Earth beside being neglected, onely one piece thereof, no better then the rest, nor bigger then the smallest seed, should be inhabited? The same may be said also of the compass of the Aire; and therefore it is necessary to enlarge their Territories, and confidently to pronounce there are *Aethereal Animals*, as well as *Terrestrial* and *Aereal*.

4. It is plain therefore that these three *Congruities* are to be found in several Subjects; but that which makes most to our purpose, is to finde them in one, and that in the Soul of Man. And there will be an easy intimation thereof; if we consider the vast difference of those Faculties that we are sure are in her *Perceptive* part, and how they occasionaliy emerge, and how upon the laying asleep of one, others will spring up. Neither can there be any greater difference betwixt the highest and lowest of these *Vital congruities* in the *Plastick* part, then there is betwixt the highest and lowest of those Faculties that result from the *Perceptive*. For some Perceptions are the very same with those of *Beasts*; others little inferiour to those that belong to *Angels*, as we ordinarily call them; some perfectly brutish, others purely divine: why therefore may there not reside so great a Latitude of capacities in the *Plastick* part of the Soul, as that she may have in her all those three *Vital Congruities*, whereby she may be able livingly to unite as well with the *Celestial* and *Aereal Body* as with this *Terrestrial* one? Nay, our nature being so free and multifarious as it is, it would seem a reproach to Providence, to deny this capacity of living in these several Vehicles; because that *Divine Nemesis* which is supposed to rule in the world would seem defective without this contrivance.

But without controversy, Eternal Wisdom and Justice has forecast that which is the best: and, unless we will say nothing at all, we having nothing to judge by but our own Faculties, we must say that the Forecast is according to what we, upon our most accurate search, do conceive to be the best. For there being no Envy in the Deity, as Plato somewhere has noted, it is not to be thought but that He has framed our Faculties so, that when we have rightly prepared our selves for the use of them, they will have a right correspondency with those things that are offered to them to contemplate in the world.

And truly if we had here time to consider, I do not doubt
but it might be made to appear a very rational thing, that there
should be such an *Amphibion* as the Soul of man, that had a
5   capacity (as some Creatures have to live either in the Water or
on the Earth) to change her Element, and after her abode here
in this *Terrestrial Vehicle* amongst Men and Beasts, to ascend
into the company of the *Aereal Genii*, in a Vehicle answerable
to their nature.

10   5. Supposing then this triple capacity of *Vital Congruity*
in the Soul of Man, the manner how she may leave this Body is
very intelligible.   For the Bodies fitness of temper to retain the
Soul being lost in Death, the lower *Vital Congruity* in the Soul
looseth its Object, and consequently its Operation.   And
15   therefore as the letting goe one thought in the *Perceptive part* of
the Soul is the bringing up another; so the ceasing of one *Vital
Congruity* is the wakening of another, if there be an Object, or
Subject, ready to entertain it; as certainly there is, partly in
the Body, but mainly without it.   For there is a *vital Aire* that
20   pervades all this lower world, which is continued with the life of
all things, and is the chiefest Principle thereof.   Whence *Theon*
in his *Scholia* upon *Aratus* interprets that Hemistich,

...τοῦ γὰρ καὶ γένος ἐσμὲν.

in a secondary meaning as spoken of the *Aire*, which he calls
25   τὸν Δία or τὸν Ζῆνα τὸν φυσικὸν, the *natural Jupiter*, in whom,
in an inferiour Sense, we may be said *to live, and move, and
have our Being*: for without *Aire*, neither Fishes, Fowls, nor
Beasts can subsist, it administring the most immediate matter
of life unto them, by seeding and refreshing their Animal
30   Spirits.

Wherefore upon the cessation of the lowest *Vital
Congruity*, that *Aereal* capacity awakening into Act, and finding
so fit Matter everywhere to imploy her self upon, the Soul will
not fail to leave the Body; either upon choice, by the power of
35   her own Imagination and Will; or else (supposing the very
worst that can happen) by a natural kinde of Attraction, or
Transvection, she being her self, in that stound and confusion
that accompanies Death, utterly unsensible of all things.

For the Aire without being more *wholesome* and *vital* then
40   in the corrupt caverns of the dead Body, and yet there being a
continuation thereof with that without; it is as easy to
understand how (that Principle of joyning therewith in the

Plastick part of the Soul being once excited) she will naturally glide out of the Body into the free *Aire*, as how the Fire will ascend upwards, or a Stone fall downwards: for neither are the motions of these merely Mechanical, but vital or Magical, that cannot be resolved into *mere Matter*, as I shall demonstrate 5 in my Third Book.

6. And being once recovered into this vast Ooean of Life, and *sensible Spirit of the world*, so full of enlivening Balsame; it will be no wonder if the Soul suddainly regain the use of her *Perceptive* faculty, being, as it were in a moment, regenerate 10 into a natural power of Life and Motion, by so happy a concurse of rightly-prepared Matter for her *Plastick* part vitally to unite withall. For grosser generations are performed in almost as inconsiderable a space of time; if those Histories be true, of extemporary Salads, sown and gathered not many 15 hours before the meal they are eaten at: and of the suddain ingendring of Frogs upon the fall of rain, whole swarms whereof, that had no Being before, have appeared with perfect shape and liveliness in the space of half an houre, after some more unctuous droppings upon the dry ground; as I find not 20 onely recited out of *Fallopius*, *Scaliger*, and others, but have been certainly my self informed of it by them that have been eye-witnesses thereof; as *Vaninus* also professes himself to have been by his friend *Johannes Ginochius*, who told him for a certain, that in the month of *July* he saw with his own eyes a 25 drop of rain suddenly turned into a Frog. By such examples as these it is evident, that the reason why Life is so long a compleating in Terrestrial generations, is only the sluggishness of the Matter the *Plastick* power works upon. Wherefore a Soul once united with Aire, cannot miss of being able, in a manner 30 in the twinckling of an eye, to exercise all *Perceptive functions* again, if there was ever any intercessation of them in the astonishments of Death.

7. How the Soul may live and act separate from the Body, may be easily understood out of what has been spoken. But 35 that she does so *de facto*, there are but two waies to prove it; the one by the testimony of *History* the other by *Reason*. That of *History* is either of persons *perfectly dead*, or of those that have been subject to *Ecstasies*, or rather to that height thereof which is more properly called ἀφαιρεσία. when the Soul does 40 really leave the Body, and yet return again. Of this latter sort is that Example that *Pliny* recites of *Hermotimus Clazomenius*,

whose Soul would often quit her Body, and wander up and
down; and after her return tell many true stories of what she
had seen during the time of her disjunction. The same,
Maximius Tyrius and *Herodotus* report of *Aristaeus*
5   *Proconnesius. Marsilius Ficinus* adjoyns to this rank that
narration in *Aulus Gellius,* concerning one *Cornelius*, a Priest,
who in an Ecstasie saw the Battel fought betwixt *Caesar* and
Pompey in *Thessalie*, his Body being then at *Padua*; and yet
could, after his return to himself punctually declare the Time,
10   Order and Success of the Fight. That in *Wierus*, of the *Weasel*
coming out of the Souldiers mouth when he was asleep, is a
more plain example: which, if it were true, would make
Aristaeus his *Pigeon* not so much suspected of fabulosity as
Pliny would have it. Several Relations there are in the world to
15   this effect, that cannot but be loudly laughed at by them that
think the Soul inseparable from the Body;   and ordinarily they
seem very ridiculous also to those that think it is separable,
but as firmly believe that it is never, nor ever can be, separate
but in Death.
20   8. *Bodinus* has a very great desire, notwithstanding it is
so incredible to others, that the thing should be true; it being so
evincing an Argument for the Soul' s Immortality. And he
thinks this Truth is evident from innumerable examples of the
Ecstasies of Witches: Which we must confess with him not to
25   be natural; but that they amount to a perfect ἀφαιρεσία or
carrying away the Soul out of the Body, the lively sense of
their meeting, and dancing, and adoring the Devil, and the
mutual remembrance of the persons that meet one another
there at such a time, will be no infallible *Demonstration* that
30   they were there indeed, while their Bodies lay at home in Bed.
Conformity of their Confessions concerning the same
Conventicle is onely a *shrewd probability*, if it once could be
made good that this leaving their Bodies were a thing possible.
        For when they are out of them, they are much-what in the
35   same condition that other *Spirits* are, and can imitate what
shape they please; so that many of these Transformations into
Wolves and Cats. may be as likely of the Soul having left thus
the Body, as by the Devils possessing the Body and
transfiguring it himself. And what these *aiery* Cats or Wolves
40   suffer, whether cuttings of their limbs, or breaking the Back, or
any such like mischief, that the Witch in her Bed suffers the
like, may very well arise from that *Magick Sympathy* that is

seated in the Unity of the Spirit of the World, and the continuity of the subtile Matter dispersed throughout: the Universe in some sense being, as the *Stoicks* and *Platonists* define it, one vast entire *Animal.*

9. Now that this *real Separation of the Soul* may happen in some *Ecstasies* will be easily admitted, if we consider that the Soul in her own Nature is separable from the Body, as being a Substance really distinct therefrom; and that all Bodies are alike penetrable and passable to her, she being devoid of that corporeal property which they ord*inarily call* ἀντιτυπία, and therefore can freely slide through any Matter whatsoever, without any *knocking* or *resistance*; and lastly, that she does not so properly impart Heat and Motion to the Body, as Organization: and therefore when the Body is well organized, and there be that due temper of the Blood, the Heart and Pulse will in some measure beat, and the Brain will be replenish'd with Spirits, and therewith the whole Body, though the Soul were out of it. In which case (saving that the *Spirit* of *Nature* cannot be excluded thence) it would be perfectly *Cartesius* his *Machina* without Sense, though seemingly as much alive as any animate Creature in a deep sleep. Whence it appears, that if the Soul could leave the Body, that she might doe it for a certain time without any detriment thereto, that is, so long as it might well live without Repast. Which fully answers their fears who conceit that if the Soul was but once out of the Body, perfect Death must necessarily ensue, and all possible return thither be precluded.

10. But all the difficulty is to understand how the Soul may be loosned from the Body, while the Body is in a *fit* condition to retain her. That is a very great Difficulty indeed, and in a manner impossible for any power but what is supernatural. But it is not hard to conceive that this *vital fitness* in the Body may be changed, either by way of *natural Disease*, or by *Art.* For we may not some certain Fermentation in the Body so alter the Blood and Spirits, that the powers of the *Plastick* part of the Soul may cease to operate, as well as sometimes the *Perceptive* faculties do, as in *Catalepsies, Apoplexies*, and the like? Wherefore this passing of the Soul out of the Body in *Sleep*, or *Ecstasie*, may be sometime a certain Disease, as well as that of the νυκτοβάται, those that walk in their sleep.

Now if it should happen that some such distemper should
arise in the Body as would very much change the *Vital
Congruity* thereof for a time, and in this Paroxysm that other
Disease of the *Noctambuli* should surprise the party; his
5   Imagination driving him to walk to this or that place, his Soul
may very easily be conceived in this loosned condition it lies in,
to be able to leave the Body,and pass in the Aire, as other
Inhabitants of that Element doe, and act the part of separate
Spirits, and exercise such Functions of the *Perceptive* faculty as
10   they do that are quite released from Terrestrial Matter. Onely
here is the difference, That that damp in the Body that loosned
the Union of the Soul being spent, the Soul, by that natural
Magick I have more then once intimated, will certainly return
to the Body, and unite with it again as firm as ever. But no
15   man can when he pleases pass out of his Body thus, by the
Imperium of his Will, no more then he can walk in his Sleep:
For this capacity is pressed down more deep into the lower life
of the Soul, whither neither the *Liberty of Will* nor *free
Imagination* can reach.
20   11. *Passion* is more likely to take effect in this case then
either of the other two Powers, the seat of Passions being
originally in the Heart, which is the chief Fort of these lower
Faculties; and therefore by their propinquity can more easily
act upon the first Principles of Vital Union. The effect of these
25   has been so great, that they have quite carried the Soul out of
the Body, as appears in sundry Histories of that kinde. For
both *Sophocles* and *Dionysius* the *Sicilian* Tyrant died suddainly
upon the news of a Tragick Victory; as *Polycrita* also a Noble-
Woman of the Isle of *Naxus*, the Poet *Philippides*, and *Diagoras*
30   of *Rhodes*, upon the like excess of *Joy*. We might adde
examples of sudden *Fear* and *Grief*, but it is needless.
It is known and granted Truth, that *Passion* has so much
power over the vital temper of the Body as to make it an unfit
mansion for the Soul; from whence will necessarily follow her
35   disunion from it. Now if *Passion* will so utterly change the
Harmony of the Blood and Spirits, as quite to release the Soul
from the Body by a perfect Death; why may it not sometime
act on this side that degree and only bring a present
intemperies, out of which the Body may recover and conse-
40   quently regain the Soul back again, by virtue of that *Mundane
Sympathy* I have so often spoke of?

12. Now of all *Passions* whatever, excess of *Desire* is fittest for this more harmless and momentany ablegation of the Soul from the Body; because the great strength thereof is so closely assisted with the imagination of departing to the place where the party would be, that upon disunion not amounting to 5 perfect Death, the power of Fancy may carry the Soul to the place intended; and being satisfied and returned, may re-kindle life in the Body to the same degree it had before it was infested by this excess of Desire. This is that, if any thing, that has made dying men visit their friends before their departure, at 10 many miles distance, their Bodies still keeping their sick bed; and those that have been well, give a visit to their sick friends, of whose health they have been overdesirous and solicitous. For this *Ecstasie* is really of the *Soul*, and not of the *Blood* or *Animal Spirits*; neither of which have any *Sense* or *Perception*in 15 them at all. And therefore into this Principle is to be resolved that Story which *Martinus Del-Rio* reports of a Lad who, through the strength of Imagination and Desire of seeing his Father, fell into an Ecstasie; and after he came to himself, confidently affirmed he had seen him, and told infallible 20 circumstances of his being present with him.

13. That *Cardan* and others could fall into an *Ecstasie* when they pleased, by force of *Imagination* and *Desire* to fall into it, is recorded and believed by very grave and sober Writers: but whether they could ever doe it to a compleat 25 ἀφαιρεσία or local disjunction of the Soul from the Body, I know none that dare affirm; such events being rather the chances of Nature and Complexion, as in the *Noctambuli*, then the effects of our Will. But we cannot assuredly conclude but that *Art* may bring into our own power and ordering that which natural 30 causes put upon us sometimes without our leaves. But whether those *Oyntments* of Witches have any such effect, or whether those unclean Spirits they deal with, by their immediate presence in their Bodies, cannot for a time so suppress or alter their *Vital Fitness* to such a degree as will 35 loosen the Soul, I leave to more curious Inquisitors to search after. It is sufficient that I have demonstrated a very intelligible possibility of this actual separation without *Death* properly so called.

From whence the peremptory Confessions of Witches, and 40 the agreement of the story which they tell in several, as well those that are there bodily, as they that leave their Bodies

behinde them, especially when at their return they bring something home with them, as a permanent sign of their being at the place, is (though it may be all the delusion of their *Familiars*) no contemptible probability of their being there
5   indeed where they declare they have been. For these are the greatest evidences that can be had in humane affairs: And nothing, so much as the supposed Impossibility thereof, has deterred men from believing the thing to be true.

10   ————————————————————————————————————

Chap. XVI.

I. *That Souls departed communicate Dreams. 2. Examples of*
15   *Apparitions of Souls deceased. 3. Of Apparitions in fields where pitcht Battels have been fought; as also of those in Churchyards, and other vaporous places. 4. That the Spissitude of the Air may well contribute to the easiness of the appearing of* Ghosts *and* Spectres. *5. A further proof thereof from sundry Examples. 6. Of*
20   Marsilius Ficinus *his appearing after death. 7. With what sort of people such Examples as these avail little. 8. Reasons to perswade the unprejudiced that ordinarily those Apparitions that bear the shape and person of the deceased, are indeed the Souls of them.*
25

I. The Examples of the other sort, *viz.* of the *appearing of the Ghosts of men after death*, are so numerous and frequent in all mens mouths, that it may seem superfluous to particularize in any. This appearing is either by *Dreams*, or *open Vision*. In
30   *Dreams*, as that which hapned to *Avenzoar Albumaron* an *Arabian* Physician, to whom his lately-deceased friend suggested in his sleep a very soverain Medicine for his sore Eyes. Like to this is that in *Diodorus* concerning *Isis* Queen of *Aegypt*, whom he reports to have communicated remedies to the
35   *Aegyptians* in their sleep after her death, as well as she did when she was alive. Of this kind is also that memorable story of *Posidonius* the *Stoick*, concerning two young men of *Arcadia*, who being come to *Megara*, and lying the one at a Victualler's, the other in an Inne; he in the Inne while he was asleep
40   dream'd that his Fellow traveller earnestly desired him to come and help him, as being assaulted by the Victualler, and in danger to be kllled by him: But he, after he was perfectly

awake, finding it but a Dream, neglected it. But faln asleep
again, his murdered friend appeared to him the second time,
beseeching him, that though he did not help him alive, yet he
would see his Death revenged; telling him how the Victualler
had cast his Body into a Dung-cart, and that if he would get up   5
timely in the morning, and watch at the Town-gate, he might
thereby discover the murder: which he did accordingly, and so
saw Justice done on the Murderer. Nor does the first Dream
make the second impertinent to our purpose: For as that might
be from the strength of Imagination, and desire of help in the   10
distressed *Arcadian*, impressed on the *Spirit of the World*, and
so transmitted to his friend asleep (a condition fittest for such
communications;) so it is plain that this after his Death must
fail, if his Soul did either cease to be or to act. And therefore it
is manifest that she both was and did act, and suggested this   15
Dream in revenge of the Murder. Of which kinde there be
infinite Examples, I mean of Murders discovered by Dreams,
the Soul of the person murdered seeming to appear to some or
other asleep, and to make his complaint to them.

But I will content my self onely to adde an Example of   20
Gratitude to this of *Revenge*: As that of *Simonides*, who lighting
by chance on a dead Body by the Sea side, and out of the sense
of Humanity bestowing Burial upon it, was requited with a
Dream that saved his life. For he was admonisht to desist
from his Voiage he intended by Sea, which the Soul of the   25
deceased told him would be so perillous, that it would hazard
the lives of the Passengers. He believed the Vision, and
abstaining,   was   safe;   those   others   that   went   suffered
Shipwreck.

2. We will adjoyn onely an Example or two of that other   30
kind of *Visions*, which are ordinarily called the *Apparitions of
the dead*. And such is that which *Pliny* relates at large in his
Epistle to Sura, of an house haunted at *Athens*, and freed by
Athenodorus the Philosopher, after the Body of that person that
appeared to him was digged up, and interred with dumbe   35
solemnity. It is not a thing unlikely, that most houses that are
haunted, are so chiefly from the Souls of the deceased; who
have either been murdered, or some way injured, or have some
hid treasure to discover, or the like. And persons are haunted
for the like causes, as well as houses; as *Nero* was after the   40
murdering of his Mother; *Otho* pull'd out of his bed in the night
by the Ghost of *Galba*. Such instances are infinite: as also

those wherein the Soul of ones friend, suppose Father, Mother, or Husband, have appeared to give them good counsel, and to instruct them of the Event of the greatest affairs of their life. The Ghosts also of deceased Lovers have been reported to
5   adhere to their Paramours after they had left their Bodies; taking all opportunities to meet them in Solitude, whether by day or by night.

3. There be also other more fortuitous occursions of these deceased Spirits; of which one can give no account, unless it be,
10 because they find themselves in a more easy capacity to appear. As haply it may be in Fields after great slaughters of Armies, and in publick Burial-places. Though some would ridiculously put off these *Apparitions*, by making them nothing but the reek or vapour of the Bodies of the dead, which they
15 fancy will fall into the like stature and shape with the man it comes from: Which yet *Cardan* playes the fool in as well as *Vaninus* and others; as he does also in his account of those *Spectra* that appear so ordinarily in *Iseland*, where the Inhabitants meet their deceased friends in so lively an Image,
20 that they salute them and embrace them for the same persons; not knowing of their death, unless by their suddain disappearing, or by after-information that they were then dead. This he imputes partly to the *Thickness* of the Aire, and partly to the foule food and gross spirits of the *Iselanders*; and yet
25 implies, that their fancies are so strong, as to convert the thick vaporous Aire into the compleat shape of their absent and deceased acquaintance, and so perswade themselves that they see them, and talk with them; whenas it is nothing else but an Aiery Image made out by the power of their own Fancy from
30 the ragged rudiments of these thick flying vapours, as men fancy shapes in the broken clouds. But certainly it had been better flatly to have denied the Narration, then to give to slight and unprobable reason of the *Phaenomenon*. For neither do such visible vaporous consistencies near humane stature move
35 near the Earth; nor, if they did, could men be mistaken in an object so nigh at hand.

4. That the *Spissitude* of the Aire in that place may contribute something to the frequency of these *Spectra*, is rational enough. For it being more thick, it is the more easily
40 reduced to a visible consistency: but must be shaped, not by the fancy of the Spectatour, (for that were a monstrous power) but by the Imagination of the Spirit that actuates its own Vehicle

of that gross Aire. For the same reason also in other places these *Apparitions* haply appear oftner in the Night then in the Day, the Aire being more clammy and thick after the Sun has been some while down then before. To which also that custome of the *Lappians*, a people of *Scandia*, seems something to agree; who, as *Caspar Peucerus* relates, are very much haunted with Apparitions of their deceased friends. For which trouble they have no remedy but burying them under their Hearth. Which Ceremony can have no naturall influence upon these *Lemures*, unless they should hereby be engaged to keep in a warmer aire, and consequently more rarefied, then if they were interred elsewhere. Or rather because their Bodies will sooner putrefy by the warmth of the hearth; whenas otherwise the coldness of that Clime would permit them to be sound a longer time, and consequently be fit for the Souls of the deceased to have recourse to, and replenish their Vehicle with such a *Cambium* or gluish moisture, as will make it far easier to be commanded into a *visible consistence*.

5. That this facilitates their condition of *appearing*, is evident from that known recourse these infestant Spirits have to their dead Bodies. As is notorious in the History of *Cuntius*, which I have set down at large in my *Antidote*, as also in that of the *Silesian* Shoomaker and his Maid. To which you may adde what *Agrippa* writes out of the *Cretian* Annals, How there the *Catechanes*, that is the Spirits of the deceased Husbands, would be very troublesome to their Wives, and endeavour to lie with them, while they could have any recourse to their dead Bodies. Which mischief therefore was prevented by a Law, that if any Woman was thus infested, the Body of her Husband should be burnt, and his Heart struck through with a stake. Which also put a speedy end to those stirs and tragedies the Ghost of *Cuntius* and those others caused at *Pentsch* and *Breslaw* in *Silesia*.

The like disquietnesses are reported to have hapned in the year 1567. at *Trawtenaw* a city of *Bohemia*, by one *Stephanus Hubener*, who was to admiration grown rich, as *Cuntius* of *Pentsch*, and when he died, did as much mischief to his fellow Citizens. For he would ordinarily appear in the very shape he was when he was alive, and such as he met, would salute them with so close embraces, that he caused many to fall sick and several to die by the unkind huggs he gave them. But burning his Body rid the Town of the perilous occursations of this malicious Goblin.

All which Instances do prove not only the *appearing* of
Souls after they have left this life, but also that some thickning
Matter, (such as may be got either from Bodies alive, or lately
5   dead, or as fresh as those that are but newly dead (as the Body
of this *Hubener* was, though it had lyen 20 weeks in the
Gravĕ,) or lastly from thick vaporous Air,) may facilitate much
their appearing, and so invite them to play tricks, when they
can doe it at so cheap a rate; though they have little or no end
10   in doing them, but the pleasing of their own, either ludicrous, or
boisterous and domineering humour.

6. But of any private person that ever appeared upon
design after his death, there is none did upon a more noble one
then that eximious Platonist *Marsilius Ficinus*; who, after a
15   warm dispute of the Immortality of the Soul, having (as
Baronius relates) made a solemn vow with his fellow-Platonist
Michael Mercatus, that whether of them two died first should
appear to his friend, and give him a certain information of that
Truth; (it being his fate to die first, and indeed not long after
20   this mutual resolution) was mindful of his promise when he had
left the Body. For *Michael Mercatus* being very intent at his
Studies betimes on a morning, heard an horse riding by with all
speed, and observed that he stopped at his window; and
therewith heard the voice of his friend *Ficinus* crying out aloud,
25   *O Michael, Michael, vera, vera sunt illa.* Whereupon he
suddenly opened the window, and espying *Marsilius* on a white
Steed, called after him; but he vanish'd in his sight. He sent
therefore presently to *Florence* to know how *Marsilius* did; and
understood that he died about that hour he called at his
30   window, to assure him of his own and other mens
Immortalities.

7. The Examples I have produced of the *appearing* of the
Souls of men after death, considering how clearly I have
demonstrated the separability *of them from the Body, and their*
35   *capacity of Vital Union* with an *Aiery Vehicle,* cannot but have
their due weight of Argument with them that are unprejudiced.
But as for those that have their minds enveloped in the dark
mist of Atheism, that lazy and Melancholick saying which has
dropt from the careless pen of that uncertain writer *Cardan,*
40   *Orbis magnus est, et aevum longum, et error ac timor multum in*
hominibus possunt, will prevail more with them then all the
Stories the same Authour writes of *Apparitions,* or whatever

any one else can adde unto them. And others that do admit of
these things, preconceptions from Education, That the Soul
when she departs this life is suddenly either twitched up into
the *Coelum Empyreum*, or hurried down headlong towards the
Centre of the Earth, makes the Apparitions of the Ghosts of 5
men altogether incredible to them; they alwaies substituting in
their place some Angel or Devil which must represent their
persons, themselves being not at leisure to act any such part.

    8. But *Misconceit* and *Prejudice*, though it may hinder the
force of an Argument with those that are in that manner 10
entangled, yet *Reason* cannot but take place with them that are
free. To whom I dare appeal whether (considering the *Aëreal
Vehicles* of Souls which are common to them with other *Genii*,
so that whatever they are fancied to doe in their stead, they
may perform themselves; as also how congruous it is, that 15
those persons that are most concerned, when it is in their
power, should act in their own affairs, as in detecting the
Murtherer, in disposing their estate, in rebuking injurious
Executors, in visiting and counselling their Wives and Children,
in forewarning them of such and such courses, with other 20
matters of like sort; to which you may adde the profession of
the Spirit thus appearing, of being the Soul of such an one, as
also the similitude of person; and that all this adoe is in things
very just and serious, unfit for a Devil with that care and
kindness to promote, and as unfit for a good *Genius*, it being 25
below so noble a nature to tell a Lie, especially when the affair
may be as effectually transacted without it;) I say, I dare
appeal to any one, whether all these things put together and
rightly weighed, the violence of prejudice not pulling dow the
balance, it will not be certainly carried for the present Cause; 30
and whether any indifferent Judge ought not to conclude, if
these Stories that are so frequent every where and in all Ages
concerning the Ghosts of men appearing be but true, that it is
true also that they are their Ghosts, and that therefore the
Souls of men subsist and act after they have left these Earthly 35
Bodies.

Chap. XVII.

I. *The preeminence of Arguments drawn from Reason above those
from Story.* 2. *The first step toward a Demonstration of Reason
that the Soul acts out of her Body, for that she is an* Immaterial
Substance separable there-from. 3. *The second, That the*
immediate Instruments *for Sense, Motion, and Organization of
the Body, are certain* subtile *and* tenuious Spirits. 4. *A
comparison betwixt the* Soul in the Body *and the Aëreal* Genii.
5. *Of the nature of* Daemons *from the account of* Marcus *the
Eremite, and how the Soul is presently such, having once left this
Body.* 6. *An Objection concerning the Souls of Brutes to which is
answered, First, by way of concession*; 7. *Secondly, confuting the
Arguments for the former concession.* 8. *That there is no rational
doubt at all of the Humane Soul acting after death.* 9. *A further
Argument of her activity out of this Body, from her conflicts with
it while she is in it.* 10. *As also from the general hope and belief
of all Nations, that they shall live after death.*

I. But we proceed now to what is less subject to the
evasions and misinterpretations of either the *Profane* or
Superstitious. For none but such as will profess themselves
mere Brutes can cast off the Decrees and Conclusions of
Philosophy and Reason; though they think that in things of this
nature they may, with a great deal of applause and credit,
refuse the testimony of other mens Senses, if not of their own:
all *Apparitions* being with them nothing but the strong
surprisals of *Melancholy* and *Imagination.* But they cannot
with that ease nor credit silence the Deductions of Reason, by
saying it is but a *Fallacy*, unlesse they can shew the Sophisme;
which they cannnot doe, where it is not.

2. To carry on therefore our present Argument in a
rational way, and by degrees; we are first to consider, That
(according as already has been clearly demonstrated) there is a
Substance in us which is ordinarily called *the Soul*, really
distinct from the Body, (for otherwise how can it be a
Substance?) And therefore it is really and locally separable
from the Body. Which is a very considerable step towards what
we aim at.

3. In the next place we are to take notice, That the
immediate Instrument of the Soul are those tenuious and Aëreal
particles which they ordinarily call the *Spirits*; that these are

they by which the Soul hears, sees, feels, imagines, remembers, reasons, and by moving which, or at least directing their motions, she moves likewise the Body; and by using them, or some subtile Matter like them, she either compleats, or at least contrinutes to, the Bodie's Organization. For that the Soul should be the *Vital Architect* of her own house, that close connexion and sure possession she is to have of it, distinct and secure from the invasion of any other particular Soul, seems no slight Argument. And yet that while she is exercising that Faculty she may have a more then ordinary Union or Implication with the *Spirit of Nature*, or the *Soul of the World*, so far forth as it is *Plastick* , seems not unreasonable: and therefore is asserted by *Plotinus*; & may justly be suspected to be true, if we attend to the prodigious effects of the Mother's Imagination derived upon the Infant, which sometimes are so very great, that, unless she raised the *Spirit of Nature* into consent, they might well seem to exceed the power of any Cause. I shall abstain from producing any Examples till the proper place: in the mean time I hope I may be executed from any rashness in this assignation of the Cause of those many and various Signatures found in Nature, so plainly pointing at such a Principle in the World as I have intimated before.

4. But to return, and cast our eye upon the Subject in hand. It appears from the two precedent Conclusions, That the Soul considered as invested immediately with this *tenuious Matter* we speak of, which is her inward Vehicle, has very little more difference from the *Aëreal Genii*, then a man in a Prison from one that is free. The one can onely see, and suck air through the Grates of the Prison, and must be annoyed with all the stench and unwholsome fumes of that sad habitation; whenas the other may walk and take the fresh air, where he finds it most commodious and agreeable.

This difference there is betwixt the *Genii* and an *incorporated Soul*. The *Soul*, as a man faln into a deep pit, (who can have no better Water, nor Aire, nor no longer enjoyment of the Sun, and his chearful light and warmth, then the measure and quality of the pit will permit him) so she once immured in the Body cannot enjoy any better Spirits (in which all her life and comfort consists) then the constitution of the Body after such circuits of concoction can administer to her. But those *Genii* of the Aire, who possess their Vehicles upon no such hard terms, if themselves be not in fault, may by the power of their

minds accommodate themselves with more pure and impolluted
Matter, and such as will more easily conspire with the noblest
and divinest functions of their Spirit.

5　　In brief therefore, if we consider things aright, we cannot
abstain from strongly surmising, that there is no more
difference betwixt a Soul and an aëreal *Genius*, then there is
betwixt a Sword in the scabbard and one out of it: and that a
Soul is but a *Genius* in the Body, and a *Genius* a Soul out of the
Body; as the Ancients also have defined, giving the same name,
10　　as well as nature, promsicuously to them both, by calling them
both Δαίμονες ,as I have elsewhere noted.

　　5. This is very consonant to what *Michael Psellus sets*
down, from the singular knowledge and experience of *Marcus*
the Eremite, in these matters; who describes the nature of
15　　these Δαίμονες. *as being* throughout *Spirit* and *Aire*; whence
they hear and see and feel in every part of their Body. Which
he makes good by this reason, and wonders at the ignorance of
men that do not take notice of it, viz. τὸ μὴ ἐπι τινος ὀστοῦν ἤ
νεῦρον εἶναι τὸ ἀισθανόμενον, ἀλλὰ τὸ ἐν τούτοις ἐνυπάρχον πνεῦμα
20　　,*that is neither Bones, nor Nerves, nor any gross or visible part of
the Body or of any Organ thereof, whereby the Soul immediately
exercises the functions of Sense; but that it is the Spirits that are
her nearest and inmost instrument of these operations*: Of which
when the Body is deprived; there is found no Sense in it,
25　　though the gross Organs and parts are in their usual
consistency, as we see in *Syncopes* and *Apoplexies*. Which
plainly shews, that the immediate Vehicle of Life are the
Spirits, and that the Soul's connexion with the Body is by
these; as the most learned Physicians do conclude with one
30　　consent. Whence it will follow, that this *Vinculum* being broke,
the Soul will be free from the Body, and will as naturally be
carried out of the corrupt carkass that now has no harmony
with the Soul, into that Element that is more congenerous to
her, the vital Aire, as the Fire will mount upwrds; as I have
35　　already noted. And so Principles of Life being fully kindled in
this thinner Vehicle, she becomes as compleat for Sense and
Action as any other Inhabitants of these Aiery regions.

　　6. There is onely one perverse Objection against this so
easie and natural Conclusion, which is this; That by this
40　　manner of reasoning, the Souls of Brutes, especially those of
the perfecter sort, will also not onely subsist, (for that difficulty
is concocted pretty well already) but also live and enjoy

themselves after death. To which I dare boldly answer, That it
is a thousand times more reasonable that they do, then that the
Souls of Men do not. Yet I will not confidently assert that they
do, or do not; but will lightly examine each Hypothesis. And
first, by way of feigned concession, we will say, They do; and 5
take notice of the Reasons that may induce one to think so.
Amongst which two prime ones are those involved in the
Objection, That they do subsist after death; and, That the
immediate instrument of their Vital Functions is their Spirits,
as well as in Man. To which we may adde, That for the 10
present we are fellow-inhabitants of one and the same Element,
the Earth, subject to the same fate of Fire, Deluges and
Earthquakes. That it is improbable that the vast space of Aire
and Aether, that must be inhabited by living creatures, should
have none but of one sort, that is the Angels or Genii, good or 15
bad. For it would seem as great a solitude as if Men alone
were the Innabitants of the Earth, or Mermaids of the Sea.
That the periods of *Vital Congruity*, wound up in the Nature of
their Souls by that eternal Wisdome that is the Creatress of all
things, may be shorter or longer, according as the property of 20
their essence and relation to the Universe requires; and that so
their Descents and Returns may be accordingly swifter or
slower. That it is more conformable to the Divine goodness to
be so then otherwise, if their natures will permit it: And that
their existence would be in vain, while they were deprived of 25
vital operation when they may conveniently have it. That they
would be no more capable of Salvation in the other state, then
they are here of Conversion. That the intellectual Inhabitants
of the Aire having also external and corporeal Sense, variety of
Objects would doe as well there, as here amongst us on Earth. 30
Besides that Histories seem to imply, as if there were such kind
of Aëreal Animals amongst them, as Dogs, Horses, and the
like. And therefore to be short, that the Souls of Brutes cease
to be alive after they are separate from this Body, can have no
other reason then *Immorality* the Mother of *Ignorance*, (that is, 35
nothing but narrowness of Spirit, out of over-much self-love,
and contempt of other Creatures) to embolden us so confidently
to adhere to so groundless a Conclusion.

7. This Position makes indeed a plausible shew, insomuch
that if the Objection drove one to acknowledge it for Truth, he 40
might seem to have very little reason to be ashamed of it. But
this Controversy is not so easily decided. For though it be plain

that the Souls of Beasts be Substances really separable from
their Bodies; yet if they have but one *Vital congruity*, namely
the *Terrestrial* one, they cannot recover life in the Aire. But
their having one or two, or more Vital congruities, wholy
5   depends upon his wisdome and counsel that has made all
things. Besides, the Souls of Brutes seem to have a more
passive nature then to be able to manage or enjoy this escape
of Death, that free & commanding Imagination belonging onely
to us, as also Reminiscency. But Brutes have onely a passive
10   Imagination, and bare Memory; which failing them in all
likelihood in the shipwreck of their Body, if they could live in
the Aire, they would begin the World perfectly on a new score,
which is little better then Death: so that they might in this
sense be rightly deemed mortall. Our being Co-inhabitants of
15   the same element, the Earth, proves nothing: for by the same
reason, Worms and Fleas should live out of their Bodies, and
Fishes should not, who notwithstanding, their shape, it may be,
a little changed (for there is no necessity that these creatures in
their Aiery Vehicles should be exactly like themselves in their
20   Terrestrial ones) might act and live in the more moist tracts of
the Aire.

    As for the supposed solitude that would be in the Aire, it
reaches not this matter. For in the lower Regions thereof, the
various Objects of the Earth and Sea will serve the turn. The
25   winding up of those several circuits of *Vital Congruity* may
indeed pass for an ingenious invention, as of a thing possible in
the Souls of Brutes: but, as the Schools say well, *A posse ad
esse non valet consequentia.* As for that Argument from *Divine
Goodness*, it not excluding his Wisdome, which attempers it self
30   to the natures of things, and we not knowing the nature of the
Souls of Brutes so perfectly as we do our own, we cannot so
easily be assured from thence what will be in this case. A
Musician strikes not all strings at once; neither is it to be expected that every thing in Nature at every time should act: but
35   when it is its time, then touched upon it will give its sound; in
the interim it lies silent.   And so it may be with the Souls of
Brutes for a time, especially when the vital temper of Earth
and Aire and Sea shall fail; yea and at other times too, if none
but Intellectual Spirits be fit to manage *Aëreal* Vehicles.

40   I confess indeed, that Salvation can no more belong to the
Souls of Brutes then Conversion; but that is as true of the
Souls of Plants, (if they have any distinct from the *Universal*

Spirit of Nature) but yet it does not prove that the Souls of Vegetables shall live and act in Aiery Vehicles, after an Herb or Tree is dead and rotten here. To that of conveniency of variety of Objects for the Aiery Inhabitants I have answered already. And for the Apparitions of Horses, Doggs and the 5 like, they may be the transformation of the Aërial *Genii* into these shapes: Which though it be a sign that they would not abhor from the use and society of such Aërial Animals, if they had them; yet they may the better want them, they being able so well themselves to supply their places.   10

We will briefly therefore conclude, that from the mere light of Reason it cannot be infallibly demonstrated, That the Souls of Brutes do not live after death, nor that it is any Incongruity in Nature to say they do. Which is sufficient to enervate the present Objection.   15

8. But for the life and activity of the Souls of Men out of this Body, all things goe on hand-smooth for it, without any check or stop. For we finding the Aërial *Genii* so exceeding near-a-kin to us in their Faculties, we being both *intellectual Creatures*, and both using the same immediate Instrument of 20 Sense and Perception, to wit, *Aërial Spirits*, insomuch that we can scarce discover any other difference betwixt us then there is betwixt a man that is naked and one clad in gross thick cloathing; it is the most easy and natural inference that can be, to conclude, that when we are separate from the Body, and are 25 invested only in Aire, that we shall be just like them, and have the same life and activity they have. For though a Brute fall short of this Privilege, it ought to be no disheartning to us, because there is a greater cognation betwixt the *Intellectual* Faculties and the *Aiery* or *Aethereal* Vehicle, then there is 30 betwixt such Vehicles and those more low and sensual powers common to us with Beasts. And we finde, in taking the fresh aire, that the more fine and pure our *Spirits* are, our thoughts become the more noble and divine, and the more purely intellectual.   35

Nor is the step greater upwards then downwards: For seeing that what in us is so *Divine* and *Angelical* may be united with the body of a *Brute*, (for such is this Earthly cloathing) why may not the Soul, notwithstanding her *Terrestrial* Congruity of life, (which upon new occasions may be easily 40 conceived to surcease from acting) be united with the Vehicle of an *Angel*? So that there is no puzzle at all concerning the Soul

of Man, but that immediately upon Death she may associate
her self with those Aërial Inhabitants, the *Genii* or *Angels*

9. Which we may still be the better assured of, if we
consider how we have such Faculties in us as the Soul finds
5   entangled and fettered, clouded and obscured by her fatal
residence in this prison of the Body. Insomuch that, so far as it
is lawful, she falls out with it for those incommodations that
the most confirmed brutish health brings usually upon her.
How her Will tuggs against the impurity of the Spirits that stir
10   up bestial Passions, (that are notwithstanding the height and
flower of other Creatures enjoyments) and how many times her
whole life upon Earth is nothing else but a perpetual warfare
against the results of her union with this lump of Earth that is
so much like to other terrestrial Animals. Whence it is plain
15   she finds her self in a wrong condition, and that she was
created for a better and purer state; which she could not attain
to, unless she lived out of the Body: which she does in some
sort in *divine Ecstasies* and *Dreams*; in which case she making
no use of the Bodies Organs, but of the purer Spirits in the
20   fourth Ventricle of the Brain, she acts as it were by herself,
and performs some preludious Exercises, conformable to those
in her Aiery Vehicle.

10. Adde unto all this, that *the Immortality of the Soul* is
the common, and therefore natural, hope and expectation of all
25   Nations; there being very few so barbarous as not to hold it for
a Truth: though, it may be, as in other things, they may be
something ridiculous in the manner of expressing themselves
about it; as that they shall retire after Death to such a Grove
or Wood, or beyond such a Hill, or unto such an Island, such as
30   was Δρόμος Αχιλλέως, *the island where Achilles* his Ghost was
conceived to wander, or the *Insulae Fortunatae* the noted
Elysium of the Ancients. And yet, it may be, if we should tell
these of the *Coelum Empyreum*, and compute the height of it,
and distance from the Earth, and how many solid Orbs must be
35   glided through before a Soul can come thither; these simple
Barbarians would think as only of the *Scholastick* Opinion as
we do of theirs: and it may be some more judicious and
sagacious Wit will laugh at us both alike.

It is sufficient, that in the main all Nations in a manner
40   are agreed that there is an *Immortality* to be *expected*, as well
as that there is a *Deity* to be *worshipped*; though ignorance of
circumstances makes Religion vary, even to Monstrosity, in

many parts of the world. But both Religion, and the belief of
the Reward of it, which is a blessed state after Death, being so
generally acknowledged by all the Inhabitants of the Earth; it
is a plain Argument that it is true according to the Light of
Nature. And not onely because they believe so, but because 5
they do so seriously either desire it, or are so horribly afraid of
it, if they offend much against their Consciences: which
Properties would not be in men so universally, if there were no
Objects in Nature answering to these Faculties, as I have
elsewhere argued in the like case. 10

Chap. XVIII.

15

I. *That the* Faculties *of our* Souls, *and the nature of the
immediate Instrument of them, the* Spirits, *do so nearly symbolize
with those of* Daemons, *that it seems reasonable, if God did not
on purpose hinder it, that they would not fail to act out of this
earthly Body.* 2. *Or if they would, his Power and Wisdome* 20
could easily implant in their essence a double or triple Vital
Congruity, *to make all sure.* 3. *A further demonstration of the
present Truth from the Veracity of God.* 4. *An Answer to an
Objection against the foregoing Argument.* 5. *Another
Demonstration from his Justice.* 6. *An Answer to an Objection.* 25
7. *An Answer to another objection.* 8. *Another Argument from
the Justice of God.* 9. *An objection answered.* 10. *An invincible
Demonstration of the Soul's immortality from the Divine
Goodness.* 11. *A more particular enforcement of that Argument,
and who they are upon whom it will work least.* 12. *That the* 30
*Noblest and most Vertuous Spirit is the most assurable of the
Soul's Immortality.*

I. But finally, to make all sure, let us contemplate the
Nature of *God,* who is the Author and Maker of all things, 35
according to whose *Goodness, Wisdome* and *Power* all things
were *created,* and are ever *ordered*; and let us take special
notice how many steps towards this Immortality we now treat
of are impressed upon the very nature of the Soul already; and
then seriously consider, if it be possible that the *Sovereign Deity* 40
should stop there, and goe no further, when there are so great
reasons, if we understand any thing, that He perfect our

expectations. For we have already clearly demonstrated,
That the Soul of man is a Substance actually separable from
the Body, and that all her Operations and Functions are
immediately performed, not by those parts of the Body that are
5   of an earthly and gross consistency, but by what is more Aërial
or Aethereal, the *Vital* and *Animal Spirits*; which are very
congenerous to the Vehicles of the Angels or *Genii*.
Insomuch that if the Divine power did but leave Nature to
work of it self, it might seem very strange, considering those
10   Divine and Intellectual Faculties in us, (as conformable to the
essences or Souls of Angels as our Animal Spirits are to their
Vehicles) if it would not be an immediate sequel of this
Priviledge that our Souls once separate from the Body should
act and inform the Air they are in with like facility that other
15   *Genii* do, there being so very little difference betwixt both their
natures.

2. Or if one single *Plastick* power in a Subject so near a-kin
to these Aërial people, will not necessarily suffice for both
states, certainly it must be a very little addition that will help
20   out: and how easy is it for that Eternal Wisdome to contrive a
double or triple Vital Congruity, to wit, *Aërial* and *Aethereal*, as
well as *Terrestrial*, in such an Essence, whose Faculties and
Properties do so plainly symbolize with those purer Inhabitants
of both the *Aether* and *Air*?

25   3. But this is not all we have to say. For if there be one
thing more precious in the Deity then another, we shall have it
all as a sure and infallible pledge of this present Truth, *That
our Souls will not fail to prove Immortal.* And for my own part,
I know nothing more precious in the Godhead then his *Veracity*,
30   *Justice* and *Goodness*; and all these Three will assure me and
secure us, that we shall sustain no loss or damage by our
departure out of these Earthly Bodies, in either Life or
Essence. For it were a very high reproach to that Attribute of
God which we call his *Veracity*, he so plainly and universally
35   promising to all the Nations, of the World, where there is any
Religion at all, a happy state after this life; if there should in
reality be no such thing to be expected. For he does not onely
connive at the Errour, if it be one, by not declaring himself
against it, (as any upright person should, if another should take
40   upon him, in his presence or hearing, to tell others that he
intended to bestow such and such gifts and revenues upon
them, when there was no such matter:) but he has, as a man

may say, on set purpose indued men with extraordinary parts
and powers, to set this Opinion on foot in the Earth; all
Prophets and *Workers of Miracles* that have appeared in the
world, having one way or other assured to Mankind this so
weighty Truth. And the most *Noble* and *Vertuous* Spirits in all 5
Ages have been the most prone to believe it. And this not onely
out of a sense of their own Interest; but any one that ever had
the happiness to experience these things may observe, That
that Clearness and Purity of temper that most consists with
the Love and admiration of God and Vertue, and all those 10
divine Accomplishments that even those that never could attain
to them give their highest approbation of, I say, that this more
refined temper of Mind does of it self beget a wonderful
proneness, if not a necessity, of presuming of the Truth of this
Opinion we plead for. And therefore if it be not true, God has 15
laid a train in Nature, that the most Vertuous and Pious men
shall be the most sure to be deceived: Which is a contradiction
to his Attribute of *Veracity.*

4. Nor can the strength of this Argument be evaded by
replying, That God may deceive men for their good, as Parents 20
do their Children; and therefore His *Wisdome* may contrive
such a naturall Errour as this, to be serviceable for States and
Polities, to keep the people in awe, and so render them more
faithfull and governable, I must confess that there does result
from this divine Truth such an *Usefulness*, by the by, for the 25
better holding together of Commonweals: But to think that this
is the main use thereof, and that there is nothing more in it
then so, is as Idiotical and Childish as to conclude, that because
the Stars, those vast lights, doe some small offices for us by
Night, that therefore that is all the meaning of them, and that 30
they serve for nothing else.

Besides, there is no Father would tell a Lye to his Child,
if he were furnisht with Truth as effectual for his purpose; and
if he told any thing really good as well as desirable to his Child,
to induce him to Obedience, if it lay in his power, he would be 35
sure to perform his promise. But it is in the power of God to
make good whatever he has propounded for reward; nor need
he make use of any falshood in this matter, Wherefore if he do,
he has less *Veracity* then an ordinary honest man; which is
blasphemous, and *contradictious* to the nature of the Deity.   40

5. Again upon point of *Justice*, God was engaged to contrive the Nature and Order of things so, that the Souls of Men may live after death, and that they may fare according to their behaviour here upon earth. For the Godhead, as the
5   Philosopher calls him, is Νόμος ἰσοκλινὴς. and does immutably and inevitably distribute Justice, both *Reward & Punishment*, in the world, the common practice and complaint of all men do confess with one consent; and that it is exceeding hard to perswade any one to doe that violence to their own natures, as
10   to endeavour after a due degree and right sense of Vertue (for Craft and Policy are easy enough, and other things there are that, set against the contrary Vices look like Vertues but are not:) But to perswade to those that truly are is I say exceeding hard, if not impossible, without the inculcation of this grand
15   concernment, *the State of the Soul after Death*, and the *Reward* that will then follow a *Vertuous* life. Of which hopes if we be frustrated by the Soul' s Mortality, we are defrauded of our Reward, and God of the honour of *Justice*.

6. Nor can the force of this Argument be enervated by
20   either that high pretension of *Stoicism*, *That Vertue to it self is a sufficient reward*; or that the very hopes of this Immortality, it being accompanied with so much joy, tranquility and contentment, will countervail all the pain and trouble of either acquiring, or keeping close to Vertue once acquired. For as for
25   the first, It is one thing to talk high, and another thing to practice. And for my own part, I think in the main, that *Epicurus*, who placed the chiefest good in *Pleasure*, philosophized more solidly then the paradoxical *Stoicks*. For questionless that is that which all men ought to drive at, if they
30   had the true notion of it, and knew wherein to place it, or could arrive to the purest and most warrantable sense of it. But there can be no *Pleasure*, (without a perfect Miracle) while our Spirits are disturbed and vitiated by sordid and contemptible Poverty, by Imprisonments, Sicknesses, Tortures, ill Diet, and
35   a number of such Adversities, that those that are the most exactly Vertuous have been in all Ages most lyable to. Besides the care and sollicitude of perpetually standing upon their guard, the stings of Calumny and Defamation, and a continual vexation to see the baseness and vileness of mens tempers and
40   ugly oblique transactions of affairs in the world. Which inquietudes cannot be avoided by any other remedy but what is as ill as the disease, or worse, (it being altogether incompetible

to a true *Heroical* tenour of mind,) I mean their *Stoical Apathy*;
of which the best that can be said is, that it is a kind of
constant and safe piece of sulleness, stating us onely in the
condition of those that are said to have neither wonne nor lost:
So poor a reward is persecuted and distressed Vertue of it self, 5
without the hope of future Happiness.

7. But to say, the Hope thereof without Enjoyment is a
sufficient compensation, is like that mockery *Plutarch* records
of *Dionysius* towards a Fidler, whom he caused to play before
him, promising him a reward, but when he demanded it of him 10
for his pains, denied it him, or rather said it was paid already,
putting him off with this jest, ὅσον χρόνον εὔφαινες ἀιδῶν,
τοσοῦτον ἔχαιρες ἐλπίζων, i.e. *So long as you pleased me with
playing, so long you rejoyced your self with hoping after the
reward; so that you are sufficiently paid already.* Which piece of 15
injurious mirth may be passable in a ludicrous matter, and
from a Tyrant, where height of Fortune makes proud and
forgetful Mortality contemn their inferiours: But in a thing of
this nature, that concerns not onely this transient life, but the
sempiternal duration of the Soul, *Injustice* there is unspeakably 20
grievous; and so much the more harsh and uncomely, if we
consider that it is supposed to be committed, not by a frail
earthly Potentate, (the height of whose Honours may make him
regardless of smaller affairs and meaner persons,) but by the
God of Heaven, who can with the like ease attend all things as 25
he can any one thing, and who is perfectly and immutably just,
not doing nor omitting any thing by changeable humours, as it
happens in vain Men, but ever acting according to the
transcendent Excellency and Holiness of his own Nature.

8. Neither is *Divine Justice* engaged onely to *reward*, but 30
also to *punish*; which cannot be, unless the Souls of men subsist
after Death. For there are questionless many thousands that
have committed most enormous Villanies, persecuted the Good,
taking away their possessions, liberties, or lives, adding
sometimes most barbarous tortures and reproachful abuses; 35
and in all this highly gratified their covetousness, ambition and
revenge; nay, it may be the bestial ferocity of their own spirits,
that have pleased themselves exceedingly to bring the truly
religious into disgrace, and have laughed at all vertuous actions
as the fruits of Ignorance and Folly; and yet for all this have 40
died in peace on their beds, after their Lives have been as thick
set with all sensual enjoyments of Honour, Riches and

Pleasure, as their Story is with Frauds, Rapines, Murders, Sacriledges, and whatever crimes the impious boldness of lawless persons will venture on.

9. Such things as these happen proportionably through all the ranks and orders of men. Nor is it sufficient to reply that their own Consciences, as so many Furies, do lash them and scorch them in this life: For we speak of inveterate and successful wickedness, where that Principle is utterly laid asleep; or if it at any time wake and cry, the noise of the affairs of the world, and hurry of business, and continual visits of friends and flatterers, false instructions of covetous Priests or mercenary Philosop hers (who for gain will impudently corrupt and pervert both the Light of Nature and Sense of Religion,) the sound and clatter of these, I say, will so possess the ear of the prosperously wicked, that the voice of Conscience can be no more heard in this continual tumult, then the vagient cries of the Infant *Jupiter* amidst the rude shuffles and dancings of the *Cretick Corybantes*, and the tinckling and clashing of their brazen Targets. And therefore if there be no Life hereafter, the worst of men have the greatest share of happiness, their passions and affections being so continually gratified, and that to the height, in those things that are so agreeable, and, rightly circumstantiated, allowable to humane Nature: such as are the sweet reflexion on the success of our political management of the affairs of the World; the general tribute of Honour and respect for our Policy and Wit, and that ample testimony thereof, our acquisitions of Power or Riches; that great satisfaction of foiling and bearing down our Enemies, and obliging and making sure our more serviceable Friends; to which finally you may adde all the variety of Mirth and Pastime that flesh and blood can entertain it self with, from either *Musick, Wine,* or *Women*.

10. Thirdly and lastly, The Mortality of the Soul is not onely inconsistent with the *Veracity* and *Justice* of God, but also with his *Goodness*, the most soveraign and sacred Attribute in the Deity, and which alone is enough to demonstrate, *That the Soul of man cannot perish in Death.* For suppose that God had made no promise to us, either by any extraordinary Prophet, or by the suggestion of our own natural Faculties, that we shall be Immortal, and that there was neither Merit nor Demerit in this life, so that all plea from either the Divine *Veracity* or *Justice* were quite cut off; his *Goodness* alone (especially if we consider

how capable the Soul is of after-subsistence) is a sufficient
assurance that we shall not fail to live after Death. For how
can that soveraign *Goodness* assisted by an Omnipotent
Knowledge, fail to contrive it so; it being so infinitely more
conformable to His Transcendent Bounty to ordain thus then   5
otherwise? that is to say, so soon as he created the World, to
make it so compleat, as at once to bring into Being not onely all
Corporeal Substance (according as all men confess he did) but
also all Substances *Immaterial* or *Incorporeal* and as many of
them as can partake of Life, and of enjoyment of themselves   10
and the Universe, to set them upon living and working in all
places and Elements that their Nature is able to operate in; and
therefore amongst other Beings of the Intellectual Order, to
ordain that the Souls of men also, whereever they were, or
ever should be, especially if it were not long of themselves,   15
should have a power of Life and Motion, and that no other
Nemesis should follow them then what they themselves lay the
trains of; nor this to utter annihilation, but by way of
chastisement or punishment: and that they being of so
multifarious a nature, as to have such Faculties as are nearly   20
a-kin to Brutes, as well as such as have so close an affinity
with those of the Aëreal *Genii* and Celestial Angels their *Vital
Congruity* should be as multifarious, and themselves made
capable of a living Union with either *Celestial, Aëreal,* or
Terrestrial Vehicles; and that the leaving of one should be but   25
the taking up of another, so long as the Elements continue in
their natural temper, and as soon as the Laws of Generation
will permit.

    11. These, and a long series of other things consonant to
these, represent themselves to their view that have the favour   30
of beholding the more hidden treasures of *the Divine Benignity.*
But they being more then the present occasion requires, I shall
content my self with what precisely touches the matter in
hand, which is, That the Soul of Man being capable to act after
this life in an *Aëreal Vehicle,* as well as here in an *Earthly*; and   35
it being *better* that she do live and act, then that she be idle and
silent in death; and it depending merely upon the Will of God
whether she shall or no; He ordering the natures of things
infallibly according to what is *best,* must of necessity ordain
that the Souls of men live and act after death. This is an   40
unavoidable Deduction of Reason to those that acknowledge the
Being of God, and rightly relish that transcendent Attribute in

the Divine Nature. For those that have a true sense thereof, can as hardly deny this Conclusion as the Existence of the Deity. Nor can they ever be perswaded, that He who is so *perfectly Good* in himself, and to whom they have so long
5 adhered in faithful obedience and amorous devotion, has made them of such a nature, that when they hope most to enjoy him, they shall not be able to enjoy him at all, nor any thing else; as not being in a capacity to act but in an *Earthly* Body. But to those that be of a mere animal temper, that relish no love but
10 that of themselves and their own interest, nor care for any but those that are serviceable to them and make for their profit, these being prone to judge of God according to the vileness of their own Spirit, will easily conceit, that God' s care of us and tenderness over us is onely proportionable to the fruit he reaps
15 by us; which is just none at all.

   12. And therefore this Arugment especially, and also the Two former though they be undeniable Demonstrations in themselves, yet they requiring a due resentment of Morality, that is of *Veracity, Justice* and *Goodness*, in him that is to be
20 perswaded by them; it will follow, that those whose Mindes are most blinded and debased by Vice, will feel least the force of them; and the *Noblest* and most *generous Spirit* will be the *most firmly assured of the Immortality of the Soul.*

The
IMMORTALITY
of
THE SOUL

5

The Third Book

10

Chap. I.

I. *Why the Author treats of the state of the Soul after Death, and
in what Method.* 2. *Arguments to prove that the Soul is ever
united vitally with some Matter or other.* 3. *Further Reasons to* 15
evince the same. 4. *That the Soul is capable of an* Aiery *and*
Aethereal *Body, as well as a* Terrestrial. 5. *That she ordinarily
passes out of an* Earthly *into an* Aëreal *Vehicle first.* 6.*That in
her Aiery Vehicle she is capable of* Sense, Pleasure, *and* Pain.
7. *That the main power of the Soul over her* Aëreal *Vehicle is the* 20
direction of Motion in the particles thereof. 8. *That she may also
adde or diminish Motion in her* Aethereal. 9. *How the purity of
the Vehicle confers to the quickness of Sense and Knowledge.* 10.
Of the Soul's power of changing the temper of her Aëreal *Vehicle*;
11.*As also the shape thereof.* [12.] 13. *The plainness of the last* 25
Axiome.

     I. We have, I hope, with undeniable evidence demonstrated
The Immortality of the Soul to such as neither by their slowness
of parts, nor any prejudice of Immorality, are made 30
incompetent Judges of the truth of Demonstrations of this kind
: so that I have already perfected my main Design. But my
own curiosity, and the desire of gratifying others who love to
entertain themselves with Speculations of this nature, do call
me out something further; if the very Dignity of the present 35
Matter I am upon doth not justly require me, as will be best
seen after the finishing thereof: which is *concerning the State of
the Soul after Death.* Wherein though I may not haply be able to
fix many foot so firmly as in the foregoing part of this Treatise,
yet I will assert nothing but what shall be reasonable, though 40
not demonstrable, and far preponderating to whatever shall be
alledged to the contrary, and in such clear order and Method,

that if what I write be not worthy to convince, it shall not be able to deceive or entangle by perplexedness and obscurity; and therefore I shall offer to view at once the main Principles upon which I shall build the residue of my Discourse.

5

AXIOME XXVII.

The Soul *separate from this* Terrestrial *Body is not released from all* Vital Union *with* Matter.

10   2. This is the general Opinion of the *Platonists. Plotinus* indeed dissents, especially concerning the most divine Souls, as if they at last were perfectly unbared of all Matter, and had no union with any thing but God himself: which I look upon as a fancy proceeding from the same inequality of temper, that

15   made him surmise that the most degenerate Souls did at last sleep in the bodies of Trees, and grew up merely into *Plantal life.* Such fictions as these of fancyfull men have much depraved the ancient *Cabbala* and sacred Doctrine which the *Platonists* themselves do profess to be θεοπαράδοτον, a holy

20   *Tradition* received from the mouth of God or Angels. But however *Plotinus* himself does not deny but till the Soul arrive to such an exceeding height of purification, that she acts in either an *Aiery* or *Celestial* Body.

But that she is never released so perfectly from all Matter,

25   how pure soever and tenuious, her condition of operating here in this life is greater presumption then can be fetcht from any thing else that she ever is. For we find plainly that her most subtile and most Intellectual oparations depend upon the *fitness of temper* in the *Spirits*; and that it is the *fineness* and *purity* of

30   them that invites her and enables her to love and look after *Divine* and *Intellectual* Objects: Which kind of Motions if she could exert immediately by her own proper power and essence, what should hinder her but that, having a will; she should bring it to effect? which yet we find she cannot if the *Spirits* be

35   *indisposed.* But, as I said, the Soul cannot be hindred by the undue temper of the Spirits in these Acts, if they be of that nature that they belong to the bare essence of the Soul quite prescinded from all Union with *Matter.* For then as to these Acts it is all one where the Soul is, that is, in *what Matter* she

40   is (and she must be in some, because the Universe is every where thick-set with *Matter)* whether she be raised into the purest regions of the Aire, or plunged down into the foulest

Receptacles of Earth or Water; for her *Intellectual* actings would be alike in both; this Conjunction in all likelihood engaging onely the *Plastick* and *Sensitive* powers of the Soul even when she is vitally united with *Matter*. What then is there imaginable in the *Body* that can hinder her in her nobler 5 Operations?

Wherefore it is plain that the nature of the Soul is such, as that she cannot act but in dependence on *Matter*, and that her Operations are some way or other alwaies modified thereby. And therefore if the Soul act at all after death, (which we have 10 demonstrated she does) it is evident that she is not released from all *vital union* with all kind of *Matter* whatsoever: Which is not onely the Opinion of the *Platonists*, but of *Aristotle* also, as may be easily gathered out of what we have above cited out of him. 15

3. Besides, it seems a very wilde leap in nature, that the Soul of Man, from being so deeply and muddily immersed into Matter as to keep company with Beasts, by vitall union with gross flesh and bones, should so on a suddain be changed, that she should not adhere to any Matter whatsoever, but ascend 20 into an ἀϋλότης *competible haply to none but* God himself; unless there be such Creatures as the *Platonists* call Νόεσ or *pure Intellects*. This must seem to any indifferent man very harsh and incongruous, especially if we consider what noble Beings there are on this side the Νόοι *or* Νόες, *that all the Philosophers* 25 that ever treated of them acknowledge to be vitally united with either *Aëreal* or *Aethereal* Vehicles. For of this condition are all the *Genii* or Angels.

It is sufficient therefore that the Soul never exceed the immateriality of those Orders of Beings; the lower sort whereof 30 that they are vitally united to Vehicles of *Aire*, their ignorance in Nature seems manifestly to bewray. For it had been an easy thing, and more for their credit, to have informed their followers better in the Mysteries of Nature; but that themselves were ignorant of these things, which they could not 35 but know, if they were not thus bound to their *Aiery* bodies. For then they were not engaged to move with the whole course of the *Aire*, but keeping themselves steddy, as being disunited from all Matter, they might in a moment have perceived both the *diurnal* and *annual motion* of the *Earth*, and so have saved 40 the Credit of their followers, by communicating this Theory to them; the want of the knowledge whereof spoils their repute

with them that understand the Systeme of the world better
then themselves, for all they boast of their Philosophy, so as if
it were the Dictate of the highest Angels.

5   AXIOME XXVIII.
There is a Triple Vital Congruity *in the Soul, namely* Aethereal,
Aëreal, *and* Terrestrial.

      4. That this is the common Opinion of the *Platonists*, I
10 have above intimated. That this Opinion is also true in it self,
appears from the foregoing Axiome. Of the *Terrestrial
Congruity* there can be no doubt; and as little can there be but
that at least one of the other two is to be granted, else the Soul
would be released from all *vital union with Matter* after Death.
15 Wherefore she has a *Vital aptitude* at least to unite with *Aire*:
But *Aire* is a common Receptacle of bad and good Spirits, (as
the *Earth* is of all sorts of men and beasts) nay indeed rather of
those that are in some sort or other bad, then of good, as it is
upon Earth. But the Soul of Man is capable of very high
20 refinements, even to a condition *purely Angelical*. Whence
Reason will judge it fit, and all Antiquity has voted it, That the
Souls of men arrived to such a due pitch of purification must at
last obtain *Celestial* Vehicles.

25   AXIOME XXIX.
*According to the usual custome of Nature, the Soul awakes
orderly into these* Vital Congruities, *not passing from one
Extreme to another without any stay in the middle.*

30   5. This Truth, besides that at first sight it cannot but
seem very reasonable, according to that known Aphorism,
Natura non facit saltum; so if it be further examined, the
solidity thereof will more fully appear. For considering how
small degrees of purification the Souls of almost all men get in
35 this life, even theirs who pass vulgarly for honest and good
men; it will plainly follow that very few arrive to their
Aethereal Vehicle immediately upon quitting their *Terrestrial*
Body; that being a priviledge that has appertained to none but
very Noble and *Heroical* Spirits indeed, of which History
40 records but very few. But that there may be degrees of purity
and excellency in the *Aëreal* Bodies, *is a thing that is not to be
denied, so that a just Nemesis* will finde out every one after

death.

AXIOME XXX.

The Soul in her Aëreal *Vehicle is capable of* Sense *properly so callad, and consequently of* Pleasure *and* Pain .   5

6. This plainly appears from the 27 and 28 Axioms. For there is a necessity of the resulting of *Sense* from Vital Union of the Soul with any Body whatsoever: and we may remember that the immediate Instrument of *Sense*, even in this *Earthly* 10 Body, are the *Spirits*; so that there can be no doubt this Truth. And *Pleasure* and *Pain* being the proper modification of *Sense*, and there being no Body but what is *possible*, it is evident that these *Vehicles of Aire* are subject to *Pain* as well as *Pleasure*, in this Region where ill things are to be met with as well as good.   15

AXIOME XXXI.

The Soul can neither impart to nor take away from the Matter of her Vehicle of Aire *any considerable degree of Motion, but yet can direct the particles moved which way she pleases by the* Imperium 20 *of her Will.*

7. The reasonableness of this Axiom may be evinced, partly out of the former; for considering the brushiness and angulosity of the parts of the *Air*, a more then ordinary Motion 25 or compressive Rest may very well prove painful to the Soul, and dis-harmonius to her touch: and partly from what we may observe in our own Spirits in this Body, Which we can onely direct, not give Motion to, nor diminish their Motion by our Imagination or Will, (for no man can imagine himself into Heat 30 or Cold, the sure consequences of extraordinary Motion and Rest, by willing his Spirits to move faster or slower; but he may direct them into the Organs of spontaneous Motion, and so by moving the grosser parts of the Body, by this direction he may spend them, and heat these parts in the expence of them; 35 and this is all we can doe:) and partly from that Divine Providence that made all things, and measures out the Powers and Faculties of his Creatures according to his own Wisdome and Counsel, and therefore has bound that state of the Soul to streighter conditions, that is competible to the bad as well as to 40 the good.

AXIOME XXXII.

Though the Soul can neither confer nor take away any considerable degree of Motion from the Matter of her Aiery *Vehicle, yet nothing hinders but that she may doe both in her* Aethereal.

8. The reason hereof is, because the particles of her *Aethereal* Vehicle consist partly of smooth spherical Figures, and partly of tenuious Matter, so exceeding liquid that it will without any violence comply to any thing: whenas the *Aire*, as may be observed in Winde-Guns, has parts so stubborn and so stiff, that after they have been compressed to such a certain degree that the barrel of the Piece grows hot again, they have not lost their shapes nor virtue; but like a spring of Steel, liberty being given, they return to their natural posture with that violence, that they discharge a Bullet with equal force that Gun-power does. Besides that *the Goodness* of that Deity on whom all Beings depend may be justly thought to have priviledged the *Aethereal Congruity of Life* (which awakes onely in perfectly-obedient Souls, such as may be trusted as throughly faithful to his Empire) with a larger power then the other, there being no incompetibleness in the Subject. For it is as easy a thing to conceive that God may endow a Soul with a power of moving or resting Matter, as of determining the motions thereof.

AXIOME XXXIII.

The purer the Vehicle is, the more quick and perfect are the Perceptive *Faculties of the Soul.*

9. The truth of this we may in a manner experience in this life, where we find that the quickness of Hearing, Seeing, Tasting, Smelling, the nimbleness of Reminiscency, Reason, and all other *Perceptive* Faculties, are advanced or abated by the clearness, or foulness and dulness of the *Spirits* of our Body; and that Oblivion and Sottishness arise from their thickness and earthiness, or waterishness, or whatsoever other gross consistency of them: which distemper removed, and the Body being replenished with good Spirits in sufficient plenty and purity, the Mind recovers her activity again, remembers what she had forgot, and understands what she was before uncapable of, sees and hears at a greater distance; and so of

the rest.

AXIOME XXXIV.

The Soul has a marvellous power of not onely changing the temper of her Aiery Vehicle, but also of the external shape thereof.

10. The truth of the first part of this Axiome appears from daily experience; for we may frequently observe how strangely the *Passions* of the Mind will work upon our Spirits in this state; how Wrath, and Grief, and Envy will alter the Body, to say nothing of other Affections. And assuredly the finer the Body is, the more mutable it is upon this account: so that the *Passions* of the Mind must needs have a very great influence upon the Soul's *Aëreal Vehicle*; which though they cannot change into any thing but Air, yet they may change this *Air* into qualifications as vastly different as *Vertue* is from *Vice*, *Sickness* from *Health*, *Pain* from *Pleasure*, *Light* from *Darkness*, and the *stink* of a Gaol from the *Aromatick odours* of a flourishing *Paradise*.

11. The truth of the latter part is demonstrable from the latter part of the 31 Axiome. For supposing a power in the Soul of directing the motions of the particles of her fluid Vehicle, it must needs follow that she will also have a power of shaping it in some measure according to her own Will & Fancy. To which you may adde, as no contemptible pledge of this Truth, what is done in that kind by our Will and Fancy in this life: as, onely because I will and fancy the moving of my Mouth, Foot, or Fingers, I can move them, provided I have but Spirits to direct into this motion; and the whole Vehicle of the Soul is in a manner nothing else but Spirits. The *Signatures* also of the *Foetus* in the Womb by the Desire and Imagination of the Mother is very serviceable for the evincing of this Truth: but I shall speak of it more fully in its place.

AXIOME XXXV.

It is rational to think, that as some Faculties are laid asleep in Death or after Death, so others may awake that are more sutable for that state.

12. The truth of this Axiome appears from hence, That
our Souls come not by chance, but are made by an All-wise
God, who foreseeing all their states, has fitted the *Excitation* or
Consopition of Powers and Faculties sutably to the present
5   condition they are to be in.

AXIOME XXXVI.

Whether the Vital Congruity *of the Soul expire, as whose period
beingquite unwound, or that of the Matter be defaced by any*
10   *essential Disharmony,* Vital Union *immediately ceases.*

13. This last Axiome is plain enough of it self at first sight,
and the usefulness thereof may be glanced at in its due place.
These are the main Truths I shall recurre to, or at least
15   suppose, in my following Disquisitions: others will be more
seasonably delivered in the continuation of our Discourse.

20   Chap. II.

1.*Of the* dimensions *of the Soul considered barely in her self.* 2.
Of the Figure of the Soul's Dimensions. 3. *Of the* Heterogeneity
of her essence 4. *That there is an* Heterogeneity *in her* Plastick
25   part *distinct from the* Perceptive. 5. *Of the acting of this* Plastick
part in her framing of the Vehicle. 6. *The excellency of* Des-
Cartes *his Philosophy.* 7. *That the* Vehicles of Ghosts *have as
much of* solid corporeal Substance *in them as the* Bodies of Men.
8. *The folly of the contrary Opinion evinced.* 9. *The advantage*
30   *of the Soul, for matter of Body in the other state, above this.*

I. That we may now have a more clear and determinate
apprehension of *the nature and condition of the Soul out of the
Body*, let us first consider her a while, what she is in her own
35   Essence, without any reference to any *Body* at all, and we shall
find her *a Substance extended and indiscerpible*, as may be
easily gathered out of what we have above written. And it is a
seasonable Contemplation here (where we consider the Soul as
having left this *Terrestrial* Body) that she hath as ample, if not
40   more ample, *Dimensions* of her own, then are visible in the
Body she has left. Which I think worth taking notice of, that it
may stop the mouths of them that, not without reason, laugh

at those unconceivable and ridiculous fancies of the Schools; that first rashly take away all *Extension* from *Spirits*, whether *Souls* or *Angels*, and then dispute how many of them booted and spurr'd may dance on a needles point at once. Fooleries much derogatory to the Truth, and that pinch our Perception 5 into such an intolerable streightness and evanidness, that we cannot imagine any thing of our own Being; and if we do, are prone to fall into despair, or contempt of our selves, by fancying our selves such unconsiderable Motes of the Sun.

2. But as it is very manifest that *the Soul has Dimensions*, 10 and yet *not infinite*, and therefore that she is necessarily bounded in some *Figure* or other; so it is very uncertain whether there be any *peculiar Figure* natural to her, answerable to *animal shape*, or whether she be of her self of either a *Round* or *Oval* figure, but does change her shape 15 according as occasion requires. It is not material to define any thing in this Question more then thus, That when the Soul acts in *Terrestrial Matter*, her *Plastick* part is determined to the Organization of the Body into humane form; and in the *Aëreal* or *Aethereal*, that she is neither more nor less determined to 20 any shape then the *Genii* or Angels; and that if their Vehicles are more naturally guided into one shape then another, that hers is in the same condition; so that in her visible Vehicle she will bear the ordinary form of *Angels*, such a countenance, and so cloathed, as they. 25

3. That which is more material, I think is more easie to be defined, and that is, whether the Soul be one *Homogeneal* Substance, or whether it be in some manner *Heterogeneal*. That the latter is in some measure true, is manifest from what we have elsewhere written, namely, That the *Perceptive* faculty 30 reaches not throughout the whole Soul, but is confined to a certain part, which we called the *Centre* or *Eye of the Soul*, as also her *Perceptive part*; but all the rest *Plastick*. But here arises a further Scruple, whether there be not an *Heterogeneity* in the very *Plastick* part also of the Soul. The *Aristoteleans* 35 seem to be confident there is not, and do affirm that if there were an Eye in the Toe, the Toe would see as well as the Head. Of which I very much doubt: For hence it would follow that some Creatures would have a glimmering Light all over, they being in a manner all over transparent, and some thin and 40 clear Complexions might haply have the perception of Light betwixt the lower parts of their Fingers, which are in some

good measure pellucid; and therefore Life and Spirits being
continued from thence to the *Conarion*, as they are, or to the
fourth Ventricle of the Brain, it would follow that the Soul
would have a perception of some glimmerings of Light from
5   thence, which were to *see* there as well as to *feel*.

    4.   Wherefore it seems more rational to admit an
Heterogeneity in the *Plastick* part of the Soul also, and to
acknowledge that every removal from the Seat of Common
Sense, that is to say, every Circle that surrounds the *Centre of*
10 *the Soul*, has not the same bounds of power, neither for number
nor extent.   But that as concerning the former, there is a
gradual falling off from the first excellency, which is the
Perceptive part of the Soul; the closest Circle to which is that
part of the *Plastick* that is able to convey Objects of *Sight* as
15 well as of *Touch* and *Hearing*, and what other Senses else there
may be in the Soul.   The next Circle is *Hearing* without *Seeing*
though not without *Touch*:   for *Touch* spreads through all.   But
in its exteriour region, which is excessively the greatest, it
transmits the circumstantiated Perceptions of no Objects those
20 that are *Tactile*; but to others it is onely as a dead Medium, as
the Circle of *Hearing* is but as a dead medium to the Objects of
Sight.   So that if we would please our Imagination with *Ficinus*,
in fancying the Soul as a Star, we shall doe it more perfectly if
we look upon her in her Circles, as having an *Halo* about her:
25 For the Soul to our *Reason* is no more *Homogeneal* then that
Spectacle is to our *Sight*.

    5. But if we look upon the Soul as ever propending to some
personal shape, the direction of the *Plastick* rayes must then
tend to a kind of Organization, so far as is conducent to the
30 state the Soul is in, whether in an *Aiery* or *Aethereal* Vehicle.
For that the *Plastick* power omits or changes as she is drawn
forth by the nature of the Matter she acts upon, is discoverable
in her Organization of our Bodies here.   For in all likelihood the
Soul in her self is as much of one sex as another; which makes
35 her sometimes sign the *Matter* with both, but that very
seldome: and therefore it is mananifest that she omits one part
of her *Plastick* power, and makes use of the other in almost all
efformations of the *Foetus*.

    Whence it is easie to conclude, that supposing her *Plastick*
40 power naturally work the *Aethereal* or *Aëreal* Vehicle into any
animal shape, it may put forth onely such strokes of the
efformative virtue as are convenient and becoming the

Angelical Nature.

But according to this Hypothesis haply all Objects of Sense will not arrive to the *Centre of the Soul* from every part of the Horizon; no not though this Organization were not natural, but merely arbitrarious. But be the Soul conceived either bound up 5 thus into *animal form*, or spread loose into any careless round shape, according as her rayes shall display themselves in her *Vehicle of Aire* or *Aether*, yet the *Seat of sight* will be duely restrained, which is a consideration of no contemptible consequence.   10

6. This in general may suffice concerning the very Nature of the Soul it self, her *Extension* and *Heterogeneity*. I shall onely adde to this one Observable concerning her *Aiery* and *Aethereal Vehicle*, and then I shall descend to more particular disquisitions. Rash fancies and false deductions from 15 misunderstood Experiments have made some very confident that there is a *Vacuum* in Nature, and that every Body by how much more light it is, so much less substance it has in it self. A thing very fond and irrational, at the first sight, to such as are but indifferently well versed in the incomparable 20 Philosophy of *Renatus Des-Cartes*, whose dexterous wit and through insight into the nature and laws of *Matter* has so parfected the reasons of those *Phaenomena* that *Democritus*, *Epicurus, Lucretius*and others have puzzled themselves about, that there seems nothing now wanting as concerning that way 25 of Philosophizing, but patience and an unprejudiced judgment to peruse what he has writ.

7. According therefore to his Philosophy and the Truth, there is ever as much Matter or Body in one consistency as another; as for example, there is as much Matter in a Cup of 30 Aire as in the same Cup filled with Water, and as much in this Cup of Water as if it were filled with Lead or Quicksilver. Which I take notice of here, that I may free the imagination of men from that ordinary and idiotick misapprehension which they entertain of *Spirits* that appear, as if they were as evanid 35 and devoid of Substance as the very Shadows of our Bodies cast against a Wall, or our Images reflected from a River or Looking-glass; and therefore from this errour have given them names accordingly, calling the Ghosts of men that present themselves to them, Εἴδωλα and *Umbrae, Images* and *Shades*. 40 The which, the more visible they are, they think then the more substantial; fancying that the *Aire* is so condensed, that there

is not onely more of it, but also that simply there is more
Matter or Substance, when it appears thus visible, then there
was in the same space before. And therefore they must needs
conceit that Death reduces us to a pitiful thin pittance of Being,
5   that our Substance is in a manner lost, and nothing but a
tenious reek remains; no more in proportion to us, then what a
sweating horse leaves behind him as he gallops by in a frosty
morning.   Which certainly must be a very lamentable
consideration to such as love this thick and plump Body they
10 bear about with them, and are pleased to consider how many
pounds they outweighed their Neighbour the last time they
were put in the balance together.

　　8. But if a kinde of dubious Transparency will demonstrate
the *deficiency* of Corporeal Substance, a Pillar of *Crystal* will
15 have less thereof then one of *Tobacco-smoak*; which though it
may be so doubtful and evanid an Object to the Eye, if we try it
by the Hand, it will prove exceeding solid: as also these *Ghosts*
that are said to appear in this manner have proved to them
that have touched them, or have been touched by them. For it
20 is a thing ridiculous and unworthy of a Philosopher, to judge
the measure of *corporeal Matter* by what it seems to our sight;
for so Aire would be nothing at all: or what it is to our *handing*
or weighing of it; for so indeed a Cup of Quick-silver would
seem to have infinitely more Matter in it then one fill'd with
25 Aire onely, and a vessel of Water less when it is plung'd under
the water in the River, then when it is carried in the Aire. But
we are to remember, that let *Matter* be of what consistency it
will, as thin and pure as the flame of a candle, there is not less
of *corporeal Substance* therein then there is in the same
30 dimensions of Silver, Lead, or Gold.

　　9. So that we need not bemoan the shrivell'd condition of
the deceased, as if they were stript almost of all Substance
corporeal, and were too thinly clad to enjoy themselves as to
any Object of Sense. For they have no less Body then we our
35 selves have, only this Body is far more active then ours, being
more *spiritualized*, that is to say, having greater degrees of
Motion communicated to it: As it does also in that which is the
effect of Motion, to wit the tenuity and subtilty of its particles,
whereby it is enabled to imitate, in some sort, the proper
40 priviledge of Spirits that pass through all Bodies whatsoever.
And these Vehicles of the Soul, by reason of the tenuity of their
parts, may well pass through such Matter as seems to us

impervious, though it be not really so to them. For Matter reduced to such fluid subtilty of particles as are invisible, may well have entrance through Pores unperceptible.

Whence it is manifest that the Soul, speaking in a natural sense loseth nothing by Death, but is a very considerable 5 gainer thereby. For she does not onely possess as much Body as before, with as full and solid dimensions, but has that accession cast in, of having this Body more invigorated with Life and Motion then it was formerly. Which consideration I could not but take notice of, that I might thereby expunge that 10 false conceit that adheres to most mens fancies, of that *evanid* and *starved* condition of the other state.

15

Chap. III.

I. *That the natural abode of the Soul after death is the* Air. 2. *That she cannot quit the* Aëreal Regions *till the* Aethereal Congruity *of life be awakened in her.* 3. *That all Souls are not* 20 *in the same Region of the Aire.* 4. Cardan's *conceit of placing all* Daemons *in the upper Region.* 5. *The use of this conceit for the shewing the reason of their seldome appearing.* 6. *That this* Phaenomenon *is salved by a more rational Hypothesis.* 7. *A further confutation of* Cardan's *Opinion.* 8. *More tending to the* 25 *same scope.* 9. *The Original of* Cardan's *errour concerning the remote operations of* Daemons. 10. *An Objection how* Daemons *and Souls separate can be in this lower Region, where Winds and Tempests are so frequent.* 11. *A preparation to an Answer from the consideration of the nature of the Winds.* 12. *Particular* 30 *Answers to the Objection.* 13. *A further Answer from the nature of the* Statick Faculty *of the Soul.* 14. *Another from the suddain power of actuating her vehicle.* 15. *What incommodations she suffers from haile, rain, etc.*

35

I. Those more particular Enquiries we intend to fall upon, may be reduced to these few Heads: viz. *The place of the Soul's abode, Her Employment,* and *Her Moral condition after Death.* That the *place of her abode* is the *Aire,* is the constant opinion of the ancient Philosophers and natural Theologers, 40 who do unanimously make *that* Element the Receptacle of Souls departed: which therefore they called ἅιδης ,that is ἅιδης

,because men deceased are in a state of *invisibility*, as the place
they are confined to is an Element utterly *invisible* of its own
nature, and is accloy'd also with caliginous mists, and enveloped by vicissitudes with the dark shadow of the Earth. The
5   truth of this Opinion of theirs is plainly demonstrable from the
29 and 31 Axiomes. For Nature making no enormous jumps, it
must needs follow, that Separate Souls must take their first
station in the *Aire*, because that *Vital Congruity* that fits an
Aëreal Vehicle does of order awaken immediately upon the
10   quitting of the *Earthly Body*.

2. Wherefore the Soul being thus vitally united with a
Body or *Vehicle of Aire*, it is impossible that she should drive
out of those Regions: because her motions are only according to
the capacity of her Vehicle, she being not able to alter the
15   consistency thereof into any more subtile or purer temper then
the *Aire* will admit, keeping still its own Species. Only she
may *conspissate* the *Aire* by directing the motion thereof
towards her, and so squeezing out a considerable part of the
first and second Element may retain more Aire then ordinary:
20   But she cannot command the Air from her so entirely, as to
actuate these two Elements alone, or any considerable part of
them, because the *Aethereal Congruity* of life is as yet wholly
asleep; nor is it in the power of the Soul to awake it as she
pleases: and therefore it would be Pain and Death to her to
25   attempt the removal of the *Aëreal* matter quite from her.
Besides that it would require such a force as would imply a
contribution of motion to it, as well as direction of it, to make it
able to bear against other parts of the Aire that love not to be
streightned nor crouded: which though it may haply be done in
30   some measure, yet that she may by this force of direction
recover a whole *Vehicle of Aether*, seems excessively
improbable, as is plain from the 31. Axiome.

3. Wherefore it is necessary that the Soul departed this life
should be somewhere in the *Aire*, though it be not at all
35   necessary that they should inhabit all of them the *same Region*
thereof. For as some Souls are *more purified* then others when
they leave the Body, so a *more pure* degree of *Vital Congruity*
will awake in them: whence by that Divine *Nemesis* that runs
through all things, they will be naturally conveyed to such
40   places and be associated to such company as is most congruous
to their Nature; and will be as distinctly sorted by that Eternal
Justice that God has so deeply ingrafted in the very essential

contexture of the Universe, as humane Laws dispose of persons with us, sending some to Prisons, some to Pest-houses, and others to the *Prytaneum.*

4. It will therefore, in all likelinood, fall to some of their shares to be fatally fettered to this *lower Region of the Aire,* as 5 I doubt not but many other Spirits are; though *Cardan* much pleases himself with a peculiar conceit of his own, as if the *supreme Region of the Aire* was the only habitation of all *Daemons* or Spirits whatever, and that their descent to us is as rare as the diving of Men into the bottome of the Sea, and 10 almost as difficult, this *thick Aire* we breath in being in a manner as unsutable to their tenuious consistencies as the *Water* is to us; in which we are fain to hold our breath, and consequently to make a very short stay in that Element.

Besides that he fancies the passage of the *Middle Region* 15 tedious to them, by reason of its Coldness; which therefore he saith is as it were a fence betwixt us and them, as the Sea is betwixt the Fishes and us; whom though we exceed much in Wit and Industry, and have a great desire to catch them and kill them, yet we get very few into our hands in comparison of 20 those that scape us: And so these *Daemons,* though they bear us no good will, by bodily conflict they can hurt none of us (it being so difficult a thing to come at us) and very few of us by their Art and Industry.

For this fancyfull Philosopher will have them only attempt 25 us as we do the Fishes, by Baits, and Nets, and Eel-spears, or such like Engines which we cast into the bottom of the Water: So, saith he, these Aëreal *Genii,* keeping their station above in the third Region of the Aire (as we do on the bank of the River, or in a Boat on the Sea, when we fish) by sending down *Dreams* 30 and *Apparitions,* may entangle some men so, that by affrightments and disturbances of mind at last, though at this distance, they may work their ruine and destruction.

5. This Hypothesis, I suppose, he has framed to give an account why the appearing of the *Genii* is so seldome, and why 35 so little hurt is done by them as there is. For an Answer would be ready, that this lower Aire is no Element for them to abide in: and that it is as foolishly argued by those that say there are no Spirits, because they are so seldome seen, as if the Fishes, upon a concession of Speech and Reason to their mute Tribe, 40 should generally conclude, that there are such Creatures as Men or Horses, because it happens so very seldome that they

can see them; and should contemn and laugh at those Fishes
that, having had the hap to meet with them, should say they
have seen such Creatures, as if they were fanatick and
lunatick, and not well in their wits, or else too much in them,
5   and that they contrived such fictions for some political design.

6. Which Parable may hold good, though not upon the
same grounds, only by substituting *difference of condition* for
distance of place; and the similitude will prove as sound as
before. For, for a Spirit to *condensate* his Vehicle to almost a
10   Terrestrial grossness and Visibility, is as rare and uncouth as
for Terrestrial animals to dive to the bottom of the Sea, and it's
likely every jot as difficult: and so the reason as obvious why so
few are seen, and the confident denial of their existence as rash
and foolish, by them that have not seen them themselves. For
15   it is as if the Fishes should conceit amongst themselves about
the existence of Men, and their diving into the Water, and
whether there were any places haunted in the Sea; as those
would be the most famous where they fish for Pearls, or that
cause the most frequent Shipwrecks, or are most pleasant to
20   swim in. And some notable occasion, mischance, or weighty
design, such as occurre more rarely, must be reasonably
conceived the only invitements to the *Genii* to expose
themselves to our view.

7. That there is so little hurt done by them, need not be
25   resolved into the *distance of their habitation*, but into the *Law of
the Universe*, whose force penetrates through all Orders of
Beings. Besides, it is too trivial and idiotick a conceit, and far
below the pitch of a Philosopher, to think that *all* Aëreal Spirits
are Haters of Mankind, so as to take delight merely in
30   destroying them. For Men do not hate Fishes because they live
in another Element different from theirs, but catch them
merely in love to themselves, for gain and food; which the
Aiery *Genii* cannot aim at in destroying of us. But to doe
mischief merely for mischief's sake, is so excessive an
35   Enormity, that some doubt whether it be competible to any
Intellectual Being. And therefore *Cardan* ought to have proved
that first: as also, if there be any so extremely degenerate,
that there be many of them, or rather so many that they
cannot be awed by the number of those that are less depraved.
40   For we may observe that men amongst our selves that are
sufficiently wicked, yet they abhor very much from those
things that are grossly and causlesly destructive to either Man

or Beast; and themselves would help to destroy, punish, or at least hinder the attempters of such wild and exorbitant outrages that have no pretence of Reason, but are a mere exercise of Cruelty and Vexation to other Creatures.

He also ought to have demonstrated, that all Mankind are 5 not the *Peculium* of some Spirits or other, and that there are not invisible Governours of Nations, Cities, Families, and sometime of particular Men, and that at least a *Political Goodness*, such as serves for the safety of Persons and what belongs to them, is not exceedingly more prevalent even in 10 these Kingdomes of the *Aire*, then *gross Injustice*. For all this may be on this side of the *Divine Life*: so that there is no feate of making these Aëreal Inhabitants over-perfect by this Supposition. In a word, he should have proved that *Political Order*, in the full exercise thereof, did not reach from *Heaven* to 15 *Earth*, and pierce into the *Subterraneous Regions* also, if there be any *Intellectual Creatures* there. For this will suffice to give a reason that so little hurt is done, though all places be full of *Aëreal Spirits*.

8. Adde unto all this, that though they may not be 20 permitted to doe any gross evil themselves, and to kill men at pleasure without their consents, yet they may abet them in such wayes, or invite them to such courses, as will prove destructive to them: but, it may be, with no greater plot then we have when we set Doggs together by the eares, fight Cocks, 25 bait Beares and Bulls, run Horses, and the like; where often, by our occasion, as being excited and animated by us, they pursue their own inclinations to the loss of their lives.

But though we do not care to kill a Dog or a Cock in this way yet there are none so barbarous as to knock these 30 Creatures on the head merely because they will doe so. So these worser kind of *Genii*, acording as their tempers are, may haply follow some men prone to such or such vices, in which they may drive them in way of contest, or to please their own fancies, to the utmost they can doe in it; and, taking their parts 35 sport themselves in making one man overcome another in duelling, in drinking, in craft and undermining, in wenching, in getting riches, in clambering to honours; and so of the rest. Where it may be their pastime to try the Victory of that Person they have taken to; and if he perish by the hurry of their 40 temptations and animations, it is a thing they intended no more, it may be, then he that sets his Cock into the pit desires his neck should be broke: but if it happen so, the sorrow is much alike in both cases.

Wherefore these Spirits may doe mischief enough in the world, in abetting men that act it, though haply they neither 5 take pleasure in doing of it upon any other termes, nor if they did, are able to doe it, there being so many watchful eyes over them. For these *Aëreal Legions* are as capable of *Political Honesty*, and may as deeply resent it, as the nations of the Earth do, and it may be more deeply.

10   9. But if these Creatures were removed so far off as *Cardan* would have them, I do not see how they could have any communion at all with us, to doe us either good or hurt. For that they are able to send *Apparitions* or *Dreams* at this distance, is it self but a Dream, occasioned from that first 15 Errour in the *Aristotelean* Philosophy, that makes God and the Intelligences act from the heavenly sphears, and so to produce all these Effects of Nature below; such as can never be done but by a present *Numen* and *Spirit of Life* that pervades all things.

20   10. This conceit therefore of his shall be no hindrance to our concluding, That this *lower Region of the Aire* is also replenisht with *Daemons*. Which if it be, it is not unlikely but that the *Impurer Souls* wander there also; though I have taken all this pains to bring still greater trouble upon my self. For it 25 is obvious to object that which *Lucretius* has started of old, that this Region being so obnoxious to *Windes* and *Tempests*, the Souls will not be able to keep their *Vehicles of Aire* about them, but that they will be blown in pieces by the roughness of these storms. But we may be easily delivered of this solicitude, if we 30 consider the Nature of the *Windes*, the nature of these *Vehicles*, and the *Statick* power of the Soul. For to say they will make as good shift as the *Genii* here, is not fully satisfactory, because a man would also willingly understand how the *Genii* themselves are not liable to this inconvenience. My Answer therefore shall 35 reach both.

11. That *Windes* are nothing else but Watery particles at their greatest agitation, *Cartesius* has very handsomely demonstrated in his *Meteors*: Which particles do not so much drive the Aire before them, as pass through it, as a flight of 40 arrows and showers of haile or rain. One part of the Aire therefore is not driven from another; but it is as if one should conceive so many little pieces of haire twirling on their middle

point as at quarter-staffe, and so passing through the Aire; which motion would pass free, without carrying the Aire along with it. This therefore being the nature of *Winde*, the Aire is not torn apieces thereby, though we finde the *impetus* of it moving against *us*, because it cannot penetrate *our* Bodies with 5 that facility that it does the *Aire*.

12. But the *Vehicles* of the *Genii* and Souls deceased are much what of the very nature of the *Aire*; whence it is plainly impossible that the *Winde* should have any other force on them then what it has on the rest of that Element; and therefore the 10 least thing imaginable will hold all the parts together. Which is true also if the *Winde* did carry along the *Aire* with it: for then the Vehicles of the *Genii* would move along with the stream, suffering little or no violence at all, unless they would force themselves against it. Which they are not necessitated to doe, 15 as indeed not so much as to come into it, or not at least to continue in it, but may take shelter, as other living Creatures doe, in houses, behind walls, in woods, dales, caverns, rocks and other obvious places; and that maturely enough, the change of Aire and prognostick of storms being more 20 perceptible to them then to any terrestrial animal.

13. And yet they need not be so cautious to keep out of danger, they having a power to grapple with the greatest of it, which is their *Statick* faculty; which arises from the power of *directing the motion* of the particles of their Vehicle. For they 25 having this power of *directing the motion* of these particles which way they please, by Axiome 31. it necessarilly follows, that they can determinate their course inwards, or toward the Centre; by which direction they will be all kept close together, firm and tight: which ability I call the *Statick* power of the Soul. 30 Which if it can direct the whole agitation of the particles of the Vehicle, as well those of the first and second Element as those of the Air, and that partly towards, the Centre, and partly in a countertendency against the storms, this force and firmness will be far above the strongest *Windes* that she can possibly 35 meet with.

14. Wherefore the Soul's Vehicle is in no danger from the boisterousness of the *Winds*, and if it were, yet there is no fear of cessation of Life. For as the wind blows off one part of Aire, it brings on though there be no need to take refuge in so large 40 an Hypothesis. And it is more probable that she is more peculiarly united to one part of the Aire then another, and that

she dismisses her Vehicle but by degrees, as our Spirits leasurely pass away by insensible Perspiration.

15. We see how little the Soul's Vehicle can be incommodated by storms of *Winde*. And yet *Rain, Hail, Snow* and *Thunder* will incommodate her still less. For they pass as they do through other parts of the *Aire*, which close again immediately, and leave neither wound nor scarre behinde them. Wherefore all these *Meteors* in their Mediocrity may be a pleasure to her and refreshment; and in their excess no long pain, nor in their highest rage any destruction of life at all. From whence we may safely conclude, that not only the *Upper* Region, but this *Lower* also, may be inhabited both by the *deceased Souls* of *Men* and by *Daemons*.

Chap. IV.

I. *That the Soul once having quitted this Earthly Body becomes a* Daemon 2. *Of the* External Senses *of the Soul separate, their number and limits in the Vehicle.* 3. *Of* Sight *in a Vehicle* organized *and unorganized.* 4. *How* Daemons *and* separate Souls hear *and* see *at a vast Distance: and whence it is that though they may so easiiy* hear *or* see us, *we may neither* see *nor* hear them. 5. *That they have* Hearing *as well as* Sight. 6. Of the *Touch, Smell, Tast, and* Nourishment *of* Daemons. 7. *The external employment that the* Genii *and Souls deceased may have out of the Body.* 8. *That the actions of Separate Souls, in reference to us, are most-what comformable to their life here on Earth.* 9. *What their Entertainments are in reference to themselves.* 10. *The distinction of Orders of* Daemons *from the places they most frequent.*

I. The next thing we are to enquire into is *the Employment of the Soul after Death*; how she can entertain her self, and pass away the time, and that either in *Solitude*, in *Company*, or as she is *a Political member of some Kingdome or Empire.* Concerning all which in the general we may conclude, that it is with her as with the rest of the Aëreal *Genii,* ἡ γὰρ ψυχὴ ἀποδυσαμένη τὸ σῶμα δαιμόνιόν ἐστι. *for the Soul having once put off this Terrestrial Body becomes a* Genius *her self; as Maximus Tyrius, Xenocrates, Philo and others expressly affirm.* But we shall consider these things more particularly.

2. As for those *Employments* wherewith she may entertain her self in *solitude*, they are either *Objects* of the *External Senses*, or of the *Inward Minde*. Concerning the *former* whereof it is more easie to move Questions then satisfie them; as 5 Whether she have the same number of Senses she had in this life. That she is endued with *Hearing, Sight* and *Touch*, I think there can be no scruple, because there will fall to her share necessarily, whether her *Vehicle* be organized or not; and that of *Seeing* and *Touch* is the most uncontrovertible of all. For the 10 sense of visible Objects being discovered to us by transmission of Motion through those Spherical particles that are continued along from the Object through the Aire to our very Organ of Sight (which sees merely by reason of these particles being vitally united with the Soul) the same particles pervading all 15 the Soul's Vehicle, it is impossible but that she should *see*. But the Question is, whether she *sees* in every part thereof. To which I must answer, No: partly from what I have already declared concerning the *Heterogeneity* of her *Plastick part*; and partly from a gross inconvenience that would follow this 20 Supposition. For if we should grant that the Soul saw in every part of her Vehicle, every Object that is near would not only seem double, but centuple, or millecuple; which would be a very ugly enormity and defacement of *Sight*. Wherefore we have, with very good reason, restrained the *Visive faculty* of the soul 25 in this state of *Separation*, as well as it was in the *Terrestrial Body*.

3. But this hinders nothing but that the Soul, when she lies in one *Homogeneal* orb of Aire, devoid of organization, may *see* round about her, behinde, before, above, beneath, and every 30 way. But if she organize her Vehicle, *Sight* may haply be restrain'd, as in us who cannot see behinde us. Which Consideration we toucht upon before.

4. It is plain therefore that these *Aëreal Spirits*, though we cannot see them, cannot miss of *seeing* us; and that, it may be, 35 from a mighty distance, if they can transform their Vehicle, or the Organ of Sight, into some such advantageous Figure as is wrought in Dioptrick Glasses. Which power will infinitely exceed the contracting amd dilating of the pupil of our Eye, which yet is a weaker and more defectuous attempt towards so 40 high a Priviledge as we speak of: which notwithstanding may seem very possible in *Spirits*, from 31 and 34 Axiomes. The

same also may be said of their *Hearing*. For the same principle
may enable them to shape themselves Organs for the receiving
of *Sounds*, of greater art and excellency then the most accurate
Acoustick we read of, or can excogitate.

5   Wherefore it is a very childish mistake to think, that
because we neither *see* the shape nor *hear* the discourse of
Spirits, that they neither *hear* nor *see us* .For soft Bodies are
impressible by hard ones, but not on the contrary; as melted
Wax will receive the Signature of the Seal, but the Seal is not
10   at all impressed upon by the Wax. And so a solid Body will
stop the course of the Aire, but the Aire will not stop the course
of a solid Body; and every inconsiderable terrestrial consistency
will reflect Light, but Light scarce moves any terrestrial Body
out of its place, but is rebounded back by it. That therefore
15   that is most tenuious and thin, is most passive, and therefore if
it be once the Vehicle of Sense, is most sensible.

Whence it will follow, that the reflexion of Light from
Objects being able to move our Organs, that are not so fine,
they will more necessarily move those of the *Genii*, and at a
20   greater distance. But their Bodies being of *diaphanous Aire*, it
is impossible for us to *see* them, unless they will give
themselves the trouble of reducing them to a more *terrestrial
consistency*, whereby they may reflect light. Nor can we easily
hear their ordinary speech, partly because a very gentle motion
25   of the Aire will act upon their Vehicles, and partly because
they may haply use the finer and purer part of that Element in
this exercise, which is not so fit to move our Sense. And
therefore unless they will be heard *datâ operâ* (of which the
Devil of *Mascon* is a notorious example) naturally that impress
30   of the Air in their usual discourse can never strike *our* Organ.

5. And that we may not seem to say all this for nought;
that they will have *Hearing* as well as *Seeing*, appears from
what I have intimated above, that *this Faculty* is ranged near
the Common *Sensorium* in the Vehicle, as well as that of *Sight*;
35   and therefore the Vehicle being all Air, such percussions of it
as cause the sense of Sound in us will necessarily doe the like
in them; but more accurately, haply, if they organize their
Vehicle for the purpose, which will answer to the arrection of
the Ears of Animals, for the better taking in the Sound.

40   6. That they have the sense of *Touch* is inevitably true,
else how could they feel resistance, which is necessary in the
bearing of one Body against another, because they are

impenetrable? And to speak freely my mind, it will be a very hard thing to disprove that they have not something analogical to *Smell* and *Tast*, which are very near a-kin to *Touch* properly so called. For *Fumes* and *Odours* passing so easily through the Air, will very naturally insinuate into their Vehicles also: 5 which *Fumes*, if they be grosser and humectant, may raise that diversification of *Touch* which we Mortals call *Tasting*: if more subtle and dry, that which we call *Smelling*. Which if we should admit, we are within modest bounds as yet in comparison of others; as *Cardan*, who affirms downright that 10 the Aëreal *Genii* are nourished, and that some of them get into the Bodies of Animals to batten themselves there in their Bloud and Spirits. Which is also averred by *Marcus* the *Mesopotamian Eremite* in *Psellus*, who tells us that the purer sort of the *Genii* are nourished by drawing in the Air, as our 15 Spirits are in the Nerves and Arteries; and that other *Genii*, of a courser kinde, suck in moisture, not with the Mouth as we do, but as a Sponge does water. And *Moses Aegyptius* writes concerning the *Zabii*, that they eat of the blood of their Sacrifice, because they thought it was the food of the *Daemons* 20 they worshipped, and that by eating thereof they were in a better capacity to communicate with them. Which things if they could be believed, that would be no such hard Probleme concerning the *Familiars* of Witches, why they *suck* them. But such curiosities, being not much to our purpose, I willingly 25 omit.

7. The conclusion of what has been said is this, That it is certain that the *Genii*, and consequently the Souls of men departed, who *ipso facto* are of the same rank with them, have the sense of *Seeing, Hearing* and *Touching*, and not improbably 30 of *Smelling* and *Tasting*. Which Faculties being granted, they need not be much at a loss how to spend their time, though it were but upon external Objects; all the furniture of Heaven and Earth being fairly exposed to their view. They see the same Sun and Moon that we do, behold the persons and converse of 35 all men, and, if no special Law inhibit them, may pass from Town to Town, and from City to City, as *Hesiod* also intimates,

Ἠέρα ἐσσάμενοι πᾶσαν φοιτῶσιν ἐπ' αἶαν.

There is nothing that we enjoy but they may have their fees out of it; fair Fields, large and invious Woods, pleasant 40 Gardens, high and healthful Mountains, where the purest gusts of Air are to be met with, Crystal Rivers, mossy Springs, solemnity of Entertainments, Theatrick Pomps and Shews, publick and private Discourses, the exercises of Religion, whether in Temples, Families, or hidden Cells.

5   They may be also (and haply not uninteressed) Spectators of the glorious and mischievous hazards of War, whether Sea-fights or Land-fights; besides those soft and silent, though sometimes no less dangerous, Combats in the Camps of *Cupids*; and a thousand more particularities that it would be too long to reckon up, where they haply are not *mere* Spectators but
10   Abettors, as *Plutarch* writes: Like old men that are past Wrestling, Pitching the Barre, or playing at Cudgels themselves, yet will assist and abet the young men of the Parish at those Exercises. So the Souls of men departed, though they have put off with the Body the capacity of the
15   ordinary functions of humane Life, yet they may assist and abet them, as pursuing some design in them; and that either for evil or good, according as they were in the Body.

8. In brief, whatever is the *Custome* and *Desire* of the Soul in this life, that sticks and adheres to her in that which is to
20   come; and she will be sure, so farre as she is capable, either to act it, or to be at least a Spectator and Abettor of such kinde of actions.

> *... Quae gratia currûm*
> *Armorúmque fuit vivis, quae cura nitentes*
25 > *Pascere equos, eadem sequiitur tellure repostos.*

Which rightly understood is no poetical fiction, but a professed Truth in *Plato*'s Philosophy.And *Maximus Tyrius* speaks expresly even of the better sort of Souls, who having left the body, and so becoming τῶι αὐτῶι χρόνωι καὶ νόμωι δαίμονες ἀντ᾽
30   ἀνθρώπων i.e. *being made* ipso facto *Genii in stead of men*, that, beside the peculiar happiness they reap thereby to themselves, they are appointed by God, and have a mission from him, to be Overseers of humane affairs: but that every Genius does not perform every office, but as their natural Inclinations and
35   Customes were in this life, they exercise the like in some manner in the other. And therefore he will have *Aesculapius* to practise Physick still, and *Hercules* to exercise his strength, *Amphilochus* to prophesy, *Castor* and *Pollux* to navigate, *Minos* to hear causes, and *Achilles* to war. Which opinion is as likely
40   to hold true in Bad Souls as in Good; and then it will follow, that the Souls of the wicked make it their business to assist and abet the exercise of such Vices as themselves were most

addicted to in this life, and to animate and tempt men to them. From whence it would follow, that they being thus by their separate state *Daemons*, as has been said already, if they be also tempters to evil, they will very little differ from mere *Devils.*   5

9. But besides this employment in reference to us, they may entertain themselves with *Intellectual* Contemplations, whether Natural, Mathematical, or Metaphysical. For assuredly *Knowledge* is not so easy and cheap in this state of Separation, but that they may advance and improve 10 themselves by exercise and Meditations. And they being in a capacity to forget by reason of desuetude, it will be a new pleasure to them to recall to minde their almost obliterate speculations. And for those that take more pleasure in *outward sense* then in the operations of their *Understanding*;there being 15 so much change in Nature, and so various qualifications of the Aire and these inferiour Elements, which must needs act upon their *Aëreal* Bodies to more or less gratification or dislike, this also will excuse them from being idle, and put them upon quest after such refreshments and delights as nature will afford the 20 multifarious presages and desires of their flitting Vehicles.

10. Not but that they keep constant to some general inclination, which has divided these Aëreal Wanderers into so many Orders or Tribes; the ancient Philosophers and Poets (which are Philosophers of the ancientest standing of all) 25 having assigned places proper to each Order: the Sea, Rivers and Springs to one, Mountains and Groves to others, and so of the rest. Whence they imposed also those names of the *Nereides, Naiades, Oreades, Dryades*, and the like: to which you may adde the *Dii tutelares* of Cities and Countries, and those 30 that love the warmth of Families and homely converse of Men, such as they styled *Lares familiares.* All which, and hundreds more, which there is no need to recite, though they be engaged ever in one natural propension, yet there being so great variety of occasions to gratify it more or less, their thoughts may be 35 imployed in purchasing and improving those delights that are most agreeable to their own nature. Which particularities to run over would be as infinite as useless.

These short intimations are sufficient to make us understand that the *Genii* and *Separate Souls* need want no 40 *Employment*, no not in *Solitude*: for such must their stay also amongst us be esteemed, when they do not sensibly and personally converse with us.

5   Chap. V.

I. *That the Separate Soul spends not all her time in Solitude.* 2.
*That her converse with us seems more intelligible then that with
the Genii.* 3. *How the* Genii *may be visible one to another,*
10   *though they be to us invisible.* 4. *Of their approaches, and of the
limits of their swiftness of motion:* 5. *And how they far exceed us
in celerity.* 6. *Of the figure or shape of their Vehicles, and of
their privacy, when they would be invisible.* 7. *That they cannot
well converse in a mere simple Orbicular forme.* 8. *That they*
15   *converse in Humane shape, at least the better sort of them.* 9.
Whether the shape they be in proceed merely from the Imperium
of their Will *and* Fancy, *or is regulated by a natural Character of
the* Plastick *part of the Soul.* 10. *That the personal shape of
a Soul or* Genius *is partly from the Will,* and partly from the
20   Plastick *power.* 11. *That considering how the Soul organizes the*
Foetus *in the Womb, and moves our limbs at pleasure, it were a
wonder if Spirits should not have such command over their
Vehicles as is believed.* 12. *A further Argument from an
excessive virtue some have given to* Imagination.
25

I. But the *Separate* state of the Soul does not condemn her
to this *Solitude,* but being admitted into the Order of the *Genii,*
she is possessed of their Priviledges, which is to converse
personally with this *Aëreal people,* and also upon occasion with
30   the Inhabitants of the Earth; though the latter with far more
difficulty.
2. As for her converse with the Aëreal *Genii* and other
Souls Separate, it must be in all reason concluded to be
exceeding much more frequent then that with Men, and yet
35   this latter is in some sort more intelligible; because it is certain
she can see us, light being reflected from our Opake Bodies
unto her Sense, and by conspissating her Vehicle she may
make her self *visible* to us. But the Vehicles of the *Genii* and of
Souls being in their natural consistence purely *Aëreal,* and Air
40   being a transparent Body, it will transmit the light wholly; and
so no reflexion being made from these *Aiery* Bodies, they can
have no perception of one anothers presence, and therefore no

society nor communion one with another.

3. This seems a shrewd Difficulty at the first view. But it is easily taken off, if we consider that *Aire* will admit of many degrees of *Rarefaction* and *Condensation*, and yet still appear unto us alike invisible, as one may observe in the *Weather-* 5 *glass*. But it were more proper to propose in this case the Experiment of the *Wind-gun*, wherein the *Aire* is compressed to a great number of degrees of *Condensation* beyond its natural state; within the compass of many whereof there is no doubt, if not in the utmost, that the *Aire* does remain invisible to us. 10 But there is no scruple to be made but that in the progress of these degrees of *Condensation* the *Aire*, if it were in a *Glass-barrel*, might become visible to the *Genii*, by reason of the tenderness and delicacy of their Senses, before it would be so to us. 15

Whence it follows, that the Vehicles of the *Genii* may have a consistency different from the *Aire*, and perceptible to them, that is to say, to one anothers sight, though it be as unperceptible to us as the rest of the *Aire* is. As, it may be, a man that has but bad eyes would not be able to distinguish Ice 20 immersed in the Water from the Water it self by his sight, though he might by his Touch. Or if their Vehicles could be supposed purer and finer then the rest of the *Aire*, their presence might be perceptible by that means too. For this vaporous *Aire* having without question a confused reflexion of 25 light in it, every way in some proportion like that in a Mist, or when the Sun shines waterishly and prognosticks rain; these repercussions of light being far more sensible to the *Genii* then to us, the lessening of them would be more sensible, and therefore the diminution of reflexion from their Vehicles would 30 be sufficient to discover their presence one to another: and for the illustrating of this Hypothesis, the experiment of the *Weather-glass* is more proper.

But the other supposition I look upon as the more likely to be true; and that as the *aquatil Animals* that live in the *Sea* 35 have a consistency grosser then the Element they move in, so it is with these that live in the *Aire*, though there be nothing near so great a difference here as in that other Element.

4. It is plain therefore, that the Persons of the *Genii* and Separate Souls are visible one to another: But yet not at any distance, and therefore there is necessity of approaching to one 40 another for mutual converse: which enforces us to say

something of their *Local Motion*. Which is neither by Fins nor
Wings, as in Fishes or Birds, who are fain to sustain
themselves by these instruments from sinking to the bottome of
either Element: but it is merely by the direction of the agitation
5   of the particles of their Vehicle toward the place they aime at;
and in such a swiftness or leasureliness as best pleases
themselves, and is competible to their natures. For they can
goe no swifter then the whole summe of agitation of the
particles of their Vehicle will carry so much Matter, nor indeed
10   so swift; for it implies that their Vehicles would be turned into
an absolutely-hard Body, such as Brass or Iron, or whatever
we find harder; so that necessarily they would fall down to the
Earth as dead as a Stone. Those therefore are but phantastick
conceits that give such agility to Spirits, as if they could be
15   here and there and every where at once, skip from one Pole of
the World to another, and be on the Earth again in a moment:
whenas in truth they can pass with no greater swiftness then
the direction of such a part of the agitation of the particles of
their Vehicles will permit, as may be spared from what is
20   employed in keeping them within a tolerable compass of a due
Aëreal fluidity.

5. And this alone will suffice to make them exceed us in
activity and swiftness by many degrees. For their whole
Vehicle is haply at least as thin and moveable as our *Animal*
25   *Spirits*, which are very few in comparison of this luggage of an
earthly Body that they are to drive along with them. But the
spiritual Bodies of the *Genii* have nothing to drive along with
them but themselves; and therefore are more free and light,
compared to us, then a mettl'd Steed that has cast his Rider,
30   compared with a Pack-horse loaden with a sack of Salt.

6. The next thing to be considered, touching the *mutual
conversation* of these Aëreal *Genii*, is the shape they appear in
one to another, of what *Figure* it is, and whether the Figure be
Natural, or *Arbitrarious*, or *Mixt*. For that they must appear in
35   some *Figure* or other is plain, in that their Vehicles are not of
an infinite extension. It is the more general Opinion, that there
is no particular Figure that belongs unto them naturally, unless
it be that which of all Figures is most simple, and most easy to
conform to, even by external helps, which is the equal
40   compression of the Aire on every side of the Vehicle, by which
means drops of Dew and Rain and pellets of Hail come so
ordinarily into that shape. Which also will more handsomely

accord with the nature of the Soul, supposing she consist of
Central and *Radial* essence, as I have above described, and the
Common *Sensorium* be placed in the midst. In this Figure may
the Soul reside in the Aire, and haply melt herself, I mean her
Vehicle, into near so equal a liquidity with that part of that   5
Element adjacent to her, that it may be in some measure like
our retiring into secrecy from the sight of men, when we desire
to be private by our selves.

   7. But she may, if she will, and likely with far more ease,
change this consistency of her *Aëreal* Body into such a degree of 10
thickness, that there may be a dubious discovery of her, as in
the glimpse of a Fish under the water, and may still make her
self more visible to her fellow-*Genii*, though keeping yet this
simple *Orbicular* form. But what converse there can be betwixt
two such heaps of living Aire, I know not. They may indeed 15
communicate their *Affections* one to another in such a way as is
discovered in the *Eye*, wherein the *motions of the Spirits* do
plainly indicate the *Passions of the Mind*: so that it may seem
possible, in this simple Figure, to make known their *joy or grief,*
peaceableness or wrath, love or dislike, by the modification of the 20
motion of the Spirits of their Vehicle. But how there can well
be entertained any *Intellectual* or *Rational Conference*, without
any further organization of their Aiery Bodies, I profess my
self at a loss to understand.

   8. Wherefore the *Genii* and *Separate Souls*, whatever their 25
shape be in private, appear in a more operose and articulate
form when they are to converse with one another. For they
can change their *Figure* in a manner as they please, by Axiome
34. Which power, I conceive, will be made use of not onely for
service, but ornament amd pulchritude.   And the most 30
unexceptionable Beauty, questionless, is that of *Man* in the
best patterns (chuse what Sex you will) and far above the rest
of Creatures; which is not our judgement onely, but His that
made us. For certainly he would give to the *Principal of*
terrestrial Animals the *noblest form* and shape; which though it 35
be much obscured by our unfortunate Fall, yet questionless the
defacement is not so great, but that we may have a near guess
what it has been heretofore. It is most rational therefore to
conclude, that the Aëreal *Genii* converse with one another in
Humane shape, at least the better sort of them.   40

9. But the difficulty now is, whether that *Humane shape* that the Soul transforms her Vehicle into be simply the Effect of the *Imperium* of her *Will* over the Matter she actuates, or that her Will may be in some measure limited or circumscribed in its effect by a concomitant exertion of the *Plastick* power; so that wnat proceeds from the *Will* may be onely more general, that is, That the Soul's *Will* may onely command the Vehicle into an *Animal form*; but that it is the form or shape of a *Man*, may arise in a more natural way from the concomitant exertion of the *Plastick* virtue: I say, in a more easy and natural way; For vehemency of desire to alter the Figure into another representation may make the appearance resemble some other creature: But no forced thing can last long.

The more easy and natural shape therefore that, at least, the better *Genii* appear in, is *Humane*: which if it be granted, it may be as likely that such a determinate *Humane shape* may be more easy and natural then another, and that the Soul, when she *wills* to appear in personal Figure will transform her Vehicle into one constant likeness, unless she disguise her self on set purpose. That is, the *Plastick power* of every Soul, whether of Men, or of the other *Genii*, does naturally display it self into a different modification of the *Humane shape*, which is the proper Signature of every particular or individual person: which though it may be a little changed in Generation by virtue of the Imagination of the Parents, or quality of their seed, yet the Soul set free from that Body she got here, may exquisitely recover her ancient form again.

10. Not that the *Plastick* virtue, awakened by the *Imperium* of her *Will*, shall renew all the lineaments it did in this *Earthly Body* (for abundance of them are useless and to no purpose, which therefore, Providence so ordaining, will be silent in this *Aiery* figuration, and onely such operate as are fit for this separate state; and such are those as are requisite to perfect the visible feature of a Person, giving him all parts of either ornament or use for the pleasure of Rational converse;) nor that this *Efformative* power does determine the whole appearance alone (for these *Aëreal* Spirits appear variously clad, some like beautiful Virgins, others like valiant Warriours with their Helmets and Plumes of feathers, as *Philostratus* would make us believe *Achilles* did to *Apollonius*:) But there is a mixt action and effect, resulting partly from the freeness of the *Will* and *Imagination*, and partly from the natural

propension of the *Plastick* virtue, to cast the Vehicle into such a personal shape.

11. Which Prerogative of the Soul, in having this power thus to shape her Vehicle at will, though it may seem very strange, because we do not see it done before our eyes, nor often think of such things; yet it is not much more wonderful then that she *organizes* the *Foetus* in the womb, or that we can *move* the parts of our Body merely by our *Will* and *Imagination*. And that the *Aëreal* Spirits can doe these things, that they can thus shape their Vehicles, and transform themselves into several Appearances, I need bring no new instances thereof. Those Narrations I have recited in my *Third Book against Atheism* do sufficiently evince this Truth. And verily, considering the great power acknowledged in *Imagination* by all Philosophers, nothing would seem more strange, then that these *Airey* Spirits should not have this command over their own Vehicles, to transform them as they please.

12. For there are some, and they of no small note, that attribute so wonderful effects to that Faculty armed with *Confidence* and *Belief* (to which Passion *Fear* may in some manner be referred, as being a strong belief of an imminent evil, and that it will surely take effect, as also vehement *Desire*, as being accompanied with no small measure of perswasion that we may obtain the thing desired, else *Desire* would not be so very active) I say, they attribute so wonderful force to *Imagination*, that they affirm that it will not onely alter a mans own Body, but act upon anothers, and that at a distance; that it will inflict diseases on the sound, and heal the sick; that it will cause Hail, Snows and Winds; that it will strike down an Horse or Camel, and cast their Riders into a ditch; that it will doe all the feats of Witchcraft, even to the making of Ghosts and Spirits appear, by transforming the adjacent Aire into the shape of a person that cannot onely be felt and seen, but heard to discourse, and that not onely by them whose *Imagination* created this aiery spectrum, but by other by-standers, whose *Fancy* contributed nothing to its existence. To such an extent as this have *Avicenna, Algazel, Paracelsus, Pomponatius, Vaninus* and others, exalted the power of *humane Imagination*: which if it were true, this transfiguration of the Vehicles of the separate Souls and *Genii* were but a trifle in comparison thereof.

Chap. VI.

I. But I shall contain my belief within more moderate
bounds, that which the most sober Authors assent to being
20 sufficient for our turn; and that is *the power of Imagination* on
our own Bodies, or what is comprehended within our own, *viz.*
the *Foetus* in the Womb of the Mother. For that *Imagination*
will bring real and sensible effects to pass is plain, in that some
have raised diseases in their own Bodies by too strongly
25 imagining of them; by fancying bitter or sour things, have
brought those real sapours into their mouths; at the
remembring of some filthy Object, have faln a vomiting; at the
imagining of a Potion, have faln a purging; and many such
things of the like nature. Amongst which, that of prefixing to
30 ones self what time in the morning we will wake, is no less
admirable then any. Which alterations upon the Spirits for the
production of such qualities is every jot as hard as the ranging
them into new figures or postures.

But the hardest of all is, to make them so determinately
35 active, as to change the shape of the Body, by sending out
knobs like horns, as it hapned to *Cyppus*, of which *Agrippa*
speaks in his *Occult. Philosoph.* Which I should not have
repeated here, had I not been credibly informed of a later
Example of the like effect of *Imagination*, though upon more
40 fancyfull grounds. That *Fear* has killed some, and turned
others gray, is to be referred to *Imagination* also: the latter of
which examples is a sign that the *Plastick* power of the Soul

has some influence also upon the very hairs: which will make it
less marvellous that the Soul's Vehicle may be turned into the
live effigies of a Man; not a hair, that is necessary to the
perfecting of his representation, being excluded, free
Imagination succeeding or assisting the *Plastick* power in the 5
other state.

2. But of all Examples, those of the *Signatures* of the
Foetus by the *Imagination of the Mother* come the nearest to our
purpose. For we may easily conceive, that as the *Plastick*
power in the *Foetu s* is directed or seduced by the force of the 10
Mothers Fancy; so the *Efformative* virtue in Souls separate and
the *Genii* may be governed and directed or perverted by the
force of their *Imagination*. And so much the more surely by
how much the union is more betwixt the *Imagination* of the
Soul and her own *Plastick* faculty, then betwixt her and the 15
Plastick power of another Soul; and the capacity of being
changed, greater in the yielding *Aëreal* Vehicle, then in the
grosser rudiments of the *Foetus* in the Womb.

3. And yet the Effects of the force of the Mothers
Imagination in the signing of the *Foetus* is very wonderful, and 20
almost beyond belief, to those that have not examined these
things. But the more learned sort both of Physicians and
Philosophers are agreed on the truth thereof, as *Empedocles,*
Aristotle, Pliny, Hippocrates, Galen, and all the modern
Physicians, being born down into assent by daily experience. 25
For these *Signatures* of less extravagance and enormity are
frequent enough, as the simulitude of Cherries, Mulberries, the
colour of Claret-wine spilt on a woman with child, with many
such like instances. And if we stand but to what *Fienus* has
defined in this matter, who has, I think, behaved himself as 30
cautiously and modestly as may be, there will be enough
granted to assure us of what we aim at. For he does
acknowledge that the *Imagination* of the Mother may change
the figure of the *Foetus* so as to make it bear a resemblance,
though not absolutely parfect, of an Ape, Pig, or Dog, or any 35
such like Animal. The like he affirms of colours, hers, and
excresencies of several sorts: that it may produce also what is
very like or analogous to horns and hoofs, and that it may
encrease the bigness and number of the parts of the Body.

4. And though he does reject several of the Examples he 40
has produced out of Authors, yet those which he admits for
true are Indications plain enough, what we may expect in the

Vehicle of a *departed Soul* or *Daemon*. As that of the Hairy
girle out of *Marcus Damascenus;* that other out of *Guilielmus
Paradinus*, of a Child whose skin and nails resembled those of a
Bear; and a third out of *Balduinus Ronsaeus*, of one born with
5   many excrescencies coloured and figured like those in a Turky-
cock; and a fourth out of *Pareus*, of one who was born with an
head like a Frog; as lastly that out of *Avicenna*, of Chickens
with Hawks heads. All which deviations of the *Plastick* power
hapned from the force of *Imagination* in the Females, either in
10   the time of Conception, or gestation of their young.

5. But he scruples of giving assent to others, which yet are
assented to by very learned Writers. As that of Black-moors
being born of white Parents, and white Children of black, by
the exposal of pictures representing an Aethiopian or
15   European: which those two excellent Physicians, *Fernelius*
and *Sennertus*, both agree to. He rejects also that out of
Cornelius Gemma, of a Child that was born with his Forehead
wounded and running with blood, from the husbands threatning
his wife, when she was big, with a drawn sword which he
20   directed towards her Forehead. Which will not seem so
incredible, if we consider what *Sennertus* records of his own
knowledge, viz. That a Woman with child seeing a Butcher
divide a Swines head with his Cleaver, brought forth her Child
with its face cloven in the upper jaw, the palate, and upper lip
25   to the very nose.

6. But the most notorious instances of this sort are those
of *Helmont De injectis materialibus*. The one of a Taylor's wife
at *Mechlin*, who standing at her door, and seeing a souldiers
hand cut off in a quarrel, presently fell into labour, being struck
30   with horrour at the spectacle, and brought forth a child with
one hand, the other arm bleeding without one, of which wound
the infant died by the great expense of blood. Another woman,
the wife of one *Marcus De Vogeler* Merchant of *Antwerp*, in the
year 1602. Seeing a souldier begging who had lost his right
35   arm in *Ostend-siege*, which he shewed to the people still bloody,
fell presently into labour, and brought forth a Daughter with
one arm struck off, nothing left but a bloody stump to employ
the Chirurgions skill: this woman married afterwards to one
Hoochcamer Merchant of *Amsterdam*, and was yet alive in the
40   year 1638. as *Helmont* writes. He adds a third example, of
another Merchants wife which he knew, who hearing that on a
morning there were thirteen men to be beheaded (this hapned

at *Antwerp* in Duke *D'Alva* his time) she had the curiosity to
see the execution.   She getting therefore a place in the
Chamber of a certain widow-woman, a friend of hers that dwelt
in the market-place, beheld this Tragick spectacle; upon which
she suddainly fell into labour, and brought forth a perfectly- 5
formed infant, only the head was wanting, but the neck bloody
as their bodies she beheld that had their heads cut off.   And
that which does still advance the wonder is, that the hand,
arm, and head of these infants, were none of them to be found.
From   whence   *Van-Helmont*   would   infer   a   penetration of 10
corporeal dimensions; but how groundlessly I will not dispute
here.

7. If these Stories he recites be true, as I must confess I
do not well know how to deny them, he reporting them with so
honest and credible circumstances; they are notable examples 15
of the *power of Imagination*, and such as do not onely win belief
to themselves, but also to others that *Fienus* would reject, not
of this nature onely we are upon, of wounding the body of the
Infant, but also of more exorbitant conformation of parts, of
which we shall bring an instance or two anon.   20

In the mean time, while I more carefully contemplate this
strange virtue and power of the Soul of the Mother, in which
there is no such measure of purification or exaltedness, that it
should be able to act such *miracles*, as I may call them, rather
then *natural effects* I cannot but be more then usually inclinable 25
to think that the *Plastick* faculty of the Soul of the Infant, or
whatever accessions there may be from the *Imagination* of the
Mother, is not the adequate cause of the formation of the
Foetus: a thing which *Plotinus* somewhere intimates by the bye,
as I have already noted, viz. That *the Soul of the World*, or *the* 30
Spirit of Nature, assists in this performance.   Which if it be
true, we have discovered a Cause proportionable to   so
prodigious an effect.   For we may easily conceive that the
deeply-impassionated Fancy of the Mother snatches away *the*
Spirit of Nature into consent: which Spirit may rationally be 35
acknowledged to have a hand in the efformation of all vital
Beings in the World, and haply be the only Agent in forming of
all manner of *Plants*.

In which kind whether she exert her power in any other
Elements then *Earth* and *Water*, I will conclude no further, then 40
that there may be a possibility thereof in the calmer Regions of
Aire and *Aether*.   To   the   right   understanding   of   which

conjecture, some light will offer it self from what we have said
concerning the *Visibility* and *Consistency* of the Aëreal *Daemons*
in their occursions one with another.

8. But this is not the onely Argument that would move
5 one to think that this *Spirit of Nature* intermeddles with the
Efformation of the *Foetus*. For those *Signatures* that are
derived on the Infant from the Mothers fancy in the act of
Conception cannot well be understood without this Hypothesis.
For what can be the Subject of that Signature? Not the
10 *Plastick* part of the Soul of the Mother; for that it is not the
Mothers Soul that efforms the *Embryo*, as *Sennertus*
ingeniously conjectures from the manner of the efformation of
Birds, which is in their Eggs, distinct from the Hen, and they
may as well be hatched without any Hen at all, a thing
15 ordinarily practised in *Aegypt*; nor the *Body* of the *Embryo*, for
it has yet no Body; nor *its Soul*, for the Soul, if we believe
Aristotle, is not yet present there. But the *Spirit of Nature* is
present every where, which snatcht into consent by the force of
the *Imagination* of the Mother, retains the Note, and will be
20 sure to seal it on the Body of the Infant.

For what rude inchoations the *Soul of the World* has begun
in the Matter of the *Foetus*, this *Signature* is comprehended in
the whole design, and after compleated by the presence and
operation of the particular *Soul of the Infant*, which co-operates
25 conformably to the pattern of the Soul of the World, and insists
in her footsteps; who having once begun any hint to an entire
design, she is alike able to pursue it in any place, she being
every where like, or rather the same to her self. For as our
Soul being one, yet, upon the various temper of the Spirits,
30 exerts her self into various imaginations and conceptions; so
the Soul of the World, being the same pefectly every where, is
engaged to exert her *Efformative* power every where alike,
where the Matter is exactly the same.

Whence it had been no wonder, if those Chickens above-
35 mentioned with Hawks heads had been hatched an hundred
miles distant from the Hen, whose Imagination was disturbed
in the act of Conception: because the *Soul of the World* had
begun a rude draught, which it self would as necessarily pursue
every where, as a *Geometrician* certainly knows how to draw a
40 Circle that will fit three Points given.

9. This Opinion therefore of *Plotinus* is neither irrational nor unintelligible, That the *Soul of the World* interposes and insinuates into all generations of things, while the Matter is fluid and yielding. Which would induce a man to believe that she may not stand idle in the transfiguration of the Vehicles of the *Daemons*, but assist their fancies and desires, and so help to cloath them and attire them according to their own pleasures: or it be may sometimes against their wills, as the unwieldiness of the Mothers Fancy forces upon her a Monstrous birth.

Chap. VII.

I. *Three notable Examples of* Signatures, *rejected by* Fienus: 2. *And yet so farre allowed for possible, as will fit our design.* 3. *That* Helmont's *Cherry and* Licetus *his Crab-fish are shrewd arguments that the Soul of the World has to doe with all Efformations of both Animals and Plants.* 4. *An Example of a most exact and lively Signature out of* Kircher: 5. *With his judgement thereupon.* 6. *Another Example out of him of a Child with gray hairs.* 7. *An application of what has been said hitherto, concerning the* Signatures *of the* Foetus, *to the transfiguration of the Aiery Vehicles of* Separate Souls *and* Daemons. 8. *Of their personal transformation visible to us.*

I. Those other Examples of the *Signation* of the *Foetus* from the Mothers *Fancy*, which *Fienus* rejecteth, the one of them is out of *Wierus*, of a man that threatened his Wife when she was bigge with child, saying, she bore the *Devil* in her womb, and that he would kill him: whereupon, not long after, she brought forth a Child well shaped from the middle downwards, but upwards spotted with black and red spots, with eyes in its forehead, a mouth like a *Satyre*, ears like a Dog, and bended horns on its head like a Goat. The other out of *Ludovicus Vives*, of one who returning home in the disguise of a *Devil*, whose part he acted on the Stage, and having to doe with his wife in that habit, saying he would beget a *Devil* on her, impregnated her with a Monster of a shape plainly *diabolical*. The third and most remarkable is out of *Peramatus*, of a Monster born at *S. Laurence* in the *West-Indie*s, in the

year 1573. the narration whereof was brought to the Duke of
Medina Sidonia from very faithful hands. How there was a
Child born there at that time, that besides the horrible
deformity of its mouth, ears and nose, had two horns on the
5 head, like those of young Goats, long hair on the body, a fleshy
girdle about his middle, double, from whence hung a piece of
flesh like a purse, and a bell of flesh in his left hand, like those
the *Indians* use when they dance, white boots of flesh on his
leggs, doubled down: In brief, the whole shape was horrid and
10 *diabolical,* and conceived to proceed from some fright the
Mother had taken from the antick dances of the *Indians,*
amongst whom the *Devil* himself does not fail to appear
sometimes.

2. These Narrations *Fienus* rejecteth, not as false, but as
15 not being done by any natural power, or if they be, that the
description are something more lively then the truth. But in
the mean time he does freely admit, that by the mere power of
Imagination there might be such excrescencies as might
represent those things that are there mentioned; though those
20 *diabolical* shapes could not have true horns, hoofs, tail, or any
other part specifically distinct from the nature of Man. But so
farre as he acknowledges is enough for our turn.

3. But *Fortunius Licetus* is more liberal in his grants,
allowing not onely that the Births of women may be very
25 exquisitely distorted in some of their parts into the likeness
of those of Brutes, but that Chimaerical imaginations in
Dreams may also effect it, as well as Fancies or external
Objects when they are awake. Of the latter sort whereof he
produces an Example that will more then match our purpose,
30 of a *Sicilian* matron, who by chance beholding a *Crab* in a
Fishermans hand new caught, and of a more then ordinary
largeness, when she was brought to bed, brought forth a *Crab*
(as well as a *Child*) perfectly like those that are ordinarily
caught in the Sea. This was told him by a person of credit,
35 who both knew the Woman, and saw the *Crab* she brought
forth.

Helmont's Cherry he so often mentions, and how it was
green, pale, yellow, and red, at the times of year other Cherries
are, is something of this nature; that is to say, comes near to
40 the perfect species of a *Cherry,* as this did of a *Crab,* the
plantal life of a Cherry being in some measure in the one, as
the life of an Animal was perfectly in the other. Which

confirms what we said before, that strength of our *Desire* and *Imagination* may snatch into consent the *Spirit of Nature*, and make it act: which once having begun, leaves not off, if *Matter* will but serve for to work up-on; and being the same in all places, acts the same upon the same *Matter*, in the same 5 circumstances. For the *Root* and *Soul* of every *Vegetable* is the Spirit of Nature; *in virtue whereof this* Cherry *flourisht and ripened*, according to the seasons of the Country where the party was that bore that live Signature.

These two instances are very shrewd arguments that the 10 *Soul of the World* has to doe with all Efformation of either *Plants* or *Animals*. For neither the Childs Soul nor the Mothers, in any likelihood, could frame that *Crab*, though the Mother might, by that strange power of *Desire* and *Imagination*, excite the *Spirit of the World*, that attempts upon 15 any Matter that is fitted for generation, some way or other, to make something of it; and being determined by the fancy of the Woman, might sign the humid materials in her Womb with the image of the Minde.

4. Wherefore if *Fienus* had considered from what potent 20 causes *Signatures* may arise, he would not have been so scrupulous in believing that degree of exactness that some of them are reported to have: or if he had had the good hap to have met with so notable an example thereof, as *Kircher* professes himself to have met with. For he tells a story of a 25 man that came to him for this very cause, to have his opinion what a certain strange *Signature*, which he had on his Arm from his birth, might portend; concerning which he had consulted both *Astrologers* and *Cabbalists*, who had promised great preferments, the one imputing it to the Influence of the 30 Stars, the other to the favour of the *sealing* Order of Angels. But *Kircher* would not spend his judgement upon a mere verbal description thereof; though he had plainly enough told him, it was *the Pope sitting on his Throne, with a Dragon under his feet, and an Angel putting a Crown on his head.*   35

Wherefore the man desirous to hear a further confirmation of these hopes (he had conceived from the favourable conjectures of others) by the suffrage of so learned a man, was willing in private to put off his doublet, and shew his Arm to *Kircher*: who having viewed it with all possible care, does 40 profess that the *Signature* was so perfect, that it seemed rather the work of *Art* then of exorbitating *Nature*; and yet by certain

observations he made, that he was well assured it was the
work of *Nature*, and not of *Art*, though it was an artificial piece
that Nature imitated, *viz*. the picture of Pope *Gregory* the
thirteenth, who is sometimes drawn according as this *Signature*
5   did lively represent, namely on a Throne, with a Dragon under
his feet, leaning with one hand on his Seat, and bearing the
other in that posture in which they give the Benediction, and an
Angel removing a Curtain and reaching a Crown towards his
head.

10   5. *Kircher* therefore leaving the superstitions and fooleries
of the spurious *Cabbalists* and *Astrologers*,told him the truth,
though nothing so pleasant as their lies and flatteries, *viz*. That
this *Signature* was not impressed by any either influence of the
Stars, or Seals of Angels, but that it was the effect of the
15   *Imagination* of his Mother that bore him, who in some more
then ordinary fit of affection towards this Pope, whose picture
she beheld in some Chappel or other place of her devotion, and
having some occasion to touch her Arm, printed that image on
the Arm of her Child, as it ordinarily happens in such cases.
20   Which doubtless was the true solution of the mystery.

         6. The same Author writes, how he was invited by a
friend to contemplate another strange miracle (as he thought
that did invite him to behold it) that he might spend his
judgement upon it. Which was nothing else but an exposed
25   Infant of some fourteen days old, that was *gray-hair'd*, both
head and eye-brows. Which his friend, an Apothecary, look'd
upon as a grand Prodigy, till he was informed of the cause
thereof: That the Mother that brought it forth, being married
to an old man whose head was all white, the fear of being
30   surprized in the act of Adultery by her snowy-headed husband
made her imprint that colour on the Child she bore. Which
Story I could not omit to recite, it witnessing to what an exact
curiosity the power of *Fancy* will work for the fashioning and
modifying the Matter, not missing so much as the very *colours*
35   *of the hair*, as I have already noted something to that purpose.

         7. To conclude therefore at length, and leave this
luxuriant Theme. Whether it be the *Power of Imagination*
carrying captive *the Spirit of Nature* into consent, or the *Soul of
the Infant*, or both; it is evident that the Effects are notable,
40   and sometimes very accurately answering the *Idea* of the
Impregnate, derived upon the moist and ductile matter in the
Womb: Which yet not being any thing so yielding as the soft

Aire, nor the Soul of the Mother so much one with that of the
Infant as the separate Soul is one with it self, nor so peculiarly
united to the Body of the Infant as the Soul separate with her
own Vehicle, nor having any nearer or more mysterious
commerce with the *Spirit of Nature* then she has when her   5
Plastick part, by the *Imperium* of her *Will* and *Imagination*, is
to organize her Vehicle into a certain shape and form, which is
a kind of a momentaneous Birth of the distinct Personality, of
either a *Soul separate*, or any other *Daemon*; it follows, that we
may be very secure, that there is such a power in the *Genii* and   10
Separate Souls, that they can with ease and accuracy
transfigure themselves into shapes and forms agreeable to their
own temper and nature.

8. All which I have meant hitherto in reference to their
Visible congresses one with another. But they are sometimes   15
visible to us also, under some Animal shape, which questionless
is much more difficult to them then that other Visibility is. But
this is also possible, though more unusual by far, as being more
unnaturall. For it is possible by Art to *compress Aire* so, as to
reduce it to visible opacity, and has been done by some, and   20
particularly by a friend of *Des-Cartes*, whom he mentions in his
Letters as having made this Experiment; the Aire getting this
opacity by squeezing the *Globuli* out of it. Which though the
Separate Souls and *Spirits* may doe by that directive faculty,
Axiome 31, yet surely it would be very painful. For the first   25
Element lying bare, if the *Aire* be not drawn exceeding close, it
will cause an ungratefull heat; and if it be, as unnatural a cold;
and so small a moment will make the first Element too much or
too little, that it may, haply, be very hard, at least for these
inferiour Spirits, to keep steddily in a due mean. And   30
therefore, when they appear, it is not unlikely but that they
soak their Vehicles in some vaporous or glutinous moisture or
other, that they may become visible to us at a more easy rate.

                                                                35

Chap. VIII.

I. *That the Better sort of* Genii *converse in Humane shape, the*
Baser sometimes in Bestial. 2. *How they are disposed to turn*   40
themselves into several Bestial forms. 3. *Of* Psellus *his* αὐγαὶ
πυρώδεις. *or* Igneous splendours *of* Daemons, *how they are made.*

4. *That the external Beauty of the* Genii *is according to the degree of the inward Vertue of their Minds.* 5. *That their Aëreal form need not be purely transparent, but more finely opake, and coloured.* 6. *That there is a distinction of Masculine and Feminine beauty in their personal figurations.*

I. After this Digression, of shewing the facility of the figuring of the Vehicles of the *Genii* into personal shape, I shall return again where we left; which was concerning the *Society* of these *Genii* and *Souls Separate*, and *under what shape they converse one with another*; which I have already defined to be *Humane*, especially in the *Better* sort of Spirits. And as for the *Worst* kind, I should think that they are likewise for the most part in Humane form, though disguised with ugly circumstances, but that they figure themselves also in *Bestial* appearances; it being so easie for them to transform their Vehicle into what shape they please, and to imitate the figures as dexterously as some *men* will the voices of brute beasts, whom we may hear sing like a Cuckow, crow like a Cock, bellow like a Cow and Calf, bark like a Dog, grunt and squeak like a Pig, and indeed imitate the cry of almost any Bird or Beast whatsoever. And as easie a matter is it for these lower *Genii* to resemble the shapes of all these Creatures, in which they also appear visibly oftentimes to them that entertain them, and sometimes to them that would willingly shun them.

2. Nor is it improbable, but the variety of their impurities may dispose them to turn themselves into one *brutish* shape rather then another; as envying, or admiring, or in some sort approving and liking the condition and properties of such and such *Beasts*: as *Theocritus* merily sets out the Venereousness of the Goatheard he describes,

Ω᾽ πολος ὅκκ᾽ ἐσορῆι τὰς μηκάδας οἶα βατοῦνται.
τάκεται ὀφϑαλμὼς, ὅτι οὐ τράγος ἀυτὸς ἔγεντο.

As if he envied the happiness of the he-Goats, and wisht himself in their stead, in their acts of carnal Copulation. So according to the several *Bestial* properties that symbolize with the uncleanness and vitiousness of the tempers of these *Daemons*, they may have a propension to imitate their shape rather then others, and appear ugly, according to the manner and measure of their internal turpitudes.

3. As it is likely also that those ϑεοπτίαι *or* αὐγαὶ πυρώδεις, those *Igneous Splendours Psellus* makes mention of, (as the end and scope of the nefarious ceremonies those wicked wretches, he describes, often used) were coloured according to the more or less feculency of the Vehicle of the *Daemon* that did appear in 5 this manner, viz. in no personal shape, but by exhibiting a light to the eyes of his abominable Spectatours and Adorers: which, I suppose, he stirred up within the limits of his ow Vehicle; the power of his *Will* and *Imagination*, by Axiome 31, commanding the grosser particles of the Aire and terrestrial 10 vapours, together with the *Globuli,* to give back every way, from one point to a certain compass, not great, and therefore the more easy to be done. Whence the first Element lyes bare in some considerable measure, whose activity cannot but lick into it some particles of the Vehicle that borders next 15 thereto, and thereby exhibit, not a pure star-like light (which would be, if the first Element thus unbared), and in the midst of pure Aire, were it self ummixt with other Matter) but by the feculency of those parts that it abrades and converts into fewel, and the foulness of the ambient Vehicle through which it 20 shines, exhibit a show red and fiery like the Horizontal Sun seen through a thick throng of vapours.

Which *Fiery splendour* may either onely slide down amongst them, and so pass by with the Motion of the *Daemons* Vehicle, which *Psellus* seems mainly to aime at; or else it may 25 make some stay and discourse with them it approaches, according as I have heard some Narrations. The reason of which *lucid appearances* being so intelligible out of the Principles of *Cartesius* his Philosophy, we need not conceit that they are nothing but the prestigious delusions of *Fancy,* and no 30 real Objects, as *Psellus* would have them; it being no more uncompetible to a *Daemon* to raise such a light in his Vehicle, and a purer then I have described, then to a wicked man to light a candle at a tinderbox.

4. But what we have said concerning the purity and 35 impurity of this light, re-mindes me of what is of more sutable consequence to discourse of here, which is the *Splendour and Beauty of personal shape* in the *Better* sort of the *Genii.* Which assuredly is greater or lesser, according to the degrees of *Vertue and Moral affections* in them. For even in this Body, 40 that is not so yielding to the powers of the Mind, a man may observe, that according as persons are better or worse inclined,

the aire of their visage will alter much; and that vicious
courses, defacing the inward pulchritude of the Soul, do even
change the outward countenance to an abhorred hue.

   Which must therefore necessarily take place, in a far
5 greater measure, in the other state; where our outward form is
wholy framed from the inward *Imperium* of our Mind: which
by how much more pure it self is, it will exhibit the more
irreprehensible pulchritude in the outward feature and fashion
of the Body, both for proportion of parts, the spirit and aire of
10 the Countenance, and the ornament of cloaths and attirings:
there being an indissoluble connexion in the Soul of the Sense of
these Three things together, *Vertue, Love,* and *Beauty*; of all
which she her self is the first Root, and especially in the
Separate state, even of *outward Beauty* it self: whence the
15 converse of the most Vertuous there must needs afford the
highest pleasure and satisfaction; not onely in point of rational
communication, but in reference to external and personal
complacency also. For if *Vertue* and *Vice* can be ever seen with
outward eyes, it must be in these Aëreal Vehicles, which yield
20 so to the Will and Idea of good and pure affections, that the
Soul in a manner becomes perfectly transparent through them,
discovering her lovely *Beauty* in all the efflorescencies therefore,
to the ineffable enravishment of the beholder.

   5. Not that I mean, that there is any necessity that their
25 Vehicle should be as a Statue of fluid *Crystal*; but that those
Impresses of *Beauty* and *Ornament* will be so faithfully and
lively represented, according to the dictates of her inward
Sense and Imagination, that if we could see the Soul her self,
we could know no more by her then she thus exhibits to our
30 eye: which personal figuration in the extimate parts thereof,
that represent the Body, Face and Vestments, may be
attempered to so fine an opacity, that it may reflect the light in
more perfect colours then it is from any earthly body and yet
the whole Vehicle be so devoid of weight, as it will necessarily
35 keep its station in the Aire. Which we cannot wonder at, while
we consider the hanging of the *Clouds* there, less *Aëreal* by far
then this consistency we speak of: to say nothing of *Aëreal*
Apparitions as high as the *Clouds*, and in the same colours and
figures as are seen here below, and yet no reflexions of
40 terrestrial Objects, as I have proved in my Third Book against
Atheism.

6. The *exact Beauty* of the personal shapes and becoming habits of these Aiery Beings, the briefest and safest account thereof that Philosophy can give, is to refer to the description of such things in Poets: and then, when we have perused what the height and elegancy of their Fancy has penn'd down, to 5 write under it, *An obscure Subindication of the transcendent pulchritude of the Aëreal* Genii, whether *Nymphs* or *Heroes*. For though there be neither Lust, nor difference of Sex amongst them (whence the kindest commotions of Mind will never be any thing else but an exercise of *Intellectual love*, whose Object 10 is *Vertue* and *Beauty*;) yet it is not improbable but that there are some *general* strictures of discrimination of this Beauty into *Masculine* and *Feminine*: partly because the temper of their Vehicles may encline to this kind of pulchritude rather then that; and partly because several of these *Aëreal Spirits* have 15 sustained the difference of Sex in this life, some of them here having been *Males*, others *Females*: and therefore their History being to be continued from their departure hence, they ought to retain some charactere, especially so *general* a one, of what they were here. And it is very harsh to conceit that *Aeneas* 20 should meet with *Dido* in the other World in any other form then that of a *Woman*: whence a necessity of some slighter distinction of habits, and manner of wearing their hair, will follow. Which dress, as that of the *Masculine* mode, is easily fitted to them by the power of their *Will* and *Imagination*: as 25 appears from that Story out of *Peramatus*, of the *Indian* Monster that was born with fleshy boots, girdle, purse, and other things that are no parts of a Man, but his cloathing or utensils; and that merely by the Fancy of has Mother, disturb'd and frighted, either in sleep or awake, with some such ugly 30 appearance as that *Monster* resembled.

Chap. IX.   35

I. *A general account of the mutual entertains of the* Genii *in the other World.* 2. *Of their Philosophical and Political Conferences.* 3. *Of their Religious Exercises.* 4. *Of the innocent Pastimes and Recreational of the Better sort of them.* 5. *A confirmation* 40 *thereof from the Conventicles of Witches.* 6. *Whether the purer* Daemons *have their times of repast or no.* 7. *Whence the Bad*

Genii *have their food.* 8. *Of the food and feastings of the Better sort of* Genii.

I. We have now accurately enough defined in what form
5   or garb the Aëreal *Genii* converse with one another. It remains
we consider *how they mutually entertain one another* in passing
away the time. Which is obvious enough to conceive, to those
that are not led aside into that blind Labyrinth which the
generality of men are kept in, of suspecting *that no*
10 *representation of the state of these Beings is true, that is not so*
confounded and unintelligible that a man cannot think it sense,
unless he wink with the inward eyes of his Minde, and command
silence to all his Rational Faculties. But if he will but bethink
himself, that the immediate Instrument of the Soul in this life
15 is the *Spirits*, which are very congenerous to the body of
Angels; and that all our *Passions* and *Conceptions* are either
suggested from them, or imprest upon them; he cannot much
doubt but that all his Faculties of *Reason, Imagination* and
Affection, for the general, will be in him in the other state as
20 they were here in this: namely, that he will be capable of *Love*,
of *Joy*, of *Grief*, of *Anger*; that he will be able to *imagine*, to
discourse, to remember, and the rest of such operations as were
not proper to the Fabrick of this Earthly Body, which is the
Officine of Death and Generation.
25   2. Hence it will follow, that the Souls of men deceased,
and the rest of the Aëreal *Daemons*, may administer much
content to one another in mutual Conferences concerning the
nature of things, whether *Moral, Natural,* or *Metaphysical.* For
to think that the quitting the earthly Body entitles us to an
30 *Omnisiciency*, is a Fable never enough to be laugh'd at. And
Socrates, somewhere in *Plato*, presages, that he shall continue
his old Trade when he comes into the other World; convincing
and confounding the idle and vain-glorious *Sophists* whereever
he went. And by the same reason *Platonists, Aristoteleans,*
35 *Stoicks, Epicureans,* and whatever other sects and humors are
on the Earth, may in likelihood be met with there, so far as
that estate will permit; though they cannot doubt of all things
we doubt of here. For these *Aëreal* Spirits know that
themsleves *are*, and that the Souls of men *subsist* and *act* after
40 death, unless such as are too deeply tinctured with *Avenroism.*
But they may doubt whether they will hold out for ever, or
whether they will perish at the conflagration of the World, as

the *Stoicks* would have them.

It may be also a great controversie amongst them, whether *Pythagoras*'s or *Ptolemie*'s Hypothesis be true concerning the Motion of the Earth; and whether the Stars be so big as some define them. For these lower *Daemons* have no 5 better means then we to assure themselves of the truth or falshood of these Opinions. Besides the discourse of News, of the affairs as well of the *Earth* as *Aire*. For the *Aëreal Inhabitants* cannot be less active then the *Terrestrial*, nor less busie, either in the performance of some solemn exercises, or in 10 carrying on designs party against party; and that either more Private or more Publick; the Events of which will fill the *Aëreal Regions* with a quick spreading fame of their Actions. To say nothing of prudential conjectures concerning future successes aforehand, and innumerable other entertains of Conference, 15 which would be too long to reckon up, but bear a very near analogy to such as men pass away their time in here.

3. But of all *Pleasures*, there are none that are comparable to those that proceed from their joynt exercise of *Religion* and *Devotion*. For their Bodies surpassing ours so much in tenuity 20 and purity, they must needs be a fitter soil for the *Divinest* thoughts to spring up in, and the most delicate and most enravishing affections towards their Maker. Which being heightned by *sacred Hymns* and *Songs*, sung with voices perfectly imitating the sweet passionate relishes of the sense of 25 their devout Minds, must even melt their Souls into Divine Love, and make them swim with joy in God. But these kinds of Exercises being so highly rapturous and Ecstatical, transporting them beyond the ordinary limits of their Nature, cannot in Reason be thought to be exceeding frequent; but as a 30 solemn repast, after which they shall enjoy themselves better for a good space of time after.

4. Wherefore there be other Entertainments, which though they be of an inferiour nature to these, yet they far exceed the greatest pleasure and contentments of this 35 present state. For the *Animal life* being as essential to the Soul as union with a Body, which she is never free from; it will follow that there be some fitting gratifications of it in the other World. And none greater can be imagined then *Sociableness* and *Personal complacency*, not onely in rational discourses, 40 which is so agreeable to the Philosophical Ingeny, but innocent Pastimes, in which the *Musical* and *Amorous* propension may

be also recreated. For these Three dispositions are the flowr of
all the rest, as *Plotinus* has somewhere noted: And his
reception into the other World is set out by *Apollo'* s Oracle
from some such like circumstances as these.

5   ... μεθ' ὁμήγυριν ἔρχεαι ἤδη
       Δαιμονίην ἐρατοῖσιν ἀναπνείουσαν ἀήταις·
       ἐνὺ' ἔνι μὲν φιλότης, ἔνι δ' ἵμερος ἀβρὸς ἰδέσϑαι
       εὐφροσύνης πλείων καϑαρῆς πληρούμενος ἀιὲν
       ἀμβροσίων ὀχετῶν ϑεόϑεν· ὅϑεν ἐστὶν ἐρώτων
10   πείσματα καὶ γλυκερὴ πνοιὴ καὶ νήνεμος αἰϑήρ
Of the meaning of which Verses that the Reader may not quite
be deprived, I shall render their sense in this careless
paraphrase:
       Now the blest meetings thou arriv'st unto
15   *Of th' Aiery Genii, where soft winds do blow,*
       Where Friendship, Love, and gentle sweet Desire
       Fill their thrice-welcom guests with joys entire,
       Ever supply'd from that immortal spring
       Whose streams pure Nectar from great Jove do bring:
20   *Whence kind Converse and amorous Eloquence*
       Warm their chast minds into the highest sense
       Of Heav'nly Love whose Myst'ries they declare
       'Midst the fresh breathings of the peaceful Aire.
And he holds on, naming the happy company the Soul of
25 *Plotinus* was to associate with, viz. *Pythagoras*, *Plato*, and the
purer Spirits of the Golden Age, and all such as made up the
Chorus of immortal *Love* and *Friendship*.

       These sing, and play, and dance together, reaping the
lawful pleasures of the very *Animal life*, in a far higher degree
30 then we are capable of in this World. For every thing here
does as it were tast of the cask, and has some courseness and
foulness with it. The sweet motions of the Spirits in the
passion of *Love* can very hardly be commanded off from too
near bordering upon the shameful sense of *Lust*; the Fabrick of
35 the *Terrestrial* Body almost necessitating them to that
deviation. The tenderer Ear cannot but feel the rude
thumpings of the wood, and gratings of the rosin, the
hoarsness, or some harshness and untunableness or other, in
the best consorts of Musical Instruments and Voices. The
40 judicious *Eye* cannot but espy some considerable defect in
either the proportion, colour, or the aire of the face, in the
most fam'd and most admired beauties of either Sex: to say

nothing of the inconcinnity of their deportment and habits. But in that other state, where the Fancy consults with that First Exemplar of Beauty, *Intellectual Love* and *Vertue*, and the Body is wholly obedient to the imagination of the Mind, and will to every Punctilio yield to the impresses of that inward Pattern; nothing there can be found amiss, every touch and stroke of motion and Beauty being conveyed from so judicious a power through so delicate and depurate a Medium. Wherefore they cannot but enravish one anothers Souls, while they are mutual Spectators of the perfect pulchritude of one anothers persons & comely carriage, of their graceful dancing, their melodious singing and playing, with accents so sweet and soft, as if we should imagine the Aire here of it self to compose Lessons, and send forth Musical sounds without the help of any terrestrial Instrument. These, and such like Pastimes as these, are part of the Happiness of the Best sort of the Aëreal *Genii*.

5. Which the more certain knowledge of what is done amongst the inferiour *Daemons* will further assure us of. For it is very probable that their Conventicles, into which Witches and Wizzards are admitted, are but a depraved adumbration of the friendly meetings of the superiour *Genii*. And what *Musick*, *Dancing* and *Feasting* there is in these, the free confession of those Wretches, or fortuitous detection of others, has made manifest to the World, *viz.* How *Humane* and *Angelical Beauty* is transformed there into *Bestial Deformity*, the chief in the company ordinarily appearing in the Figures of *Satyres*, *Apes*, *Goats*, or such like *ugly* Animals; how the comely deportments of Body, into ridiculous gesticulations, perverse postures and antick dances; and how innocuous love and pure friendship degenerates into the most brutish lust and abominable obscenity that can be imagined: of which I will adde nothing more, having spoke enough of this matter in the Appendix to my *Antidote*.

6. What is most material for the present, is to consider, whether as the *Musick* and *Dancing* of these lower and more deeply lapsed Daemons are a distorted imitation of what the higher and more pure *Daemons* doe in their Regions; so their *Feasting* may not be a perverted resemblance of the others Banquetings also: that is to say, it is worth our enquiring into, whether they do not *eat* and *drink* as well as these. For the rich amongst us must have their repast as well as the poor, and Princes feed as well as Prisoners, though there be a great

difference in their diet. And I must confess, there is no small difficulty in both, whence the good or bad *Genii* may have their food; though it be easy enough to conceive that they may feed and refresh their Vehicles.

5   For supposing they do vitally actuate some particular portion of the Aire that they drive along with them, which is of a certain extent, it is most natural to conceive, that partly by local motion, and partly by the activity of their thoughts, they set some particles of their Vehicles into a more then usual

10   agitation, which being thus moved, scatter and perspire; and that so the Vehicle lessens in some measure, and therefore admits of a recruit: which must be either by formal repast, or by drawing in the crude Aire onely, which haply may be enough; but it being so like it self alwaies, the pleasure will be

15   more flat. Wherefore it is not improbable but that both may have their times of Refection, for pleasure at least, if not necessity, which will be the greater advantage for the *Good*, & the more exquisite misery for the *Bad*, they being punishable in tnis regard also.

20   7. But, as I said, the greatest difficulty is to give a rational account whence the Bad *Genii* have their food, in their execrable Feasts, so formally made up into dishes. That the materials of it is a *vaporous Aire*, appears as well from the faintness and emptiness of them that have been entertained at

25   those Feasts, as from their forbidding the use of *Salt* at them, it having a virtue of dissolving of all aqueous substances, as well as hindering their congelation. But how the *Aire* is moulded up into that form and consistency, it is very hard to conceive: whether it be done by the mere power of Imagination upon

30   their own Vehicles, first dabled in some humidities that are the fittest for their design, which they change into these forms of Viands, and then withdraw, when they have given them such a fibre, colour, and consistency, with some small touch of such a sapour or tincture: or whether it be the priviledge of these

35   *Aëreal Creatures*, by a sharp Desire and keen Imagination, to pierce the *Spirit of Nature*, so as to awaken her activity, and engage her to the compleating in a moment, as it were, the full design of their own wishes, but in such matter as the Element they are in is capable of, which is this crude and vaporous Aire;

40   whence their food must be very dilute and flashie, and rather a mockery then any solid satisfaction and pleasure.

8. But those Superiour *Daemons*, which inhabit that part of the Aire that no storm nor tempest can reach, need be put to no such shifts, though they may be as able in them as the other. For in the tranquillity of those Upper Regions, that *Promus-Condus* of the *Universe, the Spirit of Nature,* may silently send forth whole Gardens and Orchards of most delectable fruits and flowers, of an equilibrious ponderosity to the parts of the *Aire* they grow in, to whose shape and colours the transparency of these Plants may adde a particular lustre, as we see it is in precious Stones. And the *Chymists* are never quiet till the heat of their Fancy have calcined and vitrified the Earth into a crystalline pellucidity, conceiting that it will be then a very fine thing indeed, and all that then grows out of it: which desirable Spectacle they may haply enjoy in a more perfect manner, whenever they are admitted into those *higher Regions* of the Aire.

For the very Soile then under them shall be transparent, in which they may trace the very Roots of the Trees of this *Superiour Paradise* with their eyes, and if it may not offend them, see this opake Earth through it, bounding their sight with such a white faint splendour as is discovered in the Moon, with that difference of brightness that will arise from the distinction of Land and Water; and if they will recreate their palats, may tast of such Fruits, as whose natural juice will vie with their noblest Extractions and Quintessences. For such certainly will they there find the blood of the Grape, the rubie-coloured Cherries, and Nectarines.

And if, for the compleating of the pleasantness of these habitations, that they may look less like a silent and dead solitude, they meet with Birds and Beasts of curious shapes and colours, the single accents of whose voices are very grateful to the Ear, and the varying of their notes perfect Musical harmony; they would doe very kindly to bring us word back of the certainty of these things, and make this more then a *Philosophical Conjecture.*

But that there may be *Food* and *Feasting* in those higher Aëreal Regions, is less doubted by the *Platonists*; which makes *Maximus Tyrius* call the Soul, when she has left the Body, ϑρέμμα αἰϑέριον and the above-cited Oracle of *Apollo* describes the Felicity of that Chorus of immortal Lovers he mentions there, from feasting together with the blessed *Genii,*

κέαρ ἐν ϑαλίηισιν

5

10

15

20

25

30

35

40

Λιὲν εὐφροσύνῃσιν ἰαίνεται...

So that the *Nectar* and *Ambrosia* of the Poets may not be a mere fable. For the *Spirit of Nature*, which is the immediate Instrument of God, may enrich the fruits of these *Aëreal*
5 *Paradises* with such liquors, as being received into the bodies of these purer *Daemons*, and diffusing it self through their Vehicles, may cause such grateful motions analogical to our tast, and excite such a more then ordinary quickness in their minds, and benign chearfulness, that it may far transcend the
10 most delicate Refection that the greatest Epicures could ever invent upon Earth; and that without all satiety and burdensomeness, it filling them with nothing but Divine Love, Joy, and Devotion.

15 ────────────────────────────────────

Chap. X.

I. *How hard it is to define any thing concerning the* Aëreal *or*
20 Aethereal Elysiums. *2.That there is Political Order and Laws amongst these* Aiery Daemons. *3. That this Chain of Government reaches down from the highest* Aethereal *Powers through the* Aëreal *to the very* Inhabitants *of the* Earth. *4. The great security we live in thereby. 5. How easily detectible and*
25 *punishable wicked Spirits are by those of their own Tribe. 6. Other reasons of the security we find our selves in from the gross infestations of evil Spirits. 7. What kind of punishments the* Aëreal Officers *inflict upon their Malefactours.*

30   I. I Might enlarge my self much on this Subject, by representing the many *Concamerations* of the *Aëreal* and *Aethereal Elysiums*, depainting them out in all the variety of their Ornaments: but there is no prudence of being lavish of ones pen in a matter so lubricous and Conjectural. Of the bare
35 existence whereof we have no other ground, then that otherwise the greatest part of the Universe by infinite measure, and the most noble, would lye as it were uncultivate, like a desart of Sand, wherein a man can spie neither Plant nor living Creature. Which though it may seem as strange as if
40 Nature should have restrained all the Varieties she would put forth to one contemptible Mole-hill, and have made all the rest of the Earth one Homogeneal surface of dry clay or stone, on

which not one sprig of Grass, much less any Flower or Tree, should grow, nor Bird nor Beast be found once to set their foot thereon: yet the *Spirits* of us *Mortals* being too pusillanimous to be able to grapple with such vast Objects, we must resolve to rest either ignorant, or Sceptical, in this matter.   5

2. And therefore let us consider what will more easily fall under our comprehension, and that is the *Policy* of the *Aiery Daemons*. Concerning which, that in general there is such a thing among them, is the most assuredly true in it self, and of the most use to us to be perswaded of. To know their 10 particular *Orders* and *Customes* is a more needless Curiosity. But that they do lye under the restraint of *Government*, is not onely the opinion of the *Pythagoreans* (who have even to the nicety of *Grammatical Criticisme* assigned distinct names to the Law that belongs to these Three distinct ranks of Beings, 15 ἀνϑρωποι. δαίμονες and ϑεοί. calling the Law that belongs to the first Νόμος. the second Δίκη and the third ϑέμις) but it is also the easy and obvious suggestion of ordinary Reason, that it must needs be so, and especially amongst the Aëreal *Genii* in these lower Regions, they being a mixt rabble of good and bad, 20 wise and foolish, in such a sense as we may say the Inhabitants of the Earth are so, and therefore they must naturally fall under a Government, and submit to Lawes, as well and for the same reasons as Men do. For otherwise they cannot tolerably subsist, nor enjoy what rights may some way 25 or other appertain to them.

For the Souls of men deceased and the *Daemons* being endued with corporeal Sense, by Axiome 30, and therefore capable of *Pleasure* and *Pain*, and consequently of both *Injury* and *Punishment*, it is manifest, that having the use of Reason, 30 they cannot fail to mould themselves into some *Political* form or other; and so to be divided into Nations and Provinces, and to have their Officers of State, from the King on his Throne to the very lowest and most abhorred Executioners of Justice.

3. Which invisible Government is not circumscribed 35 within the compass of the *Aiery* Regions, but takes hold also on the Inhabitants of the *Earth*, as the Government of Men does on several sorts of brute Beasts, and the *Aethereal* powers also have a Right and Exercise of Rule over the *Aëreal*. Whence nothing can be committed in the World against the more 40 indispensable Laws thereof, but a most severe and inevitable punishment will follow: every Nation, City, Family and

Person, being in some manner the *Peculium*, and therefore in
the tutelage, of some invisible Power or other, as I have above
intimated.

    4. And such Transgressions as are against those Laws
5   without whose observance the Creation could not subsist, we
may be assured are punished with Torture intolerable, and
infinitely above any Pleasure imaginable the evil *Genii* can take
in doing of those of their own Order, or us Mortals, any
mischief. Whence it is manifest that we are as secure from
10 their gross outrages (such as the firing of our houses, the
stealing away our Jewels or more necessary Utensils,
murdering our selves or children, destroying our cattel, corn,
and other things of the like sort,) as if they were not *in rerum
natura*. Unless they have some special permission to act, or we
15 our selves enable them by our rash and indiscreet tempering
with them, or suffer from the malice of some person that is in
league with them. For their greatest liberty of doing mischief
is upon that account; which yet is very much limited, in that all
these Actions must pass the consent of a visible person, not
20 hard to be discovered in these unlawful practices, and easy to
be punished by the Law of Men.

    5. And the Aëreal *Genii* can with as much ease inflict
punishment on one another, as we Mortals can apprehend,
imprison, and punish such as transgress against our Laws.
25 For though these *Daemons* be invisible to us, yet they are not
so to their own Tribe: nor can the activity and subtilty of the
Bad over-master the Good Commonwealths-men there, that
uphold the Laws better then they are amongst us. Nor may
the various Transfiguration of their shapes conceal their
30 persons, no more then the disguises that are used by fraudulent
men. For they are as able to discern what is fictitious from
what is true and natural amongst themselves, as we are
amongst our selves. And every *Aëreal* Spirit being part of
some *Political Subdivision*, upon any outrage committed, it will
35 be an easy matter to hunt out the Malefactor; no *Daemon* being
able so to transfigure himself, but upon command he will be
forced to appear in his natural and usual form, not daring to
deny upon examination to what particular *Subdivision* he
belongs. Whence the easy discovery of their miscarriages, and
40 certainty of insupportable torment, will secure the World from
all the disorder that some scrupulous wits suspect would arise
from this kinde of Creatures, if they were in Being.

6. To which we may adde also, That what we have is useless to them, and that it is very hard to conceive that there are many Rational Beings so degenerate as to take pleasure in ill, when it is no good to themselves. That *Socrates* his Aphorism, πᾶς ὁ μοχϑηρὸς ἀγνοεῖ ,may be in no small measure 5 true in the other World, as well as in this. That all that these evil Spirits desire, may be onely our lapse into as great a degree of Apostasy from God as themselves, and to be full partakers with them of their false Liberty; as debauched persons in this life love to make Proselytes, and to have 10 respect from their Nurslings in wickedness. And several other Considerations there are that serve for the taking away this Panick fear of the incursations and molestations of these Aëreal Inhabitants, and might further silence the suspicious Atheist; which I willingly omit; having said more then enough of this 15 Subject already.

7. If any be so curious, as to demand what kind of ‧ *Punishment* this *People of the Aire* inflict upon their Malefactors, I had rather refer them to the Fancies of *Cornelius Agrippa* then be laugh'd at many self for venturing to descend 20 to such particularities. Amongst other things he names their Incarceration, or confinement to most vile and squalid Habitations. His own words are very significant: *Accedunt etiam, vilissimorum ac teterrimorum locorum habitacula, ubi Aetnaei ignes, aquarum ingluvies, fulgurum et tonitruorum* 25 *concussus, terrarum voragines, ubi Regio lucis inops, nec radiorum Solis capax, ignaraque splendoris siderum, perpetuis tenebris et noctis specie caligat.* Whence he would make us believe, that the subterraneous caverns of the Earth are made use of for Dungeons for the wicked *Daemons* to be punished in 30 as if the several *Volcano's*, such as *Aetna*, *Vesuvius*, *Hecla*, and many others, especially in *America*, were so many Prisons or houses of Correction for the unruly *Genii*.

That there is a *tedious restraint* upon them upon villanies committed, and that intolerable, is without all question; they 35 being endued with *corporeal Sense*, and that more quick and passive then ours, and therefore more subject to the highest degrees of torment. So that not onely by incarcerating them, and keeping them in by a watch, in the caverns of burning Mountains, where the heat of those infernal Chambers and the 40 stream of Brimstone cannot but excruciate them exceedingly; but also by commanding them into sundry other Hollows of the

ground, noisome by several fumes and vapours, they may
torture them in several fashions and degrees, fully
proportionable to the greatest crime that is in their power to
commit, and farre above what the cruellest Tyranny has
5   inflicted here, either upon the guilty or innocent. But how
these *Confinements* and *Torments* are inflicted on them, and by
what Degrees and *Relaxations*, is a thing neither easy to
determine, nor needful to understand.

   Wherefore we will surcease from pursuing any further so
10 unprofitable a Subject, and come to the Third general Head we
mentioned, which is, *What the Moral condition of the Soul is
when she has left this Body.*

15

Chap. XI.

I. *Three things to be considered before we come to the* Moral
condition of the Soul after Death: namely, her Memory of
20 *transactions in this Life.* 2. *The peculiar feature and individual*
Character of her Aëreal Vehicle. 3. *The Retainment of the same*
Name. 4. *How her ill deportment here lays the train of her*
Misery hereafter. 5.*The unspeakable torments of Conscience*
worse then Death, and not to be avoided by dying 6. *Of the*
25 *hideous tortures of external sense on them whose searedness of*
Conscience may seem to make them uncapable of her Lashes 7.
Of the state of the Souls of the more innocent and conscientious
Pagans. 8. *Of the natural accruments of* After-happiness *to the*
morally good in this life. 9. *How the Soul enjoys her actings or*
30 *sufferings in* this Life *for an indispensable Cause, when she has*
passed to the other. 10. *That the reason is proportionably the*
same in things of less consequence. 11. *What mischief men may*
create to themselves in the other world by their zealous mistakes
in this. 12. *That though there were no Memory after Death, yet*
35 *the manner of our Life here may sow the seeds of the Soul's future*
happiness or misery.

   I. For the better solution of this Question, there is another
first in nature to be decided; namely, *Whether the Soul*
40 *remembers anything of this Life after Death.* For *Aristotle* and
Cardan seem to deny it; but I do not remember any reasons in
either that will make good their Opinion. But that the contrary

is true, appears from what we have already proved in my second Book, viz. *That the immediate seat of Memory is the Soul her self, and that all Representations with their circumstances are reserved in her, not in the Spirits,* (a thing which *Vaninus* himself cannot deny) *nor in any part of the Body.* And that the Spirits are onely a necessary Instrument whereby the Soul works,; which we they are too cool and gross and waterish, Oblivion creeps upon her in that measure that the Spirits are thus distempered; but the disease being chased away, and the temper of the Spirits rectified, the Soul forthwith recovers the memory of what things she could not well could before, as being now in a better state of Activity. Whence, by the 33 Axiome, it will follow, that her *Memory* will be rather more perfect after Death, and *Conscience* more nimble to excuse or accuse her according to her Deeds here.

2. It is not altogether beside the purpose to take notice also, That the natural and usual Figure of the Soul's *Aëreal Vehicle* bears a resemblance with the feature of the party in this life; it being most obvious for the *Plastick part* (at the command of the Will to put forth into personal shape) to fall as near to that in this life as the new state will permit. With which act the *Spirit of Nature* haply does concurre, as in the figuration of the *Foetus*; but with such limits as becomes the *Aëreal* Congruity of life, of which we have spoke already: as also how the proper Idea or Figure of every Soul (though it may deflect something by the power of the Parent's Imagination in the act of Conception, or Gestation, yet) may return more near to its peculiar semblance afterwards, and so be an unconcealable Note of *Individuality*.

3. We will adde to all this, the Retainment of the same Name which the deceased had here, unless there be some special reason to change it: so that their persons will be as punctually distinguisht and circumscribed as any of ours in this life. All which things, as they are most probable in themselves that they will thus naturally fall out, so they are very convenient for administration of Justice and keeping of Order in the other State.

4. These things therefore premised, it will not be hard to conceive how the condition of the Soul after this life depends on her *Moral* deportment here. For *Memory* ceasing not, *Conscience* may very likely awake more furiously then ever; the Mind becoming a more clear Judge of evil Actions past then

she could be in the Flesh, being now stript of all those
circumstances and concurrences of things that kept her off from
the opportunity of calling her self to account, or of perceiving
the ugliness of her own ways. Besides, there being that
5   communication betwixt the *Earth* and the *Aire*, that at least the
same of things will arrive to their cognoscence that have left
this life; the after ill success of their wicked enterprises and
unreasonable   transactions   may   arm   their   tormenting
Conscience with new whips and stings, when they shall either
10 hear, or see with their eyes, what they have unjustly built up,
to run with shame to ruine, and behold all their designs come to
nought, and their same blasted upon Earth.

5. This is the state of such Souls as are capable of a sense
of dislike of their past-actions: and a man would think they
15 need no other punishment then this, if he consider the mighty
power of the Mind over her own Vehicle, and how vulnerable it
is from her self. These *Passions* therefore of the Soul that
follow an ill Conscience, must needs bring her Aiery body into
intolerable distempers, worse then Death it self. Nor yet can
20 she die if she would, neither by fire, nor sword, nor any means
imaginable; no not if she should fling her self into the flames of
smoaking *Aetna*. For suppose she could keep her self so long
there, as to indure that hideous pain of destroying the *vital
Congruity* of her Vehicle by that sulphureous fire; she would be
25 no sooner released, but she would catch life again in the Aire,
and all the former troubles and vexations would return, besides
the overplus of these pangs of Death. For *Memory* would
return, and an ill Conscience would return, and all those busie
Furies, those disordered Passions which follow it. And thus it
30 would be, though the Soul should kill her self a thousand and a
thousand times; she could but pain and punish her self, not
destroy her self.

6. But if we could suppose some means Consciences *seared*
in the next state as well as this, (for certainly there are that
35 make it their Business to obliterate all sense of difference of
Good and Evil out of their minds; and hold it to be an high
strain of wit (though it be nothing else but a piece of bestial
stupidity) to think there is no such thing as *Vice* and *Vertue*,
and that it is a principall part of perfection, to be so degenerate
40 as to act according to this Principle without any remorse at all;)
these men may seem to have an excellent priviledge in the
other world, they being thus armour-proof against all the fiery

darts of that domestick Devil: As if the greatest security in the other life were, to have been compleatly wicked in this.

But it is not out of the reach of mere Reason and Philosophy to discover, that such bold and impudent wretches as have lost all *inward* sense of Good and Evil, may there against their wills feel a lash in the *outward*. For the Divine *Nemesis* is excluded out of no part of the Universe; and *Goodness* and *Justice*, which they contemn here, will be accounted with them in that other state, whether they will or no. I speak of such course Spirits that can swallow down Murder, Perjury, Extortion, Adultery, Buggery and the like gross crimes, without the least disgust, and think they have a right to satisfy their own Lust, though it be by never so great injury against their Neighbour. If these men should carry it with impunity, there were really no Providence, and themselves were the truest Prophets and faithfullest Instructers of mankind, divulging the choicest *Arcanum* they have to impart to them, namely *That there is no God*.

But the case stands quite otherwise. For whether it be by the importunity of them they injure in this life, who may meet with them afterward, as *Cardan* by way of Objection suggests in his Treatise of this Subject; or whether by a general desertion by all of the other world that are able to protect, (such Monsters as I describe being haply far less in proportion to the number of the other state, then these here are to this;) they will be necessarily exposed to those grim and remorseless *Officers of Justice*, who are as devoid of all sense of what is Good as those that they shall punish. So that their penalty shall be inflicted from such as are of the same Principles with themselves, who watch for such booties as these, and when they can catch them, dress them and adorn them according to the multifarious petulancy of their own unaccountable humours; and taking a special pride and pleasure in the making and seeing Creatures miserable, fall upon their prey with all eagerness and alacrity, as the hungry Lions on a condemned malefactour, but with more ferocity and insultation by far. For having more wit, and, if it be possible, less goodness then the Soul they thus assault, they satiate their lascivient cruelty with all manner of abuses and torments they can imagine, giving her only so much respite as will serve to receive their new inventions with a fresher smart and more distinct pain. Neither can any Reason or Rhetorick prevail with them, no

Expostulation, Petition or Submission. For to what purpose
can it be, to expostulate about injury and violence with them
whose deepest reach of wit is to understand this one main
Principle, *That every ones Lust, when he can act with impunity is*
5 *the most sacred and soveraign Law?* Or what can either
Petitions or Submissions doe with those who hold it the *most*
contemptible piece of fondness and silliness that is, to be intreated
to recede from their own Interest? And they acknowledging no
such thing as *Vertue* and *Vice*, make it their onely interest to
10 *please* themselves in what is agreeable to their own desires:
and their main *pleasure* is, to excruciate and torture, in the
most exquisite ways they can, as many as Opportunity delivers
up to their power.

And thus we see how, in the other life, the proud conceited
15 *Atheist* may at last feel the sad inconvenience of his own
Practices and Principles.   For even those that pleased
themselves in helping him forward, while he was in this life, to
that high pitch of wickedness, may haply take as much
pleasure to see him punish'd by those *grim Executioners* in the
20 other.   Like that sportful cruelty (which some would
appropriate to *Nero*'s person) of causing the *Vestal* virgins to be
ravish'd, and then putting them to death for being so.

7. But this Subject would be too tedious and too Tragical to
insist on any longer. Let us cast our eyes therefore upon a
25 more tolerable Object; and that is The state of the Soul that
has, according to the best opportunity she had of knowledge,
liv'd vertuously and conscientiously, in what part or Age of the
world soever. For though this *Moral Innocency* amongst the
Pagans will not amount to what our Religion calls *Salvation*; yet
30 it cannot but be advantageous to them in the other state,
according to the several degrees thereof; they being more or
less *Happy* or *Miserable*, as they have been more or less
Vertuous in this life. For we cannot imagine why God should
be more harsh to them in the other world then in this, noting
35 having happened to them to alienate his affections but Death;
which was not in their power to avoid, and looks more like a
punishment then a fault: though it be neither to those that are
well-meaning and conscientious, and not professed contemners
of the wholsome suggestions of the Light of Nature, but are
40 lovers of Humanity and Vertue. For to these it is onely an
entrance into another life.

... Ad amoena vireta

Fortunatorum nemorum, sedésque beatas.
Which Truth I could not conceal, it being a great prejudice to
Divine Providence to think otherwise. For to those that are
free, her wayes will seem as unintelligible in overloading the
simple with punishment, as in not rewarding the more perfectly 5
righteous and illuminate. For from a fault in either they will
be tempted to a misbelief of the whole, and hold no Providence
at all.

8. Let there therefore be peculiar Priviledges of *Morality*,
every where, to those that pass into the other state. For unless 10
God make a stop on purpose, it will naturally follow, That
Memory after Death suggesting nothing but what the *Conscience*
allows of, much Tranquilliity *of Minde* must result from thence,
and a certain *Health* and *Beauty* of the *Aëreal* vehicle; also
better Company and Converse, and more pleasant Tracts and 15
Regions to inhabit. For what *Plotinus* speaks of the *extreme*
degrees, is also true of the *intermediate*, else Divine Justice
would be very maime. *For a man*, saith he, *having once appro-
priated to himself a pravity of temper, and united with it, is
known well what he is; and according to his nature is thrust* 20
*forward into what he propends to, both here, and departed hence,
and so shall be pulled by the drawings of Nature into a sutable
place. But the Good man his Receptions and Communications
shall be of another sort, by the drawing as it were of certain
hidden strings transposed and pulled by Natures own fingers. So* 25
*admirable is the power and order of the Universe, all things being
carried on in a silent way of Justice, which none can avoid, and
which the Wicked man has no perception nor understanding of,
but is drawn, knowing nothing whither in the Universe he ought
to be carried. But the Good man both knows and goes whither he* 30
*ought, and discerns before he departs hence where he must
inhabit, and is full of hopes that it shall be with Gods.* This
large Paragraph of *Plotinus* is not without some small Truth in
it, if rightly limited and understood; but seems not to reach at
all the Circumstances and accruments of *Happiness* to the Soul 35
in the other state, which will naturally follow her from her
transactions in this life.

9. For certainly, according to the several degrees of
Benignity of Spirit, and the *desire of doing good* to mankinde in
this life, and the more ample opportunities of doing it, the 40
Felicity of the other World is redoubled upon them; there being
so certain communication and entercourse betwixt both. And

therefore they that *act* or *suffer* deeply in such Causes as God
will maintain in the World, and are *just* and *holy* at the
bottome, (and there are some Principles that are indispensably
such, which Providence has countenanced both by Miracles,
5   the suffrages of the Wisest men in all Ages, and the common
voice of Nature;) those that have been the most Heroical Abet-
ters and Promoters of these things in this life, will naturally
receive the greater contentment of Minde after it, being
conscious to themselves how seriously they have assisted what
10   God will never desert, and that Truth is mighty and must at
last prevail; wnich they are better asssured of out of the Body,
then when they were in it.

    10. Nor is this kinde of access of Happiness to be confined
onely to our furtherance of what is of the highest and most
15   indispensable consideration here, but in proportion touches all
transactions that proceed from a vertuous and good Principle,
whereof there are several degrees: amongst which those may
not be esteemed the meanest that refer to a *National* good and
therefore those that, out of a natural generosity of Spirit and
20   successful fortitude in Warre, have delivered their Country
from bondage, or have been so wise and understanding in
Politicks, as to have contrived wholsome Laws; for the greater
happiness and comfort of the People; while such a Nation
prospers and is in being, it cannot but be an accrument of
25   Happiness to these so considerable Benefactors, unless we
should imagine them less generous and good in the other
World, where they have the advantage of being Better. And
what I have said in this more notable instance, is in a degree
true in things of smaller concernment, which would be infinite
30   to rehearse. But whole Nations, with their Laws and Orders of
Men, and Families may fail, and therefore these accessions be
cut off: but he that laies out his pains in this life for the
carrying on such designs as will take place so long as the World
endures, and must have a compleat Triumph at last; such a
35   one laies a train for an Everlasting advantage in the other
World, which, in despite of all the tumblings and turnings of
unsetled fortune, will be sure to take effect.

    11. But this matter requires Judgement as well as Heat
and Forwardness. For pragmatical Ignorance, though
40   accompanied with some measure of Sincerity and well-
meaning, may set a-foot such things in the World, or set upon
record such either false, or impertinent and unseasonable,

Principles, as being made ill use of, may very much prejudice
the Cause one desires to promote; which will be a sad spectacle
for them in the other State. For though their simplicity may be
pardonable, yet they will not fail to finde the ill effect of their
mistake upon themselves. As he that kills a friend instead of 5
an enemy, though he may satisfy his Conscience that rightly
pleads his innocency; yet he cannot avoid the sense of shame
and sorrow that naturally follows so mischievous an error.

    12. Such accruencies as these there may be to our
Enjoyments in the other World from the durable traces of our 10
transactions in this, if we have any *Memory* of things after
Death, as I have already demonstrated that we have. But if we
had not, but *Aristotle*'s and *Cardan*'s Opinion were true, yet
Vertue and *Piety* will not prove *onely* useful for this present
state. Because according to our living here, we shall hereafter, 15
by a hidden concatenation of Causes, be drawn to a condition
answerable to the purity or impurity of our Souls in this life:
that silent *Nemesis* that passes through the whole contexture of
the Universe ever fatally contriving us into such a state as we
our selves have fitted our selves for by our accustomary 20
actions. Of so great consequence is it, while we have
opportunity, to aspire to the Best things.

25

Chap. XII.

I. *What* The Spirit of Nature *is*. 2. *Experiments that argue its
real Existence; such as that of two Strings tuned Unisons*. 3.
Sympathetick *Cures and Tortures*. 4. *The* Sympathy *betwixt* 30
the Earthly *and* Astral *Body*. 5. *Monstrous Births*. 6. *The
Attraction of the Load-stone and Roundness of the Sun and Stars*.

    I. We had now quite finished our Discourse, did I not
think it convenient to answer a double Expectation of the 35
Reader. The one is touching *The Spirit of Nature*, the other the
producing of *Objections* that may be made against our
concluded Assertion of the Soul's Immortality. For as for the
former, I can easily imagine he may well desire a more
punctual account of that Principle I have had so often recourse 40
to, then I have hitherto given, and will think it fit that I should
somewhere more fully explain what I mean by the terms, and

shew him many strongest grounds why I conceive there is any
such Being in the World. To hold him therefore no longer in
suspence, I shall doe both in this place. *The Spirit of Nature*
therefore, according to that notion I have of it, *is, A substance*
5   *incorporeal, but without Sense and Animadversion, pervading the*
whole Matter of the Universe, and exercising a Plastical power
therein according to the sundry predispositions and occasions in
the parts it works upon, raising such Phaenomena *in the World,*
by directing the parts of the Matter and their Motion, as cannot be
10   *resolved into mere Mechanical powers.* This rude Description
may serve to convey to any one a conception determinate
enough of the nature of the thing. And that it is not a mere
Notion, but a real Being, besides what I have occasionally
hinted already (and shall here again confirm by new instances)
15   there are several other Considerations may perswade us.

2. The first whereof shall be conoerning those Experiments
of *Sympathetick* Pains, Assuagements and Cures; of which
there are many Examples; approved by the most scrupulous
Pretenders to sobriety and judgment, and of all which I cannot
20   forbear to pronounce, that I suspect them to come to pass by
some such power as makes Strings that be tuned *Unisons,*
(though on several Instruments) the one being touched, the
other to tremble and move very sensibly, and to cast off a
straw or pin or any such small thing laid upon it. Which
25   cannot be resolved into any *Mechanical* Principle, though some
have ingeniously gone about it. For before they attempted to
shew the reason, why that String that is not *Unison* to that
which is struck should not leap and move, as it doth that is,
they should have demonstrated, that by the mere *Vibration of*
30   *the Aire* that which is *Unison* can be so moved; for if it could,
these Vibrations would not faile to move other Bodies more
movable by farre then the string it self that is struck a small
thred of silk or an hair with some light thing at the end of it,
they must needs receive those reciprocal Vibrations that are
35   communicated to the *Unison* string at a far greater distance, if
the mere motion of the material Aire caused the subsultation of
the string tuned *Unison*: Which yet is contrary to experience.

Besides that, if it were the mere *Vibration of the Aire* that
caused this *tremor* in the *Unison* string, the effect would not be
40   considerable, unless both the strings lay well-nigh in the same
Plane, and that the Vibration of the string that is struck be
made in that Plane they both lie in. But let the string be

struck so as to cut the Plane perpendicularly by its tremulous excursions, or let both the strings be in two several Planes at a good distance above one another, the event is much-what the same, though the Aire cannot rationally be conceived to *vibrate* backwards and forwards, otherwise then wellnigh in the very 5 Planes wherein the strings are moved.

All which things do clearly shew, that pure *Corporeal* causes cannot produce this effect: and that therefore we must suppose, that *both* the strings are united with some one *Incorporeal* Being, which has a different *Unity* and *Activity* from 10 *Matter*, but yet a *Sympathy* therewith; which affecting this *Immaterial* Being, makes it affect the Matter in the same manner in another place, where it does symbolize with that other in some predisposition or qualification, as these two strings do in being tuned *Unisons* to one another: and this, 15 without sending any particles to the Matter it does thus act upon; as my thought of moving of my Toe being represented within my Brain, by the power of my Soul I can, without sending Spirits into my Toe, but onely by making use of them that are there, move my Toe as I please, by reason of that 20 *Unity* and *Activity* that is peculiar to many Soul as a Spiritual substance that pervades my whole Body. Whence I would conclude also, that there is some such Principle as we call *The Spirit of Nature*, or *the inferiour Soul of the World*, into which such *Phaenomena* as these are to be resolved.   25

3. And I account *Sympathetick* Cures, Pains and Asswagements to be such, As for example, when in the use of those *Magnetick* Remedies, as some call them, they can make the wound dolorously hot or chill at a great distance, or can put it into perfect ease, this is not by any agency of *emissary* 30 *Atoms*. For these *hot Atoms* would cool sufficiently in their progress to the party through the frigid aire; and the *cold Atoms*, if they could be so active as to dispatch so fast, would be warm enough by their journey in the Summer Sun. The inflammation also of the Cowes Udder by the boiling over of the 35 milk into the fire, the scalding of mens entrails at a distance by the burning of their excrements, with other pranks of the like nature, these cannot be rationally resolved into the recourse of the Spirits of Men or Kine mingled with fiery Atoms, and so re-entring the parts thus affected, because the minuteness of 40 those Atoms argues the sudainness of their extinction, as the smallest wires made red hot soonest cool.

To all which you may adde (if it will prove true) that notable example of the Wines working when the Vines are in the flower, and that this *Sympathetick* effect must be from the Vines of that Country from which they came: whence these exhalations of the Vineyards must spread as far as from *Spain* and the *Canaries* to *England*, and by the same reason must reach round about every way as far from the *Canaries*, besides their journey upwards into the Aire. So that there will be an Hemisphere of vineal Atoms of an incredible extent, unless they part themselves into trains, and march only to those places whither their Wines are carried. But what *corporeal* cause can guide them thither? Which question may be made of other *Phaenomena* of the like nature, Whence again it will be necessary to establish the principle I drive at, though the effects were caused by the transmission of Atoms.

4. The notablest examples of this *Mundane Sympathy* are in histories more uncertain and obscure, and such as, though I have been very credibly informed, yet, as I have already declared my self, I dare only avouch as possible, viz. the Souls of men leaving their Bodies, and appearing in shapes, suppose, of *Cats, Pigeons, Weasels*, and sometimes of *Men*; and that whatever hurt befalls them in these *Astral* bodies, as the *Paracelsians* love to call them, the same is inflicted upon their *Terrestrial* lying in the mean time in their beds or on the ground. As if their *Astral bodies* be scalded, wounded, have the back broke, the same certainly happens to their *Earthly bodies*.

Which things if they be true, in all likelihood they are to be resolved into this Principle we speak of, and that *The Spirit of Nature* is snatcht into consent with the Imagination of the Souls in these *Astral bodies* or *Aiery Vehicles*. Which act of *imagining* must needs be strong in them, it being so set on and assisted by a quick and sharp pain and fright in these scaldings, woundings, and strokes on the back; some such thing happening here as in women with child, whose Fancies made keen by a suddain fear, have deprived their children of their arms, yea and of their heads too; as also appears by two remarkable stories Sr. *Kenelme Digby* relates in his witty and eloquent *Discourse of the Cure of Wounds by the powder of Sympathy*, besides what we have already recited out of *Helmont*.

5. Which effects I suppose to be beyond the power of any humane Fancy unassisted by some more forceable Agent; as also that prodigious birth he mentions of a woman of *Carcassona*, who by her overmuch sporting and pleasing her self with an *Ape*, while she was with Child, brought forth a Monster exactly of that shape. and if we should conclude with that learned Writer, that it was a real Ape, it is no more wondeful, nor so much, as that birth of a *Crab-fish* or *Lobster* we have above mentioned out of *Fortunius Licetus*; as we might also other more usual, though no less monstrous births for the wombs of women to bear. Of which the Soul of the Mother cannot be suspected to be the cause, she not so much as being the Efformer of her own *Foetus*, as that judicious Naturalist Dr. *Harvey* has determined. And if the Mother's Soul could be the Efformer of the *Foetus*, in all reason her *Plastick* power would be ever Particular and Specifick as the Soul it self is Particular.

What remains therefore but the *Universal Soul of the World* or *Spirit of Nature* that can doe these fears? who, *Vertumnus*-like, is ready to change his own Activity and the yielding Matter into any mode and shape indifferently as occasion engages him, and so to prepare an edifice, at least the more rude strokes and delineaments thereof, for any Specifick Soul whatsoever, and in any place where the Matter will yield to his operations. But the time of the arrival thither of the particular guest it is intended for, though we cannot say how soon it is, yet we may be sure it is not later then a clear discovery of *Sensation* as well as *Vegetation* and *Organization* in the Matter.

6. The *Attraction of the Load-stone* seems to have some affinity with these instances of *Sympathy*. This mystery *Des-Cartes* has explained with admirable artifice as to the immediate Corporeal causes thereof, to wit, those wreathed particles which he makes to pass certain screw-pores in the *Load-stone* and *Iron*. But how the efformation of these particles is above the reach of the mere Mechanical powers in *Matter*, as also the exquisite direction of their motion, whereby they make their peculiar *Vortex* he describes about the Earth from Pole to Pole, and thread an incrustated Star, passing in a right line in so long a journey as the Diameter thereof without being swung to the sides; how these things, I say, are beyond the powers of *Matter*, I have fully enough declared and proved in a large Letter of mine to *V.C.* and therefore that I may not *actum*

agere, shall forbear speaking any farther thereof in this place.
To which you may adde, That mere corporeal motion in Matter,
without any other guide, would never so much as produce a
round Sun or *Star*, of which figure notwithstanding *Des-Cartes*
5   acknowledges them to be.   But my reasons why it cannot be
effected by the simple *Mechanical* powers of *Matter*, I have
particularly set down in my Letters to that excellent
Philosopher.

10 ───

Chap. XIII.

I. *That the Descent of heavy Bodies argues the existence of* The
15   Spirit of Nature, *because else they would either hang in the Aire
as they are placed,* 2. *Or would be diverted from a perpendicular
as they fall near a Plate of Metall set slooping.*   3. *That the
endeavour of the Aether or Aire from the Centre to the Circumference is not the Cause of Gravity, against Mr.* Hobbs. 4. *A full
20   confutation of Mr.*Hobbs *his Opinion.* 5. *An ocular Demonstration of the absurd consequence thereof.*   6. *An absolute
Demonstration that Gravity cannot be the effect of mere
Mechanical powers.*   7. *The Latitude of the operations of* The
Spirit of Nature, *how large and whether bounded.* 8. *The reason
25   of its name.* 9. *Of Instinct, whether it be, and what it is.* 10. *The
grand office of the Spirit of Nature in transmitting Souls into
rightly prepared Matter.*

I. And a farther confirmation that I am not mistaken
30   therein, is what we daily here experience upon Earth, which is
the descending of heavy Bodies, as we call them. Concerning
the motion Whereof I agree with *Des-Cartes* in the assignation
of the immediate corporeal cause, to wit, the *Aethereal* matter,
which is so plentifully in the Air over it is in grosser Bodies;
35   but withall do vehemently surmise, that there must be some
Immaterial cause, such as we call *The Spirit of Nature* or
Inferiour Soul of the World, that must direct the motions of the
Aethereal particles to act upon these grosser Bodies to drive
them towards the Earth. For that surplusage of Agitation of
40   the *globular* particles of the *Aether* above what they spend in
turning the Earth about, is carried every way indifferently,
according to his own concession; by which motion the drops of

liquors are formed into *round* figures, as he ingeniously concludes. From whence it is apparent, that a bullet of iron, silver or goid placed in the Aire is equally assaulted on all sides by the occursion of these Aethereal particles, and therefore, will be moved no more downwards then upwards, but hang *in* 5 *aequilibrio*, as a piece of Cork rests on the water, where there is neither winde nor stream, but is equally plaied against by the particles of water on all sides.

2. Nor is it imaginable how the occursions of this Aethereal Element here against the surface of the Earth, being 10 it is so fluid a Body, should make it endeavour to lift it self from the Earth at so great a distance as the middle Region of the Aire and further. Besides, that this is not the cause of the descent of heavy Bodies is manifest, because then a broad Plate of the most solid Metall and most perfectly polisht, such as is 15 able to reflect the Aethereal particles most efficaciously, being placed slooping, would change the course of the descent of things, and make them fall perpendicularly to it, and not to the Plane of the Horizon; as for example, not from A to B, but from A to C; which is against experience. For the heavy Body will 20 alwaies fall down from A to B, though the recession of the Aethereal Matter must needs be from C to A according to this Hypothesis.

3. Nor can the endeavour of the Celestial Matter from the centre to the circumference take place here. For besides that 25 *Des-Cartes*, the profoundest Master of Mechanicks, has declin'd that way himself (though Mr. *Hobbs* has taken it up,) it would follow, that near the Poles of the Earth there would be no descent of heavy Bodies at all, and in the very Clime we live in none perpendicular. To say nothing how this way will not 30 salve the union of that great Water that adheres to the body of the Moon.

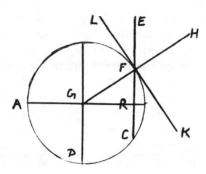

4. But to make good what I said, by undeniable proof that heavy Bodies in the very Clime where we live will not descend perpendicularly to the Earth, if Mr.*Hobbs* his solution of the
5 *Phaenomenon* of *Gravity* be true; we shall evidently *demonstrate* both to the Eye and to Reason the proportion of their declination from a perpendicular in any Elevation of the Pole. In the Circle therefore A B C, let the Aequator be B D, and from the point C draw a line to E, parallel to B D: which line C
10 E will cut the circle in F 60. degrees, suppose, from B. Imagine now a heavy Body at E; according to Mr. *Hobbs* his solution of the Probleme of *Gravity*, it must fall towards the Earth in a line parallel to the *Aequator, viz.* in the line E F; which, say I, declines from the line H F drawn perpendicular to the Horizon
15 L K two third parts of a right angle, that is to say, 60. degrees. For the angle E F H is equal to G F R; which again is equal to the alternate angle B G F, which is two third parts of a right angle *ex thesi*. Whence it is plain that E F declines from a perpendicular no less than 60. degrees. By the same reason, if
20 we had drawn the Scheme for the elevation of 50. which is more Southern then our Clime, we might demonstrate that the descent of heavy Bodies declines from a perpendicular to the Horizon 50 degrees, or 5/9 of a right angle, and so of the rest. From whence it will follow, that men cannot walk upright, but
25 declining, in the elevation suppose of 60. degrees, as near to the ground as E F is to F L, and much nearer in the more remote parts of the North, as in *Norway, Russia, Frisland, Island, Scricfinnia, Greenland* and others; and there is proportionably the same reason in other Climes less Northern.
30 So that Mr. *Hobbs* need not send us so farre off as to the Poles to make the experiment.

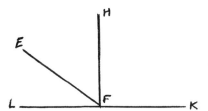

5. For if for example we drew a Scheme for the Parallel
under which we live, suppose about 52. degrees of Elevation, 5
we might represent truly to the eye in what posture men would
walk at *London* or *Cambridge,* according to Mr. *Hobbs* his
determination of the causes of *Gravity.* For it is plain from
what has been above demonstrated, that the natural posture of
their Bodies upon the Horizon L K would be in the line E F, out 10
of which if they did force themselves towards the perpendicular
H F, it would be much pain to them, neither could they place
themselves in the line H F, without being born headlong to the
ground, and laid flat upon the Horizon F K; the force of the
Aire or whatever more subtle Elements therein pressing in 15
lines parallel to E F, and therefore necessarily bearing down
whatever is placed loose in the line H F, as is plain to any one
at first sight.

But we finding no such thing in experience, it is evident
that Mr. *Hobbs* his solution is false; nay I may say that he has 20
not rendred so much as a possible cause of this so ordinary a
Phaenomenon. A thing truly much to be lamented in one who,
upon pretence that all the Appearances in the Universe may re
resolved into mere Corporeal causes, has with unparallell'd
confidence, and not without some wit, derided and exploded all 25
Immaterial Substance out of the World; whenas in the mean
time he does not produce so much as possible Corporeal causes
of the most ordinary effects in Nature. But to leave Mr.
Hobbs to his own ways, and to return to *Des-Cartes.*

6. Adde unto all this, that if the motion of gross Bodies 30
were according to mere Mechanical laws, a Bullet suppose of
Lead or Gold, cast up into the Aire, would never descend again,
but would persist in a rectilinear motion. For it being far more
solid then so much Aire and Aether put together as would fill
its place, and being moved with no less swiftness then that 35
wherewith the Earth is carried about in twenty four hours, it
must needs break out in a straight line through the thin Aire,

and never return again to the Earth, but get away as a *Comet*
does out of a *Vortex*. And that *de facto* a Cannon-Bullet has
been shot so high that it never fell back again upon the ground,
Des-Cartes does admit of as a true experiment. Of which, for
5   my own part, I can imagine no other unexceptionable reason,
but that at a certain distance *The Spirit of Nature* in some
regards leaves the motion of *Matter* to the pure laws of
Mechanicks, but within other bounds checks it, whence it is
that the Water does not swill out of the Moon.
10   7. Now if the pure Mechanick powers in *Matter* and
Corporeal motion will not amount to so simple a *Phaenomenon*
as the falling of a stone to the Earth, how shall we hope they
will be the adequate cause of sundry sorts of *Plants* and other
things, that have farre more artifice and curiosity then the
15   direct descent of a stone to the ground?
    Nor are we beaten back again by this discovery into that
dotage of the confounded *Schools*, who have indued almost
every different Object of our Senses with a distinct *Substantial
form*, and then puzzle themselves with endless scrupulosities
20   about the generation, corruption, and mixtion of them. For I
affirm with *Des-Cartes*, that nothing affects our Senses but
such Variations of *Matter* as are made by difference of Motion,
Figure, Situation of parts, &c. but I dissent from him in this,
in that I hold it is not mere and pure Mechanical motion that
25   causes all these sensible Modifications in Matter, but that
many times the immediate Director thereof is this *Spirit of
Nature* (I speak of) one and the same every where, and acting
alwaies alike upon like occasions, as a clear-minded men and of
a solid judgement gives alwaies the same verdict in the same
30   circumstances.
    For this *Spirit of Nature* intermedling with the efformation
of the *Foetus* of Animals (as I have already shewn more then
once) were notwithstanding there seems not so much need,
there being in them a more particular Agent for that purpose;
35   'tis exceeding rational that all *Plants* and *Flowers* of all sorts (in
which we have no argument to prove there is any particular
Souls) should be the effects of this *Universal Soul of the World*.
Which Hypothesis, besides that it is most reasonable in it self,
according to that ordinary Axiome *Frustra fit per plura quod*
40   *fieri potest per pauciora*, is also very serviceable for the
preventing many hard Problems about the *Divisibility* of the
Souls of *Plants*, their *Transmutations* into other *Species*, the

growing of *Slips*, and the like. For there is one Soul ready every where to pursue the advantages of prepared Matter. Which is the common and onely λόγος σπερματίτης *of all* Plantal appearances, or of whatever other *Phaenomena* there be, greater or smaller, that exceed the pure Mechanical powers of *Matter*. We except onely *Men* and *Beasts*, who having all of them the càpacity of some sort of enjoyments or other, it was fit they should have particular Souls for the multiplying of the sense of those enjoyments which the transcendent Wisdome of the Creatour has contrived.

8. I have now plainly enough set down what I mean by *The Spirit of Nature*, and sufficiently proved its existence. Out of what has been said may be easily conceived why I give it this name, it being a Principle that is of so great influence and activity in the *Nascency*, as I may so call it, and *Coalescency* of things: And this not onely in the productioin of *Plants*, with all other *Concretions* of an inferiour nature, and yet above the mere *Mechanical* lawes of *Matter*; but also in respect of the birth of *Animals*, whereunto it is preparatory and assistent.

I know not whether I may entitle it also to the guidance of Animals in the chiefest of those actions which we usually impute to *natural Instinct*. Amongst which none so famous as the Birds making their Nests, and particularly the artificial structure of the Martins nests under the arches of Church-windows. In which there being so notable a design unknown to themselves, and so small a pleasure to present Sense, it looks as if they were actuated by another, inspired and carried away in a natural rapture by this *Spirit of Nature* to doe they know not what, though it be really a necessary provision and accommodation for laying their Eggs and hatching their young, in the efformation whereof this *Inferiour Soul of the World* is so rationally conceived to assist and intermeddle: and therefore may the better be supposed to over-power the Fancy, and make use of the menbers of the Birds to build these convenient Receptacles, as certain shops to lay up the Matter whereon she intends to work, namely the Eggs of these Birds whom she thus guides in making of their nests.

9. For that this building of their nests in such sort should not be from *natural Instinct*, but from acquired Art and observation, or from the instruction of the old ones, there is no reason or ground for any one to conceit. For in that their actions tend to so considerable a scope, that is no argument

that they know it or ever consulted about it, no more then that
Ivy or *Bindweed*, that winde about the next plant that can
support them, cast up with themselves aforehand the either
necessity or convenience of such close embraces. Nor does it at
5   all follow, because the young ones might see the old ones make
their nests before they begin to make theirs, that they do see
them or take notice of them. Nay, who can produce any one
example of the old one tutouring or teaching her young ones in
this kind of Architecture: or has spide the young one of her self
10   to apply her mind to learn that art by observing what the old
one does? Wherefore a man may as well argue, yea much
better, that the *Notes* of Birds are not by *Instinct*, but by
learning and art, because they may have heard the old ones
sing or whistle before them: whenas they will take up naturally
15   of themselves such notes as belong to their kind, without
hearing of the oid ones at any time. So that it is not from any
ground of Reason, but a mere vain and shallow surmise, to
think that the Architecture of Birds in building their nests is
not *natural Instinct*, but acquired *Art* and *Imitation*.
20   But on the other side, there are very plain and positive
Reasons to convince us, that this Architecture of theirs is
from *Instinct*, and no *acquired faculty*. And that first, because
in general brute Animals are of such a nature as is devoid of
that free and reflexive reason which is requisite to acquired Art
25   and Consultation. For if they had any such principle, some of
them would be able to speak. The want of which power is the
only plausible presumption for *Des-Cartes* his conceit of their
being mere *Machina's*. Which though it will not reach to so
enormous a Paradox, yet it may justly exclude them from the
30   participation of such a free Reason as will make them able for
consultation and learning of Arts and Mysteries.
       Secondly, The hatching of their eggs being by mere
Instinct, & not out of any deliberate Knowledge, it is reasonable
to think, that the making of their nests, which is but in order
35   thereto, is *mere Instinct* also.
       Thirdly, That which is specifical is not acquired, but is by
Nature or Instinct; but to make their nests thus or thus is
specifical to this or that kinde of Bird, even as their note is, and
therefore is plainly natural.
40   Fourthly, The peculiar Indocility of those Birds that are
the most ingenious Architects in building their nests is a plain
indication that it is not *free Reason* but *Instinct* that guides

them. And *Pliny* observes in the *Swallow*, how indocil she is, and yet how admirable in framing her little mansions of mudd.

Fifthly, That this Architecture is not a piece of learning derived from the old ones in succession, but the immediate effect of Nature, is further manifest, in that in all parts of the 5 World the same kinde of Birds make the same kinde of nests, when it cannot be well supposed that they learned it from those in remote countries, whom the vastness of the Seas kept from mutual converse.

Sixthly and lastly, There is no man can well think or 10 discourse of examples of natural Architecture, but *the Martin's Nest*, the *Combes of Bees*, the *Webs of Spiders* and the *Bags of Silk-worms* will one bring in another, as being wholly congenerous and of the same nature. Which makes *Plinie*, *Cardan* and *Nierembergius* joyn them in one Catalogue as 15 examples of one suite, and may well induce us to conclude them of so near a-kin, as that if one be *natural Instinct*, all the rest must be so too. And our foregoing Argument is infinitely pressing in the three last Instances. For we may be sure that all the *Bees* in the World came not out of one Hive, and therefore 20 could not derive their Architectonical skill from the same teachers, and yet they all make their Combes with the same artifice, as I may so call it, and with the same exactness of Geometry. And as for *Spiders*, it is evident that they are of the τὰ αὐτομάτως γενόμενα. as *Aristotle* phrases it, and are 25 generated of mere fluttery and putrefaction. And yet these Insects so soon as they are bred, can set up shop and fall to their trade of weaving without any Teacher or Instructer.

But the noblest and most apposite instance is that last of the *Silk-worm*, who works so concealedly within her *folliculus* 30 or little bag, as if she either envied the communication of her skil to her fellows, who of themselves are very dim-sighted, or ought him a shame that should be so injudiciously bold as to impute the *natural Instinct* of such like Animals to external observation and imitation. And yet there is a great affinity 35 betwixt the *Nidifications* of *Birds* and these *Conglomerations* of the threads of the *Silk-worm*: not only in regard of the outward Figure of those clues of silk, as I may so call them, which are not unlike the Nests of Birds, but also in regard of the end and designe of them both. Which is not the accommodating of the 40 *Individual*, but a plot for the propagation of the *Species*. For that Insect we call the *Silk-worm* after she has run through

multifarious changes and names, as, of σκώληξ, κάμπη, βομβύλιος, χρυσαλὶς, νύμφη, νεκύδαλος, ψυχὴ , in this last title and change ends all with a plentiful provision for the continuation of the kinde. For when she has arrived to her third change,
5 wherein she is called βομβύλιος, from her mouth and with her fore-feet she works that *Folliculus* or clue of silk above named, building thus her own tombe, which yet is the *wombe or cradle of her self when* having passed the state of a χρυσαλὶς (wherein she does ἀκινητίζειν, as *Aristotle* speaks, and approaches near to
10 the shape and nature of an egg) she emerges after to a nearer tendency toward her purposed animal delineaments, and is called νύμφη *and after this acquiring* a greater degree of life and motion is styled νεκύδαλος ,as if her dead body had catched vital fire again. In this state she does not lye loose, but sticks
15 again to the cavity of the Clue, and grown to full maturity breaks through, and shews herself in the compleat forme of a Butterfly. To which pitch of perfection when they are arrived they enjoy but a very small time. For after three or four daies indulgence to the delightful usages of Venus, the Male
20 immediately bids the world adieu; whom soon after the Female follows, but yet so as that she leaves behinde her some hundreds of eggs, small like the grains of millet, as a numerous pledge and provision for the continuation of their kinde. How then according to this account can the old one ever teach the
25 young ones their trade of spinning or weaving?

And yet the *Silk-worms Bag* is as great a piece of Artifice and of as great designe, or rather the same as the *nests* of *Swallows* or *Martins*. The making of which notwithstanding *Aristotle* calls μιμήματα τῆς ἀνθρωπίνης ζωῆς. *Imitations of*
30 *humane Reason;* which they having not themselves, some Principle distinct from them must be their Guide in these performances: whence I have rightly concluded in my *Antidote,* That the *Nidification* of Birds as well as their *Incubation* is no obscure argument of a Divine Providence. Which I understand
35 mainly of the *structure of their Nests*; though the choice of the places where they build them may not be merely from the lightness of their bodies and their assuefaction to Edifices, Trees, or Bushes, but partly from the dictate of that *Instinct* which suggests to them everywhere what is most for their
40 safety, and makes them many times sagacious above our apprehension. As it appears in what *Pliny* writes concerning a kind of *Swallows* that use to build their nests near *Coptos* in

Aegypt, who do either not make or forsake their nests many daies before, *si futurum est ut auctus amnis attingat.*

That there is such a thing therefore as *Instinct* in Brute Animals I think is very plain, that is to say, That there is an *Instigation* or *Impetus* in them to doe such things without counsel, deliberation, or acquired knowledge, as according to our reason and best consultation we cannot but approve to be fittest to be done. Which Principle in general *Scaliger* seems to parallel to Divine Inspiration. *Instinctus dicitur à Natura, sicut à Diis Afflatio.* But methinks it is most safely and most unexceptionably applied where the *Instinct* respects not so much the welfare of the *Individual* as the common good of this or that *Species.* For if there be any *Impulse* from an Exptrinsecal Principle upon any particular Animal, it is most sure to be then, when that Animal is transported from the pursuance of its own particular accommodation to serve a more publick end. For from whence can this motion be so well as from that which is not a particular Being, but such as in whose Essence the scope & purpose of the general good of the World and of all the Species therein is vitally comprized, and therefore binds all Particulars together by that common Essential Law, which is it self, occasionally impelling them to such actions and services (either above their Knowledge or against their particular Interests) as is most conducing to the Conservation of the Whole? And this is that which we have styled the *Spirit of Nature*, which goes through and assists all corporeal Beings, and is the *Vicarious power of God* (who is that Νόμος ἰσοκλινὴς, as the Philosopher calls Him) upon the Universal Matter of the World. This suggests to the *Spider* the fancy of spinning and weaving her Web, and to the *Bee* of the framing of her Hony-combs, but especially to the *Silk-worm* of conglomerating her both funeral and natal Clue, and to the *Birds* of building their Nests and of their so diligent hatching of their Eggs. But I have insisted upon this Argument too long.

10. The most notable of those offices that can be assigned to *The Spirit of Nature*, and that sutably to his name, is the Translocation of the Souls of Beasts into such Matter as is most fitting for them, he being the common *Proxenet* or *Contractor* of all natural *Matches* and *Marriages* betwixt *Forms* and *Matter*, if we may also speak Metaphors as well as *Aristotle*, whose Aphorisme it is, that *Materia appetit formam ut foemina virum.*

This *Spirit* therefore may have not onely the power of
directing the motion of Matter at hand, but also of *transporting*
of particular Souls and Spirits in their state of *Silence* and
Inactivity to such Matter as they are in a fitness to catch life in
5   again. Which *Transportation* or *Transmission* may very well be
at immense distances, the effect of this *Sympathy* and *Coactivity*
being so great in *the working of Wines*, as has been above
noted, though a thing of less concernment, or, (which is a more
unexceptionable instance) in conducting the *magnetick* particles
10   from one Pole of the Earth to the other.

Whence, to conclude, we may look upon this *Spirit of
Nature* as the great *Quartermaster-General* of Divine providence,
but able alone, without any under-Officers, to lodge every Soul
according to her rank and merit whenever she leaves the Body:
15   And would prove a very serviceable Hypothesis for those
that fancy the *Praeexistence* of humane Souls, to declare how
they may be conveyed into Bodies here, be they at what
distance they will before; and how Matter haply may be so
fitted, that the best of them may be fetcht from the purest
20   *Aethereal* Regions into an humane Body, without serving any
long Apprentiship in the intermediate *Aire*: as also how the
Souls of Brutes, though the Earth were made perfectly inept
for the life of any Animal, need not lye for ever useless in the
Universe.

25   But such Speculations as these are of so vast a
comprehension and impenetrable obscurity, that I cannot have
the confidence to dwell any longer thereon; especially they not
touching so essentially our present designe, and being more fit
to fill a volume themselves, then to be comprised within the
30   narrow limits of my now almost-finish'd Discourse.

Chap. XIV.

35

I. *Objections against the* Soul's Immortality *from her condition
in* Infancy, Old Age, Sleep *and* Sicknesses. 2. *Other Objections
taken from Experiments that seem to prove her* Discerpibility.
3. *As also from the seldome appearing of the Souls of the*
40   *deceased;* 4. *And from our natural fear of Death.* 5. *A
subterfuge of the adverse party, supposing but one Soul common
to all Creatures.* 6. *An Answer concerning the Littleness of the*

Soul in Infancy: 7. *As also concerning the weakness of her
Intellectuals then, and in Old Age.* 8. *That Sleep does not at all
argue the Soul's Mortality, but rather illustrate her Immortality.*
9. *An Answer to the Objection from Apopplexies and Catalepsies:*
10. *As also to that from Madness.* 11. *That the various* 5
*depravations of her Intellectual Faculties do no more argue her
Mortality, then the worser Modifications of Matter its natural
Annihilability. And why God created Souls sympathizing with
Matter.*

10

I. As for the *Objections* that are usually made *against the
Immortality of the Soul*; to propound them all, were both tedious
and useless, there being scarce above one in twenty that can
appear of any moment to but an indifferent Wit and Judgment.
But the greatest difficulties that can be urged I shall bring into 15
play, that the Truth we do maintain may be the more fully
cleared, and the more firmly believed. The most material
Objections that I know *against the Soul's Immortality* are these
five. The first is from the consideration of the condition of the
Soul in *Infancy*, and *Old Age*, as also in *Madness, Sleep*, and 20
Apoplexies. For if we do but observe the great difference of our
Intellectual operations in *Infancy* and *Dotage* from what they
are when we are in the prime of our years; and how that our
Wit grows up by degrees, flourishes for a time, and at last
decayes, keeping the same pace with the changes that Age and 25
Years bring into our Body, which observes the same lawes that
Flowers and Plants; what can we suspect, but that the Soul of
Man, which is so magnificently spoken of amongst the learned,
is nothing else but a Temperature of Body, and that it grows
and spreads with it, both in bigness and virtues, and withers 30
and dies as the Body does, or at least that it does wholly
depend on the Body in its Operations, and therefore that there
is no sense nor perception of any thing after death? And when
the Soul has the best advantage of years, she is not then
exempted from those Eclipses of the powers of the Mind that 35
proceed from *Sleep, Madness, Apoplexies*, and *other Diseases* of
that nature. All which shew her condition, whatever more
exalted Wits surmise of her, that she is but a poor mortal and
corporeal thing.

2. The Second Objection is taken from such Experiments 40
as are thought to prove the Soul *divisible* in the grossest sense,
that is to say, *discerpible* into pieces. And it seems a clear case

in those more contemptible Animals which are called *Insects*, especially the τὰ μακρὰ καὶ πολύποδα, as *Aristotle* describes them, and doth acknowledge that being cut into pieces, each segment will have its motion and sense apart to it self. The

5   most notable Instance of this kind is in the *Scolopendra*, whose parts *Aristotle* affirms to live a long time divided, and to run backwards and forwards; and therefore he will have it to look like many living Creatures growing together, rather then one single one, Εοίκασι γὰρ τὰ τοιαῦτα τῶν ζώων πολλοῖς ζώοις

10   συμπεφυκόσι. But yet he will not afford them the priviledge of Plants, whose Slips will live and grow, being set in the Earth. But the instances that belong to this Objection ascend higher, for they pretend that the parts of perfect Animals will also live asunder.

15   There are two main instances thereof. The one, that of the Eagle *Fromondus* mentions, whose *Head* being chopt off by an angry Clown, for quarreling with his dog, the Body flew over the barn near the place of this rude execution. This was done at *Fromondus* his fathers house: nor is the story improbable, if

20   we consider what ordinarily happens in Pigeons and Ducks, when their heads are cut off. The other instance is, of a Malefactour beheaded at *Antwerp*, whose *Head* when it had given some few jumps into the crowd, and a Dog fell a licking the blood, caught the Dogs eare in its teeth, and held it so fast,

25   that he being frighted ran away with the mans head hanging at his eare, to the great astonishment and confusion of the people. This was told *Fromondus* by an eye-witness of the fact. From which two Examples they think may be safely inferred, that the Souls of Men, as well as of the more perfect kinde of

30   Brutes, are also *discerpible*.

That example in the same Authour out of *Josephus Acosta*, if true, yet is smally to this purpose. For the speaking of the sacrificed Captive, when his *Heart* was cut out, may be a further confirmation indeed that the *Brain* is the Seat of the

35   Common Sense, but no argument of the *Divisibility* of the Soul, she remaining at that time entire in the Body, after the cutting out of the *Heart*, whose office it is to afford *Spirits*, which were not so far yet dissipated, but that they sufficed for that suddain operation of life.

40   3. The Third Objection is from the seldome appearance of the Souls of the deceased. For if they can at all appear, why do they not oftner? if they never appear, it is a strong suspicion

that they are not at all in Being.

4. The Fourth is from the Fear of Death, and an inward downbearing sense in us at some times, that we are utterly mortal, and that there is nothing to be expected after this life.

5. The Fifth and last is rather a Subterfuge then an 5 Objection, That there is but *One Common Soul* in all Men and Beasts, that operates according to the variety of Animals and Persons it does actuate and vivificate, bearing a seeming particularity according to the particular pieces of Matter it informs, but is *One* in all; and that this particularity of Body 10 being lost, this particular Man or Beast is lost, and so every living creature is properly and intirely mortal. These are the reallest and most pertinent *Objections* I could ever meet with, or can excogitate, concerning the Soul' s Immortality: to which I shall answer in order.   15

6. And to the First, which seems to be the shrewdest, I say, That neither the *Contractedness* of the Soul in *Infancy*, nor the *Weakness* of her Intellectual Operations either *then* or in *extreme Old age*, are sufficient proofs of her *Corporeity* or *Morality*. For what wonder is it that the Soul, fain into this low 20 and fatal condition, where she must submit to the course of Nature, and the laws of other Animals that are generated here on Earth, should display her self by degrees, from smaller dimensions to the ordinary size of men; whenas this faculty of *contracting* and *dilating* of themselves is in the very essence 25 and notion of all *Spirits*? as I have noted already. So she does but that leisurely and naturally now, being subjected to the laws of this terrestrial Fate, which she does, exempt from this condition, suddainly and freely: not growing by *Juxtaposition* of parts, or *Intromission* of Matter, but inlarging of her self with 30 the Body merely by the *dilatation* of her own Substance, which is one and the same alwaies.

7. As for the *Debility* of her Intellectuals in *Infancy* and *Old Age*, this consideration has less force to evince her a *mere corporeal* essence then the former, and touches not our 35 Principles at all, who have provided for the very worst surmise concerning the operations of the Mind, in acknowledging them, of my own accord, to depend very intimately on the temper and tenour of the Soul's immediate instrument, the *Spirits*; Which being more torpid and watry in *Children* and *Old men*, must 40 needs hinder her in such Operations as require another constitution of Spirits then is usually in *Age* and *Childhood:*

though I will not profess my self absolutely confident, that the
Soul cannot act without all dependence on Matter. But if it
does not, which is most probable, it must needs follow, that its
Operations will keep the laws of the Body it is united with.
5   Whence it is demonstrable how necessary *Purity* and
Temperance is to preserve and advance a mans Parts.

  8. As for *Sleep*, which the dying Philosopher called *the
Brother of Death*, I do not see how it argues the Soul's
Mortality, more then a mans inability to wake again: but
10 rather helps us to conceive, how that though the stounds and
agonies of Death seem utterly to take away all the hopes of the
Soul' s living after them; yet upon a recovery of a quicker
Vehicle of Aire, she may suddainly awake into fuller and
fresher participation of life then before. But I may answer
15 also, that *Sleep* being onely the ligation of the outward Senses,
and the interception of motion from the external world, argues
no more any radical defect of Life and Immortality in the Soul,
then the having a mans Sight bounded within the walls of his
chamber by Shuts does argue any blindness in the immured
20 party; who haply is busie reading by candle-light, and that with
ease, so small a print as would trouble an ordinary Sight to
read it by day. And that the Soul is not perpetually employed
in *Sleep*, is very hard for any to demonstrate; we so often
remembring our dreams merely by occasions, which if they had
25 not occurred, we had never suspected we had dreamed that
night.

  9. Which Answer, as also the former, is applicable to
Apoplexies, Catalepsies, and whatever *other Diseases* partake of
their nature; and witness how nimble the Soul is to act upon
30 the suppeditation of due Matter, and how *Life* and *Sense* and
Memory and *Reason* and all return, upon return of the fitting
temper of the Spirits, suitable to that *vital Congruity* that then
is predominant in the Soul.

  10. And as for *Madness*, there are no Apprehensions so
35 frantick but are arguments of the *Soul's Immortality*, not as
they are *frantick*, but as *Apprehensions*. For *Matter* cannnot
apprehend any thing, either wildly or soberly, as I have already
sufficiently demonstrated. And it is as irrational for a man to
conclude, that the depraved Operations of the Soul argue her
40 Mortality, as that the worser tempers, or figures, or whatever
more contemptible modifications there are of Matter, should
argue its annihilation by the mere power of Nature; which no

man that understands himself will ever admit.

The Soul indeed is indued with several Faculties, and some of them very fatally passive, such as those are that have the nearest commerce with *Matter*, and are not so absolutely in her own power, but that her levity and mindlessness of the divine 5 light may bring her into subjection to them; as all are, in too sad a sort, that are incarcerate in this *Terrestrial* Body, but some have better luck then other some in this wild and audacious ramble from a more secure state. Of which Apostasy if there be some that are made more Tragick 10 examples then others of their stragling from their soveraign Happiness, it is but a merciful admonition of the danger we all have incurr'd, by being where we are; and very few so well escaped, but that if they could examine their Desires, Designs, and Transactions here, by that Truth they were once masters 15 of, they would very freely confess, that the mistakes and errours of their life are not inferiour to, but of worse consequence then, those of natural Fools and Madmen, whom all either hoot at for their folly, or else lament their misery. And questionless the Souls of Men, if they were once reduced to 20 that sobriety they are capable of, would be as much *ashamed* of such *Desires* and *Notions* they are not wholly engaged in, as any madman, reduced to his right Senses, is of those freaks he played when he was out of his wits.

11. But the variety of degrees, or kindes of depravation in 25 the Intellective faculties of the Soul, her Substance being *Indiscerpible*, cannot at all argue her *Mortality* not more then the different modifications of *Matter* the *Annihilability* thereof, as I have already intimated. Nor need a man trouble himself how there should be such a sympathy betwixt Body and Soul, 30 when it is so demonstrable that there is. For it is sufficient to consider, that it is their immediate nature so to be by the will and ordinance of Him that has made all things. And that if *Matter* has no *Sense* nor *Cogitation* it self, as we have demonstrated it has not, it had been in vain, if God had not 35 put forth into Being that Order of *Immaterial* Creatures which we call *Souls*, vitally unitable with the *Matter*: Which therefore, according to the several modifications thereof, will necessarily have a different effect upon the Soul, the Soul abiding still as unperishable as the *Matter* that is more mutable then *she*. For 40 the *Matter* is *dissipable*, but she utterly *indiscerpible*.

Chap. XV.

5 I. *An Answer to the experiment of the* Scolopendra *cut into pieces:*
2. And to the flying of an headless Eagle over a barn, as also to
that of the Malefactour's head biting a Dog by the eare. 3. A
superaddition of a difficulty concerning Monsters born with two
or more Heads and but one Body and Heart. 4. A solution of the
10 *difficulty. 5. An answer touching the seldome appearing of the*
deceased: 6. As also concerning the fear of Death; 7. And a
down-bearing sense that sometimes so forcibly obtrudes on us the
belief of the Soul's Mortality. 8. Of the Tragical Pomps and
dreadful Preludes of Death, with some corroborative Consider-
15 *ations against such sad spactacles. 9. That there is nothing*
really sad and miserable in the Universe, unless to the wicked
and impious.

I. Nor do those Instances in the second Objection prove
20 any thing to the contrary, as if the Soul it self were *really*
divisible. The most forcible Example is that of the *Scolopendra*,
the motion of the *dividend* parts being so quick and nimble, and
so lasting. But it is easy to conceive, that the activity of the
Spirits in the Mechanical conformation of the pieces of that
25 Insect, till motion has dissipated them, will be necessarily make
them run up and down, as Gunpowder in a squib will cause its
motion. And therefore the Soul of the *Scolopendra* will be but
in one of those Segments, and uncertain in which, but likely
according to the Segments be made. For cut a Wasps head off
30 from the Body, the Soul retires out of the Head into the Body;
but cut her in the wast, leaving the upper part of the Body to
the Head, the Soul then retires into that forepart of the Wasp.
And therefore it is no wonder that the Head being cut off, the
Body of the wasp will fly and flutter so long, the Soul being still
35 in it, and haply conferring to the direction of the Spirits for
motion, not out of Sense, but from custome or nature: as we
walk not thinking of it, or play on the Lute though our minde
be running on something else, as I have noted before. But
when the Wast is left to the Head, it is less wonder, for then
40 the Animal may not be destitute of sense and fancy, to
conveigh the Spirits to move the wings.

2. The former case will fit that of the headless Eagle that flew over the Barn. But the mans *Head* that catch'd the Dog by the ear would have more difficulty in it (it not seeming so perfectly referrible to the latter case of the Wasp) did not we consider how hard the teeth will set in a swoon. As this *Head* therefore wes gasping while the Dog was licking the blood thereof, his ear chanced to dangle into the mouth of it, which closing together as the ear hung into it, pinched it so fast that it could not fall off.

Besides it is not altogether improbable, especially considering that some man die upwards, and some downwards, that the Soul may as it happens, sometimes retire into the *Head*, and sometimes into the *Body*, in these decollations, according as they are more or less replenish'd with *Spirits*; and by the lusty jumping of this *Head*, it should seem it was very full of them. Many such things as these also may happen by the activity of the *Spirit of Nature*, who, it's like, may be as busie in the ruines of Animals, while the Spirits last, as it is in the fluid rudiments of them when they are generated. But the former Answers being sufficient, it is needless to enlarge our selves upon this new Theme.

3. To this second Objection might have been added such *monstrous births*, as seem to imply the *Perceptive part* of the Soul divided actually into two or more parts. For *Aristotle* seems expresly to affirm, that that monstrous birth that has two Hearts is two Animals, but that which has but one Heart is but one. From whence it will follow that there is but one Soul also in that one-hearted Monster, though it have two or more Heads; whence it is also evident, that the *Perceptive part* of that one Soul must be actually divided into two or more. This opinion of *Aristotle Sennertus* subscribes to, and therefore conceives that that monstrous child that was born at *Emmaus*, in *Theodosius* his time, with two Heads & two Hearts, was two persons; but that other born *Anno* 1531. with two Heads and but one Heart, who lived till he was a man, was but one person. Which he conceives appears the plainer, in that both the Heads professed their agreement perpetually to the same actions, in that they had the same appetite, the same hunger and thirst, spoke alike, had the same desire to lie with their wife, and of all other acts of exonerating nature. But for that other that had two Hearts, and was divided to the Navel, there was not this identity of affection and desire, but sometimes one

would have a mind to a thing, and sometimes another,;
sometimes they would play with one another, and sometimes
fight.

4. But I answer, and first to *Aristotle*'s authority, that he
5 does not so confidently assert that every Monster that has but
one Heart is but one *Animal*. For his words run thus. ἓν δε
εἶναι τὸ ζῶον τὸ τερατῶδες ἢ πλείω συμπεφυκότα δεῖ νομίζειν κατὰ
τὴν ἀρχὴν, οἷον εἰ τοιοῦτόν τί ἐστιν ἡ καρδία μόριον, τὸ μὲν μίαν
ἔχον καρδίαν ἓν ζῶον. Where he onely speaks hypothetically,
10 not peremptorily, that the Heart is that part where the first
Principle of life is, and from which the rest of life in Soul or
Body is to be derived. For indeed he makes it elsewhere the
seat of Common Sense; but that it is a mistake we have
already demonstrated, and himself seems not confident of his
15 own Opinion; and therefore we may with the less offence
decline it, and affirm (and that without all hesitancy) that a
Monster is either one or more Animals according to the number
of the Heads of it, and that there are as many distinct Souls as
there are Heads in a monstrous Birth. But from the Heads
20 downwards the Body being but one, and the Heart but one, that
there must needs be a wonderful exact concord in the sense of
affections in these Heads, they having their Blood and Spirits
from one fountain, and one common seat of their passions and
desires. But questionless whenever one Head winked, it could
25 not then see by the eyes of the other; or if one had pricked one
of these Heads, the other would not have felt it: though
whatever was inflicted below, it is likely they both felt alike,
both the Souls equally acting the Body of this Monster, but the
Heads being actuated by them onely in several. Which is a
30 sufficient Answer to *Sennertus*.

5. The weakness of the third Objection is manifest, in that
it takes away the Existence of all Spirits, as well as the Souls
of the deceased. Of whose being notwithstanding none can
doubt that are not dotingly incredulous. We say therefore that
35 the Souls of men, being in the same condition that other Spirits
are, *appear sometimes*, though but *seldome*. The cause in both
being, partly they having no occasion so to doe, and lastly it
being not permitted to them to doe as they please, or to be
where they have a minde to be.

40   6. As for the *Fear of Death*, and that *down-bearing sense*
that sometimes so uncontroulably suggests to us that we are
wholly mortal: To the first I answer, That it is a necessary

result of our union with the Body, and if we should admit it one
of the imperfections or infirmities we contract by being in this
state, it were a solid Answer. And therefore this fear and
presage of ill in Death is no arguments that there is any ill in
it, nor any more to be heeded then the predictions of any   5
fanatical fellow that will pretend to prophecie. But besides this,
it is fitting that there should be in us this fear and abhorrency,
to make us keep this station Providence has plac'd us in;
otherwise every little pet would invite us to pack our selves out
of this World, and try our fortunes in the other, and so leave   10
the Earth to be inhabited onely by Beasts whenas it is to be
ordered and cultivated by Men.

   7. To the second I answer, That such peremptory
conclusions are nothing but the impostures of Melancholy, or
some other dull and fulsome distempers of blood that corrupt   15
the Imagination; but that Fancy proves nothing, by Axiome 4.
And that though the Soul enthroned in her *Aethereal Vehicle* be
a very magnificent thing, full of Divine, Love, Majesty and
Tranquillity; yet in this present state she is in, clogg'd and
accloy'd with the foulness and darkness of this *Terrestrial Body*,   20
she is subject to many fears and jealousies, and other
disturbing passions, whose Objects though but a mockery, yet
are a real disquiet to her mind in this her Captivity and
Imprisonment

   Which condition of hers is lively set out by that   25
incomparable Poet and Platonist, in his *Aeneid.* where,
comparing that more free and pure state of our Souls in their
Celestial or Fiery Vehicles with their restraint in this Earthly
Dungeon, he makes this short and true description of the whole
matter.   30

    Igneus est ollis vigor, et coelestis origo
    Seminibus;quantum non noxia corpora tardant,
    Terrenique hebetant artus, moribundáque membra:
    Hinc metuunt, cupiúntque, dolent, gaudentque nec auras
    Respiciunt, clausi tenebris et carcere caeco.   35
            To this sense,
    A fiery vigour from an heavenly source
    Is in these seeds, so far as the dull force
    Of noxious Bodies does not them retard,
    In heavy earth and dying limbs imbar'd.   40
    Hence, fool'd with fears, foul lusts, sharp grief, vain joy,
    In this dark Gaol they low and groveling lie,

Nor with one glance of their oblivious mind
Look back to that free Aire they left behind.
This is the sad estate of the more deeply-lapsed Souls upon
Earth; who are so wholly mastered by the motions of the Body,
5 that they are carried headlong into an assent to all the
suggestions and imaginations that it so confidently obtrudes
upon them; of which that of our *Mortality* is not the weakest.

But such melancholy fancies, that would bear us down so
peremptory that we are utterly extinct in death, are no more
10 argument thereof, then those of them that have been
perswaded they were dead already, while they were alive; and
therefore would not eat, because they thought the dead never
take any repast, till they were cheated into an appetite, by
seeing some of their friends disguised in winding-sheets feed
15 heartily at the table, whose example then they thought fit to
follow, and so were kept alive.

8. I cannot but confess that the *Tragick pomp and*
preparation to dying, that layes wast the operations of the
Minde, putting her into fits of dotage or fury, making the very
20 visage look ghastly and distracted, and at the best sadly pale
and consumed, as if Life and Soul were even almost quite
extinct, cannot but imprint strange impressions even upon the
stoutest Mind, and raise suspicions that all is lost in so great a
change. But the Knowing and Benign Spirit though he may
25 flow in tears at so dismal a Spectacle, yet it does not at all
suppress his hope and confidence of the Soul's safe passage into
the other world; and is no otherwise moved then the more
passionate Spectatours of some cunningly-contrived Tragedy,
where persons, whose either Vertue, or misfortunes, or both,
30 have wonne the affection of the beholders, are at last seen
wallowing in their blood, and after some horrid groans and
gasps lye stretcht stark dead upon the stage: but being once
drawn off, find themselves well and alive, and are ready to tast
a cup of wine with their friends in the attiring room, to solace
35 themselves really, after their fictitious pangs of death, and
leave the easy-natur'd multitude to indulge to their soft
passions for an evil that never befell them.

9. The *fear* and abhorrency therefore we have *of Death*,
and the *sorrow* that accompanies it, is no argument but that we
40 may live after it, and are but due affections for those that are
to be Spectatours of the great *Tragick-Comedy* of the World; the
whole plot whereof being contrived by Infinite Wisdom and

Goodness, we cannot but surmise that the most sad representations are but a *shew*, but the delight *real* to such as are not wicked and impious; and that what the ignorant call *Evil* in this Universe is but as the shadowy strokes in a fair picture, or the mournful notes in Musick, by which the Beauty 5 of the one is more lively and express, and the Melody of the other more pleasing and melting.

10

Chap. XVI.

I. *That that which we properly* are *is both* Sensitive *and* Intellectual. 2. *What is the true Notion of* a Soul being One. 3. *That if there be* but One Soul *in the world, it is both* Rational 15 *and* Sensitive. 4. *The most favourable representation of their Opinion that hold* but One. 5. *A confutation of the foregoing representation.* 6. *A Reply to the Confutation.* 7. *An Answer to the Reply.* 8. *That the Soul of Man is not properly any Ray either of God or the Soul of the World.* 9. *And yet if she were so, it* 20 *would be no prejudice to her Immortality: whence the folly of* Pomponatius *is noted.* 10. *A further animadversion upon* Pomponatius *his folly, in admitting a certain number of remote* Intelligencies, *and denying* Particular Immaterial Substances *in* Men *and* Brutes. 25

I. As for the last Objection, or rather Subterfuge, of such as have no minde to finde their Souls immortal, pretending indeed they have none dislinct from that *one Universal Soul* of the World, whereby notwithstanding they acknowledge that the 30 Operations we are conscious to ourselves of, of Reason and other Faculties, cannot be without one; we shall easily discover either the falseness or unserviceableness of this conceit for their design, who would so fain slink out of Being after the mad freaks they have played in this Life. For it is manifestly true, 35 that a Man is most properly that, whatever it is, that *animadverts* in him; for that is such an operation that no Being but himself can doe it for him. And that which *animadverts* in us, does not onely perceive and take notice of its *Intellectual* and *Rational* operations, but of all *Sensations* whatsoever that we 40 are conscious of, whether they terminate in our Body or on some outward Object. From whence it is plain, that *That which we are* is both *Sensitive* and *Intellectual*.

2. Now if we rightly consider what is comprehended in the true and usual Notion of the *Unity* of a Soul, it is very manifest that it mainly consists in this, that the *Animadversive* thereof is
5   *but one*, and that there is no *Sensation* nor *Perception* of any kind in the Soul, but what is communicated to and perceived by the whole *Animadversive*.

3. Which things being premised, it necessarily follows, that if there be *but one Soul* in the World, that Soul is both
10 *Rational* and *Sensitive*, in one mans Soul, but the same would be in all; nay that a man cannot lash a Dog, or spur a Horse, but himself would feel the smart of it: which is flatly agaInst all experience, and therefore palpably false. Of this wilde Supposition I have spoken so fully in my *Poems*, that I need
15 adde nothing here in this place, having sufficiently confuted it there.

4. But not to cut them so very short, let us imagine the most favourable contrivance of their Opinion we can, and conceit that though this *Soul of the World* be of it self every
20 where alike, and that the *Animadversive* faculty is in it all in like vigour; yet it being engaged in severally-tempered Bodies, *Animadversion* is confin'd to that part of Matter onely which it actuates; and is stupid and unsensible of all other operations, whether Sensitive or Intellectual, that are transacted by her
25 without, in other persons: a thing very hard to conceive, and quite repugnant to the Idea of the *Unity* of a Soul, not to be conscious to her self of her own perceptions. But let it pass for a possibility, and let us suppose that one part of the *Soul of the World* informs one man, and another, or at least some vital
30 Ray there; yet notwithstanding, this opinion will be incumbred with very harsh difficulties.

For if several parts of the *Soul of the World* inform several parts of the Matter, when a man changes has place, he either tears one part of the *Soul of the World* from another, or else
35 changes Souls every step; and therefore it is a wonder that he changes not his Wits too, and loses his Memory. Unless they say that every part of the *Soul of the World*, upon the application of a new Body, acts just so in it as that part acted which it left, if there be no change or alteration thereof: whence
40 every part of the *Soul of the World* will have the self-same Thoughts, Errours, Truths, Remembrances, Pains, Pleasures, that the part had the Body newly left. So that a man shall

always fancy it is himself, whereever he goes, though this self be nothing but the *Soul of the World* acting in such a particular Body, and retaining and renewing to her self the Memory of all Accidents, Impressions, Motions and Cogitations, she had the perception of in this particular piece of organized Matter. This 5 is the most advantageous representation of this Opinion that can possibly be excogitated. But I leave it to those that love to amuse themselves in such Mysteries, to try if they can make any good sense of it.

5. And he that can fancy it as a thing possible, I would 10 demand of him, upon this supposition, who *himself* is; and he cannot deny but that he is a Being *Perceptive* and *Animadversive*, which the *Body* is not, and therefore that himself is not the *Body*; wherefore he is that in him which is properly called *Soul*: But not its *Operations* for the former 15 reason; because they perceive nothing, but the Soul perceives them in exerting them: nor the *Faculties*, for they perceive not one anothers Operations; but that which is a mans *Self* perceives them all: Wherefore he must say he is the *Soul*; and there being but one Soul in the World, he must be forc'd to 20 vaunt himself to be the *Soul of the World*. But this boasting must suddainly fall again, if he but consider that the *Soul of the World* will be every mans personal *Ipseity* as well as his; whence every *one* man will be *all* men, and *all* men but *one* Individual man: Which is a perfect contradiction to all the 25 Laws of *Metaphysicks* and *Logick*.

6. But re-minded of these inconveniences, he will pronounce more cautiously, and affirm that he is not the *Soul of the World* at large but onely so far forth as she expedites or exerts her self into the Sense and Remembrance of all those 30 Notions or Impresses that happen to her whereever she is joyned with his Body; but that so soon as this Body of his is dissipated and dissolved, that she will no longer raise any such determinate Thoughts or Senses that refer to that Union; and that so the Memory of such Actions Notions and Impressions, 35 that were held together in relation to a particular Body, being lost and laid aside upon the failing of the Body to which they did refer, this *Ipseity* or *Personality*, which consisted mainly in this, does necessarily perish in death.

This certainly is that (if they know their own meaning) 40 which many Libertines would have, who are afraid to meet themselves in the other World, for fear they should quarrel

with themselves there for their transactions in this. And it is
the handsomest Hypothesis that they can frame in favour of
themselves, and far beyond that dull conceit, *That there is
nothing but mere Matter in the World*; which is infinitely more
5   liable to confutation.

7. And yet this is too scant a covering to shelter them and
secure them from the sad after-claps they may justly suspect in
the other life. For first, it is necessary for them to confess that
they have in this life as particular and proper sense of
10   Torment, of Pleasure, of Peace, and Pangs of Conscience, and
of other impressions, as if they had an individual Soul of their
own distinct from that of the World, and from every ones else;
and that if there be any *Daemons* or *Genii*, as certainly there
are, that it is so with them too. We have also demonstrated,
15   that all *Sense* and *Perception* is immediately excited in the Soul
by the Spirits; wherefore with what confidence can they
promise themselves that the death of this earthly Body will
quite obliterate all the tracts of their Being here on earth?
whenas the subtiler ruines thereof, in all likelihood, may
20   determine the Thoughts of the *Soul of the World* to the same
tenour as before, and draw from her the memory of all the
Transactions of this life, and make her exercise her judgment
upon them; and cause her to contrive the most vital exhalations
of the Terrestrial Body into an Aëreal Vehicle, of like nature
25   with the ferment of these material rudiments of life, saved out
of the ruines of death.

For any slight touch is enough to engage her to perfect the
whole Scene; and so a man shall be represented to himself and
others in the other state whether he will or not, and have as
30   distinct a personal *Ipseity* there as he had in this life. Whence
it is plain, that this false *Hypothesis, That we are nothing but
the Soul of the World acting in our Bodies*, will not serve their
turns at all that would have it so; nor secure them from future
danger, though it were admitted to be true. But I have
35   demonstrated it false already, from the Notion of the *Unity* of a
Soul.

Of the truth of which Demonstration we shall be the better
assured, if we consider that the subtile Elements, which are the
immediate conveyers of *Perceptions* in our Souls, are continued
40   throughout in the *Soul of the World*, and insinuate into all living
Creatures. So that *the Soul of the World* will be necessarily
informed in every one, what she thinks or feels every where, if

she be the onely Soul that actuates every Animal upon Earth. Whence the Sun, Stars and Planets would appear to us in that bigness they really are of, they being perceiv'd in that bigness by those parts of the *Soul of the World* that are at a convenient nearness to them.   5

8. That other conceit, of our Souls being *a Vital Ray of the Soul of the World*, may gain much countenance by expressions in ancient Authors that seem to favour the Opinion as that of *Epictetus*, who saith that the Souls of men are συναφεῖς τῶι θεῶι, ἄτε αὐτοῦ μόρια οὖσαι καὶ ἀποσπάσματα. And *Philo* calls the 10 Minde of Man, τῆς θείας ψυχῆς ἀπόσπασμα οὐ διαιρετὸν and Trismegist ὁ νοῦς οὐκ ἔστιν ἀποτετμημενος τῆς οὐσιότητος τοῦ θεοῦ, ἀλλ' ὥσπερ ἥπλωμένος καθάπερ τὸ τοῦ ἡλίου φῶς. All which expressions make the Soul of man *a Ray* or *Beam of the Soul of the World* or *of God*. But we are to take notice that 15 they are but Metaphorical phrases, and that what is understood thereby, is, *that there is an emanation of a secondary substance from the several parts of the Soul of the World; resembling the Rayes of the Sun.* Which way of conception, though it be more easy then the other, yet it has difficulties 20 enough. For this *Vital Ray* must have some head from whence it is stretched, and so the Body would be like a Bird in a string, which would be drawn to a great length when one takes long voyages, suppose to the East or West *Indies*; which yet are nothing so long as our yearly sailing on the Earth from *Libra* to 25 *Aries*. Or if you will not have it a *linear* Ray, but an *Orb* of particular life; every such particular *Orb* must be hugely vast, that the Body may not travel out of the reach of the Soul. Besides, this *Orb* will strike through other Bodies as well as its own, and its own be in several parts of it; which are such 30 incongruities and inconcinnities as are very harsh and unpleasing to our Rational faculties.

Wherefore that Notion is infinitely more neat and safe, that proportions the Soul to the dimensions of the Body, and makes her independent on any thing but the Will and Essence 35 of her Creator; which being exactly the same every where, as also his Power is, her emanative support is exactly the same to what she had in the very first point of her production and station in the World. In which respect of dependence she may be said to be a *Ray* of Him, as the rest of the Creation also; but 40 in no other sense that I know of, unless of likeness and similitude, she being the *Image* of *God*, as the *Rays* of Light are of the *Sun*.

9. But let every particular Soul be so many *Rayes* of the *Soul of the World*, what gain they by this, whenas these *Rayes* may be as capable of all the several congruities of life, as the Soul is in that sense we have described? and therefore *Personality, Memory and Conscience* will as surely return or continue in the other state, according to this Hypothesis, as the other more usual one. Which also discovers the great folly of *Pomponatius* (and of as many as are of the same leven with him) who indeed is so modest and judicious as not to deny *Apparitions*; but attributes all to the influence of the Stars, or rather the *Intelligencies* of the Celestial Orbs. For they giving life and animation to brute Animals, why may they not also, upon occasion, animate and actuate the Aire into shape and form, even to the making of them speak and discourse one shape with another? For so *Pomponatius* argues in his Book of the *Immortality of the Soul*, from *Aquinas* his concession, that Angels and Souls separate may figure the Aire into shape, and speak through it; *Quare igitur Intelligentiae moventes corpora coelestia haec facere non possunt cum suis instrumentis quae tot ac tanta possunt, quae faciunt Psittacos, Picos, Corvos et Merulas, loqui?* And a little after, he plainly reasons from the power the *Intelligencies* have of generating Animals, that it is not at all strange that they should raise such kinde of *Apparitions* as are recorded in History.

But if these Celestial *Intelligencies* be confined to their own Orbs, so as that no *secondary Essence* reach these inferiour Regions, it is impossible to conceive how they can actuate the Matter here below. But if there be any such *essential Emanations* from them, whereby they actuate the Matter into these living *Species* we see in the World, of Men and Brutes; nothing hinders but the same *Emanations* remaining, may actuate the Aire when this earthly fabrick fails, and retains the memory of things transacted in this life, and that still our *Personality* will be conserved as perfect and distinct as it was here.

10. But this conceit of *Pomponatius* is farre more foolish then theirs that make onely one *Anima Mundi* that passes through all the Matter of the World, and is present in every place, to doe all feats that there are to be done. But to acknowledge so many several *Intellectual Beings* as there be fancied Celestial Orbs, and to scruple, or rather to seem

confident, that there are not so many particular Souls as there
be Men here on Earth, is nothing but Humour and Madness.
For it is as rational to acknowledge eight hundred thousand
Myriads of *Intellectual* and *Immaterial Beings*, really distinct
from one another, as eight; and an infinite number, as but one, 5
that could not create the Matter of the World. For then two
Substances, wholly independent on one another, would be
granted, as also the Infinite parts of Matter that have no
dependence one on the other.

Why may not there be therefore Infinite numbers of 10
Spirits or Souls that have as little dependence one on another,
as well as there should be eight *Intelligencies?* whenas the
motions and operations of every Animal are a more certain
argument of an *Immaterial Being* residing there, then the
motions of the Heavens of any distinct *Intelligencies* in their 15
Orbs, if they could be granted to have any: And it is no
stranger a thing to conceive an Infinite multitude of *Immaterial*,
as well as *Material, Essences*, independent on one another, then
but two, namely the Matter and the Soul of the World. But if
there be so excellent a Principle existent as can *create* Beings, 20
as certainly there is; we are still the more assured that there
are such multitudes of Spiritual Essences, surviving all the
chances of this present life, as the most sober and knowing men
in all Ages have professed there are.

25

Chap. XVII.

I. *That the Author having safely conducted the Soul into her* 30
Aëreal condition through the dangers of Death, might well be
excused from attending her any further. 2. *What reasons urge*
him to consider what fates may befall her afterwards. 3. *Three*
hazzards the Soul runs after this life, whereby she may again
become obnoxious to death, according to the opinion of some. 4. 35
That the Aëreal Genii *are mortal, confirmed by three testimonies.*
5. *The one from the Vision of* Facius Cardanus, *in which the*
Spirits that appeared to him profest themselves mortal. 6. *The*
time they stayed with him, and the matters they disputed of. 7.
What credit Hieronymus Cardanus *gives to his Father's Vision.* 40
8. *The other testimony out of* Plutarch, *concerning the Death of*
the great God Pan. 9. *The third and last of* Hesiod, *whose*

opinion Plutarch *has polisht and refined.* 10. *An Enumeration of the several Paradoxes contained in* Facius Cardanus *his Vision.* 11. *What must be the sense of the third Paradox, if those Aëreal Spaculatours spake as they thought.* 12. *Another* Hypothesis *to the same purpose.* 13. *The craft of these* Daemons, *in shuffling in poisonous Errour amongst solid Truths.* 14. *What makes the story of the death of* Pan *less to the present matter, with an addition of* Demetrius *his observations touching the* Sacred Islands *near* Britain. 15. *That* Hesiod *his opinion is the most unexceptionable, and that the harshness therein is but seeming, not real.* 16. *That the* Aethereal Vehicle *instates the Soul in a condition of perfect Immortality.* 17. *That there is no internal impediment to those that are* Heroically good, *but that they may attain an everlasting Happiness after Death.*

I. We have now, maugre all the oppositions and Objections made to the contrary, safely conducted the Soul into the other state, and installed her into the same condition with the *Aëreal Genii.* I might be very well exceed, if I took leave of her here, and committed her to that fortune that attends those of the Invisible World: it being more seasonable for them that are there, to meditate and prefigure in their mindes all futurities belonging to them, then for us that are on this side the passage. It is enough that I have demonstrated, that neither the Essence nor Operations of the Soul are extinct by Death; but that they either not intermit, or suddainly revive upon the recovery of her Airey Body.

2. But seeing that those that take any pleasure at all in thinking of these things can seldome command the ranging of their thoughts within what compass they please, and that it is obvious for them to doubt whether the Soul can be secure of her permanency in life in the other world, (it implying no contradiction, That her *Vital Congruity* ,appropriate to this or that Element, may either of it self expire, or that she may by some carelessness debilitate one *Congruity,* and awaken another, in some measure, and so make her self obnoxious to Fate;) we cannot but think it in a manner necessary to extricate such difficulties as these, that we may not seem in this after-game to lose all we won in the former; and make men suspect that the Soul is not at all Immortal, if her Immortality will not secure her against all future fates.

3. To which she seems liable upon three accounts. The one we have named already, and respects an intrinsecal Principle, the *Periodical terms* of her *Vital Congruity*, or else the Levity and Miscarriage of her own Will. Which obnoxiousness of hers is still more fully argued from what is affirmed of the 5 Aëreal *Genii* (whose companion and fellow-Citizen she is) whom sundry Philosophers assert to be *Mortal*. The other two hazards she runs are from without, to wit the *Conflagration of the World*, and the *Extinction of the Sun*.

4. That the Aëreal *Genii* are mortal, three main 10 Testimonies are answered for it. The Vision of *Facius Cardanus*, the Death of the great God *Pan*, in *Plutarch*, and the Opinion of *Hesiod*. I will set them all down fully, as I finde them, and then answer to them. The Vision of *Facius Cardanus* is punctually recited by his son *Hieronymus* in his *De* 15 *Subtilitate*, in this manner.

5. That his Father *Facius Cardanus*, who confessed that he had the society of a familiar Spirit for about thirty years together, told him this following Story often when he was alive, and after his death he found the exact relation of it committed 20 to writing, which was this. *The 13. day of August 1491. after I had done my holy things, at the 20. houre of the day, there appeared to me, after their usual manner, seven men cloathed in silk garments, with cloaks after the Greek mode, with purple stockings and crimson Cassocks, red and shining on their* 25 *breasts; nor were they all thus clad, but onely two of them who were the chief. On the ruddier and taller of these two other two waited, but the less and paler had three attendants; so that they made up seven in all. They were about fourty years of age, but looks as if they had not reacht thirty. When they were asked who* 30 *they were, they answered that they were* Homines Aërii, *Aëreal Men, who are born and die as we; but that their life is much longer then ours, as reaching to 300 years. Being asked concerning the Immortality of our Souls, they answered,* Nihil quod cuique proprium esset superesse: *That they were of a* 35 *nearer affinity with the* Divi *then we; but yet infinitely different from them: and that their happiness or misery as much transcended ours, as ours does the brute Beasts. That they knew all things that are hid, whether Monies or Books. And that the lowest sort of them were the* Genii *of the best and noblest men, as* 40 *the basest men are the trainers up of the best sort of* Dogs. *That the tenuity of their Bodies was such, that they can doe us neither*

good nor hurt, saving in what they may be able to doe by
Spectres and Terrours, and impartment of Knowledge. That they
were both publick Professors in an Academy and that he of the
lesser stature had 300. disciples, the other 200. Cardan's
5 *Father further asking them why they would not reveal such*
treasures as they knew unto men; they answered, that there was
a special law against it, upon a very grievous penalty.

6. *These Aëreal Inhabitants stai'd at least three hours with*
Facius Cardanus, *disputing and arguing of sundry things,*
10 *amongst which one was* The Original of the World. *The taller*
denied that God made the world ab aeterno: *the lesser affirmed*
that he so created it every moment, that if he should desist but one
moment, it would perish. Whereupon he cited some things out of
the Disputations of Avenroes, *which Book was not yet extant,*
15 *and named several other Treatises, part whereof are known, part*
not, which were all of Avenroes *his writing, and withall did*
openly profess himself to be an Avenroist.

7. The record of this Apparition *Cardan* found amongst his
Fathers Papers, but seems unwilling to determine whether it be
20 a true history or a Fable, but disputes against it in such a
shuffling manner, as if he was perswaded it were true, and had
a mind that others should think it so. I am sure he most-what
steers his course in has Metaphysical adventures according to
this *Cynosura*, which is no obscure indication of his assent and
25 belief.

8. That of the Death of the great God *Pan*, you may read
in *Plutarch* in his *De defectu Oraculorum*; where *Philippus*, for
the proof of the Mortality of *Daemons*, recites a Story which he
heard from one *Aemilianus* a Roman, and one that remov'd far
30 enough from all either stupidity or vanity: *How his Father*
Epitherses *being shipt for* Italy, *in the evening, near the*
Echinades, *the winde failed them; and their ship being carried by*
an uncertain course upon the Island Paxae, *that most of the*
Passengers being waken, many of them drinking merrily after
35 *Supper, there was a voice suddainly heard from the Island, which*
called to Thamus *by name, who was an Aegyptian by birth, and*
the Pilot of the Ship: which the Passengers much wondred at, few
of them having taken notice of the Pilots name before. He was
twice called to before he gave any sign that he attended to his
40 *voice, but after giving express attention, a clear and distinct voice*
was heard from the Island, uttering these words, ὅταν γένῃ κατὰ
τὸ Γαλῶδες. ἀπάγγελον. ὅτι Πὰν ὁ μέγας τέϑνηκεν. *The company*

was much astonisht at the hearing of the voice: and after much debate amongst themselves, Thamus *resolved that, if the wind blew fair much debate amongst themselves,* Thamus *resolved that, if the wind blew fair, he would sail by and say nothing; but if they were becalmed there, he would doe his Message: and therefore they being becalmed when they came to* Palodes, *neither winde nor tide carrying them on,* Thamus *looking out of the poop of the Ship toward the shore, delivered his Message, telling them that the great* Pan *was dead. Upon which was suddainly heard as it were a joynt groaning of a multitude together, mingled with a murmurous admiration.*

9. The opinion of *Hesiod* also is, that the *Genii* or *Daemons* within a certain period of years do die; but he attributes a considerable Longaevity to them, to wit of nine thousand seven hundred and twenty years, which is the utmost that any allow them, most men less. *Plutarch,* under the person of others, has polisht this Opinion into a more curious and distinct dress: for out of the mortality of the *Daemons,* and the several ranks which *Hesiod* mentions of *Rational Beings,* viz. θεοὶ. δαίμονες. ἥρωες. and ἄνθρωποι. he has affixed a certain manner and law of their passing out of one state *into* another, making them to change their Elements as well as Dignities; Ἕτεροι δὲ. saith he, μεταβολὴν τοῖς τε σώμασιν ὁμοίως ποιοῦσι καὶ ψυχαῖς. ὥσπερ ἐκ γῆς ὕδωρ. ἐκ δ᾽ ὕδατος ἀὴρ. ἐκ δ᾽ ἀέρος πῦρ γεννώμενον ὁρᾶται. τῆς οὐσίας ἄνω φερομένης· οὕτως ἐκ μὲν ἀνθρώπων εἰς ἥρωας, ἐκ δ᾽ ἡρώων εἰς δαίμονας αἱ βελτίονες ψυχαὶ τὴν μεταβολὴν λαμβάνουσιν. ἐκ δὲ δαιμόνων ὀλίγαι μὲν ἔτι χρόνωι πολλῶι δι᾽ ἀρετῆς καθαρθεῖσαι παντάπασι θεότητος μετέσχον. But other, *he saith,* μὴ κρατοῦσαι ἑαυτῶν. *not having sufficient command of themselves,* are again wrought down into humane Bodies, *to live there an evanid and obscure life,* ἀλαμπῆ καὶ ἀμυδρὴν ζωὴν ἴσχουσαι. as he phrases it.

10. These are the most notable Testimonies for the Mortality of *Daemons* that I have met withall, and therefore the more worth our reviewing. That Vision of *Facius Cardanus,* if it be not a Fable, contains many Paradoxes.

As first *That these* Aëreal Genii *are born at set times as well as we.* Not that any she-*Daemons* are brought to bed of them, but that they seem to have a beginning of their Existence, from which they may be reckoned to have continued, some more years and some less. A thing unconceivable, unless we should imagine that there is *still* a lapse or descent of Souls out of the

higher Regions of the Aire into these loftier or that these that
leave these Earthly Bodies pass into the number of the Aiery
Daemons. As neither their *death* can so well be understood,
unless we should fancy that their Souls pass into more pure
5   *Vehicles*, or else descend into *Terrestrial* Bodies. For *Cardan*
himself acknowledges they perish not; which also is agreeable
with his Opinion of the Praeexisstence of our Souls.

Secondly, *That these Aëreal* Genii *live but about* 300. *years*,
which is against *Hesiod* and the greatest number of the
10   *Platonists*, unless they should speak of that particular Order
themselves were of; for it is likely there may be as much
difference in their ages as there is in the ages of several kinds
of Birds and Beasts.

Thirdly, *That our Souls are so farre mortal, as that there is*
15   *nothing proper to us remaining after death.*

Fourthly, *That they were nearer allied to the Gods then we*
by farre, and that there was as much difference betwixt them and
us, as there is betwixt us and Beasts. Which they must
understand then concerning the excellency of their Vehicles,
20   and the natural activity of them, not the preeminency of their
Intellectual Faculties. Or if they do, they must be understood
of the better sort ot those *Aëreal Spirits* Or if they mean it of all
their Orders, it may be a mistake out of pride: as those that
are rich and powerful as well as speculative amongst us, take it
25   for granted that they are more judicious and discerning then
the poor and despicable, let them be never so wise.

Fifthly, *That they know all secret things, whether hidden*
Books or Monies: which men might doe too, if they could stand
by concealedly from them that hide them.
30   Sixthly, *That the lowest sort of them were the Genii of the*
Noblest men, as the baser sort of Men are the Keepers and
Educators of the better kinde of Dogs and Horses. This clause of
the Vision also is inveloped with obscurity, they having not
defined whether this meanness of condition of the Tutelar *Genii*
35   be to be understood in a *Political* or *Physical* sense; whether the
meanness of rank and power, or of natural wit and sagacity; in
which many times the Groom exceeds the young Gallant who
assigns him to keep his Dogs and Horses.

Seventhly, *That such is the thinness and lightness of their*
40   *Bodies, that they can doe neither good nor hurt thereby, though*
they may send strange Sights and Terrors, and communicate
Knowledge; which then must be chiefly of such things as belong

to their Aëreal Region. For concerning matters in ths Sea, the
Fishes, if they could speak, might inform men better then they.
And for their corporeal debility, it is uncertain whether they
may not pretend it, to animate their Confabulators to a more
secure converse, or whether the thing be really true in some 5
kindes of them. For that it is not in all, may be evinced by that
Narration that *Cardan* a little after recites out of *Erasmus*, of
the Devil that carried a Witch into the Aire, and set her on the
top of a Chimney, giving her a Pot, and bidding her turn the
mouth downwards, which done the whole Town was fired, and 10
burnt down within the space of an hour. This hapned *April* the
10. *Anno* 1553. The Towns name was *Schiltach*, eight
German miles distant from *Friburg*. The Story is so well
attested,   and   guarded   with   such   unexceptionable
circumstances, that though *Cardan* love to shew his wit in 15
cavilling at most he recites, yet he finds nothing at all to
quarrel at in this.

   Eighthly, *That there are Students and Professors of
Philosophy in the Aëreal World, and are divided into Sects and
Opinions there, as well as we are here.* Which cannot possibly 20
be true, unless they set some value upon Knowledge, and are
at an eager loss how to finde it, and are fain to hew out their
way by arguing and reasoning as we do.

   Ninthly and lastly, *That they are reduced under a Political
Government, and are afraid of the infliction of punishment.*   25

   11. These are the main matters comprehended in *Facius*
his Vision, which how true they all are, would be too much
trouble to determine. But one clause, which is the third, I
cannot let pass, it so nearly concerning the present Subject, and
seeming to intercept all hopes of the Soul's Immortality. To 30
speak therefore to the summe of the whole business; we must
either conceive these Aëreal Philosophers to instruct *Facius
Cardanus* as well as they could, they being guilty of nothing
but a foward pride, to offer themselves as dictating Oracles to
that doubtful Exorcist (for his son *Cardan* acknowledges that 35
his Father had a form of Conjuration that a Spaniard gave him
at his death;) or else we must suppose them to take the liberty
of equivocating, if not of downright lying.

   Now if they had a mind to inform *Facius Cardanus* of
these things directly as they themselves thought of them, it 40
being altogether unlikely but that there appeared to them, in
their Aëreal Regions, such sights as represented the persons of

men here deceased, it is impossible that they should think
otherwise then as we have described their Opinion, in the foregoing Chapter, that hold there is but one Soul in the World, by
Which all living Creatures are actuated. Which, though but a
5   mere possibility, if so much, yet some or other of these Aëreal
Speculators may as well hold to it as some do amongst us. For
Pomponatius and others of the *Avenroists* are as ridiculously
pertinacious as they.

And   therefore   these *Avenroistical Daemons* answered
10   punctually according to the Conclusions of their own School,
Nihil proprium cuiquam superesse post mortem. For the Minde
or Soul being a Substance common to all, and now disunited
from those Terrestrial Bodies which it actuated in *Plato*,
suppose, or *Socrates*, and these Bodies dead and dissipated and
15   onely the common Soul of the World surviving, there being
nothing but this Soul and these Bodies to make up *Socrates* and
Plato; they conclude it is a plain case, that nothing that is
proper survives after death. And therefore, though they see
the representation of *Socrates* and *Plato* in the other World,
20   owing also their own personalities with all the Actions they did,
and accidents that befell them in this life; yet according to the
sullen subtilties and curiosities of their School, they may think
and profess, that to speak accurately and Philosophically it is
none of them, there being no Substance proper to them
25   remaining after death, but only *the Soul of the World*, renewing
the thoughts to her self of what appertained to those parties in
this life.

12. This is one Hypothesis consistent enough with the
veracity of these *Daemons*; but there is also another, not at all
30   impossible, viz. That the Vehicles of the Souls of men departed
are as invisible to this Order of the *Genii* that confabulated
with *Facius Cardanus* as that Order is to us: and that
therefore, though there be the appearance of the Ghosts of Men
deceased to them as well as to us: yet it being but for a time, it
35   moves them no more then our confirmed *Epicureans* in this
world are moved thereby: especially it being prone for them to
think that they are nothing but some ludicrous spectacles that
the universal Soul of the World represents to her self and other
Spectatours, when, and how long a time she pleases, and the
40   vaporous reliques of the dead body administer occasion.

Now that the Vehicles of the Souls of men departed this life, after they are come to a setled condition, may be farre thinner and more invisible then those of the fore-named *Daemons*, without committing any inconcinnity in Nature, may appear from hence: For the excellency of the inward Spirit is 5 not alwaies according to the consistency of the Element with which it does incorporate; otherwise those Fishes that are of humane shape, and are at set times taken in the Indian Sea, should have an higher degree of Reason and Religion then we that live upon Earth, and have bodies made of that Element. 10 Whence nothing hinders but that the Spirit of man may be more noble then the Spirit of some of the Aëreal *Daemons*. And Nature not alwaies running in Arithmetical, but also in Geometrical Progression, one Remove in one may reach far above what is before it for the present in the other degrees of 15 Progression. As a creeping worm is above a cad-worm, and any four-footed beasts above the birds, till they can use their leggs as well as they; but they are no sooner even with them, but they are straight far above them, and cannot onely goe, but fly. As a Peasant is above an imprison'd Prince, and has more 20 command; but this Prince can be no sooner set free and become even with the Peasant in his liberty, but he is infinitely above him. And so it may be naturally with the Souls of men when they are freed from this prison of the Body, their steps being made in Geometrical progression, as soon as they seem equal 25 to that Order of *Daemons* we speak of, they may mount far above them in tenuity and subtilty of Body, and so become invisible to them; and therefore leave them in a capacity of falsly surmising that they are not at all, because they cannot see them.   30

13. But if they thought that there is either some particular Ray of the Soul of the World, that belongs peculiarly (suppose) to *Socrates* or *Plato*, or that they had proper Souls really distinct, then it is evident that they did either equivocate or lye. Which their pride and scorn of mankinde (they looking 35 upon us but as Beasts in comparison of themselves) might easily permit; they making no more conscience to deceive us, then we do to put a dodge upon a dog, to make our selves merry. But if they had a design to winde us into some dangerous errour, it is very likely that they would shuffle it in 40 amongst many Truths, that those Truths being examined, and found solid at the bottome, we might not suspect any one of

their dictates to be false. Wherefore this Vision being ill meant, the poison intended was, that of the Soul's Mortality; the dangerous falseness of which opinion was to be covered by the mixture of others that are true.

5   14. As for the Relation of *Aemilianus*, which he heard from his Father *Epitherses*, it would come still more home to the purpose, if the conclusion of the Philologers at *Rome*, after *Thamus* had been sent for, and averred the truth thereof to *Tiberius Caesar* could be thought authentick, namely, That this

10   *Pan*, the news of whose death *Thamus* told to the *Daemons* at *Palodes*, was the Son of *Mercury* and *Penelope*; for then 'tis plain that *Pan* was an humane Soul, and therefore concerns the present question more nearly. But this Narration being applicable to a more sacred and venerable Subject, it loses so

15   much of its force and fitness for the present use. That which *Demetrius* adds, concerning certain Holy Islands near *Britain*, had been more fit in this regard. Whither when *Demetrius* came, suddainly upon his arrival there happened a great commotion of the air, mighty tempests and prodigious

20   whirlwinds. After the ceasing whereof, the Inhabitants pronounced, Ὅτι τῶν κρειττόνων τινὸς ἔκλειψις γέγονεν. *That some of a nature more then humane was dead.* Upon which *Plutarch*, according to his usual Rhetorick, descants after this manner, Ὡς γὰρ λύχνος ἀναπτόμενος φάναι δεινὸν οὐδὲν ἔχει. σβεννύμενος δὲ

25   πολλοῖς λυπηρός ἐστιν· οὕτως αἱ μεγάλαι ψυχαὶ τὰς μὲν ἀναλάμψεις εὐμενεῖς καὶ ἀλύπους ἔχουσιν. αἱ δὲ σβέσεις αὐτῶν καὶ φθοραὶ πολλάκις μὲν, ὡς νυνὶ, πνεύματα καὶ ζάλας τρέφουσι, πολλάκις δὲ καὶ λοιμικοῖς πάθεσιν ἀέρα φαρμάττουσιν. i.e. *As the lighting of a lamp brings no grievance with it, but the extinction of it is*

30   *offensive to many; so great Souls, while they remain kindled into life, shine forth harmlesly and benignly, but their extinction or corruption often stirs up windes and tempests, as in this present example, and often infects the Aire with pestilential annoiances.*

      15. But the last Testimony is the most unexceptionable,

35   though the least pretending to be infallible, and seems to strike dead both waies. For whether the Souls of men that goe out of these *Earthly* bodies be Vertuous or Vitious, they must die to their *Aëreal* Vehicles. Which seems a sad story at first sight, and as if *Righteousness* could not *deliver from Death*. But if it

40   be more carefully perused, the terrour will be found onely to concern the *Wicked*. For the profoundest pitch of *Death* is the *Descent into this Terrestrial Body*, in which, besides that we

necessarily forget whatever is past, we do for the present lead ἀλαμπῆ καὶ ἀμυδρὴν ζωὴν, *a dark and obscure life*, as *Plutarch* speaks, dragging this weight of *Earth* along with us, as Prisoners and Malefactours do their heavy shackles in their sordid and secluse confinements.   But in our return back 5 from this state, *Life* is naturally more large to them that are prepared to make good use of that advantage they have of their *Aiery Vehicle*. But if they be not masters of themselves in that state, they will be fatally remanded back to their former prison in process of time; which is the most gross *Death* imaginable. 10 But for the *Good* and *Vertuous* Souls, that after many Ages change their *Aëreal Vehicle* for an *Aethereal* one, that is no *Death* to them, but an higher ascent into *Life*.   And a man may as well say of an Infant, that has left the dark Wombe of his Mother, that this change of his is *Death*, as that a *Genius* 15 dies by leaving the gross *Aire*, and emerging into that Vehicle of *Light* which they ordinarily call *Aethereal* or *Celestial*.

     16. There may be therefore, by Axiome 36, a dangerous relapse out of the *Aëreal* Vehicle into the *Terrestrial*, which is properly the *Death* of the Soul that is thus retrograde. But for 20 those that ever reach the *Aethereal state*, the periods of Life there are infinite; and though they may have their *Perige's* as well as *Apoge's*, yet these Circuits being of so vast a compass, and their *Perige's* so rare and short, and their return as certain to their former *Apsis* as that of the Celestial Bodies, and their 25 *Aethereal* sense never leaving them in their lowest touches towards the Earth; it is manifest that they have arrived to that *Life* that is justly styled *Eternal*.

     17. Whence it is plain, that *Perseverance in Vertue*, if no *external Fate* hinder, will carry Man to an *Immortal life*. But 30 whether those that be thus *Heroically good*, be so by discipline and endeavour, or θέιαι τινὶ μοίραι, by a special favour and irresistible design of God, is not to be disputed in this place; though it be at large discussed somewhere in the Dialogues of *Plato*.   But in the mean time we will not doubt to conclude, 35 that there is no *Internal impediment* to those that are highly and *Heroically vertuous* but that, in process of time, they may arrive to an everlasting security of *Life* and *Happiness*, after they have left this *Earthly* Body.

                                                                                40

Chap. XVIII.

I. The Conflagration of the World *an Opinion of the* Stoicks. 2.
Two ways of destroying the World the Ancients have taken notice
5   *of, and especially that by* Fire. 3. *That the* Conflagration *of the*
World, *so far as it respects us, is to be understood onely of the*
burning of the Earth. 4. *That the Ends of the* Stoicks
Conflagration *are competible onely to the* Earth's *burning.* 5. *An*
acknowledgement that the Earth may be burnt, though the proof
10   *thereof be impertinent to this place.* 6. *That the* Conflagration
thereof will prove very fatal to the Souls of wicked men and
Daemons. 7. *Five several Opinions concerning their state after*
the Conflagration; *whereof the first is,* That they are quite
destroy'd by Fire. 8. *The second,* That they are annihilated by
15   a special act of Omnipotency. 9. *The third,* That they lye
sensless in an eternal Death. 10. *The fourth,* That they are in
a perpetual furious and painful Dream. 11. *The fifth and last,*
That they will revive again, and that the Earth and Aire will
be inhabited by them. 12. *That this last seems to be fram'd*
20   *from the fictitious* παλιγγενεσία *of the Stoicks who were very sorry*
Metaphysicians, *and as ill Naturalists.* 13. *An Animadversion*
upon a self-contradicting sentence of Seneca. 14. *The*
unintelligibleness of the state of the Souls of the Wicked after the
Conflagration. 15. *That the* Aethereal Inhabitants *will be safe.*
25   *And what will then become of* Good Men *and* Daemons *on the*
Earth and in the Aire. And how they cannot be delivered but by
a supernatural power.

I. As for the External impediments, we shall now examine
30   them, and see of what force they will be, and whether they be
at all. The former of which is *The Conflagration of the World.*
Which is an ancient Opinion, believed and entertain'd, not only
by Religions, but by Philosophers also, the *Stoicks* especially,
who affirm that the Souls of Men do subsist indeed after Death,
35   but cannot continue any longer in Being then to the
Conflagration of the World. But it is not so much material what
they thought, as to consider what is the condition indeed of the
Souls of Men and Daemons after that sad Fate.
      2. Those that will not have the World eternal, have found
40   out two ways to destroy it, ἐξυδατώσει or ἐκπυρώσει. *by* Water *or*
by Fire. Which, they say, does as naturally happen in a vast
Period of Time, which they call *Annus Magnus,* as Winter and

Summer doe in our ordinary year. *Inundatio non secus quàm Hyems, quàm Aestas lege Mundi venit.* But for this ἐξυδάτωσις. it not being so famous, nor so frequently spoken of, nor so destructive, nor so likely to end the World as the other way, nor belonging so properly to our enquiry, we shall let it pass. 5 The general prognostick is concerning *Fire* now, not onely of the *Stoicks*, as *Zeno, Cleanthes, Chrysippus Seneca*; but of several also of different Sects, as *Heraclitus, Epicurus, Cicero, Pliny, Aristocles, Numenius*, and sundry others.

3. But though there be so great and unanimous consent 10 that the *World shall be burnt*, yet they do not express themselves all alike in the business. *Seneca's* vote is the most madly explicit of any, making the very Stars run and dash one against another, and so set all on fire. But *Posidonius* and *Panaetius* had more wit, Who did not hold that ἐκπύρωσις τῶν 15 ὅλων which the other *Stoicks* did. Fo the destroying of the *Aethereal* Regions by Fire is as foolish a fancy as the sentencing of the Eele to be drown'd, because the matter of the *Aether* is too fine and subtile for *Fire* to rage in, it being indeed nothing but a pure Light or Fire it self. And yet this *Aethereal* Matter 20 is infinitely the greatest portion of the World. Wherefore the World cannot be said properly to be lyable to the destruction of *Fire* from any natural causes, as the *Stoicks* would have it. Which is demonstratively true upon *Des-Cartes* has Principles, who makes Fire nothing but the motion of certain little 25 particles of Matter, and holds that there is no more motion at one time in the World then at another because one part of the Matter cannot impress any agitation upon another, but it must lose so much it self. This hideous noise therefore of the *Conflagration of the World* must be restrain'd to the firing of the 30 *Earth* onely, so farre as it concerns us. For there is nothing else *combustible* in the Universe but the *Earth*, and other *Planets*, and what *Vapours* and *Exhalations* arise from them.

4. This *Conflagration* therefore that *Philosophers, Poets, Sibyls*, and all have fill'd the World with the fame of, is nothing 35 but the burning of the *Earth*. And the ends the *Stoicks* pretend of their ἐκπύρωσις may be competible to it, but not to the burning of the *Heavens* or *Aether* at all; as any but meanly skilled in Philosophy cannot but acknowledge. For their nature is so simple that they cannot corrupt, and therefore 40 want no renovation, as the *Earth* does. Nor do the Inhabitants of those Heavenly Regions defile themselves with any vice; or if

they do, they sink from their *material* station as well as *moral*,
and fall towards these terrestrial dreggs. And therefore that
part of the happy ἀποκατάστασις *Seneca* speaks of, *Omne animal
ex integro generabitur, dabitúrque terris homo inscius scelerum,*
5 *et melioribus auspiciis natus*, will take no place with those
Aethereal Creatures.

   5. We are willing then to be born down, by this common
and loud cry of *Fire* that must burn the World, into an
acknowledgment that the *Earth* may within a certain Period of
10 time be *burnt*, with all those things that are upon it or near it.
But what concurse of natural causes may contribute to this
dismal spectacle, is not proper for me to dispute, especially in
this place. I shall only take a view of what sad effects this
Conflagration may have upon the *Souls* of *Daemons* and *Men*.
15 For that those that have recovered their *Aethereal* Vehicles are
exempt from this fate, is evident; the remoteness of their
habitation securing them from both the rage and noisomness of
these sulphureous flames.

   6. The most certain and most destructive execution that
20 this *Fire* will doe, must be upon the unrecovered *Souls of
Wicked Men* and *Daemons*; those that are so deeply sunk and
drown'd εἰς γένεσιν, that the very consistency of their Vehicles
does imprison them within the confines of this thick caliginous
Aire.   These Souls or Spirits therefore that have so
25 inextricably entangled themselves in the Fate of this lower
World, giving up all their Senses to the moment any pleasures
of the most luxurious Principle, which is the very seat of
Death, these, in the Mystical Philosophy of the Ancients, are
the *Nymphs*, to whom though they allot a long Series of years,
30 yet they do not exempt them from mortality and fate. And
Demetrius in *Plutarch* pronounces expresly out of *Hesiod*, that
their Life will be terminated with the *Conflagration* of the
World, from wnat the Poet intimates *Aenigmatically*, καὶ ὁ
λόγος ὅλος ἠνίχϑαι δοκεῖ τῶι Ἡσιόδωι πρὸς τὴν ἐκπύρωσιν. ὁπηνίκα
35 συνεκλείπειν τοῖς ὑγροῖς εἰκός ἐστι τὰς Νύμφας.
            ... Ἇι τ᾽ ἄλσεα καλὰ νέμονται
              καὶ πηγὰς ποταμῶν καὶ πείσεα ποιήεντα.
   7. But to leave these Poetical Riddles, and take a more
serious and distinct view of the condition of the Soul after the
40 *Conflagration* of the Earth; we shall finde five several sorts of
Opinions concerning it. The first hold, *That this unmerciful heat
and fire will at last destroy and consume the Soul as well as the*

Body. But this seems to me impossible, that any created Substance should utterly destroy another Substance, so as to reduce it to nothing. For no part of *Matter*, acting the most furiously upon another part thereof, does effect that. It can onely attenuate, dissipate and disperse the parts, and make 5 them invisible. But the Substance of the Soul is *indissipable* and *indiscerpible*, and therefore remains entire, whatever becomes of the Body or Vehicle.

8. The second Opinion is, *That after long and tedious torture in these flames, the Soul by a special act of Omnipotency is* 10 *annihilated.* But, methinks, this is to put Providence too much to her shifts, as if God were so brought to a plunge in his creating a Creature of it self Immortal, that he must be fain to *uncreate* it again, that is to say, to *annihilate* it. Besides that that Divine *Nemesis* that lies within the compass of Philosophy, 15 never supposes any such forcible eruptions of the Deity into extrtraodinary effects, but that all things are brought about by a wise and infallible or inevitable train of secondary Causes, whether natural or free Agents.

9. The third therefore, to avoid these absurdities, denies 20 both *absumption by Fire* and *annihilation*; but conceives, *That tediousness and extremity of pain makes the Soul at last, of her self, shrink from all commerce with Matter*: the *immediate* Principle of Union, which we call *Vital Congruity*, consisting of a certain modification of the Body or Vehicles as well as of the 25 Soul, which being spoiled and lost, and the Soul thereby quite loosned from all sympathy with Body or Matter, *she becomes perfectly dead, and sensless to all things*, by Axiome 36, *and*, as they say, *will so remain for ever.* But this seems not so rational; for, as *Aristotle* somewhere has it, ἕκαστον, οὗ ἐστιν 30 ἐνέργεια, ἔστιν ἕνεκα τοῦ ἔργου. Wherefore so many entire Immaterial Substances would be continued in Being to all Eternity to no end nor purpose, notwithstanding they may be made use of, and actuate Matter again as well as ever.

10. A fourth sort therefore of Speculators there is, who 35 conceive that after this solution of the Souls or Spirits of *Wicked Men* and *Daemons* from their Vehicles, *That their pain is continued to them even in that separate state, they falling into an unquiet sleep, full of furious tormenting Dreams, that act as fiercely upon their Spirits as the external Fire did upon their* 40 *Bodies.* But others except against this Opinion as a very uncertain Conjecture, it supposing that which to them seems

not so sound, *viz.* That the Soul can act when it has lost all
vital Union with the Matter; which seems repugnant with that
so intimate and essential aptitude it has to be united therewith.
And the Dreams of the Soul in the Body are not transacted
5 without the help of the Animal Spirits in the Brain, they
usually symbolizing with their temper. Whence they conclude,
that there is no certain ground to establish this Opinion upon.

    11. The last therefore, to make all sure, that there may
be no inconvenience in admitting that the Souls or Spirits as
10 well of *evil Daemons* as *wicked Men,* disjoyned from their
Vehicles by the force of that fatal *Conflagration,* may subsist,
have excogitated an odde and unexpected Hypothesis, *That
when this firing of the World has done due execution upon that
unfortunate Crue, and tedious and direful torture has wearied
15 their afficted Ghosts into an utter recess from all Matter, and
thereby into a profound sleep or death; that after a long Series of
years, when not onely the fury of the Fire is utterly slaked, but
that vast Atmosphere of smoak and vapours, which was sent up
during the time of the Earth' s Conflagration, has returned back
20 in copious showres of rain* (which will again make Seas and
Rivers, will binde and consolidate the ground, and falling
exceeding plentifully all over, make the soil pleasant and
fruitful, and the Aire cool and wholsome) *that Nature recovering
thus to her advantage, and becoming youthful again, and full of
25 genital salt and moisture, the Souls of all living Creatures
belonging to these lower Regions of the Earth and Aire will
awaken orderly in their proper places: The Seas and River; will
be again replenished with Fish; the Earth will send forth all
manner of Fowls, four-footed Beasts, and creeping things, and the
30 Souls of Men also shall then catch life from the more pure and
balsamick parts of the Earth, and be clothed again in terrestrial
Bodies; and lastly, the Aëreal* Genii, *that Element becoming
again wholsome and vital, shall, in due order and time, awaken
and revive in the cool rorid Aire.* Which Expergefaction into life
35 is accompanied, say they, with propensions answerable to those
resolutions they made with themselves in those fiery torments,
and which they fell into their long sleep.

    12. But the whole Hypothesis seems to be framed out of
that dream of the *Stoicks,* concerning the ἀποκατάστασις or
40 παλιγγενεσία of the World after the ἀνάστασις or ἐκπύρωσις
thereof. As if that of *Seneca* belonged to this case,
*Epist.*36.*Mors,quam pertimescimus ac recusamus, intermittit*

vitam, non eripit. Veniet iterum quinos in lucem reponet dies,
quem multi recusarent, nisi oblitos reduceret. But how coursely
the Stoicks Philosophize when they are once turned out of their
rode-way of *moral Sentences,* any one but moderately skilled in
Nature and Metaphysicks may easily discern. For what Errors   5
can be more gross then those that they entertain of *God,* of the
Soul, and of the *Stars?* they making the two former Corporeal
Substances, and feeding the latter with the Vapours of the
Earth; affirming that the Sun sups up the water of the great
Ocean to quench his thirst, but that the Moon drinks off the   10
lesser Rivers and Brooks; which is as true as that the Ass
drunk up the Moon, Such conceits are more fit for *Anacreon* in
a drunken fit to stumble upon, who to invite his Companions to
tipple, composed that Catch,

Πίνει θάλασσασ δ᾿ αὔρας   15

Ο δι᾿ ἥλιος θάλασσαν.

then for to be either found out or owned by a serious and sober
Philosopher. And yet *Seneca* mightily triumphs in this notion of
foddering the Stars with the thick foggs of the Earth, and
declares his opinion with no mean strains of eloquence: but I   20
loving solid sense better then fine words, shall not take the
pains to recite them.

13. At what a pitch his Understanding was set, may be
easily discerned by my last quotation, wherein there seems a
palpable contradiction. *Veniet iterum qui nos in lucem reponet* 25
dies, quem multi recusarent, nisi oblitos reduceret. If *nos,* how
oblitos? If *oblitos,* now *nos?* For we are not we, unless we
remember that we are so. And if mad-men may be said, and
that truly, to be besides themselves or not to be themselves,
because they have lost their wits; certainly they will be far   30
from being themselves that have quite lost the Memory of
themselves, but must be as if they had never been before. As
Lucretius has excellently well declared himself;

Nec, si materiam nostram conlegerit aetas
Post obitum, rursumque redegerit ut sita nunc est,   35
Atque iterum nobis fuerint data lumina vitae
Pertineat quicquam tamen ad nos id quoque factum
Interrupta semel cum sit retinentia nostri.

Where the Poet seems industriously to explode all the hopes of
any benefit of this *Stoical* παλιγγενεσία, and to profess that he is 40
as if he had never been, that cannot remember he has ever
been before. From whence it would follow that though the Souls

of men should revive after the *Conflagration* of the World, yet
they have not escaped a perpetual permanent death.

14. We see therefore how desperately undemonstrable the
condition of the Soul is after the *Conflagration* of the Earth, all
these five Opinions being accompanied with so much lubricity
and uncertainty. And therefore they are to be looked upon
rather as some Night-landskap to feed our amused Melancholy,
then a clear and distinct draught of comprehensible Truth to
inform our Judgment.

15. All that we can be assured of is, That those Souls that
have obtained their *Aethereal Vehicles* are out of the reach of
that sad fate that follows this *Conflagration*; and That the
wicked Souls of *Men* and *Daemons* will be involved in it. But
there are a middle sort betwixt these, concerning whom not
only curiosity but good will would make a man sollicitous. For
it is possible, that the *Conflagration* of the World may
surprise many thousands of Souls, that neither the course of
Time, nor Nature, nor any higher Principle has wrought up
into an *Aethereal Congruity* of life, but yet may be very holy,
innocent and vertuous.

Which we may easily believe, if we consider that these
very *Earthly Bodies* are not so great impediments to the
goodness and sincerity of the Mind, but that many, even in this
life, have given great examples thereof. Nor can that *Aëreal*
state be less capable of, nor well be without, the *good Genii*, no
more then the Earth without *good men*, who are the most
immediate Ministers of the Goodness and Justice of God. But
exemption from certain fates in the world is not alwaies
entailed upon *Innoceny*, but most ordinarily upon *natural power*.
And therefore there may be numbers of the *good Genii*, and of
very holy and innocuous Spirits of men departed, the
consistency of whose Vehicles may be such, that they can no
more quit these Aëreal Regions, then we can fly into them, that
have heavy bodies, without wings. To say nothing of those
vertuous and pious men that may haply be then found alive,
and so be liable to be overtaken by this storm of Fire.

Undoubtedly, unless there appear, before the approach of
this fate, some visible Ζεὺς σωτήριος or *Jupiter Sospitator*, as the
heathens would call him, they must necessarily be involved in
the ruine of the wicked. Which would be a great eye-sore in
that exact and irreprehensible frame of Providence, that all
men promise to themselves who acknowledge That there is a

God. Wherefore according to the light of Reason, there must be some Supernatural means to rescue those innocuous and benign Spirits out of this common calamity. But to describe the manner of it here how it must be done, would be to entitle natural Light and Philosophy to greater abilities then they are 5 guilty of; and therefore that Subject must be reserved for its proper place.

10

Chap. XIX.

I. *That the* Extinction of the Sun *is no* Panick *feare, but may be rationally suspected from the Records of History and grounds of Natural* Philosophy. 2. *The sad Influence of this Extinction upon* 15 *Man and Beasts, and all the Aëreal* Daemons *imprison'd within their several* Atmospheres *in our* Vortex, 3. *That it will doe little or no damage to the Aethereal Inhabitants in reference to heat or warmth.* 4. *Nor will they find much what of his light.* 5. *And if they did, they may pass out of one* Vortex *into another, by the* 20 *priviledge of their Aethereal Vehicles*; 6. *And that without any labour or toile, and as maturely as they please.* 7.*The vast incomprehensibleness of the tracts and compasses of the waies of Providence.* 8. *A short Recapitulation of the whole Discourse.* 9. *An Explication of the* Persians *two Principles of* Light and 25 Darkness. *which they called* Θεὸς and Δαίμων. *and when and where the Principle of* Light *gets the full victory.* 10. *That Philosophy, or something more sacred then Philosophy is the onely Guide to a true* Ἀποθέωσις.

30

I. The last danger that threatens *the Separate Soul* is the *Extinction of the Sun*; which though it may seem a mere *Panick* fear at first sight, yet if the matter be examined, there will appear no contemptible reasons that may induce men to suspect that it may at last fall out, there having been, at 35 certain times, such near offers in Nature towards this sad accident already. *Pliny*, though he instances but in one example, yet speaks of it as a thing that several times to pass. *Fiunt*, saith he, *prodigiosi et longiores Solis defectus, qualis occiso Dictatore Caesare, et Antoniano bello, totius anni pallore* 40 *continuo*. The like happened in *Justinian*'s time, as *Cedrenus* writes; when, for a whole year together, the Sun was of a very

dim and duskish hue, as if he had been in a perpetuall Eclipse.
And in the time of *Irene* the Empress it was so dark for
seventeen dayes together, that the ships lost their way on the
sea, and were ready to run against one another, as
5   *Theophanes* relates. But the late accurate discovery of *the*
Spots of the Sun by *Shiner*, and the appearing & disappearing
of fixt Stars, & the excursions of Comets into the remoter parts
of our *Vortex*, as also the very intrinsecal contexture of that
admirable Philosophy of *Des-Cartes*, do argue it more then
10   possible that, after some vast periods of time, the Sun may be
so inextricably inveloped by the *Maculae* that he is never free
from, that he may quite lose his light.

2. The Preambles of which *Extinction* will be very hideous,
and intolerable to all the Inhabitants of the Planets in our
15   *Vortex*, if the Planets have then any Inhabitants at all. For
this defect of light and heat coming on by degrees, must needs
weary out poor mortals with heavy languishments, both for
want of the comfort of the usual warmth of the Sun, whereby
the Bodies of men are recreated and also by reason of his
20   inability to ripen the fruits of the Soil; whence necessarily must
follow Famine, Plagues, Sicknesses, and at length an utter
devastation and destruction of both *Man* and *Beasts*.

Nor can the *Aëreal Daemons* scape free, but that the *vital*
tye to their Vehicles necessarily confining them to their several
25   *Atmospheres*, they will be inevitably imprisoned in more then
Cimmerian darkness. For the *Extinction of the Sun* will put out
the light of all their *Moons*, and nothing but Ice, and Frost, and
flakes of Snow, and thick mists, as palpable as that of *Aegypt*,
will possess the Regions of their habitation. Of which sad
30   spectacle though those twinkling eyes of heaven, the Stars,
might be compassionate spectatours; yet they cannot send out
one ray of light to succour or visit them, their tender and
remote beams not being able to pierce, much less to dissipate,
the clammy and stiff consistency of that long and fatal Night.
35   3. Wherefore calling our mind off from so dismal a sight,
let us place it upon a more hopeful Object; and consider the
condition of those Souls that have arrived to their *Aethereal*
Vehicle, and see how far this fate can take hold of them. And it
is plain at first sight, that they are out of the reach of this
40   misty dungeon, as being already mounted into the secure
mansions of the purer *Aether*.

The worst that can be imagined of them is, that they may find themselves in a condition something like that of ours when we walk out in a clear, starlight, frosty night, which to them that are found is rather a pleasure then offence. And if we can bear it with some delight in these Earthly Bodies, whose parts 5 will grow hard and stiff for want of due heat, it can prove nothing else but a new modification of tactual pleasure to those *Aethereal Inhabitants* whose bodies are not constipated as ours, but are themselves a kinde of *agile light and fire.*

All that can be conceived is, that the spherical particles of 10 their Vehicles may stand a little more closely and firmly together then usual, whence the triangular intervalls being more straight, the subtilest element will move something more quick in them, which will raise a sense of greater vigour and alacrity then usual. So little formidable is this fate to them in 15 this regard.

4. But their light, you'l say, will be obscured, *the Sun being put out,* whose shining seems to concern the *Gods* as well as Men, as *Homer* would intimate,

Ὄρνιθ᾽ ἵν᾽ ἀθανάτοισι φάος φέρηι ἠδὲ βροτοῖσι   20

But I answer, that that of *Homer* is chiefly to be understood of the *Aëreal Daemons,* not the *Aethereal Deities,* who can turn themselves into a pure actual Light when they please. So that there is no fear but that their personal converse will be as chearful and distinct as before, white letters being as legible 25 upon black paper as black upon white. But this is to suppose them in the dark, which they are not, but in a more soft and mild light, which is but a change of pleasure, as it is to see the Moon shine fair into a room after the putting out of the Candle. And certainly the contribution of the light of the Stars 30 is more to their quick and tender Senses, then the clearest Moon-shine night is to ours; though we should suppose them no nearer any Star then we are. But such great changes as these may have their conveniences for such as Providence will favour, as well as their inconveniencies. And the *Extinction of* 35 *our Sun* may be the Augmentation of Light in some Star of a neighbouring *Vortex.* Which though it may not be able to pierce those *Cimmerian* Prisons I spake of before, yet it may give sufficient light to these *Spirits* that are free. Besides that the Discerption and spoil of our *Vortex,* that will then happen, will 40 necessarily bring us very much nearer the Centre of some other, whose Star will administer sufficient light to the

Aethereal Genii, though it be too weak to relieve the *Aëreal*.

And that so remote a distance from these central Luminaries of the *Vortices* is consistent with the perfectest happiness, we may discern partly, in that the Celestial Matter
5   above *Saturn*, till the very marge of the *Vortex*, is more strongly agitated then that betwixt him and the Sun, and therefore has less need of the Sun's beams conserve its agility and liquidity; and partly, in that those huge vast Regions of *Aether* would be lost, and in vain in a manner, if they were not
10 frequented by *Aethereal Inhabitants*, which in all reason and likelihood are of the noblest kind, according to the nature of their Element. And therefore all the *Aethereal People* may retire thither upon such an exigency as this, and there rest secure in joy ard happiness, in these true *Intermundia Deorum*
15 which *Epicurus* dream'd of.

5. Which we may easily admit, if we consider the grand Priviledges of the *Aethereal Vehicle*, wherein so great a power of the Soul is awakened, that she can moderate the motion of the particles thereof as she pleases, by adding or diminishing
20 the degrees of agitation, Axiome 32. whereby she is also able to temper the solidity thereof, and, according to this contemperation of her Vehicle, to ascend or descend in the *Vortex* as she lifts her self, and that with a great variety of swiftness, according to her own pleasure. By the improvement
25 of which Priviledge she may also, if she please, pass from one *Vortex* into another, and receive the warmth of a new *Vesta*, so that no fate imaginable shall be ever able to lay hoid upon her.

6. Nor will this be any more labour to her then sailing down the stream. For she, having once fitted the agitation and
30 solidity of her *Vehicle* for her Celestial voiage, will be as naturally carried whither she is bound, as a stone goes downward, or the fire upward. So that there is no fear of any lassitude, no more then by being rowed in a Boat, or carrired in a Sedan. For the Celestial Matter that environs her Vehicle
35 works her upward or downward, toward the Centre or from the Centre of a *Vortex*, at its own proper pains and charges. Lastly, such is the tenuity and subtilty of the Senses of the *Aethereal* Inhabitants, that their prevision and sagacity must be, beyond all conceit, above that of ours; besides that there
40 will be warnings and premonitions of this future disafter, both many, and those very visible and continued, before the Sun shall fail so far as that they shall at all be concerned in his

decay; so that the least blast of misfortune shall never be able
to blow upon them, nor the least evil imaginable overtake
them.

7. This is a small glance at the Mysteries of Providence,
whose fetches are so large, and Circuits so immense, that they 5
may very well seem utterly incomprehensible to the
Incredulous and *Idiots,* who are exceeding prone to think that
all things will ever be as they are, and desire they should be so:
though it be as rude and irrational, as if one that comes into a
Ball, and is taken much with the first Dance he sees, would 10
have none danced but that, or have them move no further one
from another then they did when he first came into the room;
whenas they are to trace nearer one another, or further off,
according to the measures of the Musick, and the law of the
Dance they are in. And the whole Matter of the Universe, and 15
all the parts thereof, are ever upon Motion, and in such a
Dance, as whose traces backwards and forwards take a vast
compass; and what seems to have made the longest stand,
must again move, according to the modulations and accents of
that Musick, that is indeed out of the hearing of the acutest 20
ears, but yet perceptible by the purest Mi nds and the sharpest
Wits. The truth whereof none would dare to oppose, if the
breath of the gainsayer could but tell its own story, and declare
through how many *Stars* and *Vortices* it has been strained
before the particles thereof met, to be abused to the framing of 25
so rash a contradiction.

8. We have now finisht our whole *Discourse,* the summary
result whereof is this; *That there is an Incorporeal Substance,*
and that in Man, which we call his Soul. That this Soul of his
subsists and acts after the death of his Body, and that usually 30
first in an Aëreal Vehicle, as other Daemons *do; wherein she is*
not quite exempt from fate, but is then perfect and secure when
she has obtain'd her Aethereal *one, she being then out of the*
reach of that evil Principle whose dominion is commensurable
with misery and death. Which power the *Persian Magi* termed 35
Arimanius, and resembled him to *Darkness,* as the other good
Principle, which they called *Oromazes,* to *Light,* styling one by
the name of Δαίμων. the other by the name of ϑεός.

9. Of which there can be no other meaning that will prove
allowable, but an adumbration of those two grand parts of 40
Providence, the one working in the *Demoniacal,* the other in the
Divine Orders. Betwixt which natures there is perpetually

more or less strife and contest, both inwardly and outwardly. But if *Theopompus* his prophecy be true in *Plutarch* who was initiated into these *Arcana*, the power of the *Benign Principle* will get the upper hand at last, Τέλος δ᾽ ἀπολείπεσθαι τὸν Ἅιδην.

5 etc. At length *Hades* or *Arimanius* will be left in the lurch, who so strongly holds us captive, καὶ τοὺς μὲν ἀνθρώπους εὐδαίμονας ἔσεσθαι, μήτε τροφῆς δεομένους, μήτε σκιὰν ποιοῦντας, *and men shall then be perfectly happy, needing no food, nor casting any shadow.* For what *shadow* can that Body cast that is a pure

10 and transparent light, such as the *Aethereal Vehicle* is? And therefore that Oracle is then fulfilled, when the Soul has ascended into that condition we have already described, in which alone it is out of the reach of *Fate* and *Mortality*.

10. This is the true Ἀποθέωσις, to speak according to the

15 *Persian* Language, with whose empty title Emperours and great Potentates of the Earth have been ambitious to adorn their memory after death; but is so high a Priviledge of the Soul of Man, that mere *Political* vertues, as *Plotinus* calls them, can never advance her to that pitch of Happiness. Either

20 Philosophy, or something more sacred then Philosophy, must be her Guide to so transcendent a condition. And not being curious to dispute, whether the *Pythagoreans* ever arrived to it by living according to the precepts of their Master, I shall notwithstanding with confidence averre, that what they aimed

25 at, is the sublimest felicity our nature is capable of; and being the utmost Discovery this *Treatise* could pretend to, I shall conclude all with a *Distich* of theirs (which I have elsewhere taken notice of upon like occasion) it comprehending the furthest scope, not onely of their Philosophy, but of this present

30 Discourse.

Ἢν δ᾽ ἀπολείψας σῶμα ἐς αἰθέρ᾽ ἐλεύθερον ἔλθῃς,
Ἔσσεαι ἀθάνατος, θεὸς ἄμβροτος, οὐκέτι θνητός.
To this sense,
Who after death once reach th' Aethereal Plain,

35 *Are straight made Gods, and never die again.*

The CONTENTS of the Several Chapters
contained in this Treatise

Book I.

---

* [The original folio numbers have been altered to suit the pagination of the present edition-Ed.]

59

Book II.

*by his own Sophistry. 9. That one part of this first Argument of his
is groundless, the other sophistical. 10. The plain proposal of his
Argument, whence appears more fully the weakness and sophistry
thereof. 11. An Answer to his second Argument. 12. An Answer to
the third.13. An Answer to a difficulty concerning the Truth and
Falshood of future Propositions. 14. An Answer to Mr Hobbs his
fourth Argument, which, though sighted by himself, is the strongest
of them all. 15. The difficulty of reconciling Free-will with Divine
Prescience and Prophecies. 16. That the faculty of Free-will is
seldome put in use. 17. That the use of it is properly in Moral
conflict. 18. That the Soul is not invincible there neither. 19. That
Divine decrees either finde fit Instruments or make them. 20. That
the more exact Divine Prescience, even to the comprehension of any
thing that implies no contradiction in it self to be comprehended, the
more clear it is that mans Will may be sometimes free. 21. Which is
sufficient to make good my last Argument against Mr.* Hobbs.

*Chap.IV. I. An Enumeration of sundry Opinions concerning the Seat
of Common Sense. 2. Upon supposition that we are nothing but
mere Matter, That the whole Body cannot be the Common
Sensorium; 3. Nor the Orifice of the Stomach; 4. Nor the Heart; 5.
Nor the Brain; 6. Nor the Membranes; 7. Nor the* Septum *lucidum;
8. Nor* Regius *his small and perfectly-solid Particle. 9. The
probability of the* Conarion *being the common Seat of Sense.*

*Chap.V. I. How Perception of external Objects, Spontaneous Motion,
Memory and Imagination, are pretended to be performed by the*
Conarion, *Spirits and Muscles, without a Soul. 2. That the*
Conarion, *devoid of a Soul, cannot be the* Common Percipient,
demonstrated out of Des-Cartes *himself.3. That the* Conarion, *with
the Spirits and organization of the Parts of the Body, is not a
sufficient Principle of Spontaneous motion, without a Soul. 4. A
description of the use of the* Valvulae *in the Nerves of the Muscles
for spontaneous motion. 5. The insufficiency of this contrivance for
that purpose. 6. A further demonstration of the insufficiency thereof,
from whence is clearly evinced that Brutes have Souls. 7. That
Memory cannot be salved the way above described; 8. Nor
Imagination. 9. A Distribution out of* Des-Cartes *of the Functions in
us, some appertaining to the Body, and others to the soul. 10. The
Author's Observations thereupon.*

Commentary Notes

The editions and translations used in these notes are those listed in the Bibliography. Where no translator is acknowledged, the translation is mine. The symbol [M] denotes the extent of More's own citations of references in his marginal notes to the 1662 edition. The form of More's marginal notes has, in many cases, been slightly adapted for the sake of clarity.* Where the original form has been preserved, it is reproduced within quotation marks.

Title page

Page/Line

/1   Πάντα...νομίζεσθαι: More's epigraph is adapted from Diogenes Laertius,VIII,32: εἶναι τε πάντα τὸν ἀέρα ψυχῶν ἔμπλεων καὶ ταύτας δαίμονας τε καὶ ἥρωας ὀνομάζεσθαι.
[The whole air is full of souls which are called genii or heroes.]
As the entire section on the opinion of Pythagoras on the soul from which this line is taken (VIII, 30-32) has a bearing on the psychological and metaphysical themes developed by More in this treatise, I shall quote it in full here:
'The soul of man, [Pythagoras] says, is divided into three parts,intelligence, reason, and passion. Intelligence and passion are possessed by other animals as well, but reason by man alone. The seat of the soul extends from the heart to the brain; the part of it which is in the heart is passion, while the parts located in the brain are reason and intelligence. The senses are distillations from these. Reason is immortal all else mortal. The soul draws nourishment from the blood; the faculties of the soul are winds, for they as well as the soul are invisible, just as the aether is invisible. The veins, arteries, and sinews are the bonds of the soul . But when it is strong and settled down into itself, reasonings and deeds become its bonds. When cast out upon the earth it wanders in

---

* i.e. The Latin forms of the names of the various authors have been replaced by the English, and abbreviations of titles have been expanded.

the air in the body. Hermes is the steward of souls, and for that reason is called Hermes the Escorter, Hermes the Keeper of the gate, and Hermes of the Underworld, since it is he who brings in the souls from their bodies both by land and sea, and the pure are taken into the uppermost region, but the impure are not permitted to approach the pure or each other, but are bound by the Furies in bonds unbreakable. The whole air is full of souls which are called genii or heroes; these are they who send men dreams and signs of future disease and health, and not to men alone but to sheep also and cattle as well; and it is to them that purifications,and instructions, all divinations, omens, and the like, have reference. The most momentous thing in human life is the act of winning the soul to good or to evil. Blest are the men who acquire a good soul; (if it be bad) they can never be at rest, nor ever keep the same course two days together.' (Tr. R.S. Hicks, Loeb Classical Library)

/13   *Quid ... vicissitudines?*: 'What is more pleasant than to know what we are, what we were, and what we will be; and, with these, the supreme,divine things which follow death and the changes of the world?' I have not been able to identify this quotation in Cardano's voluminous writings, but the sentiment it expresses is obviously a deeply felt one. In *De Libriis Propriis*, for instance, we find another variant of the same concern: 'Quam dulce est atque iucundum, scire quae ante nos, et quae supra nos sint, quaeque futura sint cum animus hinc discesserit: neque molesta vita, nec quae post mortem formidolosa, ipse solus transitus naturae lege gravis est.'

Epistle Dedicatory

1/2   Edward: Third Viscount of Conway and husband of Anne, More's pupil and friend (see Biographical Introduction p.ix).

2/4   handsome: clever

2/7   *Ragley*: Ragley Hall was acquired by the first Viscount Conway in 1591. Situated twenty miles south of Birmingham, it is now the seat of the Marquess of Hertford.

2/8   civil ... Mother: Frances Conway, Dowager Viscountess Conway -- More 's affection and gratitude for her kindness to him is constantly evidenced in his letters to the Conways. cf. More's letter of 1664 [?] to Anne Conway: 'I pray you Madame, present my very humble service to my lady your Mother with my very hearty acknowledgements for her great civilitys at Ragley' (*Conway Letters*, ed. M.H. Nicolson, New Haven: Yale Univ. Press 1930, p. 234.)

Preface

5/7   *Christianity ... Light*: cf. II Tim. 1:10: 'But is now made manife st by the appearing of our Saviour Jesus Christ, who hath abolished death, and hath brought life and immortalitie to light, through the Gospel.'

5/20   set: 'Book 3, Chap 14' [M].

6/3   *spinosities*: Arguments of a 'difficult and unprofitable character' (OED)

6/6   Mystery: 'Book 5, Ch. 1, 2 and 3, Also Book 6, Ch. II, sect. 13 and Book 8, Ch. 17' [M].

6/31   indiscerpible: the property of being incapable of being divided into parts.

7/37   *extuberancy*: protuberancy

8/13   Hedrae: bases

8/21   Epictetus: *Encheiridion*, 43: πᾶν πρᾶγμα δύο ἔχει λαβάς, τὴν μὲν φορητήν, τὴν δὲ ἀφόρητην.
[Everything has two handles, by one of which it ought to be carried and by the other not (Tr. W.A. Oldfather, Loeb Classical Library)].

9/11   Pomponatius: Pietro Pomponazzi (1462-1525) was a Neo-Aristotelian philosopher associated with the universities of Padua, Ferrara, and Bologna. His chief works concern immortality, miracles, and freewill. The three treatises on immortality are *De immortalitate animae* (1516), *Apologia*(1518), and *Defensiorium* (1519). Based on Aristotelian epistemology and psychology, his theory of the mortality of the soul along with the death of the body was balanced by a subtle scholastic resort to faith which assures us nevertheless of the soul's immortality. In *De immortalitate animae* and *De Incantationibus* (1556), a treatise on miracles, Pomponazzi suggested that miracles could be explained as being produced by the Intelligences which move the heavenly bodies. *De immortalitate animae* provoked both philosophers and theologians and began the immortality controversy, which was one of the most important debates prior to the Reformation. The controversy reached such proportions that Pope Leo X demanded a retraction frcm Pomponazzi in 1518, and his final work, the *Defensorium*, was allowed to be published only with an appended list of orthodox conclusions supporting the immortality of the soul, (*Dictionary of Scientific Biography*, XI:71-74)

9/12   Cardan: Girolamo Cardano (1501-1576). After a wide-ranging education under the guidance of his father, Cardano received his doctorate in medicine in 1526, and was second only to Vesalius among the doctors of Europe. In 1570, he was arrested by the Inquisition for having cast the horoscope of Christ and having attributed the events of His life to the influence of the stars. In 1571, he obtained the favour of Pope Pius V, who gave him a life annuity. Cardano wrote more than 200 books on medicine, mathematics, music, physics, philosophy, and religion. The two works which More constantly refers to are his encyclopediae of natural science, *De Subtilitate libri XXI*(1550), and its supplemanent, *De rerum varietate*,(1557). These include articles on everything from cosmology to the construction of machines, from the usefulness of natural sciences to the evil influence of demons, from the laws of mechanics to cryptology. (*Dictionary of Scientific Biography*, III:64-67)

9/12   Vaninus: Giulio Cesare Vaninus, (1585-1619) was a Carmelite friar who was also doctor of laws in the University of Naples. His first book, *Amphitheatrum Aeternae Providentiae* (1615), was a critique of traditional beliefs about Divine Providence. He insisted that the immortality of the soul could not be demonstrated by physical principles. His own proofs are that 1. the soul being a simple substance cannot decompose; 2. the soul is, besides, a celestial substance which is not subject to corruption; and 3. if nothing can be made out of nothing, something cannot disintegrate into nothing. His second work, *De Admirandis naturae reginae deaeque mortalium arcanis* (1616), is composed of four sets of dialogues between Alexander and Julius Caesar that deal with the planets and the elements, sublunar matters, man, and the pagan church, respectively. Though directed against atheists, the work is blatantly impious. Vanini was arrested as an atheist at Toulouse in 1618, and, in February 1619, has tongue was cut off before he was strangled, burned, and his ashes were scattered to the winds. (*Dictionary of Scientific Biography*, XIII: 573)

10/11   *allision*: collision

10/37   species intentionales: cf. Descartes, *La Dioptrique*, Discours Premier: Having enunciated his own theory of light, and colours, Descartes adds: 'Et par ce moyen votre esprit sera delivré de toutes ces petites images voltigeantes par l'air, nommées *des espèces intentionelles*, qui travaillent tant l'imagination des philosophes.'

11/12   the *Schools*: More seems to refer here to S. Thomas Aquinas' theory of the angelic nature in *Summa Theologiae*, 1a 50, 1-2, and 1a 51, 1, where he maintains that 'Angels are not by nature conjoined with bodies.'

11/31   Vaninus: Vanini, *De admirandis naturae*, Dialogue L: 'An cum Pomponatio nostri seculi Philosophorom Principe afferemus, visiones has admirabiles confici a supernis mentibus immaterialibus Coelorum motricibus, homines quos ipse fideliter custodiant, ita instruendo, dirigendoque, ut futuros eis eventus praeostendant: nunquam haec apparuisse legimus apud his toricos, quin caedes, vel fames vel pestis, vel Regum, legumque subsecutei fuerint mutationes.'
[We affirm with Pomponazzi, the chief of our secular philosophers, that these admirable visions were produced by

the immaterial celestial intelligences of the Heavens which constantly guard men, guiding them in such a way that they reveal future events to them: indeed we read in the historians that they have never appeared without being followed by massacres, famines, plagues or changes of kings and laws.]

12/2   Psychopannychyites: 'All-night sleep of the soul, a state in which ... the soul sleeps between death and the day of judgement' (OED). The term was used as the title of one of Calvin's tracts, *Psychopannychia, qua refellitur eorum error, qui animas post mortem usque ad ultimum iudicium dormire putant* (1545).

12/25   *Book*: 'Chap 5, 6, 7' [M].

13/9   Canoa: the original, Spanish name for a canoe.

13/39   Mahometan *Paradise*: See the *Koran*, LV, 46-78 for a description of the sensual delights awaiting the blessed in Heaven.

14/10   Plotinus: See *Enneades*, I, VI, 3.

14/28   *the* Sicilian *Tyrants*: See Strabo, *Geography*, VI, i, 8 for a vivid description of the sexual maltreatment of the Locri Epizephyrii by Dionysius the Younger.

15/2   *confuted*: 'Book 3, chap. 16' [M].

15/5   *there*: 'Chap. 16, sect. 4' *[M]*.

15/33   Avenroists: More refers to the mediaeval Aristotelian tradition based on the commentaries of Averroes or Ibn Rushd (1126-1198) who held that the possible or 'material' intellect as well as the active or 'agent' intellect was a separated substance and one for all men. In Averroes ' view, the individual has no spiritual intellect; rather, imagination, memory, and cogitation within the brain merely provide data for the separated intellect, which actuates the intelligible species present potentially in the individual and is thus the real subject in which all knowledge occurs (See

Commentarium magnum in Aristotelis De anima libros III).
This concept of a single spiritual entity in the universe was
considered dangerous by church authorities and, in 1256, St.
Albert attacked it in *De Unitate intellectus contra
Averroem.*The first person to use the term 'Averroists' was
St. Thomas Aquinas in *De Unitate Intellectus contra
Averroistas* (1270) which condemned the divergence of their
philosophy from the Christian faith: 'For if we deny to men a
diversity of intellect, which alone among the parts of the soul
seems to be incorruptible and immortal, it follows that after
death nothing of the souls of men would remain except that
single substance of intellect; and so the recompense of
rewards and punishments and also their diversity would be
destroyed' (*De unitate*, Proem 2). Finally in 1270, the Bishop
of Paris, Etienne Tempier condemned thirteen propositions
traceable to Averroes' interpretations of Aristotle -- these
included the oneness of the intellect, the eternity of the world
and the human species, the mortality of the human soul, the
denial of providence and freewill, and the necessitating
influence of the heavenly bodies on the sublunar world.

15/33   *those* ... Cardanus. see Note to Bk. III, Ch. 17, sect. 5 below.

15/38   *already*: 'Book 3, ch 16, sect 2' [M].

16/34   *Discourse*: 'Book 2, ch. 5, sect 7, also Ch. 11, sect. 4, 5, 6'
         [M].

18/34   Treatise: 'Book 3, ch. 12' [M].

18/41   *tenour*: See More, *An Antidote Against Atheism*, Bk. 2, Ch 9
         [not 10, as More indicates] sect.12 [M]: 'It is but some rude
         and general congruity of vital preparation that sets this
         Archeus on work rather then another: As mere *Choler*
         engages the phansie to dream of firing of guns and fighting
         of armies, *Sanguine* figures the Imagination into the
         representation of fair Women and beautiful children; *Phlegm*
         transforms her into Water and Fishes; and the shadowy
         Melancholy intangles her in colluctation with old Hags and
         Hobgoblins and frights her with dead men's faces in the
         dark.'

20/20   deprehension: discovery

Book I

22/29   most certain ... *Happiness*: cf. Descartes, *Discours de la methode*, 3ème Partie: 'La première maxime était d'obéir aux lois et aux coutumes de mon pays,retenant constamment la religion en laquelle Dieu m'a fait la grace d'être instruit dès mon enfance, et me governant, en toute autre chose, suivant les opinions les plus modérées, et les plus éloignées de l'excès, qui fussent communément reçues en pratique par les mieux sensés de ceux avec lesquels j'aurais à vivre.

23/6   Cocks ... Cherry-stones: children's games

24/39   Consectary: corollary

25/1   *Scepticisme*: 'See *Antidote*, Book I, Ch. 2, and 9 [M].

25/40   *Perplexiveness of Imagination*: 'See *Antidote*, Book I, Ch 4, sect 2' [M].

25/42   *Euclide:Elements*,Bk.III, Prop. 16: 'The straight line drawn at right angles to the diameter of a circle from its extremity will fall outside the circle, and into the space between the straight line and the circumference. Another straight line cannot be interposed; further, the angle of the semicircle is greater, and the remaining angle less, than any acute rectilineal angle.' The perplexity of this proposition is attested by the long controversy related to it from antiquity to the 17th century. Sir Thomas Heath indicates in his edition of *The Thirteen Books of Euclid's Elements* (London, 1926) -- to which I refer the reader for full details of the controversy -- that the main dispute was about the nature of the 'angle of a semicircle' and the 'remaining angle' between the circumference of the semicircle and the tangent at its extremity (p. 39) as well as about the nature of contact between straight lines and circles. It involved such mathematicians as Proclus, Johannes Campanus -- the 13th century editor of Euclid -- Cardano, Peletier -- the 16th century French editor -- Viète, and John Wallis. One of the

most interesting contributions to the controversy was that of
Peletier who, according to Heath, held that the 'angle of
contact' was not an angle at all, that the 'contact of two
circles touching one another internally or externally' is not a
entity, and the 'contact of a straight line with a circle' is not
a quantity either (p. 41).

26/39   *The Subject ... Faculties*: More's denial of the mind's ability to
apprehend the essence of things seems to be a shift from his
earlier position in 'Antipsychopannychia' II, 22ff, where he
had insisted on the "innate *idee*/ Essentiall forms created
with the mind" (29). But it is not so certain that these
innate ideas that the mind contains are of the 'substance' of
things as much as of the "forms" or "shapes" of external
objects:
> ...If she doth not ken
> These shapes that flow from distant objects,then
> How can she know those objects?
>
> (31)

His later examples of innate ideas are of universal common
notions such as those of geometrical relations and qualities
(37-38). In the 'Interpretation Generall' to the 1647 edition
of *A Platonick Song of the Soul*, he describes 'Innate Idees' as
"the soul's nature it self, her uniform essence, able by her
Fiat to produce this or that phantasm," where the
representational quality of the innate ideas is to be noted as
well as the representing activity of the soul (see also Note to
p.56,l.18).

Shortly after the publication of *A Platonick Song*, in his
letter of 5 March 1649 to Descartes, More points to the
inscrutability of essences, "radix rerum omnium ac essentia
in aeternas defossa lateat tenebras" [the root and essence of
all things is hidden and buried in eternal darkness]. In the
present axiom, it is important to note that, while denying the
apprehension of 'things in themselves', More yet declares
that the mind possesses the "*Idea*" of an undiversificated
substance -- only, the idea is, in this case, an undifferentiated
one. In fact, by More's logic, the essence of things is the
same as the essence of the mind itself, which , too, is
ultimately an undiversificated substance. It is only when we
recognize the 'immediate' attributes of spirit and matter (*viz.*
penetrability/   indiscerpibility   and   impenetrability/

discerpibility) that we obtain distinct ideas, or representations, of them.

28/13   *Spissitude*: orginally, density or corpactness

29/15   *Pythagoras*: Iamblichus of Chalcis, *Vita Pythagorica*, Ch 28[M]: Iambl ichus gives this story as an example of the marvellous virtues possessed by Pythagoras: 'once passing over the river Nessus with many of his associates, he spoke to it, and the river in a distinct and clear voice, in the hearing of all his followers, answered, "Hail Pythagoras!"' (Tr.Thomas Taylor, *Iamblichus' Life of Pythagoras*, London, 1818). Iamblichus of Chalcis (ca. 250-325 A.D.) studied under Porphyry in Ro me, or Sicily, and later founded his own School in Syria. As a Neoplatonist he emphasized theurgy rather than the Plotinian ecstasy as a means of achieving enlightenment. His Περὶ πυϑαγόρου αἱρέσεως was an elaborate exposition of Pythagorean philosophy meant as a preparation for the study of Plato. In the Περὶ μυστηρίων Iamblichus defended the divine origin of Egyptian and Chaldean theology.

29/17   *Apollonius*: Flavius Philostratus, *Vita Apollonii*, Bk VI [M] Ch 10: '"Heigh! You tree yonder," he cried, pointing to an elm tree, the third in the row from that under which they were talklng, "just salute the wise Apollonius, will you?" And forthwith the tree saluted him, as it was bidden to do, in accents which were articulate and like those of a woman.'(Tr. F. C. Conybeare, Loeb Classical Liorary) The story of Apollonius -- a sage who had lived a century before Philo-stratus -- being saluted by a tree at the command of Thespasian, the head of the gymnosophists of Ethiopia, whom the sage was visiting, is a strange example to give of supernatural powers, for Thespasian, in this meeting with Apollonius, actually derides tricks of this sort, in order to dissuade the latter from excessive admiration of the wonder-working powers of the Indian sages whom he venerated above all others.
Philostratus (ca. 170-247 A.D.) studied at Athens and later joined the philosophical circle patronized by Septimus Severus and his wife, Julia Domna. It was at her insistence that he wrote the life of Apollonius of Tyana.

32/2   λόγοι σπερματικοί: The term is originally Stoic in conception and appears in, among other works, Antoninus, IV, 14 and 21.

34/12   though... them: 'See Book 3, Ch. 12, and 13' [M].

34/14   Antidote: 'Book I, ch. 4, sect. 3' [M].

35/10   Those: 'See further in my *Antidote*, Bk I, ch. 4, sect.2. Also the *Append[ix]* chap. 3 *ad* 10' [M].

35/19   elsewhere: '*Append[ix]* c. 3 [not 13 as More indicates], sect. 2 [M].

35/25   *Scaliger: Exercitationes Exotericarum,*Exer. CCC. More is probably thinking of this passage:. 'At nullo infinitas successione infinita est. Quin habet multos fines: et quovis momento temporis finiuntur. Quin hoc ipsum infinitum sub sua cognoscitur ratione: quia cognoscitur non finiri. Sic lineam, cuius finem non videt oculus: hoc ipsa de caussa cognoscit hoc, quod cognoscere non potest: scilicet infinitatem.
[No infinity is such by succession, for it would have many terminations and end at any moment of time. This Infinity is apprehended by one's reason for it is *known* not to finish -- for example, a line whose end is not visible. Thus, what cannot be really apprehended - namely, infinity - is apprehended causally.]

37/12   Besides ... *Indiscerpible*: This criticism of the mathematical point was made even by Plato, according to Aristotle, *Metaphysica*, 992a.

37/30   in Magnitude ... great: cf.the Greek quotation from *Ethica Nichomachea* in Sec. 4 below.

38/2   Now... *in infinitum*: cf. *An Appendix to the foregoing Antidote*, chap 1 sect.4[M]. More here elaborates on the priority of motion to matter: 'But you'l say that this *Matter* that moved *ab Aeterno* was moved of *it self*. Be it so, yet no part of it can move in this full Ocean of *Matter* that is excluded out of no space, but it must hit some other part of matter so soon as it moves, and that another, and so on. And thus there might be a *Succession* of Motions *ab Aeterno* or *infinite*, and yet a *first* in order of causality. For that primordial Motion of the *Matter* is plainly first and cause of all the rest.'

39/42   transcursion: permeation.

40/5   Aristotle: *Ethica Nichomachea*, X, 7 [M]: 'For though this be small in bulk, in power and value it far surpasses all the rest.' (Tr. H. Rackham, Loeb Classical Library). More's use of Aristotle's conception of the mind is significant since he, like Aristotle, (ϑεῖον ὁ νοῦς πρὸς τὸν ἄνϑρωπον) considers it to be divine. However, More's mathematical elaboration of the power of spirit in Axiom 19 is far beyond Aristotle's intentions in the last book of his *Ethica*.

45/7   competible: applicable

45/25   Appendix... Antidote: Chap 3, sect. 7 and 8 [M]: In first examining the reason why there is 'in some kindes of matter almost an invincible union of parts, as in steel, adamant, and the like,' More suggests, 'If you'l say some inward substantial form, we have what we look'd for, a substance distinct from the matter,' thereby revealing the affinity of his conception of spirit to the Aristotelian form. But his spirit is a real substance and the penetration of matter by spirit is explained by its ὑλοπάϑια which he defines as 'A power in a Spirit of offering so near to a corporeal emanation from the center of life, that it will so perfectly fill the receptivity of matter into which it has penetrated, that it is very difficult or impossible for any other spirit to possess the same, and therefore of becoming hereby so firmly and closely united to a body as both to actuate and to be acted upon, to affect and be affected thereby. The difference between the *union* of matter and Spirit and the *conjunction* of matter and matter is that the former 'pervades through all' whereas the latter 'is only in a common superficies.' What is more interesting is that More declares this 'hylopathia' in a finite spirit or soul to be analogous to 'that power of creating matter which is necessarily included in the idea of God.' (See Bk I, ch 4, sect. 3). More is obviously careful to reserve for God a special

position distinct from the other spirits, but his definition of
God in Bk. I, Ch. 4, sect. 2 as 'a *Spirit* Eternal, infinite in
Essence' makes us wonder why the process of 'creation' must
be different in any way from the 'emanation ' peculiar to
spirits except in the duration and extent of the resulting
substances. This is confirmed, I think, indirectly by More's
earlier differentiation of the two phenomena in the *Appendix*,
Ch. 3, sect. 3: 'both the central and secondary substance of a
spirit were created at once by God and ... these free active
spirits have only a power in them of contracting their vital
rays and dilating of them, not of annihilating or creating of
them. This juxtaposition of annihilating and creating to
contracting and dilating shows that creation differs from
emanation only in range of activity rather than in kind.

46/39   ἰδέα *possibilis*:   possible idea.

47/18   if ... *Particular*:   'See Book 3, Ch. 12,   13' [M].

50/21   *Leviathan*:   'Chap. 34' [M].

51/1   *Physicks*:   'Part 4, chap. 25,   Article 9' [M].

51/16   the same Book: 'Part 1, chap. 5, Article 4' [M].

51/21   Humane Nature: 'Chap. 11, Article 4 [M].

51/31   Excerption: excerpt

51/32   Leviathan: *'Leviathan*, chap. 12' [M].

52/8   Humane Nature: 'Chap 11, Article 5' [M].

52/14   Chap 45: *'Leviathan*, chap 45' [M].

52/36   the same book: *'Leviathan*, chap 46' [M].

54/2   Ambages: *circumlocutions*

54/34   but ...Beings: 'See my *Antidote against Atheism*, the whole
        second Book' [M].

54/41   *Apparitions*: 'See my *Antidote*, the whole third Book.' [M].

55/5   *Operations* ... Soul: '*Antid[ote]*, Book I, chap. 11' [M].

55/33   my Letters ... *Des-Cartes*: More, *Epistolae Quatuor Henrici Mori ad Renatum Descartes*, especially Epist. Prima,11 December 1648: Quod aliam innuit materiae sive corporis conditionem, quam appellare poteris impenetrabilitatem nempe, quod nec penetrare alia corpora, nec ab illis penetrari possit. Unde manifestissisum est discrimen inter Naturam divinam ac corpoream, cum illa hanc, haec vero seipsam penetrare non possit.
[This reveals another condition of matter or body, which you might call impenetrability, in that it cannot penetrate the bodies nor be penetrated by them. Whence the difference between Divine nature and corporeal is evident, for the former can penetrate bodies but the latter cannot indeed penetrate itself.]

55/35   present Treatise: 'Book I, ch 2 &   3' [M].

56/18   I have: In *Antidote*, Book I, ch.6 and *Appendix*, ch.2, sect.4, 5, 6, etc.[M]: Both these sections give several Socratic examples of relative notions as well as mathematical ones such as cause and effect, like and unlike, whole and part, etc., which are 'no external Impresses upon the Senses, but the Souls own active manner of conceiving those things which are discovered by the outward Senses' (*Antidote*, Bk I, Ch 6, sect. 4). The transformation of Platonic innate ideas into innate ideational activity in More is easily explained by More's emphasis on the self-motion of the soul (see my Introduction, p.lvi).

56/18   its due place: 'Book 2, ch 2, sect 9,10,11' [M].

56/40   eminency ... *Politicks*: Hobbes, *Elements of Philosophy*, Epistle Dedicatory: After briefly tracing the development of the sciences, mathematical, physical and physiological, from Greek antiquity to 'the College of Physicians in London,' Hobbes adds: 'Natural Philosophy is therefore but young; but Civil Philosophy yet much younger, as being no older ... than my own book *De Cive*.'

58/6   *Hobbs: Elements of Philosophy*, part II, Ch 8, Art 5: ' That
        space, by which I have understand imaginary space, which is
        coincident with the magnitude of any body, is called the *place*
        of that body.'

58/33   Plato: *Timaeus*,35a. More's quotation seems to be a
        condensation of this passage: τῆς ἀμερίστου καὶ ἀεὶ κατὰ
        ταὐτὰ ἐχούσης οὐσίας καὶ τῆς αὖ περὶ τὰ σώματα γιγνομένης
        μεριστῆς, τρίτον ἐξ ἀμφοῖν ἐν μέσωι συνεκεράσατο οὐσίας
        εἶδος, τῆς τε ταὐτοῦ φύσεως [αὖ περὶ] καὶ τῆς θατέρου, καὶ
        κατα ταὐτὰ ξυνέστησεν ἐν μέσωι τοῦ τε ἀμεροῦς αὐτῶν καὶ
        τοῦ κατὰ τὰ σώματα μεριστοῦ.
        [Midway between the Being which is indivisible and remains
        always the same and the Being which is transient and
        divisible in bodies, He blended a third form of Being
        compounded out of the twain, that is to say, out of the Same
        and the Other; and in like manner He compounded it midway
        between that one of them which is indivisible and that one
        which is divisible in bodies. (Tr. R.G. Bury, Loeb Classical
        Library)]
        cf. also Plotinus, *Enneades*, IV, ii, 1.

59/36   *Antidote*: Book 1, chap 7, 8 [M]. More develops in these two
        chapters his rational notion of God and the necessity of his
        existence respectively.

61/19   This matter ... entire: This is the view held by Descartes in
        Principia ,II, 40. 'Si un corps qui se meut en rencontre un
        autre plus fort que soi, il ne perd rien de son mouvement, et
        s'il en rencontre un plus faible qu' il puisse mouvoir, il en
        perd autant qu' il lui en donne.'

63/24   *Numen*: divine power or presence

64/6   *Antidote*: Book 2, ch 2, sect 8 [M]: More gives as an example
        of the impossibility of any matter, even air, being endowed
        with reason two experiments (the second and thirty-second)
        recorded by Robert Boyle in his *New Experiments Physico-
        Mechanical touching the air*, (Oxford, 1660): 'For whereas in
        the first of those Experiments, the Brass Key or Stopple of
        the Cover of the Receiver, after the Receiver is emptied well

of Aire is with much difficulty lifted up; and in the other, if
you apply a tapering Valve of brass to the lower branch of
the Stop-cock of the Receiver well emptied of Aire, as before,
and turn the key of the Stop-cock, the external Aire beating
like a forcible stream upon the Valve to get in there, will
suddenly both shut the Valve, and keep it shut so strongly,
that it will bear up with it a ten-pound weight ... it is
apparent from hence that neither the Aire it self, nor any
more *subtile* and *Divine* Matter (which is more throngly
congregated together in the Receiver upon the pumping out of
the Aire) has any *freedome of will*, or any *knowledge* or
perception to doe any thing, they being so puzzel'd and acting
so fondly and preposterously in their endeavours to replenish
the Receiver again with Aire.'

64/10   More's use of motion as an evidence of "*some incorporeal
Essence distinct from the Matter*" (Ch 12, sec 1) is due to his
reification of motion as spirit (see my Introduction p.liv).

65/24   *Elements*: Chap 25 [M] Art 2: 'Sense, therefore, in the
sentient, can be nothing else but motion in some of the
internal parts of the sentient; and the parts so moved are
parts of the sentient; and the parts so moved are parts of the
organs of sense.'

66/3   *Compages*: the compaction of parts into a whole.

66/38   Mr. *Hobbs*: see *Leviathan*, Part I, Ch.12.

68/5   tergiversations: equivocations

68/33   *Aristotle: Metaphysica*, XII, 8, 1073a: ὁρῶμεν δὲ παρὰ τὴν
τοῦ παντὸς τὴν ἀπλῆν φοράν.ἣν κινεῖν φαμὲν τὴν πρώτην
οὐσίαν καὶ ἀκίνητον. ἄλλας φορὰς οὔσας τὰς τῶν πλανήτων
ἀϊδίους ... ἀνάγκη καὶ τούτων ἑκάστην τῶν φορῶν ὑπ'
ἀκινήτου τε κινεῖσθαι καθ' αὐτὴν καὶ ἀϊδίου οὐσίας.
[Since we can see that besides the simple spatial motion of
the universe (which we hold to be excited by the primary
immovable substance) there are other spatial motions ...
those of the planets are eternal ... then each of these spatial
motions must also be excited by a substance which is
essentially immovable and eternal. (Tr. G.C. Armstrong)]

cf. also *De Coelo*, II, xii, 292a: δεῖ δ᾽ ὡς μετεχόντων
ὑπολαμβάνειν πράξεως καὶ ζωῆς.
[The fact is that we must consider them as partaking of life
and act (Tr. G.C. Armstrong, Loeb Classical Library)]

68/33   *Avenroes*: Averroes (See Note to Preface, sect. 10, above) held
that there are many Intelligences and that their number and
rank are determined by the number and physical conditions
(i.e. the size and speed) of the celestial bodies they move (cf.
De Substantia orbis and his commentaries on Aristotle's
Metaphysica and *De Coelo*).

69/3   Sadducees: The Sadducees were a conservative Jewish
priestly sect that flourished for about two centuries before the
destruction of the Second Temple in 70 A.D. They were
doctrinally opposed to the Pharisees and the Essenes, and
refused to go beyond the written Torah. Thus they denied the
immortality of the soul (cf. Josephus, *Antiquities of the Jews*,
Bk I, Ch. Art 4), the resurrection of the body, and the
existence of angels and spirits (cf. Acts: 23, 8). They
probably subscribed to a literal interpretation of Gen II: 3
and Eccl. XII: 7,which distinguish the spirit from the soul so
that while the latter constitutes the individual personality of
the body, the former is a continuous breath of life from God
which, on death, returns to its source without bearing the
traces of any personal individuation. More's reference to the
Sadducees is misleading since he uses the term to mean
materialists in general. More's association of the Sadducees
with the Epicureans may be traced back to John Smith's
treatise 'Of the Immortality of the Soul' (*Select Discourses*
,ed. J. Worthington, London, 1660, Sig. I2): "For the
Sadducees, the Jewish writers are wont commonly to reckon
them among the *Epicureans*, because though they had a God,
yet they denied the *Immortality of mens Souls*. " Interestingly,
More's view of the soul corresponds rather closely to the
belief of the Epicureans that apparitions are produced by the
aerial fusion of the delicate ἀπόρροιαὶ or images that are
constantly emitted by bodies.(cf. Lucretius, *De Rerum Natura*,
Bk IV, 724-748, and More, 'The Praeexistency of the Soul',
18-29.)

69/9   this ... treatise: 'Book 3, Ch. 16[M].

69/10   *Influenciaries*: objects or persons that exercise influence. The OED gives More's use here as the only example of the term.

69/31   *Namque ... orbis*: Virgil, *Eclogues*, 6 [M], ll. 31-34: This eclogue begins with a description of the encounter between the shepherds, Chromis and Mnasylus and the old satyr, Silenus. When the shepherds find Silenus besotted with wine, they bind him with his own garlands hoping to obtain a song from him. They succeed in their endeavour and Silenus sings to them of the formation of the world according to the Epicurean philosophy: ' For he sang how, through the great void, were brought together the seeds of earth, and air, and sea, and streaming fire withal; how from these elements came all beginnings and even the young globe of the world grew unto a mass.' (Tr. H.R. Fairclough, Loeb Classical Library)
cf. Lucretius, *De Rerum Natura*, Bk II, 11. 184 ff.

70/32   *Pomponatius: De Immortalitate Animae*, Ch 14 [M]: Pomponazzi, following Aristotle (*Metaphysica*, XII, 8) and Alexander of Aphrodisias *(De Fato)* maintains that all Intelligences necessarily move spheres and that they can thus produce miracles using these heavenly bodies as their instruments: 'Neque mirandum est si talia a corporibus coelestibus figurari possunt, cum animata sint nobilissima anima. quaeque omnia inferiora generent et gubernent.' Pomponazzi goes on to defend the Peripatetic notion of natal stars against the demonology of the Platonists: 'Quodque Platonici genium sive demonem familiarem appellant, apud Peripateticos est eius genitura: quia talis natus est cum tali constellatione. ille vero cum alia. Si sine illa multiplicatione daemonum et geniorum salvare possumus. supervacaneum videtur illa ponere: cum hoc quod illa etiam rationi non consonat.'
[And what the Platonists call the genius or familiar demon, is with the Peripatetics his natal star; because such a man is born under such a constellation, but another under another. If we can do without that multiplication of demons and genii, it seems superfluous to assume them; besides the fact that it is also contrary to reason.(Tr. W.H.Hay II)]

More not only denies any possibility of stellar influence on human action (Bk I, Ch 14) but also develops his own sophisticated version of Neoplatonist demonology (Bk. III, *passim*).

71/16   *Increpation*: Reproof

71/27   *Paracelsus*: See More, *Enthusiasmus Triumphatus*, sect 45 [M]: The whole of this section is a catalogue of the various powers attributed to the stars by Paracelsus who maintained 'that a man has a sydereall body besides this terrestriall which is joyned with the Stars; and so when this body is more free from the Elements, as in sleep, this body and the stars confabulating together, the Mind is informed of things to come.

That the Stars are struck with terrour or horrour of the approach of any mans death, Whence it is that no man dies without some sign or notice from them, as the *dances of dead men*, some *noise in the house*, or the like.'
cf. Paracelsus, *Explicatio Totius Astronomiae*,'Probatio in *Scientiam Divinationis*': Quicquid enim vivit, Spiritum sydereum in se continet et ubicunque operationes sunt, ibi manifestantur ... Iam, vero nullus hominum moritur, nisi id per praegressos prodromos aut signa praeindicetur. Si enim moriturus homo est, tunc Sidus in ipso suam operationem perdit, et perdito seu amissio illa fit per Signum et magnam mutationem ... Sic mortuorum salsationes visae, Luridem futuram pestem indicrunt. In domibus non-nullis interdum etiam audiuntur, qui instar hominum laborent ac operentur, Paulo post obire solent illi qui similia opificia exercent. Et sciat hoc loco homo illa minima esse spectra, sed operationes naturales, quae taliterin hominibus per astra perficiantur.
Paracelsus, the pseudonym of Theophrastus Philipus Aureolus Bombastus von Hohenheim (ca.1493-1541) was a German doctor and alchemist whose anti-Galenic approach to medicine paved the way for many modern medical concepts. In his vitalistic natural philsophy, the *astra* denoted not only the stars but also the essential virtues of individual objects which shared specific qualities with their celestial counterparts. One of Paracelsus' principal works was the *Opus Paramirum*, while the *Archidoxis* (published posthumously around 1570) was an important handbook of

Paracelesian chemistry.

72/32   cogitabundly: thoughtfully

74/3   *Alcibiades* his Patrimony, Aelian, *Varia Historia*, III, 28:
         ὁρῶν ὁ Σωκράτης τὸν Ἀλκιβίαδην τετυφωμένον ἐπὶ τῶι
         πλούτωι, καὶ μέγα φρονοῦντα ἐπὶ τῆι περιουσίαι καὶ ἔτι
         πλέον ἐπὶ τοῖς ἀγροῖς, ἤγαγεν αὐτον εἴς τινα τῆς πόλεως
         τόπον,ἔνϑα ἀνέκειτο πινάκιον ἔχον γῆς περίοδον, καὶ
         προσέταξε τῶι Ἀλκβιάδηι τὴν Ἀττικὴν ἐνταῦϑ᾽ ἀναζητεῖν.Ὡς
         δ᾽ εὗρε προσέταξεν αὐτῶι τοὺς ἀγροὺσ τοὺς ἰδίους διαϑρῆσαι.
         τού δε εἰπόωτος, Ἀλλ᾽ οὐδαμοῦ γεγραμμένοι εἰσίν, ἐπὶ τούτοις
         οὖν, εἶπε, μέγα φρονεῖς οἵπερ οὐδὲν μέρος τῆς γῆς εἰσίν;
         [Seeing Alcibiades conceited on account of his wealth and
         lands, Socr ates led him to a certain part of the city where
         there was a tablet with a map of the world, and asked
         Alcibiades to look for Athens in it. When he had found it, he
         asked him to trace the extent of his estates, and Alcibiades
         said , "But they are not depicted here: " To which Socrates
         replied, "Do you then pride yourself so on that which forms
         no part of the earth?"]

74/9   *Lansbergius*: Phillipe van Lansberge, *Uranometriae*, Bk II.,
         Elementum 12: 'Sol major est terra quadrigenties et trigesies
         quater fere. Luna autem est sole minor deciesnonies millies,
         septingenties et septuagesies.'
         [The sun is almost 434 times larger than the earth. The
         moon, however, is 19,770 times smaller than the sun.]
         Philippe van Lansberge (1561-1632) was a mathematician
         and astronomer whose works include *Cyclometriae* (1616),
         Triangulorum geometriae (1631), *Commutationes in motum
         terrae diurnum et annum* (1630) and *Tabulae motuum
         coelestium perpetuae (1630).*

75/17   fridging: rubbing

75/30   already: 'Chap 12, sect 4,5.'[M].

76/11   *in rerum Naturâ*: in the nature of things

Book II

78/14 Elements: 'Chap 25, Artic 2' [M]. See Note to Bk. I, Ch. 12, sect 3
       above.

79/12 its due place: 'Chap 6, sect 4, 5, 6'[M].

80/3   which ... Godhead: 'See Book 4, Ch 11, sect 8' [M].

80/11 Demonstration: 'See Preface, sect. 5' [M].

80/34 Antidote: 'Book 2, ch 2, sect 8' [M].

80/37 already: 'Book I, ch 6' [M].

83/6   Meteors: Descartes, *Les Météores*, Discours huitième, Article
       4,5,6,7, 8[M]: where he describes light as being due to
       'l'action ou le mouvement d'une certaine matière fort subtile,
       dont il faut imaginer les parties ainsi que de petites boules
       qui roulent dans les pores des corps terrestres ...' Similarly,
       the nature of colours 'ne consiste qu'en ce que les parties de
       la matière subtile, qui transmet l'action de la lumière,
       tendent a tournoyer avec plus de force qu'a se mouvoir en
       ligne droite; en sorte que celles qui tendent à tourner
       beaucoup plus fort causent la couleur rouge et celles qui n'y
       tendent qu'un peu plus fort causent le jaune.' cf. also, the
       more detailed explanation in La Dioptrique, Discours
       premier.

86/23 *Principia*: Descartes, *Principia Philosophiae*, II [not I as More
       indicates] 37 [M]: 'Prima lex naturae: quid unaquaeque res,
       quantum in se est, semper in eodem statu perseveret, sicque
       quod semel movetur, semper moveri pergat. '
       [The first law of nature is that every thing as far as it can,
       continues in the state in which it is always and what is once
       moved continues to move always.]

87/17 *Catochus*: catalepsy

87/27 Hobbs: 'See his *Elements of Philosophy*, Chap 25, Article
       5'[M]: 'B ut though all sense, as I have said, be made by
       reaction, nevertheless it is not necessary that every thing

that reacteth should have sense unless those bodies had organs, as living creatures have, fit for the retaining of such motion as is made in them, their sense would be such, as that they should never remember the same.'

87/37   his philosophie: Hobbes,*op.cit.*, Ch 25, Artic 7, 8 [M]: *'Imagination* therefore is nothing else but *sense decaying, or weakened,* by the absence of the object.'

88/15   τὸ αὐτεξούσιον: freedom of choice. cf. Plotinus, *Enneades*, II, ii, 10, and Proclus, *In Platonis Alcibiadem*, 143 c.

89/1   Bullet: 'A small round ball'(OED).

89/2   Spur-rowels: 'the rowel or revolving pricking wheel of a spur' (OED).

89/23   it may be: 'But why it may not be something is suggested in the fore - going chapter, sect. 3[M].

89/26   Whence ... perception: cf. Galen, *De Placitis Hippocratis et Platonis*, Bk 7, 606: ἐκ τούτῶν οὖν τῶν φαινομένων, ἴσως ἄν τις ὑπονήσειε τὸ κατὰ τὰς κοιλίας τοῦ ἐγκεφάλου πνεῦμα δυοῖν θάτερον, εἰ μὲν ἀσώματος ἐστιν ἡ ψυχή, τὸ πρῶτον αὐτῆς ὑπάρχειν, ὡς ἂν εἴποι τισ, οἰκητήριον, εἰ δὲ σῶμα, τοῦτο αὐτὸ τὸ πνεῦμα τὴν ψυχὴν εἶναι.
[From these phenomena it is possible to infer one of two things: either the soul is incorporeal and that spirit which is contained in the ventricle of the brain is its principal habitation, or else it is corporeal and that very spirit is the soul].

92/30   *Similitudo* and ὁμοιτης, ἀναλογία and *Proportio*, λόγος and *Ratio*: Greek and Latin terms for similitude, proportion, and reason.

97/17   Illation: Inference

98/25   lank: hollow

99/6   captiositie: Sophistry

99/13   *Quicquid ... esse*: Whatever is, as long as it is, must necessarily be.

100/14   *Cras Socrates disputabit*: Tomorrow Socrates will dispute.

100/25   *Aristotle*: see *De Interpretatione*, 9: ὁρῶμεν γὰρ ὅτι ἔστιν ἀρχὴ τῶν ἐσομένων καὶ ἀπὸ τοῦ βουλεύσθαι καὶ τοῦ πρᾶξαί τι, καὶ ὅτι ὅλως ἔστιν ἐν τοῖς μὴ ἀεὶ ἐνεργοῦσι τὸ δυνατὸν εἶναι, καὶ μὴ ὁμοίως· ἐν οἷς ἄμφω ἐνδέχεται, καὶ τὸ εἶναι καὶ τὸ μὴ εἶναι, ὥστε καὶ τὸ γενέσθαι καὶ τὸ μὴ γενέσθαι ... φανερὸν ἄρα ὅτι οὐκ ἄπαντα ἐξ ἀνάγκης οὔτ ἔστιν οὔτε γίνεται.
[We know from our personal existence that future events may depend on the counsel and actions of men, and that speaking more broadly, those things that are not uninterruptedly actual exhibit a potentiality, that is, a "may or may not be". If such things may be or may not be, events may take place or may not ... thus it is clear that not everything is or takes place of necessity. (Tr. H.P. Cooke, Loeb Classical Library)]

103/7   *External Sense* See chap.1, sect. 8,9,10,11,12,13,14 and Chap.2, sect 3,4,5,6'[M].

104/38   the *Arabians*: This was the doctrine of the 10th c. Neophythagorean sect called the Brethren of Purity (Ikhwan al-Safa) whose major philosophical document is the *Epistles* (*Rasa-il*). See Ikhwan-al-safa, *Rasa-il*, Beirut, 1957, vol. II, pp. 189f.

105/2   *Antidote*: Book I, Ch 11, sect 5,6,7 [M]: More dismisses the possibility of the physical substance of the brain being capable of reason, imagination, and spontaneous motion on account of the fact that the softness of the brain implies that 'it is in some measure *liquid*, and *liquidity* implies a severall *Motion* of loosned parts.' (Sect. 7) This being so, the faculty of active intellection must reside either in one of its parts or in all of them together. The former results in the absurdity of many contending animadversions that render both the unity of thought and the direction of animal spirits under a common impulse extremely difficult . The latter contradicts the phenomenon of memory as there will be no 'distinct Notes and places for the several *Species* of things there represented.' (Sect. 5)

105/15   *Septum lucidum*: This is the opinion of Sir Kenelm Digby, cf.
Two Treatises, ('The Nature of Bodies') Ch. 35: '[The brain]
containeth, towards the middle of its substance, foure
concavities, as some do count them; but in truth, these foure,
are but one great cavity, in which, foure, as it were, divers
roomes, may be distinguished ... Now, two roomes of this
great concavity, are divided by a little body, somewhat like a
skinne (though more fryable) which of it selfe is cleere; but
there it is somewhat dimmed, by reason that hanging a little
slacke, it somewhat shriveleth together, and this,
Anatomistes do call *Septum lucidum*, or *Speculum*; and is a
different body from all the rest that are in the braine. This
transparent body, layeth as it were straightwardes, from the
forehead towards the hinder part of the head, and divideth
the hollow of the braine, as farre as it reacheth, into the
right and the left ventricles.

This part seemeth to me ... to be that, and only that, in
which the fansie or common sense resideth, though Monsieur
des Cartes hath rather chosen a kernell to place it in.'
Sir Kenelm Digby (1603-65) was educated at Oxford and
spent most of his life travelling in Europe. He settled in
France, where he met Hobbes, Mersenne, and corresponded
with Descartes (whom he met in Holland). Digby was both
an occultist and a natural philosopher and apart from the
Aristotelian *Two Treatises, in one of which, the Nature of
Bodies; in the other, the Nature of Mans Soule, is looked into in
way of discovery, of the immortality of Reasonable Soules*
(1644), his most popular work was the *Discours fait en une
célèbre assemblé par le Chevalier Digby ... touchant la guérison
des playes par le poudre de sympathie (1658).*

105/19   *Regius*: Henri de Roy, *Philosophia Naturalis*, Bk V,Ch 1[M]:
'Cum mens humana, ut jam patet, sit substantia incorporea
sive non extensa, eaque in solo sensoria communi, quae est
parva quaedam cerebri particula, antehac designata,
actiones cogitativas immediate exerceat; cumque ea ex nullis
effectis, in ulla alia corporis humani parte se prodat (nam
alitura, ut et generatio, a solo corpore humano peragitur)
nulla est causa cuream in ulla alia parte, quam in solo
sensorio communi, existere ullamque extensionem ibi habere

statuamus.'
[We declare that the human mind, as has been made clear, is
an incorporeal substance, and unextended, and exercises its
cogitative actions immediately from a single common
sensorium, which is a small particle of the brain designated
above. And since it, on no account, extends itself in any
other part of the human body (for nourishment and generation are effected solely through the body), there is no reason
for it to exist in any other part but in the common sensorium
and have any extension except in that place.]
This 'small particle of the brain' is earlier in the same
chapter referred to as a 'minima atomus' characterized by its
'parvitatem et soliditatem.'
Henri de Roy (1598-1679) was Professor of medicine and
botany at the University of Utrecht and for some time an
ardent disciple of Descartes. His scientific and philosophical
works include the *Fundamenta Physices* (1646), *Brevis
explicatio mentis humunae,sive animae rationalis* (1657) as
well as the comprehensive *Philosophia Naturalis* (1661).

105/31   *Conarion*: the *glandula pinealis* situated behind the third
         ventricle of the brain. The term is derived from κωνάριον,
         'little pine cone.'

105/31   *Des-Cartes*: Descartes, *La Dioptrique*, Discours cinquième,
         Article 3 [M]: 'Et de là je pourrais encore la [l'image d'un
         object] transporter jusques à une certaine petite glande, qui
         se trouve environ le milieu de ces concavités, et est
         proprement le siège du sens commun.'
         Also, *Les Passions de l'âme*, Première partie, Artic.11-16[M]
         detail the different ways in which the animal spirits, with or
         without the help of the *conarion*, produce spontaneous
         motion.

106/24   For ... *double*: Descartes,*op. cit.*, Première partie, Artic.32
         [M]

106/34   Moreover ... removed: Descartes, *op. cit.*, Première partie,
         Artic. 21
            [M].

107/19   in ... *Soul*: Descartes, op. cit., Première partie, Artic.35[M].

107/22   Whence ... thereof: See Book 2, ch 2, sect 6 [M].

107/36   that ... thereof: 'See the *Appendix* to my *Antidote*, ch 10, sect
         6' [M]: More concludes this section dealing with the debility
         of the conarion with the reminder that 'in *Motion corporeal* it
         is an acknowledged Maxime, "*Whatever is moved, is first
         moved by another.*" So demonstrable is it every way that the
         first principle of our *spontaneous motion* is not nor can be
         seated in any part of our *Body*, but in a substance really
         distinct from it, which men ordinarily call the Soul.'

108/24   *Regius*: Henry de Roy, *Philosophia Naturalis*, Bk IV, Ch 17
         (not 16 as More indicates) [M].

108/26   *Des-Cartes*: Descartes, *op. cit.*, Première partie, Artic. 11 [M].

109/30   *Des-Cartes*: Descartes, *op. cit.*, Première partie , Artic. 42
         [M].

110/26   how ... upwards: Descartes, *op. cit.*, Première partie , artic.
         43 [M]

110/30   already: Chap 2, sect 8[M].

110/39   *Cogitations*: Descartes, *op. cit.*, Première partie, Artic. 17,18
         [M].

111/6   He distinguishes ... Body: *Ibid.*, Artic 19,20[M].

111/11   Imagination ... *Conarion: Ibid.*, Artic 21 [M].

111/17   *Perceptions ... Nerves: Ibid.*, Artic 22-25 [M].

111/22   *Perceptions* ... Cause: *Ibid.*, Artic 19-20, 42 [M].

111/32   he holds: Descartes, *Discours de la méthode*, Artic. 5 and
         Passions, Première partie, Artic. 16 [M].

112/1   vellication: irritation or stimulation by means of small or
         sharp points.

112/1   Tunicles: membranes enclosing bodily organs.

113/25   before: Chap. 2, sec. 3,4,5,6,7,8. [M].

114/20   as if ... *cano*: The two verses that More uses here are the opening lines of the *Iliad* and the *Aeneid* respectively.

115/12   colourable: plausible

115/41   *dissipability*: capability of being disintegrated or scattered. The OED gives More's use of the term here as a unique example.

118/35   *Van-Helmont*'s Opinion: Jan Baptista van Helmont, *de Sede Animae [M]* Art 6: 'Creator (cui sit omnis honos) servavit quendam progressum a simili, qui nos animae solium instruit, ut a crassioribus consideremus magis abstracta. Etenim cernitur in arbore (argumentum ab arbore peculiariter desumtum ob praerogativam arboris vitae) radix, initium vitale sui. Si quidem in radice, velut culina, peregrinus succus terrae cognitur, alteratur, a pristina simplicitate aquae alienatur, subitque dispositionem fermenti vitalis, ibidem locati. Coctus autem unde distribuitur, ut magis magisque cognatur, simile evadat, juxta ulterioris eujusque coquinae necessitatem, quae inhabitanti spiritui sanxit leges. Sic in hominis medio corporis trunco est stomachus, quinedum saccus vel pera est, ut ciborum olla: Sed stomacho, praesertim ejus Orifico, tanquam centrali puncto, atque radice, stabilitur evidentissime principium vitae, digestionis ciborum et dispositionis eorundem ad vitam.'
[The creator (to whom all honour) hath kept a certain progress from a like thing, who instructs as in the seat-royal of the soul, that from the more grosse things we may consider more abstracted. For in a tree (an argument is peculiarly drawn from a tree, by reason of the prerogative of the Tree of Life) is seen a root, the vital beginning of itself. For truly,in the root as it were in a kitchin, a foreign juyce of the earth is cocted, altered, is alienated from its simplicity of water, and undergoes the disposition of a vital ferment there placed. But being cocted, it is distributed from thence, that it may more and more be constrained, and become like, according to the

necessity of every further cookroom, which hath established lawes for the spirit inhabiting. So in the middle trunck of the body of man is the stomach which is not onely the sack or scrip, or the pot of the food; but in the stomach, especially in its orifice or upper mouth, as it were in a central point and root, is the principle of life, of the digestion of meals, and the disposing of the same unto life, most evidently established.(Tr. J.C., *Van Helmont's Works*, London, 1664)]

Jan Baptista van Helmont (1579-1644) was a Flemish physician and chemist who first formulated the chemistry of gases and physiological chemistry . Influenced by Neoplatonism and Paracelsian science, Helmont's physiology was that of an iatrochemist. He believed that life results from a vegetative soul (*archaeus influus*) and every organ of the body has it own *archaeus insitus* that determines its special function. His collected works were edited posthumously by his son, Frans Mercurius, as *Ortus Medicinae* (1684).

119/12   *Des-Cartes*: Descartes, *Passions*, Première partie, Art 33.

119/20   *Pathemata:*   παθήματα, pains

119/23   καρδιαλγία and καρδωγμοὶ: pains and aches of the heart

19/39   lethiferous: lethal

120/6   Hobbs: Hobbes, *Elements of Philosophy*, Part 4, ch 25, artic 4[M]: 'Now these parts [the instruments of sense] in the most of living creatures are found to be certain spirits and membranes, which proceeding from the *pia mater*, involve the brain and all the nerves, also the brain itself, and the arteries which are in the brain; and such other parts, as being stirred, the heart also, which is the fountain of all sense, is stirred together with them.'

120/16   *Aristotle: De Juventute et Senectute*, Ch 3[M]: 'Moreover in all sanguineous animals the supreme organ of the sense-faculties lies in the heart; for in this part must lie the common sensorium of all the sense-organs.' (Tr. W.S. Hett) See Note to Bk III, ch 15, sects 3,4, below.

120/29 *Aristotle:* De Anima, *Bk II, Ch 11, 424a:* τὸ γὰρ μέσον κριτικόν· γίνεται γὰρ πρὸς ἑκάτερον αὐτῶν θάτερον τῶν ἄκρων.

Aristotle expounds in this section his theory that all sensation is the actualization of sense objects that are already potentially in the organs of sense. This necessarily implies that sense itself can be neither one extreme nor another but a mean which can assume either of two opposite qualities such as hot and cold, hard and soft, white and black, and so on. More's interpretation of Aristotle is irreproachable and it serves as further evidence of the inconsistency that More observes in Aristotle's location of the common sensorium in the heart, which is described in *De Juventute et Senectute,* Ch. 4, 469b, as τὴν ἀρχὴν τῆς θερμότητος.

120/41 *Calcidius:* Chalcidius, *Timaeus in Platonis translatus item eiusdem in eundem commentarius:* 'Illud etiam in corde negant; crocodilis enim avulsis cordibus, aliquandiu vivere, et resistere adversum violentiam. Hoc idem in testudinibus observatum marinis, et terrestibus capris.'
[They [the atomist philosophers] deny that it [the principal power of the soul] is in the heart, for crocodiles live a little while, even after their heart has been removed, and resist violence. This is also observed in the case of sea-tortoises and mountain goats.]

120/42 Galen: More is paraphasing *De placitis Hippocratis et Platonis,* Bk. II [M] 238: γίνεται μὲν οὖν τοῦτο καὶ κατὰ πολλὰς θυσίας ἐξ ἔθους οὕτως ἐπιτελουμένας καὶ φαίνεται τὰ ζῶια τῆς καρδίας ἤδη κατὰ τῶν βωμῶν ἐπικειμένης οὐκ ἀναπνέοντα μόνον ἢ κεκραγότα συντόνως, ἀλλὰ καὶ φεύγοντα, μέχρι περ ἂν ὑπὸ τῆς αἱμορραγίας ἀποθάνηι.

121/6 exenterated: eviscerated

121/14 *Hobbs:* Hobbes, *Ibid.* [M]: 'Also if the motion be intercepted between the brain and the heart by the defect of the organ by which the action is propagated, there will be no perception of the object.'

121/25 *Laurentius:* André DuLaurens, *Historia anatomica,* Bk IV, quaest 7 [M]: 'Praeterea maior apparet continuatio nervi cum cerebro, quam cum corde si enim ligetur nervus in medio, pars superior cerebrum versus, sentiet et movebitur, pars vero cordi vicinior insensibilis erit et immobilis.'

[Further the continuity of the nerves with the cerebrum seems greater than their continuity with the heart, for if a nerve were to be bound in the middle, the upper part towards the cerebrum will be sentient and move, while the lower part near the heart will be insentient and immobile.]

André Du Laurens (1558-1609) was doctor of medicine, Royal Physician, and Chancellor of the University of Montpellier. His comprehensive *Historia Anatomica* (1600) was one of the most widely used anatomical textbooks of the seventeenth century. The twelve books of the *Historia* include not only descriptions of the structures, actions, and uses of the parts but also 178 "controversies" in which are discussed disputed questions such as whether there is a natural spirit and whether the brain is the seat of the principal faculty.

122/23 Galen: *op. cit.*, Bk VII, 605: οὐ μὴν οὐδὲ εἰ τὸν ἐγκέφαλον αὐτὸν ὁπωσοῦν ἐκτέμνοις. οὐδὲ οὕτω τὸ ζῷον ἀκίνητον ἢ ἀναίσθητον γίνεται, πρὶν ἐπί τινα τῶν κοιλιῶν αὐτοῦ τὴν τομὴν ἐξικέσθαι.

[If the brain is injured in some way, the animal does not lose motion or sense unless the cut penetrates one of the ventricles.]

122/38 *Trepan*: 'A small surgical instrument ... for cutting out small pieces of bone, especially from the skull'(OED).

123/19 Author: Thomas Wharton, *Adenographia*, Ch 23[M]: Repeating the four objections of Caspar Bertholin guoted by More, Wharton adds, ' Nam incongruam videtur, ne dicam ridiculum, principes animae operationes parti adscribere quae nullam conmunionem cum externis organis obtinet, quomodo enim species ab iisdem excipiat, aut mandata motum imperantia eisdem communicet? '

[Indeed it is incongruous, if not ridiculous, to ascribe the principal operations of the soul to a part which has no communication with any external organs; how, then, can the ruling command [i.e. of the soul] draw images out of them or communicate motion to them?]

Thomas Wharton (1614-1673) was doctor of medicine and Fellow of the Royal College of Physicians. His *Adenographia* (1656) was the first thorough account of the glands of the body, which he classified as excretory, reductive,and nutrient. Caspar Bartholin (1585-1629): Danish doctor who first studied philosophy and theology at Copenhagen and Wittenberg and, later, medicine at Leiden, and anatomy at Padua. His great work on anatomy, *Anatomicae institutiones corporis humani*, was published in 1611. An enlarged and illustrated version was brought out by his son posthumously in 1641.

123/42 which... *remember*: 'See chap 11 sect. 4,5' [M].

124/3 *Arx ... Atomus*: citadel, or mountain ... atom

124/31 above: 'Chap 5, sect 3,4,5,6' [M].

124/33 net ... *Arteries*: cf. Caspar Bartholin, *Institutiones Anatomicae*, Bk III, Ch. 6: 'glandula... pinealis dicta estque substantia durioris coloris sublutei non numquam subobscuri et membrana tenui obducitur ... glandulam hanc ... nerveus funiculus utrinque firmat.
[The so-called pineal gland is of a harder substance and a yellowish colour,and covered with a thin membrane ... A small net of nerves hold s this gland firmy on both sides.]

124/36 Author: Wharton, *Adenographia*, Ch.23[M] 'Sunt enim duo illa crura, superiora atque etiam inferiora, sita in ipso concursu nervorum omnium gui intra calvariam oriuntur, et propter continuitatem cum spinali medulla, e qua alii omnes nervi oriuntur, dici possunt eorum quasi cen trum. Cum actiones et passiones omnes totius corporis per imagines suas ad hanc partem primo opellant, credibile est in ipso confino ejusdem cum cerebro communem sensum perfici.'
[There are two of those limbs, superior and inferior, situated in the same concourse of all the nerves that originate from within the skull and which, on account of its continuity with the spinal marrow from which all other nerves arise, can be called their centre. As all the actions and passions of the entire body go towards this part first by virtue of their images, it is likely that in this very connection between it and

the cerebrum consists the common sensorium.]

126/28   Γνώμη...αἵματος: Hippocrates, *De Corde* [M], 10-11.

127/8   *Lucretius: De Rerum Natura*, Bk III [M], 11. 203-206: 'Now,
         therefore, since the nature of the mind has been found to be
         moved with unusual ease, it must consist of bodies
         exceedingly small and smooth and round.' (Tr. W.H.D.
         Rouse, Loeb Classical Library)

127/31   *Ficinus*: Marsilio Ficino, *In Plotinum Philosophum ... In*
         librum de Coelo commentarius, Ch. 7: Proinde ubi totam
         civitatem [coelestem] ait [Platon] factum ex aero puro
         fulgorem hunc ignem per omnia vult esse diffusum.
         [Therefore where [Plato] says the [heavenly] city is made of
         pure gold he means that this brilliant fire is diffused
         throughout.]
         The Platonic allusion is to *Phaedo* 110C.
         Marsilio Ficino (1433-1499) was the founder of the Florentine
         Academy which served as the center of Platonist learning in
         the Renaissance. After his early studies in humanities,
         medicine, philosophy, and Greek, Ficino received, in 1462, a
         house in Careggi near Florence, and several Greek
         manuscripts, from Cosimo de Medici with whose family he
         was closely associated. The first of Ficino's major
         translations from the Greek was his version of Hermes
         Trismegistus (1463). This was followed by the first complete
         translation of the dialogues of Plato (1484) and the
         translation and commentary on Plotinus (1492). Ficino's
         translations of Porphyry, Iamblichus, Proclus, and other
         philosophers appeared in 1497. Ficino's major philosophical
         work was the *Theologia Platonica de immortalitate animorum*
         (1482), though his apologetic treatise, *De Christiane Religione*
         (1474), his medical and astrological work, *De Vita Libri tres*
         (1489), and his letters (1495) are also important for an
         understanding of his Neoplatonist system. Borrowing
         Plotinus' hierarchical framework, Ficino posited a gradation
         of being constituted of five degrees: God, the angelic mind,
         the rational soul, quality, and body. The central position of
         the Soul allowed it to move upwards as well as downwards,
         and its ascent to God was facilitated by contemplation and
         love. The divinity of the Soul was ensured by its immortality,

which Ficino proved through an elaborate, scholastic, series of arguments in his *Theologia Platonica* -- a work that More drew upon in the argumentation of many parts of his *Platonick Song of the Soul*(1647). While Ficino defended the Christian religion as the true one, his love of Platonist philosophy impelled him to emphasize the continuity of the philosophical tradition as a venerable counterpart of the religious.

127/32 *Trismegist*: Hermes Trismegistus,*Poemander*, Libellus ix, sive Clavis [M]: νοῦς δὲ ὀξύτατος ὢν πάντων τῶν [θείων] νοη[μα]τῶν, καὶ τὸ ὀξύτατον πάντων τῶν στοιχείων ἔχει σῶμα τὸ πῦρ. δημιουργὸς γὰρ ὢν [πάντων] ὁ νοῦς ὀργάνωι τῶι πυρὶ πρὸς τὴν δημιουργίαν χρῆται
[But mind, which is the keenest of all things incorporeal, has for its body fire, the keenest of all material elements. Mind is the maker of things, and in making things it uses fire as its instrument. (Tr. Walter Scott)]

127/38 *Regius*: Henri de Roy, *Philosophia Naturalis*, Bk IV, [not Ch 16 as More indicates] [M] Ch 17: 'Quod autem motus spontaneus per influxum spirituum fiat, id ad oculum aliqumodo conspici potest in limace ... phiale vitrea ... inclusa,
[The spontaneous motion that is produced by the influx of spirits can in a way be observed even by the eyes in the case of a snail ... kept ... in a glass phial.]

128/18 but ... it: See More, *Antidote*, Bk. 3, Ch. 13, sect.6 [not Ch 3, sect.8 as More indicates] [M]: More relates here Bodin's account of the assistance he received from a good genius (recorded in *De la démonomanie des Sorciers*, Bk I, Ch 2) which would not speak to him but merely strike objects around him every time it wished to communicate with him.

128/22 Galen: *De Placitis Hippporatis et Platonis*, Bk 7, 614:. ὅτι μὲν οὖν φέρεταί τι πνεῦμα διὰ τῶν πόρων τούτων ἐπὶ τοὺς ὀφθαλμούς, ἥ τε κατασκεύι σε διδάσκει καὶ προσέτι τὸ κλεισθέντος μὲν αὐτῶν ἑνὸς εὐρύνεσθαι θατέρου τὴν κόρην, ἀνοιχθέντος δὲ παραχρῆμα πάλιν εἰς τὸ κατὰ φύσιν ἐπανέρχεσθαι μέγεθος. ὅτι τε γὰρ ὑπό τινος οὐσίας διατεινομένου τοῦ ῥαγοειδοῦς χιτῶνος ἐν τῶι πληροῦσθαι τὴν ἔνδον αὐτοῦ χώραν ἀναγκαῖόν ἐστιν εὐρύνεσθαι τὸ κατὰ τὴν κόρην τρῆμα καὶ ἄλλως ἀμήχανον, ὅτι τε τὸ τάχος τῆς κενώσεώς τε καὶ πληρώσεως οὐχ ὑγροῦ τινος ἐπιρρέοντος, ἀλλα μόνης ἐστὶ πνευματικῆς ἔργον οὐ καλεπὸν συνιδεῖν. ἐπεὶ δὲ ἐς ταὐτὸ ἀμφότεροι οἱ πόροι παραγίνονται, καὶ γὰρ καὶ τοῦτο ἐναργῶς φαίνεται διὰ τῆς ἀνατομῆς, εἰκός ἐστι τὴν κοινὴν χώραν ἐξ ἀμφοτέπων τῶν πόρων τὸ πνεῦμα δεχομένην ἐν τῶι μῦσαι τὸν ἕτερον ὀφθαλμὸν ἐπὶ πέμπειν τῶι λοιπῶι σύμπαν αὐτο.

[That some spirits are transmitted through these passages to the eyes is demonstrated by the fact that when one eye is closed, the other pupil is dilated and, if it is opened again, the other pupil returns to its normal size. It is necessary that the *acinosa tunica* be distended with some other substance which dilates the pupil by filling the aperture inside it, which is not possible any other way but is effected by a spiritual substance alone, just as the speed with which this emptying and filling takes place is difficult to understand if there is an influx of a humour of any kind. For the two passages are united into one -- and this is seen clearly from anatomy -- so that it is likely that when the spirits enter the place where the two passages join, and when one eye shuts, the spirits are transmitted entirely into the other.]

128/34 *Boeotum ... natum*: Horace, *Epistulae*, II, i, 44: ' You would swear he was born in the dense air of Boetia.' The section that this line is taken from refers to Alexander's lack of artistic discrimination:

> ... Idem rex ille, poema
> qui tam ridiculum tam care prodigus emit,
> edicto vetuit ne quis se praeter Apellem
> pingeret aut alius Lysippo duceret aera
> fortis Alexandri vultum simulantia.Quodsi
> iudicium subtile videndis artibus illud
> ad libros et ad haec Musarum dona vocares,
> Boetûm in crasso iurares aere natum.

129/9 *Dionysius: Orbis Descriptio*, ll. 839-842:

> οὐ μὰν οὐδὲ γυναῖκας ὀνόσσεαι, αἵ περὶ κεῖνο
> θεῖον ἔδος, χρυσοῖο κατ᾿ ἰξύος ἄμμα βαλοῦσαι,
> ὀρχεῦνται, θηητὸν ἐλισσόμεναι περὶ κύκλον,
> εὖτε Διωνύσοιο χοροστασίας τελέοιεν·

σὺν καὶ παρθενικαὶ νεοθηλέες, οἶά τενεβροί,
σκαίρουσιν· τῆσιν δὲ περισμαράγεῦωτες ἀῆται
ἱμερτοὺς δονέουσιν ἐπὶ στήθεσσι χιτῶνας

More himself translates the verse in his Notes to the 1713
edition thus:

Nor shall the Women that with Loins girt round
With golden Ties dance on that Sacred Ground
Be blam'd; Strange Rings they form while on this wise
Great Bacchus Rites with Trips they Solemnize
At the same time the Virgins of the Place
Leap too as Kids, and with the rest keep pace.
While the soft Winds around them briskly blow,
And make the Vestments on their Breasts to flow.

129/25   Hippocrates: Epidemiae, Bk VI[M]7: The line in Hippocrates
reads τὰ ἴσχοντα ἢ ὁρμῶντα ἢ ἐνισχόμενα. Palladius'
scholium on the Epidemiae reads: τὰ ἴσχοντα (ἢ ὁρμῶντα)
καὶ τὰ ἐνισχόμενα σώματα ἢ ἐνορμῶντα.
cf. also Kircher, Magnes, sive de Arte Magnetica, Bk III, Part
7, 7: 'Quae ideo fusius hic prosecutus sum, ut videas qui
spiritus hi ominum anime functionum organum necessarium
sint. Unde non immerito ab Hippocrates σώματα ἐναρμοῦντα
dicuntur.'
[I have described them at such length so that you may see
that these spirits are necessary for all the organic functions
of the soul.   Whence they have been appropriately called
'active bodies' by Hippocrates.]

129/28   Spigelius: Adriaan van der Spiegel, De Humani Corporis
fabrica, Bk V II, Ch 1[M]: 'Re vera enim ipsius spiritus
substantiam a cerebro per nervos diduci, exeo videtur
perspicuum, quod partes compressae et stupentes ubi motum
recipiunt, aliquid formicarum instar repentium persentire
videntur, id enim profecto neutiquam contingeret, nisi pars
affluxionem spirituum interceptam antea redire ad se
perciperet.'
[Indeed that the substance of these spirits is distributed from
the cerebrum through the nerves is clearly observed from the
fact that, when those parts that have been compressed and
stupefied receive motion, they seem to feel suddenly
something like ants; this would not indeed happen unless the
part felt an influx of spirits that were hitherto intercepted

returning to it.]
Adriaan van der Spiegel (1578-1625) was born in Brussels and was first, a student of botany, and later, professor of anatomy and surgery in Venice. His important anatomical work, *De humani corppris fabrica* (1627) was published posthumously by Daniel Rindfleisch.

129/33 Pismires: ants

131/4 two Enquiries:'See chap 6,Sect. 9'[M].

131/29 Hofman: Kasper Hofman, *De Thorace eiusque partibus commentarius tripartitus*, Bk II, Ch 28: 'Interim dum animalum illum spiritum in ventriculis cerebri fabricat, quod absurda incurrit ... fiunt Spiritus in ventriculis et e ventriculis nervos ingrediuntur? An non probabilis hic metus subest, ut quemadmodum sanguis, vasis suis elapsus, definit esse sanguis ita etiam fiat de spiritibus? Tanto magis, quod finis trium ventriculorum est in palato? Ibi, ubi excrementorum cloaca est, ut sic dicam: Quae vero affinitas est corpori huic purissimo cum excrementis, quorum receptacula esse ventriculos, ne ipsa quidem Galen ausit negare?'
[That the animal spirits are produced in the ventricles of the brain is a theory that runs into many absurdities ... are the spirits made in the ventricles and, from the ventricles, do they enter the nerves? Is this not a valid doubt... for, does not blood cease to be blood once it is removed from its vessels? Is it the same with the spirits? So much more so, indeed, that the end of the true ventricles is in the "palate" -- where the drain of the excrements, as I may call it, is! What affinity can there be between this pure entity and the excrements whose receptacle is the ventricles -- a fact which Galen himself does not dare deny?]
Kasper Hofman (1572-1648) was a medical doctor and humanist who spent twenty years of his life preparing a new edition of Galen. Hofman studied medicine in Altdorf and, later, in Padua. In 1606 he was appointed Professor of Medicine in Basel. His works include the *Commentarius in Galeni de usu partium corporis humanis* (1625), *De Thorace eiusque partibus commentarius tripartitus* (1627), *De Generatione Homini* (1629) and *Institutionum Medicarum*

(1645).

131/40 *Infundibulum*: a funnel-shaped prolongation downwards and forwards of the third ventricle of the brain, at the extremity of which is the pituitary body.

132/14 some ... pure: cf. Bartholin, *Institutiones Anatomicae*, Bk III, Ch 6 : 'Usus cavitatum vel ventriculorum cerebri est esse excrementorum conceptacula quod apparet: 1. Ex structura: Nam foramen abit a cavitatibus ad glandulam pituitariam. 2. Superficies ventriculorum semper aqueo humore oblinitur. 3. Saepe toti repleti pituitam reperiuntur.'
[The use of the cavities or the ventricles of the cerebrum is to be the receptacle of excrements, which is evident from 1. the structure, for the hole goes from the cavities to the pituitary gland, 2. the fact that the superficies of the ventricles are always filled with an aqueous humour, and 3. that they are often found to be filled with pituite.]

133/13 *Rete Mirabile*: 'an elaborate network or plexus of blood-vessels ... which is formed by the intra-cranial part of the internal carotid artery in some animals, and was supposed to exist also in man.' (OED)

133/14 *Plexus Choroides*: 'a plexus of blood-vessels connected by a thin membrane derived from the *pia mater*, in each lateral ventricle of the brain forming a cord-like border on each side of the *velum interpositum* also applied to similar structures in the third and fourth ventricles' (OED)

133/30 *Bartholine*: Bartholin, *op. cit.*, Bk III, Ch.4 [M]: 'In principio hujus medullae, dum adhuc in calvaria est, insculptus visitur, sinus vel cavitas, cum Galenus cerebelli ventriculum vocat, alii quartum cerebri ventriculum, cum tamen in cerebro non sit. Nos ventriculum medullae nobilem vocabimus. Hic solidissimus est, purissimus subtilissimus set minimus, nam rem majorum virium et facultates continent, ut ait Galenus.'
[One sees at the beginning of the medulla which is in the cranium, a sinus or a cavity which Galen calls the ventricle of the cerebellum, and others the fourth ventricle of the cerebrum, though it is not in the cerebrum. We shall call it

the noble ventricle of the medulla. It is very solid, very pure, and very fine, but very small, since, as Galen says, it contains a substance of great power and virtue.]

and Bk III, Ch. 5: 'Usus hujus ventriculi a nobis statuitur, ut sit locus generationis, et elaborationis animalium spirituum. Hic enim ventriculus 1. est purissimus et subtilissimus, 2. Cavitatem que ad id sufficientem obtinet, 3. In eo denique loco est situs, ut undique circa se in omnes nervos spiritum animalium effundere possit recte ergo Herophilus hunc ventriculum principalissimum existimavit.'

[We consider the use of this ventricle is to be the place of generation and elaboration of the animal spirits. For, this ventricle is 1. very pure and subtle, 2. it has a sufficient cavity for this purpose, 3. it is placed in a convenient situation to spread the animal spirits around it everywhere into the nerves. Hierophil was, therefore, right in believing this ventricle to be the most important of all.]

134/11 *Regius*: Henri de Roy, *op. cit.*, Bk 5, Ch.2 [M]: 'Itaque, quicunque motus, fibrillis nervorum impressis, ad cerebrum diffunditur, is necessario et iam contiguis spiritibus, in ventriculis cerebro existentibus,imprimitur ac, illorum ope, glandulae pineali et ibidem animae, inter partes ejus in unum ibi coeuntes existentis communicatur.'

[Thus, whatever motion that is impressed on the fibrillae of the nerves and is diffused to the cerebrum is necessarily impressed also on the contiguous spirits which exist in the ventricles of the brain, and, through their force, is communicated to the pineal gland and, there, to the soul, which, exists amidst its parts collected in one point.]

134/31 it ... fault: 'See my *Antidote*, Book 2, chap 12, sect 2ff'[M]: More considers in these sections the providential design evident in the constitution of the various parts of the body.

135/3 she... Efformation:'Plotinus calls them προϋπογραφὴν and προδρόμους ἐλλάμψεις εἰς ὕλην. *Enneades*,VI, vii, 7 [M]: τί γὰρ κωλύει τὴν μὲν δύναμιν τῆς τοῦ παντὸς ψυχῆς προϋπαγράφειν, ἅτε λόγον πάντα οὖσαν, πρὶν καὶ παρ' αὐτῆς ἥκειν τὰς ψυχικὰς δυνάμεις, καὶ τὴν προϋπογραφὴν οἷον προδρόμους ἐλλάμψεις εἰς τὴν ὕλην εἶναι, ἤδη δὲ τοῖς τοιούτοις ἴχνεσιν ἐπακολουθοῦσαν τὴν ἐξεργαζομένην ψυχὴν

κατὰ μέρη τὰ ἴχνη διαρθροῦσαν ποιῆσαι καὶ γενέσθαι
ἑκάστην τοῦτο ὦι προσῆλθε, σχηματίσασα ἑαυτὴν ὥσπερ τὸν
ἐν ὀρχήσει πρὸς τὸ δοθὲν αὐτῶι δρᾶμα.
[The power of the All-Soul, as reason-Principle of the
universe may be considered as laying down a pattern before
the effective separate powers go forth from it: this plan
would be something like a tentative illumining of matter; the
elaborating Soul would give minute articulation to those
representations of itself; every separate effective Soul would
become that towards which it tended assuming that
particular form as the choral dancer adapts himself to the
action set down for him.'(Tr. S. Mackenna)]

135/13　My Opinion ...: cf. Marsilio Ficino, *Theologia Platonica de
Immortalitate Animorum*, Bk 18, Ch 7: 'Anima quae est
medium rerum, iussu Dei, qui est mundi centrum, in
punctum cordis medium, quod est centrum corporis, primum
infunditur. Inde per univers sui corporis membra se fundit,
quando currum suum naturali iungit calori; per calorem
spiritui corporis; per hunc spiritum immergit humoribus;
membris inserit per humores.'
[The soul, which is at the center of things, at the order of
God, who is the center of the universe, infuses itself into the
central point of the heart, which is the center of the body.
From there, it spreads into all the parts of the body when it
unites itself through its vehicle to the natural heat of the
body; then, through the heat, to the spirit of the body;
through this spirit, it immerses itself into the humors and,
through these humors, into the parts of the body.]

135/22　*Enthusiasmus Triumphatus*: ' Enthus Triumph, sect, 3,4,5'
[M].

135/29　*Libration*: 'swaying to and fro' (OED)

135/29　*Tensility*: Ductility

135/34　*Regius*: Henri de Roy, *op. cit.*, Bk 4, Ch 16 [M]: 'Spiritus
cerebri, qui vulgo animales appellantur, sunt halitus subtiles
et celerrime agitati, qui e sanguine cordis calidissimo, in
plexum choroidem et vasa conorium involventia, a corde in
ejus diastole perpetuo impulso, in cavitates ventriculorum,

per vasorum poros, exhalantes, inde, per interstitia
fibrillarum cerebri, in nervos et totium corpus magna vi
diffunduntur.
     Spiritibus his, per diastolem cordis, in ventriculos
cerebri exhalantibus atollitur cerebrum; iis vero in cerebro,
ob systolem cordis et frigidum per nares inspiratum aerem,
intepescentibus subsidit illud. Atque ita eodem tempore fit
alternata cordis et cerebri intumescentia et subsidentia.'
[The spirits of the brain, which laymen call animal spirits,
are subtle vapours that are rapidly agitated, which,
orginating from the hot blood of the heart, course into the
plexum choroidem and the *vasa conarium* impelled by the
heart in its perpetual diastole into the cavities of the
ventricles through the pores of the vessels and, evaporating,
are diffused with great force from there through the
interstices of the fibrillae of the brain into the nerves and the
entire body.
     Those spirits that are effused into the ventricles of the
brain by the diastole of the heart raise the cerebrum. Then,
turning lukewarm there on account of the systole of the heart
and the cold air inhaled through the nose, the spirits cause it
to subside. Thus, at the same time is provided an alternating
tumescence of the heart and a subsidence of the cerebrum.]

136/11 For ... *Credulity*: See Descartes, *Passions*, Première Partie,
        Artic 36 [M].

136/23 For ... intermedling: *Ibid.*, Artic. 13[M].

137/9   Such ... temper: cf. Sir Kenelm Digby's *A late Discourse ...*
        concerning the curing of wounds by the powder of Sympathy.
        Digby's treatise on sympathetic cures revolves around a cure
        he effected of a wound that was suffered by one Mr. Howel
        while the latter was trying to part two of his friends engaged
        in a duel. Digby healed the deep cuts in Howel's hand by
        immersing his bloodstained garter in a basin of water mixed
        with powder of vitriol. After giving a detailed naturalistic
        explanation of this cure, Digby adds: 'The same cure is
        performed by applying the remedy to the blade of a sword
        which hath wounded a person ... Now the reason why the
        sword may be dressed in order to the cure, is, because the
        subtil spirits of blood do penetrate the substance of the blade,

as far as the extent which the sword made within the body of the wounded party, where they use to make their residence ... Now then, while the spirits lodge in the sword, they may serve as great helps for the cure of the patient' (p. 148). The powder Digby used worked through the phenomenon of attraction, for 'the aire is ful of Atomes, which are drawn from bodies by meanes of the light which reflects thereon or which sally out by the interior naturall heat of those bodies which drive them forth' (p.44) and 'the body which attracts them to it selfe, draws likewise after them that which accompanies them [i.e. the healing power]' (p.68). Digby even recognizes that 'The *Chymists* do assure us that it is no other then a corporification of the universall spirit which animates and perfects all that hath existence in this sublunary world ... But to anatomise as we ought the nature of this transcendent individuall, which nevertheless in some fashion may be said to be universall and fundamentall to all bodies, it would require a Discourse far more ample then I have yet made' (p.142).

137/15   *Unity ... Universe*: 'See Book 3, Chap 6, sect 7,8,9[M].

137/18   *Plotinus:* Η ἀληϑινὴ μαγεία ἡ ἐν τῶι παντὶ φιλία καὶ τὸ νεῖκος αὖ. καὶ ὁ γόης ὁ πρῶτος καὶ φαρμαεὺς οὗτος ἐστιν. Plotinus, *Enneades*, IV, iv, 40[M].
[There is much drawing and spell-binding dependent on no interfering machination; the true magic is internal to the all, its attractions and, not less, its repulsions. Here is the primal mage and sorcerer.]
Interestingly, Plotinus further calls it, in an Empedoclean manner, Love: 'Love is given in Nature; the qualities inducing love induce mutual approach.' (Tr. Stephen MacKenna, *The Enneads*, London, 1956)

137/23   *Gamaieu's*: marriages

137/25   its due place: 'Book 3, chap. 12, & 13' [M].

138/29   decussation: the crossing of lines so as to form a figure like the letter X.

140/2   *Plutarch*: Pseudo-Plutarch, *De placitis philosophorum*, Bk IV,

901c: Πλάτων, κατὰ συναύγειαν, τοῦ μὲν, ἐκ τῶν ὀφθαλμῶν φωτὸς ἐπι ποσόν ἀπορρέοντος εἰς τὸν ὁμογενῆ ἀέρα· τοῦ δ' ἀπὸ (μὲν) τῶν σωμάτων [ἀντι]φερομένου, τοῦ δε περὶ τὸν μεταξὺ ἀέρα, εὐδιάχυτον ὄντα, καὶ εὐτρεπτον, συνεκτειμένου τῶι πυρώδει τῆς ὄψεως. Αὕτη λέγεται Πλατωνικὴ συναύγεια.

[Plato on the 'concourse of light rays': light rays from the eyes flow through a certain amouont of space to congenerous air, while other light flows in the opposite direction from bodies so that the light of the air in the middle, being readily diffused and tunned round, is blended with the fiery light of vision. This phenomenon is called by the Platonists the 'concourse of light rays'.]

140/28   which ... proposed: 'See chap 6, sect 9' [M].

140/36   third Querie: 'Ch. 6, sect. 9' [M].

141/21   already: See Chap 5, sect. 7; also ch,2, sect,7,8 [M]\.

141/23   *Brachygraphie*: Shorthand

142/28   *Sennertus*: Deniel Sennert, *Institutiones Medicinae*, Bk II, Part 3, Sec2, Ch4[M]: 'Frigus itaque et humiditas, imprimis si coniungantur, memoriae obsunt et praecipue si humor similis, nimirum frigidus et humidus, qualis est pituita, accedat ... Omnia enim illa quae cerebrum refrigerant,eius calidum innatum absumunt aut dissipant, humores ac pituitam in illo coacervant, causa laesae memoriae esse possunt.'

[Therefore, if cold and humidity are combined together, memories fade, and especially if a fluid which is quite cold and humid such as the pituite reaches it ... All things which cool the cerebrum and consume or dissipate its innate heat and fill it with fluids and pituite can be the cause of a lesion of memory.]

Daniel Sennert (1572-1637) was Professor of medicine at the University of Wittenberg from 1602 to 1637. He published several important scientific works including *Institutionum medicinae libri V*, (1611), *Epitome scientiae naturalis*, (1618), *De Chymicorum cum Aristotelicis et Galenicis consensu et dissensu liber I*, *(1619)*, and the *Practicas medicinae*

(1628-36).

143/36 Chalcidius: *op.cit.*: 'Idem negant animae vim principalem consistere in capite; propterea quid pleraque animalia, capite secto, vivant ad tempus, et agant solita, tanquam nullo damno allato corporis univers itati, ut apes, et item fuci, quae licet capitibus abscisis ad momentum vivunt, et volant.'
[They deny that the principal power of the soul is contained in the head; for many animals live for a while after their head has been cut off, and move by themselves as if they had suffered no damage to the body -- so bees and drones continue to live and fly for a moment after their head has been cut off.]

144/37 *Synesius*: Hymnus I , ll.168-173:
πνευματοεργὲ
καὶ ψυχοτρόφε,
παγὰ παγῶν,
ἀρχῶν ἀρχά,
ῥιζῶν ῥίζα
[Creator of Spirits
And sustainer of Souls,
Source of Sources,
Principle of principles,
Root of roots;]
Synesius (see Note to Ch 12, Art 11 below) is credited with four hymns written before 408, of which the first three exhibit the influence of Iamblichus, the Chaldean oracles and the Orphic hymns.

145/12 lusorious: playful

146/14 *Appendix*: Ch 10, sect 7[M]. Interestingly, one of More's major rea sons for his denial of immortality to the souls of brutes is that his admission of incorporeal souls in brutes is really nothing more than 'what all Philosophers and School men, that have held *Substantial forms*, have either expressly or implicitly acknowledged to be true.' The only immortality he is willing to grant this type of morphic soul is one akin to that of matter itself: 'If they mean by *Immortal*, unperishable, as *Matter* is, why should they not be so well as *Matter* it self; this active substance of the *Soul*, though but of a *Brute*, being a more noble Essence, and partaking more of its Makers perfection, then the dull amd dissipable *Matter*? But if they mean by *Immortality*, a capacity of eternal life and bliss after the dissolution their Bodies, that's a ridiculous consequence of their own ...'

147/15   *Traduction*: The doctrine that the human soul is originated from the parents as the result of the process of generation and that it is transmitted along with the body. Materialistic traducianism was taught by Tertullian (*De Anima*, 9-41) and favored by other Fathers such as Gregory of Nyssa and Faustus of Riez.

147/15   *Creation*: "Creationism," the doctrine that God creates for each human individual a new soul at the moment of its union with the body during conception. The majority of the Church Fathers, especially the Eastern ones, and medieval theologians maintained this theory, which was close to the Aristotelian opinion that the infusion of the soul takes place during the development of the embryo (40th day for the male and 80th for the female).
         In their most literal sense, both traducianism and creationism are opposed to the spirituality and simplicity of the soul.

148/3   concinnity: conformity

148/5   *à mundo condito*: made from the earth.

149/4   this Hypothesis: cf. Origen, *De Principiis*, Bk II, Ch 8-9.

150/6   fragments of *Trismegist*: Revelatory writings of Egyptian Gnostic origin (lstc.- 3rd c. A.D.) attributed to Hermes Trismegistus. Influenced by Plato's *Timaeus* as well as such commentation as Posidonius, they included dialectical as well as mystical treatises and thus form an epitome of eclectic Neoplatonism, both scholastic and popular.

150/15   *Oracles ... Chaldaical*: A collection of mystical writings dating to about 200 A.D. which probably formed part of the pagan Gnostic tradition. It resembles the Hermetic writings in its mixture of Orphism, Pythagoreanism, Platonism, and

Stoicism, though it is characterised also by a strong
emphasis on theology. The cosmology and psychology of both
the Chaldaic Oracles and the Hermetic writings as well as
their vocabulary are directly employed by More in
'Psychozoia' and echoed in the other poems of the *Psychodia
Platonica.*

150/16 *Pletho*: George Gemistos Plethon (ca. 1355-1452) was a late
Byzantine philosopher and humanist. Educated at
Constantinople, he opened a school of esoteric religion and
philosophy at Mistra in the Peloponessus, near Sparta. He
was greatly influenced by Psellus and his aim was to
establish Neoplatonism as a new social as well as spiritual
order.His numerous writings served as a stimulus to the
establishment of the Florentine Academy. His commentaries
on the Chaldaic Oracles were edited along with Psellus' by J.
Opsopoeus, *Oracula magica Zorastris cum scholiis Plethonis et
Pselli* (Paris, 1599).

150/16 *Psellus*: Michael Psellus (1018-1078): Born in
Constantinople, Psellus was head of the imperial secretariat
under Michael V. Calaphates, and head of the Philosophy
faculty at Constantinople between l045 and 1054. In 1054, he
became a monk, though he was actively associated with
imperial politics for the rest of his life. Psellus wrote several
treatises on grammar, rhetoric, law, philosophy, and science
as well as a history of Byzantium from 976 to 1078,
Chronographia. He was concerned to promote Neoplatonism
and its theurgical aspect and preserved various works of
Iamblichus and Proclus and one version of the *Corpus
Hermeticum.* His longest commentary on the Chaldaic oracles
is the Εξήγησις είς τά χαλδαικά λόγια.

150/18 *Cabbala*: The generic term for the esoteric Jewish mysticism
that developed from the twelfth century onwards. Akin to
Gnosticism in its earliest origins, it first involved magical
notions along with ideas on cosmology and angelology,
though the speculative elements were separated from the
occult in medieval times. The most famous Cabbalist text is
the *Sefer ha Zohar* written by Moses ben Shem Tov de Leon
in Guadalajara between 1280 and 1286. The Cabbalists
employed the psychological doctrines of Neoplatonism and

maintained the preexistence of the soul and its descent into this world through a process of emanation.

150/36 *Synesius*: Synesius of Cyrene (ca. 370-414 A.D.) studied in Alexandria under Hypatia and, after visits to Athens and Antioch, settled in Cyrenaica. In 410, he was chosen by the people of Ptolemais to be their bishop, but he refused consecration citing in particular his Origenistic belief in the preexistence of the soul (cf. *Epist.* 105), the eternity of the world, and his allegorical ideas concerning the Resurrection. However, Theophius of Alexandria consecrated him in 411.

150/36 *Origen*: Origen (ca. 184 - ca. 254 A.D.) was born in Alexandria and probably studied under Clement of Alexandria and Ammonius Saccus, the father of Neoplatonism. Most of his writings were exegetical, though the most remarkable of his works was the early treatise *De Principiis* which deals with the Trinity, the world, and rational creation. Its controversial claims resulted in Origen's excommunication from the Church of Alexandria in 231 A.D. Origen's heretic principles are maintained in most points by More. These include the notion that the souls of men and even that of Christ preexisted as pure intelligences. All these intelligences, except Christ's, grew cold in their divine fervour and became souls (Origen derives the term ψυχή from ψῦχος. However, the material bodies with which the erring souls have been punished will be transformed by spiritual purgation in this life into absolutely ethereal ones at the resurrection. (cf. *De Principiis*, Bk 11, Ch 8-10).

151/5 *De ... Causis*: Jean Fernel, *De abditis rerum causis*, Bk II, Ch 4[M]: Quoting the authority of Hippccrates in the *Liber de Carnibus*, Fernel, through the persona of Eudoxus, declares '
His etiam Hippocrates ani mae coelestem facit originem: illius vero substantiam quam caloris nomine appelat, immortalem. '
Jean Francois Fernel (1497-1558) was a physician with a philosophical cast of mind whose works included *De naturalis parte medicinae* (1542) and *De abditis rerum causis* (1548). His physiology was largely the humoral medicine of his time and he believed that the spirit enters the foetus on the _ fortieth day of pregancy, though the substance of the soul is

ever hidden from us. *De abditis rerum causis* is written in the
form of a conversation among three educated citizens,
Brutus, Philiatros, and Eudoxus, who represents Fernel
himsel. The subjects discussed include God, nature, the Soul,
and the preternatural. Matter according to Fernel is a
substance composed of the traditional four elements, while
the soul is the principle of life and reason derived from the
stars. Fernel's Aristotelian identification of the soul with the
celestial element was clearly congenial to More.

151/5   *Cardan*: Cardano, *De Animorum Immortalitate*, 'Aristotelis de
animorum immortalitate opinio' [M]: Cardano interprets
Aristotle as having implicity differentiated the individual
souls of men in his discussion of the active and passive
intellect in *De Anima*, Bk.III, Ch 5: 'Si vero unum
intellectum censuit, cur non potius, quod in promptu erat,
addubitavit scilicet cur unus alterius non habet scientiam:
neque enim hoc alibi quaesivit qui sciam.'
[If indeed he held that the intellect was a simple entity, why
did he not rather doubt what was uncertain, namely, why a
person does not have the knowledge of another -- this person
never wonders who he is in another place.]
Cardano's further exegesis of the last lines of this chapter
which deal with the soul's pre-existence is, I think, an
interesting gloss on More's own notions of the soul: 'voluit
tamen [Aristoteles] et per haec verba ut intelligeremus posse
etiam [intellectum agentem] non denuo ingredi in corpora sed
in unum coire et ad unum, ut opinio Plotini erat. Sic tamen
ut essent diversa in numero et unum in principio, et essentia
sicut partes lucis in Sole, quae numero diversas sunt ita quod
una non est alia: habent tamen idem principium et eandem
essentiam. Quia ergo solae hae duae opiniones verae esse
poterant, per haec verba utranque declaravit, esse posse, sed
tamen ei quae diceret, denuo animas in corpora reverti magis
assentiri.'
[Aristotle intended that we understand by these words that
the agent intellect cannot once again enter into bodies but
that it can be collected into one, which was the opinion of
Plotinus. Thus, they are many in number and one in origin
and essence, as the parts of light in the sun which are many
in number in that one is not another, though they have
nevertheless the same origin and essence. Since these two

opinions of the sun can be true, he declared through these words, that both might be possible, but it is preferable to assent to the opinion that states that souls return once again into bodies.]

cf. More's opinion in Bk III, Ch 16, Sec 2: 'Now if we rightly consider what is comprehended in the true and usual notion of the unity of a soul, it is very manifest that it mainly consists in this, that the animadversive thereof is but one and that there is no sensation nor perception of any kind in the soul but what is communicated to and perceived by the whole animadversive,' and the subtle, Christian, modulation of Plotinianism in Sec 8: 'Wherefore that Notion is in finitely more neat and safe, that proportions the Soul to the dimensions of the Body and makes her independent on any thing but the Will and Essence of her Creator; which being exactly the same every where, as also his Power is, her emanative support is exactly the same to what she had in the very first point of her production and station in the world. In which respect of dependence she may be said to be a *Ray* of Him, as the rest of the creation also, but in no other sense that I know of, unless of likeness and similitude, she being the *Image* of *God* as the *Rays* of *Light* are of the *Sun.'*

151/15   *De Anima*: Aristotle, *De Anima*, Bk I, Ch 3 [M]: Aristotle does indeed restrict the soul to the specific form of any living creature in this passage and in Bk II, Ch 1,412a: ἀναγκαῖον ἄρα τὴν ψυχὴν οὐσίαν εἶναι ὡς εἶδος σώματος φυσικοῦ δυνάμει ζωὴν ἔχοντος.
[So the soul must be substance in the sense of being the form of a natural body, which potentially has life (Tr. W.S. Hett,Loeb Classical Library)].
But it is not so certain as More makes out that Aristotle allowed transmigration of souls even within the same species. Rather, his notion of immortality was confined to 1. the divinity of the rational soul (*De Gen. Anim.*, II, 3, 736 b), and 2. the vicarious immortality of individuals through their images, which are identical to them not numerically but specifically (*De Anima*, II, 4, 415 b).

151/27   *Cardan*: Cardano, *Ibid.*[M]: 'Haud dubium opinor, hanc illum transmutationem   non   reprehendere   verum   corporum dissimilitudem.'

[I am quite sure that he does not reprehend this transmutation but only the dissimilarity of bodies into which the soul passes.]

151/34 *De ... Animal*: Aristotle, *De Generatione animalium*, Bk III, Ch 11 [M],762a. Although the exact meaning of ψυχὴ in Aristotle is not easy to ascertain, More is quite right in maintaining that Aristotle here actually means that each living creature is necessarily possessed of a soul or vital principle. For, as he says in *De Anima* Bk II, Ch 4: ἔστι δὲ ἡ ψυχὴ τοῦ ζῶντος σώματος αἰτία καὶ ἀρχή [The soul is the cause and the principle of the living body.]

151/41 *Sennertus*: Sennert, *Thirteen Books of Natural Philosophy*, 5th Discourse, Ch 2: More appropriately adduces the authority of Sennert to reinforce his interpretation of Aristotle's statement in *De generatione Animalium*, Bk III, Ch 11, 762a, that τρόπον τινὰ πάντα ψυχῆς εἶναι πλήρη (see Note above). For, Sennert's explanation of the spontaneous generation of living things is based on a notion of pervasive vegetative substance that lends support to More's own *Spiritus Naturae* and the plastic power of the soul: ' For in the first place, which no man denies, there is a twofold act of the soul: one essential, called the First Act and is the bare essence of the soul. The other accidental, which is called the Second, and is the operation proceeding from the soul. And therefore the participation of the soul is also twofold, the first is the participation of the simple substance of the soul as of a form perfecting its matter; the second is the participation of the soul operating. The second participation is when organs are provided for the perfomance of the actions, to the first there needs only a disposition of the matter that the soul may thereby be fit to perform the office of an efficient cause and to form the body. But besides these two manners there is yet a third, and the soul may yet after another manner be in some kind of matter, so as neither to inform the same and vivifie it, nor to perform the proper operations of such a living thing. So the seeds of plants and animals may be in the water and in the earth and the soul may be in them and yet they neither inform nor vivifie the water nor the earth. Hence Aristotle said, not without reason, *De generatione animalium*, *Cap*. 11, that things are ful of souls, while he thus writes:

"Now animals and plants are bred in the earth and water because there is moisture in the earth, spirit in the water, animal heat in the universe, so that all things are in some sort ful of souls. And therefore they come speedily to a consistence when that heat is comprehended or received" which very thing manifestly appears from things putrid, out of which sundry kinds of worms are everywhere bred and in plants which grow in common fields and gardens where no seed hath been cast. And scarce any place is so barren but that plants and animals will breed therein of their own accord. Now this speech of Aristotle is thus to be understood, not that all things do live and are animated; for which cause he did not simply say that all things are ful of souls, but in some sort, viz. in all things in a manner there is such a like substance, which when all impediments being removed it hath got a fitting matter, it rouses itself and performs the office of a soul. For, to live is not to have and contain a soul after any fashion, but to participate the same and be informed by it, and as that which frames and preserves the original body.' (Tr. N. Culpepper and A. Cole, *Thirteen Books of Natural philosophy*, London,1659)

152/19   the same Treatise: Aristotle, *De Generatione Animalium*, Bk II, Ch 3[M]: More's conclusion that "the Soul of man is *Immortal*" from Aristotle's distinction between the rational element in the soul and the sensitive and nutrient souls is rather unconvincing. For, Aristotle suggests here that only the rational soul is immortal and not the entire soul -- the theory, in fact, held by Pomponazzi, whom More is constantly decrying as an atheist. More himself is little concerned throughout this treatise with the rational soul *per se* but concentrates, rather, on the connexion between it and the sensitive soul.

154/27   *Messala Corvinus*: The incident of Messala's losing his memory in the dotage of his last years is recounted in Pliny, *Historia Naturalis*, VII ,Ch 24: 'Sui vero nominis Messala Corvinus cepit oblivionem.'

154/32   *Thucydides: History*, II, 49: 'In some cases the sufferer was attacke d immediately after recovery by loss of memory, which extended to every object alike, so that they failed to recognize either themselves or their friends.' (Tr. C.F. Smith Loeb Classical Library)

154/39 *Lucretius: De Rerum Natura*, Bk VI[M] ll. 1213 -1214: As More indicates, Lucretius' harrowing description of the plague of Athens (ca. 430 B.C.) is derived from Thucydides' account.

155/4 *Aristotle: De Generatione Animalium*, II, iii, 736b: λείπεται δὴ τὸν νοῦν ... θύραθεν ἐπεισιέναι καὶ θεῖον εἶναι.
[It remains then, that Reason ... enters in, as an additional factor, from outside, and that it ... is divine. (Tr. A.L. Peck)]

156/27 *De ... Animal*: Aristotle, *De Generatione Animalium*, Bk II, Ch 3[M] , cf also Sec. 6.

157/7 elsewhere: 'In this 2,Book, chap. 8' [M].

157/38 *Chariot*: For the *locus classicus* where the divine souls are described as heavenly chariots, τὰ μὲν θεῶν ὀχήματα, see Plato, *Phaedrus*, 247b.

158/13 εἰς γένεσιν: towards generation

158/24 *Crassities*: materiality

160/23 hereafter: 'Book 3, ch 13, sect 9.'[M].

161/31 *Regius*: Henri de Roy, *Philosophia Naturalis*, V, Ch l[M] ' Vinculum quo anima cum corpore conjuncta manet est lex immutabilitatis naturae, quo unumquodque manet in eo statu in quo est donec ab alio inde deturbetur. Cum enim anima humana, ut jam patet, sit substantia incorporea, nullus motus, quies, situs, figura, vel magnitudo, ullave alia partium corporis dispositio, ad eam cum corpore conjungendam vel retinendam, quicquam valere potest. Atque ideo, ubi ea in generatione per creationem Divinam in corpore humano semel est producta, eique per utilem necessitatem qua corpore ad actiones suas peragendas indiget, est unita, ex sola illa lege necessario in unione naturaliter perseverare debet: ab eoque tantum per legem aliquam supernaturalem separatur. Neque enim solutio

continui, vel intemperies, vel alius similis morbis, hic per se
quicquam potest, quippe quae non mentem, sed corporis
motum, situm, quantitatem, et figuram tantum spectent.
Atque hoc satis clare arguit Lucas Evangelista Cap 16.22
cum dicit Lazari mortui animam ab Angelis, sive causis
supernaturalibus, portam fuisse in sinum Abrahae.'
[The link which maintains the soul joined to the body is the
immutable law of nature which preserves every thing in that
condition in which it is until it is disturbed from it by
something else. As the human soul is an incorporeal
substance, as has been shown, no motion, rest, position,
figure, magnitude or any other disposition of the parts of a
body is sufficient to join it with the body and retain it there.
So that, when once it is introduced by the divine creation into
the human body, it is united to it by the need that the body
has of it to accomplish its own actions, and, by that
necessary law, it must naturally persist in this union; and it
is separated from it only by some supernatural law. Nor can
any weakening of the connection be effected by distemper or
any other similar disease by itself since these relate not to
the mind but to the motion, situation, quantity, and figure of
the body. And this has been sufficiently shown by St. Luke's
Gospel, Ch. 16:33, where it says the soul of the dead Lazarus
was borne to the bosom of Abraham by an angel, that is, a
supernatural cause.]
The resemblance of Henri le Roi's 'lex immutabilitatis
naturae ' to Leibniz's 'pre-established harmony' is striking --
in spite of Leibniz's distrust of miracles.

161/38 *Aristotle: Physica*, II, ii, 194b: ἔτι τῶν πρός τι ἡ ὕλη ἄλλωι
γαρ εἴδει ἄλλη ὕλη.
[And again, the conception of material is relative, for it is
different material that is suited to receive the several forms.
(Tr. F.M. Crawford)]

162/33 Δαίμονες: daemons, genii

162/35 θεοί: Gods

163/39 *Plato: Timaeus*,29e: ἀγαθὸς ἦν. ἀγαθῶι δὲ οὐδεὶς περὶ
οὐδενὸς οὐδέποτε. ἐγγίγνεται φθόνος, τούτου δ᾽ ἐκτὸς ὢν
πάντα ὅτι μάλιστα γενέσθαι ἐβουλήθη παραλήσια ἑαυτῶι.

[He was good, and in him that is good no envy ariseth ever concerning anything; and being devoid of envy he desired that all should be, so far as possible, like unto himself. (Tr R.G. Bury, Loeb Classical Library)]

164/22 *Scholia*: Theon, Scholia on the *Phaenomena* of Aratus. The hemistich referred to is the last line of the opening verse of Aratus' poem:

Εκ Διὸς ἀρχώμεσϑα, τὸν οὐδέποτ᾽ ἄνδρες ἐῶμεν
ἄρρητον μεσταὶ δὲ Διὸς πᾶσαι μὲν ἀγυιαί,
πᾶσαι δ᾽ ἀνϑρώπων ἀγοραί, μεστὴ δὲ ϑάλασσα,
καὶ λιμένες. πάντη δὲ. Διὸς κεχρήμεσϑα πάντες·
τοῦ γὰρ καὶ γένος εἰμεν.

[From Zeus let us begin; him do we mortals never leave unnamed; full of Zeus are all the streets and all the market-places of men; full is the sea and the havens thereof; always we all have need of Zeus. For we are also his offspring (Tr. G.R. Mair, Loeb Classical Library)]

Theon's scholium on the last line is: πρὸς τὸ "πατὴρ ἀνδρῶν τε ϑεῶν τε" εἰ γὰρ αὐτὸς ταῦτα ἐδημιούργησε πρὸς τὸ τοῖς ἀνϑρόποις βιωφελὲς. αὐτοῦ ἂν κληϑείμεν, αὐτὸν πατέρα καὶ δημιουργὸν ἐπιγραφόμενοι. δύναται δὲ καὶ ἐπι τοῦ ἀερος· αὐτὸν γὰρ ἐπι σπώμενοι, ὡς ἐξ αὐτοῦ ζῶμεν ,ὄντος ζωητικοῦ, καὶ τῆς πνοῆς ἡμῶν αἴτιου.

[Regarding 'the Father of men and of gods'; if he created them for the benefit of men, we would have been called His, addressing Him as father and creator. It is possible to so term the air, for we adhere to it in that we live from it, which is the principle of life and the cause of our vital breath.]

Aratus of Soli (ca. 315-240 B.C.) studied in Athens and imbibed Stoicism from Zeno. His astronomical poem, *Phaenomena*, was undertaken at the request of Antigonus of Macedonia. The poem is a versification of a prose treatise of Eudoxus of Cnidus (ca. 390-377 B.C.) and begins with a proem to Zeus (1-18).

Theon of Alexandria (fl. 364 A.D.) was a mathematician and astronomer. Apart from his commentary on Aratus, he also wrote commentaries on Ptolemy's *Almagest* and *Manual Tables* and prepared an edition of Euclid.

164/37 Transvection: transportation

165/6   Third Book: 'Chap 13, sect 6'[M]

165/8   Balsame: healing balm

165/21   *Fallopius*: Gabriele Fallopio, *Tractatus de Metallis et Fossilibus*, Ch 9: 'Nam et imputrescentibus dum fit fermentatis, excitatur quidam vapor, et spiritus, et fit animal: et prout spiritus excitatur a materia vel perfectiori vel imperfectiori, ita perfectione, vel minus imperfecta generantur animalia unde aliquando vidi concidisse guttas quasdam aquae magnas in pulverem, et statim obortas esse ranunculas.Unde haec? Certe ex spiritu excitato ex fermentatione facta a gutta ille aquae cum pulvere.'
[For when there is a fermentation in putrefying things, a certain vapour and spirits are engendered and produce an animal. Just as spirits are produced from matter either perfect or imperfect, so animals are generated either perfect or less perfect. How is it that large drops of rain are seen sometimes scattered in the dust and, soon after, turned into frogs? How indeed? Surely,from the spirits produced from the fermentation arising from that drop of water and the dust.]
Gabriele Fallopio (1523-62) held the chair of pharmacy at the Unive rsity of Ferrara and, later, the chair of anatomy in the Universities of Pisa and Padua. His most important work was the *Observationes Anatomicae*(1561), an illustrated commentary of Vesalius' *De humani corporis fabrica(1542)*. Fallopius sought to correct the errors of Vesalius as well as present new material. Vesalius answered Fallopio's criticisms in his *Anatomicorum Gabriellis Falloppii observationum examen*(1564).

165/21   *Scaliger: Exotericarum Exercitationum*, Exercitatio 323[M]:Replying to Cardano, Scaliger says 'Sed et ranarum ovis in aerem sublatis ranunculas excludi scribis: quibus pluat. Quod aeque vanum est. Quippe deductis ex hiatu novo rupium limpidissimis aquis: ut postridie non gyrinos, sed perfectas ibi ranas vidimus in lapidea fossa, quae ante villam erat, nullius pridie ovis apparentibus; sic in aere licet eidem Naturae non ex ovis generare. Nam si Mus non semper e parentum femine sed e quisquiliis in navi, sic in aere ranae, haud ex ovo, sed ex aqua genitali caelesti calore condensata,

conformataque.'
[But you have written that the eggs of frogs taken up into the
air pro duce frogs, which then rain down. This is quite
absurd. For, once, limpid water was drawn out of a new
gash in the rocks and the next day we saw, not tadpoles but
full-fledged frogs in the stony pit which was in front of the
town, although no eggs had been seen the previous day; thus,
it is possible for them to be born in the air and not out of
eggs. Just as mice are not always born from the female
parent but from rubbish in ships, so, in the air, frogs are
condensed and formed not from eggs but from life-bearing
water and celestial heat.]
And he gives the following story to prove his point: 'Miram
bellum oppidum est Santonicae praeturae. In eius agro
tantum pluit ranarum: ut cumulatim totae viae tegerentur.
Oppidani neque domo effere pedem neque ubi vestigium
ponerent, haberent. Quo si totius pene Aquitaniae ranina
ova convecta essent, vix ille numerus expleri potuerit.'
[Miram is a pleasant town in the province of Santonica. In
its fields there was such a rain of frogs that all the roads
were quite covered up The townspeople could not go out of
their houses nor set foot anywhere. Even if almost all of
Aquitaine were heaped with eggs of frogs, it would be
difficult to explain that number.]
Giulio Cesare Scaliger (1484-1558) studied Aristotelian
philosophy in the University of Padua and was taught
mathematics by Pomponazzi. His later studies in botany
resulted in editions of three ancient treatises on plants by
Aristotle and Theophrastus. He was also a medical doctor,
and physician to the king of Navarre. His *Exotericarum
Exercitationes* (1557) was a spirited critique of Cardano's *De
Subtilitate*. Cardano's reply was not published until two years
after Scaliger's death.

165/23 *Vaninus*: Vanini, *De admirandis naturae*: Dial X , 'De
Fulgure, Nive, et Pluvia': 'J.C.: Quemadmodum mus non
semper e parentum femine, sed a navalibus quisquilis
procedit, sic in aere genuit Natura ranas non ex ovis, sed ex
aqua genitali, coelesti calore condensata, et conformata, idem
de lapideis, ac ferreis imbribis dictum volumus. Quid mirum?
nonne sulphur in aere generatur? quippe fulmine, quod in
aere gignitur, vitiata corpora sulphureum odorem naribus

offundunt.'
[As a mouse is not always produced from its female parent
but from rubbish in ships, so, frogs are born naturally in the
air, not from eggs but from genital water, condensed and
formed in the heat of the skies. We maintain the same about
stones and metals produced in rain. Why not? Is sulphur
not generated in the air? For indeed bodies produced in the
air that are decayed by lightning fill our nostrils with a
sulphureous odor.]
Vanini does not refer to Johannes Ginochius in the section,
and when he does relate an anecdote concerning the
theologian (Dial. LV) it is with no connection to the mode of
generation of frogs. Besides, Vanini's ironical mode is plainly
evident in Dial.XLIX, 'DeDeo': 'J.C.: Venetiis cum essem
novi impurissimum impostorem Hebraeum, qui suis
persuadebat, Messiam primo vere nova pluvia sese demi-
ssurum: cum ranunculis, addebam ego.'
[When I was at Venice, I saw a Jewish impostor who was
persuading his people that the Messiah was to appear at the
next rainfall in spring -- along with the tadpoles, I added.]

165/40 ἀφαιρεσία: See More's definition in sect 8.

165/42 *Pliny: Naturalis Historia*, Bk VII, Ch 52[M]: This section of
Pliny's work deals with, among other things, the different
ways in which death visits human beings, along with some
examples of extraordinary psychic phenomena such as the
story of Hermotimus: 'Reperimus inter exempla Hermotimus
Clazomenii animam relicto corpore errare solitam vagamque
e longinquo multa adnuntiare quae nisi a praestante nosci
non possent, corpore interim semianimi, donec crematoeo
inimici qui Cantharidae vocabantur remeanti animae veluti
vaginam ademerint.'
[Among other instances we find that the soul of Hermotimus
of Clazomenae used to leave his body and roam abroad, and
in its wanderings report to him from a distance many things
that only one present at them could know of -- his body in the
meantime being only half-conscious; till finally some enemies
of his named the Cantharidae burned his body and so
deprived his soul on its return of what may be called its
sheath. (Tr. H. Rackham, Loeb Classical Library)].

166/4   *Maximus Tyrius*: Maximus of Tyre, *Dissertationes*, 28: Tyrius discussing the Platonic question ἐι ἀι μαϑήσεις ἀναμνήσεις refers to Pythagoras as the first among the Greeks to have maintained the immortality of the soul and its preexistence. He gives as an example of this doctrine the story of Aristeas as narrated by Pliny (see Note above).

Maximus of Tyre (ca 125-185 A.D.) was an itinerant orator and eclectic Platonist whose most important work is the *Dissertationes* consisting of 41 essays which deal with theological, ethical, and philosophical subjects.

166/4   *Herodotus: History*, IV [M] 14,15: Herodotus' tale of Aristeas is different from that recounted by Pliny: 'It is said that this Aristeas , who was as nobly born as any of his townsmen, went into a fuller's shop at Proconnesus and there died; the fuller shut his workshop and went away to tell the dead man's kinsfolk, and the report of Aristeas' death being now spread about in the city, it was disputed by a man of Cyzicus, who had come from the town of Artace, and said that he had met Aristeas going towards Cyzicus and spoken with him. While he vehemently disputed, the kinsfolk of the dead man had come to the fuller's shop with all that was needful for burial; but when the house was opened there was no Aristaeas there, dead or alive. But in the seventh year after that Aristeas appeared at Proconnesus and made that poem which the Greeks now call the Arimaspeia after which he vanished once again. Such is the tale told in these two towns. But this, I know, befell the Metapontines in Italy, two hundred and forty years after the second disappearance of Aristeas, as reckoning made at Proconessus and Metapontum shows me. Aristeas, so the Metapontines say, appeared in their country and bade them set up an altar to Apollo, and set beside it a statue bearing the name of Aristeas, the Proconnesian, for he said, Apollo had come to their country alone of all Italiot lands, and he himself -- who was now Aristeas but then when he followed the god had been a crow -- had come with him. Having said this, he vanished away. The Metapontines, so they say, sent to Delphi and inquired of the god what the vision of the man might be, and the Pythian priestess bade them obey the vision, saying that their fortune would be the better, having received which answer they did as commanded.' (Tr. A.D. Godley, Loeb Classical Library).

166/5   *Ficinus*: Marsilio Ficino, *Theologia Platonica*, Bk 13, Ch 2 [M]:
In this chapter 'De Sacerdotibus,' Ficino relates various
stories drawn from classical authors illustrating the ecstatic
powers of priests. The example More refers to is from Aulus
Gellius, Bk 15, Ch 18[M]: 'Cornelium Sacerdotem
castissimum scribit Aulus Gellius Patavi mente motum
fuisse, eo tempore quo Caesar et Pompeius in Thessalio,
confligebant, adeo ut et tempus et ordinem et exitum pugnae
videret.'
Aulus Gellius (ca 123-169 A.D.) is famous for his twenty
books of *Noctes Atticae*, a miscellany of numerous extracts
from Greek and Roman writers on history, philosophy,
philology, and antiquities, interspersed with original remarks
and discussions.

166/10   *Wierus*: Johann Weyer, *De Praestigiis daemonum*, Bk I, Ch
14: ' Refert Helimandus monachus, [*Libro Chronicorum* 13]
se audisse ab ebando patruo suo, qui a cubiculis erat Henrico
Remensi archiepiscopo, Ludovici Gallorum regis fratri: quod
Henrico archiepiscopo aestate quadam in itinere somnum
meridianum capiente, miles quidam caeteros aperto et hiante
ore ost prandium dormiret, e cuius ore visa est ab alijs vigi-
lantibus quaedem alba bestiola mustelae similis exijsse,
atque ad vicinum ibi rivulum procurrisse. Cumque sursum
deorsum in ripa rivuli anxia cucurrisset, nec transeundi viam
inveniret, quidam ex astantibus accedens evaginatum
gladium rivulo angusto veluti pontem faciens, imponit.
Bestiola ilico rivulum super gladium transgrediens, longitus
procurrit, et sese subduxit. Paulo post redire visa, cum
iterum notum pontem quaereret, atque eo iam sublato
discurrens transire non valeret, idem ille qui,antea, rursum
rivuli ripas imposito gladio coniungit, atque abscedit. Tum
transit bestiola, et ad dormientis adhuc patulum os rediens,
videntibus omnibus ingreditur: acilico qui dormierat
expergiscitur, rogatusque num quid in somno passus esset
respondit, se sessum esse, et fatigatum, tanquam ex difficili
& longo itinere; in quo bis super pontem ferreum, flumen
transivisset. Unde socij collegerunt, eum, quae ipsi viderant
vere somniasse.'
In *An Antidote against Atheism*, Bk III, Ch XI, Sec 7[M] to
which More directs us in his marginal note here, he gives the

same story from Weyer in greater detail and adds: 'Wierus
acknowledgeth the truth of the Relation, but, will by all
means have it to be the *Devil*, not the *Soul* of the Man,'
referring to Weyer's comment, 'Mihi vero diaboli ludibrium
esse videtur, qui ut vigilantes socios falleret, aut animam
hominis corpoream esse, ideoque interituram cum corpore,
ipsis   ostenderet   persuaderetque,   idolum   hoc,   exiens
dormientis corpus, & ingrediens, oculis obiecit.'
Johann Weyer (1515-1588) was a German doctor of medicine
who studied in France and travelled extensively in N. Africa
and the East before settling in his native land. His
publications include medical works such as *De morbo gallico*
and *De irae morbo* (1577), but his most remarkable treatises
were *De praestigiis daemonum et incantationibus ac veneficiis*
(1563) and its sequel, *De Lamiis* (1577). Although Weyer
believed in the existence of the Devil,and the magical arts, he
was much more sympathetic to the victims of sorcery than
the bigoted witch-hunters of his age such as Martin Del Rio
and Jean Bodin. He pleaded pathological infirmity on the
part of the women who were possessed by the Devil or his
human agents so that they might be spared the persecution.
Bodin promptly published a *Réfutation des opinions de Jean
Wier*(1580) which discounted Weyer's scientific explanations
of witchcraft and cast asper sions on both Weyer and his
teacher, Agrippa von Nettesheim, as being, themselves,
agents of the Devil.

166/14   *Pliny: Naturalis Historia*, Bk VII, Ch 52[M]: Pliny's allusion
to thee story of Aristeas shows him, indeed, to be less
credulous than More. For, having stated that we learn of
'Aristeae etiam visam evolantem ex ore in Proconneso corvi
effigie,' he adds 'cum magna quae sequitur hanc
fabulositate.' More, besides, inaccurately refers to a 'pigeon'
instead of a 'raven.'

166/20   *Bodinus*: 'See my *Antidote*, Book 3, Chap 11, sect 2-3'[M].
There Mo re cites Jean Bodin, *De la démonomanie des
sorciers*, Bk II, Ch. 5, 'De Ravissement, ou Ecstase des
Sorciers, et des fréquentations ordinaires, qu'ils ont avec les
demons' and Ch 6 'De la Lycanthropie et si le Diable peut
changer les hommes en bestes.' More's preference for Bodin
over Weyer is readily understandable since Bodin's literal

acceptance of all supernatural stories, ancient or modern, too, was motivated by his desire to establish the immortality of the soul: 'Or combien que nous ayons des tesmoignages très certains et demonstrations indubitables de l'immortalité de l'ame si est-ce que celuy-cy me semble des plus forts, et des plus grands, et qui peut suffire estant averé, comme il a esté par infinies histoires, jugemens, recolemens, confrontations, convictous les Epicuriens et atheistes, que l'esprit humain est une essence immortelle. Car l'hipothese d'Aristote au second livre de l'Ame est par ce moyen très bien verifée, et demonstrée en ce qu'il dit que l'ame est immortelle si elle peut quelqua chose sans l'ayde du corps. Mais les infideles, qui ne croyent ny la puissance de Dieu, ny l'essence des esprits disent que ce que nous appelons ame est une liaison harmonieuse et forme universelle resultant des formes particulieres des humeurs et autres parties du corps humain: qui est une incongruité bien lourde de composer la forme de l'homme, que tous philosophes confessent estre pure et simple, de plusieurs formes.' (Ch 5).

Jean Bodin (1530-96) was a French philosopher, statesman, and one of the earliest writers on economics. His first systematic work, *Methodus ad Facilem Historiarum Cognitionem*(1566) was similar in conception to Descartes' in the Preface to his *Principia*. In the *Six Livres de la République*(1576) Bodin defended French monarchy, as in his last work *Heptaplomeres*, he defended the Catholic Church. His *Universae Naturae Theatrum* (1576) expounds his physics and metaphysics in a curious combination of Aristotelian materialism and Neoplatonist idealism. The soul, in Bodin's view, is a unity and its function is to vivify the extended matter of the body. It is also separable from the body both during life and at death. But, at the same time, it is the corporeal form of the body and acts directly on the body without any intermediary. The work More quotes from, *La Démonomanie des sorciers* (1580), is a strong plea for the repression of witchcraft and offers its own demonology derived from the Bible.

166/29 no ... Demonstration: See *Enthusiasmus Triumphatus*, Sect 5-28[M]. More discusses in sect. 5 the reason why the representations of our dreams can seem preternaturally real: 'Because the *Brains, Animal Spirits*, or whatever the

Soul works upon within in her Imaginative operations, are not considerably moved, altered or agitated from any external motion, but keep intirely and fully that figuration or modification which the Soul *necessarily* and *naturally* moulds them into in our sleep: so that the opinion of the truth of what is represented to us in our *Dreams* is from hence, that *Imagination* then (that is, the inward figuration of our *Brain* or *Spirits* into this that representation) is far *stronger* then any motion or agitation from *without*, which to them that are awake dimmes and obscures their inward Imagination, as the light of the Sun doth the light of a Candle in a room.'

168/27 *Sophocles*: Anon., Σοφοκλεους Γενος Και Βιος: τελετῆσαι δ᾽ αὐτον ... φασὶ τοῦτον τὸν τροπον ... ὅι δὲ ὅτι μετὰ τὴν τοῦ δραματος ἀνάγνωσιν, ὅτε νικῶν ἐκηρύλϑη χαρᾶι νικηϑεῖς ἐξέλιπεν.
[Some say that he died ... in this way: on hearing about his play that it had won, he was so delighted, he died out of joy in the victory.]

168/27 *Dionysius*: see Diodorus Siculus, *Bibliotheca Historica*, Bk XV, 74: In Diodorus' account of the death of Dionysius, the tyrant dies from his excessive consumption of liquor in celebration of the victory of his mediocre play: ἑστιῶν δὲ λαμπρῶς τοὺς φίλους, καὶ κατὰ τοὺς ποτούς, φιλοτιμότερον τῆι μέϑηι δοὺς ἑαυτόν εἰς ἀρρωστίαν σφοδοτέραν, ἐνέπεσε διὰ τὸ πλῆϑος τῶν ἐμφορηϑέντων ὑγρῶν.
[As he entertained his friends lavishly and during the bout applied himself overzealously to drink, he fell violently ill from the quantity of liquor he had consumed. (Tr. C.L. Sherman, Loeb Classical Library)]

168/28 *Polycrita ...Philippides ... Diagoras*: see Aulus Gellius, *Noctes Atticae*, Bk III, Ch 15: 'Cognito repente insperato gaudio expirasse animam refert Aristoteles philosophus Polycritam, nobilem feminam Naxo insula. Philippides quoque, comoediarum poeta haut ignobilis, aetate iam edita cum in certamine poetarum praeter spem vicisset et laetissime gauderet, inter illud gaudium repente mortuus est. De Rodio etiam Diagora celebrata historia est. Is Diagoras tris filios adulescentes habuit, unum pugilem, alterum pancratiastem, tertium luctatorem. Eos omnis vidit vincere

coronarique Olympiae eodem die et, cum ibi eum tres
adulescentes amplexi coronis suis in caput patris positis
saviarentur, cum populus gratulabundus flores undique in
eum laceret, ibidem in stadio inspectante populo in osculis
atque in manibus filiorum animam efflavit.'
[Aristotle the philosopher relates that Polycrita, a woman of
high rank in the island of Naxos, on suddenly and
unexpectedly hearing joyful news, breathed her last.
Philippides too, a comic poet of no little repute, when he had
unexpectedly won the prize in a contest of poets at an
advanced age, and was rejoicing exceedingly, died suddenly
in the midst of his joy. The story also of Diogoras of Rhodes
is widely known. This Diogoras had three young sons, one a
boxer, the second a pancratist, and the third a wrestler. He
saw them all victors and crowned at Olympia on the same
day, and when the three young men were embracing him
there and having placed their crowns on their father's head
were kissing him, and the people were congratulating him
and pelting him from all sides with flowers, there in the very
stadium, before the eyes of the people, amid the kisses and
embraces of his sons, he passed away. (Tr. J.C. Rolfe, Loeb
Classical Library)].

168/39 *intemperies*: disorder.

169/16 Story: see Jan Baptista van Helmont, *De Magnetica
Curatione Vulnerum* [M]: After the narration of the story
drawn from Martin del Rio's *Disquisitionum Magicarum libri
VI* (1599-1600), Helmont explains: 'Igitur in sanguine est
quaedam potestas ecstatica, quae si quando ardenti desiderio
excita fuerit, etiam ad absens aliquod objectum, exterioris
hominis spiritum deducendo sit: ea autem potestas in
exteriori homine latet, velut in potentia; nec ducitur ad
actum, nisi excitetur, accensa imaginatione ferventi
desiderio, vel arte aliqua pari. Porro uti sanguis
quadammodo corrumpiter, tunc se ejus potestates omnes,
sine praevia imaginationis excitatione, quae antea in
potentia, erant, sponte in actum deducuntur. Corruptione
namque grani, virtus seminalis, alias torpeus et sterilis, in
actum erumpit.'
[There is therefore in the blood, a certain ecstatical or
transporting power, the which, if it shall at any time be

stirred up by an ardent desire, is able to derive or conduct the spirit of the more outward man, even into some absent object. But that power lies hid in the more outward man, as it were in *potentia*, or by way of possibility, rouzed up by the imagination enflamed by a fervent desire, or some art like unto it. Moreover, when as the blood is after some sort corrupted, then indeed all the powers thereof which without a fore-going excitation of the imagination were before impossibility, are of their own accord drawn forth into action, for through corruption of the grain the seminal virtue, otherwise drowsie and barren, breaks forth into act. (Tr. J.C.)].

170/30   *Avenzoar Albumaron*: see Ficino, *op. cit.*, Bk 16, Ch 5[M]: 'Avenzoar Albumaron, medicus Arabs, scribit se a medico nuper defuncto per somnum accepisse optimum oculo suo aegrotanti remedium.'

170/33   *Diodorus: Bibliotheca Historicae*, Bk I M: As for Isis, the Egyptians say that she was the discoverer of many health-giving drugs and was greatly versed in the science of healing; consequently, now that she has attained immortality,she finds her greatest delight in the healing of mankind and gives aid in their sleep to those who call upon her, plainly manifesting both her very presence and her beneficence towards men who ask her help. In proof of this, as they say, they advance not legends, as the Greeks do, but manifest facts; for practically the entire inhabited world is their witness, in that it eagerly contributes to the honours of Isis because she manifests herself in healings. For standing above the sick in their sleep she gives them aid for their disease and works remarkable cures upon such as submit themselves to her; and many who have been cured of by their physicians because of the difficult nature of their malady are restored to health by her, while numbers who have altogether lost the use of their eyes or of some other part of their body, whenever they turn for help to this goddess, are restored to their previous condition. Furthermore, she discovered also the drug which gives immortality, by means of which she not only raised from the dead her son, Horus, who had been the object of plots on the part of the Titans and had been found dead under the water, giving him his soul again, but also

made him immortal. And it appears that Horus was the last
of the gods to be king after his father Osiris departed from
among men. Moreover, they say that the name Horus, when
translated, is Apollo, and that, having been instructed by his
mother Isis in both medicine and divination, he is now a
benefactor of the race of men through his oracular responses
and his healings.' (Tr. C.H. Oldfather)
Diodorus Siculus, who was a contemporary of Caesar and
Augustine, spent most of his life working on a universal
history from the earliest times to the Gallic wars of Caesar.
The result of his endeavours was the 40 books of history
called *Bibliotheca Historica* (ca 60-30 B.C.).

170/37 *Posidonius*: see Ficino, *Ibid.* [M]: 'Confirmat Platonis
sententia Posidonius Stoicus ex eo quod duo quidam Arcades
familares cum Megaram venissent, alter ad cauponem
divertit, alter ad hospitem. Qui ut coenati quieverunt, nocte
visus est in somnis ei, qui erat in hospitio , ille alter orare ut
subveniret, quod sibi a caupone interitus pararetus. Hic
primo perterritus somno surrexit, deinde cum se collegisset
idque visum pro nihilo habendum esse duxisset, recubuit.
Tum ei dormienti ille idem visus est rogare, ut quoniam sibi
vivo non subvenisset, mortem suam saltem ne inultam esse
pateretur, se interfectum a caupone in plaustrum esse
coniectum, et supra stercus iniectum, petere ut mane ad
portam adesset, priusquam plaustrum ex oppido exiret. Hoc
ergo insomnio is commotus, mane bubulco proesto ad portam
affuit. Quaesivit ex eo quid esset in plaustro. Ille perterritus
fugit, mortuus erutus est. Caupo re patefacta poenas dedit.'

171/21 *Simonides*: see Ficino, *Ibid.*[M]: 'Beneficii quoque memores
esse animas defunctorum ex hoc coniiciunt Stoicorum
nonnulli, quod Simonides cum ignotum quemdam projectum
mortuum vidisset eumque humavisset haberetque in animo
navem conscendere, moneri visus est, ne id faceret, ab eo
quem sepultura affecerat, si navigasset, eum naufragio
periturum. Rediit Simonides, caeteri naufragium fecerunt.
Haec omnia docent aliquid in nos agere animas defunctorum.'

171/32 *Pliny*: Pliny the younger, *Epistulae*, VII, 27: In this letter to
Sura , Pliny presents his friend with three stories, two from
hearsay and one from personal experience, that seem to lend

substance to the belief in ghosts. The story that More refers
to is the second of these three. Although Pliny is not entirely
credulous, he appears to be inclined to such a belief and
earnestly requests his friends views on the subject.

171/40   *Nero*: see Suetonius, *De Vita Caesarum*, Nero, XLVI.

171/41   *Otho*: see Suetonius, *op. cit.*, Otho, VII.

172/16   *Cardan*: Cardano, *De Subtilitate*, Bk 18[M]. Cardano begins
his explanation of apparitions by declaring that it is the
same as Averroes': 'Pulcherrime igitur mihi in Collectaneis
Averrois causam reddere visus est, dicens: Cùm spiritus
imaginationi serviens, formas imaginando exceperit, soni aut
qualitatis cuiuspiam, quo odore aut tactu dignoscatur, aut
mortui vel daemonis, illaque imbutus transferetus ad
sensum, qui in actioni correspondet, in odoribus quidem ad
instrumentu m proprium olfactus, in auditu ad aures, in
spectris ad oculus, necessariò olfaciet, aut audiet, aut videbit
nullo assistente objecto: nam si visio nihil aliud est, qùm
speciei in spiritu in perceptio, seu species illa ab objecto
decidatur, seu non, pater quotiescunque contigerit hoc, illum
videre vere. Atque ita vigilando contigit daemones ac
mortuos videre, tum etiam cognitorum audire voces,
odoresque sentire, ac tangere, velut in succubis, incubisque.
Ob id vero rariùs ista videntur, quàm audiantur,
tangantúrve: quoniam in caetaris sensibus cùm unicam
sufficiat observasse differentiam, unicus spiritus translatus
ad sensum cum illa imagine hoc referre potest, in oculis cum
plures sint differentiae necessariae, magnitudo, forma, calor,
plures spiritus transferri necessarium est; ob id etiam natura
cavos fecit nervos, qui ad oculum feruntur, solósque tales,
quod ipsi in suis operationibus longe pluribus indigeant
spiritibus; multoque etiam ob id plus fatiganmur intente
intuendo quàm ullum aliorum sensuu m exercendo. Hinc
igitur multorum problematum solutio contingit quae cùm
verissima sint tamen adeo fatigarunt plerosque ut ad
miracula transferre alij ad daemonas, alij negare non
dubitarint.'
[I have seen the reason explained very finely in a Collection
of Averroes', where he says: As the spirits serving the
imagination draw for the imagination forms of the sounds --

or of the qualities by which odour and touch are effected -- of spirits and of the dead, they are imbibed and transferred to the sense which corresponds in action -- in the case of odours to the olfactory instrument, in the case of hearing to the ears, in the case of vision to the eyes; and the sense will necessarily smell or hear or see without any assisting object. Now, if vision is nothing else but perception of an image in the mind in crystalloid form, whether that inage has been exuded by an object or not, it is clear that as often as it touches it i.e. the visual faculty, it indeed sees it. Thus, it has happened that a person awake has seen spirits or dead people and has even heard the voices or smelt the odours of their acquaintances, or touched them as in the case of succubi and incubi. They are seen more rarely than they are heard or touched since, in the other senses, one spirit carried to the sense with that image can produce it. As many differentiae are necessary in the case of sight -- magnitude, form, and heat -- it is necessary for many spirits to be carried. That is why nature has made hollow only the nerves which are coneccted to the eyes, since they need many spirits for a long time in their operations. This is the reason why we are tired more easily by looking intently than by exercising any other senses. Here then is reached the solution of many problems which tire most people so easily that some relegate them to miracles and others to demons, while still others deny them completely.]
He then gives the story of the Icelanders that More refers to.

172/17   *Vaninus*: Vanini, *op. cit.*: 'An dicemus corpora nostra pro sua magnitudine emittere vaporem, qui illorum refert effigiem quae in denso aere complicata a ventis in altum elevari potest, atque ita humanum imaginem oculis nostris subijciet: quapropter in Ecclesiasticis cimiterijs mortuororum figurae visae sunt a nonullis (si vera referunt) quia a paucis diebus nec in profundo lectulo cum esset sepultum emisit idcirco olim, quia cremabantur cadaveres, et scitissime quidem ad aeris corruptionem prohibendam, nihil tale videbatur.'
[We should maintain that our bodies, on account of their volume, emit a vapor which transports their image, which can be raised to higher levels by breezes along with the dense air in which it is mixed, and offer to our view human images. It is in this way that in church cemeteries shapes of the dead

have been seen by some (if they speak the truth) since the buried corpse interred for a few days and in a grave that is not very deep, has emitted a vapour corresponding to its shape. It is for this reason that formerly, since they wisely burnt corpses in order to prevent corruption of the air, nothing of this sort was seen.]

172/17 others. Gaffarel, *Unheard-of Curiosities*, Part 2, Ch 5 [M]: 'From hence we may draw this conclusion, that the ghosts of dead men which are often seen to appeare in churchyards are naturall effects being only the formes of the bodies which are buried in those places, or their outward shapes or figures; and not the souls of those men or any such like apparition, caused by evil Spirits, as the common opinion is.'
Jacques Gaffarel (1607-1681) was Librarian to Cardinal Richelieu. Adept at several Oriental languages, he was deeply interested in the occult sciences and the Cabala. His book *Curiositez inouies sur la sculpture talismanique des Persans, Horoscope des Patriarches et lécture des étoiles* (1629) caused a scandal since it maintained that taslismans or constellated figures had the power to render people rich or healthy. Being a doctor of theology who held public religious offices, Gaffarel had to retract his opinions. He nevertheless continued to enjoy the favour of Cardinal Richelieu who sought to use his services for his grand project of the reunion of religions. His writings include many works on Hebraic culture and the Cabala. More also refers us in his marginal note here to his *Antidote*, Book 3, chap 16, sect 2,3 [M].

173/5 *Caspar Peucerus*: De ϑεομαντείαι, in Henning Grosse, *Magica de Spectris et apparationibus spiritum*, Sect 104 (Not 140 as More indicates)[M]
Henning Grosse (1553-1621) was an editor and printer in Leipzig.

173/9 *Lemures*: ghosts

173/16 *Cambium*: one of the alimentary humours supposed to nourish the bodily organs.

173/22 *Antidote*: Book 3, Chap 8 and 9 [M]. Chapter 8 deals with the story of the Silesian shoemaker, and chapter 9 with that of

Cuntius.

173/24 what *Agrippa* writes: *De Occulta Philosophia*, Bk IV, Ch 41:
'Legimus etiam in Cretensium annalibus, manes quas ipsi
Catechanes vocant, in corpora remuere solitos, et ad relictas
Uxores ingredi, libidinemque, perficere: ad quod evitandum,
et quo amplius uxores non infestent, legibus municipalibus
cautum est, surgentium corclavo transfigere totumque;
cadaver exurere.'

173/35 *Stephanus Hubener*: see Henning Grosse, *op. cit.*, Sec 184
[M].

174/14 *eximious* : eminent

174/16 *Baronius*: Cesare Baronio, *Annales Ecclesiastici*, Annus 411,
para 49: ' Haud namque inexplorata referram, sed quae
complurium eruditorum virorum scimus assertione firmata,
immo et a religiosis viris ad populum pro concione saepè
narrata. Ego vero a quo accepi, auctorem proferam, nempe
integerrimae fidei virum, Michaelem Mercatum Miniatensem
S.R.E.Protonotarium, probitate morum atque doctrina
spectatum: ipse enim narravit de avo suo, eodem quo ipse
nomine nuncupato, Michaele Mercato Seniore, cui cum
Marsilio Ficino nobilissimi ingenij viro summa intercedebat
amicitiae consuetudo, parta et aucta philosophicis
facultatibus, in quibus Platonem ambo affectabantur
auctorem. Accidit autem aliquando, ut ex more, quidnam
post obitum supersit homini, ex eiusdem Platonis sententia:
sed non sine tamen trepidatione deducerent, quae labantia
Christianae fidei sacramentis suffulcienda essent: eo enim
argumento extat eiusdem Marsilij ad ipsum Michaelem
Mercatum erudita quidem epistola, de animi et Dei
immortalitate. Cum vero inter differendum eorum progressa
longius fuisset disputatio; eam ad calcem perductam illo
clauserunt corollario, ut iuncta simul dextera pacti fuerint,
uter eorum ex hac vita prior decederet (si liceret) alterum de
alterius vitae statu redderet certiorem. Quibus inter se
conventis, ambo iurati ab invicem discessere. Interlapso
autem haud brevi temporis spatio, evenit, ut cum summo
mane idem Michael Senior in philosophicis speculationibus
vigilaret: ex inopinato strepitum velociter currentis equi,

eiusdemque ad ostium domus cursum sistentis audiret,
vocemque simul Marsilij clamantis: 'O Michael, O Michael,
vera vera sunt illa.' Ad vocem amici Michael admiratus,
assurgens, fenestramque aperiens, quem audierat, vidit post
terga ad cursum iterum acto equo candido, candidatum:
prosecutus est eum voce "Marsilium, Marsilium," invocans;
prosecutus et oculis, sed ab eis evanuit. Sic ipse novi casus
stupore affectus, quid de Marsilio Ficino esset, solicitius
perquirendum curavit (degebat ille Florentiae, ubi diem
clausit extremum) invenitque eundem illa ipsa hora
defunctum, qua eo medo auditus & visus est sibi.'
Cesare Baronio (1538-1607) was a Roman cardinal and
Church historian. His 12-volume *Annales Ecclesiastici*
(1598-1607), written in response to the *Centuriae
Magdeburgenses* (1559-74), a polemical Lutheran history of
the Church conceived by Matthias Flacius Ilyricus, was based
on a careful examination of innumerable textual sources,
coins, and inscriptions.

174/17   whether: whichever

174/39   *Cardan*: Cardano, *De Subtilitate*, Bk 18: 'The world is large
and time long, and error and fear can work many things in
men.' Cardano continues: 'Eadem vero ratione qua in
Islandia, in arenae solitudinibus Aegypti, et Aethiopiae,
Indiaeque, ubi Sol ardet, eadem imagines, eadem spectra
viatores ludificare solent.'
[For the same reason as in Iceland, in the solitary deserts of
Egypt, Ethiopia and India, where the sun burns, these shades
and spectres are wont to fool travellers.]

176/34   already...demonstrated: 'Chap 2,4,5,6.'[M].

176/42   *Spirits*: 'Chap 8, 9'[M].

177/13   *Plotinus: Enneades* VI, vii, 7.

177/22   before: 'Chap 10, sect.7'[M].

178/5   there ... it: 'See Chap 8, sect.13'[M].

178/12   *Michael Psellus: De Operatione Daimonum*[M]: When the

Thracian asks Marcus the Mesopotamian hermit how daemons that are constituted of spirits alone may feel sensations, Marcus replies: θαυμάζω ... ὅτι τοῦτο ἠγνόηται, τὸ μὴ ἐπὶ τινος ὀστοῦν ἢ νεῦρον εἶναι τὸ αἰσθανόμενον, ἀλλά τὸ ἐν τούτοις ἐνυπάρχον πνεῦμα· διὸ κ'ἂν θλίβηται τὸ νεῖρον, κ'ἂν ψύχηται, κ'ἂν ἄλλο τοῖον δήτοι πάθοι, τοῦ πνεύματος εἰς τὸ πνεῦμα πεμπομένου τὴν ὀδύνην εἶναι.
[I am amazed, said he, you should be ignorant of the fact, that it is not the bone or nerve of any is endowed with the faculty of sensation, but the spirit inherent in them, therefore, whether the nerve be pained or refreshed, or suffer any other affection, the pain proceeds from the immission of spirit into spirit.]
He substantiates his point by revealing that even in composite bodies it is the spirits that cause sensation: καθ' ἑαυτὸ γὰρ οὐκ ἂν ὀδυνῶτο τὸ σύνθετον ,ἀλλὰ τὸ μετέχον τοῦ πνεύματος, ἐπεὶ παραλελυμένον ἢ νεκρωθὲν ἀνεπαίσθητόν ἐστι, τοῦ πνεύματος γυμνωθὲν.
[For a compound body is not capable of being pained by virtue of itself, but by virtue of its union with spirit, for when dissected or dead, it is incapable of suffering, because deprived of the spirit. (Tr. M. Collison
On the Operation of Daemons, Sydney, 1843)].

178/33 congenerous: congenial

178/35 already: 'Chap 15, sect. 5' [M]

178/42 concocted: discussed and resolved

180/27 *A posse ... consequentia*: 'There is no valid consequence from "can be" to "is".'

182/31 *Insulae Fortunatae*: cf. Hesiod, *Works and Days*, 171, and Pindar, Olympian Ode, II, 72.

182/33 *Coelum Empyreum*: The sphere of fire, or highest heaven.

183/10 elsewhere: *Antidote*, Book I, Ch 10, sect 9 [M]. More explains *universal Religious Worship* as a natural, instinctive, faculty in man with God as its proper object: 'For as the plying of a *Dog*'s feet in his sleep, as if there were some game before

him, and the butting of a young Lamb before he has yet
either horns or enemies to encounter, would not be in nature,
were there not such a thing as a *Hare* to be coursed, or an
horned Enemy to be encountred with horns; so there would
not be so *universal* an exercise of *Religious Worship* in the
world, though it be done never so ineptly and foolishly, were
there not really a due Object of this Worship, and a capacity
in Man for the right performance thereof; which could not be
unless there were a *God.'*

184/2   *separable*: 'Chap 2,3,4,5,6' [M].

184/6   *Animal Spirits*: 'Chap 8,9' [M].

187/8   *Plutarch: De recta ratione audiendi*, 41d-e,cf. also *De
         Alexandre magni fortuna aut virtute*, 333f-334a, where
         Plutarch employs the same story in another context.

188/16   vagient ... Targets: See Lucretius *,De Rerum Natura*, Bk II,
         ll. 629-639:
                    Hic armata manus, Curetas nomine Grai
                    Quos memorant, Phrygias inter si forte catervas
                    Ludunt in numerumque exultant sanguine laeti,
                    Terrificas capitum quatientes numine cristas,
                    Dictaeos referunt Curetas qui Iovis illum
                    Vagitum in Creta quondam occultasse feruntur,
                    Cum pueri circum puerum pernice chorea
                    Armati in numerum pulsarent aeribus aera,
                    Ne Saturnus eum malis mandaret adeptus
                    Aeternumque daret Matri sub pectore volnus.
         [Here an armed group, whom the Greeks name the Curetes,
         whenever they sport among the Phrygian bands and leap up
         rhythmically, joyful with blood, shaking their awful crests
         with the nodding of their heads, recall the Dictaean bands,
         who are said once upon a time to have concealed that infant
         wailing of Jupiter in Crete; when, boys round a boy in rapid
         dance, clad in armour, they dashed bronze upon bronze to a
         measure, that Saturn might not catch him and cast hin into
         his jaws and plant an everlasting wound in the Mother's
         heart. (Tr. M.F. Smith, Loeb Classical Library)]

188/16   vagient: squalling

188/19 Targets: Shields

Book III

192/10 *Plotinus: Enneades*, III, iv, 2: εἰ δὲ μηδ᾽ αἰσθήσει μετὰ τούτων, ἀλλὰ νωθείαι αἰσθήσεωσ μετ᾽ αὐτῶν, καὶ φυτά· μόνον γὰρ τοῦτο ἢ μάλιστα ἐνήργει τὸ φυτικόν, καὶ ἦν αὐτοις μελέτη δενδρωθῆναι.
[Those who in their pleasures have not even lived by sensation, but have gone their way in a torpid grossness became mere growing things, for only, or mainly, the vegetative principle was active in them, and such men have been busy be-treeing themselves.' (Tr. S. Mackenna)]

192/19 θεοπαράδοτον: given by God

192/21 *Plotinus: Enneades*, III, v, 6: τοὺς δὲ, δαίμονας τι΄; Ἆρά γε ψυχῆς ἐν κόσμωι γενομένης τὸ ἀφ᾽ ἑκάστης ἴχνος ; Διά τί δὲ τῆς ἐν κοσμωι; ὅτι ἡ καθαρά θεὸν γεννᾶι
[What, then, are these spirits? A celestial spirit is the representative generated by each Soul when it enters the Cosmos. And why, by a Soul entering the Cosmos? Because Soul pure of the Cosmos generates not a celestial spirit but a God. (Tr. S. Mackenna)]

193/14 above: 'Book 2, Ch 14, sect. 4, 5' [M].

193/21 ἀϋλότης: immateriality. The term is used by Plotinus, *Enneades*,I, ii, 7: καὶ γὰρ ἡ νόησις ἐκεῖ ἐπιστήμη καὶ σοφία τὸ δὲ πρὸς αὐτὸν ἡ σωφροσύνη. τὸ δὲ οἰκεῖον ἔργον ἡ οἰκειοπραγία, τὸ δὲ οἷον ἀνδρία ἡ ἀυλότης καὶ τὸ ἐφ᾽ αὐτοῦ μένειν καθαρόν.
[In the Supreme, Intellection constitutes knowledge and wisdom; selfconcentration is Sophrosyny: Its proper Art is its Dutifulness; Its Immateriality, by which it remains inviolate within itself, is the equivalent of Fortitude. (Tr. S. Mackenna).]

193/32 bewray: betray

194/10   above: 'Book 2, Chap 14, sect. 1' [M].

194/32   *Natura ... saltum*:   Nature does not make a leap

195/18   *The Soul ... Motion*: The soul's inability to generate motion in her aerial vehicle may be due to the fact that motion has originally been imparted in a fixed quantity to matter by God, according to Bk I, Ch, sec 9. Yet, in the following axiom, 32, More declares that the soul in her ethereal vehicle *can* increase or reduce motion. He attributes this superior ability to the fact that the soul in an ethereal state is "perfectly obedient" to God, showing that the more purified and god-like a soul is, the more powerful it becomes in controlling its motion.

197/34   place: 'Chap 5, sect. 11, 12; Ch. 6' [M].

198/4   *Consopition*:   a lulling to sleep

198/37   above: 'Book 1, Ch 3,5,8: Also Book 2, Chap. 1,2' [M].

199/6   evanidness: weakness

199/30   elsewhere: 'Book 2, Ch 11, sect 10, 11' [M].

200/22   *Ficinus*: Ficino, *op. cit.*, Bk XVII, Ch 2: More is probably referring to this passage: 'animam ideo "currum" vocant, quia motus efficit circulares ... in ea lineam ponunt quodammodo rectam, quantum corpora movet et respicit, deinde circulum quendam inferiorem, quasi planetarum orbem. quando redit in semetipsam, circulum qunque superiorem, quasi stellarum orbem fixarum, quatenus ad superiora convertitur.
[They [the Platonists] call the soul a chariot since it effects circular movements ... they postulate a straight line in it when it moves and regards bodies, and an inferior circle, such as the orbit of the planets, when it returns to itself, and a superior circle, such as the orbit of the fixed stars, when it turns to superior things. In the *Commentarium in Phedrum*, Ch. 7, Ficino defines the Phaedran term "chariot" thus: \Currum vero proprie corpus celeste vocamus: cum immortali qualibet anima sempiternum sphericumque natura motuve

celerrimum.
[Strictly, I call 'chariot' a celestial body i.e. a star which is sempiternal, spherical, and exceedingly swift in its motion, and endowed with an immortal soul.]

203/10   expunge: destroy

203/42   ἄιδης: Hades

203/42   ἄιδης: invisible

204/17   *conspissate*: condense

205/3   *Prytaneum*: a ceremonial public hall.In ancient Athens the prytaneum was the hall where those who had performed distinguished service to the state were entertained.

205/6   *Cardan*: Cardano, *De Varietate rerum*, Bk 16, Ch 93[M]: 'Principio igit ur illud animadvertendum, daemonas in suprema aeris regione generari, & habitare: ubi scilicet aer & purior, & siccior, & minus frigidus existat. Neque plus illos ad nos solere descendere, quam homines ad maris imum: non solum, quod acrem hunc crassiorem ferre nequeant, ubi neque respirare, nec agere quicquam possint, sed quod descendendo transitus sit per regionem frigidissimam, quae nobis proxima circumstat. Ut sit quasi septum inter nos, & daemonas, velut maris aqua inter nos ac pisces. Et licet nos ingenio, & industria valeamus, cupiamusque pisces enixe perdere, paucos tamen admodum licet: nec nisi illos, qui quasi ultro se nobis obiiciunt: qui, pro tanto numero eorum, qui in mari sunt, nulli dici possunt. Ita quamvis daemones oderint nos, corpore tamen nullo, industria per paucos perdere possunt. Et sicut si pisces loquerentur, dicere iure marito possent, existimare nulla alia esse animalia, quam quae in aqua degunt, nec tamen vera dicerent: ita iure etiam existimare homines possunt, demones non esse: cum tamen proculdubio sint, & tanto verius, quanto homines piscibus. Ergo demones in alto regione habitant, hominesque imaginibus admonent, ac terrent, presertim per somnum, quod in vigilia vis nos afficere possint. Genij igitur, non corpore, sed vi nobis astant, aliquidque in nobis possunt, si nos consenserimus. Rarissime enim ad nos veniunt, & si veniant, vix manere possunt: breve tamen tempus, longum videri faciunt sua arte, varietateque imaginum volubilitateque formarum & actionum. Verum vocati quandoque veniunt, aut venientis imaginem praeferunt; tunc mitiores, & sapientiores, & ex pacto futura quaedam docent mille ambagibus involuentes, mendaciisque miscentes: alij vero strangulant; vel si id non possunt, in desperationem agunt; aliquibus videntur in corpora inseri aliorum itros occidunt, non per se; sed arte quadam, non secus ac homines in fundo maris fuscina, & reti pisces opprimunt. Quod si omnino corpora hominum, verique ingrediuntur, & non ex alto imaginem solam immittunt: ob caloris similitudinem, & fomentum id contingere potest. Oportet autem tales daemones non generosos esse: nec venire sed mitti. Optimum est igitur eorum generi haud commisceri: uti neque tyrannis, aut potentioribus, aut feris: in quibus tam perniciosa est inimicitia, qmam familiaritas periculosa.'

207/6   *Peculium*: exclusive possession

208/37   *Cartesius*: Descartes, *Les Météores*, Discours Quatrième: 'Toute l' agitation d'air qui est sensible se nomme vent, et tout corps invisible et impalpable se norme air. Ainsi, lorsque l'eau est fort rarefiée et changée en vapeur fort subtile, on dit quelle est convertie en air, nonobstant que ce grand air que nous respirons ne soit, pour le plupart, composé que de parties qui ont des figures fort differentes de celles de l'eau, et qui sont beaucoup plus deliées. Et ainsi l'air, estant chassé hors d'un soufflet, ou poussé par un eventail, se nomme vent, nonobstant que ces vens plus étendus, qui regnent sur la face de la mer et de la terre, ne soient ordinairement autre chose que le mouvement des vapeurs qui, en se dilatant, passent, du lieu où elles sont, en quelque autre ou elles trouvent plus de commodité de s'estendre.'

210/41   *Maximus Tyrius*: Maximus of Tyre, *Dissertationes*, 27[M]:See note to Sec 8, below.

210/42   *Xenocrates*: see Plutarch, *De Defectu oraculorum*, ch 13.

210/43   *Philo: De Somnis*, I, 139-140.

211/8 already: 'Chap 2, sect 3,4'[M]

211/33 before:'Chap 2, sect. 5'[M]

212/28 *datâ operâ*: in given cases

212/29 the Devil of *Mascon*: see More, *Antidote*, Book 3, Chap 3, sect 8 [M] 'Amongst which that relation of *Mr. Francis Perreand*, concerning an unclean Spirit that haunted his house at *Mascon* in *Burgundy*, *both* for the variety of manatter and the Authentickness of the Story, is of prime use. For though this *Daemon* never appear'd visible to the eye yet his presence was palpably deprehensible by many freaks and pranks that he play'd.' The story of the Devil of Mascon first reported in Fr. Perreand's *Démonologie ou Traitté des Demons et Sorciers*(1653) was supported by Robert Boyle in a letter to Joseph Glanvill in 1678 (see *Works*, ed. T. Birch, V, 245)

212/33 above: 'Chap 2, sect 4'[M]

212/38 arrection: erection

213/6 humectant: moistening

213/10 *Cardan*: Cardano, *De Rerum Varietate*, Bk 16, Ch 93 [M]: 'aliquibus videntur in corpora inseri.'

213/14 *Psellus: De operatione daemonum* [M]: κίνδυνος αὐτοις καὶ τρεφεσϑαι καϑ᾽ ἡμᾶς τρέφονται. ὁ Μάρκος εἶπεν. ὃι μὲν δὶ εἰς πνοῆς, ὡς τὸ ἐν ἀρτηρίαιας καὶ ἐν νεύροις πνεῦμα. ὃι δὲ δι᾽ ὑγρότητος᾽. ἀλλ᾽ ὀυ στόματι καϑ᾽ ἡμας. ἀλλ᾽ ὥσπερ σπόγγοι καὶ ὠστρακόδερμα σπῶντες μὲν τῆς παρακειμένης ὑγρότητος ἔξωϑεν.
[Marcus... replied, Some derive it by inhalation, as for instance a spirit resident in lungs and nerves, and some from mosture, but not as we do, with the mouth, but as sponges and testaceous fishes do, by draining nourishment from the extraneous moisture lying around them. (Tr. M. Collison)].

213/18 *Moses Aegyptius*: Moses Maimonides, *Guide for the Perplexed*, Part 3, Ch 46[M]: 'Although blood was very unclean in the eyes of the Sabeans, they nevertheless partook of it, because they thought it was the food of the spirits; by eating it man has something in common with the spirits, which join him and tell him future events, according to the notion which people generally have of spirits.' The laws of the Pentateuch forbade such rituals, "for the eating of blood leads to a kind of idolatry, to the worship of spirits." (Tr. M. Friedländer from the original Arabic).

Moses ben Maimon(1158-68),one of the most significant of post-Talmudic Jewish philosophers,was born in Cordoba and earned his living first as a physician. His philosophical and theological interests were consolidated in an important commentary on the Mishnah, *Siraj* (1158-68), in his codification of Jewish Law, *Mishneh Torah* (1180), and in the *Dalalat al-Harin* (1190), translated into Hebrew 1202 as *More Nevochim*, or *Guide for the Perplexed*. The *Guide* was written to show the student of philosophy perplexed by the anthopormorphism of the Bible that the Biblical vocabulary is capable of bearing spiritual as well as literal connotations. Its topics vary from a discussion of God and creation to an exposition of the Law of Moses and its usefulness for incluating moral virtue.

213/37 *Hesiod: Works and Days,* 125. This line is part of the description o f the δαιμονες ἁγνοι ἐπιχϑονιοι -- spirits of the first, golden, of men created by the Olympian gods -- who are

ἐσϑλοί. ἀλεξίκακοι.φύλακες ϑνητῶν ἀνϑρώπων
ὅι ῥαφυλάσσουσιν τε δίκας καὶ σχέτλια ἔργα
ἠέρα ἑσσάμενοι πάντη φοιτῶντες ἐπ᾿ αἶαν

[kindly, delivering from harm, and guardians of mortal men; for they roam everywhere over the earth, clothed in mist and keep watch on judgements and cruel deeds. (Tr. H.L. Evelyn-White, Loeb Classical Li brary)]

213/40 *invious*: pathless

214/4   uninteressed: disinterested

214/10 *Plutarch: De Genie Socratis,* 593d-594a: Theanor, the Pythagorean stranger who gives the final account of the actions of gods and daemons in this dialogue refers only to the encouragement that the daemons offer to the virtuous.

There is no mention of the daemons abetting the wicked in their evil pursuits.

214/23 *Quae ... repostos*: Virgil, *Aeneid*, Bk VI 11. 653-55: Aeneas, accompanied by the Cumaean Sibyl, travels through the underworld and finally reaches the 'locos laetos et amoena virecta/Fortunatorum Nemorum Sedesque beatas,' where the blessed disport themselves, indulging in their favorite earthly pastimes: 'The selfsame pride in chariot and arms that was theirs in life,the selfsame care in keeping sleek steeds, attends them when hidden beneath the earth.' (Tr. H. R. Fairclough, Loeb Classical Library)

214/27 *Maximus Tyrius*: Maximus of Tyre, *op.cit.*[M]: προστέτακται δὲ αὐτὴ ὑπὸ τοῦ θεοῦ ἐπιφοιτᾶν τὴν γῆν ἀναμίγνυσθαι πάσηι μὲν ἀνδρῶν φύσει, πάσηι δὲ ἀνθρώπων τυχηι καὶ γνώμηι καὶ τέχνηι· καὶ τοῖς μὲν χρηστοῖς συνεπιλαμβάνειν,τοῖς δὲ ἀδικουμένοις τιμωρεῖν,τοῖς δὲ ἀδικοῦσι προστιθέναι τὴν δίκην. Ἀλλ᾽ ουχὶ δαιμόνων πᾶς πάντα δρᾶ ἀλλ᾽ αὐτοῖς διακέκριται κἀκεῖ τὰ ἔργα, ἄλλο ἄλλωι. καὶ τοῦτό ἐστιν ἀμέλει τὸ ἐμπαθὲς ὧι ἐλαττοῦται δαίμων θεοῦ.
[But the soul is ordered by divinity to descend to earth, and become mingled with every kind of men, with every human fortune, disposition, and art; so as to give assistance to the worthy, avenge those that are injured, and punish those that are injured. Every daemon, however, does not effect all things; but there, also, different works are assigned to different demons. And this indeed, is the passivity by which a daemon is inferior to a god. (Tr. T. Taylor, *The Dissertations of Maximus Tyrius*, London,1804)]

219/26 operose: elaborate

220/39 *Philostratus: Vita Apollonii*, Bk 4, Ch 11, 16: In Ch. 11 Apollonius tells his friends that he is not afraid of encountering the ghost of Achilles since he is not one of the Trojans whom Achilles must hate and since, in his previous apparition to Odysseus, Achilles 'made himself so gracious that Odysseus thought him more handsome than terrible' wearing 'his shield and his plumes.' But when later, in Ch. 16, Apollonius actually sees Achilles, the latter appears merely 'wearing a cloak in Thessalian fashion.' (Tr. F.C.

Conybeare, Loeb Classical Library)

221/6   yet ... *Imagination*: The notion that the imagination of the mother is capable of altering the foetus in different ways is widely discussed by scientists, natural historians, and philosophers in the Renaissance, as the numerous references in More's work attest. According to K. Svoboda, (*La démonologie de Michel Psellos*, Brno, 1927, p. 22), it may be traced back to the treatise, *On the animation of embryos*, attributed to Po rphyry.

222/37 *Occult Philosoph*: Agrippa, *De Occulta Philosophia*, Bk I, Ch 64[M]: 'Nonnunquam etiam ipsa humana corpora transformant transfiguranturque, et transportantur, saepe quidem in somniis nonnunquam etiam in vigilia. Sic Cyppus qui postea electus est rex Italiae dum taurorum pugnam victoriam que, vehementius admirans meditatur, in illa cura obdormiens noctem, mane corniger repertus est, non aliundeque virtute vegetativa vehementi imaginatione stimulata, corniferos humores in caput elevante, et cornua producente. Vehemens enim cogitatio dum species vehementer movet, in illis rei cogitatae figuram depingit, quam illi in sanguine effingunt, ille nutritis a se imprimit membris, cum propriis tum aliquando etiam alienis.'
[And sometimes men's bodies are transformed, and transfigured, and also transported; and this oft times when they are in a dream, and sometimes when they are awake. So Cyprus [*sic*] after he was chosen king of Italy, did very much wonder at and meditate upon the fight and victory of bulls, and in the thought thereof did sleep a whole night, and in the morning he was found horned, no otherwise than by the vegetative power, being stirred up by a vehement imagination, elevating cornific humors into his head and producing horns. For a vehement cogitation, whilst it vehemently moves the species, pictures out the figure of the thing thought on, which they represent in their blood, and the blood impresseth the figure on the members that are nourished by it; as upon those of the same body, so upon those of another.' (Tr. W.F. Whitehead, *Three Books of Occult Philosophy*,Chicago,1898)]
Agrippa von Nettesheim (1486-1535) was a German diplomat, lawyer, medical doctor, theologian, cabalist, and

occultist. In 1506 he joined a secret group of theosophists in Paris and immersed himself in Cabalistic, Gnostic, and Hermetic writings. The result of these researches was the three books *De Occulta philosophia*, written between 1509 and 1510 but published 1531-33. His Cabalistic and Pythagorean interpretation of the universe maintained that the three worlds -- the domain of the elements, the celestial world of the stars, and the intelligible cosmos of the angels -- were endowed with a *spiritus mundi* which represents a germinating force comparable to the λόγος σπερματίκος of the Stoics. Agrippa's later work, *De Incertitudine et Vanitate de Scientiarum et Artium* (1530), however , was a critique of all types of intellectual endeavor, including occult researches, aimed at revealing the superiority of Scriptural knowledge.

223/29 *Fienus*: Thomas Feyens, *De Viribus Imaginationis*, Quaestio 22 [M]: Feyens gives a natural, physiological, explanation of the production of mons trous features in foetuses: 'Dico tertio phantasiam posse mutare secundam quid figuram foetus, seu aliquam partium ejus, et dico phantasiam facere posse ut foetus aliquo modo et ruditer ad figuram alicuijus animalis permutetur, puta simiae, porcelli, canis, etc., id est, potest facere ut mulier deterrita a cane vel simia producat foetum habentum caput quod quidem principaliter sit simile capiti humano sed tamen aliquo modo referat caput canis aut simiae, ut quod sit prominens aut oblongum aut alicubi pilis consitum sicut caput canis vel planum, certis quibusdam lineamentis promenentiis aut cavitatibus simiae effigiens referens. Hoc enim non est contra naturam conformatrices humanae. Quia est tale caput habeat aliquam similitudinem cum capiti illorum animalium, principaliter tamen est caput humanum. Formatrix enim humana non est praecise determinata aut alligata ad aliquam certam figuram sed habet suam latitudinem sub qua potest formare capita cum varis figuris, alia sic alia aliter, et faciem unius hominis sic alterius aliter. Et ita saepe etiam citra concursum phantasiae, facit in uno homine aliquando faciem habentem similitudinem alioquam cum simia, in alio cum cane, in alio cum rostro acciptrino, etc. Et ideo, quando a phantasia seducta aliquando efformat ad similitudinem illorum animalium, nihil facit contra naturam inclinationem aut potentiam suam; et id eo potest tales figuras aliquando ruditer imitari.'

[I say, thirdly, that the imagination can cause the foetus to
alter somehow, and in a rough manner, to the figure of some
animal,for example, a monkey or a pig or a dog; that is, it
can cause a girl who has been frightened by a dog or monkey
to produce a foetus having a head which is in most part like
a human head but still in some way resembles the head of a
dog or a monkey in that it might be prominent or oblong or
covered all over with hair as the head of a dog, or flat and
having certain prominent lineaments and cavities resembling
the figure of a monkey. This is indeed not contrary to the
nature of the conformation of human beings. Since, though
this head may have some similarity with the head of another
animal, it is still primarily a human head. The formative
part of the human being is not precisely determined and
directed to any particular figure but has a certain latitude
within which it can form a head with varying features and a
face resembling one man in one way and another in another.
And often, even without the help of the imagination, it causes
one man to have a face resembling, in some respects, a
monkey, in other, a dog, and yet in others, a beaked bird of
prey. And so, when led by the imagination, it sometimes
forms itself in the likeness of those animals, it does nothing
contrary to its natural inclination or power, and thus it can
sometimes roughly imitiate such figures.]

Thomas Feyens (1567-1631) was a medical doctor whose
works include *De Cauteris* (1598), *Libri Chirurgici XII* (1602),
De formatione foetus(1620), and *De Viribus Imaginationis
Tractatus*(1608).

224/1   As that ... heads: Feyens, op. cit., quaest. 13, exempl
        5,7,18,19,27, and quaest. 22[M].

224/12 As ... forehead: *Ibid* ., quaest 13, exempl. 14[M].

224/20 *Sennertus*: Sennert, *De Viribus Imaginationis*, Ch 14[M].

224/27 *Helmont*:   Jan   Baptista   van   Helmont,   'De   Injectis
        Materialibus'[M] : After relating the stories cited by More,
        Helmont goes on to attribute these extraordinary phenomena
        to the 'Archeus': 'Equidem in rerum seminibus adhuc
        consistet primaeva illa penetrandi corporum energia, non

autem vi, arte, aut arbitrio humano subjecta ... Hocque agunt
semina, vi spiritus cujusdam Archei. Archeus enim tam in
praefatio seminibus, quia in nobis, tametsi corporens
ipsemet; dum tamen agit actione regiminis, et materiam in
se absorbet, edit plures effectus, incantamentis non
absimiles: quia proprie loquendo Archeus non imitatur
incantamenti sed incantamenta sequuntur normam ab
Archaeo praescriptam, quatenus scilicet operata longe aliter
quam corpora in unicum. Ut in uterinus affectibus, ne vi
sponte distenditur, dissiliunt tendines extra locum, rursusque
resiliunt. Ossa item dislocantur nullo motore visibili, collum,
ad menti attitudinem surgit, praecluditur aere pulmo: venena
inauspicata obnascuntur, cruorque insolitos sordium vultus
ludit. Quantum autem penetrationes corporum spectat,
Archeus noster corpora in se absorbet, ut fiant quasi
spiritus.'
[Indeed that primitive efficacy of piercing Bodies doth as yet
consist in the seeds of things; but is not subjected by human
force, art, or will, or judgment ... And the Seeds do act this by
virtue of a certain Spirit, the Archeus. For although the
Archeus himself, as well in the aforesaid seeds, as in us, be
corporeal, yet while he acts by an action of government ... he
utters many effects not unlike unto enchantments, but
enchantments do follow the rule prescribed by the Archeus:
to wit as he doth operate far otherwise then bodies do on each
other, as in affects of the womb, the sinewes are voluntarily
extended, the tendons do burst forth out of their place, and do
again leap back; the bones likewise are displaced by no
visible mover; the neck riseth swollen into the height of the
chin, the lungs are stopped up from air, unthought of poysons
are engendered, and the venal blood masks itself with the
unwonted countenances of filths. But as to what doth belong
unto the penetration of bodies, our Archeus sups up bodies
into himself that they may be made as it were Spirits. (Tr.
J.C.)]

225/30 already: Book 2, Chap 10, sect,2 [M].

226/11 *Sennertus*: Daniel Sennert, *Institutionum Medicinae*, Bk V,
        Part 3, Sect. 3, Ch 9[M]:Sennert -- arguing against the
        opinion of Jacob Schegk(1 511-87) who had defended the
        Aristotelian notion of the formative power of the semen in *De*

Plastica Seminii Facultatibus (1580) -- insists that the
principle of generation and formation is the soul in the seed:
'quomodo ab eo quod actu non est fieret generatio nisi ipsi
semini actus atque animae essentia tribuatur? Et quomodo
generatio esset univoca, aut unde anima deduceretur, nisi
generans ad huc vivens semini animae essent immisisset,
dum scilicet ex ovo, etiam fornacis calore, pullus excluditur.
aut dum in plantis et animalibus semine ad generationem in
communi cato generans moritur?

Quod vero Schegkius peculiarem hic λὸγον πλαστικόν
actum substantialem, οὐσίαν οὐσιας efficientem ἀυτον qui
tamen anima non sit, introducit nae ille frustra nobis videtur
multiplicere entia. Cum enim huic substantiali actui
operationes animae tribuat; cur non concedat eundem
animam esse? Et cur actum hunc alium ab anima statuere
sit necessarium cum anima in semine sufficere possit?'
[How can there be generation from that which is not act
unless act and the essence of soul be attributed to the seed?
And how can generation be univocal and from where would
the soul be draw unless the generating and vivifying power of
the soul be in the seed, as for example a chicken is hatched
frcm an egg solely by the heat of a furnace and in plants and
animals the generating power of the seed dies when the seed
is not imparted for the sake of generation.

That Schegk introduces a peculiar plastic λόγον a
substantial act which itself effects its being and is yet not the
soul is I think a vain multiplication of entities. As he
attributes to this substantial act the operations of the soul,
why does he not concede that it is the soul itself? And why is
it necessary to posit this act as different from the soul where
the soul in the seed suffices?]
More's reference to the practice of hatching eggs without the
aid of the hens "in Aegypt" is taken from the discussion of
the same point in Sennert's *Epitome Naturalis Scientiae*, Bk
VIII, Ch 9: 'Primo enim ova quod attinet in iis animam
futuri animalis iam inesse docit illud quod quam-primum ova
a calore debite foventur se, in iis anima exserit et animal
simile ei a quo ova sunt exclusa format ... Imo Cairi calore
fornacis pullos excludi Jul. Caes. Scaliger, *Exerc.*23, refert.
[First of all, that the soul of the future animal is contained in
the eggs is seen from the fact that, as soon as eggs are
warmed by heat, the soul is stirred and forms an animal

similar to that from which the eggs were removed ... Indeed
J.C. Scaliger, *Exerc.* 23, reports that in Cairo chickens were
hatched by the heat of a furnace.]

Like More, Sennert sought to reconcile the theories of
Aristotle, Galen, Paracelsus and the supporters of the atomic
hypotheses. He accepted Paracelsus' notion that all natural
bodies contain a vis seminalis that bestows life on them.
And, whereas Aristotle considered the soul to be only
potentially in the seed, Sennert maintained that it was a real
substance actually in the seed before the latter reaches its
final perfection. More's opinion on this matter is midway
between Aristotle's and Sennert's in that he believed that the
rational soul, though a real substance, is not propagated
along with the seed -- which contains only the sensitive soul
in conjunction with the Spirit of Nature.

226/21 inchoations: beginnings

227/1   Plotinus: *Enneades*, V, i, 2: οἷον σκοτεινὸν νέφος ἡλίου
        βολαὶ φωτίσασαι λάμπειν ποιοῦσαι χρυσοειδῆ ὄψιν διδοῦσαι.
        οὕτω τοι καὶ ψυχὴ ἐλθοῦσα εἰς σῶμα οὐρανοῦ ἔδωκεμὲν
        ζωήν ... ἔσχε τε ἀξίαν οὐρανὸς ψυχῆς εἰσοικισθείσης ὢν πρὸ
        ψυχῆς σῶμα νεκρόν. γῆ καὶ ὕδωρ.
        [As the rays of the sun throwing their brilliance upon a
        louring cloud make it gleam all gold, so the Soul entering the
        material expanse of the heavens has given life ... the Soul
        domiciled within, the heavenly system takes worth where,
        before the Soul, it was stark body -- clay and water.(Tr. S.
        Mackenna)].
        cf. also *Enneades*, VI, vii, 7-12 [M].

227/30 *Wierus*: Weyer, *op.cit.*, Bk IV, Ch 18 [M].

227/36 The other ... *diabolical*: Feyens, *op. cit.*, quaest. 13 (not 15
        as More indicates)exempl.8 [M].

227/41 The third... hands: *Ibid.*, quaest. 22 [M].

228/14 *Fienus: Ibid.* 22[M].

228/24 *Fortunius Licetus*: Fortunio Liceti, *De Monstrorum Causis*, Bk
        II, Ch 6 [M]: 'Et quia quae in somnis phantasiae observantur

spectra, plerumque chimerica sunt ex diversissimorum animalium partibus turpiter conficta; proinde nullum est tam horribile, ac multiforme monstrum, cui sola imaginatio caussam suppeditare nequeat; sed monstra brutali figura horrido gignere parereque mulieres, ex eventu compertissimum esse potest, quo superioribus annis matrona Sicula quum utero gerens mirabunda conspexisset in manu piscatoris ingentem astacum nuper e mari captum; tempore partus cum humano foetu simul et astacum marinum peperit marino nil prorsus dissimilem, quam historiam testis oculatis non iter pridem mihi retulit D. Franciscus Maria Delmonaco Siculus Drepraritanus Clericus regularis, vis spectatae doctrinae, ac integerrimae fide; qui et mulierem novit, et ex ea natum astacum perspexit.'

228/37 *Helmont*'s Cherry: Jan-Baptista van Helmont , *De Magnetica vulnerum curatione*, 33 [M]:' Serio notandum est, exemplum praegnanti, quae si cerasum violenter animo conceperit, mox ejus vestigium foetui imprimitur, parte ea, qua sibi praegnans manum admoverit. Nec est quidem otiosum dumtaxat cerasi simulacrum, ac macula; sed quod suo tempore, cum caeterus arboribus florescit et maturescit, mutati nimirum colorum et figurarum signaturis: ardua ac sacra prosecto vis microcosmici spiritus qui extra truncum arboreum, verum cerasum, id est, interioris cerasi proprietatibus, et dynami, in signatam carnem solo conceptu profer t.'
[We must seriously note the example of a Woman great with Child, who, if she hath violence of desire, conceived a Cherry in her Mind, the Footstep thereof is presently imprinted on her young, in that part whereon the great-bellied Woman shall lay her hand: Nor is it indeed only an idle Image or spot of a Cherry, but that which flowers, and grows to Maturity with the other Trees in their season; to wit, the Signatures of Colours, and Figures being changed: Truly, high and sacred is the force of the Microcosmical Spirit, which without the Trunck of a Tree, brings forth a true Cherry, that is, Flesh ennobled with the Properties and Powers of the more inward or real Cherry, by the Conception of Imagination alone. (Tr. J.C.)].
cf. also *De Mens Idea*, 37, *Vis Magnetica* and *Tractatus De Animae*,7 [M].

229/24   *Kircher*: Athanasius Kircher, *Magnes sive De Arte Magnetica*,
Bk III, Part 7, Ch 7[M]: These stories do not appear in the
first edition and were added in the third edition of 1654 under
the heading 'Historia memorabilis de signo et nota humano
corpori impressa.'
Athanasius Kircher (1601/2-1680) was a polymath and
disseminator of knowledge. He joined the Society of Jesus in
1616 and was Professor of philosophy and mathematics at
the University of Wurzburg from 1628. His diverse studies
include magnetism, optics, astronomy, harmony, medicine,
geology, archaeology, philology, philosophy, and theology.
His first book, *Ars Magnesia* (1651) was based on his own
experiments and elaborated in *Magnes, Sive de arte
Magnetica* (1641). His late work, *Ars magna sciendi* (1668)
was a didactic, encyclopedic treatise.

229/42   exorbitating: deviating

231/22   Letters: see Descartes, Lettre à Mersenne, 2 février, 1643,
where he broaches the subject: 'Je ne puis deviner si l'air
ordinaire se peut plus rarefier que condenser par les forces
naturelles, mais par force Angelique on Surnaturelle, au lieu
qu'il peut estre rarefié a l'infiny au lieu qu'il ne peut estre
condensé que jusques a ce qu'il n'ayt plus de pores, et que
toute la matière subtile, qui les remplit, en soit chassée.' But
in his letter of 23 février, 1643, he expresses doubt regarding
the experiment reported by Mersenne: 'Je vous remercie de
l'experience de l'air pesé dans une arquebuse a vent, lors
qu'il y est condensé mais je croy que c'est plustost l'eau
meslée parmy l'air ainsy condensé qui peze tant, que non pas
l'air mesme.' (*Oeuvres de Descartes*, Correspondance, vol. III,
pp. 612, 634).

232/11   already: 'Chap 5, sect 8, 9'[M].

232/31   *Theocritus*: Idyll I: Priapus, visiting Thyrsis, the shepherd,
who is enervated by his defiance of Eros, tries to revive him
by reminding him of his sexual desires:
βούτας μὲν ἐλέγευ .νῦν δ' αἰπόλωι ἀνδρὶ ἐοίκας·
ὡιπόλος, ὄκκ' ἐσορῆι τὰς μηκάδας οἷα βατεῦνται,
τάκεται ὀφθαλμώς ὅτι οὐ τράγος αὐτος ἔγεντο.

[Neatherd, forsooth? 'tis goatherd now, or 'faith, 'tis like to be; When goatherd in the rutting-time the skipping klds doth scan, His eye grows soft, his eye grows sad, because he's born a man' (Tr. J.M. Edmonds, Loeb Classical Library)].

233/2 *Psellus: De Operatione daimonum* [M]: ἀφικνοῦνται μὲν γὰρ ἀπ᾽ αὐτῶν ἐπὶ τοὺς θρησκεύοντας αὐγαι πυρώδεις. οἷαι δή τινες αἱ τῶν Διὰ τούτων ὑποδρομαὶ ἅς θεοπτίας οἱ μεμηνότες ἀξιοῦσι καλεῖναι. οὐδὲν ἐχούσας ἀληθές.οὐδ᾽ ἐστηκος οὐδὲ βέβαιον. τί γὰρ ἐν δαίμοσιν ἐξοφωμένοις οὖσι φωτοειδές; ἀλλὰ παίγνια τούτων οὔσας. οἷα τὰ τοῖς τῶν ὀμμάτων παραγωγαῖς. ἤ τὰ περὶ τῶν καλουμένων θαυμαζοποιῶν. ἐπ᾽ ἐξαπάτῃ τῶν ὁρώντων γιγνόμενα.

[However fiery meteors, such as are usually called falling stars, descend from them on their worshippers, which the madmen have the hardihood to call visions of god, though they have no truth, nor certainty, nor stability about them, (for what of a luminous character, could belong to the darkened demons) and though they are but ridiculous tricks of such things as are effected by optical illusions, or by means called miraculous,but really by imposing on the spectators.(Tr. M. Collison)].

234/30 extimate: outmost. The OED gives More's use of the word here as the first evidence of it.

234/40 Third Book: More, *Antidote*, Book 3, Chap 16, sect 4ff. [M]: More demonstrates the impossibility of these apparitions being due to cloud reflections of earthly objects by pointing to the great distance between the clouds and the earth, the rough surface of the clouds, and their inability to reflect even the image of a star, when 'not onely glasse but every troubled pool or dirty plash of water in the high-way does usually doe it.' (sec. 5)

236/24 Officine: workshop

236/31 *Plato: Apologia*,41b: καὶ δὴ τὸ μέγιστον τοὺς ἐκεῖ ἐξετάζοντα καὶ ἐρευνῶντα ὥσπερ τοὺς ἐνταῦθα διάγειν. τίς αὐτῶν σοφός ἐστιν καὶ τίς οἴεται μέν ἔστιν δ᾽ οὔ.

[And the greatest pleasure would be to pass my time in the other world in examining and investigating the people there, as I do those here, to find who among them is wise and who thinks he is when he is not. (Tr. H.N. Fowler, Loeb Classical Library)].

237/41 Ingeny: temperament, genius

238/2   *Plotinus: Enneades*, I, iii, 1-3, which comments on *Phaedrus* 248d, where the highest type of human soul is said to be manifest in the philosopher (or lover of Ideal beauty), the musician, and the lover.

238/2   And ... these: see Porphyry, *Vita Plotini*, Ch 22.

239/37 rosin: resin, used as a varnish or adhesive

239/5   Punctilio: minute detail

239/8   depurate: rarefied, purified

239/19 Conventicles: assemblies

239/32 Appendix: 'Chap. 12, sect. 3'[M].

241/5   *Promus-Condus*: one who stores and dispenses things.

242/31 *Concamerations*: divisions into chambers. The term was also used astronomically to indicate the celestial spheres.

243/13 the *Pythagoreans*: see Iamblichus, *De Vita Pythagorica*, Ch 9: From Pythagoras' counsel to the leaders of Croton: τοὺς γὰρ ἀνθρώπος εἰδότας, ὅτι τόπος ἅπας προσδεῖται δικαιοσύνης μυθοποεῖν τὴν αὐτὴν τάξιν ἔχειν παρά τε τῶι Διὶ τὴν Θέμιν καὶ παρὰ τῶι πλούτωνι τὴν Δίκην καὶ κατὰ τὰς πόλεις τὸν νόμον ἵν' ὁ μὴ δικαίως ἐφ' ἀτέτακται ποιῶν ἅμα φαίνηται πάντα τὸν κόσμον συναδικῶν.
[For men, knowing that every place requires justice, have asserted in fables that Themis has the same order with Jupiter, that Dice, i.e. justice, is seated by Pluto, and that Law is established in cities; in order that he who does not act justly in things which his rank in society requires him to perform,may at the same time appear to be unjust towards the whole world. (Tr. T. Taylor)]

244/2   above: 'Chap. 3, sect. 7' [M].

245/5   Πᾶς ... ἀγνοεῖ: Every wicked man is ignorant.

245/12   incursations: Incursions. The OED gives More's use here as the only example.

245/16   already: 'Chap 3, sect 7, 8' [M].

245/20   *Agrippa: De Occulta Philosophia*, Bk III, Ch 4l[M]: 'They reach habitations in the most vile and frightful places where abound the fires of Aetna, gulfs of water, the striking of lightning and thunder, chasms of the earth, and where there is no reign of light, incapable as they are of receiving the rays of the sun, never having known the splendor of the stars, and darkened by perpetual darkness and the cloak of night.'
In this chapter, which deals with the after-life of the soul, grottoes, volcanoes, and the Cimmerian night of the North are described as the halting places of the soul in its post-mortem peregrinations. Interestingly, More's conclusion of this chapter is much like Agrippa's : 'Illum quippe divitem in ardore poenarum et illum pauperem in refrigerio gaudiorum intelligendos esse non dubito [referring to traditional Christian eschotalogical notions discussed earlier]: Sed quomodo intelligenda illa flamina inferni, ille sinus Abrahe, illa divitis lingua, ille digitus pauperis, illa sitis tormenti, illa stilla refrigerii vix a mansuete quaerentibus a contentiose autem certantibus nunquam invenitur.'

247/2   second Book: Chap 11, sect.4,5,6'[M].

247/4   *Vaninus:* Guilio Cesare Vanini, *De admirandis naturae*, Dial. LX: During their discussion of dreams, Alexander, Vanini's interlocutor, asks the author where the images that appear in dreams reside, and the latter replies: ' In sensu dixere aliqui: quod mihi non placet, ea namque aliquando somniamus, quae nec audita nobis, nec visa sunt umquam. In spiritibus dixit Galenus, Incitissime tamen, qua enim fieri potest, ut qui novi quotidie spiritus innobis generantur, et intereunt, visas a longe tempore verum imagines in somno

representent? At representantur, non igitur in spiritibus verum simulachra immovantur. Aristoteles censuit illas rerum Ideas in anima conservari.'
[Some say that it is in the senses, but I do not agree, for we often dream what has never been heard by us nor seen. Galen said that it is in the spirits, but unwisely, for how can it be that spirits which are produced afresh daily in us and die represent in dreams the images of things seen a long time ago? And if they are represented in the spirits, they do not remain firmly there. Aristotle believes that these Ideas of things are conserved in the soul.]

247/24   already: 'Chap 9, 10'[M].

249/17   *Arcanum*: secret

249/21   *Cardan*: Cardano, *De Animorum immortalitate*, Object. 3 [M]: 'Nec credendum est; reges ac tyrannos tam parvam in hominum caede habere dubitationem, si illorum animos existimarent esse superstes, quandoquidem exuti et ipsi regno simul ac vita, tot hostes mertito sint habituri.'

249/36   insultation: injurious conduct

250/20   some ... *Nero*'s person: This incident is not found in Suetonius or Dio Cassius. Dio, however, makes a similar charge against Domitian: 'He did not spare even the Vestal Virgins, but punished them on the charge of having had intercourse with men' (*Roman History*, Bk 67,Tr. E. Cary).

250/42   *Ad ... beatas*: Virgil, *Aeneid*, Bk VI, ll.638-39: 'to ... the green{ pleasances and happy seats of the Blissful Groves.' (Tr. H.R. Faircl ough).See Note to Ch. 4, sec. 8 above.

251/16   *Plotinus: Enneades*, IV, iv, 45 [M]. Plotinus' concern here is to reveal the "common sensitiveness" linking the parts of the universe and the Natural Law that assigns a proper place in the universe to every being according to its particular quality.

254/21   Some such power... it: cf. Digby *op. cit.*, p. 112: 'In the like manner also it happens, that when one Lute doth sound, it makes the strings of the other to shake by the motions and tremblings which it causeth in the aire, though it be not touched at all.'

254/36 *subsultation*: jumping

256/19 the Souls ... *Men*: 'See Book 2, Chap 15, sect 8,9,10' [M].

256/23 *Paracelsians*: see Paracelsus, *Explicatio Totius Astronomiae*, 'Practica in Scientiam Divinationis': 'Constellationem hominis in sua cogitatione tam magnam esse posse ut sydereum spiritum in somno alio amandere possit, sine ope corporis Elementaris. Astrale, id corpus vim habet veneno, inficiendi infirmandi, distorquandi, excoecendi, occidendi, affendi, et aspirandi, et verberandi idque sine momento, et postea ad Elementare suum corpus redeundi. Notorium namque est, per tam fortem hostes suos multa huiusmodi molitos esse et praestitisse ita ut nonnulli derepente in lecto paralytica redderentur, nulla naturali causa concurrente. [The constellation of a man could be so great during the process of cogi tation that it could send forth his sydereal body to another place during sleep without the help of the elemental body. This astral body has the power to infect bodies with poison, to debilitate, distort, blind, strike, scald and scourge them, and then return to its elemental body, all in a moment. Notorius, indeed, is the example of the ancients who, through strong imaagination and the power of the astral body contrived and effected many such things against their enemies so that some were suddenly rendered paralyzed in bed without the operation of any natural cause.]

256/37 Sir *Kenelme Digby*: *op. cit.*, p. 189: 'I need not tell you ... of the woman of St. Maixent who could not forbear going to see an unfortumate child of a poor passenger woman, that was born without arms, and she herself was delivered afterwards of such a Monster; who yet had some small excrescence of flesh upon the shoulders, about the place whence the arms should have come forth. As also of her who was desirous to see the execution of a Criminal, that had his head cut off according to the laws of France: whereof her affrightment made so deep a print upon her Imagination that presently falling in labour, before they could carry her to her lodging, she was brought to bed, before her time, of a Child who had his head sever'd from his body, both the parts yet shedding fresh blood, besides that which was abundantly shed in the womb; as if the heads-man had done an execution also upon the tender young body within the Mother's wombe.' Digby's explanation of such phenomena is that 'the Imagination of the Mother is ful of corporeal atoms ... and her Imagination being ... surprized with an emotion, by the suddenness of the accident, it follows necessarily, that she must send some of these atoms also to the Brain of the Infant, and so to the same part of the body which her imagination has focussed upon... The infant also having his parts tuned in an harmonious consonance with the Mothers cannot fail to observe the same movement of spirits, twixt his Imagination and [the parts focussed on by the Mother's imagination], as the Mother did 'twixt hers' p.97).

256/39   already: 'Chap. 6, sect. 6' [M].

257/13   Dr. *Harvey*: Sir William Harvey, *Exercitationes Anatomicae de generatione Animalium*, Exer. 25: 'Si itaque ovum a propria anima foecundum redditur, sive proprio principio foecundante insito praeditum est ... certe concludendum est, ovum (etiam in ovario dum est) matris anima non vivere; sed esse instar filii emancipati, a prima statim origine: sicut arborum glandes, et semina a plantis ablata, haud ulterius earundem partes aestimanda sunt, set sui juris facta; quae propria insitaque potentia vegetativa, jam vitam degant. '
[If therefore the egg is rendered fertile by its own proper soul, or is endowed with its own proper innate principle of fecundation ... it must of a surety be concluded that the egg, even while it is in the ovary, does not live by the soul of its mother, but that it is immediately from its very beginning like an emancipated child, in the same way in which acorns removed from trees and seeds from plants are no longer to be accounted as parts of those trees and plants, but individuals in their own right, already enjoying their own life by reason of their own proper innate vegetative faculty (Tr. G. Whitteridege, *Disputations touching the generation of Animals*, London, 1981).]

257/19   *Vertumnus*-like: like the god of change, Vertumnus.

257/38   incrustated: covered with a crust.

257/42   Letter ... *V.C.*: More, *Epistola ad V.C.* [M]: This epistle was
         meant to serve as an apology for Descartes and an
         introduction to his philosophy. The explanation of the
         attraction of the "load-stone" by Descartes is to be found in
         Principia, Part IV, Art. 133.

257/42   *actum agere*: make a show of it.

258/7   Letters ... Philosopher: More, *Epistolae Quatuor ad Renatum
         Descartes* Epistola Tertia, 23 July 1649 [M]: More argues
         that if matter moves it self, matter being homogeneous, and
         motion, consequently, equal everywhere, it would follow that
         matter would be divided into infinitely small particles all
         equal to one another in size and shape and movement. This
         leads to the absurd conclusion that there would be no
         differentiated parts in the universe :' Si naturaliter igitur
         moveretur materia, nec Sol nec coelum, nec Terra esset, nec
         vortices ulli, nec heterogeneum quicquam, sive sensibile sive
         imaginibile, in rerum natura. Ideoque periret tuum condendi
         caelos, terrasque, caeteraque sensibilia mirificum artificium.'
         Descartes' theory of the formation of the sun and the stars
         and the cause of their round figure is detailed in *Principia*,
         Part III, Arts 54-56.

258/39   For ... particles: see Descartes, *Principia*, IV, Art 15-20 [M].

259/9   the occursions ... further: see Descartes, *op. cit.*, Art 22, 23
         [M].

260/4   *Hobbs: Elements of Philosophy*, Part 4, Chap 30 Art 4: 'The
         possible cause therefore of the descent of heavy bodies under
         the equator, is the diurnal motion of the earth ... But because
         this motion hath, by reason of its greater slowness, less force
         to thrust off the air in the parallel circles than in the
         equator, and no force at all at the poles, it may well be
         thought (for it is a certain consequent) that heavy bodies
         descend with less and less velocity, as they are more and
         more remote from the equator; and that at the poles

themselves, they will either not descend at all, or not descend by the axis.'

260/27 *Frisland*: Imaginary island southwest of Iceland, first reported in a work by Nicolo Zeno entitled *The Discovery of the Islands of Frislandia, Eslanda, Engroenlanda, Estotilanda, and Icaria* (Venice, 1558). The island seems to have been created out of a miscalculation of the exact position of places actually situated in the Faroes. Peter Heylyn's edition of *Cosmography* (London, 1657) states 'Southwest of Iseland is another, and as cold an Isle, commonly called by the name of Freezland, from the continued frosts unto which it is subject. By the Latins it is called Frislandia, to distinguish it from the Frisia or Friesland in Germany. It is situated under the North Frigid Zone; but not so much within the Arctick as Iseland is ...' However, by the end of the seventeenth century, the island had disappeared from most maps and the 1701 edition of *Cosmography*, while repeating Heylyn's account of the island, added the caution: 'It is much disputed whether there be any such Island in the world, and by some positively denied.' For a full discussion of this mysterious island, see R.H. Ramsay, *No Longer on the Map* (N.Y.: Ballantine Books, 1973, pp. 39-59).

260/28 *Scricfinnia*: Renaissance name for part of the Scandinavian lands near the North Cape.

262/32 already: 'Chap 6,7,8; chap 7, sect. 3'[M].

262/39 *Frustra ... pauciora*: What can be done by few is done uselessly by many.

264/2   *Bindweed*: climbing plant of the species *convolvulus*.

265/1   *Pliny: Historia Naturalis*[M]: The sections dealing with the elusive nature and the nesting habits of swallows are X, 35: 'Volucrum soli hirundini flexuosi volatus velox celeritas quibus ex causis neque rapinae ceterarum alitum obnoxia est.'
[The swallow is the only bird that has an extremely swift and swerving flight, owing to which it is also not liable to capture

by the other kinds of birds. (Tr. H. Rackham)]

265/14 *Plinie*: Pliny, *op. cit.*[M]: For "the martin's nest," see Bk X,49
for "the combes of bees," Bk X, 5; for "the webs of spiders, Bk
XI,28; and for "the bags of silk-worms," Bk X. 25.

265/15 *Cardan*: Cardano, *De Subtilitate*, Bk 14 M: 'Inscia igitur
omnia anim lia esse compositionis ... carereque iudicio ex hoc
primum constat, quod quae maxime solertia videntur
artificiis ut bombyces, apes, et formicae, palam est quod his
carent. Itaque et hirundines eodem modo verisimile est
nidum construere, quo apes, quo bombyces.'
[That all animals are ignorant of the art of construction ...
and lack discernment is proved above all by the fact that
those seen to have most skill in artifice, such as silk worms,
bees and ants, clearly lack it. Thus, swallows, too, probably
have the same way of constructing nests as bees and silk
worms.]

265/15 *Nierembergius*: Juan Eusebio Nieremberg, *Historia Naturalis*,
Bk 3, Ch 2 8 [M]: 'Nec enin animalium instinctum aliud reor
quam operationem phantasiae ad iudicium commodi vel
incommodi determinatem, determinantem que appetitum ad
impetum vel fugam. Judicium non propriè intelligo sed
histrionem quandam eius, Differt autem instinctus, licet
brutorum phantasia in eamdem speciem coear pro formarum
et temperamentorum diversitate, quae bases indoles sunt;
inde tanta operum varietas, ut bombyx lanam, apis favos,
formica   horrea,   araneus   telam,   hirundo   nidum
architectentur.'
[I deem animal instinct to be nothing but the operation of the
imagina tion directed to the discernment of the pleasant and
the unpleasant and determining the desire for motion or
flight. I do not really mean dis cernment as such, but merely
an imitation of it. Instincts differ, that is, the imagination of
animals works in each species according to the diversity of
forms and temperaments, whose bases are natural. Thus,
there is such a great variety of operations that a silkworm
builds a cocoon, a bee a hive, an ant a hill, and a spider a
web.]
Juan   Eusebio   Nieremberg(1595-1658)   was   Professor   of
physiology at the University of Madrid.

265/25 *Aristotle: Historia Animalium*, Bk. V, Ch 19: More's classification of spiders as τὰ αὐτομάτως γενόμενα is inaccurate as is evident from the passage in Aristotle: γίνεται δ᾽ αὐτῶν τὰ μὲν ἐκ ζώιων τῶν συγγενῶν οἶον φαλάγγία τε καὶ ἀράχνια ἐκ φαλαγγίων καὶ ἀραχνίων.καὶ ἀττέλβοι καὶ ἀκρίδες καὶ τέττιγες τὰ δ᾽ οὐκ ἐκ ζώιων, ἀλλ᾽ αὐτόματα τὰ μὲν ἐκ τῆς δρόσου τῆς ἐπι τοῖς φύλλοις πιπτούσης ... τὰ δ᾽ ἐν βορβόρωι καὶ κόπρωι σηπομένοις, τὰ δ᾽ ἐν ξύλοις, τὰ μὲν φυτὼν, τὰ δ᾽ ἐν αὕοις ἤδη.

[Some insects are produced from animals of the same kind as themselves e.g. venom spiders are produced from venom spiders, ordinary spiders from ordinary spiders, so too are locusts, grasshoppers and cicadas. Some, however, are not produced from animals at all, but spontaneously some out of the dew which falls on foliage ... others are produced in putrefying mud and dung, others in wood, green or dry. (Tr. A.L. Peck, Loeb Classical Library)]

265/26 fluttery: rubbish, from 'flutter', meaning an untidy condition.

265/38 clues: balls of thread

266/1 σκώληξ ... ψυχὴ: *i.e. Vermis, Eruca, Aurelia, Nympha, Necudalus, Papilio*. See Aristotle, *De Historiae Animal.*, Bk 5, Ch. 19 [M], 551 a-b, the section dealing with butterflies and silkworms.

266/13 νεκύδαλος: More refers in his marginal note here to the derivation of νεκύδαλος by Mattias Martini in his *Lexicon Philologicum* from νέκυς and δαίω: 'An quod ex campe mortua velut accendatur νέκυς mortuus, δαίω accendo, unde δαλός titio.' [M].

266/29 *Aristotle: op. cit.*, Bk 9, Ch 7 [M], 612b: ὅλως δὲ περὶ τοὺς βίους πολλὰ ἂν θεωρηθείη μιμήματα τῶν ἄλλων ζώιων τῆς ἀνθρωπίνης ζωῆς.
[Many imitations of human life are observed in the mode of life of othe r animals.]

266/32 *Antidote*: 'Book 2, ch 9, sect. 9' [M].

266/37 assuefaction: habituation

266/41 *Pliny: op. cit.*, Bk X, Ch 45 [M] (ch. 49 in the Loeb edition):
'Non faciunt hae nidos migrantque multis diebus ante si
futurum est ut auctus amnis attingat' .
[These birds do not build their proper nests, and if a rise of
the river threatens to reach their holes, they migrate many
days in advance. (Tr . H. Rackham)]

267/8 *Scaliger: Exotericarum Exercitationum*, Exercitatio 307 [M]:
'Nam vol untas est ἐν τῶι λογικωι in homine. Itaque bruta
non dicuntur velle sed instigari: unde instinctus dicitur a
Natura. Sicut a Diis afflatio apud M. Tullium.'
[For will is in the reasoning faculty in man. Thus, brutes are
not said to will but to be moved. So that, instinct is said to
be from Nature "a divine afflation," as Tully says.]

267/27 Νόμος ἰσοκλινὴς : Pseudo-Aristotle, *De Mundo*, 6, 400 b:
νόμος μὲν γὰρ ἡμιν ἰσοκλινὴς ὁ θεός.
More's use of this definition is particularly appropriate since
Aristotle in fact depicts, in this section, the total control that
God, as ruler of the cosmos has over the ordering of every
part of the universe:. ἡγουμένου δὲ ἀκινήτως αὐτοῦ καὶ γῆς,
μεμερισμένος κατὰ τὰς φύσεως πασας διὰ τῶν οἰκείων
σπερμάτων εἴς τε τὰ φυτὰ καὶ ζῶια κατὰ γένη τε καὶ εἴδη.
[Under his motionless and harmonious guidance all the
orderly arrange ment of heaven and earth is administered,
extending over all things through the seed proper to their
kind, to plants and animals by genus and species.]
That God works through a "vicarious power" distinct from
his essence is also the opinion of Aristotle who attributes all
motion to the " δύναμις " of God (398b): σεμνότερον δὲ καὶ
πρεπωδέστερον αὐτὸν μὲν ἐπὶ τῆς ἀνωτάτω χώρας
ἰδρῦσθαι,τὴν δὲ δύναμιν διὰ τοῦ σύμπαντος κόσμου
διήκουσαν ἥλιόν τε κινεῖν καὶ σελήνην καὶ τὸν πάντα
οὐρανὸν περιάγειν αἴτιόν τε γίνεσθαι τοῖς ἐπὶ τῆς γῆς
σωτηρίας.
[It is more noble, more becoming, for him to reside in the
highest place, while his power, penetrating the whole of the
cosmos, moves the sun and moon and turns the whole of the
heavens and is the cause of preservation for the things upon
the earth. (Tr. D.J. Frley, Loeb Classical Library)]

267/38 *Proxenet*: a match maker. OED gives More's use of the term here as the earliest example.

267/41 *Materia ... virum*: Aristotle, *Physica*, I, 9, 192 a: ἀλλα τοῦτ' ἐστιν ἡ ὕλη [ἐφίεσθαι τὸ εἶδος]. ὥσπερ ἄν εἰ ὑῆλυ [ἐφίεσθαι] ἄρρενος καὶ αἰσχρὸν καλοῦ.

270/2 *Aristotle: Historia Animalium*: Bk 4, Ch 7 [M], 532a: ὅσα δὲ μακρὰ καὶ πολύποδά ἐστι πολὺν χρόνον ζῆι διαρούμενα, καὶ κινεῖται τὸ ἀποτμηθὲν ἐπ' ἀμφότερα τὰ ἔσχατα· καὶ γὰρ ἐπὶ τὴν τομὴν πορεύεται καὶ ἐπὶ τὴν οὐράν, οἷαν ἡ καλουμένη σκολόπενδρα.
[The long insects with numerous feet live a long time after division, and the severed portion can move in either direction. The portion can move either toward the cut or toward the tail-end, as happens with the millipede as it is called.(Tr. A.L. Peck)]

270/6 *Aristotle: Ibid.*[M].

270/9 Εοίκασι ... συμφεπυκόσι: Aristotle, *De Juventute et Senectute*, Ch 2 [M]:' Animals of this kind are like a concretion of several animals.' After the line quoted by More,Aristotle goes on: τὰ δ' ἄριστα συνεστηκότα τοῦτ' οὐ πάσχει τῶν ζώιων διὰ το εἶναι τὴν φύσιν αὐτῶν, ὡς ἐνδέχεται μάλιστα μίαν.
[But the best constituted aninals do not show this defect because their nature is one in so far as it can be. (Tr.W.B. Hett)]
The beginning of Ch. 3 refers to the generation of plants by grafting and slip-taking.

270/16 *Fromondus*: Libert Froidmont, *De Anima*, Bk I, Ch 4 (The 1649 edition contains this story in Art. 3, not Art. 13 as More indicates)[M]
Libert Froidmont (1587-16535) was Professor Regius in the Liège seminary as well as Professor of theology at the University of Louvain. One of his earliest works was the *Meteorologicorum libri sex*(1627). His opposition to the Copernican theory is expressed in his *Ant-Aristarchus sive orbis terrae immobilis* (1631) and *Vesta, sive Ant-Aristarchi*

vindex adversus Jac. Lansbergius Philippi (1634).

270/35 no... Soul: 'see Book 2, ch 7, sect 9' [M].

271/26 already: Book I, chap.5 [M].

271/30 *Intromission*: "The action of sending, letting, or putting in" (OED)

272/7 the dying Philosopher: Aelian, *Varia Historia*, Bk II, Ch 35 [M]: Γοργίας δι Λεοντῖνος ἐπὶ τέρματι ὢν τοῦ βίου καὶ γεγηρακώς εὖ μάλα ὑπό τινος ἀσθενείας καταληφθείς, κατ᾿ ὀλίγον εἰς ὕπνον ὑπολισθάνων ἔκειτο. ἐπεὶ δὲ τις αὐτὸν παρῆλθε τῶν ἐπιτηδείων ἐπισκοπούμενος καὶ ἤρετο, ὅ τι πράττοι, ὁ Γοργίας ἀπεκρίνατο, Ἤδη με ὁ ὕπνος ἄρχεται παρακατατίθεσθαι τἀδελφῶι.
[When Georgias Leontinus was at the end of his life, very old and devastated by some illness, he gradually fell into a sleep. When one of his attendants reached him and, observing him, asked him how he was, Georgias replied, "Already in me sleep has begun to give place to his brother."]
Aelian (ca 170-235 A.D.) is remembered chiefly for his miscellaneous history *Varia Historia* which includes anecdotes, historical and biographical, drawn from other writers, and aims at inculating moral and religious virtues of a largely Stoic sort.

272/10 stounds: shocks

272/30 suppeditation: the act of supplying

272/37 already: 'Book 2, ch 2,3,4,5,6' [M].

273/30 Sympathy ... Soul: 'See Book 2, chap,10, sect.9' [M].

274/38 before: 'Book 2, ch.11, sect.8'M].

275/24 *Aristotle*: *De Generatione Animalium*, see Note to Sec. 4 below.

275/31 *Sennertus*: Daniel Sennert, *Epitome Naturalis Scientiae*, Bk 6, Ch 1: 'Deinde illud membrorum praecipuum est, cujus

unitatem vei multitudinem sequitur unitas vel multitudo animalis. Quia enim animal per unam animam unu est; per duas duplex, illud membrum quo duplicato animal fit duplex, animae sedes omnino est constituenda. Tale ante cor esse docet Aristotelis l. 4. *De gen. an.* c. 4.'
[Thus, that is the chief of all organs whose singleness or plurality results in the singleness or plurality of the animal. Since an animal is one by virtue of having one soul and two by virtue of having two souls, that organ whose duplication causes the animal to be two is indeed to be considered the seat of the soul. Such, above all, is the heart, as Aristotle teaches in *De Gen. Animal*,IV, 4.]

276/4   *Aristotle's* Authority: *De Generatione Animalum*, Bk 4, Ch 4 [M]: More's suggestion regarding Aristotle's hesitancy on the question of the heart's being the principle of life is valid with respect to the passage quoted from this Aristotelian work. But see Note below.

276/6   Ἐν ... ζῶον : 'Whether an animal which is a monstrosity is to be reckoned as one or as several grown together depends upon its "principle"; thus assuming that the heart is a part answering to this description, a creature which possesses one heart will be one animal. (Tr. A.L. Peck)

276/12 elsewhere: *De Juventute et Senectute*, Ch 3[M]: Aristotle is, here, rather more confident of the location of the seat of the common sensorium in the heart: ἀλλὰ μὴν τό γε κύριον τῶν αἰσθήσεων ἐν ταύτηι τοῖς. ἐναίμοις πᾶσιν· ἐν τούτωι γὰρ ἀναγκαῖον εἶναι τὸ πάντων τῶν αἰσθητηρίων κοινόν. αἰσθητήριον ... εἰ τὸ ζῆν ἐν τούτωι τῶι μορίωι πᾶσιν ἐστι. δῆλον ὅτι καὶ τὴν αἰσθητικὴν ἀρχὴν ἀναγκαῖον· ἧι μὲν γὰρ ζῶιον ταύτηι καὶ ζῆν φαμέν. ἧι δ' αἰσθητητικόν. ταύτηι τὸ σῶμα ζῶιον εἶναι λέγομεν.
[Moreover, in all sanguineous animals the supreme organ of the sense faculties lies in the heart; for in this part must lie the common sen sorium of all the sense-organs ... if in all creatures life resides in this part clearly so too must the origin of sensation; for we say that a creature is alive in so far as it is an animal, and an animal in so far as it is sensitive],
as well as of the source of life-giving warmth in it: τὴν

ἀρχὴν ἐντεῦθεν τῆς θερμότητος ἠρτῆσθαι πᾶσι καὶ τῆς ψυχῆς ὥσπερ ἐμπεπυρευμένης ἐν τοῖς μορίοις τούτοις, τῶν μὲν ἀναίμων ἐν τῶι ἀνάλογον ἐν δὲ τῆι καρδίαι ἐναίμων.
[The principle of heat in all other parts depends on the heat therein , and the soul is so to speak fired in this organ, which in sanguineous animals is the heart, and in the bloodless that which corresponds to the heart.(Tr.W.S.Hett)]

276/13 already: 'Book 2, Ch,7, sect 8,9'[M].

277/9 pet: a fit of ill-humour or peevishness

277/11 whenas: 'See [More, *Conjectura Cabbalistica*] *Cabb.Philos. cap.* 3, *v.*20,21,22'[M].

277/26 *Aeneid*: VI[M] 730ff: This passage is taken from Anchises' speech to Aeneas about the destination of the souls hovering about the river Lethe in the Blissful groves. In the course of this discourse, Anchises tells his son how heaven and earth and all the planets were originally informed by a "spiritus intus," while "totamque infusa per artus mens agitat molem et magno se corpore miscet." And it is from this infusion of spirit in the primal matter of the world that men and animals were generated. Virgil seems to retain the Stoic conception of λόγοι σπερματικοὶ in his allusion to the vital spirit as being constituted "ollis ... seminibus," while his further description of it as possessing "igneus ... vigor", and "coelestis origo" points farther back to pre-Socratic sources.

282/13 as... are: [see More,]*Antidote*, Book 3 ch 3,4,5,6,7,8,9,10 &c' [M].

282/16 Spirits: More, *op. cit.*,' Book 2, chap 8,9' [M].

283/9 *Epictetus*: Joest Lips, *Physiologiae Stoicorum Libri tres*, Bk 3, Dissertatio 8 [M]: The quote from Epictetus is from *Dissertationes*,I,Ch. 14: ἀλλ' αἱ ψυχαὶ μὲν οὕτως εἰσὶν ἐνδεδεμέναι καὶ συναφεῖς τῶι θεῶι ἅτε αὐτοῦ μόρια οὖσαι καὶ ἀποσπάσματα. Lips translates this as 'Animae ita illigata et coniunctae deo sunt ut particulae sint eius et decerpta.' More, apparently, did not read the original text of Epictetus since, if he had, he would have noticed that

Epictetus arrives at at a notion of the soul's divinity from a
consideration of the sympathetic unity that pervades the life
of the universe: ἀλλὰ τὰ φυτὰ μὲν καὶ τὰ ἡμέτερα σώματα
οὕτως ἐνδέδεται τοῖς ὅλοις καὶ συμπέπονθεν αἱ ψυχαὶ δ' αἱ
ἡμέτεραι οὐ πολὺπλέον.

[But are the plants and our own bodies so closely bound up
with the universe, and do they so intimately share its
affections, and is not the same much more true of our own
souls? (Tr. W.A. Oldfather, Loeb Clas sical Library)].

Joest Lips (1547-1606) was a Flemish humanist, philologist,
and foremost interpreter of Stoicism in the later renaissance.
His *De Constantia*(1584) was written as an introduction to
Stoicism, while the *Manuductio ad Stoicam Philosophiam*
(1604) was a miscellany of Stoic moral doctrines. The
Physiologia Stoicorum (1604), from which More quotes, is a
careful study of Stoic logic and physics in which he
attempted to demonstrate the compatibility between Stoic
fatum and Christian freewill.

283/10   *Philo*: 'A fragment of the Divine Soul and not separated.' I
have not been able to trace the exact quotation cited by More,
but the idea occurs in more then one place in Philo. cf., for
example, *De opificio mundi, 146:* πᾶς ἄνθρωπος κατὰ μὲν
τὴν διάνοιαν ωικείωται λογωι θείωι τῆς μακαρίας φύσεως
ἐκμαγεῖον ἢ ἀποσμασμα ἢ ἀπαύγασμα γεγονώς.

[Every man , in respect of his mind, is allied to the divine
Reason, having come into being as a copy or fragment or ray
of that blessed nature. (Tr. F. H. Colson,G. H. Whitaker,
Loeb Classical Library)]

cf. also *De Somniis*, 34:   νοῦς ἀπόσπασμα θεῖον ων.

283/12   *Trismegist*: Hermes Trismegistus, *Poemander*, XII, I, i ὁ νοῦς
οὖν οὐκ ἔστιν ἀποτετμημένος τῆς οὐσιότητος τοῦ θεοῦ. ἀλλ'
ὥσπερ ἡπλωμένος, καθάπερ τὸ τοῦ ἡλίου φῶς.

[Mind then is not severed from the substantiality of God, but
is, so to speak, spread abroad from that source, as the light
of the sun is spread abroad. (Tr. W. Scott)]

284/9   *Pomponatius*: Pomponazzi, *De Immortalitate Animae*, Ch
14[M]: See note to Bk I, Ch 13, sect. 8, above. More once
again attacks the Aristotelian theory that all universal
movements posterior to the first eternal movement of the

Frime Mover, must be derived from the stellar bodies which represent, in their circular movements, a model of eternity (*Metaphysica*, X, 8) and Pomponazzi's inference therefrom that all supernatural phenomena are due to celestial influence. In his attempt to demonstrate the immortality of individual souls, More is obliged to deprive the stars of some of their power and transfer it to the countless human spirits with their attributes of " *Personality, Memory,* and *Conscience.*"

284/9 leven: persuasion, derived from the obsolete 'leveness' meaning "faith, confidence" (OED). The OED records no instance of the use of this particular form.

287/15 *Hieronymus*: Cardano, *De Subtilitate*, Bk 19 [M].

287/34 Nihil ... superesse: that nothing remained of what was peculiar to a person.

287/36 Divi: gods

288/19 but seems ... so: Cardano, *De rerum varietate*, Bk 16, Ch 93 [M]: After narrating the story told him by his father, Cardano adds, 'Haec seu historia, seu fabula sit, ita se habuit. Quod fabula videatur, satis argumento esse debet, quod placita haec non satis cum religione consentiunt, quodque pater meus cum suls daemonibus nihilo aut felicior, aut ditior, aut notior hominibus fuerit quam ego qui daemones nunquam vidi.'
[Whether this be a real story or a fairy tale, thus did he relate it. If it is considered a fairy tale, it must be by a strong argument, for these opinions are not sufficiently in accord with religion, and my father with his daemons was neither happier or richer or more famous than I who have never seen any daemons.]

288/24 *Cynosura*: something that serves for guidance or direction, a guiding star.

288/27 *Plutarch: De defectu oraculorum*, 419 b-d.

289/16 *Plutarch: op. cit.* [M] 415 b-c: The classification of Hesiod is from *Works and Days*,106-201 (See note to Ch 4, Art 7 above). The opinion of the "others" can be traced back to Heraclitus, cf. *Die Fragmente der Vorsokratiker*, Heraclitus, Fr. 76.

290/5   *Cardan*: Cardano, *Ibid.*: 'Aeterni mente et immortales.'

291/7   *Cardan*: Cardano, *De Subtilitate*, Bk 19 [M].

291/35 *Cardan: Ibid.* [M].

293/7   those fishes ... Sea: Jan Jonston, *Historiae naturalis de piscibus et cetis*, Bk IV, iii, 1[M]: Quoting Athanasius Kircher, *De Arte Magnetica* , Bk 3, Part 6, as his source, Jonston relates the following story: 'Capitur certis anni temporibus in mari orientali Indiae ad insulas Vissajas, quas insulas Pictorum vocant, sub Hispanorum dominio, piscis quidam ἀνϑρωπομορφος. id est, humana prorsus figura'
[In some seasons of the year,in the E. Indian ocean, near the island Vissajas, which is called the Artist's Island, under Spanish dominion, is caught a certain anthropomorphic fish, that is, with an absolutely human form.]
Jan Jonston (1603-1675) was a Polish scientist who wrote several encyclopedic works including an *Idea universae medicina practicae* (1648) a *Historia universalis civilis et ecclesiasticis* (1638) and the *Historiae naturalis libri VI* (1650/53).

293/14 cad-worm: "The larva of the May-fly and other species of *Phryganea* which lives in water and ... is used as bait by anglers" (OED)

294/22 *Plutarch: op. cit.* [M], 419 E.

295/5   secluse: secluded

295/22 *Perige's*: The point in the orbit of a heavenly body at which it is nearest to the earth.

295/23 *Apoge's*: The point in the orbit of a heavenly body at which it is at the greatest distance from the earth.

295/25   Apsis: Apogee, (the term 'apsis' may be used for both apogee
         and perigee)

295/30   But whether ... *Plato*: The reference is most probably to the
         Phaedo 58e where Socrates is referred to as μηδ᾽ εἰς Ἅιδου
         ἰόντα ἄνευ θείας μοίρας ἰέναι. The discussion on the need to
         purify the soul by disciplining the sensual concerns of the
         body follows in 63e-69e.

297/1   *Inundatio ... venit*: Seneca, *Naturales Quaestiones*, Bk III, Ch
         29 *apud* Joest Lips, *op. cit.*, Bk 2, Dissertation 21 [M].

297/12   *Seneca's vote*: Seneca, [*Consolatio ad Marciam*, Ch. 26] *apud*
         Joest Lips, *op. cit.*, Bk 2, Dissertation 22[M]: 'Cum tempus
         advenerit, quo se renovatur, mundus exstinguat, viribus ista
         suis se caedant, et sidera sideribus incurrent et omni
         flagrante materia, uno igne, quidquid nunc ex disposito jucet,
         ardebit.'
         [And when the time shall come for the world to be blotted out
         in order that it may begin its life anew, these things will
         destroy themselves by their own power, and stars will clash
         with stars, and all the fiery matter of the world that now
         shines in orderly array will blaze up in a common
         conflagration. (Tr. J.W. Basore, Loeb Classical Library)]

297/24   *Des-Cartes*: For Descartes' explanation of fire see *Principia*,
         IV, 80. For his theory of the conservation of motion in the
         universe, see *Principia*, II, 36.

298/3   *Omne ... natus*: [Seneca, *Naturales Quaestiones*, Bk 3, Ch. 30
         apud] Lips,*op. cit.*, Bk 2, Ch. 22[M]: 'Every living creature
         will be created anew and the earth will be given men
         ignorant of sin, and born under new auspices.' (Tr. T.H.
         Corcoran). After a description of the flood that will destroy
         all life on earth, Seneca predicts the παλιγγενεσία in these
         words.

298/29   *Nymphs*: cf. More, *The Defense of the Philosophick Cabbala*,
         Ch. 1 Art 6: '*Demetrius* also in *Plutarch* makes the Souls
         involved in *generation* to be so many *Water-Nymphs*. And it
         is not a mere Metaphor, but aimes also at a Physical truth,
         namely at the moisture of the Vehicles of such Souls or

Spiritual Powers as are engaged in *Generation.*' More substantiates his theory of the nymphs as spirits steeped in "genital moisture" by citing Porphyry, *De Antro Nympharum*; Synesius, Hymnus II, and Virgil, *Georgics*, IV,334-349.

298/31   *Plutarch: op. cit.* 415f: 'The whole matter as stated by Hesiod seems to contain as veiled reference to the "conflagration", when the disappearance of all liquids will most likely be accompanied by the extinction of the Nymphs "who in the midst of fair woodlands, sources of rivers and grass-covered meadows have their abiding."'(Tr. F.C.Babbit, Loeb Classical Library)

299/30   *Aristotle*: cf.*Metaphysica*, IX, viii, 1050a: τέλος δ᾽ ἡ ἐνέργεια, καὶ τούτου χάριν ἡ δύναμις λαμβάνεται ... τὸ γὰρ ἔργον τέλος, ἡ δὶ ἐνέργεια τὸ ἔργον.
[And the actuality is the end, and it is for the sake of this that the potentiality is acquired ... For the activity is the end, and the actuality is the activity. (Tr. H. Tredennick, Loeb Classical Libra ry)]

300/34   *rorid*: dewy

300/34   Expergefaction: arousing, awakening

300/39   ἀποκατάστασις ... παλιγγενεσία ... ἀνάστασις ... ἐκπύρωσις: reconstitution ... regeneration ... destruction ... conflagration.

300/41   *Seneca*: Epistula 36: 'Death, which we fear and shrink from, merely interrupts life, but does not steal it away, the time will return when it shall be restored to the light of day; and many men would object to this, were they not brought back in forgetfulness of the past.' (Tr. R.N. Gummere, Loeb Classical Library)

301/3   the *Stoicks* ... *God*: see Joest Lips, *op. cit.*, Bk. 1, Dissert
         6[M]: 'Stoici viri et vitam omnem mundi, atque ipsum adeo Deum in igne ponebant, imo Deum esse. Sed ignem non quem-cumque, non hunc nostrum corruptorem et corruptibilem sed artificiosum, id est, artificem atque opificem, condentem ratione et velut arte, vegetantem et

servantem.'
[The Stoics consider the life of men and all the world and
even of god to be in fire which they think to be god. But not
any fire, not our destroying and destructible fire, but
formative, that is, fire that organizes and constructs,
produces, vegetates and preserves, as if by reason or art.]

301/6 *Soul*: see Joest Lips, *op.cit.*, Bk 3, Dissertation 13 [M]:Omnino
est ipsi et Stoicis est enim Spiritus. Laertius ψυχὴν πνεῦμα
εἶναι δίο καὶ σῶμα εἶναι animam Spiritum ergo et corpus
esse.'
[The Soul to him and the Stoicks is spirit. As Laertius says,
the soul is spirit and, therefore, corporeal.]

301/6 *Stars*: See Joest Lips, *op. cit.*, Bk 2, Dissertation 14 [M]: 'Set
et Stoici pastum in sideribus agnoscunt atque ali vaporibus
et aere ferridam illam naturam volunt.'
[But the Stoicks deny that there is pasture in the stars and
maintain that its solid substance is fed by other vapours and
air.]
Then quoting Laertius in the Greek, he translates: 'Nutriri
atque ali et haec ignita, solem et lunam et cetere astra.
Solem quidem e magno mari quod sit fax et accensio
quaedam intellectu praedita, Lunam autem ex aquis dulcibus
et potabilis, quod sit aeri permixta et vicinior terrae.'
[These fiery bodies, the sun and the moon and the other stars
have different nourishments, the sun from the great ocean,
which is fiery and somewhat furnished with intellect, the
moon from the sweet and drinkable waters which are mixed
with air and closer to the land.]

301/11 Ass ... Moon: More identifies this anecdote in the Notes to
the 1713 edition as follows: 'I allude to the known Story of a
foolish person, w ho, when he saw the Moon shining in the
water, but that, clouds intervening, it was gone suddenly
from his Sight, while the Ass on which he rode was drinking,
conceited that the Ass had swallowed up the Moon, and took
it clear away out of all Being.'

301/12 *Anacreon*: Ode XIX:
ἡ γῆ μέλαινα πίνει.
πίνει δὲ δένδρὲ αὐτὴν.

πίνει ϑάλασσα δ᾽ αὔρας,
ὁ δ᾽ ἥλιος ϑάλασσαν,
τόν δ᾽ ἥλιον σελήνη.
τί μοι μάχεσϑ᾽ ἑταῖροι
κ᾽ αὐτῶι ϑέλοντι πίνειν;

[The earth drinks the rain The trees drink of the earth, The sea drinks the breezes, The sun drinks the sea, The moon drinks the sun. Why, then, my friends, do you protest Against my desire to drink?]

301/33 *Lucretius: De rerum natura*, Bk III[M] ll.847-851: 'Even if time should gather together our matter after death and bring it back again as it is now placed, and if once more the light of life should be given to us, yet it would not matter one bit to us that even this had been done, when the recollection of ourselves has once been broken asunder. (Tr. M. F. Smith, Loeb Classical Library)

302/37 Ζεὺς ... *Sospitator*: Zeus the preserver

303/37 *Pliny: Historia Naturalis*, Bk II, Ch. 30[M]: Pliny's examples of solar eclipses are part of his series of extraordinary astronomical phenomena that have portended great historical events.

303/41 *Cedrenus: Historiarum Compendium*, [A.D. 531, during the war conducted by Justinian's general, Belisarius, in Africa]: ἐν τούτωι τῶι χρόνωι ὁ ἥλιος ὥσπερ ἡ σελήνη, χωρὶς ἀκτίνων τὴν αἴγλην ἐστύγναζεν ἅπαντα τὸν ἐνιαυτὸν ἐπι πλεῖστον δὲ ἐκλείποντι ἐώικει· ἐν τούτῶι τῶι χρόνωι οὔτε πόλεμος οὔτε ϑάνατος ἐπιφερόμενος τοῖς ἀνϑρώποις ἐπέλιπε. [Throughout this year the sun shone with a pale light, like the moon, as if without rays and suffering a total eclipse. In the same year, wars and death did not cease their visitation upon men.]

304/5 *Theophanes: Chronographia*, [A.D. 789, when Irene blinded her son{ Constantine and became Empress of the Romans]: ἐσκοτίσϑη δὲ ὁ ἥλιος ἐπὶ ἡμέρος 17 καὶ οὐκ ἔδωκε τὰς ἀκτῖνας αὐτοῦ ὥστε πλανᾶσϑαι τὰ πλοῖα καὶ φέρεσϑαι, καὶ πάντας λέγειν καὶ ὁμολεγεῖν ὅτι διὰ τὴν τοῦ βασιλέως τύφλωσιν ὅ ἥλιος τὰς ἀκτῖνας ἀπέϑετο· καὶ οὕτως κρατεῖ

Εἰρήνη ἡ μήτηρ αὐτοῦ.
[At that time the sun was so dimmed for seventeen days
without any rays that ships lost their way and were thrown
off their course and everybody was convinced that the sun
had withdrawn its rays on account of the blinding of the
emperor. Thus did Irene his mother gain power.]

304/6' *Shiner*: Christoph Scheiner, *De Maculis Solaribus ...
accuratior disquisitio. In the letter dated April 14, 1612, he
observes: 'et reliqui Iovis asseclae utrunque insinuant cum
repente alij evanescant ad eum fere modum quo umbrae in
Sole.'
[When the remaining satellites of Jupiter enter [our field of
vision through the telescope], some of the fixed stars suddenly
appear, while others disappear, in the same way as the spots
on the sun.]
and *Rosa Ursina*, Bk II, Part II, Ch. 27: 'Qui enim fieri
potest ut Cometae huc illuc per caeli spatia discurrant, et
usque ad Veneris altitudinem aut etiam maiorem evehantur
nisi caeli aeris fluidi constituantur?'
[How could it be that the comets wander from place to place
through the expanse of the heavens and are borne to the
height of Venus and farther, unless the skies are constituted
of air-like fluids?]
Christoph Scheiner (1573-1650) was mathematician and
astronomer in Ingolstadt. In 1611, Scheiner constructed a
telescope with which he made astronomical observations, and
in March of that year he detected the presence of spots in the
sun. His letters to his friend, Marc Welser, maintaining that
these spots were small planets circling the sun, were
published by Welser in 1612 as *Tres epistolae de maculis
solaribus*. In a second series of letters, which Welser
published in the same year as *De maculis solaribus ...
accurator disquitio*, Scheiner discussed the individual motion
of the spots, their period of revolution and the appearance of
brighter patches, or faculae, on the sun's surface. His
voluminous *Rosa ursina sive Sol*, (1626-1630), criticized
Galileo for failing to mention the inclination of the axis of
rotation of the sun spots to the plane of the ecliptic.
Scheiner, a Jesuit priest, upheld the tradition that the earth
was at rest and refuted the Copernican system in *Prodromus
de sole mobili et stabili terra contra Galilaeum*, published

posthumously.

304/11 *Maculae*: spots

305/19 *Homer: Iliad*, Bk.XIX, l. 2: This is from the majestic opening of the book which describes the appearance of Thetis to her son, Achilles, at daybreak, bearing the armour fashioned for him by Hephaestus:

ἠὼς μὲν κροκόπεπλος ἀπ᾽ Ὠκεανοῖο ῥοάων
ὄρνυϑ᾽ ἵν᾽ ἀϑανάτοισι φόως φέροι ἠ δὲ βροτοῖσιν
ἠ δ᾽ ἐς γῆας ἵκανε ϑεοῦ πάρα δῶρα φερουσα.

[Now Dawn the saffron-robed arose from the streams of Oceanus to bring light to immortals and to mortal men, and Thetis came to the ships bearing the gifts from the god. (Tr. A.T. Murray, Loeb Classical Library)]

306/14 *Intermundia Deorum*: See Cicero, *De natura deorum*, I, viii, and Lucretius, *De rerum natura*, III, 11. 16-18, for references to the Epicurean notion that the Gods dwelt aloof from men in the spaces betwee n the material worlds.

307/35 Which power ... *Oromazes*: The reference is to the dualistic religion developed in ancient Persia by the prophet Zarathustra who lived probably in the sixth century B.C. Zarathustra's teachings were centered on the conflict between the forces of good and evil represented by Ahura-Mazda ("The Wise Lord") and Angra Mainyu, the chief agent of Druj ("The Lie"). In the later Pahlavi language, these two entities were named Ormazd and Ahriman, respectively. During the Sassanian period (2nd c.-7th c. A.D.) Zoroastrianism developed an influential cosmology which divided historical time into four eras. In the first Ahura Mazda creates, by means of thought, angelic spirits and the eternal prototypes of creatures. Since he foresees Angra Mainyu too the latter comes into existence at the same time. The peaceful coexistence of good and evil during the second era is disturbed by Angra Mainyu's assault on the archetypes, which results in a mixture of good and evil in the third era. The final era is marked by Zarathustra's ministry, which will culminate in the victory of good over evil, effected partly through the agency of Soshyans, a semidivine Saviour. The universe will then be restored to its original purity and the saved will be rendered immortal.

308/2 Plutarch: *De Iside et Osiride* [M] 369d-370c. 'And finally Hades shall pass away.'

308/18 *Plotinus: Enneades*, I, ii, 7: ἐπὶ μείζους δὲ ἀρχὰς ἥκων καὶ ἄλλα μέτρα κατ' ἐκεῖνα πράξει· οἷον τὸ σωφρνεῖν οὐκ ἐν μέτρωι ἐκείνωι τιθείς, ἀλλ' ὅλως κατὰ τὸ δυνατὸν χωρίζων καὶ ὅλως ζῶν οὐχὶ τὸν ἀνθρώπον βίον τὸν τοῦ ἀγαθοῦ, ὂν ἀξιοῖ ἡ πολιτικὴ ἀρετή (διαζῆν), ἀλλὰ τοῦτον μὲν καταλιπών, ἄλλον δὲ ἑλόμενος τὸν τῶν θεῶν.
[And as he reaches to loftier principles and other standards, these in turn will define his conduct: for example, restraint in its earlier form will no longer satisfy him; he will work for the final Disengagement; he will live, no longer, the human life of the good man -- such as Civic Virtue commends -- but, leaving this beneath him, will take up instead another life, that of the Gods. (Tr. S. Mackenna)]

308/27 A *Distich* of theirs: Verses 70 and 71 of the 'Golden Verses of Pythagoras.' cf. Hierocles, *Commentarius in aureum carmen Pythagoreorum*, 27: τοῦτο πέρας τῶν πόνων τὸ κάλλιστον, τοῦτο ὡς Πλάτων φησίν, ὁ μέγας ἀγὼν καὶ ἐλπὶς ἡ μεγάλη, τοῦτο φιλοσοφίας ὁ τελειότατος καρπός, τοῦτο τῆς ἐρωτικῆς καὶ τελεστικῆς τέχνης τὸ μέγιστον ἔργον.
[This is the most glorious end of all our labours. This, as Plato says, is the great struggle and the great hope, this is the most perfect fruit of philosophy and the most sublime achievement of Love and the art of the Mysteries.]

Textual Notes

Recorded here are all the substantive variants between the 1662 edition and the first edition of 1659. These do not include differences in spelling, capitalization, italicization, punctuation, paragraphing, or contractions of Greek and Latin words.

Page/Line 1662] 1659

1/21   this your averseness,] this averseness of your Lordship,

2/8   abode ... there] abode with your Lordship

2/8   treatment from] treatment there, from

2/28   Your Vertues] your Lordships Vertues

2/31   Your Modesty;] Your Lordships modesty;

2/37   you] your L

3/10   *Your Lordships*] Your Honours

5/20   *what ... them,] What I have set down* (Lib.3.Cap.14)

12/25   *Book*] *Book*, Cap. 5, 6, 7

13/11   *Saving ... Light.*] not in 1659

15/2   *have ... Book]* *have confuted* Lib. 3, cap. 16.

15/5   *I ... it.] I have made of it*

16/11   *Nor can ...* Phaenomena.] not in 1659

18/34   *Against ... interposed]* *not in 1659*

24/42   Conclusion.] Conclusion see my *Antidote against Atheisme*, lib.1.Cap.2, and 9.

26/1   contradiction.] contradiction. See my Antidote lib.1.Cap.4.

34/14   Antidote] Antidote, Lib. 1. Cap. 4

35/19   I elsewhere call it] I call it

35/40   This *inmost life*] Wherefore this inmost center of life

40/4   μικρόν] μικρὸν

40/4   δυνάμει] δυνᾳμει

40/4   τὶμιότητι] τιμιότητι

42/13   Chap.2] Cap. 2

45/25   Antidote.] Antidote, Cap. 3

50/21   his *Leviathan*] his *Leviathan*, Chap. 34

51/1   his *Physicks*] his *Physicks*, Part 4, Chap. 25. Article 9

51/16   Book] book, Part I. Chap. 5. Art. 4.

51/21   Nature] Nature, Chap. 11. Art. 4.

51/32   Leviathan] *Leviathan*, Chap. 12

52/8   Nature] Nature, Cap. 11. Art. 5

52/38   *Formes*, writes] *Formes*, he writes

55/35   writ ... treatise] writ, Cap. 2, and 3

56/18   I have ... place] I shall in it's due place

59/21   8. *The last ... answered.*] not in 1659

59/21   9.] 8.

59/36   my *Antidote*] my *Antidote*, Lib. I. Cap. 7, 8

61/34   grain of sand] apple

62/3   seems] is

63/4   For ... inferred] not in 1659

63/22   8. The utmost ... *Atheism*] not in 1659

64/8   9.] 8.

64/8   no matter ... any] Matter of its own Nature has no

65/23   (as Mr ... *Elements* of Philosophy:)] as *Mr* ... his Physics.Chap. 25.

69/8   and shall ... Treatise] not in 1659

75/16   way; yet they] way; they

77/16   *as well as ... Preface*] not in 1659

77/16   3, 4. That Demonstration ... Evasion] not in 1659

77/18   5.] 3.

77/18   6.] 4.

77/19   7.] 5.

77/20   8.] 6.

77/21   9. *A further ... thereof.*] 7. *A further proof thereof.* 8. A third Argument of the Truth thereof.

77/21   10.] 9.

77/22   11.] 10.

77/22   12. A further ... thereto.] 11. *A further Answer thereto*

77/23   13.] 12.

77/23   *second] third*

77/24   14.] 13.

77/24   *third] fourth*

77/25   15.] 14.

77/26   16.] 15.

78/13   his Elements of Philosophy.] his Elements of Philosophy. Cap.25.Art.2

78/31   3. Against which ... all.] not in 1659.

81/5   5.] 3.

81/16   6.] 4.

81/38   7.] 5.

82/22   8.] 6.

82/23   The *least* ... already.)] the *least* Reality of which Matter can consist concerning which I have already spoke. Lib.1.Cap.6

82/24   Which being] This being

82/31   But this ... bodies.] 7. I acknowledge indeed that the Pupil of the Eye is very small in comparison of those vast objects that are seen through it, as also that through a Hole exceedingly much less, made suppose in brass or lead, large objects are transmitted very clearly; but I have observed with all that you may lessen the hole so far, that an unclouded day at noon will look more obscure than an ordinary moonshine might. Wherefore Nature has bounds, and reducing her to the least measure imaginable the effect must prove insensible.

82/39   9.] 8.

83/14   10.] 9.

83/30   11.] 10.

84/12   12.] 11.

85/1   13.] 12.

85/16   14.] 13.

85/30   also, especially ... is] also, by reason of the instability of that particle that is plaied upon from all parts thereof. At least it is

87/42   *perception.*] *perception*; see Mr. *Hobbs* his Elements of Philos. Chap. 25

89/23   homogeneity, ... imperceptibility] homogeneity and imperceptibility

91/5   (if ... all:)] not in 1659

101/27 Secondly, That] That

104/32 steddily ... place] steddily resting in the same place.

106/27 as well of] both

106/28 as] and

108/24 as Regius ... *Philosophy*] as Regius has, Philosop. Natural.Lib.4.Cap. 16.

108/26 Book of Passions] book of Passions Artic. 11.

110/21 some (suppose) ... how] not in 1659

113/25 brought before] brought Chap. 2. Sect. 3.

114/30 that is the Cause thereof] not in 1659

127/10 choice;] choice, *De rerum Nat lib.* 3

127/38 brings into view] brings *Philos. Natur. lib.* 4 *Cap.* 16

130/24 so likewise is it plain] so it is plain likewise

130/29 And so ... body.] not in 1659

135/22 Enthusiasmus Triumphatus] *Enthusiasmus Triumphatus* Artic.3,4,5.

136/23 Theorem] Theorem, Artic. 13.

137/15 Which is ... powers,] not in 1659.

137/38 Sense) the Soul] Sense) that the Soul

138/10 The consideration ... demonstrated] not in 1659

140/28 which is... proposed] not in 1659

142/3   Wherefore] And therefore

144/38 ῥιζαν. so)] ῥιζαν)

146/14 *Appendix ... Antidote,*] *Appendix to my Antidote* &. Cap.10.

151/15 Treatise *De Anima*] Treatise *De Anima* Lib. I. Cap. 3.

151/34 *De Generat. Animal.*] *De Generat. Animal.* Lib. 3. Cap.   11.

152/19 clear, out of ... Treatise] clear, Lib. 2. Cap. 3.

156/27 De Generat. Animal.] De Generat Animal. Lib. 2. Cap. 3.

172/33 For ... hand] not in 1659.

173/22 *Antidote ... of*] *Antidote*, Lib. 3. Cap. 9 and of

173/23 Maid] Maid in the foregoing chapter

174/14 who, after ... whether] who having, as *Baronius* relates, made a solemn vow with his fellow-Platonist *Michael Mercatus* (after they had been pretty warmly disputing of the Immortality of the Soul out of the Principles of their Master *Plato*) that whether

174/19 his Fate] *Ficinus* his fate

175/6 they] it

182/5 entangled] hoppled

182/30 *Achilles* his ghost] *Achilles* ghost

193/2 this ... *Matter.*] not in 1659

193/14 out of him.] out of him, Lib. 2. Cap. 14.

198/13 its] his

198/37 have above written] written, *Lib.* 1. *Cap.* 3, 5, 8, as also *Lib.2. Cap.1, 2.*

199/30 elsewhere written, namely,] written *Lib.* 2, *Cap.* 11. viz.

201/40 Εἴδωλα]Εἰδωλα

205/28 Saith he] not in 1659

208/3 Wherefore] And therefore

212/28 (of which ... example)] not in 1659

239/33 *Antidote,*] *Antidote* Chap. 12.

241/21 white faint splendour] white splendour

241/21 in the Moon] in the full Moon

245/16 already.] already. See *Cap.* 3. *Sect.* 7, 8

247/1 proved ... Book,] proved *Lib.* 2 *Cap.* 11.

251/17 degrees,] degrees, *Ennead.* 4. *Lib.* 4. *Cap.* 45.

256/1 (if it ... true)] not in 1659

256/40　*Helmont*] *Helmont* See *Lib*. 2. *Cap*. 15. *Sect*. 8, 9, 10.

258/25　9. *Of Instinct ... is*.] not in 1659

258/25　10. *The grand ... in*] 9. *Its grand office of*

263/38　9. For ... Eggs.] not in 1659

267/33　But I have ... long.] But this argument being too lubricous, I will not much insist upon it.

267/35　10.] not in 1659

268/8　or ... other.] not in 1659.

270/7　*Aristotle*] *Aristotle* (*Histor. Animal. Lib* 4. *Cap*. 7)

270/10　συμπεφυκόσι] συμπεφυκόσι. *De Juvent. & Senect. Cap*. 2

271/26　already.] already *Lib*. 1. *Cap*. 5

275/25　affirm] affirm, *De Generat. Animal. Lib*. 4. *Cap*. 4.

276/3　fight] fight. See *Sennert. Epitom. Scient. Natural. Lib*. 6. *Cap*. 6.

277/19　in, clogg'd] inclogg'd

283/2　Whence ... then] not in 1659.

283/24　which ... *Aries*] not in 1659.

283/36　which ... World] not in 1659.

287/15　*De Subtilitate*] *De Subtilitate Lib*. 19

301/33　himself;] himself, *De rerum natura Lib*. 3.

Bibliography

I. Henry More

A. Primary Sources

This list includes the first editions of More's works published during his lifetime, as well as all the posthumous editions and collections of his writings.

Psychodia Platonica, or A Platonicall Song of the Soul, Consisting of Foure Severall Poems, viz, Psychozoia, Psychathanasia, Antipsychopannnychia, Antimonopsychia, Cambridge, 1642.

Democritus Platonissans, or An Essay upon the Infinity of Worlds out of Platonick Principles, Cambridge, 1646.

Philosophicall poems, Cambridge, 1647.

Observations upon Anthroposophia Theomagica and Anima Magica Abscondita, London, 1650.

The Second Lash of Alazonomastix;Concerning a Solid and Serious Reply to a very Uncivill Answer to Certain Observations upon Anthroposophia Theomagica, and Anima Magica Abscondita, Cambridge, 1651.

An Antidote Against Atheisme, or An Appeal to the Naturall Faculties of the Minde of Man, whether there be not a God, London, 1653.

Conjectura Cabbalistica, or A Conjectural Essay of Interpreting the Minde of Moses according to a Threefold Cabbala: viz. Literal, Philosophical, Mystical, or Divinely Moral, London, 1653.

The Defense of the Threefold Cabbala, London, 1653.

An Appendix to the late Antidote against Atheism, London, 1655.

Enthusiasmus Triumphatus; or, A Discourse of the Nature, Causes, Kinds, and Cure of Enthusiasme, London, 1656.

The Immortality of the Soul, So farre forth as it is demonstrable from the knowledge of Nature and the Light of Reason, London, 1659.

An Explanation of the Grand Mystery of Godliness, or, a true and faithfull representation of the Everlasting Gospel of our Lord and Saviour Jesus Christ, London, 1660.

Free-Parliament Quaeres: proposed to tender consciences, London, 1660.

Henrici Mori Epistolae Quatuor ad Renatum Des-Cartes in *A Collection* below.

Epistola H. Mori ad V.C. in *A Collection* below.

A Collection of Several Philosophical Writings of Dr. Henry More, London, 1662.

A Modest Enquiry into the Mystery of Iniquity, London, 1664.

Synopsis prophetica; or, The Second Part of the Enquiry into the Mystery of Iniquity, London, 1664.

The Apology of Dr. Henry More, London, 1664.

Enchiridion Ethicum, London, 1668.

Divine Dialogues, Containing Sundry Disquisitions and Instructions Concerning the Attributes of God and His Providence in the World, London, 1668.

An Exposition of the Seven Epistles to the Seven Churches, London, 1669.

Enchiridion Metaphysicum, sive, De Rebus Incorporeis Succincta et Luculenta Dissertatio, London, 1671.

An Antidote against Idolatry, London, 1672.

An Appendix to the late Antidote against Idolatry, London, 1672.

A brief Reply to a late Answer... to H. More his Antidote against Idolatry, London, 1672.

Antidotus Adversus Idolatrium, London, 1674.

De Anima Ejusque Facultatibus, London, 1675.

Remarks upon two late ingenious discourses: the one, An essay touching the gravitation and non-gravitation of fluid bodies: the other, Observations touching the Toricellian experiment; so far forth as they may concern any passages in his Enchiridion Metaphysicum, London, 1676.

Ad clarissimum ... virum N.N. in Knorr von Rosenroth, C., ed., Kabbala *Denudata*, Frankfurt, 1677.

Aditus tentatus rationem reddendi nominum et ordinis decem Sephirotharum in above.

Fundamenta philosophiae, sive Cabbalae Aeto-paedo-melissaeae in above.

Quaestiones et considerationes paucae brevesque in Tractatum primum libri Druschim in above.

Visiones Ezechieliticae, sive Mercavae expositio in above.

H. Mori Cantabrigiensis Opera Omnia, tum quae Latine, tum quae Anglice Scripta Sunt; Nunc Vero Latinate Donata, 3 vols., London, 1675-79.

Philosophematum eruditi Authoris Difficulium Nugarum, and Adnotamenta in duas ingeniosas Dissertationes in above.

Epistola altera ad V.C. and *Demonstrationis duarum propositionum* in above.

Apocalypsis Apocalypseos; or the Revelation of St. John the Divine unveiled, London, 1680.

An Answer to a letter of a learned psychopyrist concerning the true notion of a spirit in Glanvill, J. Sadducismus Triumphatus, *London,1681.*

A Continuation of [Joseph Glanvill's] Collection; or, An addition of some few more stories of apparitions and witchcraft in above.

The easie, true and genuine notion and explication of the nature of a spirit [translated from Bk. I, Ch. 27 and 28 of *Enchiridion Metaphysicum*] in above.

A Plain and continued Exposition of the Several Prophecies or Divine Visions of the Prophet Daniel, London, 1681.

Tetractys Anti-Astrologica; or, the four chapters in the explanation of the grand Mystery of godliness, which contain a ... confutation of Judiciary Astrology, London, 1681.

Annotations on Two Choice and useful Treatises: The One Lux Orientalis; or, An Enquiry into the Opinion of the Eastern Seges Concerning the Praeexistence of souls ... [by Joseph Glanvill] the other, A Discourse of Truth ... [by George Rust], London, 1682.

Answer to "Remarks upon his Expositions of the Apocalpse and Daniel, etc. by S.E. Mennonite," annexed, *Arithmetica apocalyptica, and Appendicula apocalyptica,* London, 1684.

An Illustration of those two abstruse books ... the Book of Daniel, and the Revelation of S. John, London, 1685.

Paralipomena Prophetica, London, 1685.

Some cursory reflexions impartially made upon Mr. Richard Baxter, his way of writing notes on the Apocalypse, and upon his advertisement and postscript, London, 1685.

A brief Discourse of the Real Presence of the Body and Blood of Christ in the celebrating of the Holy Eucharist, London, 1686.

Letters Philosophical and Moral between the author and Dr. Henry More in Norris, J., The Theory and Regulation of Love, *London, 1688*.

An account of virtue; or, Dr. Henry More' s abridgement of morals, put into English [by E. Southwell], London, 1690.

Discourse on Several texts of Scripture, ed. J. Worthington, London, 1692.

Letters on several subjects, edited by E. Elys London 1694.

A Collection of Aphorisms, In Two Parts, London, 1704.

Divine Hymns, London, 1706.

The Theological Works of the most pious and learned Henry More, D.D. ... According to the author's improvements in his Latin edition, London, 1708.

"Select letters written upon Several Occasions" in Ward,R. *The Life of theLearned and Pious Dr. Henry More*, London, 1710.

A Collection of Several Philosophical Writings of Dr. Henry More, 4th edition, London, 1712.

Select Sermons, in Wesley, J., *A Christian Library*, London, 1819-27.

Letters from More to Dr. Worthington, in *The Diary and Correspondence of Dr. John Worthington* ,2 vols. in 3, Chetham Society Series, Vols. XIII,XXXVI CXIV, Manchester, 1847, 1855, 1886.

The complete Poems of Dr. Henry More, ed. A. B. Grosart, Edimaburgh, 1878.

Philosophical Writings of Henry More, ed. F. I. MacKinnon, N.Y., 1925.

"Psychozoia", ed. R. B. Botting, doctoral diss., Cornell University, 1930.

Letters from More to Lady Conway, in *Conway Letters: The Correspondence of Anne, Viscountess Conway, Henry More, and their Friends, 1642-1684*, ed. M.H.Nicolson, New Haven, 1930.

Philosophical Poems of Henry More, ed. G. Bullough, Manchester, 1931.

Correspondence between More and Descartes, in Descartes, *Correspondance avec Arnauld et Morus*, ed. G. Lewis, Paris, 1953.

"Henry More's Psychathanasia and Democritus Platonissans, A Critical Edition," ed. L. Haring (unpub. doctoral diss. Columbia University, 1961).

Enthusiasmus Triumphatus, intro. by M.V.D. Porte, the Augustan Reprint Society, Los Angeles, 1966.

Democritus Platonissans, intro by P.G. Stanwood, The Augustan Reprint Society, Los Angeles, 1968.

'The Purification of a Christian Man's Soul' and *An Antidote Against Atheism*, Bk. I and II in *The Cambridge Platonists*, ed. C.A. Patrides, Cambridge, Mass., 1970.

"Lettres sur Descartes" (1650-1651) in A Gabbey, "Anne Conway et Henry More," *Archives de Philosophie*, 40 (1977), 379-404.

'The Praexistency of the Soul' and Other Poems in *The English Spenserians*, ed W.B. Hunter, Jr., Salt Lake City, 1977.

B. Secondary Sources

Adams, C.V., "An Introduction to the *Divine Dialogues* of Henry More (unpub. doctoral dissertation, Univ. of Cincinnati, 1934).

Anderson, P.R., *Science in Defense of Liberal Religion: A Study of Henry More's attempt to link seventeenth century religion with science*, N.Y.: G. Putnam's Sons, 1933.

Allen, D.C., *Doubt's Boundless Sea: Skepticism and Faith in the Renaissance*, Baltimore: The John *Hopkins Press, 1964.*

Argyle, A.W., "The Cambridge Platonists," *Hibbert Journal*, 53(1955) 255-61.

Amstrong, R.L.A., *Metaphysics and British Empiricism*, Lincoln: Univ. of Nebraska Press, 1970.

Austin, E.M., *The Ethics of the Cambridge Platonists*, Philadelphia: Univ. of Pennsylvania, 1935.

Baker, H., *The Wars of Truth: Studies in the Decay of Christian Humanism in the Earlier Seventeenth Century*, Cambridge, Mass., H.U.P., 1952.

Baker, J.T., *An Historical and. Critical Examination of English Space an Time Theories from Henry More to Bishop Berkeley*, Bronxville: Sarah Lawrence College: 1930.
"Henry More and Kant: A Note to the Second Argument on Space in the Transcendental Aesthetic," *Philosophical Review*, 49 (1937), 298-306.

Baxter, Richard, *Of the Nature of Spirits, especially Mans Soul, in a placid collation with Dr. Henry More, in a reply to his answer to a{ private letter, printed in his second edition of Mr. Glanviles Sadducismus Trimphatus*, London, 1682.

Beach, J.W., *The Concept of Nature in Nineteenth Century English Poetry*, N.Y.: Russell and Russell, 1936.

Beaumont, J., *Some observations upon the Apologie of Dr. Henry More*, Cambridge, 1665.
The complete poems of Dr. Joseph Beaumont, ed., A.B. Grosart, Edinburgh, 1880, pt. N.Y.: AMS Press, 1967.

Benson, A.C., "Henry Moore the Platonist," in *Essays*, London: W.Heinemann 1896, 35-67.

Bréhier, E., *La Philosophie et son passé*, Paris, Alcan, Presses Universitaires de France, 1940.

Brown, C.C., "Henry More's 'Deep Retirement': New Material on the Years of the Cambridge Platonist, " *Review of English Studies, (N.S)., XX, 80 (1969),445-454.* 445-454.

"The Mere Numbers of Henry More's Cabbala," *Studies in English Literature, 1500-1900, X, (1970) 143-153.*

Burnham, F. B., "The More-Vaughan Controversy: The Revolt Against Philosophical Enthusiasm," *JHI*, 35(1974) 33-49.

Burtt, E.A., *The Metaphysical Foundations of Modern Science*, N.Y.: Harcourt, Brace, and Co., 1925, 2nd rev. ed., 1932.

Bush,D., *English Literature in the Earlier Sevententh Century, 1600-1660*, Oxford, Clarendon Press, 1962.

Cassirer, E., *The Platonic Renaissance in England*, tr. J.P. Pettegrove, Edinburgh: Thomas Nelson and Sons, 1953.

Cohen, L.D., "Descartes and Henry More on the Beast Machine: A Translation of their Correspondence pertaining to Animal Automation," *Annals of Science* I (1936), 48-61

Colby, F.L., "Thomas Traherne and Henry More," *MLN*, LXII(1947) 490-492.

Coleridge, S.T., *Coleridge on the Seventeenth Century*,ed R. F.Brinkley, Durham:Duke Univ. Press, 1955.

Colie, R.L., *Light and Enlightenment: A Study of the Cambridge Platonists and the Dutch Arminians*, Cambridge: C.U.P.,1959.

Copenhaver, B.P., "Jewish Theologies of Space in the Scientific Revolution: Henry More, Joseph Raphson, Isaac Newton and their predecessors," *Annals of Science*, 37(Sept.1980), 489-548.

Cragg, G.R., *From Puritanism to the Age of Reason: A Study of Changes in Religious Thought within the Church of England 1660 to 1700*, Cambridge: *C.U.P., 1950.*

Craig, G.A., "Umbra Dei: Henry More and the Seventeenth Century Struggle for Plainness" (unpub. doctoral dissertation, Harvard Univ., 1947).

Cristofolini, P., *Cartesiani e Sociniani: Studio su Henry More*, Urbino: Argalia, 1974.

De Boer, J.J., *The Theory of Knowledge of the Cambridge Platonists*, Madras: Methodist Publishing House, 1931.

De Pauley, W.C., *The Candle of the Lord: Studies in the Cambridge Platonists*, London: Society for promoting Christian knowledge, 1937.

Dolson, G.N., "The Ethical System of Henry More," *Philosophical Review,6(1897), 593-607.*

Feilchenfeld, W., "Leibniz and Henry More: Ein Beitrag zur Entwicklung der Monadologie, " *Kantstudien*, 28(1923), 323-334.

Gabbey, A., "Philosophia Cartesiana Truimphata, Henry More (1646-1671)," in *Problems of Cartesianism*, ed., T.M. Lennon, J.M. Nicholas J.W. Davis Kingston: McGill-Queen's Univ.Press, 1982.

Galbralth, J.K., "Henry More's Divine Dialogues: A Critical Analysis" (unpub. doctoral dissertation, Univ. of N. Carolina, 1969).

George, E.A., *Seventeenth Century Men of Latitude*, N.Y.: Charles Scribner's Sons, 19 08.

Greene, R.A., "Henry More amd Robert Boyle on the Spirit of Nature," *JHI*, XXIII(1962), 451-74.

Harrison, A.W., "Henry More, the Cambridge Platonist, " *London Quarterly and Holborn Review*, 158 (1933) 485-492.

Harrison, C.T., "The Ancient Atomists and English Literature of the Seventeenth Century," in *Harvard Studies in Classical Philology*,45 (1934), *1-79*.

Howard, C., *Coleridge's Idealism: A Study of its Relationship to Kant and the Cambridge Platonists*, Boston: R. G.Badger, 1924.

Hoyles, J., *The Waning of the Renaissance, 1640-1740*, The Hague:Martinus Nijhoff, 1971.

Hunter, W.B.Jr., "The Seventeenth Century Doctrine of Plastic Nature," *Harvard Theological Review*, 43(1950), 197-213.

Hutin, S., *Henry More: Essai sur les doctrines théosophiques chez les platoniciens de Cambridge*, Hildesheim: Georg Olms, 1966.
Trois études sur Henry More,Torino: Edizioni di Filosofia, 1964.
"Rationalisme, Empirisme, Théosophie: La théorie de la connaisance chez Henry More," *Filosofia*, XII, 1962, 570-583.
"Leibniz a-t-il subi l'influence d'Henry More?" *Studia Leibnitiana*, II/1, 1979, 59-62.

Inge, W.R., *The Platonic Tradition in English Religious Thought* N.Y.: Longmans, Green and Co., 1926.

Jacob, A., "Henry More's *Psychodia Platonica* and its relationship to Marsilio Ficino's *Theologia Platonica*," *JHI*, 46(198 5),pp.503-22.

Jaeger, J.W., *Examen Theologiae mystica veteris et novae (Dissertio de Enthusiasmo. De J. Boehmio judicum H. Mori)*, Frankfurt and Leipzig, 1709.

Jammer, M., *Concepts of Space: The History of Theories of Space in Physics*, Cambridge, Mass., H.U.P.,1954.

Jentsch,H.A., *Henry More in Cambridge*, Göttingen, University of Göttingen,1935.

Jordan,W.K., *The Development of Religious Toleration in England*, Cambridge, Mass., 1940, Vol. IV.

Klawitter, G.A., "The Poetry of Henry More" (unpub. doctoral dissertation, Univ. of Chicago, 1981)

Laird, J., "L'influence de Descartes sur la philosophie anglaise du XII siècle," *Revue Philosophique*, 122 (1937), 226-256.

Lamprecht, S. P., "Innate Ideas in the Cambridge Platonists," *Philosophical Review*, 35 (1926), 553-573.

"Locke's Attack upon Innate Ideas," *Philosophical Review*,36 (1927), 145-165.

"The Role of Descartes in Seventeenth Century England," *Studies in the History of Ideas*, 3, N.Y. 1935, 181-240.

Lichtenstein, A., *Henry More, The Rational Theology of a Cambridge Platonist*, Cambridge, Mass.: H.U.P., 1962.

Lovejoy, A.O., "Kant and the English Platonists,"*Essays Philosophical and Psychological in Honor of William James*, N.Y.: Longmans, Green, and Co., 1908, 265-302.

Lowery, W. R., "John Milton, Henry More and Ralph Cudworth: A Study in Patterns of Thought "(unpub. doctoral dissertation, Northwestern Univ., 1970).

Masson, David, *The Life of John Milton*, 6vols., London: Macmillan, rev. ed. 1877-1896.

McAdoo, H.R., "The Cambridge Platonists," in *The Spirit of Anglicanism: A Study of Anglican Theological Method in the Seventeenth Century*, N.Y.: Charles Scribner's Sons, 1965.

Mintz, S.I. *The Hunting of Leviathan: Seventeenth Century Reactions to the Materialism and Moral Philosophy of Thomas Hobbes*, Cambridge: H.U.P., 1962.

Mullinger, J.B., *The University of Cambridge*, Cambridge: C.U.P., 1873 - 1911, Vol.III.

Nicolson,M.H. *The Breaking of the Circle: Studies in the effect of the New Science upon Seventeenth Century Poetry*, Evanston: Northwestern Univ. Press, 1950.

Mountain Gloom and Mountain Glory: The Development of the Aesthetics of the Infinite, Ithaca: Cormell Univ. Press, 1957.

"The Life and Works of Henry More: A Study in Cambridge Platonism" (unpub. doctoral dissertation, Columbia Univ.1920).

"More's Psychozoia," *Modern Language Notes*, 37 (1922),*141-148*.

"The Spirit World of Milton and More," *Studies in Philology*, 22 (1925), 433-452.

"Milton and the Conjectura Cabbalistica," *Philosophical Quarterly*, 6 (1927), 1-18.

"Christ's College and the Latitude Men," *Modern Philology*, 27 (1929), 35-53.

"The Early Stages of Cartesianism in England," *Studies in Philology*, 26 (1929) 356-374.

"George Keith and the Cambridge Platonists," *Philosophical Review*, 39 (1930),36-55.

Osmond, P., *Mystical Poets of the English Church*, London: Society for Promoting Christian Knowledge, 1919.

Pacchi,Arrigo, *Cartesio in Inghilterra*, Roma-Bari:Laterza,1973.

S.P.[Simon Patrick] *A Brief Account of the New Sect of Latitude-Men together with some reflections upon the New Philosophy*, London, 1662.

Pawson, G.P.H., *The Cambridge Platonists and their Place in Religibus Thought*, London: Society for Promoting Christian Knowledge, 1930.

Peile, J., *Biographical Register of Christ's College, 1505-1905*, Cambridge, C.U.P . 1910, Vol. I.

Power, L.E., "Henry More and Isaac Newton on Absolute Space," *JHI*, 31 (1970), 289-296.

Powicke, F. J., *The Cambridge Platonists: A Study*, London: J.M. Dent and Sons, 1926.

Reimann, H., *Henry Mores Bedeutung für die Gegenwart*, Basel: R.Geering,1941.

Rémusat, C., *Histoire de la philosophie en Angleterre*, Paris; Didier et cie., 1875, Vol. II.

Røstvig, M., "The Hidden Sense," in *Norwegian Studies in English*, 9, Oslo; Universitetsforlaget, 1963, 1-112.

Saveson, J.E., "Differing Reactions to Descartes among the Cambridge Platonists," *JHI*, 21(1960), 560-567.

Sherer, G.R., "More and Traherne," *Modern Language Notes*, 34(1919), 49-50.

Shorey, P., *Platonism: Ancient and Modern*, Berkeley: Univ. of California Press, 1938.

Snow, A.J., *Matter and Gravity in Newton's Physical Philosophy*, London: O.U.P., 1926.

Sorley, W.R., *A History of English Philosophy*, N.Y.: G.P. Putnam's Sons,1921.

Staudenbaur, C.A., "The Metaphysical Thought of Henry More" (unpub. doctoral dissertation, John Hopklns Univ., 1961).

"Galileo, Ficino, and Henry More's Psychathanasia," *JHI*, 29 (1968), 567-578.

"Platonism, Theosophy, and Immaterialism: Recent Views of the Cambridge Platonists," *JHI*, 35 (1974), 157- 169.

Tulloch, J., *Rational Theology and Christian Philosophy in England in the Seventeenth Century*, Edinburgh: W. Blackwood, 1872, Vol. II.

Tuveson, E.L., *Millenium and Utopia: A Study in the Background of the Idea of Progress*, Berkeley; Univ. of California Press,1949.

Vaughan, T., *Anima Magica Abscondita*, London, 1650.
Anthroposophia Magica, London, 1650.
The Man-Mouse taken in a trap, London, 1650.
The Second Wash, or the Moore scour'd once more, London, 1651.

Ward, R., *The Life of the Learned and Pious Dr. Henry More*, London, 1710, (ed. M. F. Howard, London, 1911).

Webster, C., "Henry More and Descartes, some new sources," *BJHS*, IV, No. 16(1969) 359-377.

Webster, C.M., "Swift and Some Earlier Satirists of Puritan Enthusiasm," *PMLA*, 48(1933),1141-1153.

Wiley, B., *The Seventeenth Century Background*, London: Chatto and Windus, 1934.

Williamson, G., "The Restoration Revolt Against Enthusiasm," *Studies in Philology*, 30(1933), 571-603.

Yates, F., *Giordano Bruno and the Hermetic Tradition*, London: Routledge and Kegan Paul, 1964.

Zimmerman,R., "Henry More und die Vierte Dimension des Raumes," *Sitzungsberichte der Philosophisch-Historischen Classe der Kaiserlichen Akademie der Wissenschaften*, 98(1881),403-448.

II. Intellectual Relations

A. Primary Sources

Aelian, Claudius, *De Natura Animalium, Varia Historia, Epistolae et Fragmenta, etc.*, ed. R. Hercher, Paris, 1858.

Agrippa von Nettesheim, Cornelius, *De Occulta Philosophia Libri tres, Cologne, 1533.*
Three Books of Occult Philosophy or Magic, tr. W.F.Whitehead, Chicago: Hahn and Whitehead, 1898.

Anacreon, *Anacreon Teius, Poeta Lyricus,* ed. Joshua Barnes, Cambridge, 1705.

Aquinas, St. Thomas *On the Unity of the Intellect against the Averoists,* tr. B. H. Zedler, Milwaukee, Wisconsin, 1968.
Summa Theologiae, 60 vols., ed. T. Gilby, London:Blackfriars, 1964-66.

Aratus, Solensis, *Phaenomena et Diosemea,* ed. Johann Bühle,*Leipzig,* 1793-1801.
Phaenomena in Callimachus, *Hymns and Epigrams,* Loeb Classical Library, Cambridge, Mass., 1955.

Aristotle, *Works,* 23 vols., Loeb Classical Library, Cambridge,Mass., 1926-1970.

Aurelius, Marcus, *The Commumings with himself,* tr. C. R. Haines, Loeb Classical Library, Cambridge, Mass., 1930.

Averroes, *Commentarium Magnum in Aristotelis de anima libros,* ed. F. S. Crawford, Cambridge, Mass., 1953.

Bartholin, Caspar, *Anatomicae Institutiones corporis humani,* Oxford, 1633.

Baronio, Cesare, *Annales Ecclesiastici,* Cologne, 1624.

Berkeley, George, *Siris* in *The Works of George Berkeley ,Bishop of Cloyne,* Vol. V, ed. T. E. Jessop, London: Thomas Nelson and Sons, 1953.

Bible, *The Holy Bible, conteyning the Old Testment and the New,* London, 1611-1613.

Bodin, Jean, *De la Démonomanie des Sorciers,* Paris, 1587.

Boehme, Jacob *Theosophia Revelata: Das ist, Alle Göttliche Schriften ... Jacob Bohmens,* 10 vols., ed., J. W. Ueberfeld, Amsterdam, 1730.

The Works of Jacob Behmen, 4 vols., tr. J. Sparrow, J. Ellistone, H. Blunden, London, 1764-81.

Boyle, Robert, *The Works of the Honourable Robert Boyle*, 6 Vols., ed. Thomas Birch, London, 1772.

Browne, Sir Thomas, *Works*,4 Vols. ed. Sir Geoffrey Keynes, 2nd ed.,Chicago,1964.

Burthogge,Richard, *An Essay on Reason and the Nature of Spirits*,London, 1694.
Of the Soul of the World; and of Particular Souls, London, 1699.

Cardano, Girolamo, *Opera Omnia*, Lyons, 1663.

Cedrenus, *Historiarum Compendium*, in *Patrologiae Cursus Completus, Series Graeca*, ed. J.P. Migne, Vol. 121.

Chalcidius *Timaeus de Platonis translatus item eiusdem in eundem commentarius*, Leiden, 1617.

Chaldaic oracles, *The Chaldaick Oracles of Zoroaster and his followers with the expositions of Pletho and Psellus*, London, 1661.

Charleton, Walter, *The Immortality of the human soul*, London, 1657.

Conway, Anne, *The Principles of the most ancient and modern philosophy*, London, 1692, (ed. with an introduction by Peter Loptson, the Hague: Martinus Nijhoff, 1982).

Cudworth, Ralph, *The True Intellectual System of the Universe*, 4 vols., ed. T. Birch, London, 1820.

Davies, Sir John, *The Poems of Sir John Davies*, ed. R. Krueger, Oxford, 1975.

DeRoy, Henri, *Philosophia Naturalis*, Amsterdam, 1661.

Descartes, René, *Oeuvres de Descartes*, pub. par Charles Adam et Paul Tannery, Nouvelle Présentation, 11 vols., Paris: J.Vrin, 1964-1974.
The Philosophical Writings of Descartes, 2 vols., tr J. Cottingham, R. Stoothoff, D. Murdoch, Cambridge: *C.U.P.*, *1985.*

Digby, Sir Kenelm, *Two Treatises*, Paris, *1644.*
A Late Discourse ... Touching the Cure of Wounds by the Powder of Sympathy, London, 1658.

Diodorus Siculus, *Library of History*, 12 vols., Lceb Classical Library Cambridge, Mass., 1933-1967.

Diogenes, Laertius, *Lives of Eminent Philosophers*, 2 vols., Loeb Classical Library, Cambridge, Mass., 1925, 1938.

Dionysius Periegetes, *Orbis Descriptio*, in *Geographi Graeci Minores*, Vol. II, Paris, 1882.

Du Laurens, André, *Historia anatomica humani corporis*, Frankfurt, 1600.

Epictetus, *Works*, 2 vols., Loeb Classical Library, Cambridge, Mass., 1925, 1928.

Euclid, *The Thirteen Books of Euclid's Elements*, ed. Thomas Heath, London, 1926.

Fallopio, Gabriele, *Opera quae adhuc extant omnia*, Frankfurt, 1584.

Fernel, Jean, *Universa Medicina*, Utrecht, 1656.

Feyens, Thomas *De Viribus Imaginationis Tractatus*, Leyden, 1635.

Ficino, Marsilio, *Opera Omnia*, Basel, 1576.
   Théologie platonicienne de l'immortalité des âmes, tr. R. Marcel, Paris: Société d'édition 'Les Belles Lettres,' 1964-1970.

Froidmont, Libert, *Philosophia Christiana de Anima*, Louvain, 1649.

Gaffarel, Jacques, *Unheard-of Curiosities concerning the Talismanical Scripture of the Persians, the horoscope of the Patriarkes and the reading of the stars*, tr. Edmund Chilmead, London, 1650.

Galen, *De Placitis Hippocratis et Platonis*, ed. J. Mueller, Leipzig, 1874.

Gassendi, Pierre, *Syntagma Philosophicum* in *Opera Omnia*, Lyons, 1658.

Gellius, Aulus, *Attic Nights*, 3 vols., Loeb Classical Library, Cambridge, Mass., 1927.

Grosse, Henning, *Magica, de spectris et apparationibus spiritum*, Leiden, 1656.

Harvey, Sir William, *Exercitationes de generatione animalium*, London, 1651.
   Disputations touching the generation of animals, tr. G. Whitteridge, Oxford: Blackwell Scientific Publications, 1981.

Helmont, Jan Baptista van, *Opera Omnia*, Frankfurt, 1707.
   Van Helmont's Works, tr. J.C., London, 1664.
   A Cabbalistical Dialogue, London, 1682.

Hermes Trismegistus, *Hermetica*, ed., Walter Scott, Oxford, 1924.

Herodotus, *Historiae*, 4 Vols., Loeb Classical Library,Cambridge, Mass., 1920-1924.

Hesiod, *Poems, Homeric Hymns and Homerica*, Lceb Classical Library, Cambridge, Mass., 1914.

Hierocles, *In Aureum Pythagoreorum Carmen Commentarius*, ed. F.W. Koehler, Stuttgart, 1974.
The Commentaries of Hierocles on the Golden Verses of Pythagoras, London: Theosophical Publishing Co.,1906.

Hippocrates, *Opera Omnia*, 10 vols., ed. E. Littré, Paris, *1839-1861*.

Hobbes, Thomas, *The English Works*, ed. Sir William Molesworth,

Homer, *The Iliad*, 2 vols., Loeb Classical Library, Cambridge, Mass., 1924-1925.

Horace, *Satires, Epistles, Ars Poetica*, Loeb Classical Library, Cambridge, Mass., 1926.

Iamblichus, *De Vita Pythagorica*, ed. L. Deubner, Stuttgart, 1975
Iamblichus' Life of Pythagoras, tr. T. Taylor, *London, 1818*.

Jonston, Jan, *Historia Naturalis de Piscibus et Cetis*, Frankfurt, *1650*.

Josephus, Flavius *Works*, 9 vols., Loeb Classical Library, Cambridge, Mass., 1926-1965.

Kircher, Athanasius, *Magnes, sive de Arte Magnetica*, Rome, 1654.

Lansberge, Philippe van, *Uranometriae*, Middleburg, 1631.

Leibniz, G.W. von, *De Philosophischen Schriften von Gottfried Wilhelm Leibniz*, 7 vols., ed. C. J. Gerhardt, Berlin, 1875-1890.
Sämtliche Schriften und Briefe, Darmstadt, 1923-1938

Liceti, Fortunio, *De Monstrorum Caussis*, Padua, 1634.

Lips, Joest, *Physiologia Stoicorum libri tres L. Annaes Senecae Aliisque Scriptoribus, Illustrandis*, Paris, 1604.

Locke, John, *An Essay Concerning Human Understanding*, ed. P.H. Nidditch, Oxford, 1975.

Lucretius, *De Rerum Natura*, Loeb Classical Library, Cambridge, Mass.,1924.

Maimonides, Moses, *The Guide for the Perplexed*, Tr. N. Friedländer, N.Y.: 1956.

Martini, Matthias, *Lexicon Philologicum*, Utrecht, 1711.

Maximus Tyrius, *Dissertationes* in *Theophrasti Characteres, etc.*, ed. Fred Dübner, Paris, 1877.
The dissertations of Maximus Tyrius, tr. Thomas Taylor, London, 1804.
Nieremberg, Juan Eusebio, *Historia naturae*, Antwerp, 1635.
Origen *De Principiis* in *Patrologiae Cursus Completus, Series Graeca*, ed. J.P. Migne, Vol. 11.
De Principiis, tr. F. Crombie in *The Ante-Nicene Fathers*, ed. A. Roberts and J. Donaldson, N.Y.: 1926, vol. IV.
Paracelsus, *Opera Omnia*, Geneva, 1658.
Philo, *Works*, 12 vols., Loeb Classical Library, Cambridge, Mass., 1929-1962.
Philostratus, Flavius, *De Vita Apolonii*, 2 vols., Loeb Classical Library, Cambridge, Mass., 1912.
Plato, *Works*, 12 vols., Loeb Classical Library, Cambridge,Mass., 1914-1935.
Pletho, George, *Zoroastrea* in *Patrologiae Cursus Completus, Series Graeca*, ed., J. P. Migne, Vol. 160.
Pliny the Elder, *Natural History*, 10 vols., Loeb Classical Library, Cambridge, Mass., 1938-1962.
Pliny the Younger, *Letters and Panegyrics*, 2 vols., Loeb Classical Library, Cambridge, Mass., 1969.
Plotinus, *Opera*, 3 vols., ed. P. Henry and H. R. Schwyzer, Paris, Desclée de Brouwer, 1951-1973.
The Enneads, tr. Stephen Mackenna, London, 1956.
Plutarch, *Moralia*, 16 vols., The Loeb Classical Library, Cambridge, Mass., 1927-1969.
Scripta Moralia, 2 vols., ed. F. Dübner, Paris, 1890.
Pomponazzi, Pietro, *Tractatus de immortalitate animae* in *Opera*,Basel,1567.
On the immortality of the soul (Tr. W.H. Hay II) in *The Renaissance Philosophy of Man*, ed. E. Cassirer, P.O. Kristeller, J. H. Randall, Jr., Chicago,1948.
Porphyry, *Vita Plotini* in Plotinus, *Opera*, ed. Henry et Schwyzer.
On the life of Plotinus and the arrangement of his work in *Plotinus, The Enneads*, tr. S. MacKenna.
Pre-Socratics, *Die Fragmente der Vorsokratiker*, ed. H. Diels and W. Kranz, Berlin, 1951-1952.
Ancilla to the pre-Socratic Philosophers: a complete translation of the fragments in Diels, Fragmente der Vorsokratiker, tr. K. Freeman, Cambridge, Mass., 1948.

Proclus, *The Commentaries of Proclus on the Timaeus of Plato*, tr. T. Taylor, London, 1820.

The Elements of Theology, tr. E.R. Dodds, Oxford, 1962.

The Six Books of Proclus the Platonic succesor, on the theology of Plato, tr. T. Taylor, London, 1816.

Psellus, Michael, *De Operatione Daemonum*, ed. Gilbert Gaulmin, Paris,1615.

On the operation of Daemons, tr. M. Collison, Sydney, 1843.

Expositio in Oracula Chaldaica in *Patrologiae cursus Completus, Series Graeca*, ed. J. P. Migne, Vol. 122.

Scaliger, Guilio Cesare, *Exotericarum Exercitationes ... De subtilitate*, Paris, 1557.

Scheiner, Christoph, *Tres epistolae de maculis solaribus*, Augsburg, 1612.

Rosa Ursina sive sol, Braciani, 1630.

Seneca, *Epistulae Morales*, 3 vols., Loeb Classical Library, Cambridge, Mass., 1917-1925.

Moral Essays, 3 vols., Loeb Classical Library, Cambridge, Mass., 1928-1935.

Naturales Quaestiones, 2 vols., Loeb Classical Library, Cambridge, Mass., 1971, 1972.

Sennert,Daniel, *Opera Omnia*,Paris, 1641.

Thirteen Books of Natural Philosophy, tr. N. Culpepper and A. Cole, London,1659.

Smith, John, *Select Discourses*, ed. John Worthington, London, 1660.

Sophocles, Σοφοκλεους Γενος Και Βιος in *Sophocle*, ed.Paul Masqueray, Paris, 1946, *Vol. I*.

Spiegel, Adriaan van der, *De humani corporis fabrica*, Venice, 1626.

Spinoza, Benedict de, *Opera*, ed., van Vloten and Land, Amsterdam, 1882-3.

Suetonius, *The Lives of the Caesars*,2 vols., Loeb Classical Library, Cambridge, Mass., 19 51.

Synesius, *Epistolae, Hymni*, in *Patrologiae Cursus Completus, Series Graeca*, ed. J.P. Migne, Vol. 66.

Theocritus, *Poems* in *The Greek Bucolic Poets*, Lceb Classical Library, Cambridge, Mass., 1912.

Theophanes, *Chronographia* in *Patrologiae Cursus Completus, Series Graeca*, ed. J.P. Migne, Vol. 108.

Thucydides *Historia*, 4 vols., Loeb Classical Library, Cambridge, Mass., 1919-1923.

Vanini Lucilio, 'Guilio Cesare,' *De admirandis Naturae reginae deaeque mortalium arcanis*, Paris, 1616.

Virgil, *Works*, 2 vols., Loeb Classical Library, Cambridge, Mass., 1934, 1935.

Wharton, Thomas, *Adenographia, sive glandularum totius corporis descriptio*, London, 1656.

Weyer, Johann, *De Praestigiis Daemonum*, Basel, 1577.

Zohar, *The Zohar*, tr. H. Sperling and M. Simon, London, 1931-34.

B. Secondary Sources

This is a select list.

Aiton, E.J., "The Cartesian Theory of Gravity," *Annals of Science*, 15(1959), 27-49.

Armstrong, A.H., *The Cambridge History of later Greek and early Medieval Philosophy*, Cambridge: C.U.P., 1967.
The Intelligible Universe in Plotinus, Cambridge, *C.U.P*, *1940*.

Aspelin, Gunnar, 'Ralph Cudworth' s Interpretation of Greek Philosophy *A Study in the History of English Philosophical Ideas,' Göteborgs Högskolas Årsskrift*, XLIX (1943),

Beare, J. I. *Greek Theories of Elementary Cognition from Alcmaeon to Aristotle*, Oxford: Clarendon Press, 1906.

Bloch, O.R., *La Philosophie de Gassendi: Nominalisme, Matérialisme et Métaphysique*, The Hague: Martinus Nijhoff,*1971*.

Boswell, James, *Life of Johnson*, ed. R.W. Chapman, London: O.U.P.,1953.

Bréhier, Émile, *The Philosophy of Plotinus*, tr. J. Thomas, Chicago: Univ. of Chicago Press 1958.

Buckley, G.T., *Atheism in the English Renaissance*, Chicago: Univ. of Chicago Press, 1932.

Dodds, E.R., *Pagan and Christian in an age of anxiety*, Cambridge, *C.U.P.*, *1965*.

Fakhry, M., *A History of Islamic Philosophy*, N.Y.: C.U.P., *1970*.

Foster, Sir Michael, *Lectures on the History of Physiology during sixteenth, seventeenth and eighteenth centuries,* Cambridge, C.U.P., 1901.

Gaye, R. K., *The Platonic Conception of Immortality and its connexion with the Theory of Ideas,* London: C.J. Clay and Sons,1902.

Geffcken, Johann, *The last days of Greco-Roman paganism,* tr. Sabine MacCormack, Amsterdam: North-Holland Publishing Co.,*1978*.

Gibson, A.B., *The Philosophy of Descartes,* London: Methuen & *Co.,1932*.

Gysi, Lydia, *Platonism and Cartesianism in the Philosophy of Ralph Cudworth,* Bern: Herbert Lang, 1962.

Klibansky, Raymond, *The Continuity of the Platonic Tradition in the Middle Ages,* London: The Warburg Institute, 1939.

Kristeller, P.O., *Eight Philosophers of the Italian Renaissance,* Stanford, Stanford Univ. Press, 1964.
The Philosophy of Marsilio Ficino, tr. V. Conant, N.Y. Columbia Univ. Press. 1943.

Laird, J., *Hobbes,* London: Ernest Benn, 1934.

Merton, E.S., *Science and Imagination in Sir Thomas Browne,* N.Y.:King's Crown Press, 1949.

Meyer, R.W., *Leibniz and the Seventeenth Century Revolution,* tr. J.P. Stern, Cambridge: Bowes and Bowes, 1952.

Moore, C.H., *Ancient beliefs in the immortality of the soul with some account of their influence on later views,* N.Y.: Cooper Square Publishers, 1963.

Muirhead, J.M., *The Platonic Tradition in Anglo-Saxon Philosophy* London: George Allen and Unwin, 1931.

Niebyl, P. H., "Sennert, Van Helmont and Medical ontology," *Bulletin of the History of Medicine,* 45(1971)115-137.

Notestein, Wallace, *A History of Witchcraft in England from 1558 to 1718,* Washington: The American Historical Association,1911.

Passmore, J.A., *Ralph Cudworth: An Interpretation,* Cambridge, *C.U.P.,1951*.

Ramsay, R.H., *No longer on the Map,* N.Y.: Ballantine Books, 1973.

Robinson T.M., *Plato's Psychology,*Toronto: Univ. of Toronto Press, 1970.

Rohde, Erwin, *Psyche:The cult of souls and belief in immortality among the Greeks*, tr. W.B. Hillis, N.Y.: Harcourt, Brace and Co., 1925.

Roberts, Sr., J.D., *From Puritanism to Platonism in Seventeenth Century England*, The Hague: Martinus Nijhoff, 1968.

Ryan, J.K., "John Smith: Platonist and Mystic," *The New Scholasticism*, XX(1946), 1-25.

Sanderson, J.L., *Sir John Davies*, Boston: Twayne Publishers, 1975.

Sherrington, Sir Charles, *Man on his nature*, Cambridge, C.U.P., 1941.

Shumaker, Wayne, *The Occult Sciences in the Renaissance*, Berkeley: Univ. of California Press, 1972.

Soury, Guy, *La démonologie de Plutarque*, Paris: Société d' édition' Les Belles Lettres', 1942.

Stendhal, Krister,ed., *Immortality and Resurrection*, N. Y.: Macmillan,*1965*.

Stewart, J.A., *The Myths of Plato*, Carbondale: Southern Illinois Univ. Press, 1960.

Svoboda, K., *La démonologie de Michel Psellos*, Brno: Faculty of Philosophy, Univ. of Masarykiana, 1927.

Temkin Owsei, *Galenism: Rise and Decline of a Medical Philosophy*, Ithaca: Cornell Univ. Press, 1973.

Walker, D.P., *The Ancient Theology: Studies in Christian Platonism from the Fifteenth to the Eighteenth Century*, Ithaca: Cornell Univ. Press, 1972.

The Decline of Hell: Seventeenth Century Discussions of Eternal Torment, Chicago: Univ. of Chicago Press*1964*.

"The Astral Body in Renaissance Medicine," *Journal of the Warburg and Courtauld Institutes*, XXI*(1958)*, *119-133*.

Webster, Charles, *From Paracelsus to Newton: Magic and the Making of Modern Science*, Cambridge: C.U.P., 1982.

West, R.H., *Milton and the Angels*, Athens: Univ. of Georgia Press,1955.

Wild, John, *George Berkeley: A Study of his life and Philosophy*, Cambridge, Mass.: H.U.P., 1936.

William, G., "Milton and the Mortalist Heresy," *Studies in Philosophy*, 32(1935), pp.553-79.

Zeller, Edward *Aristotle and the earlier Peripateties*, tr. B. F. C. Costelloe and J.H. Muirhead, London: Longmans, Green and Co., 1897.

A History of Eclecticism in Greek Philosophy, tr. S. F. Alleyne, London: Longmans, Green, and Co.,1883.
Plato and the older Academy, tr. S.F. Alleyne and Goodwin, London: Longmans, Green, and Co., 1888.
Socrates and the Socratic Schools, tr. O.J. Reichel, London: Longmans, Green, and Co., 1885.
The Stoics, Epicureans, and Sceptics, tr. O. J. Reichel, London: Longmans, Green, and Co., 1879.

C. *Tertiary Sources*

Dictionaire historique et critique, ed. Pierre Bayle, Rotterdam, R. Leers, 1697.
Dictionary of Greek and Roman Biography and Mythology, 3 vols., ed. William Smith, London: Taylor, Walton, and Maberly, 1849.
Dictionary of Scientific Biography, 16 vols., N.Y.: Scribner, 1970-1980.
Encyclopedia Judaica, 16 vols., N.Y.: Macmillan, 1971-1972.
Encyclopedia of Islam, 5 vols., London: Luzac and Co., 1913-1938.
Encyclopedia of Philosophy, 8 vols., N.Y.: Macmillan, 1967.
Oxford Classical Dictionary, ed. N.G.L. Hammond and H.H. Scrillard, Oxford: Clarendon Press, 1970.
New Catholic Encyclopedia, 16 vols., N.Y.: McGraw-Hill, 1967-1979.
Paulys Real-Encyclopedie der classischen Altertums-Wissenschaft, 49 vols., Stuttgart, J.B. Metzler, 1894-1967.